VIRAL ONCOGENESIS AND CELL DIFFERENTIATION

THE CONTRIBUTIONS OF CHARLOTTE FRIEND

CHARLOTTE FRIEND
1921-1987

ANNALS OF THE NEW YORK ACADEMY OF SCIENCES
Volume 567

VIRAL ONCOGENESIS AND CELL DIFFERENTIATION

THE CONTRIBUTIONS OF CHARLOTTE FRIEND

Edited by Leila Diamond and Sandra R. Wolman

The New York Academy of Sciences
New York, New York
1989

Library of Congress Cataloging-in-Publication Data

Viral oncogenesis and cell differentiation.

(Annals of the New York Academy of Sciences, ISSN 0077-8923 ; v. 567)
Papers presented at a conference held by the New York Academy of Sciences on Sept. 29-Oct. 1, 1988, in New York, N.Y.
Includes bibliographical references.
1. Viral carcinogenesis—Congresses. 2. Friend virus—Congresses. 3. Cell differentiation—Congresses. 4. Oncogenes—Congresses. 5. Friend, Charlotte, 1921-1987—Congresses. I. Friend, Charlotte, 1921-1987. II. Diamond, Leila. III. Wolman, Sandra R. IV. New York Academy of Sciences ; v. 567. V. Series: Annals of the New York Academy of Sciences ; v. 567.
[DNLM: 1. Cell Differentiation—congresses. 2. Hematopoietic Stem Cells—congresses. 3. Oncogenes—congresses. 4. Oncogenic Viruses—congresses. W1 AN626YL v.567 / QW 166 V8125 1989]
Q11.N5 vol. 567 500 s 89-14488
[RC268.57] [616.99'4071] 89-14488
ISBN 0-89766-549-X (alk. paper)
ISBN 0-89766-550-3 (pbk. : alk. paper)

Cover (paperbound edition): A Friend leukemia virus budding from the surface of a Friend leukemia cell in culture and viewed with high-resolution transmission electron microscopy. Magnification: 475,000 ×, reproduced at 128%. Photograph courtesy of Dr. E. de Harven, University of Toronto, Canada. Reproduced from Advances in Virus Research *(1974), volume 19, page 236, with permission from Academic Press.*

PCP
Printed in the United States of America
ISBN 0-89766-549-X (cloth)
ISBN 0-89766-550-3 (paper)
ISSN 0077-8923

ANNALS OF THE NEW YORK ACADEMY OF SCIENCES

Volume 567
August 4, 1989

VIRAL ONCOGENESIS AND CELL DIFFERENTIATION: THE CONTRIBUTIONS OF CHARLOTTE FRIEND [a]

Editors and Conference Organizers
LEILA DIAMOND AND SANDRA R. WOLMAN

CONTENTS

[a]This volume contains papers from a conference entitled Viral Oncogenesis and Cell Differentiation: The Contributions of Charlotte Friend, which was held by the New York Academy of Sciences on September 29-October 1, 1988, in New York, New York.

Part III. Oncogenes

Part IV. Hematopoiesis: Normal and Abnormal

Part V. Growth and Differentiation of Normal and Malignant Cells

Part VI. Molecular and Genetic Control of Cell Proliferation

Closing Remarks

Poster Papers

Keynote Address

Financial assistance was received from:

- AMERICAN CANCER SOCIETY
- BETHESDA RESEARCH LABORATORIES, LIFE TECHNOLOGIES, INC.
- BRISTOL-MYERS COMPANY/PHARMACEUTICAL RESEARCH AND DEVELOPMENT DIVISION
- BURROUGHS WELLCOME COMPANY
- CENTOCOR
- HOFFMANN-LA ROCHE/CELL BIOLOGY
- HOFFMANN-LA ROCHE/CLINICAL INVESTIGATION
- MERCK SHARP & DOHME RESEARCH LABORATORIES
- NATIONAL CANCER INSTITUTE/NIH
- PFIZER CENTRAL RESEARCH
- SEARLE RESEARCH AND DEVELOPMENT
- SMITH KLINE & FRENCH LABORATORIES
- THE MOUNT SINAI MEDICAL CENTER

INTRODUCTORY REMARKS

Charlotte Friend, Ph.D. 1921-1987

A Scientist's Life

LEILA DIAMOND [a,b] AND SANDRA R. WOLMAN [c]

[a] *The Wistar Institute*
Philadelphia, Pennsylvania 19104
and
[c] *Michigan Cancer Foundation*
Detroit, Michigan 48201

The conference on which this volume is based was organized to honor the memory of Charlotte Friend. Many of those attending the conference knew Charlotte and loved and respected her as a person and as a scientist. However, probably few knew her background and the events in her life that brought her to the position of eminence she achieved. And so we begin this volume with a short biographical sketch of her personal history and her early scientific accomplishments.

Charlotte Friend was a born-and-bred New Yorker—she adored this city. She was proud to have been a recipient of the First Annual Mayor's Award in Science and Technology, presented by Mayor Edward Koch in 1985. So it's fitting that a conference in her honor be held in New York City and be sponsored by the New York Academy of Sciences.

Charlotte Friend was born on Houston Street in lower Manhattan and, in fact, lived most of her adult life not far from there, on East 14th Street. Her parents had come to New York from Russia as young adults. When Charlotte, the youngest of three daughters, was three years old and her mother was pregnant with a son, her father died of bacterial endocarditis. The cause of his death probably influenced Charlotte's choice of a career in microbiology. Shortly thereafter, her mother moved the family to Boston Post Road in the Bronx in order to be near *her* mother and the rest of the family. Charlotte often spoke about her large coterie of aunts and uncles; this extended family was clearly very supportive and important to her, both while she was growing up and in her subsequent life.

Charlotte was a graduate of Hunter High School and Hunter College in New York City. She attended college at night while working in a doctor's office during the day. Upon graduation from college, she enlisted in the Navy and was commissioned an ensign in April 1944. She was sent to the naval hospital in Shoemaker, California,

[b] Address correspondence to Dr. Leila Diamond, the Wistar Institute, Thirty-sixth Street at Spruce, Philadelphia, PA 19104-4268.

where, as a lieutenant junior grade, she was second-in-command of the hematology laboratory. Discharged in early 1946, she was admitted to Stanford Medical School but chose instead to attend graduate school at Yale; she received her Ph.D. from Yale in 1950.

Inspired by a 1949 *Time* magazine cover of Cornelius P. Rhoads, the Director of what was then the new Sloan-Kettering Institute, Charlotte wrote to him about the possibility of a postdoctoral position and was hired to work with the virologist, Alice Moore. Rhoads was extremely supportive of the members of his institute, and he and Charlotte developed a strong mutual respect and admiration, particularly after her isolation of what came to be known as the Friend leukemia virus.

With the change in atmosphere at Sloan-Kettering after Rhoads died, Charlotte decided that it was time to move on, In 1966 she accepted a position as Professor and Director of the Center for Experimental Cell Biology at the new medical school at Mt. Sinai Hospital. Peyton Rous, who had been so helpful to her in the period following the discovery of the virus, presented the dedication remarks at the opening ceremony of her new laboratory.

Charlotte won many prizes and awards for her work, including the ultimate recognition by her peers, election to the National Academy of Sciences, in 1976. Perhaps one of the most rewarding of her prizes was the Alfred P. Sloan Award in Cancer Research, in 1962. She chose to use the money for traveling around the world to visit various laboratories, which, she has written, was one of the most important experiences in her life. She said that during that journey she fulfilled her dream of working at the Pasteur Institute, which she had cherished since she was 10 years old.

Charlotte was a very warm and social person as well as a superb scientist. She had many lifelong friends and associates, and a dedicated staff that would have followed her to the ends of the earth. She took an interest in their personal lives—their families, their problems—and was always available to listen. She could frequently be found in the laboratory after six o'clock in the evening doing just that. Within her own family, she was the leader and matriarch, deeply devoted to her siblings and their children, and they to her.

Charlotte was a Renaissance woman who loved the theater, music, opera, reading, and travel. She hated sports, however, and at one point in her education was threatened with not graduating because she refused to learn how to swim. She had a good sense of humor, and one of the droll comments she made during the controversy surrounding her first report of a virus-induced leukemia became a classic. She said words to the effect that those who study the problem of cancer viruses and report positive results are thought to fall into one of two categories—either they have holes in their heads or holes in their filters.

She was a woman of strong convictions and a fighter, with no compunctions about defending ideas and causes in which she believed. She wrote letters to newspapers and spoke up without fear even during the McCarthy and Nixon eras, when doing so could jeopardize one's grants and career. She was a fervent supporter of the women's movement, and in the early 1970's, when every society and organization needed its "instant" woman, she was there. She had been there all the time, but few had called on her to see what she could do. When the calls did come, she undertook them all; during a four-five-year period she worked extremely hard as President of the Harvey Society, the American Association for Cancer Research, and the New York Academy of Sciences.

The lymphoma that was to kill her was first diagnosed in 1981 on her sixtieth birthday. She told very few people and was adamant that others not know. Despite undergoing extensive therapy, she continued to spend time in the lab, to write, to discuss work with colleagues, to send out grant applications and, when necessary, to fight with editors, reviewers, and administrators. Until the end, she did all that was required to see that her department remained viable. One of her last public appearances was at Brandeis University, where she received an honorary doctor of science degree in May 1986. Those who were there have vivid memories of Charlotte sitting in a wheelchair in the broiling sun, chatting with the other honorees and thoroughly enjoying herself.

Charlotte Friend's lifetime of publication spanned a period of 36 years, from 1951 to 1987. Her bibliography of 163[d] items includes 49 abstracts and 113 original papers, reviews, and book chapters. In these days of multiple authorship, it is worth noting that 70 of her publications were authored by her alone or with only one other person. Her thesis work on the effects of salicylates on the solubility of antigen-antibody complexes was published in 1953 in a single paper in the *Journal of Immunology.*[4] She reported that the amounts of immune precipitate formed could be decreased by exposure to salicylates before, during, or after the reaction between circulating antigen and antibody and that salicylates affected the formed complexes whether the antigen was a protein or a polysaccharide.

Even before this paper appeared, Charlotte had begun several interesting lines of investigation after her move to Sloan-Kettering in 1950. Her very first publication was an abstract in the *Federation Proceedings* in 1951.[1] It and the two papers that followed in the *Proceedings of the Society for Experimental Biology and Medicine*[2,3] concerned the effects of a purine analog on the infectivity and tumor-suppressing ability of a virus in culture and in the animal. It is somewhat startling to note the rather primitive techniques in use at the time. Virus inoculation in culture was accomplished by adding to the culture system a suspension of infected mouse brain; tumor cells were added in the form of small tissue cubes; and cell viability was monitored by removing those cubes from the culture and reinoculating them back into mice. The conclusion of those early studies was that the purine analog interfered with a metabolic process related to nucleic acid synthesis which was necessary for virus replication.

Thus, major themes for Charlotte's later work were in place, and during the next few years she explored several diverse paths before finding those which would dominate her work. She returned to the theme of purine and pyrimidine synthesis and metabolism many times: in work with Gabrielle Reem showing that Friend leukemia virus causes an increase in splenic phosphoribosyl transferases that can be inhibited by purine nucleotides *in vivo;*[52,57] in a brief report with Fred Rapp on the use of antinuclear serum to detect and study virus replication in infected cells;[33] in studies with Robert Silber and others on relationships between nucleic acid enzymes and neoplastic cell proliferation;[49] and, of course, much later, in work on the differentiation of Friend erythroleukemia cells.[89,103]

Soon after Cecily Cannon Selby's arrival at Sloan-Kettering in 1950, she and Charlotte started working together, and in 1954 they published a paper with Selby as first author.[6] It was an inconclusive report on the observation of virus-like particles in 4 of 70 samples of Ehrlich mouse ascites tumor cells. The particles were observed in resting, mitotic and degenerating cells, and it was concluded that they were unlikely to be intimately involved in the growth of the tumor but might represent an irregularly appearing mouse infection. They noted that further studies on the identity, incidence, and biological properties of the particles would require fresh tissue specimens known to contain them. Also in 1954, Charlotte reported with Herbert Braunsteiner on the co-incidence of acute viral hepatitis with a transplantable mouse leukemia.[5] They were unable to free the leukemic cells of the virus and suggested that investigation of other

[d]The complete bibliography of Charlotte Friend may be found at the end of this paper.

leukemic lines might reveal the presence of an agent which was sometimes latent in the tumor and sometimes capable of causing acute infectious disease.

In 1955-1956, Charlotte published studies with Felix Wroblewski on the liver enzymes serum glutamic oxaloacetic transaminase and serum glutamic pyruvic transaminase and on their relation to hepatitis and transplantable leukemias in the mouse.[8,13,14] Their observations, that elevation of enzyme levels depends on liver cell injury and virus release and that increases in serum enzymes are also a feature of some human leukemias, are important in clinical medicine today.

In 1957 Charlotte sent to the *Journal of Experimental Medicine* a paper[16] entitled "Cell-free Transmission in Adult Swiss Mice of a Disease Having the Character of a Leukemia." Peyton Rous was editor of the journal at the time, and he and Charlotte had many discussions about what should be included in the paper and how it should be worded. She had prepared cell-free extracts from Ehrlich ascites tumors and had inoculated them into 30 newborn Swiss mice (Ludwig Gross's earlier work had suggested that suckling mice might be more susceptible to oncogenic viruses than adult mice would be). The mice remained healthy over a 14-month period of observation but, when sacrificed, six had enlarged livers and spleens. These enlarged spleens were minced and injected intraperitoneally into adult mi e, because newborns were not immediately available. The paper describes the clinical course and pathological features of the disease produced, its transmission by inoculation of either cell suspensions or cell-free filtrates, and various characteristics of the infectious agent. Charlotte concluded that the disorder was leukemic but not clearly granulocytic or monocytic and that the causal agent had the properties of a virus—later to be known as the Friend leukemia virus. This single paper, only ten pages of text, tables and graphs, was the basis for many scientific careers, in addition to Charlotte Friend's.

The studies that followed the initial observation were perhaps predictable but nonetheless exciting. Electron microscopy was done in collaboration with Etienne de Harven; a preliminary report[18] noted "particles resembling ferritin [that] might suggest a relation with hemoglobin synthesis." Immunological investigation of the virus-host relationship and preparation of a vaccine confirmed that the disease induced by this agent was distinct from other mouse leukemias, the Ehrlich ascites tumor, and human leukemias. It was observed that the tumor cells resembled normal primitive hemopoietic cells and that the virus was sometimes present in non-leukemic cells.[27] In work with Jamil Haddad, Charlotte was able to manipulate the leukemic cells so that transplantable solid tumor masses developed; the tumors resembled reticulum-cell sarcomas.[23]

A series of studies in the latter half of the 1960s with de Harven, Giovanni Rossi, and Cecilia Patuleia revealed that these leukemic cells were able to undergo maturation to erythroid cells. When inoculated into lethally irradiated mice (the spleen-colony assay of Till and McCulloch) or grown in tissue culture, the cells became pleomorphic; some showed erythroid differentiation and hemoglobin was detectable by benzidine staining. In an extraordinarily prescient paper,[48] Patuleia and Friend reported that clonal populations derived from single cell isolates always consisted of primitive stem cells and of erythroblasts at varying stages of maturation. The procedure for cloning the cells which they described in this paper was painstaking and primitive by today's standards; the conclusions were not. The discussion section of that paper includes the comment: "It may be that only stem cells possess the ability to proliferate indefinitely. Other cells in more advanced stages of maturity may have a limited growth potential. This may account for the fact that some single cell isolates had been observed to undergo a number of divisions but did not progress to form clones."

The Friend virus leukemia was now perceived as a disorder resulting from a defect in maturation. These leukemic cells were not subject to control by normal regulators such as erythropoietin or polycythemia. In tissue culture, the tumor cells produced virus with relatively low leukemogenic activity. When others reported that dimethyl sulfoxide (DMSO) increased the infectivity of some viruses, Charlotte attempted to enhance infectivity of Friend virus with DMSO. Thus, serendipity led to the next major step in her career—the discovery that this solvent could induce differentiation of Friend erythroleukemia cells.[67] Her report of the concomitant loss of their malignant potential laid the foundation for a completely new era of experimental work and for the development of novel—and, it is hoped, less toxic—forms of cancer therapy, based on the induction of differentiation.

We have concentrated in this paper on Charlotte Friend's earlier work, but she went on to make many other important contributions. She published a number of papers on the relation of induced differentiation of Friend leukemia cells to normal erythrocyte maturation, on the interactions of co-infecting viruses, and on virus evolution through genetic recombination with endogenous viruses. Many aspects of these studies will be alluded to and expanded upon in the papers in this volume, contributed by the participants in this conference to honor the memory of Charlotte Friend.

The program for the conference is perhaps the best evidence that Charlotte Friend made far-reaching contributions. The outstanding panel of speakers shows that the concepts she helped to evolve are in the forefront of current cancer research and attract the interest and attention of the leading cancer scientists of our time. She would have loved to be at these lectures, sitting up front as usual, and jumping up to ask questions with that great New York accent we remember so well.

BIBLIOGRAPHY OF CHARLOTTE FRIEND, Ph.D.

1. MOORE, A. & C. FRIEND. 1951. Effect of 2,6-diaminopurine on the multiplication of the virus of Russian encephalitis. Fed. Proc. **10:** 365(Abstract).
2. FRIEND, C. 1951. Effect of 2,6-diaminopurine on virus of Russian spring-summer encephalitis in tissue culture. Proc. Soc. Exp. Biol. Med. **78:** 150-153.
3. MOORE, A. & C. FRIEND. 1951. Effect of 2,6-diaminopurine on the course of Russian spring-summer encephalitis infection in the mouse. Proc. Soc. Exp. Biol. Med. **78:** 153-157.
4. FRIEND, C. 1953. A study of the effect of sodium salicylate and some structurally related compounds on antigen-antibody reaction in vitro. J. Immunol. **70:** 141-146.
5. BRAUNSTEINER, H. & C. FRIEND. 1954. Viral hepatitis associated with transplantable mouse leukemia. 1. Acute hepatic manifestations following treatment with urethane or methylformamide. J. Exp. Med. **100:** 665-674.
6. SELBY, C. C., C. E. GREY, S. LICHTENBERG, C. FRIEND, A. MOORE & J. J. BIESELE. 1954. Submicroscopic cytoplasmic particles occasionally found in the Ehrlich mouse ascites tumor. Cancer Res. **14:** 790-794.
7. FRIEND, C. & M. YUCEOGLU. 1955. A study of the effects of urethan and other compounds on a viral hepatitis of mice. Proc. Am. Assoc. Cancer Res. **2:** 18(Abstract).
8. FRIEND, C., F. WROBLEWSKI & J. S. LADUE. 1955. Glutamic-oxaloacetic transaminase activity of serum in mice with viral hepatitis. J. Exp. Med. **102:** 699-704.
9. STERNBERG, S. S. & C. FRIEND. 1955. Pathological study of a transmissable viral hepatitis in mice. *In* Congress (7) International de Pathologie Comparee, Lausanne, May 1955: 25.
10. WROBLEWSKI, F., C. FRIEND, I. NYDICK, P. RUEGSEGGER & J. S. LADUE. 1956. The mechanism and significance of alterations in serum glutamic oxaloacetic and serum glutamic pyruvic transaminase in liver and heart disease. Clin. Res. Proc. **4:** 102(Abstract).
11. FRIEND, C. 1956. The isolation of a virus causing a malignant disease of the hematopoietic system in adult Swiss mice. Proc. Am. Assoc. Cancer Res. **2:** 106(Abstract).

12. FRIEND, C. & M. YUCEOGLU. 1956. The conversion of several lines of transplantable leukemias to their ascitic form. Proc. Am. Assoc. Cancer Res. **2:** 106(Abstract).
13. WROBLEWSKI, F., C. FRIEND, I. NYDICK, P. RUEGSEGGER & J. S. LADUE. 1956. The mechanism and significance of alterations in serum glutamic oxaloacetic and serum glutamic pyruvic transaminase in liver and heart disease. J. Clin. Invest. **35:** 746.
14. FRIEND, C. & F. WROBLEWSKI. 1956. Lactic dehydrogenase activity of serum in mice with transplantable leukemia. Science **124:** 173-174.
15. FRIEND, C. 1957. Immunological studies on a filtrable agent causing a leukemia-like disease in mice. Proc. Am. Assoc. Cancer Res. **2:** 204(Abstract).
16. FRIEND, C. 1957. Cell-free transmission in adult Swiss mice of a disease having the character of a leukemia. J. Exp. Med. **105:** 307-318.
17. FRIEND C. 1957. Leukemia of adult mice caused by a transmissible agent. Ann. N. Y. Acad. Sci. **68:** 522-532.
18. DE HARVEN, E. & C. FRIEND. 1958. Electron microscope study of a cell-free induced leukemia of the mouse: A preliminary report. J. Biophys. Biochem. Cytol. **4:** 151-156.
19. MOORE, A. E. & C. FRIEND. 1958. Attempts at growing the mouse leukemia virus in tissue culture. Proc. Am. Assoc. Cancer Res. **2:** 328(Abstract).
20. FRIEND, C . 1959. Immunological relationships of a filterable agent causing a leukemia in adult mice. 1. The neutralization of infectivity by specific antiserum. J. Exp. Med. **10:** 217-221.
21. FRIEND, C. & J. HADDAD. 1959. Tumor formation with transplants of spleen or liver of mice with a virus-induced leukemia. Proc. Am. Assoc. Cancer Res. **3:** 21(Abstract).
22. FRIEND C., G. DIMAYORCA, & A. BENDICH. 1959. Studies on the nature and purification of the leukemia agent of Swiss mice. Fed. Proc. **18:** 567(Abstract)
23. FRIEND, C. & J. R. HADDAD. 1960. Tumor formation with transplants of spleen or liver from mice with virus-induced leukemia. J. Natl. Cancer Inst. **25:** 1279-1289.
24. DIMAYORCA, G., B. D . EDDY, S. E. STEWART, W. S . HUNTER, C. FRIEND & A. BENDICH. 1959. Isolation of infectious deoxyribonucleic acid from SE polyoma-infected tissue cultures. Proc. Natl. Acad. Sci. USA **45:** 1805-1808.
25. FRIEND, C., J. E. ULTMANN & P. FEIGELSON, Discussants; A. GELLHORN, Moderator. 1960. The lymphomas: Combined clinic at the College of Physicians and Surgeons, Columbia University, New York City. Ann. Intern. Med. **52:** 201.
26. DE HARVEN, E. & C. FRIEND. 1960. Electron microscopy of Swiss mouse leukemia virus (Presented at Symposium on Phenomena of the Tumor Viruses, New York City, March 1960). Natl. Cancer Inst. Monogr. **4:** 291-311.
27. DE HARVEN, E. & C. FRIEND. 1960. Further electron microscope studies of a mouse leukemia induced by cell-free filtrates. J. Biophys. Biochem. Cytol. **7:** 747-752.
28. FRIEND, C. 1960. Immunological studies on the leukemia agent of Swiss mice. Acta Union Int. Contre Le Cancer **5:** 1171.
29. FRIEND, C. 1960. Experimental studies on a virus-induced leukemia of mice. *In* Proceedings of the Seventh International Congress of Hematology, Tokyo, Japan: 410-415. Pan Pacific Press.
30. FRIEND, C., V. DARCHUN, E. DE HARVEN & J. R. HADDAD. 1961. The incidence and classification of spontaneous malignant diseases of the hematopoietic system in Swiss mice. Proc. Am. Assoc. Cancer Res. **3:** 227(Abstract).
31. FRIEND, C. 1962. Cancer et virus. Nouv. Rev. Fr. Hematol. **2:** 337-339.
32. FRIEND, C., V. DARCHUN, E. DE HARVEN, & J. R. HADDAD. 1962. The incidence and classification of spontaneous malignant diseases of the hematopoietic system in Swiss mice. *In* Tumour Viruses of Murine Origin. Ciba Symp. (J & A Churchill, Ltd.): 193-213.
33. RAPP. F. & C. FRIEND. 1962. Detection of cytoplasmic deoxyribonucleic acid and nucleoproteins with antinuclear serum. Virology **17:** 497-499.
34. DE HARVEN, E. & C. FRIEND. 1962. Electron microscope studies on mouse lymphomas (Abstract). *In* Fifth International Congress for Electron Microscopy, Philadelphia, PA. Academic Press. New York.
35. FRIEND, C., E. DE HARVEN & J. R. HADDAD. 1962. Pathogenesis and cytology of several lines of malignant lymphomas of mice. *In* Eighth International Cancer Congress, Moscow, USSR: 71(Abstract) Medgiz Pub. House.

36. FRIEND, C., E. DE HARVEN & J. R. HADDAD. 1962. Early detection and localization of Swiss mouse leukaemia virus. *In* Eighth International Cancer Congress, Moscow, USSR: 71(Abstract) Medgiz Pub. House.
37. FRIEND, C. 1963. Viruses and Cancer. Acta Union Int. Cancer **19:** 239-242.
38. FRIEND, C., E. DE HARVEN & J. R. HADDAD. 1963. Studies on several lines of murine lymphomas associated with intracytoplasmic particles. Acta Union Int. Cancer **19:** 344-347.
39. RAPP, F. & C. FRIEND. 1963. Early detection and localization of Swiss mouse leukemia virus. Acta Union Int. Cancer **19:** 348-350.
40. DE HARVEN, E. & C. FRIEND. 1964. Structure of virus particles partially purified from the blood of leukemic mice. Virology **23:** 119-124.
41. SILBER, R., R. P. COX, J. R. HADDAD & C. FRIEND. 1964. Enzyme studies in virus-induced neoplasms. 1. The effect of a murine leukemia on enzymes of one-carbon metabolism and on phosphomonoesterases. Cancer Res. **24:** 1892-1897.
42. FRIEND, C.. 1966. Immunologic relationships among some f the murine leukemia viruses. *In* Viruses Inducing Cancer. W. J. Burdette, Ed.: 51-60. Univ. of Utah Press.
43. FRIEND, C., M. C. PATULEIA & E. DE HARVEN. 1966. Erythrocytic maturation in vitro of murine (Friend) virus-induced leukemic cells. Natl. Cancer Inst. Monogr. **22:** 505-522.
44. DE HARVEN, E. & C. FRIEND. 1966. Origin of the viremia in murine leukemia. Natl. Cancer Inst. Monogr. **22:** 79-105.
45. FRIEND, C. & G. B . ROSSI. 1966. Erythropoietic activity in spleen colonies resulting from the inoculation of virus (Friend) -induced leukemic cells in mice. Proc. Am. Assoc. Cancer Res. **7:** 22(Abstract).
46. FRIEND, C., C. PATULEIA, G. B . ROSSI & E. DE HARVEN. 1966. Tissue culture lines of murine virus-induced (Friend) leukemic cells exhibiting erythrocytic maturation: Immunologic and histopathologic studies. *In* Ninth International Cancer Congress, Tokyo, Japan, October 1966: 23-29(Abstract).
47. FRIEND, C., M. C. PATULEIA, & J. B. NELSON. 1966. Antibiotic effect of tylosin on a mycoplasma contaminant in a tissue culture leukemia cell line. Proc. Soc. Exp. Biol. Med. **121:** 1009-1010.
48. PATULEIA, M. C. & C. FRIEND. 1967. Tissue culture studies on murine virus-induced leukemia cells: Isolation of single cells in agar-liquid medium. Cancer Res. **27:** 726-730.
49. SILBER, R., B. GOLDSTEIN, E. BERMAN, J. DECTER & C. FRIEND. 1967. The effect of a murine leukemia virus on RNA metabolism. Cancer Res. **27:** 1264-1269.
50. FRIEND, C., G. B. ROSSI, M. C. PATULEIA, & E. DE HARVEN. 1967. The cloning of tissue culture lines of murine virus-induced (Friend) leukemic cells. *In* International Symposium on Tumor Viruses: Subviral Carcinogenesis, Nagoya, Japan. Y. Ito, Ed.: 408-413.
51. ROSSI, G. B . & C. FRIEND. 1967. Inhibition of spleen colony formation of cultured leukemic cells in mice immunized with Friend virus. Fed. Proc. **26:** 314(Abstract).
52. REEM, G. & C. FRIEND. 1967. Phosphoribosylamidotransferase: Regulation of activity in virus-induced murine leukemia by purine nucleotides. Science **157:** 1203-1204.
53. ROSSI, G. B. & C. FRIEND. 1967. Erythrocytic maturation of (Friend) virus-induced leukemic cells in spleen clones. Proc. Natl. Acad. Sci. USA **58:** 1373-1380.
54. TKACZEVSKI, L., E. DE HARVEN & C. FRIEND. 1968. Structure and leukemogenic activity of a murine leukemia virus. J. Virol. **2:** 365-375.
55. ROSSI, G. B. & C. FRIEND. 1968. Further studies on the characteristics of spleen colonies formed by murine virus-induced leukemic cells. Proc. Am. Assoc. Canc. Res. **9:** 61(Abstract).
56. FRIEND, C. & G. B. ROSSI. 1968. Transplantation immunity and the suppression of spleen colony formation by immunization with murine leukemia virus preparations (Friend). Int. J. Cancer **3:** 523-529.
57. REEM, G. & C. FRIEND. 1969. Properties of 5′ phosphoribosylpyrophosphate amidotransferase in virus-induced murine leukemia. Biochim. Biophys. Acta **171:** 58-66.
58. FRIEND, C. & G. B . ROSSI. 1969. The phenomenon of differentiation in murine virus-induced leukemic cells. *In* Canadian Cancer Conferences J. F. Morgan, Ed. Vol. **8:** 171-182. Oxford, Pergamon Press. Toronto.

59. Friend, C., W. Scher & G. B . Rossi. 1969. Studies on the erythropoietic activity of murine virus-induced leukemic cells cloned *in vitro.* Proc. Am. Assoc. Cancer Res. **10:** 27(Abstract).
60. Friend, C., W. Scher & G. B. Rossi. 1970. The biosynthesis of heme in Friend virus-induced leukemic cell lines cloned *in vitro. In* The Biology of Large RNA Viruses. B. W. J. Mahy & R. Barry, Eds.: 267-275. Academic Press. London.
61. Rossi, G. B. & C. Friend. 1970. Failure to induce lymphomas in mice following the induction of a graft-versus-host reaction. Science **167:** 1383-1385.
62. Rossi, G. B., G. Cudkowicz & C. Friend. 1970. Evidence for transformation of spleen cells one day after infection of mice with Friend leukemia virus: Autonomous growth potential and expression of hybrid resistance genes. J. Exp. Med. **131:** 765-781.
63. Rossi, G. B. & C. Friend. 1970. Further studies on the biological properties of Friend virus-induced leukemic cells differentiating along the erythrocytic pathway. J. Cell. Physiol. **76:** 159-166.
64. de Harven, E., G. Rossi, J. Haddad & C. Friend. 1970. Studies on viremia (FLV) in lethally irradiated mice with or without hematopoietic reconstitution. Proc. Am. Assoc. Cancer Res. **11:** 76(Abstract).
65. Rossi, G. B., G. Cudkowicz & C. Friend. 1970. Early transformation of spleen cells by Friend virus: Enhanced expression of hybrid resistance genes and autonomous growth. Proc. Am. Assoc. Cancer Res. **11:** 268(Abstract).
66. Scher, W., J. G. Holland & C. Friend. 1971. Hemoglobin synthesis in murine virus-induced leukemic cells in vitro: Partial purification and identification of hemoglobins. Blood **37:** 428-437.
67. Friend, C., W. Scher, J. G. Holland & T. Sato. 1971. Hemoglobin synthesis in murine virus-induced leukemic cells in vitro: Stimulation of erythroid differentiation by dimethyl sulfoxide. Proc. Natl. Acad. Sci. USA **68:** 378-382.
68. Rossi, G. B., E. de Harven, J. R. Haddad & C. Friend. 1971. Studies on Friend virus-induced viremia in lethally irradiated mice with or without hematopoietic repopulation. Int. J. Cancer **7:** 303-312.
69. Goldfeder, A., E. de Harven & C. Friend. 1971. Studies on mice of a tumor resistant strain (X/Gf). VIII. Type C particles in mammary tumors of Friend leukemia virus-infected mice. Eur. J. Clin. Biol. Res. **16:** 323-328.
70. Gabelman, N., W. Scher & C . Friend. 1971. Biochemical studies on Friend leukemia virus-infected mouse embryo fibroblasts. Fed. Proc. **30:** 302(Abstract).
71. Sato, T., E. de Harven & C. Friend. 1971. An electron microscopic study of the in vitro effects of dimethyl sulfoxide (DMSO) on Friend leukemia cells. Fed. Proc. **30:** 513(Abstract).
72. Sato, T., C . Friend & E . de Harven. 1971. Ultrastructural changes in Friend erythroleukemia cells treated with dimethyl sulfoxide (DMSO). Cancer Res. **31:** 1402-1417.
73. Rossi, G. B., G. Cudkowicz & C. Friend. 1971. Requirement of live Friend leukemia virus for enhanced expression of hybrid histocompatibility genes. Proc. Soc. Exp. Biol. Med. **138:** 783-785.
74. Cudkowicz, G., G. B. Rossi, J. R. Haddad & C. Friend. 1972. Hybrid resistance to parental DBA/2 grafts: Independence from the H-2 locus. II. Studies with Friend virus-induced leukemia cells. J. Natl. Cancer Inst. **48:** 997-1003.
75. Scher, W., H. D. Preisler & C. Friend. 1972. Inhibition by bromodeoxyuridine (BUdR) of dimethyl sulfoxide (DMSO)-stimulated erythroid differentiation and hemoglobin synthesis in murine virus-induced leukemic cells. Proc. Am. Assoc. Cancer Res. **13:** 105(Abstract).
76. Sato, T., E. de Harven & C. Friend. 1972. Electron microscopic study of Friend leukemia virus (FLV) exposed to specific antiserum. Proc. Am. Assoc. Cancer Res. **13:** 111(Abstract).
77. Friend, C., W. Scher, H. D. Preisler & J. G . Holland. 1973. Studies on erythroid differentiation of Friend virus-induced murine leukemic cells. *In* Unifying Concepts of Leukemia: Proceedings of the Fifth International Symposium on Comparative Leukemia Research, Padova/Venice, 1971. R. M. Dutcher & L. Chieco-Bianchi, Eds. Bibl. Haematol. Basel No. 39: 916-922. Karger. Basel.

77a. PREISLER, H. D., C. FRIEND & W. SCHER. 1972. Patterns of polyribosomes and polysome-associated RNA of Friend leukemic cells (FLC) during DMSO-induced differentiation in vitro (Abstract). *In* American Society of Hematology Meeting, Proceedings, Hollywood, Fla., Dec. 3-6, 1972.

78. BOYER, S. H., K. D. WUU, A. N. NOYES, R. YOUNG, W. SCHER, C. FRIEND, H. D. PREISLER & A. BANK. 1972. Hemoglobin biosynthesis in murine virus-induced leukemic cells in vitro: Structure and amounts of globin chains produced. Blood **40:** 823-835.

79. SATO, T., E. DE HARVEN, C. FRIEND, W. SCHER & H. D. PREISLER. 1972. Ultrastructural changes in Friend leukemia cells after dimethyl sulfoxide (DMSO), dimethyl formamide (DMF), or 5-bromo-2′-deoxyuridine (BUdR) treatment in vitro. *In* Proceedings of the Electron Microscopy Society of America and the First Pacific Regional Conference on Electron Microscopy, Thirtieth Annual Meeting, Los Angeles, CA. C. J. Arceneaux, Ed.: 70(Abstract).

80. SATO., T., C. C. FRIEND. STACKPOLE & E. DE HARVEN. 1972. Coating of Friend leukemia virus after treatment with specific antiserum. Cancer Res. **32:** 2670-2678.

81. SCHER, W., H. D. PREISLER & C. FRIEND. 1973. Hemoglobin synthesis in murine virus-induced leukemic cells in vitro: III. Effects of 5-bromo-2′-deoxyuridine, dimethylformamide and dimethylsulfoxide. J. Cell. Physiol. **81:** 63-70.

82. PREISLER, H. D., W. SCHER & C. FRIEND. 1973. Polyribosome profiles and polyribosome-associated RNA of Friend leukemia cells following DMSO-induced differentiation. Differentiation **1:** 27-37.

83. ROSSI, G. B. G. CUDKOWICZ & C. FRIEND. 1973. Transformation of spleen cells three hours after infection in vivo with Friend leukemia virus. J. Natl. Cancer Inst. **50:** 249-254.

84. FRIEND, C. 1973. Immunologic studies with leukemogenic and non-leukemogenic strains of murine leukemia virus (FLV). *In* Virus Tumorigenesis and Immunogenesis. W. Ceglowski & H. Friedman, Eds.: 387-391. Academic Press. New York.

85. DE HARVEN, E., N. LAMPEN, T. SATO & C. FRIEND. 1973. Scanning electron microscopy of cells infected with a murine leukemia virus. Virology **51:** 240-243.

86. GABELMAN, N. W. SCHER & C. FRIEND. 1973. The infectivity and leukemogenicity of Friend leukemia virus (FLV) passaged in tissue culture. Fed. Proc. **32:** 1020(Abstract).

87. FRIEND, C., H. D. PREISLER & W. SCHER. 1973. Erythroid differentiation of murine virus-induced leukemic cells. In Vitro **8:** 399(Abstract).

88. FRIEND, C., H. D. PREISLER & W. SCHER. 1974. Studies on the control of differentiation of murine virus-induced erythroleukemic cells. *In* Current Topics in Developmental Biology. A. Monroy A. A. Moscona, Eds.: 81-101. Academic Press. New York.

89. PREISLER, H. D., D. HOUSMAN, W. SCHER & C. FRIEND. 1973. The effects of 5-bromo-2′-deoxyuridine on the production of globin mRNA in dimethyl sulfoxide-stimulated Friend leukemia cells. Proc. Natl. Acad. Sci. USA **70:** 2956-2959.

90. LEVY, S. B., M. TAVASSOLI & C. FRIEND. 1973. Prolonged survival of Friend leukemic mice following splenic auto-implantation. *In* American Society of Hematology Meeting, Proceedings, Chicago, Ill., Dec. 1-3, 1973. Blood **40:** 1014(Abstract).

91. GABELMAN, N., W. SCHER & C. FRIEND. 1974. Alterations in macromolecular synthesis and cellular growth in mouse embryo fibroblasts infected with Friend leukemia virus. Int. J. Cancer **13:** 343-352.

92. SATO, T., E. DE HARVEN & C. FRIEND. 1973. Increased virus budding from Friend erythroleukemic cells treated with dimethyl sulfoxide, dimethyl formamide and/or bromodeoxyuridine in vitro. *In* Comparative Leukemia Research, 1973: Leukemogenesis. Proceedings of the Sixth International Symposium on Comparative Leukemia Research, Nagoya/Ise-Shima, Japan, 1973. Y. Ito & R. M. Dutcher, Eds.: 143-151. Univ. of Tokyo Press.

93. FRIEND, C., H. PREISLER & W. SCHER. 1974. Hemoglobin biosynthesis in murine virus-induced leukemic cells in vitro. *In* Conference on Hemoglobins: Comparative Molecular Biology Models for the Study of Disease. H. Kitchen & S. H. Boyer, Eds. Ann. N. Y. Acad. Sci. **241:** 582-588.

94. FRIEND, C. & W. SCHER. 1975. Stimulation by dimethyl sulfoxide of erythroid differentiation and hemoglobin synthesis in murine virus-induced leukemic cells. *In* Confer-

ence on the Biological Actions of Dimethyl Sulfoxide. S. W. Jacob & R. Herschler, Eds. **243:** 155-163.
95. FOURCADE, A., C. FRIEND, F. LACOUR & J. G. HOLLAND. 1974. Protective effect of immunization with poly I·poly C—MBSA against Friend leukemia virus (FLV) in mice. Cancer Res. **34:** 1749-1751.
96. FRIEND, C. & W. SCHER. 1974. Erythroid cell differentiation of murine erythroleukemia (Abstract). *In* Fifteenth Congress of the International Society of Hematology, Proceedings, Jerusalem, Sept. 1-6, 1974.
97. MAROVITZ, W. & C. FRIEND. 1974. Fine structure of cells of established lines of Hodgkin's disease (Abstract). *In* Conference on Tumor Viruses—Human Tumors, Proceedings, Munich, 1974.
98. REEM, G. H. & C. FRIEND. 1975. Purine metabolism in murine virus-induced erythroleukemic cells during differentiation in vitro. Proc. Natl. Acad. Sci. USA **72:** 1630-1634.
99. TSUEI, D. & C. FRIEND. 1975. Comparison of biochemical and biological properties of three strains of Friend leukemia virus (FLV). (Abstract). *In* Seventy-fifth Meeting of the American Society for Microbiology, Proceedings, New York.
100. GOLDE, D. W., A. FAILLE, A. SULLIVAN & C. FRIEND. 1975. Leukocytic differentiation in Friend leukemia induced by colony-stimulating activity. Proc. Am. Assoc. Cancer Res. **16:** 13(Abstract).
101. GOLDE, D. W., A. FAILLE, A. SULLIVAN & C. FRIEND. 1976. Granulocytic stem cells in Friend leukemia. Cancer Res. **36:** 115-119.
102. DARZYNKIEWICZ, Z., F. TRAGANOS, T. SHARPLESS, C. FRIEND & M. R. MELAMED. 1976. Nuclear chromatin changes during erythroid differentiation of Friend virus-induced leukemic cells. Exp. Cell Res. **99:** 301-309.
103. REEM, G. H. & C. FRIEND. 1976. Purine and phosphoribosylpyrophosphate synthesis in differentiating murine virus-induced erythroleukemic cells in vitro. J. Cell. Physiol. **88:** 193-196.
104. LEVY, S. B., C. B. RUBENSTEIN & C. FRIEND. 1976. The spleen in Friend leukemia. 1. Prolonged survival of mice with Friend leukemia following autoimplantation of splenic tissue. J. Natl. Cancer Inst. **56:** 1183-1188.
105. GOLDE, D. W., C. FRIEND & M. J. CLINE. 1975. Induction of leukopoietic stem cell proliferation and differentiation in spleen cultures of normal and Friend leukemia virus-infected mice (Abstract). *In* International Society of Differentiation, Proceedings of Meeting, Copenhagen, Denmark, Sept. 1975.
106. TSUEI, D., C. FRIEND & W. SCHER. 1976. Production of virus in Friend leukemia (FL) cells in vitro. *In* Seventy-sixth Meeting of the American Society for Microbiology, Proceedings, Atlantic City 1976: 241(Abstract).
107. GOLDE, D. W. & C. FRIEND. 1976. Induction of leukopoietic stem cell proliferation and differentiation in spleen cultures of normal and Friend leukemia virus-infected mice. *In* Progress in Differentiation Research. N. Muller-Berat, *et al.*, Eds.: 513-520. North-Holland Pub. Co. Amsterdam.
108. TSUEI, D. & C. FRIEND. 1976. Synthesis of virus in Friend leukemia cells in vitro. *In* Cold Spring Harbor Meeting on RNA Tumor Viruses, May 1976, Collected Abstracts: 17(Abstract).
109. TSUEI, D., H. HAUBENSTOCK & C. FRIEND. 1977. Virus production and erythroid differentiation in Friend erythroleukemia cells. In Vitro **13:** 148(Abstract).
110. FRIEND, C. 1977. The coming of age of tumor virology. Cancer Res. **37:** 1255-1263.
111. REEM, G. & C. FRIEND. 1977. Stability of the azaguanine resistant phenotype in vivo. *In* Purine Metabolism in Man. Muller, *et al.*, Eds.: 181-185. Plenum Press. New York.
112. FRIEND, C. 1978. The phenomenon of differentiation in murine erythroleukemic cells. *In* The Harvey Lectures. Vol. 72: 253-281. Academic Press. New York.
113. STERN, R. H., S. H. BOYER, J.-F. CONSCIENCE, C. FRIEND, L. MARGOLET, R. E. TASHIAN & F. H. RUDDLE. 1977. Carbonic anhydrase isozymes in cultured Friend leukemic cells. Proc. Soc. Exp. Biol. Med. **156:** 52-55.
114. FRIEND, C. & H. A. FREEDMAN. 1978. Effects and possible mechanism of action of dimethyl sulfoxide (DMSO) on Friend cell differentiation. Biochem. Pharmacol. **27:** 1309-1314.

115. SCHER, W. & C. FRIEND. 1978. Breakage of DNA and alterations in folded genomes by inducers of differentiation in Friend erythroleukemic cells. Cancer Res. **38:** 841-849.
116. SCHER, W., J. PARKES & C. FRIEND. 1977. Increased carbonic anhydrase activity in Friend erythroleukemia cells during DMSO-stimulated erythroid differentiation and its inhibition by BrdU. Cell Differ. **6:** 285-296.
117. FRIEND, C., W. SCHER, D. TSUEI, J. HADDAD, J. G. HOLLAND, N. SZRAJER & H. HAUBENSTOCK. 1979. Perspectives on Friend leukemia virus: Pathogenesis in vivo and studies on the control of erythrodifferentiation in vitro. *In* Oncogenic Viruses and Host Cell Genes, Oji International Seminar on Friend Virus and Friend Cells. Y. Ikawa, Ed.: 279-301. Academic Press. San Francisco.
118. FRIEND, C., W. MAROVITZ, G. HENLE, W. HENLE, D. TSUEI, K. HIRSCHHORN, J. G. HOLLAND & J. CUTTNER. 1978. Observations on cell lines derived from a patient with Hodgkin's disease. Cancer Res. **38:** 2581-2591.
119. HAREL, L., F. LACOUR, T. HUYN, M. SEMMEL & C. FRIEND. 1978. Early inhibition of phospholipid synthesis in dimethyl sulfoxide (DMSO)-treated Friend erythroleukemic (FL) cells. Proc. Am. Assoc. Cancer Res. **19:** 59(Abstract).
120. SCHER, W. & C. FRIEND. 1978. Inhibition of DMSO-stimulated differentiation of Friend leukemia cells by lysosome stabilizing agents. Proc. Am. Assoc. Cancer Res. **19:** 174(Abstract).
121. SCHER, W., D. TSUEI, S. SASSA, P. PRICE, N. GABELMAN & C. FRIEND. 1978. Inhibition of DMSO-stimulated Friend cell erythroidifferentiation by hydrocortisone and other steroids. Proc. Natl. Acad. Sci. USA **75:** 3851-3855.
122. SCHER W., D. TSUEI, S. SASSA, P. M. PRICE & C. FRIEND. 1978. Inhibition by hydrocortisone of heme, hemoglobin and virus synthesis in dimethyl sulfoxide-stimulated Friend leukemia (FL) cells. J. Supramol. Struct. (Suppl. 2): 170(Abstract).
123. TSUEI, D., J.-F. CONSCIENCE, C. FRIEND. & F. H. RUDDLE. 1979. Co-suppression of virus production and erythroid differentiation in Friend erythroleukemic cell × non-erythroid mouse cell hybrids. Proc. Soc. Exp. Biol. Med. **160:** 164-167.
124. HAREL, L., F. LACOUR, C. FRIEND., P. DURBIN & M. SEMMEL. 1979. Early inhibition of phospholipid synthesis in dimethyl sulfoxide (DMSO) treated Friend erythroleukemic (FL) cells. J. Cell. Physiol. **101:** 25-32.
125. REVOLTELLA, R., L. BERTOLINI & C. FRIEND. 1979. In vitro transformation of mouse bone marrow cells by the polycythemic strain of Friend leukemia virus. Proc. Natl. Acad. Sci. USA **76:** 1464-1468.
126. GOLDE, D. W., N. BERSCH, C. FRIEND., D. TSUEI & W. MAROVITZ. 1979. Transformation of DBA/2 fetal liver cells infected in vitro by the anemic strain of FLV. Proc. Natl. Acad. Sci. USA **76:** 962-966.
127. TSUEI, D., H. HAUBENSTOCK, R. REVOLTELLA & C. FRIEND. 1979. Virus production and hemoglobin synthesis in variant lines of DMSO-treated Friend erythroleukemia (FL) cells. J. Virol. **31:** 178-183.
128. FRIEND, C. 1980. The regulation of differentiation in murine virus-induced erythroleukemia cells. *In* Differentiation and Neoplasia. R. G. McKinnell, M. A. DiBerardino, M. Blomenfeld & R. D. Bergad, Eds.: 202-212. Springer-Verlag. New York.
129. NAHON-MERLIN, E., F. LACOUR, C. FRIEND. & R. REVOLTELLA. 1979. Protective effect of immunization with non-viral antigens against Friend leukemia virus in mice. Proc. Natl. Acad. Sci. USA **76:** 2018-2021.
130. LACOUR, F., L. HAREL, C. FRIEND. & T. HUYNH. 1979. Induction of differentiation of erythroleukemic cells by aminonucleoside of puromycin (AMS) and its inhibition by inosine. Proc. Am. Assoc. Cancer Res. **20:** 272(Abstract).
131. GAZITT, Y. & C. FRIEND. 1979. Synthesis and accumulation of plasma membrane proteins in differentiating Friend erythroleukemia cells. Proc. Am. Assoc. Cancer Res. **20:** 273(Abstract).
132. SCHER, W., D. TSUEI & C. FRIEND. 1979. Steroids that stimulate maturation of myeloid leukemia cells inhibit DMSO-stimulated maturation of erythroleukemia cells. Proc. Am. Assoc. Cancer Res. **20:** 250(Abstract).
133. GOLDE, D., N. BERSCH, M. E. LIPPMAN & C. FRIEND. 1979. Detection of glucocorticoid receptors on Friend erythroleukemia cells. Proc. Natl. Acad. Sci. USA **76:** 3515-3517.

134. GAZITT, Y. & C. FRIEND. 1980. The possible role of polyamine biosynthetic enzymes in the induction of differentiation in Friend erythroleukemia cells. *In* In Vivo and In Vitro Erythropoiesis: The Friend System. G. B. Rossi, Ed.: 209-218. Elsevier/North Holland. Amsterdam.

135. LACOUR, F., L. HAREL, C. FRIEND., T. HUYNH & J. G. HOLLAND. 1980. Induction of differentiation of murine erythroleukemia cells by aminonucleoside of puromycin and its inhibition by purines and purine derivatives. Proc. Natl. Acad. Sci. USA **77:** 2740-2742.

136. GAZITT, Y. & C. FRIEND. 1980. Polyamine biosynthesis enzymes in the induction of FL cell differentiation. Cancer Res. **40:** 1727-1732.

137. TSUEI, D., B. G.-T. POGO & C. FRIEND. 1980. Properties of virus released from different cell lines transformed in vitro by Friend leukemia virus—anemic strain. *In* Proceedings of the Eightieth Annual Meeting of the American Society for Microbiology: 269(Abstract).

138. SCHER, W., D. TSUEI & C. FRIEND. 1980. The structural basis for steroid modulation of DMSO-stimulated erythrodifferentiation. Leuk. Res. **4:** 217-229.

139. BERTOLINI, L., D. TSUEI, J. G. HOLLAND & C. FRIEND. 1981. Variations in the response of cloned murine Friend erythroleukemia cells to different inducers. In Vitro **17:** 284-289.

140. TSUEI, D., B. G.-T. POGO & C. FRIEND. 1980. Variations in properties of virus released from morphologically different cell lines transformed in vitro by Friend leukemia virus. Proc. Natl. Acad. Sci. USA **77:** 5769-5773.

141. FRIEND, C. 1981. Murine virus-induced erythroleukemic cell lines. *In* Functionally Differentiated Cell Lines. G. Sato, Ed.: 235-249. Alan R. Liss, Inc. New York.

142. BERTOLINI, L., R. REVOLTELLA, M. BENDINELLI & C. FRIEND. 1981. Lack of correlation between in vivo and in vitro assays for the detection of virus released from clones of Friend erythroleukemia cells. Int. J. Cancer **27:** 67-72.

143. GAZITT, Y. & C. FRIEND. 1981. Synthesis and phosphorylation of plasma membrane proteins of Friend erythroleukemia cells induced to differentiate. Cancer Res. **41:** 1064-1069.

144. GAZITT, Y. & C. FRIEND. 1981. Early and late changes in the glycoproteins of Friend erythroleukemia cells induced to differentiate. Cancer Res. **41:** 1070-1075.

145. HAREL, L. C. BLAT, F. LACOUR & C. FRIEND. 1981. Altered RNA/protein ratio associated with the induction of differentiation of Friend erythroleukemia cells. Proc. Natl. Acad. Sci. USA **78:** 3882-3886.

146. STRINGER, E. A. & C. FRIEND. 1981. Translational control of protein synthesis in differentiating Friend erythroleukemia cells. Fed. Proc. **40**(6): 1749(Abstract #1209).

147. STRINGER, E. A. & C. FRIEND. 1982. Control of gene expression in Friend erythroleukemia cells induced to differentiate. *In* Expression of Differentiated Functions in Cancer Cells. R. P. Revoltella, G. M. Pontiera, C. Basilico, G. Rovera, R. C. Gallo & J. H. Subak-Sharpe, Eds.: 275-284. Raven Press. New York.

148. HAREL, L., C. GLAT, F. LACOUR, T. HUYN & C. FRIEND. 1982. Common mode of action of different inducers of FL cell differentiation. *In* Expression of Differentiated Functions in Cancer Cells. R. P. Revoltella, G. M. Pontiera, C. Basilico, G. Rovera, R. C. Gallo & J. H. Subak-Sharpe, Eds.: 509-512. Raven Press. New York.

149. ALTER, B. P., A. S. CAMPBELL & C. FRIEND. 1981. Increased mouse minor hemoglobin in vivo and in vitro: A model for hemoglobin regulation. Blood **58**(Suppl. 1): 66a(Abstract #174).

150. STRINGER, E. A. & C. FRIEND. 1982. Hemin-dependent control of globin synthesis in Friend erythroleukemia cells induced to differentiate. Proc. Natl. Acad. Sci. USA **79:** 1839-1843.

151. POGO, G. G.-T. & C. FRIEND. 1982. Persistent infection of Friend erythroleukemia cells with vaccinia virus. Proc. Natl. Acad. Sci. USA **79:** 4805-4809.

152. ALTER, B. P., A. S. CAMPBELL, J. G. HOLLAND & C. FRIEND. 1982. Increased mouse minor hemoglobin during erythroid stress: A model for hemoglobin regulation. Exp. Hematol. **10:** 754-760.

153. FRIEND, C., B. G.-T. POGO & J. G. HOLLAND. Properties of a leukemogenic virus synthesized by a new hematopoietic cell line derived from the spleen of a mouse infected

with the anemic strain of Friend leukemia virus (FLV-A). *In* Gene Expression and Cell Differentiation, R. Revoltella, Ed. Alan R. Liss, Inc. New York.

154. FRIEND, C., B. G.-T. POGO & J. G. HOLLAND. 1984. Characterization of leukemogenic virus produced by a new line of FLV-A transformed cells. Proc. Natl. Acad. Sci. USA **81:** 1831-1834.

155. BROWN, E. & C. FRIEND. 1984. Endogenous viral DNA sequences in normal murine cells are amplified in Friend leukemia virus (FLV)-transformed cells. Proc. Am. Assoc. Cancer Res. **25:** 389(Abstract).

156. BROWN, E., M. ZAJAC-KAYE, B. G.-T. POGO & C. FRIEND. 1985. Rat cells infected with anemia-inducing Friend leukemia virus contain integrated replication competent but not defective proviral genomes. Proc. Natl. Acad. Sci. USA **82:** 5925-5929.

157. FRIEND, C. & B.G-T. POGO. 1985. The molecular pathology of Friend erythroleukemia virus strains: An overview. Biochem. Biophys. **780:** 181-195.

158. OBOM, K., S. W. POPPLE, J. G. HOLLAND, B. G.-T. POGO & C. FRIEND. 1986. Vaccinia virus DNA sequences in the nucleus of persistently infected Friend erythroleukemia cells. Virus Res. **5:** 221-234.

159. FRIEND, C., M. ZAJAC-KAYE, J. G. HOLLAND & B. G.-T. POGO. 1987. Recent studies on the mechanism of induction of differentiation in murine erythroleukemia cells. Haematologica (Pavia) **72**(6 Suppl): 75.

160. ZAJAC-KAYE, M., E. BROWN & C. FRIEND. 1986. Induction of differentiation in Friend erythroleukemia cells with dimethyl sulfoxide, hexamethylene bisacetamide and sodium butyrate not accompanied by changes in proviral DNA or its expression. Virus Res. **6:** 45-55.

161. FRIEND, C., M. ZAJAC-KAYE, J. G. HOLLAND & B. G.-T. POGO. 1987. Depletion of sodium butyrate from cultures of Friend erythroleukemia cells undergoing differentiation. Cancer Res. **47:** 378-382.

162. POGO, B. G.-T., A. C.-K. LAI, J. G. HOLLAND & C. FRIEND. 1988. Differences in the susceptibility of human blood cell lines to vaccinia virus. Intervirology **29:** 11-20.

PART I. RETROVIRUSES

Genetic Basis of Disease Specificity of Nondefective Friend Murine Leukemia Virus

NANCY HOPKINS

Biology Department and
Center for Cancer Research
Massachusetts Institute of Technology
77 Massachusetts Avenue
Cambridge, Massachusetts 02139

I met Charlotte Friend just once. Sometimes it's intimidating to finally meet a scientist one has respected greatly from afar. Perhaps it's the fear that such a person will have no interest in you, or, worse, that he or she will turn out not to be as impressive as the work one has so long admired. Neither was the case with Dr. Friend. In the course of our meeting it was a pleasure to see so clearly and so quickly that Dr. Friend's revolutionary discoveries were no accident but the work of a brilliant and imaginative mind. On the personal level I had no doubt that we would become close colleagues and friends. Here I was wrong. Not long after our meeting I read of Dr. Friend's death in the *New York Times.* I still regret the loss of the friendship I had anticipated and also the missed opportunity to tell Charlotte Friend how much her courageous and independent life has meant to me.

◇

My laboratory is interested in the process by which nondefective mouse C-type retroviruses induce leukemias and lymphomas. Nondefective mouse retroviruses (murine leukemia viruses: MuLVs), which lack oncogenes, have genomes that consist of a single-stranded RNA molecule that encodes three polyproteins, the *gag, pol,* and *env* polyproteins. The fundamental mechanism by which nondefective MuLVs induce leukemia was worked out some years ago by analogy to the pioneering studies of leukemia induction by similar avian retroviruses.[1,2] Following injection into newborn mice, nondefective mouse C-type retroviruses replicate extensively, establishing a viremia in the animal. In some cases an infecting virus may also recombine with endogenous C-type viral sequences to generate a recombinant that replicates even more efficiently or that is, for other, unknown reasons more leukemogenic than its parent.[3] In either circumstance, the viruses ultimately infect appropriate target cells, and by chance, in a rare cell, proviral DNA integrates in the vicinity of a cellular proto-oncogene, thereby perturbing the structure or expression of that gene.[4–8] This perturbation initiates a train of events, probably including the activation of additional oncogenes, that leads to transformation of that cell and, ultimately, to tumor formation.

Given this fundamental mechanism of oncogene activation by provirus insertion, don't we understand the process of MuLV-induced leukemogenesis? What remains to be learned? In fact, much remains to be learned about the steps that occur between the time virus is injected into the mouse and the appearance of a tumor, for example: How does virus spread in the animal? Where are appropriate target cells for transformation located? If recombinants have to form between the infecting virus and endogenous viruses, where do they arise? In addition, there are a number of questions that arise simply from knowing that the mechanism of leukemogenesis is oncogene activation. The one that has particularly intrigued us is how disease specificity is achieved. Given the mechanism of proto-oncogene activation, what determines the type of leukemia a virus induces? Nondefective MuLVs usually have quite distinct disease specificities. The majority of isolates induce T cell lymphomas and leukemias; but some reproducibly induce tumors of B cells, others, of myeloid cells, and others, of erythroid cells. Some induce mixtures of these types. Why?

Several years ago, working in collaboration with the laboratory of Dr. Janet Hartley and the late Dr. Wallace Rowe, we obtained a somewhat surprising and simple answer to the question of what determines disease specificity of certain nondefective MuLVs. We took molecular clones of Moloney leukemia virus, which induces T cell lymphomas, and of nondefective Friend virus, which induces erythroleukemias, and exchanged fragments of their genomes in order to locate the viral gene or genes responsible for their phenotypic difference.[9–11] Although we found evidence that more than one gene probably contributes to this complex phenotype, we found that for this particular pair of viruses, the primary determinant of their different disease specificities lies in the U3 region (see below) of the LTR (long terminal repeat), in sequences that encode transcriptional signals.[12,13] Later, using the same genetic approach, we localized the determinants more precisely and found that they lie within a sequence of less than 200 nucleotides that includes the transcriptional enhancer regions of the viruses.[14]

Transcriptional enhancers were discovered first in the DNA virus SV40 and subsequently in many other types of viruses, including mouse C-type retroviruses, and also in cellular genes. In many cases, of which perhaps the best studied is SV40, they consist of an array of short sequence motifs, each of which specifically binds, one or more nuclear factors.[15,16] The goal of our current studies on disease specificity of MuLVs is to use genetic and biochemical approaches to try to understand how nuclear factors interact with enhancer sequences to determine the disease phenotype.

I will begin by describing genetic studies we have done to more precisely localize determinants of specificity within the enhancer region.[17] Then I will describe studies from our laboratory and from others to identify nuclear factors that bind the Friend and Moloney virus enhancer regions. Finally, I'll briefly describe the strategy behind genetic studies in progress or in the planning stages that are designed to determine more precisely how the complex structure of MuLV enhancers influences disease induction and specificity.

LOCATION OF DETERMINANTS OF DISEASE SPECIFICITY IN THE ENHANCER REGION

FIGURE 1 shows a schematic representation of the proviral DNA of a typical murine C-type retrovirus. The *gag, pol,* and *env* genes are flanked by direct repeats, the so-called long terminal repeats (LTRs), each about 600 nucleotides long. The LTRs are comprised of three functionally distinct segments, U3, R, and U5. U3 contains the transcriptional enhancer-promoter. The enhancer (horizontal arrows,

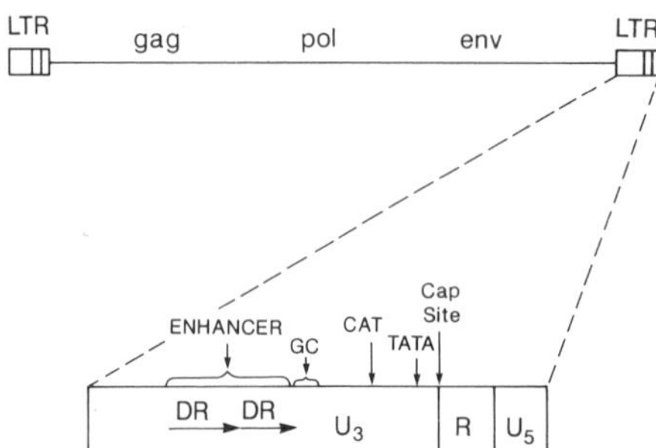

FIGURE 1. Schematic diagrams of the proviral DNA and **LTR** (long terminal repeat) of a typical nondefective mouse C-type retrovirus. *Horizontal arrows* in the U3 region of the LTR represent the direct repeat (**DR**), which has enhancer activity. Locations in the LTR of the GC-rich segment (**GC**), the CAAT (**CAT**) and TATA boxes, and the start site for transcription (**Cap Site**), as well as the U3, R and U5 regions, are indicated; see text for further details.

DR, in FIG. 1) is typically present as a direct repeat of a sequence that varies in different viruses from about 60 to 100 bases in length. This is followed by a short GC-rich segment shown by George Khoury and co-workers to have a role in transcription.[18] A typical CAAT box sequence lies about 100 bases 3′ of the enhancer, and this is followed by a TATA box and the start site for transcription. The latter defines the 5′ boundary of the R region.

It is possible to almost completely switch the disease specificity of nondefective Friend and Moloney viruses by exchanging between them about 200 nucleotides of the sequence that includes the direct repeat and the adjacent GC-rich region.[14] FIGURE 2 shows a comparison of the sequences of these two viruses in this region.[19,20] The Moloney virus direct repeat is a perfect repeat of 65 bases flanked by three copies of a nine-base sequence that corresponds to the consensus sequence of the glucocorticoid response element (GRE).[21] The Friend virus direct repeat is an imperfect copy of a sequence about 60 bases long: there is a nine-base insertion in the second copy relative to the first, as well as a few other point changes between the two copies.

We were interested in trying to define the smallest segment within the Friend virus enhancer region that could convert the Moloney virus to an erythroleukemia-inducing virus, and the smallest segment within the Moloney virus enhancer that could convert the Friend virus to a T cell lymphoma-inducing virus. From the data in FIGURE 2 it is apparent that the direct repeats of Moloney and Friend viruses are identical in sequence at their centers, around an *Eco*R V site, but have a number of base differences to either side of this conserved region. We wished to construct recombinants which would allow us to ask if the determinants of disease specificity lie in sequences to the left of the conserved sequence (in the segment designated A in FIG. 2), or to the right (segment B in FIG. 2), or in both of these segments of the direct repeat. We also wished to ask if sequences in the GC-rich segment contribute to the disease phenotype. To the extent possible, we wanted to construct recombinants with the enhancer sequences unaltered, in order to avoid unknowingly affecting the middle of a protein binding site. We used the *Eco*R V site as one recombination point, *Ava* II as another, and between the two copies of the direct repeat we made a crossover just 5′ of the central GRE site of the Moloney virus. The latter crossover was accomplished by synthesizing fragments of DNA with the desired Friend-Moloney sequence corresponding to the region between the *Eco*R V sites.

We proceeded to construct Moloney viruses into which just the A segments, just the B segments, just the GC-rich region, or any two of these segments were derived from the Friend virus, with the remainder of the genome from the Moloney virus. To determine the influence of genes outside the LTR on disease specificity, we also constructed several recombinants in which the viral genome was derived primarily from the Friend virus, with segments of the enhancer region from the Moloney virus. After being assembled, DNA constructs were transfected into cells; the viruses that emerged from the transfected cells were tested for their disease-inducing phenotype. All recombinant viruses grew efficiently and induced disease in 100% of the newborn NFS mice injected with them. What was the disease specificity of these recombinant viruses? The data on disease specificity of enhancer recombinants is shown in TABLE 1 and in simpler form in FIGURE 3.[17] Before considering the data in detail, it is helpful to understand the most important conclusions. It turns out that determinants of disease specificity are spread throughout the enhancer regions of the Friend and Moloney viruses: determinants of erythroleukemogenicity lie in the A, B, and GC-rich segments of the Friend enhancer region; determinants of T cell lymphomagenesis lie in the A and B segments of the Moloney virus and probably also in the GC-rich segment, although we have less data on this last point. Viruses with recombinant enhancer regions induce mixtures of T cell and erythroid disease. In general, single enhancer segments (A regions, B regions, or the GC-rich region) confer a rather low incidence of disease specificity. Pairs of segments are more potent, with the most potent pair being A+B, in other words, a direct repeat derived entirely from the Friend or from the Moloney sequence.

In TABLE 1, an important point to note is the number of mice that were used in the study. Although the number was substantial for this type of study, when examining the data expressed as the percentage of mice contracting a particular form of leukemia (as must be done to look at the data easily), one must remember that a low value is sometimes based on the response of just one or two mice. With that point in mind, we can look at the data in the simpler form shown in FIGURE 3. FIGURE 3A shows the frequency of different types of leukemia induced by recombinant viruses with genomes almost entirely derived from the Moloney virus, but with enhancer regions partly derived from the Friend virus. The Moloney virus itself induces only T cell lymphomas. As noted above, replacement of the entire enhancer region (the direct repeat plus the GC-rich segment) with sequences from the Friend virus converts the Moloney virus to an erythroleukemia-inducing virus [recombinant designated Mo:Fr(ABC) in FIG. 3A]. The Friend virus direct repeat alone is almost as potent a determinant of erythroleukemogenicity as the combination of the direct repeat plus the GC-rich segment [compare recombinants Mo:Fr(AB) and Mo:Fr(ABC) in FIG. 3A]. Does this mean that the GC-rich segment plays no role? Indeed, by itself, it confers only a negligible incidence of erythroleukemogenicity on the Moloney virus [recombinant Mo:Fr(C) in FIG. 3A]. However, if one looks through the data for the

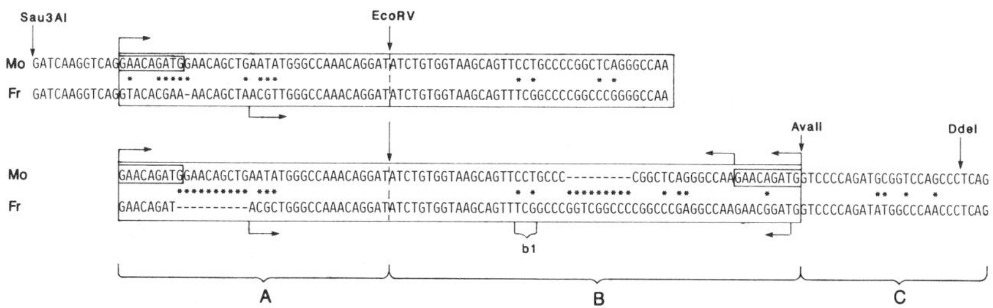

FIGURE 2. Comparison of the nucleotide sequences of Friend (**Fr**) and Moloney (**Mo**) viruses in the region of U3 whose exchange can switch their disease specificities. The sequences are aligned so that the direct repeats for each virus are located above one another. The nine-base segments enclosed in *small boxes* in the Moloney sequence correspond to the consensus sequence of the glucocorticoid response element. *Asterisks* indicate nucleotide differences between the Friend and Moloney virus sequences.

TABLE 1. Types of Leukemia Induced by Injection of Moloney, Friend, or Recombinant Viruses into Mice[a]

Virus	No. Positive[b]/ No. Inoculated	No. of Diagnosed Tumors[c]						% of Diagnosed Tumors[d]		
		Lym.	Ery.	My.	Meg.	Lym. + Ery.	Other	Lym.	Ery.	Other
Moloney (Mo)	44/44	44	0	0	0	0	0	100	0	0
Friend (Fr)	61/61	0	59	0	0	0	0	0	100	0
Recombinants[e]										
Mo:Fr(ABC)	63/63	0	63	0	0	0	0	0	100	0
Mo:Fr(AB)	31/31	2	28	0	0	1	0	9	91	0
Mo:Fr(AC)	64/64	34	21	1	0	7	1[f]	57	40	3
Mo:Fr(BC)	79/81	42	23	4	1	5	3[g]	57	34	9
Mo:Fr(A)	71/71	59	6	1	1	2	1[h]	85	11	4
Mo:Fr(B)	42/50	40	1	0	0	0	1[i]	95	2	2
Mo:Fr(b1)	32/32	25	2	0	2	1	2[j]	77	11	12
Mo:Fr(C)	35/38	33	1	0	0	0	1[k]	92	3	5
Fr:Mo(S-K)	28/28	26	0	1	0	1	0	93	3	3
Fr:Mo(AB)	72/75	57	7	2	3	1	0	82	11	7
Fr:Mo(A)	37/41	4	22	6	2	0	1[l]	11	63	26

[a] Adapted from Golemis *et al.*[17]

[b] Number of mice sacrificed with severe disease or found dead. Deaths without gross or histopathological diagnosis represented 1.8% of total.

[c] Lym., lymphoma; Ery., erythroleukemia; My., myelogenous leukemia; Meg., megakaryocytic leukemia; Lym. + Ery., both lymphoma and erythroleukemia; Other, see notes *f-l*, below.

[d] Percentages were calculated as the number of mice contracting a given type of leukemia divided by the sum of all the leukemias observed after injection of virus. For this purpose, mice diagnosed as having two distinct types of leukemias were scored twice.

[e] See FIGURE 3 for schematic diagrams of recombinants. Fr:Mo(S-K), recombinant containing *Sau* 3A–*Kpn* segment of Moloney.

[f] Ery. + My.

[g] Ery. + My. (1); Lym. + Meg. (2).

[h] Lym. + histiocytic sarcoma.

[i] Lym. + Meg.

[j] Lym. + Meg. (1); Ery. + My. (1).

[k] My. + Meg.

[l] Histiocytic sarcoma.

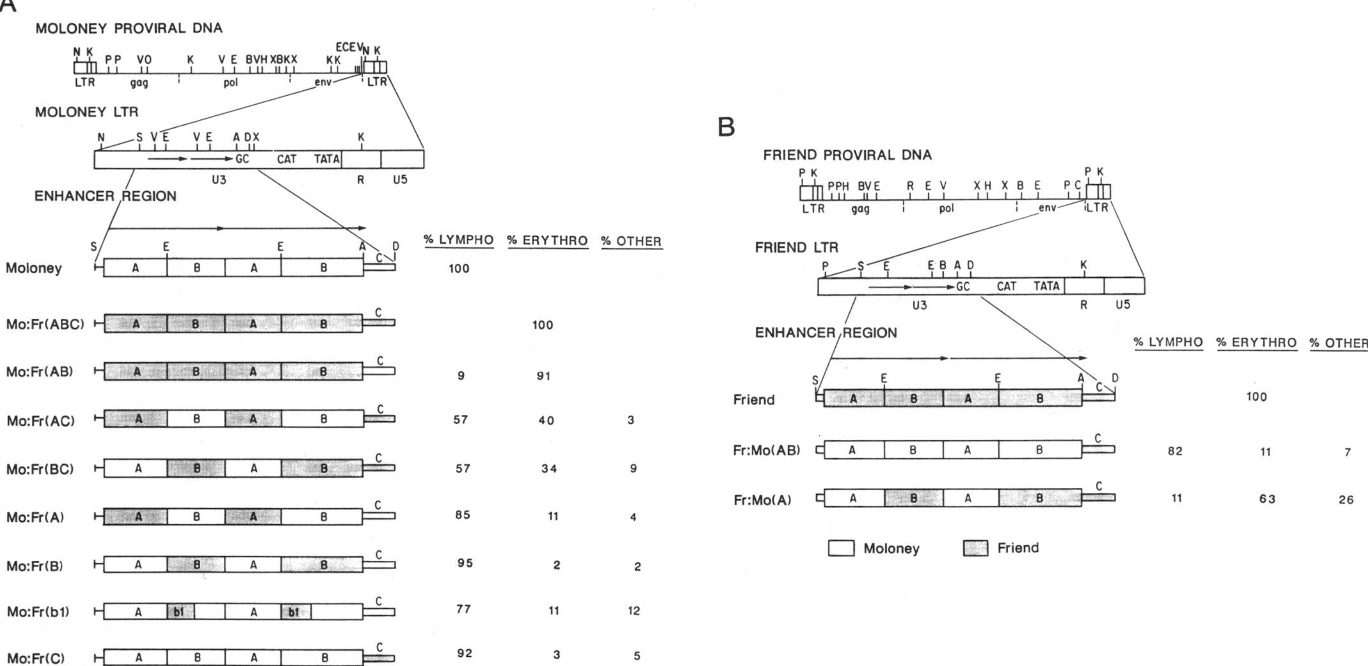

FIGURE 3. Disease specificity of the Moloney and the Friend virus and of enhancer-region recombinants between them. Schematic diagrams of the direct repeat (*arrows*) and GC-rich regions (GC) of parental viruses and enhancer-region recombinants, and the frequency of lymphoma (LYMPHO), erythroleukemia (ERYTHRO), and other types of hematopoietic tumors induced by the parental and the recombinant viruses are shown. Results are based on the data in TABLE 1, which is from Golemis *et al.*[17] (**Panel A**) Moloney virus (Mo) and recombinants that have primarily a Moloney virus genome. Fragments of the Friend virus (Fr) enhancer region that are present in recombinants are indicated by *shaded areas.* (**Panel B**) Friend virus (Fr) and recombinants that have primarily a Friend virus genome. Fragments of the enhancer derived from the Moloney virus (Mo) are indicated by *white boxes.* For sequence of each segment, see FIGURE 2.

remaining recombinants in FIGURE 3A, one sees that the GC-rich region in combination with the A or B segments of the Friend virus confers a substantial incidence of erythroleukemogenicity on the Moloney virus.

There is a temptation to say that two segments from the Friend enhancer region act cooperatively, together conferring more than an additive incidence of erythroleukemia. However, the data are borderline on this point. Of particular concern is a possible discrepancy between the potency of the Friend B and b1 segments in conferring erythroleukemogenicity on the Moloney virus [compare data for recombinants designated Mo:Fr(B) and Mo:Fr(b1) in FIG. 3A]. The b1 segment is contained within the B segment and, as shown in FIGURE 2, the Friend and Moloney viral sequences differ in only two bases within b1. Curiously, the data in FIGURE 3A suggest that the recombinant with just its b1 segments derived from the Friend virus may induce more nonlymphoid tumors than the recombinant with its entire B regions from the Friend virus. However, statistical analysis of the data shown in TABLE 1 reveals that the difference between the two recombinants may not be significant. More mice would have to be injected to produce a firm conclusion about whether segments of the Friend enhancer region increase one another's ability to confer erythroleukemogenicity.

Two additional observations of interest from these studies are (1) that some recombinants induce tumors of cell types other than those seen with either parental virus (see TABLE 1) and (2) that some combinations of enhancer segments cause an increase in the latent period of disease induction (data not shown). The increase in latent period is most pronounced in recombinants containing B segments derived from the Friend virus and A segments from the Moloney virus.

FIGURE 3B shows the disease specificity of recombinant viruses with genomes mostly derived from the Friend virus and with enhancer regions partly derived come from the Moloney virus. Qualitatively, the same conclusions noted above hold: the Moloney virus direct repeat alone, without the GC-rich segment, is a potent determinant of T cell lymphomagenesis; and a single segment (A segments alone in this case) can only weakly divert the Friend virus to T cell lymphomagenesis. Comparison of the data in FIGURES 3A and 3B reveals something else of interest. As we and others had noted in earlier studies, genes outside the U3 region also contribute to disease specificity.[12,13,22] We found that in viruses with recombinant enhancers, the influence of outside genes was greater than when the enhancer was derived entirely from one virus, and hence was a more potent determinant of disease specificity. This can be seen clearly by comparing the data for viruses designated Mo:Fr(BC) and Fr:Mo(A). The Moloney virus A enhancer segments, when lying in the Moloney virus genome, yield a virus, Mo:Fr(BC), that induces lymphoid disease 57% of the time; but the Moloney virus A enhancer segments in a genome otherwise derived from the Friend virus, i.e., recombinant Fr:Mo(A), yield a virus that induces lymphoid disease only 11% of the time.

In summary, from these studies we conclude that

1. The enhancer is the primary determinant of disease specificity in recombinants between Friend and Moloney viruses.
2. It is possible to break the enhancer up into smaller components by recombination without destroying the disease-inducing potential of the virus; the recombinants instead induce mixtures of T cell lymphomas and erythroleukemias. It should be noted that a similar conclusion was reached by Ishimoto *et al.,*[23] who constructed recombinants within the enhancer-promoter regions of Moloney virus and a Friend MCF (mink cell focus-forming) virus that induces erythroleukemia.

3. Determinants of erythroleukemogenicity (and probably T cell lymphomagenesis) lie in three separable segments of the enhancer region: the two halves of the direct repeat (A and B) and the GC-rich (C) region.
4. Single enhancer segments are quite poor at influencing disease specificity in the background of a different virus, but pairs of segments are quite good, with the two halves of the direct repeat being especially potent.
5. Genomic sequences outside the enhancer region have a minor effect on the disease specificity of viruses with intact enhancers (when at least the entire direct repeat is derived from the parental virus); but when the enhancer is split, the effect of outside sequences is more pronounced.

Finally, it is interesting to note that the array of disease specificities and latent periods shown by the viruses with recombinant enhancers in either the Friend or the Moloney virus genomic background is reminiscent of the diversity seen among naturally occurring mouse retroviruses.

IDENTIFICATION OF ENHANCER-BINDING FACTORS

It seems reasonable to imagine, and indeed there is some evidence to suggest, that enhancer elements play a role in disease specificity by augmenting transcription preferentially in particular cell types.[24–28] It is widely believed that enhancers exert their effects on transcription by interacting with nuclear factors. In this case, the factors are presumably encoded by the cells that the viruses infect, since mouse C-type viruses are not thought to encode enhancer-binding factors. We have attempted to identify and characterize nuclear factors that interact with the enhancer regions of the Friend virus. Similar studies on the Moloney virus enhancer have been done in several laboratories, most comprehensively by Nancy Speck in Baltimore's laboratory.[29]

The approach to identifying enhancer-binding factors has been the widely popular gel shift assay, in which small fragments of labeled DNA are mixed with crude or fractionated nuclear extracts and then resolved on gels. The specificity of the protein-DNA interactions in the complexes present in the bands detected by this assay is tested by competition for binding of the nuclear extracts to other DNA sequences. To more precisely localize binding sites within the DNA fragments used as probes, methylation interference assays are done, allowing identification of G residues important for the binding. The hazard of such studies is that one does not know if the factors identified by the method are the ones that actually operate on these DNA sequences *in vivo* to produce the phenotype of interest. Obviously, much more work is needed to determine if this is so. FIGURE 4 shows the results to date for this type of analysis of the Moloney virus direct repeat. Six distinct factors bind to the region. A single copy of the direct repeat is flanked by sequences that correspond to the glucocorticoid receptor binding site (GRE). Next to the 5′ GRE is a site designated LVa. This is followed by one of the two NF-1 binding sites present in each copy of the repeat. In the center of the repeated sequence, lying in the region of identity between the Friend and the Moloney virus nucleotide sequences, are two binding sites: one for a novel protein designated LVb, the other corresponding to the so-called core sequence first identified in the SV40 enhancer. This central region—whose sequence is very highly conserved in mouse, cat, and even ape C-type retroviruses (Golemis, observation from computer alignment of published sequences)—is followed by a site called LVc, then the second NF-1 and GRE sites. A third GRE follows the direct repeat.

The results of comparable studies of the Friend virus enhancer region are not yet published (Manley, O'Connell, Sharp, and Hopkins; manuscript submitted). However, relative to the Moloney virus sites shown in FIGURE 4, we can say the following: the 5′ GRE, LVa, and NF-1 sites in the Moloney virus direct repeat are absent in the Friend virus; in their place is a site designated FVa. At the location 3′ of the region of identity between the Friend and the Moloney virus, there are two new protein binding sites, FVb1 and FVb2. The FVb2 site overlaps an NF-1 site that lies in the same location as the 3′ NF-1 sites of the Moloney virus. The Friend virus is similar in sequence to the Moloney virus in the second and third GRE sites (see FIG. 2), but we do not know if the alterations in these sequences prevent the binding of the glucocorticoid receptor to the Friend virus enhancer. A surprising finding has been that the FVa and FVb1 sites cross-compete for binding of nuclear extracts, implying that they may bind the same factor. This is surprising, since their sequences are related but certainly not identical. Even more surprising are some results suggesting that the FVa and FVb1 factors may be related to the LVb factor that binds to the region of identity between the Friend and Moloney viruses (Manley, O'Connell, Sharp, and Hopkins; manuscript submitted). In other words, there seems to be a complex interaction of factors in the direct repeat region that we don't yet understand. It seems probable that we will need to understand this interaction if we are to fathom why this central region of sequence has been conserved and flanked with variable regions in mammalian C-type virus enhancers.

GENETIC STUDIES TO DETERMINE HOW ENHANCER-BINDING PROTEINS INFLUENCE DISEASE SPECIFICITY

None of the factors identified in the studies just described is reported to be present exclusively in T cells or erythroid cells. However, tumor cell lines have been employed in most of the studies examining the distribution of these factors, and it is possible the distribution observed does not apply to normal cells. Although the factors identified bind to the regions shown by genetic studies to be important to disease specificity, we can't be certain that these are the factors mediating the disease phenotype.

If they are the correct factors, how might they work? They might be positive factors that are present in higher amounts in certain hematopoietic cell lineages, thereby augmenting transcription in these cell types. They might be repressors. For example, the Moloney virus might fail to induce erythroleukemia because its transcription is depressed in cells of the erythroid lineage.

How might we address these questions? We are continuing with detailed genetic analysis as well as biochemical studies of these factors to try to explain the complex organization of the C-type retrovirus direct repeat region. In particular, we have begun to introduce mutations into G residues identified as important to the binding sites described above. Future plans include building enhancers from particular binding sites and determining the disease specificity they confer.

So far, Dr. Nancy Speck, now a postdoctoral fellow in my laboratory, has introduced mutations into the binding sites she identified in the Moloney virus direct repeat. Within a given virus, mutations were introduced into just one type of site. For example, she has made a virus with both its LVa sites mutated and another with both LVc sites mutated. For the GRE sites, she has made viruses with just one, with two, or

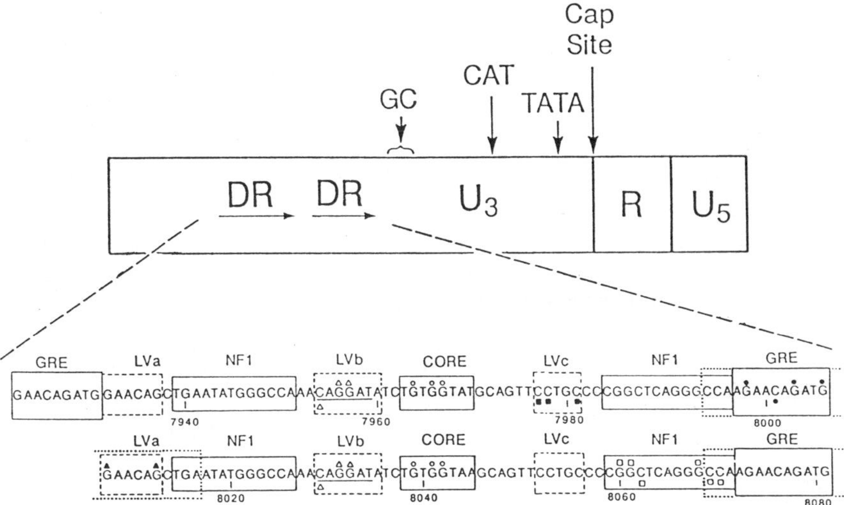

FIGURE 4. Schematic diagram indicating nuclear factors that can bind to the direct repeat (DR) region of the Moloney virus. GRE, glucocorticoid response element. See text for further details. Data adapted from Speck and Baltimore.[29]

with three sites mutated. For the NF-1 sites, she has made viruses with just two, or with all four sites mutated. The mutant enhancers were also introduced into CAT (chloramphenicol acetyltransferase) gene constructs so that the effect of the mutations on gene expression could be measured. Results with the CAT assays resemble those obtained in similar studies of the SV40 enhancer. Mutations in binding sites generally lower CAT activity 3-5-fold, and the results can vary depending on the cell line used. Most interesting to us is what will happen when the viruses with mutations in these binding sites are tested in mice. Will their leukemogenicity, latent period of disease induction, or disease specificity be altered by the mutations in enhancer-binding sites? These studies are in progress.

In all the genetic studies described above, the approach has been to construct viruses of known sequence, inject them into mice, and ask what happens. These studies do not ask what mechanism determines that a particular virus causes a particular tumor. It is widely believed that enhancers influence the disease-inducing phenotype of MuLVs by selectively affecting their replication in particular cell types. Indeed, our collaborator, Dr. Hartley, and also other investigators have shown that viruses with a Moloney virus enhancer region replicate more efficiently in the thymus than do those with the Friend virus enhancer.[30] However, this may be only part of the story. Hartley also has evidence that enhancers may have a dramatic effect on the formation of recombinant MCF viruses in the thymus, with the Moloney virus enhancer being associated with the rapid appearance of high titers of such viruses in the thymus (Golemis, Hopkins, and Hartley; unpublished results). Other studies suggest that the Moloney virus enhancer may be less active than that of the Friend virus in certain myeloid or erythroid lineages.[26,28,31] Studies in progress are continuing to dissect the multiple steps in viral leukemogenesis, and, as assays for each step are developed, the role of enhancers in these steps can be determined.

CONCLUSION

In summary, many genetic studies have shown that transcriptional enhancers are important determinants of disease induction by MuLVs. These elements influence leukemogenicity and the latent period of disease induction, as well as the type of leukemia induced.[32-35] Proceeding on the notion that enhancers exert their effects by interacting with multiple nuclear factors to influence transcription in a tissue-specific manner, we are continuing to use genetics and biochemistry to achieve a detailed understanding of how this occurs in retroviruses, particularly the erythroleukemia-inducing virus of Charlotte Friend.

Since a number of enhancer-binding proteins are inducible, their ability to bind DNA or to activate transcription being acquired in response to hormonal or other stimuli, it is interesting to consider the possibility that viral infections—that of HIV (human immunodeficiency virus) is of course of particular interest—might be controlled by regulating these proteins. Understanding which factors, and how many, are needed to control viral replication in a model system will be an important step in assessing the feasibility of such an approach.

ACKNOWLEDGMENTS

I would like to thank my collaborators on the projects that I have reviewed in this report. Dr. Pamela Chatis, in collaboration with Dr. Christie Holland, first mapped the determinants of disease specificity to the LTR region. Dr. Yen Li further identified critical determinants as the enhancer region. My graduate student Erica Golemis (now Dr. Golemis) dissected the enhancer region, showing that specificity resides in multiple segments of the enhancer. My student Nancy Manley identified proteins that bind the Friend virus enhancer region. Dr. Nancy Speck is conducting the studies that will try to establish the importance of individual enhancer-protein binding sites in determining the disease phenotype of mouse retroviruses. Lucy Pilapil has assisted in all these studies. Our collaboration with Dr. Janet Hartley and her colleagues has made it possible to perform the genetic studies described here.

REFERENCES

1. Hayward, W. S., B. Neel & S. Astrin. 1981. Nature **290:** 475-480.
2. Payne, G. S., S. A. Courtneidge, L. B. Crittenden, A. M. Fadley, J. M. Bishop & H. E. Varmus. 1981. Cell **23:** 311-322.
3. Hartley, J. W., N. K. Wolford, L. J. Old & W. P. Rowe. 1977. Proc. Natl. Acad. Sci. USA **74:** 789-792.
4. Tsichlis, P. N., P. G. Strauss & L. F. Hu. 1983. Nature **302:** 445-449.
5. Cuypers, H. T., G. Selten, W. Quint, M. Zijlstra, E. R. Maandag, W. Boelens, P. van Wezenbeek, C. Melief & A. Berns. 1984. Cell **37:** 141-150.
6. Steffen, D. 1984. Proc. Natl. Acad. Sci. USA **81:** 2097-2101.
7. Corcoran, L. M., J. M. Adams, A. R. Dunn & S. Cory. 1984. Cell **37:** 113-122.
8. Li, Y., C. A. Holland, J. W. Hartley & N. Hopkins. 1984. Proc. Natl. Acad. Sci. USA **81:** 6808-6811.

9. MOLONEY, J. B. 1960. J. Natl. Cancer Inst. **24:** 933-951.
10. FRIEND, C. 1957. J. Exp. Med. **105:** 307-318.
11. TROXLER, D. H. & E. M. SCOLNICK. 1978. Virology **85:** 17-27.
12. CHATIS, P. A., C. A. HOLLAND, J. W. HARTLEY, W. P. ROWE & N. HOPKINS. 1983. Proc. Natl. Acad. Sci. USA **80:** 4408-4411.
13. CHATIS, P. A., HOLLAND, C. A., J. E. SILVER, T. N. FREDERICKSON, N. HOPKINS & J. W. HARTLEY. 1984. J. Virol. **52:** 248-254.
14. LI, Y., E. GOLEMIS, J. W. HARTLEY & N. HOPKINS. 1987. J. Virol. **61:** 696-700.
15. ZENKE, M., T. GRUNDSTROM, H. MATTHES, M. WINTZERITH, C. SCHATZ, A. WILDEMAN & P. CHAMBON. 1986. EMBO J. **5:** 387-397.
16. HERR, W. & J. CLARKE. 1986. Cell **45:** 461-470.
17. GOLEMIS, E., Y. LI, T. N. FREDERICKSON, J. W. HARTLEY & N. HOPKINS. 1989. J. Virol. **63:** 328-337.
18. LAIMINS, L. A., P. GRUSS, R. POZZATTI & G. KHOURY. 1983. J. Virol. **49:** 183-189.
19. SHINNICK, T. M., R. A. LERNER & J. G. SUTCLIFFE. 1981. Nature **293:** 543-548.
20. KOCH, W., W. ZIMMERMAN, A. OLIFF & R. FREIDRICH. 1984. J. Virol. **49:** 828-840.
21. CHANDLER, V. L., B. A. MALER & K. R. YAMAMOTO. 1983. Cell **33:** 489-499.
22. OLIFF, A. I., K. SIGNORELLI & L. COLLINS. 1984. J. Virol. **51:** 788-794.
23. ISHIMOTO, A., M. TAKIMOTO, A. ADACHI, M. KAKUYAMA, S. KATO, K. KAKIMI, K. FUKUOKA, T. OGIU, M. MATSUYAMA. 1987. J. Virol. **61:** 1861-1866.
24. DESGROSEILLERS, L., E. RASSART & P. JOLICOEUR. 1983. Proc. Natl. Acad. Sci. USA **80:** 4203-4207.
25. CELANDER, D. & W. A. HASELTINE. 1984. Nature **312:** 159-162.
26. SHORT, M. K., S. A. OKENQUIST & J. LENZ. 1987. J. Virol. **61:** 1067-1072.
27. YOSHIMURA, F., B. DAVISON & K. CHAFFIN. 1985. Mol. Cell. Biol. **5:** 2832-2835.
28. BOSZE, Z., H. J. THIESEN & P. CHARNAY. 1986. EMBO J. **5:** 1615-1623.
29. SPECK, N. & D. BALTIMORE. 1987. Mol. Cell. Biol. **7:** 11[illegible]-1110.
30. EVANS, L. & J. MORREY. 1987. J. Virol. **61:** 1350-1357.
31. HOLLAND, C. A., P. ANKLESARIA, M. A. SAKAKEENY & J. S. GREENBERGER. 1987. Proc. Natl. Acad. Sci. USA **84:** 8662-8666.
32. LENZ, J., D. CELANDER, R. L. CROWTHER, R. PATARCA, D. W. PERKINS & W. A. HASELTINE. 1984. Nature **308:** 467-470.
33. DESGROSSEILLERS, L. & P. JOLICOEUR. J. VIROL. **52:** 945-952.
34. LUNG, M. L., J. W. HARTLEY, W. P. ROWE & N. HOPKINS. 1983. J. Virol. **45:** 275-290.
35. HOLLAND, C. A., J. W. HARTLEY, W. P. ROWE & N. HOPKINS. 1985. J. Virol. **53:** 153-165.

Genetic Resistance to Friend Virus[a]

ARTHUR AXELRAD

Department of Anatomy
University of Toronto
Toronto, Ontario, Canada M5S 1A8

The information and ideas discussed in this paper are the results of a long series of experiments carried out in several laboratories and designed to throw light on the basis for the resistance that C57BL mice inherit against the leukemia virus first isolated by Charlotte Friend in 1957.[1,2] C57BL mice are a unique breed. Presumably as a result of selection by cancer research workers, they have collected into their genome a series of genes that confer resistance to a variety of tumor-inducing viruses. Those in the C57BL genome that provide resistance to Friend leukemia virus itself and/or to the development or progress of the erythroproliferative disease induced by infection with this virus include the genes *Fv-1*,[3,4,5] *Fv-2*,[6] *Rfv-1*,[7] *Rfv-2*,[7] and *Rfv-3*.[8]

Friend leukemia virus is a complex composed of two viruses, a spleen focus-forming virus (SFFV)[9] shown to be replication-defective[10,11] and a replication-competent Friend murine leukemia virus (F-MuLV),[12] which acts as a helper for the former virus but can also have its own effects.

GENETIC RESISTANCE TO REPLICATION OF FRIEND HELPER VIRUS

The *Fv-1*[b] genotype of the C57BL mouse controls a dominant relative resistance to replication of the helper component of the Friend virus complex when the latter has the host range referred to as N-tropic.[b] Genetic restriction at the *Fv-1* locus[13] results in failure of F-MuLV DNA to integrate into the host genome,[14,15] either because of a block in the formation of covalently closed supercoiled DNA (form I, believed to be the form that becomes integrated) or because of a block in the integration event itself. The host range of the virus is transferable by phenotypic mixing; therefore, a virus-encoded protein must carry the host-range determinant which is recognized by the *Fv-1* gene product. It was found[16] that a 302-base-pair fragment coding for the 30-kDa *gag* protein (p30) was both necessary and sufficient to confer a specific host

[a] This work was supported by a grant from the National Cancer Institute of Canada.

[b] The *Fv-1* locus on chromosome 4 of the mouse has two alleles, *Fv-1*^{n} and *Fv-1*^{b}; mouse strains are said to be of the N-type or of the B-type, respectively, depending on their *Fv-1* genotype. A murine retrovirus that is not restricted in N-type mice is said to be N-tropic; a virus that is not restricted in B-type mice is B-tropic; one that is not restricted in either N-type or B-type mice is NB-tropic.

range on a viral recombinant. Nucleotide sequence analysis showed that only two consecutive amino acids in p30, Gln-Arg for the N-tropic helper virus and Thr-Gln for the B-tropic, were responsible for the host ranges of the respective viruses. NB-tropic variants,[17] such as the F-B virus used in the present work,[18] have lost the tropism determinant by mutation or recombination.[19] They thus by-pass the *Fv-1* restriction and leave the investigator free to examine genetic resistance that is determined by other mechanisms.

In genetically susceptible adult mice, Friend virus very rapidly induces an erythroproliferative disease that ultimately goes on to frank malignancy. It is the SFFV component of Friend virus that has been shown to be responsible for this condition.[20,21] The helper virus plays no role in this process except that of sustaining the replication of the SFFV and thus amplifying the number of cells engaged in erythroproliferative activity.

IMMUNOLOGICAL CONSIDERATIONS

The *H-2*^{bb} genotype of B6 mice is associated with a profound resistance to the erythroproliferative disease induced by Friend SFFV *in vivo.* This resistance, which is actually due to the *H-2*-linked genes *Rfv-1* and *Rfv-2,*[7] appears well after the initial acute erythroproliferative events and is seen as an increased incidence of recovery from the virus-induced splenomegaly. The available data indicate that cytotoxic T effector cells in the spleen may play an important role in the process of recovery from SFFV-induced splenomegaly *in vivo.* The specificities recognized by these effector cells were virus-induced cellular antigens.[22] *Rfv-3*^{r}, unlinked to *H-2,* promotes recovery from viremia, possibly by influencing the specific anti-Friend virus humoral antibody response.[8] In all these instances, host immune responses appeared to be responsible for genetic resistance against SFFV. Systematic studies on the mechanism of resistance of C57BL/6 mice to SFFV under conditions which were free of the genetic influences that operate immunologically in these mice had to await a system in which SFFV induction of erythroproliferative disease could be brought about *in vitro.* This was a long time in coming.

Odaka and Yamamoto in 1962[23] first showed that a single gene was responsible for the resistance of C57BL/6 mice to the Friend leukemia virus. Our own story begins with a pair of congenic mouse strains on a C57BL/6 background which we produced by selective breeding and which differ with respect to a small segment of chromosome 9. In this segment, a gene later identified by Lilly[6] as *Fv-2* determines either resistance or susceptibility to Friend SFFV.

B6 mice of genotype *Fv-2*^{rr} are solidly resistant to the Friend SFFV. Their congenic partner strain called B6.S are susceptible (*Fv-2*^{ss}). In these susceptible mice, low intravenous doses of the virus produce spleen foci.[24] High doses rapidly give rise to a massive splenomegaly and erythroproliferative activity[24] that is independent of erythropoietin.[25,26]

In 1985, Bondurant *et al.*[27] were able to produce erythropoietin-independent erythroid cell colonies ("bursts") in semi-solid culture *in vitro* with Friend virus-infected marrow cells from the B6.S (*Fv-2*^{ss}) but not from the B6 (*Fv-2*^{rr}) mice. This work, which utilized a culture system developed by Hankins *et al.,*[28] established that *Fv-2* (or a closely linked gene) controls resistance to SFFV induction of erythroproliferative disease *in vitro,* as had been previously shown *in vivo.*

TESTS OF HYPOTHESES TO EXPLAIN THE RESISTANCE OF B6 CELLS TO FRIEND VIRUS

Regulatory Factors

Using the Friend SFFV induction system *in vitro,* Bondurant *et al.* tested three hypotheses designed to explain the resistance of B6 cells to the induction of erythroid bursts by SFFV. They showed that the genetic resistance was not mediated by a lack of burst-promoting activity (BPA)[29] or an inability to respond to such a factor: addition of BPA did not overcome the resistance to SFFV, although the erythroid cells of the *Fv-2*^{rr} genotype could be shown to be responsive to it. It is of interest in this regard that interleukin-3 (IL-3), a burst-promoting component of pokeweed mitogen-stimulated spleen cell-conditioned medium (PWCM), enhanced cycling of CFU-GEMM,[c] BFU-E and CFU-GM *in vitro* but, administered *in vivo,* did not make B6 mice sensitive to Friend SFFV.[30]

Virus Replication

The second hypothesis that Bondurant *et al.* examined was that failure of Friend SFFV to replicate in B6 cells was responsible for the *Fv-2*-mediated resistance of B6 cells to erythroid burst induction by SFFV. Friend SFFV does not replicate in mice of the *Fv-2*^{rr} genotype *in vivo*[12,31–35] or in their cells in long-term culture *in vitro,*[36] and passage of the Friend virus complex through B6 mice results in loss of the SFFV component.[36–38] However, the cells of B6 mice are not inherently incapable of supporting replication of the virus.[34] Evans *et al.*[39] showed that a fibroblast cell line derived from the B6 strain supports the replication of SFFV *in vitro,* and Odaka[33] found *in vivo* that SFFV was able to replicate actively in B6 mice from birth to 1 week of age; from then to about 3-4 weeks of age the mice responded irregularly, and after that they failed to support replication of the virus. We have examined the effect of aging on replication of SFFV in B6 mice.[40] The results showed that 3 weeks after inoculation of NB-tropic Friend F-B virus into B6 mice of various ages, no virus was recovered from the spleens of adults of ages up to around 40 weeks. For older mice, up to at least 140 weeks of age, increasing amounts of SFFV were recovered with increasing age, in an approximately exponential manner. Thus, resistance of adult B6 mice to SFFV replication appears to be due to an acquired mechanism superimposed on an inherent capacity of the cells to replicate the virus. Titers of SFFV produced in methylcellulose cultures of B6 (*Fv-2*^{rr}) and B6.S (*Fv-2*^{ss}) cells were found by Bondurant *et al.* to be approximately equal, if low, and judging from the levels of viral RNA and gp52 (52-kDa glycoprotein) produced, B6 erythroid cells exhibited no specific restriction to SFFV penetration or to an early replicative event such as viral genomic RNA production. Nor did the *Fv-2*^{rr} genotype suppress replication of SFFV on a DDD[41] or DBA/2 background.[42]

[c]CFU-GEMM, colony-forming unit-granulocytic, erythroid, megakaryocytic, monocytic; BFU-E, burst-forming unit-erythroid; CFU-GM, colony-forming unit-granulocytic, monocytic: progenitors of the mammalian hemopoietic cell system.

The notion that *Fv-2^{rr}* directly inhibits SFFV replication was based on the observations that passage of Friend virus through SFFV-resistant mice or in long-term cultures of cells from these mice results in selective loss of the defective SFFV component,[36–38] as mentioned above, and that large quantities of SFFV are produced in *Fv-2^{ss}* animals with erythroproliferative disease.[31,32] But both of these observations could be explained if the replication of SFFV were limited to cycling erythroid cells. The relatively low numbers of such cells in B6 mice would give no positive selective advantage to SFFV during passage, and the virus would ultimately be diluted out. The presence of large numbers of cycling erythroid cells in the *Fv-2^{ss}* mice with erythroproliferative disease would provide many opportunities for the virus to replicate. In line with this interpretation is our observation on young adult B6 mice. These animals normally fail to sustain replication of SFFV. Repeated bleeding, however, which induces cycling of their BFU-E, resulted in a great increase in the yield of SFFV recovered from these animals. These B6 mice did not, however, develop erythroproliferative disease (unpublished observations). Thus *Fv-2* is not responsible for the control of SFFV replication, and genetic resistance to viral induction of erythroid bursts by B6 cells *in vitro* cannot be attributed to failure of these cells to replicate the Friend SFFV.

State of Cycle of the Erythroid Progenitor Cells BFU-E

The third hypothesis investigated by Bondurant *et al.* was that the erythroid progenitor cells (BFU-E) believed to be targets for the erythroproliferative effects of SFFV[43–45] might not be cycling under their conditions of culture. We had found that cycling of BFU-E is associated with susceptibility to the induction of erythroproliferative disease by Friend virus.[24,46] Bondurant *et al.* tested the BFU-E cycling hypothesis by using, prior to culture, a variety of manipulations of the bone marrow cells designed to induce cycling of BFU-E or to select for cycling erythroid progenitor cells from the B6 mice. Measures such as the use of fetal mouse liver cells, bone marrow or spleen cells from newborn to 6-week-old mice, regenerating marrow from BCNU-treated mice[d] or unit-gravity-separated and washed spleen and marrow cells from phenylhydrazine-treated mice, and manipulations such as washing the cells, which was shown to increase cycling of BFU-E *in vitro,*[47] all failed to overcome the resistance of B6 cells to SFFV. Bondurant *et al.* concluded that B6 resistance to SFFV-induced erythroproliferative disease was not due to lack of cycling of BFU-E.

Bondurant *et al.*[27] also, however, raised the possibility that a diffusible factor which inhibited cycling of BFU-E could be responsible for the genetic resistance to SFFV induction of erythroproliferative disease *in vitro* if regeneration of this factor *in vitro* after washing of the cells was quick enough to allow it to negate the action of the virus. Since no measurements of the proportion of BFU-E engaged in DNA synthesis were done, this possibility could not be ruled out. To test this proposal, they infected 1:1 mixtures of B6 and (B6 $\times$ DBA/2)F_1 bone marrow cells with NB-tropic Friend virus; about half as many erythroid bursts were produced as in cultures of (B6 $\times$ DBA/2)F_1 marrow cells alone. All of these bursts were shown to be derived from cells of the sensitive genotype only. Bondurant *et al.* concluded that no diffusible

[d]BCNU, *N,N*-bis(2-chloroethyl)-*N*-nitrosourea: carmustine.

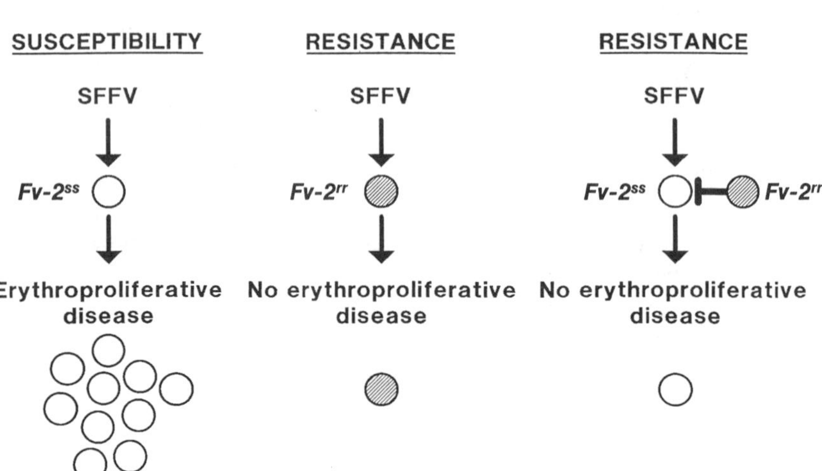

FIGURE 1. Cell-autonomous and non-cell-autonomous models for expression of resistance to induction of erythroproliferative disease by Friend spleen focus-forming virus (SFFV). In the cell-autonomous model (*left and center panels*), infection of mixtures of equal numbers of SFFV-susceptible ($Fv\text{-}2^{ss}$, **white circles**) and SFFV-resistant ($Fv\text{-}2^{rr}$, **shaded circles**) marrow cells (in bone marrow chimeras or allophenic mice) by SFFV results in proliferation only of cells of the susceptible genotype. In the non-cell-autonomous model (*right panel*), the genetically susceptible cells are rendered resistant to SFFV by some outside influence dependent on the presence of cells of the resistant genotype, as schematically depicted by the *bar* protruding from the $Fv\text{-}2^{rr}$ (**shaded**) cell.

negative regulatory influence of $Fv\text{-}2^{rr}$ cells on $Fv\text{-}2^{ss}$ cells could explain the resistance to the erythroproliferative effects of SFFV. Similar experiments *in vitro* by Silver and Teich[48] and *in vivo* by Dewey and Eldridge[49] gave the same results.

FATE OF MARKED CELLS IN HOSTS DERIVED FROM SFFV-SUSCEPTIBLE AND RESISTANT GENOTYPES

The use of bone marrow chimeras and of allophenic mice that combine marked cells from genetically susceptible mice with those from genetically resistant mice has provided new insights into the pathogenesis of Friend virus-induced erythroproliferative disease. This approach used with Hb (hemoglobin) and Gpi (glucose phosphate isomerase) markers on platelets, granulocytes, and red cells has confirmed the notion that Friend virus induces a uniquely erythroid disease, with amplification of the cell population occurring beyond the early (8-day) BFU-E stage and including the (more mature) CFU-E (erythroid colony-forming unit) stage.[50]

This approach has also been used to show that in chimeras[48] or in allophenic mice[51] composed of cells in approximately equal numbers from mice of susceptible and of resistant genotypes, cell amplification under the influence of Friend SFFV always occurred only in cells of the susceptible genotype[48,50] (FIG. 1). These results led to the conclusion that the *Fv-2* gene operates within the target cells themselves in a cell-autonomous manner, i.e., SFFV resistance is a hereditary property of the target cells and is not imposed by some influence from outside of these cells.[50] The same conclusion had been reached from cell transplantation experiments *in vivo.*[24,52,53]

However, when mixtures of cells of the two genotypes were not equal, but of the order of 85% from the resistant genotype and 15% from the susceptible genotype, an interesting thing happened: the virus failed to induce erythroproliferative disease (FIG. 2) Thus, the presence of a preponderance of *Fv-2^rr* cells protected the minority of *Fv-2^ss* cells from the action of SFFV.[54] It was also shown in this work that the administration of anti-thymocyte antiserum resulted in failure of the resistant majority to protect the sensitive minority, which was thus permitted to expand rapidly under the influence of Friend SFFV (FIG. 2). The ability of the resistant cells to confer protection indicates that *Fv-2^rr*-mediated resistance to Friend SFFV is not entirely cell autonomous, but can be imposed upon the minority of genetically susceptible target cells by the resistance gene-carrying majority. The mechanism of the influence responsible remains to be clarified. Whatever the mechanism, however, it is evident that SFFV-induced neoplastic expansion of the genetically susceptible erythroid cell population can be inhibited by some influence originating from outside of the target cells, among the bone marrow cells of the *Fv-2^rr* genotype, and apparently acting at short range.

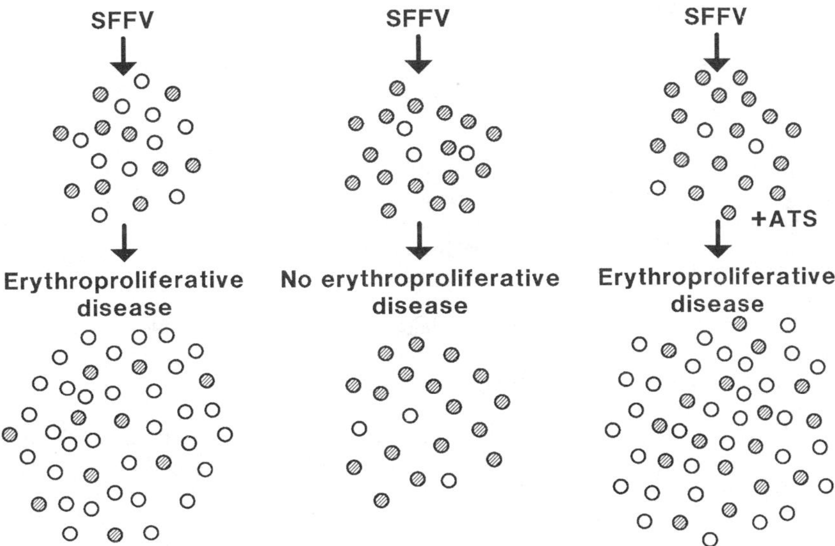

FIGURE 2. Ability of SFFV-resistant cells to protect SFFV-susceptible cells from induction of erythroproliferative disease by SFFV. When susceptible (**white circles**) and resistant (**shaded circles**) bone marrow cells are present in equal numbers, SFFV can induce proliferation of the susceptible cells (*left panel*), as previously detailed in FIGURE 1. When a preponderance of the cells present are of the resistant genotype (*center panel*), SFFV does not induce proliferation; but addition of anti-thymocyte antiserum (**ATS,** *right panel*) blocks this protective effect.

NEGATIVE REGULATION OF BFU-E CYCLING BY A GLYCOPROTEIN FROM B6 MARROW CELLS

We had found that mice congenic at the *Fv-2* locus, which differed in their susceptibility to Friend SFFV, also differed with respect to the proliferative state of their early erythropoietic progenitor cells BFU-E under normal, non-infective conditions.[46] What we wanted to do, therefore, was to investigate the proliferative state of the BFU-E. But, since in mouse bone marrow the frequency of BFU-E is ca. 1/3000, the low frequency of these cells made it impossible to study their DNA synthesis directly. However, if bone marrow cells are exposed to [^{3}H]thymidine of high specific activity, those BFU-E that are engaged in DNA synthesis will incorporate the radioisotope and be killed (commit "suicide") by internal β-radiation. Killing of the BFU-E will be seen as a reduction in number of erythroid bursts at 7 days. Since those BFU-E that are not synthesizing DNA will not pick up the radioisotope, the number of bursts they give rise to will be unchanged. Thus, the percentage of BFU-E killed serves as a measure of the proportion of BFU-E engaged in DNA synthesis.

We found that in FV-resistant mice of genotype *Fv-2^{rr}*, most of the BFU-E are in a non-DNA-synthesizing state, as judged by their invulnerability to [^{3}H]thymidine *in vivo;* in FV-susceptible mice of genotype *Fv-2^{ss}*, a high proportion of the BFU-E are normally engaged in DNA synthesis. This pattern was true not only for our mice congenic at *Fv-2* but also for other congenic partner strains, as well as for other inbred strains differing at *Fv-2.*[46] Our conclusion was that cycling of BFU-E is controlled by *Fv-2* (or by a closely linked gene on chromosome 9).

When marrow cells were removed from B6 mice and subjected to a single wash in physiological medium, their BFU-E immediately became vulnerable to [^{3}H]thymidine or to hydroxyurea,[47] cycle-active agents which operate by totally different mechanisms but have in common the ability to kill only those cells that are engaged in DNA synthesis. We therefore concluded that washing of B6 bone marrow cells must have removed something that prevents BFU-E from engaging in DNA synthesis. So, with Dr. Helena Croizat and Miss Denise Eskinazi, we went looking in the wash water. When the washed B6 cells were resuspended in supernatants obtained by washing bone marrow cells from B6 mice, only a low percentage of the BFU-E were killed by the cycle-active agents, but supernatants from B6.S cells did not have this protective effect. These results indicated that there was something in B6 but not B6.S marrow supernatants that could prevent BFU-E from engaging in DNA synthesis. Moreover, this activity protected BFU-E of both the resistant and susceptible genotypes. The genetic control of cycling was therefore not in the BFU-E itself.

We found that this activity in B6 marrow supernatants could turn off DNA synthesis rapidly, i.e., within the 20 min required to do a [^{3}H]thymidine "suicide" experiment, and that its effect was readily reversible without apparent toxicity. After bone marrow cells were kept in B6 marrow supernatant (where $< 10\%$ of the BFU-E were in DNA synthesis) for various time intervals up to 3hr, we subjected the cells to a single wash. In each instance, more than 40% of the BFU-E immediately went into DNA synthesis; this proportion was independent of the length of time that the BFU-E had been maintained in the quiescent state.

We found that the activity in the B6 marrow supernatant was apparently specific for the early BFU-E. Adding B6 bone marrow supernantant to CFU-E and regenerating CFU-S^e (both in cycle), had no effect on the proportion of these cells that engaged in DNA synthesis. We also examined the effect of washing on several types of hemopoietic cells. Washing of the B6 marrow cell suspension had no significant effect on the DNA synthesis of CFU-S, CFU-E, or CFU-GM; only the DNA synthesis of BFU-E was affected by washing. It thus seems that the negative regulatory activity in B6 marrow is both lineage-specific (erythroid) and stage-specific (early BFU-E).

Our experiments using Amicon filtration established that the activity in B6 marrow supernatants was macromolecular; we also found it to be heat stable and trypsin-sensitive.[55] We therefore concluded that it was a protein, which we named negative regulatory protein, or NRP.

The level of NRP activity in B6 marrow varied under different physiological conditions. We have already seen the genetically controlled difference in NRP activity in adult B6 and B6.S mice. In addition, we could not find NRP in baby B6 mice whose hemopoietic systems were still developing and whose BFU-E were still undergoing DNA synthesis; it was first detectable in young adults.

Bleeding is known to increase the cycling activity of early erythroid progenitor cells.[46,56] If NRP were a physiological regulator of BFU-E DNA synthesis, then this concentration in the marrow of B6 mice should be affected by bleeding. To test this prediction, we subjected young adult B6 mice to one, two or three bleedings by the orbital vein and assayed supernatants of marrow from these mice for negative regulatory activity. The results showed that repeated bleeding rendered NRP undetectable in B6 marrow, as if the absence of NRP permitted cycling of the BFU-E for the restoration of red cells lost.[57]

These data are consistent with the hypothesis that NRP, which is capable of turning off DNA synthesis of BFU-E *in vitro,* also acts *in vivo.* We believe that it is the molecule responsible for the quiescent state of BFU-E in normal adult B6 mice.

But if their BFU-E are permanently quiescent, how could B6 mice produce red blood cells (RBC) on a day-to-day basis? (And we know that B6 mice are hematologically normal.[46]) We wondered whether or not the levels of negative regulatory activity in B6 marrow remained constant throughout the day. We therefore investigated the level of this activity in supernatants of bone marrow from B6 and B6.S mice as a function of the time of day. Samples of marrow were taken at 4-hr intervals round the clock, and the supernatants were assayed on washed B6 bone marrow cells by the [^{3}H]thymidine "suicide" method. We found overall that B6 marrow supernatants showed higher levels of negative regulatory activity than B6.S marrow supernatants. Therefore, the genetic difference between these mouse strains was a quantitative difference in the level of negative regulatory activity in the marrow. *Fv-2* thus behaved like a regulatory gene. The levels of negative regulatory activity were not constant throughout the day but varied in what appeared to be a circadian rhythm in both strains (manuscript in preparation). Sharkis *et al.* had found that microscopically identifiable erythroid precursor cells show a circadian variation in their mitotic index;[58] NRP may be the basis for this phenomenon.

The peak in negative regulatory activity in B6 marrow was between 10:00 A.M. and 2:00 P.M. It thus seems that the "brake" is off at night and BFU-E are presumably then capable of synthesizing the DNA necessary for producing the cells that give rise to RBC.

If the regulation of NRP gene expression were itself negative, the action of *Fv-2* as a regulatory gene could explain the recessive nature of the inherited inhibition of BFU-E cycling. Thus, the dominant *Fv-2^s* genotype would be responsible for *inhibiting* secretion of NRP by bone marrow cells. The recessive *Fv-2^{rr}* genotype would be permissive for NRP secretion and would thus result in inhibition of BFU-E cycling.

[e] CFU-S, colony-forming unit, spleen: multipotential progenitor cell.

This scheme would also explain the unusual observation of a recessive gene being associated with the production of a protein.

The *Fv-2^r* allelic status is rare. All members of the species *Mus musculus* that have it are genetically related, being members of the C57-C58 family. The C57BL/6 subline used in the present study can be traced back[59,60] to mice received by Dr. C. C. Little of the Carnegie Institute at Cold Spring Harbor, New York, from Miss Abbie Lathrop, a knowledgeable mouse supplier in Granby, Massachusetts, in the early years of this century. From these mice Little developed a family of inbred mouse strains. In his line C, Little mated female 57 and female 58 to male 52. The descendants of female 57 became the C57BL line, which Little continued to inbreed; those of female 58 became the C58 inbred line, which E. C. MacDowell continued to inbreed. By 1921, the Black was separated from the Brown subline, and J. M. Murray inbred those that became the C57BR and its mutant, the C57L. Before 1937, at the Jackson Memorial Laboratory in Bar Harbor, Maine, sublines 6 and 10 of the C57BL line were separated. Both were brought back to the Jackson Laboratory after the fire there killed nearly all of the mice in 1947. All these mouse strains, the C57BL, the C58, the C57BR, and the C57L share the *r* allele at the *Fv-2* locus on Chromosome 9. It probably arose by mutation in male 52 or in an ancestor in C. C. Little's line C. The only other mouse that is resistant at *Fv-2* to SFFV-induced erythroproliferative disease belongs to the species *Mus spretus,* a North African mouse.[61] The rarity of the *Fv-2^r* genotype could be readily explained by a rare mutation at this locus, a mutation affecting the regulation of NRP production without impairing day-to-day erythropoiesis.[46] Our C57BL/6 (B6) and B6.S partner strains which are congenic at the *Fv-2* locus have been shown to differ by a segment of chromosome 9 that is probably nineteen recombination units in length. Ten out of ten chromosomes examined on the basis of their electrophoretic markers revealed no evidence of heterozygosity.[62]

The findings of an apparently circadian rhythm in NRP level, along with the evidence of genetic specificity, target cell specificity, reversibility without toxicity, the effect of age, and the effect of bleeding, strongly indicate that the mouse uses this mechanism physiologically to regulate negatively the proliferative behavior of the early erythroid progenitor cells.

AT WHAT POINT IN THE CELL CYCLE DOES NRP ACT?

When we continuously exposed B6.S bone marrow cells in physiological alpha medium to [^{3}H]thymidine, we found that, on the average, BFU-E entered DNA synthesis and were killed at the rate of about 13% per hour.[55] BFU-E thus have cycle times of around 8 hr, which is very fast for mammalian cells. S-phase would be a little over 3 hr long. In the presence of NRP, the proportion of BFU-E engaged in DNA synthesis was immediately reduced to less than 10%. This drop from ca. 40% to <10% [^{3}H]thymidine-vulnerable (i.e., cycling) BFU-E when NRP was added happened too quickly for the cells to have moved around the cell cycle to any extent before they were blocked. Since ca. 40% of BFU-E are normally in S-phase, this reduction could be accounted for by inhibition of DNA synthesis of the cells which were in S-phase, without accumulation of cells at any other stage in the cell cycle. This experiment was, in effect, the converse of the washing experiment in which the proportion of DNA-synthesizing BFU-E instead showed a striking *increase,* yet this happened just as quickly as the *decrease* after NRP was added. Apparently BFU-E within the S-phase of the cell cycle can still be influenced to make the decision whether DNA synthesis will proceed.

HOW DOES NRP RELATE TO OTHER GROWTH FACTORS?

Interleukin-3 (IL-3) is an "emergency" growth factor that is known to act positively on hemopoietic stem and progenitor cells to maintain their viability and their capacity for proliferation. To see if IL-3 could overcome the inhibition of DNA synthesis due to NRP, we administered a known effective dose of NRP to bone marrow cell cultures and titrated the effects of IL-3 against it. The effect of IL-3 clearly opposed the negative effect of NRP on the proportion of BFU-E engaged in DNA synthesis. These results suggest that in an emergency, IL-3 would be able to overcome the inhibition of DNA synthesis imposed by NRP. Both growth factors acted within minutes on marrow BFU-E DNA synthesis. These findings thus also strongly suggest that the actions of IL-3 and NRP are directly on the BFU-E without the involvement of an intermediate cell or factor. DNA synthesis of the BFU-E thus appears to be controlled both negatively and positively.[57]

PURIFICATION OF THE NEGATIVE REGULATORY ACTIVITY PRODUCED BY A B6 MARROW-DERIVED CELL LINE

To characterize NRP further, it was evident that we would have to first purify the protein. If we started from marrow as source, we would need myriads of mice to do the job. Fortunately, as a result of the work of a former graduate student (Dushandhan S. Vaithilingam), we have a cell line called B6 Pan, derived from the bone marrow cells of B6 mice. Its cells have been found to produce considerable quantities of a material having NRP-like activity.

Medium from B6 Pan cells served as starting material for purification of NRP.[63] The crude supernatant was concentrated, dialyzed against distilled water, and then lyophilized. This material was added onto a carboxymethyl Affi-Gel Blue (Bio-Rad) chromatographic column in phosphate buffer at pH 6, followed by a linear NaCl gradient, and fractions were collected. NRP did not bind to the carboxymethyl Affi-Gel Blue column but eluted with the running buffer. The only significant activity was in the material that did not bind to the column. This material, which we call Step I NRP, was enriched in NRP-like activity by more than 500-fold over the starting material. The next step was Sephadex G-100 (Pharmacia) gel filtration. The active fraction (Step II NRP) was found to correspond in different experiments to an average apparent M_r of ca. 79,000. This was confirmed with Superose 12 (Pharmacia) gel filtration on FPLC.

Step II NRP was loaded onto a Concanavalin A-Sepharose (Pharmacia) affinity chromatographic column. NRP (Step III) was found to elute with the unbound proteins. This step did not get rid of much protein, but it did remove contaminants that interfered with our detection of NRP. We could now obtain clean titrations of Step III NRP, and the reduction in the proportion of BFU-E engaged in DNA synthesis was related to the logarithm of the concentration of NRP added to the assay cultures. Earlier in the purification process, contamination of our preparations with positively acting factors interfered with the titration and also gave us apparent recoveries of NRP activity that were much greater than 100%. But once we eliminated the unknown positive factors, we could assay NRP more reliably. In an adult B6 mouse we found between 5 and 10 units (U)[57,63] of NRP per 2 femurs (3×10^7 cells).

For the next step in purification of NRP, we subjected the Step III material to anion exchange chromatography on a Pharmacia FPLC system with a Mono-Q (quaternary ammonium) strong anion exchange column and Tris buffer at pH 7.45. NRP activity (Step IV) did not bind to the anion exchange column. This Step IV material was then applied to an FPLC strong cation exchange column Mono-S, in which the sulfate radical is the negatively charged ion at pH 4.7. Again NRP failed to bind. The amount of protein recovered (Step V) was too low to be seen by polyacrylamide gel electrophoresis or by standard protein assay. Amino acid analysis on a Pico-tag system gave us a calculated protein content so that we could estimate an approximate specific activity. The specific activity of NRP Step V was of the order of 50,000 U/mg protein, representing an enrichment of ca. 100,000-fold over the starting material. In order to get a biological effect of NRP in our assay system, the amount of protein now required was in the order of 50 ng as opposed to 4 mg at the start.

Since NRP did not bind to the strong anion exchange column Mono-Q at pH 7.45, to the weak cation exchange carboxymethyl Affi-Gel Blue column at pH 6, or to the strong cation exchange column Mono-S at pH 4.7, NRP seems to be a neutral or weakly charged protein at physiological pH.

That this protein has carbohydrate residues was shown in another series of experiments, in which we investigated the ability of NRP to bind to Concanavalin A (Con A), soybean agglutinin (SBA), and wheat germ agglutinin (WGA). The results showed that NRP bound to WGA but not to either Con A or SBA. NRP that was bound to WGA could be eluted with 1 *M N*-acetylglucosamine (GlcNac). Thus, NRP contains either GlcNAc or sialic acid residues. Carbohydrate analysis of Step V NRP was consistent with this conclusion. On the basis of these findings, we concluded that NRP is a WGA-binding glycoprotein.

This sequence of five purification steps carried out on medium from the B6 Pan cell line greatly enriched our preparations with respect to negative regulatory activity. But they also caused great losses along the way, and they did not permit us to reach homogeneity. We are therefore at present making efforts to improve the purification protocol.

Whatever the outcome of these efforts, the experiments described here have already made it clear that from the marrow cells of B6 (*Fv-2^{rr}*) mice, a glycoprotein can be recovered which rapidly, reversibly, and specifically inhibits cycling of the early BFU-E of murine marrow. This molecule is diffusible and appears to act at short range as a physiological negative regulator of BFU-E proliferation. Since cycling of BFU-E is a necessary, if not sufficient, condition for susceptibility to Friend SFFV, it appears likely that one component of the solid resistance of B6 mice and their marrow cells to this virus is mediated by NRP molecules. Early experiments with crude NRP did in fact give suggestive evidence in favor of this hypothesis,[64] but definitive evidence for or against it must await the availability of homogeneous NRP in quantities sufficient for practical experimentation.

It is tempting to speculate that self-renewing BFU-E (presumably those responsible for the large numbers of cells in erythropoietic bursts), rather than BFU-E undergoing proliferation as part of their erythroid differentiation program, are the targets of both SFFV and NRP in marrow. That is not to say that it is these early BFU-E that express the neoplastic phenotype. Expression of the erythroproliferative phenotype occurs mainly in the spleen as unregulated proliferation of erythropoietin-independent CFU-E as well as late BFU-E. We have previously presented evidence that the normal cycling BFU-E in marrow is a proximate precursor of the normal CFU-E in spleen.[46,65]

ACKNOWLEDGMENTS

I thank Mr. H. C. Van der Gaag for excellent technical assistance and Mrs. P. Middleton for superb secretarial help.

REFERENCES

1. FRIEND, C. 1957. J. Exp. Med. **105:** 307-318.
2. FRIEND, C. & B. G.-T. POGO. 1985. Biochim. Biophys. Acta **780:** 181-195.
3. HARTLEY, J. W., W. P. ROWE & R. J. HUEBNER. 1970. J. Virol. **5:** 221-225.
4. ROWE, W. P., J. B. HUMPHREY & F. LILLY. 1973. J. Exp. Med. **137:** 850-853.
5. PINCUS, T., W. P. ROWE & F. LILLY. 1971. J. Exp. Med. **133:** 1234-1241.
6. LILLY, F. 1970. J. Natl. Cancer Inst. **45:** 163-169.
7. CHESEBRO, B. & K. WEHRLY. 1978. J. Immunol. **120:** 1081-1024.
8. CHESEBRO, B. & K. WEHRLY. 1979. Proc. Natl. Acad. Sci. USA **76:** 425-429.
9. AXELRAD, A. A. & R. A. STEEVES. 1964. Virology **24:** 513-518.
10. STEEVES, R. A. 1975. J. Natl. Cancer Inst. **54:** 289-297.
11. TROXLER, D. H., S. K. RUSCETTI & E. M. SCOLNICK. 1980. Biochim. Biophys. Acta **605:** 305-324.
12. STEEVES, R. A., R. J. ECKNER, M. BENNETT, E. A. MIRAND & P. J. TRUDEL. 1971. J. Natl. Cancer Inst. **46:** 1209-1217.
13. JOLICOEUR, P. 1979. Immunology **86:** 68-122.
14. JOLICOEUR, P. & D. BALTIMORE. 1976. Proc. Natl. Acad. Sci. USA **73:** 2236-2240.
15. SVEDA, M. M. & R. SOEIRO. 1976. Proc. Natl. Acad. Sci. USA **73:** 2356-2360.
16. DESGROSEILLERS, L. & P. JOLICOEUR. 1983. J. Virol. **48:** 685-696.
17. HARTLEY, J. W., W. P. ROWE & R. J. HUEBNER. J. Virol. **5:** 221-225.
18. LILLY, F. 1967. Science **155:** 461-462.
19. HOPKINS, N., J. SCHINDLER & R. HYNES. 1977. J. Virol. **21:** 309-318.
20. MACDONALD, M. E., G. R. JOHNSON & A. BERNSTEIN. 1981. Virology **110:** 231-236.
21. BERGER, S. A., N. SANDERSON, A. BERNSTEIN & W. D. HANKINS. 1985. Proc. Natl. Acad. Sci. USA **82:** 6913-6917.
22. CHESEBRO, B. & K. WEHRLY. 1976. J. Exp. Med. **143:** 85-99.
23. ODAKA, T. & T. YAMAMOTO. 1962. Jpn. J. Exp. Med. **32:** 405-413.
24. AXELRAD, A. A., S. SUZUKI, H. VAN DER GAAG, B. J. CLARKE & D. L. MCLEOD. 1978. *In* Hematopoietic Cell Differentiation. D. W. Golde, M. J. Cline, D. Metcalf & C. F. Fox, Eds.: 69-90. Academic Press. New York.
25. LIAO, S. K. & A. A. AXELRAD. 1975. Int. J. Cancer **15:** 467-482.
26. HOROSZEWICZ, J. S., S. S. LEONG & W. A. CARTER. 1975. J. Natl. Cancer Inst. **54:** 265-267.
27. BONDURANT, M. C., M. KOURY & S. B. KRANTZ. 1985. J. Gen. Virol. **66:** 83-96.
28. HANKINS, W. D., T. A. KOST, M. J. KOURY & S. B. KRANTZ. 1979. *In* Experimental Hematology Today 1979. S. J. Baum & G. D. Ledney, Eds.: 89-97. Springer-Verlag. New York.
29. ISCOVE, N. N. 1978. *In* Hematopoietic Cell Differentiation. D. W. Golde, M. J. Cline, D. Metcalf & C. F. Fox, Eds.: 36-52. Academic Press. New York.
30. HANGOC, G., L. LU, A. OLIFF, S. GILLIS & H. E. BROXMEYER. 1986. Exp. Hematol. **14:** 519.
31. TEICH, N., J. WYKE, T. MAK, A. BERNSTEIN & W. HARDY. 1982. *In* Molecular Biology of Tumor Viruses: RNA Tumor Viruses. R. Weiss, N. Teich, H. Varmus & J. Coffin, Eds.: 785-998. The Cold Spring Harbor Laboratory. New York.
32. STEEVES, R. A., F. LILLY, G. STEINHEIDER & K. BLANK. 1978. *In* Differentiation of Normal and Neoplastic Hemopoietic Cells. B. Clarkson, P. A. Marks & J. E. Till, Eds.: 591-600. The Cold Spring Harbor Laboratory. New York.

33. ODAKA, T. 1967. Jpn. J. Exp. Med. **37:** 71-72.
34. GEIB, R. W., M. DIZIK, R. ANAND & F. LILLY. 1987. Virus Res. **8:** 327-333.
35. STEEVES, R. A. & I. GRUNDKE-IQBAL. 1976. J. Natl. Cancer Inst. **56:** 541-546.
36. TEICH, N. M. & T. M. DEXTER. 1979. *In* Oncogenic Viruses and Host Cell Genes. Y. Ikawa & T. Odaka, Eds.: 263-276. Academic Press. New York.
37. DAWSON, P. J., W. M. ROSE & A. H. FIELDSTEEL. 1966. Br. J. Cancer **20:** 114-121.
38. STEEVES, R. A., R. J. ECKNER, M. BENNETT, E. A. MIRAND & P. J. TRUDEL. 1971. J. Natl. Cancer Inst. **46:** 1209-1217.
39. EVANS, L. H., P. H. DUESBERG & E. M. SCOLNICK. 1979. Virology **101:** 534-539.
40. CINADER, B., H. C. VAN DER GAAG, S.-Y. W. KOH & A. A. AXELRAD. 1987. Mech. Ageing Dev. **40:** 181-191.
41. ODAKA, T. 1970. Intl. J. Cancer **6:** 18-23.
42. YOOSOOK, C., R. STEEVES & F. LILLY. 1980. Intl. J. Cancer **26:** 101-106.
43. AXELRAD, A. A. & S. SUZUKI. 1980. *In* In Vivo and In Vitro Erythropoiesis: The Friend System. G. B. Rossi, Ed.: 173-182. Elsevier/North Holland. Amsterdam.
44. KOST, T. A., M. J. KOURY, W. D. HANKINS & S. B. KRANTZ. 1979. Cell **18:** 145-152.
45. SEIDEL, H. J. & L. KREJA. 1982. Int. Soc. Exp. Hematol. **10:** 459-466.
46. SUZUKI, S. & A. A. AXELRAD. 1980. Cell **19:** 225-236.
47. AXELRAD, A. A., H. CROIZAT & D. ESKINAZI. 1981. Cell **26:** 233-244.
48. SILVER, J. & N. TEICH. 1981. J. Exp. Med. **154:** 126-137.
49. DEWEY, M. J. & P. W. ELDRIDGE. 1982. Exp. Hematol. **10:** 723-731.
50. BEHRINGER, R. R. & M. J. DEWEY. 1985. Cell **40:** 441-447.
51. BEHRINGER, R. R., P. W. ELDRIDGE & M. J. DEWEY. 1983. Dev. Biol. **101:** 1-6.
52. ODAKA, T. 1969. Jpn. J. Exp. Med. **39:** 99-100.
53. ODAKA, T. & M. MATSUKURA. 1969. J. Virol. **4:** 837-843.
54. BEHRINGER, R. R. & M. J. DEWEY. PERSONAL COMMUNICATION.
55. AXELRAD, A. A., H. CROIZAT, D. ESKINAZI, S. STEWART, D. VAITHILINGAM & H. C. VAN DER GAAG. 1983. *In* Haemopoietic Stem Cells. Sv-Aa. Killman, E. P. Cronkite & C. N. Muller-Berat, Eds.: 234-251. Munksgaard. Copenhagen.
56. HANNA, I. R. A. 1967. Nature **214:** 355-357.
57. AXELRAD, A. A., H. CROIZAT, D. DEL RIZZO, D. ESKINAZI, G. PEZZUTTI, S. STEWART & H. VAN DER GAAG. *In* The Inhibitors of Hematopoiesis. A. Najman, M. Guigon, N-C. Gorin & J.-Y. Mary, Eds. Colloque INSERM Vol. 162: 79-92. John Libbey Eurotext. Paris.
58. SHARKIS, S. J., J. D. PALMER, J. GOODENOUGH, J. LOBUE & A. S. GORDON. 1974. Cell Tissue Kinet. **7:** 381-387.
59. RUSSELL, E. S. 1978. *In* Origins of Inbred Mice. H. C. Morse, III, Ed.: 33-43. Academic Press. New York.
60. MORSE, H. C., III. 1978. *In* Origins of Inbred Mice. H. C. Morse, III, Ed.: 3-21. Academic Press. New York.
61. KOZAK, C. A. 1985. J. Virol. **55:** 281-285.
62. FOX, R. 1986. (The Jackson Laboratory, Bar Harbor, Maine) Personal communication.
63. DEL RIZZO, D. F., D. ESKINAZI & A. A. AXELRAD. 1988. Proc. Natl. Acad. Sci. USA **85:** 4320-4324.
64. AXELRAD, A. A., H. CROIZAT, D. ESKINAZI, S. STEWART, D. VAITHILINGAM & H. VAN DER GAAG. 1982. J. Cell. Physiol. **1** (Suppl.): 165-173.
65. AXELRAD, A. A., D. L. MCLEOD, S. SUZUKI & M. M. SHREEVE. 1978. *In* Differentiation of Normal and Neoplastic Hematopoietic Cells. B. Clarkson, P. A. Marks & J. E. Till, Eds.: 155-163. The Cold Spring Harbor Laboratory. New York.

Genetics of Endogenous Murine Leukemia Viruses[a]

JOHN M. COFFIN, JONATHAN P. STOYE, AND WAYNE N. FRANKEL

Department of Molecular Biology and Microbiology
Tufts University School of Medicine
136 Harrison Avenue
Boston, Massachusetts 02111

INTRODUCTION

It is unlikely that the genome of any organism is free of mobile elements. In vertebrates, a major class of such elements consists of endogenous proviruses derived from past retrovirus infection of the germline. These can be conveniently grouped according to the virus or virus-like element to which they are most closely related. In mice, it has been estimated that as much as 0.5% of the genome consists of such elements, which are closely related to one of four groups: C type (i.e., related to murine leukemia virus), B type (related to mammary tumor virus), A type (encoding intracisternal A particles), and VL30 (encoding a retrovirus RNA-like sequence).[1,2] The distribution and relationships of these elements imply a recent and ongoing process of insertion into the genome. In addition, there are a large number of much older elements, clearly retroviral in origin; but they diverge highly from the sequences of known retroviruses, implying that they are fossil residues of much more ancient germline infections. Clearly, the association of endogenous retroviruses and the vertebrate genome is a long-standing one, and it is not unreasonable to suppose that endogenous proviruses (and, by extension, related exogenous retroviruses) have been present in more-or-less modern form throughout vertebrate evolution.

Despite their large numbers and their relationship to known pathogens, endogenous proviruses have relatively little effect on their host, with a few noteworthy exceptions. First, the introduction of a provirus into a coding region of the genome can have obvious disruptive effects. For example, the *d* (dilute) mutation, characteristic of several strains of inbred mice, has been shown to have been caused by insertion of an ecotropic C-type provirus.[3,4] Second, although individually benign (and often defective), the progeny of the endogenous proviruses present in some strains of mice, such as AKR, can recombine to yield viruses which can cause a lethal thymoma at a relatively young age.

Inbred strains of mice contain 40-60 endogenous C-type proviruses in a variety of chromosomal locations.[5] These can be grossly subdivided into two distinct host-range categories: ecotropic (i.e., encoding an *env* gene product capable of infecting

[a] This work was supported by Grant R35CA44385 to J. M. C. and a fellowship from the Leukemia Society of America, Inc., to W. N. F.

mice but relatively few other species) and non-ecotropic (encompassing three other host-range groups: xenotropic, polytropic, and modified polytropic). There are only a relatively small number (0-6) of ecotropic proviruses in any given strain of mice, making their genetic analysis relatively straightforward.[7] Until recently, the non-ecotropic group has remained relatively unexplored. The goals of this project were first to obtain detailed analyses of the genetic associations and evolutionary relationships of this group of viruses within inbred mice and then to identify the non-ecotropic proviruses important to the *in vivo* evolution of viruses during spontaneous oncogenesis.

RESULTS AND DISCUSSION

Structure and Distribution of Endogenous Proviruses

To approach the issue of non-ecotropic proviruses, we began by cloning as many C-type proviruses as possible from a single strain of mice. The strain chosen was HRS/J, carrying the *hr* (hairless) mutation, which results in complete loss of hair at an early age and is associated with increased incidence of AKR-like thymic lymphoma.[8] At present, we have cloned all or in some cases part (at least the 3′ half) of 33 of the 42 proviruses present in this strain. Structural analysis of a number of these revealed that they could be readily classified into one of four groups (ignoring simple deletions; FIG. 1). These provirus groups include (1) two previously reported ecotropic proviruses (*emv* 1 and 3),[7] (2) proviruses encoding a xenotropic *env* gene (xenotropic murine virus group, XMV), (3) proviruses encoding a polytropic *env* gene (polytropic murine virus group, PMV), and (4) proviruses encoding a novel *env* gene, which we have termed modified polytropic (modified polytropic murine virus group, MPMV). The latter group had not been noted previously, it encodes a host-range similar to polytropic viruses except that the relative infectivity on mink cells is substantially less (our unpublished data). All members of a group are very closely related to one another,[6] implying that their insertion into the germline is a very recent event and that they are separated from one another by only a few virus replication cycles.

In addition to differences in the *env* gene region which codes for the 70-kDa envelope glycoprotein (gp70) and the 15-kDa transmembrane protein (p15E), the groups of viruses are also distinguishable by other linked characteristics, including some restriction site polymorphisms and the insertion of a small (ca. 190-base) segment of DNA into the U3 region of PMV and MPMV proviruses. This inserted sequence is found in high copy number in the mouse genome in a non-proviral context.[9] It therefore seems to be a mobile element that inserted itself into an ancestor of the PMV and MPMV groups after divergence from the XMV group. Given all this, we can infer a pathway of evolution of these viruses as shown in FIGURE. 2. Note that the divergence between the various groups must have substantially predated the fixation of individual proviruses in inbred strains. It should also be noted that the ecotropic *env* genome is much more closely related to the others within the p15E coding region than within the gp70 coding region. This relationship suggests that the endogenous ecotropic proviruses may themselves have derived from a recombinant between an endogenous non-ecotropic provirus and an ecotropic provirus which may have been exogenous.

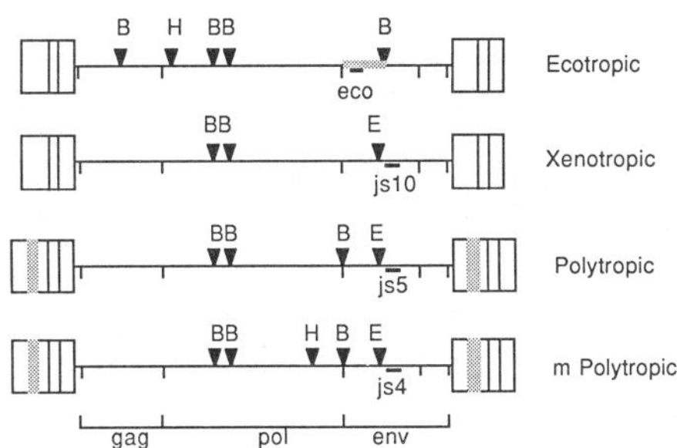

FIGURE 1. The four groups of endogenous C-type provirus structures. *Arrowheads* indicate restriction enzyme cleavage sites: B, *Bam*H I; H, *Hin*d III; E, *Eco*R I. The *split boxes* at the ends represent long terminal repeats (LTRs), in which the *shaded regions* denote a small inserted sequence. The *underlined regions* in each *env* gene show the location of the sequences reactive with the various group-specific probes (eco, js10, js5, js4). The *shaded horizontal bar* in the *env* gene (Ecotropic) indicates the region of maximal sequence diverence between ecotropic and non-ecotropic viruses. Polytropic, modified polytropic.

Acquisition of a detailed understanding of the genetic association of non-ecotropic proviruses with mice has been hindered in the past by the close nucleotide sequence relationship among these viruses that precluded the preparation of probes with sufficient specificity to distinguish individual members of the groups. Examination of the sequence of the gp70-coding region of these groups revealed a small sequence polymorphism that permitted us to prepare oligonucleotide probes specific for each group (FIG. 3). When mouse DNA is digested with a restriction enzyme (such as *Eco*R I; FIG. 1) which cuts just 5′ of the location of the polymorphic sequence recognized by the particular probe, individual proviruses are revealed on a Southern blot as distinct bands reflecting the size of the 3′ junction fragment running through the reset restriction enzyme site in the mouse DNA flanking the provirus (FIG. 4). Using this approach, we can precisely enumerate and identify the non-ecotropic proviral DNA content of inbred stains of mice (TABLE 1). All inbred stains have a distinct pattern of proviruses, some of which are shared with other strains and others of which are unique to a given strain. It appears, from the pattern of proviruses in relation to the genealogy of the mice,[10] that most of the insertions probably preceded inbreeding and represent differential fixation from a large, randomly segregating pool in the outbred progenitor mice.

Association of Proviruses and Mutations

Using the oligonucleotides probes, we have undertaken an extensive examination of the strain distribution pattern (SDP) of the proviruses in recombinant inbred (RI) strains of mice. Comparison of the SDPs for individual proviruses to those for other genetic loci permits both mapping of proviruses, by determination of genetic linkage to previously mapped markers, and identification of proviruses which might have a causal relationship with certain mutations. Using this approach, we have mapped over 100 proviruses in 7 RI sets of lines representing 7 progenitor inbred strains (TABLE 2). These mapped proviruses should provide valuable markers for use in various kinds of genetic experimentation.

The other use of this sort of data is to associate proviruses with specific mutations. This is potentially a very useful approach for accessing important genes which are

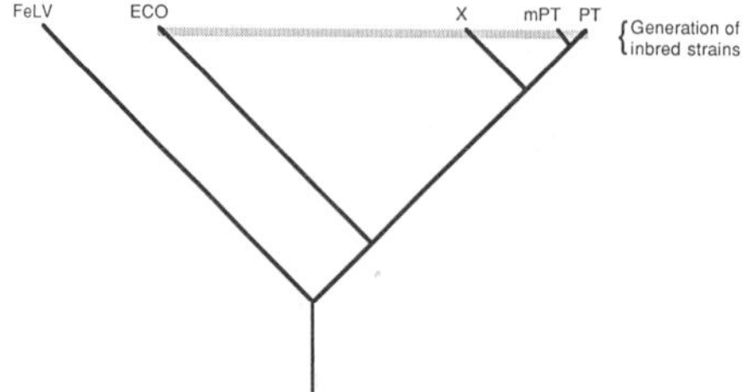

FIGURE 2. Evolutionary relationship among C-type provirus gp70 sequences. The scale is based on computer-assisted alignment among the nucleotide sequences. FeLV: feline leukemia virus; ECO, X, mPT, and PT: ecotropic, xenotropic, modified polytropic, and polytropic murine virus groups, respectively.

otherwise impossible to approach by standard cloning technology. Analysis of the RI strains as well as numerous mutant congenic and coisogenic strains carrying specific mutations has revealed close linkage of specific proviruses with a number of previously well-characterized mutations (TABLE 3). If all of these linkages reflect causality, we would estimate that some 5% of recessive mutations in mice are due to insertion of non-ecotropic proviruses (and that 5% of proviruses cause such mutations).

In one instance so far, that of the association of a provirus called MX40 and *hr*, we have been able to establish a causal relationship. A probe derived from the sequence flanking MX40 on the 3′ side of the provirus reveals the presence of the MX40 provirus in all *hr*-containing strains and its absence in all others (FIG. 5). Establishment of causality was made possible by the existence of a spontaneous hairy revertant in a mouse strain derived from HRA/Skh.[11] Analysis of this DNA shows that the revertant has lost the complete provirus but preserves in its place a sequence about 800 bp larger than that of the wild-type, indicating the presence of a residual solo long terminal repeat (LTR) from the provirus. We have confirmed the presence of the structures shown in FIGURE 5 by cloning and sequencing relevant regions. Thus, reversion at the *hr* locus (like reversion of dilute) is apparently caused by recombination of the provirus across its LTRs, leading to excision of all except a single LTR. We infer that the MX40 provirus is integrated in such a position (for example, within an intron) that the intact provirus can disrupt expression of the *hr* gene but its single LTR

VIRUS CLASS	OLIGO	
		857 884
mPT	JS4	GCAGCCTCTATA CAACCTGGGACGGGAG
		857 911
PT	JS5	GCAGCCTCTATAGTCCCTGAGACTGCCCCACCTTCTCAACAACCTGGGACGGGA
		1092 1146
X	JS6	ACGGTCTCTATGGTACCTGGGGCTCCCCCGCCTTCTCAACAACCTGGGACGGGA
X	JS10	ACGGTCTCTATGGTGCCTGGGGCTCCCCCGCCTTCTCAACAACCTGGGACGGGA

FIGURE 3. Oligonucleotide probes specific for *env* sequences of endogenous non-ecotropic proviruses. The *underlined* nucleotides correspond to the oligonucleotide probes specific for *env* genes of modified polytropic (mPT), polytropic (PT), and xenotropic (X) murine virus groups, respectively. Difference between JS6 and JS10 probes for X is indicated by *diamond.* The numbering of bases is arbitrary.

cannot. This intimate association suggests that the coding sequence of *hr* must be nearby and that MX40 can be used as a tag to identify and clone this sequence; we are currently attempting to do so.

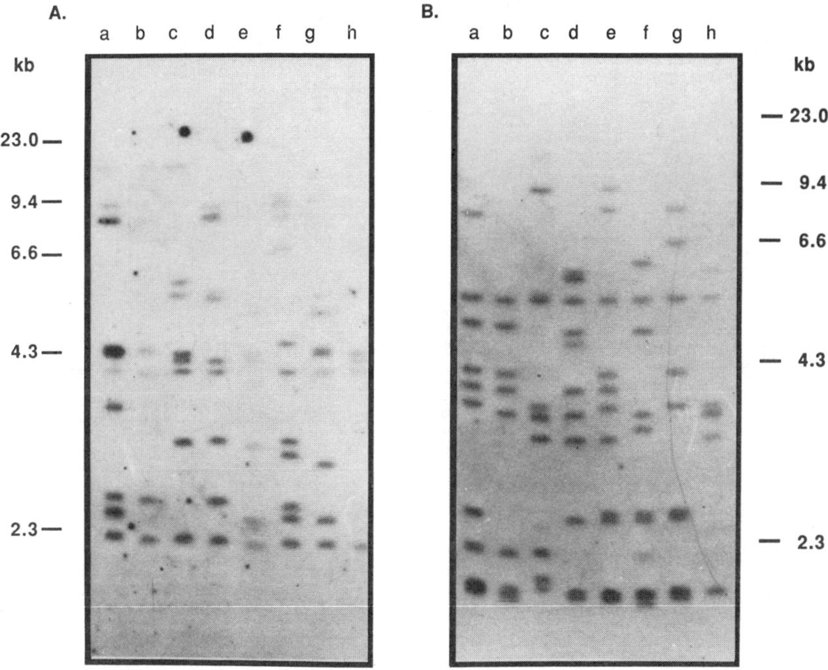

FIGURE 4. Modified polytropic provirus content of eight strains of mice. (**Panel A**) Blot hybridization analysis of *Eco*R I-digested DNAs from (**a**) HRS/J, (**b**) BALB/cJ, (**c**) A/J, (**d**) AKR/J, (**e**) C57BL/6J, (**f**) DBA/2J, (**g**) C57L/J, and (**h**) C3H/HeJ mice. (**Panel B**) Identical DNA samples as in (**A**) digested with *Pvu* II. Both blots were probed with the JS4 oligonucleotide. kb, kilobases.

Endogenous Mice and Thymomas

During the early life of AKR mice, a complex evolutionary process occurs involving at least two recombinant events and three endogenous proviral parents. The result is a virus (called MCF for mink cell focus-forming) that is intimately involved in the induction of thymic lymphoma, most likely by a mechanism involving promoter insertion.[12] The recombination events in this process involve exchange into an ecotropic virus backbone of both a new LTR and the gp70 portion of *env* derived from non-ecotropic proviruses. The use of a probe strategy similar to the one described above has allowed us to dissect some of these events. Examination of the sequence of the LTR of several MCF viruses revealed a sequence sufficiently unique to prepare a specific oligonucleotide (called JS21). The specificity of this probe is shown by the demonstration that it reacts with only one endogenous provirus in mice; this reaction

TABLE 1. Total Non-ecotropic Proviral Contents of Eight Inbred Mouse Strains

	No. of Proviral Loci		
Strain	Modified Polytropic	Polytropic	Xenotropic
HRS/J	11	23	9
BALB/cJ	8	16	12
A/J	8	17	12
AKR/J	11	17	12
C57BL/6J	13	24	20
DBA/2J	12	19	12
C57L/J	10	16	21
C3H/HeJ	8	15	8

TABLE 2. Non-ecotropic Proviruses in Recombinant Inbred (RI) Strains

			Proviruses Unique to	
RI Set[a]	No. of Strains	Common Proviruses	First Parent	Second Parent
A × B	41	24	16	36
AK × D	25	18	22	25
AK × L	18	13	26	33
B × H	12	18	39	12
B × D	26	19	38	23
C × B	7	23	34	13
L × B	3	37	9	20

[a] A, A/J; B, C57BL/6J; AK, AKR/J; H, C3H/HeJ; D, DBA/2J; C, BALB/cJ; L, C57L/J.

TABLE 3. Linkage between Proviruses and Mouse Mutations

Locus[a]	Linkage[b]	Mice[c]
Hairless	Provirus causal	CG, REV
Ichthyosis (*ic*)	Provirus 0-6.0 Cm from *ic*	CG
Retinal degeneration (*rd*)	Provirus 0-2.0 Cm from *rd*	CG, RI
Albino (*c*)	Provirus 0-1.0 Cm from *c*	RI
Non-agouti (*a*)	Provirus 0-3.1 Cm from *a*	RI
Fv-1	4 Proviruses 0-2.9 Cm from *Fv-1*^{b}	RI
t^{12}	Presence of extra provirus	CG
t^{w18}	Presence of 3 extra proviruses	CG

[a] Over 100 mouse mutations have been examined. A complete list of the mutations that did not show evidence for extra proviruses is available on request.

[b] Presented as lower and upper 95% confidence intervals calculated from the method of Silver.[15] Cm, centimorgan.

[c] Data from CG (congenic mice), RI (recombinant inbred mice), REV (revertant mice).

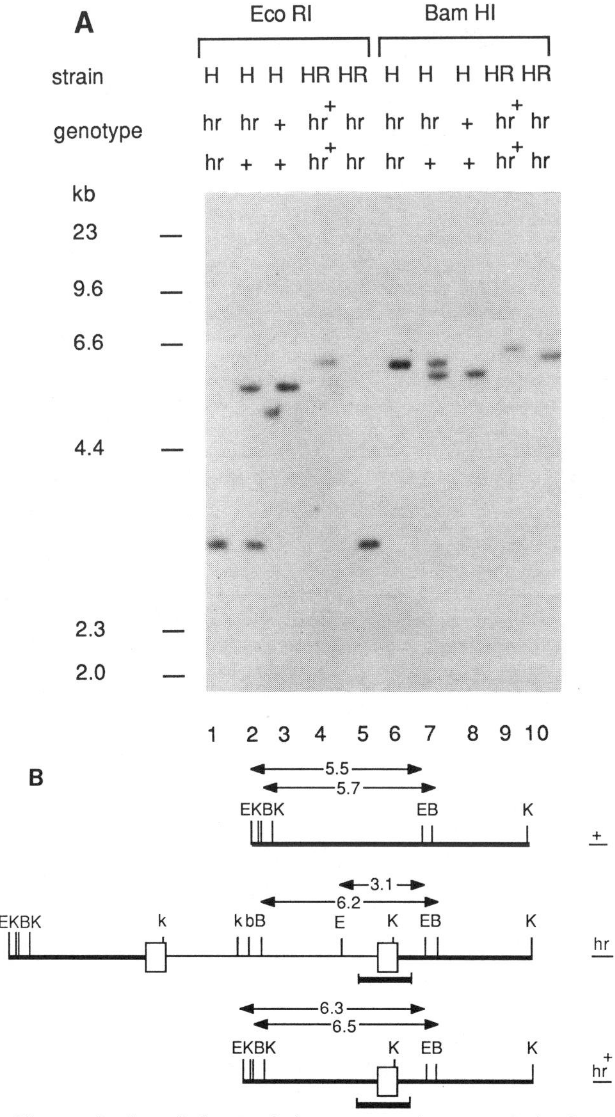

FIGURE 5. Characterization of the restriction enzyme sites around the *hr*-associated viral integration sequence in mutant and revertant mice. (**A**) Blot hybridization analysis. *Eco*R I- (*lanes 1-5*) and *Bam*H I- (*lanes 6-10*) digested DNAs (5 μg each) of HRS/J *hr/hr*, HRS/J *hr/*+, HRS/J +/+, HRA/Skh hr^+/hr^+, and HRA/Skh *hr/hr* mice were fractionated by electrophoresis, transferred to nitrocellulose, and probed with the MX40 flanking sequence probe BgX. kb, kilobases. (**B**) The predicted structures of the wild-type (+), mutant (*hr*), and revertant (hr^+) alleles of the hairless locus. Restriction sites shown are B, *Bam*H I; E, *Eco*R I; K, *Kpn* I. *Arrows* indicate restriction fragments seen in (**A**). *Lower-case letters* indicate sites presumed to be present by analogy with other endogenous polytropic viruses[5] but not demonstrated directly. *Thin lines* and *thick lines* correspond to viral and cell sequences, respectively. The *boxes* show position of the viral long terminal repeat. *Heavy bars* under the 3′ LTR of *hr* and the LTR of hr^+ indicate sequenced regions.

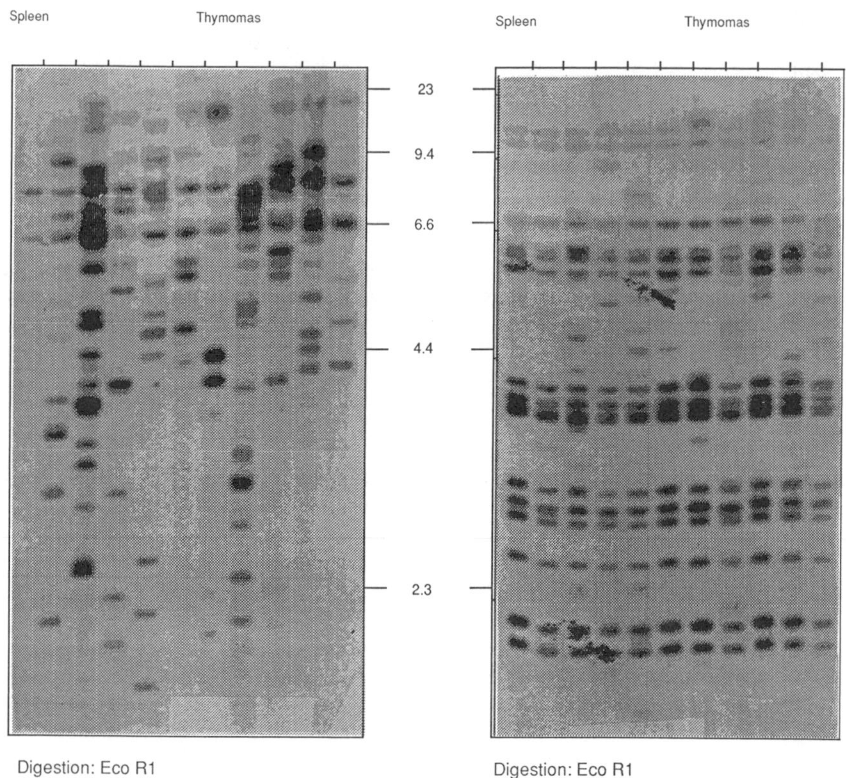

FIGURE 6. Somatically acquired proviruses in AKR thymomas. DNA from spleen (first lane on left of each panel) or 10 independent AKR thymomas was digested with *Eco*R I and, after separation on agarose gels and transfer to nitrocellulose, hybridized to the MCF LTR-specific probe JS21 (**left panel**) or to the polytropic provirus *env* probe JS5 (**right panel**). *Numbers* between panels indicate positions of size markers in kilobases. The two fragments corresponding to *Bxv-1* can be seen most clearly in the first lane of the left panel.

yields the two LTR-containing bands shown in FIGURE 6. These reactive bands belong to a provirus which has previously been termed *Bxv*-1, an endogenous provirus which can be induced to yield infectious xenotropic virus.[13] That this probe also identifies the LTR donor is shown by the dramatic amplification of the copy number of proviruses containing it in several thymomas (FIG. 6). Comparison of the same samples using a PMV probe (JS5) shows that most or all of the new proviruses are also recombinant in *env*. (To date we have been unable to identify the specific donor of this portion of the MCF genome).

Use of the JS21 probe also reveals another aspect of the evolution of MCF viruses (FIG. 7). Use of a pair of restriction enzymes that excise a portion of the LTR allows the demonstration that the LTRs of the MCF viruses in tumors are longer (by an amount varying from 70 to 150 bases) than that of the *Bxv*-1 parent. This increased length is due to the reduplication of the enhancer-containing region of the MCF

LTR.[14] We thus conclude that the evolution *in vivo* of thymomagenic viruses involves at least three events: two recombination steps and a reduplication of sequences to yield the final virus.

CONCLUSIONS

The endogenous proviruses of mice are one of the most complex, yet one of the most potentially rewarding, systems in virology. The potential both to provide access points into interesting regions of the mouse genome and to shed light on the complex interactions of viruses during pathogenesis *in vivo* has not yet been fully realized, due to the difficulties in breaking down the large numbers of elements into readily identifiable and manageable groups. The key technical advances that we have reported here are the distinction of the separate groups of these proviruses and the development of probe strategies to refine and simplify their analysis. In this way, we have begun to appreciate the role of the endogenous C-type proviruses as a force both in genetic variation and in spontaneous oncogenesis. Considering that there are other much larger groups of retrovirus-like elements in the genomes of mice and other mammals, we are optimistic that these strategies can be extended to an even greater depth of analysis of this important mechanism of genetic variation.

SUMMARY

Inbred stains of mice contain in the genome 40-60 en .ogenous proviruses related to murine leukemia virus. To assess the genetic and pathogenic consequences of these to the host, we have developed a strategy to distinguish among the three different host-range subgroups—xenotropic, polytropic and modified polytropic—by using oligonucleotide probes specific for a polymorphic region in *env.* Each of these proteins detects a relatively small number of bands in a Southern blot, thus permitting us to enumerate all individual proviruses of this group. Using this approach, we have determined the distribution of different proviruses among inbred and recombinant

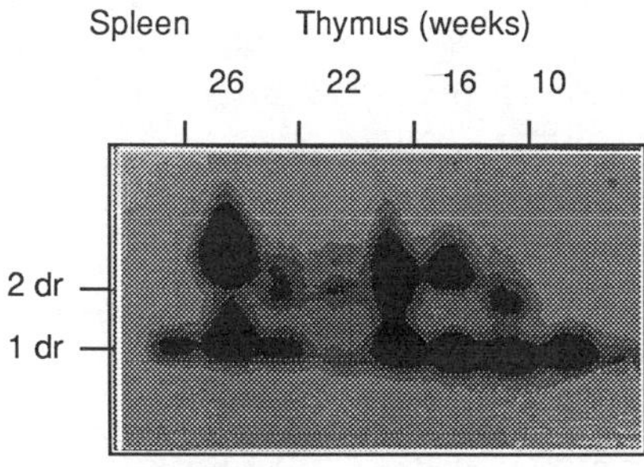

FIGURE 7. Time-course of enhancer sequence duplication in thymus of AKR mice. DNA from the spleen or from the thymus at indicated ages was taken from AKR mice and digested with *Kpn* I and *Pst* I, which cleave near the ends of the LTR, and the separated fragments were probed with the MCF LTR-specific probe. The markers show the sizes expected for the fragments containing one or two copies of the direct repeat (dr) enhancer-containing region.

inbred (RI) strains congenic or coisogenic for specific mutants. Using the RI results, we have been able to place over 100 proviruses on the mouse genetic map. A number of these are closely linked to well-characterized mutations, and we have been able to establish that at least one mutation, *hr* (hairless), was caused by a proviral insertion. If the other close linkages also prove to reflect causality, we estimate that up to 5% of recessive mutations in the mouse might be caused by insertion of proviruses of this group.

Using a similar probe strategy, we have followed the evolution of murine leukemia viruses during spontaneous leukemogenesis in AKR mice. We have found that the final leukemogenic (MCF) virus is a recombinant of three different endogenous parents; an ecotropic virus, a polytropic virus that directs the gp70 region of *env,* and a xenotropic virus (identified as the inducible element *Bxv-1*) that directs the LTR. In addition to the recombinations, all such viruses also have a reduplication of the enhancer region of the LTR, compared to the endogenous parent. MCF viruses are created by these three genetic changes, which occur in a reproducible fashion and appear in the thymus between 10 and 14 weeks of age.

ACKNOWLEDGMENTS

We thank S. Fenner for expert technical assistance and Mary Bostic-Fitzgerald for manuscript preparation.

REFERENCES

1. Coffin, J. M. 1982. Endogenous retroviruses. *In* Molecular Biology of Tumor Viruses, Part III. RNA Tumor Viruses, Vol. 1, 2nd ed. R. Weiss, N. Teich, H. E. Varmus & J. M. Coffin, Eds.: 1109-1203. Cold Spring Harbor Laboratory. Cold Spring Harbor, NY.
2. Stoye, J. P. & J. M. Coffin. 1985. Endogenous retroviruses. *In* Molecular Biology of Tumor Viruses, Part III. RNA Tumor Viruses. Vol 2, 2nd ed. R. Weiss, N. Teich, H. E. Varmus & J. M. Coffin, Eds.: 357-404. Cold Spring Harbor Laboratory. Cold Spring Harbor, NY.
3. Jenkins, N. A., N. G. Copeland, B. A. Taylor & B. K. Lee. 1981. Dilute (*d*) coat colour mutation of DBA/2J mice is associated with the site of integration of an ecotropic MuLV genome. Nature **293:** 370-374.
4. Copeland, N. G., K. W. Hutchinson & N. A. Jenkins. 1983. Excision of the DBA ecotropic provirus in dilute coat-color revertants of mice occurs by homologous recombination involving the viral LTRs. Cell **33:** 379-387.
5. Stoye, J. P. & J. M. Coffin. 1987. The four classes of endogenous murine leukemia virus: Structural relationships and potential for recombination. J. Virol. **61:** 2659-2669.
6. Stoye, J. P. & J. M. Coffin. 1988. Polymorphism of murine endogenous proviruses revealed by using virus class-specific oligonucleotide probes. J. Virol. **62:** 168-175.
7. Jenkins, N. A., N. G. Copeland, B. A. Taylor & B. K. Lee. 1982. Organization, distribution, and stability of endogenous ecotropic murine leukemia virus DNA in chromosomes of *Mus musculus.* J. Virol. **43:** 26-36.
8. Meier, H., D. D. Myers & R. J. Huebner. 1969. Genetic control by the *hr*-locus of susceptibility and resistance of leukemia. Proc. Natl. Acad. Sci. USA **63:** 759-766.
9. Schmidt, M., K. Glögger, T. Wirth & I. Horak. 1984. Evidence that a major class of mouse endogenous long terminal repeats (LTRs) resulted from recombination between

exogenous retroviral LTRs and similar LTR-like elements (LTR-IS). Proc. Natl. Acad. Sci. USA **81:** 6696-6700.
10. MORSE, H. 1978. Origins of Inbred Mice. Academic Press, Inc. New York.
11. STOYE, J. P., S. FENNER, G. E. GREENOAK, C. MORAN & J. M. COFFIN. 1988. Role of retroviruses as mutagens: The hairless mutation of mice. Cell **54:** 383-391.
12. ZIJLSTRA, M. & C. J. M. MELIEF. 1986. Virology, genetics and immunology of murine lymphomagenesis. Biophys. Biochim. Acta **865:** 197-231
13. KOZAK, C. A. & W. P. ROWE. 1978. Genetic mapping of xenotropic virus-inducing loci in two mouse strains. Science **199:** 1448-1449.
14. HOLLAND, C. A., C. Y. THOMAS, S. K. CHATTOPADHYAY, C. KOEHNE & P. V. O'DONNELL. 1989. Influence of enhancer sequences on thymotropism and leukemogenicity of mink cell focus-forming viruses. J. Virol. **63:** 1284-1292.
15. SILVER, J. 1985. Confidence limits for estimates of gene linkage based on analyses of recombinant inbred strains. J. Hered. **78:** 436-440.

Retroviral Pathogenesis: Unexpectedly High Levels of HIV-1 RNA and Protein Synthesis in a Cytocidal Infection

H. L. ROBINSON AND M. SOMASUNDARAN

Department of Pathology
University of Massachusetts Medical Center
Worcester, Massachusetts 01655

I am pleased to be able to participate in this conference honoring Dr. Friend. I first met Dr. Friend in Tokyo in 1966 when she, I, and Dr. Duesberg shared a cab. At that time I was just beginning work with avian leukosis viruses, and my interests were focused on how these viruses transformed normal cells to malignant cells. At the time of this symposium honoring Dr. Friend and her research contributions, I am again starting a new area of research, work with human immunodeficiency virus type-1 (HIV-1). It is the early work of my laboratory with HIV-1 that I am going to report on today. The work I will be describing was done by Dr. Mohan Somasundaran, a highly accomplished postdoctoral fellow in my laboratory.

◇

The question we are addressing in our work on HIV-1 is how this virus causes the depletion of helper T cells, a depletion which is in turn associated with the development of acquired immunodeficiency syndrome (AIDS). We are using as model systems cultures of continuous T cell lines and cultures of mitogen-stimulated peripheral blood lymphocytes.

At the time we initiated work with HIV, it was known that HIV-1 infections were cytopathic for T cells that display the CD4 protein, which serves as a receptor for HIV. One mechanism for this cytopathicity had been described: the induction of syncytia, or giant multinucleated cells.[1-3] As we began work with HIV-1, we rapidly came to appreciate that syncytium formation was but one mechanism by which HIV-1 infections killed cells. We found that cells of certain T cell lines, as well as mitogen-stimulated peripheral blood lymphocytes (cells of this culture system best represent the cells which become depleted in AIDS), underwent HIV-1-induced cytolysis as single, mononucleated cells.[4]

FIGURE 1 depicts the first experiment we did with HIV-1. Infections with HTLV-IIIb (human T cell leukemia virus type IIIb), a standard laboratory strain of HIV-1, or with UMA-CB, a recent HIV-1 isolate from a patient, were done in CEM cells, a cell line reported to be unusually susceptible to HIV-1-induced cytopathic effects;[5]

in H9 cells, a cell line reported to be relatively resistant to HIV-1-induced cytopathicity;[6] and in mitogen-stimulated peripheral blood lymphocytes (PBLs). Infected cultures were monitored for HIV-1-expressing cells by indirect immunofluorescent staining of fixed cells with serum from a patient and then with fluoresceinated goat anti-human immunoglobulin. Dead cells were detected by their failure to exclude trypan blue. Interestingly, infected, virus-expressing cells and dead cells appeared in each of the HTLV-IIIb-infected culture systems with fairly similar kinetics. However, syncytia occurred in only one of the culture systems, the H9 cells, where their occurrence was an early, transitory phenomenon. UMA-CB infections behaved similarly to those of HTLV-IIIb. Infection and cytolysis occurred in each of the cultures, but the induction of syncytia, which was again an early and transitory phenomenon, occurred only in the H9 cells. These results indicated that HIV-1 infections could kill cells in the absence of syncytium formation. Furthermore, they suggested that HIV-1-induced cytolysis in the absence of syncytium formation was a general and frequently occurring phenomenon. Since these initial studies, we have focused our efforts on the study of HIV-1-induced killing in cultures which are undergoing cytolysis in the absence of syncytium formation.

In the studies summarized in FIGURE 1, we had noticed that virus-expressing cells did not appear in cultures until several days after infection. Initially we assumed that this lag was because the titers of infectious virus in our viral stocks were low. However,

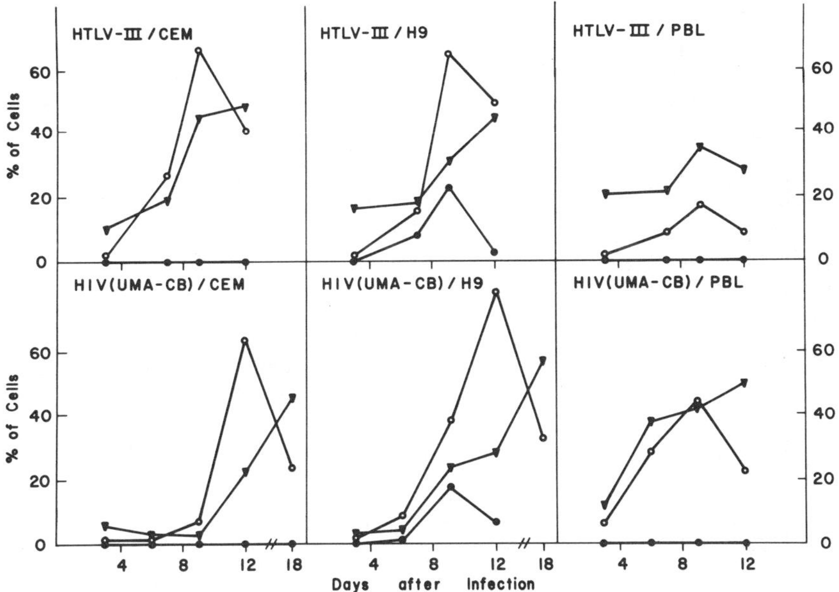

FIGURE 1. Effects of infection with HTLV-IIIb (**upper panels**) or UMA-CB (**lower panels**) on CEM cells (**left panels**), H9 cells (**center panels**), and mitogen-stimulated peripheral blood lymphocytes (PBL, **right panels**). HIV antigen-expressing cells (○) and dead cells (▼) were detected as described in Somasundaran and Robinson.[4] Syncytia (●) are cells which contained more than 4 nuclei; all syncytia were antigen-positive. (From Somasundaran & Robinson.[4] Reprinted with permission from the *Journal of Virology.*)

TABLE 1. Latency of HTLV-IIIb Infection in Various Cell Cultures

Cell Culture	% HTLV-IIIb-expressing Cells[a]
C8166	32.3
MT-2	5.2
PBL[b]	0.01
CEM	N.D.
H9	N.D.
Jurkat	N.D.
tat[+]-Jurkat	N.D.
T4[+]-HeLa	N.D.

[a] Cells were infected at a multiplicity of ≥0.2 infectious units of HTLV-IIIb per cell and examined 24 hr later by indirect immunofluorescence[4] for the expression of viral antigens. N.D., none detected.

[b] PBL, Mitogen-stimulated peripheral blood lymphocytes.

when we titered these stocks by end-point dilution, we found that our stocks had reasonable titers of infectious virus, titers which should have caused 5 to 10% of the cells to express viral antigens within 12 to 24 hr of infection (the typical eclipse period for a retrovirus infection). Since HIV-1 was known to be able to undergo latent as well as active phases of infection, we concluded that the failure of our cultures to express virus within 24 hr of infection reflected the presence of some latency phase for the HIV-1 infection in H9 cells, CEM cells, and mitogen-stimulated PBLs. There-

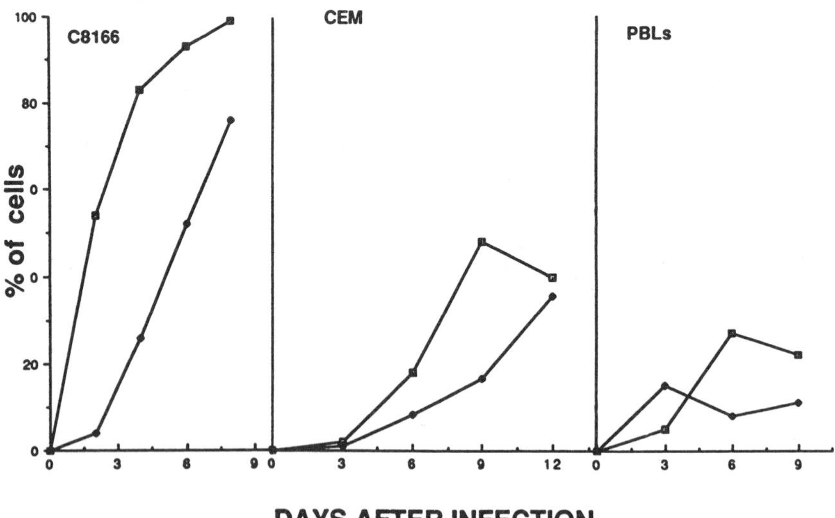

FIGURE 2. Time-course of expression of HTLV-IIIb in various cells infected with ≥ 0.2 virions/cell. Infected C8166 cells were grown in the presence of 240 ng/ml of leu3a monoclonal antibody (Becton Dickinson, Mountain View, CA). The percentages of HTLV-IIIb protein-expressing (■) and dead cells (●) are shown. PBLs, mitogen-stimulated peripheral blood lymphocytes.

fore, we set out to identify a cell line which was truly permissive for HIV-1 infections, i.e., a cell line which would express virus within 24 hr of infection.

TABLE 1 summarizes the results of this search. In this experiment, each of the cultures was infected with HTLV-IIIb at a multiplicity of infection of ca. 0.2. At 24 hr after infection, no virus-expressing cells were detected in five of the tested cell lines: CEM cells, H9 cells, Jurkat cells,[7] Jurkat cells expressing *tat,*[7] and HeLa cells expressing T4.[8] One in 10,000 (0.01%) of the mitogen-stimulated PBLs were positive, whereas 5% of the MT-2 cells[9] and 32% of the C8166 cells[10] expressed HTLV-IIIb antigens. We therefore continued work with C8166 cells to develop conditions in which we could study a synchronous active infection.

TABLE 2. Time-Course of Appearance of HTLV-IIIb Viral Products in Synchronously Infected C8166 Cells

Hours after Infection[a]	Viral Product[b]		
	DNA	RNA	Protein
2	Bg	Bg	Bg
4	Bg	Bg	Bg
6	+/−	Bg	Bg
8	+	+/−	Bg
12	+	+	+/−
24	+	+	+

[a] C8166 cells were infected with ≥ 0.2 infectious units per cell of HTLV-IIIb. Three hours after infection, 240 ng/ml of leu3a monoclonal antibody was added to the culture medium.

[b] Viral DNA was detected using Southern blots hybridized with a nick-translated HTLV-IIIb DNA probe. Viral RNA was detected using cytoblots[17] hybridized with a 675-base ^{32}P-labeled RNA probe which was complementary to all spliced as well as unspliced HTLV-IIIb RNAs. Proteins were detected by indirect immunofluorescence on fixed cells.[4] Bg, background level; +/−, barely detectable.

C8166 cells are highly susceptible to HIV-1-induced syncytia. To study HIV-1 infections in C8166 cells in the absence of syncytium formation, an anti-CD4 monoclonal antibody (leu3a), which prevents syncytium formation, was added to cultures 3 hr after infection.[11-14] When C8166 cells were infected at a multiplicity of $\geq$ 0.2 infectious units per cell and then grown in the presence of 240 ng/ml of leu3a, the majority of the cells in the culture expressed virus by two days after infection and underwent cytolysis as mononucleated cells two to three days later. As depicted in FIGURE 2, there was a nearly synchronous active infection of C8166 cells by HTLV-IIIb; the time-course of the infection in CEM cells and mitogen-stimulated PBLs infected with the same stock of virus used for the C8166 cells is shown for comparison.

To test whether HTLV-IIIb underwent a normal retroviral eclipse period in C8166 cells (the eclipse period is the time required for adsorption, penetration, reverse transcription, and expression of viral DNA), cultures were scored at several timepoints after infection for the presence of viral DNA, RNA and proteins (TABLE 2). These tests revealed viral DNA by 6-8 hr, viral RNA by 8-12 hr, and viral protein by 12-24 hr after infection. This time-course for the appearance of these viral products was consistent with the occurrence of a normal retroviral eclipse period.

TABLE 3. Steady-State Levels of Viral RNA in HTLV-IIIb-infected Cells

Cell Culture	Days after Infection[a]	% HIV-positive Cells[b]	Viral RNA Copies/ HIV-positive Cells[c] ($\times 10^5$)
C8166			
Experiment 1	2	70	4
	4	100	13
Experiment 2	2	80	25
CEM	9	46	3
PBL[d]	6	23	5.7

[a] Infections were carried out at a multiplicity of ≥ 0.2 infectious units of HTLV-IIIb per cell.

[b] HIV-positive cells were those detected by indirect immunofluorescence using serum from a patient as the primary antibody.[4]

[c] RNA copy numbers were determined on slot blots of cytoplasmic extracts prepared in the presence of 1% NP-40[17] and hybridized with 1×10^6 cpm/ml of a 675-base radiolabeled RNA probe which was complementary to sequences at the 3′ ends of all spliced as well as unspliced HTLV-IIIb RNAs. Blots were digested with RNase A (1 μg/ml) in 0.3 *M* sodium citrate/0.3 *M* NaCl for 15 min at room temperature before autoradiography. The amount of HIV-specific RNA was estimated by direct visualization of slot intensities in the radioautograph relative to the intensities of known amounts of the standard HIV-1 RNA applied to the same blot as well as by densitometric tracings. The number of copies of HIV RNA/HIV-positive cell was then calculated as

(grams HIV RNA in sample) (Avogadro's number)/(molecular weight of standard HIV-1 RNA) (number of HIV-positive cells in sample).

For example, in Experiment 1 with C8166 cells, the autoradiograph of the slot blot representing day 2 post-infection had a relative density of 44 for the slot obtained from a cytoplasmic extract of 3.3×10^4 cells and of 27 from 1.1×10^4 cells. From the standard curve obtained with known amounts of a standard HIV RNA, these optical densities were estimated to represent 4.2 ng and 2.1 ng of HIV RNA, respectively, or an average of 15.75 ng of HIV RNA for 1×10^5 cells. Since 70% of the cells in the extracts used were HIV-positive, the calculation for this sample was

$$(15.75 \times 10^{-9} \text{ g})\,(6.023 \times 10^{23} \text{ molecules})/(1097 \text{ nucleotides} \times 340 \text{ g/nucleotide})\,(7 \times 10^4 \text{ HIV-positive cells}) = 3.63 \times 10^5 \text{ molecules/cell}$$

which has been rounded to 4×10^5.

[d] PBL, mitogen-stimulated peripheral blood lymphocytes.

To get a better feel for the life cycle of HTLV-IIIb in C8166 cells, we have been quantitating and characterizing the levels of HTLV-IIIb DNA, RNA, and of protein synthesis at various times after infection. We are furthest along with our work quantitating levels of viral RNA and of viral protein synthesis. Typical retrovirus infections express steady-state levels of viral RNA in the range of 5×10^3 to 5×10^4 copies per cell.[15] These RNAs utilize 1-2% of the protein synthesizing capacity of the host cell.[16] In contrast, we have found that HTLV-IIIb-infected cells express between 2×10^5 and 2×10^6 copies of viral RNA per cell and use as much as 40% of the protein synthesizing capacity of an infected cell for the production of viral *gag* protein.

To test for steady-state levels of HTLV-IIIb RNA in virus-expressing cells, we prepared cytoplasmic extracts from HTLV-IIIb-infected C8166 cells at 2 and 4 days after infection. Dilutions of these along with dilutions of a known amount of a standard HIV-1 RNA were analyzed on slot blots to determine the amount of HTLV-IIIb RNA in each sample. To accomplish this, blots were hybridized with a 675-bp RNA complementary to sequences present at the 3′ end of all spliced as well as unspliced HTLV-IIIb mRNAs. We then calculated that the average number of copies of HTLV-IIIb RNA per virus-expressing cell was from 4×10^5 to 2.5×10^6 in virus-expressing C8166 cells (TABLE 3).

To determine whether such high copy numbers of viral RNA might also be present in other T cells which are susceptible to HIV-1 infection, cultures of HTLV-IIIb-infected CEM cells and mitogen-stimulated PBLs were harvested at the times they showed peak numbers of infected cells (9 days post-infection for CEM cells, 6 days post-infection for PBLs; see FIGURE 2). Cytoplasmic extracts were prepared and analyzed on slot blots to assay the amount of HIV-1 RNA. The results of these tests revealed an average of 3×10^5 copies of HTLV-IIIb RNA per HTLV-IIIb-expressing CEM cell and an average of 5.7×10^5 copies per HTLV-IIIb-expressing PBL. Thus, high copy numbers of viral RNA can occur in normal T cells (PBLs) as well as in at least two continuous lines of T cells (C8166 and CEM cells).

These high levels of viral RNA were unprecedented for retroviral infections, but they were reminiscent of certain lytic virus infections where viral RNAs compete for translation with host mRNAs, estimated to be present at 1×10^5 to 5×10^5 copies per cell. To test whether these high levels of HTLV-IIIb RNA were undergoing efficient translation, infected C8166 cells were grown for 30 min in the presence of [^{35}S]methionine and [^{35}S]cysteine, and total cell lysates were analyzed on polyacrylamide gels for proteins which might represent viral proteins. At 12 and 24 hr after infection, no viral proteins could be detected above the background of host cell proteins (FIG. 3). However, by 48 hr after infection, a 55-kDa protein had appeared. By 72 hr after infection, this protein and a newly appearing 41-kDa protein (visible by 60 hr; see FIG. 3) represented 40% of the newly synthesized protein. Since 55 kDa and 41 kDa are the sizes of the full-length precursor and a partial cleavage product, respectively, of the HTLV-IIIb *gag* protein, we tested monoclonal antibodies to the 24-kDa (p24) and the 17-kDa (p17) *gag* proteins of HTLV-IIIb for their ability to immunoprecipitate the 55-kDa and 41-kDa bands. Both of the bands were specifically immunoprecipitated by the anti-*gag* monoclonals (FIG. 3). Thus, by 72 hr after infection, 40% of the protein synthesis in HTLV-IIIb-expressing C8166 cells was of viral *gag* protein.

TABLE 4. Analysis of Protein Synthesis in HTLV-IIIb-infected C8166 Cells

Hours after Infection	% HIV-positive Cells	Protein Synthesis[a]	
		Inf./Uninf.	*gag*/Total
12	0	1.0	N.D.
24	18	0.8	N.D.
48	75	0.5	0.1
72	100	1.0	0.4

[a] Protein synthesis was determined on duplicate samples of cells which had been independently incubated in the presence of ^{35}S-labeled amino acids for 15 min. Labeled cells were washed in phosphate buffered saline (PBS), lysed and adjusted to a final concentration of 0.1 *N* NaOH, and incubated at 37°C for 10 min to uncharge tRNA. Proteins in the lysates were precipitated with trichloroacetic acid in the presence of bovine serum albumin (0.2 mg/ml), collected on nitrocellulose filters (0.45 μm), dried under a heat lamp, and counted in a scintillation counter with Ecolume cocktail (ICN Radiochemicals, Irvine, CA). The ratio of *gag* protein to host cell protein synthesis was determined using densitometric tracings of autoradiographs such as the one shown in FIGURE 3. Inf., infected cells; Uninf., uninfected cells; N.D., none detected.

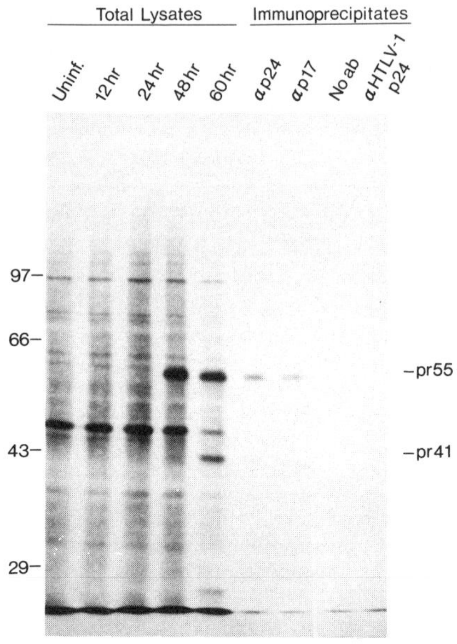

FIGURE 3. Autoradiograph of newly synthesized proteins in HTLV-IIIb-infected C8166 cells. At the indicated times (**Total Lysates,** *left*) or at 72 hr post-infection (**Immunoprecipitates,** *right*), cells (0.5×10^6) were washed in methionine- and cysteine-free medium and then incubated at 37°C for 30 min in 0.5 ml of the same medium supplemented with 50 μCi of ^{35}S-Translabel, a mixture of [^{35}S]methionine and [^{35}S]cysteine (1013 Ci/mmol; ICN Radiochemicals, Irvine, CA). Incorporation of ^{35}S was linear with time of incubation during this period. The labeled cells were washed, lysed in 0.25 *M* Tris-HCl, 2% SDS and 5% β-mercaptoethanol, and incubated at 100°C for 3-5 min. Samples containing 100,000 cpm of trichloroacetic acid-precipitable radioactivity were analyzed for ^{35}S-labeled proteins by gel electrophoresis on a 10% SDS-polyacrylamide gel either directly (**Total Lysates**) or after immunoprecipitation with the indicated monoclonal antibody (**Immunoprecipitates**). For immunoprecipitations, washed cells were lysed in phosphate-buffered saline (PBS) containing 0.001 *M* EDTA, 1% NP-40, and 0.5% sodium deoxycholate. Samples (50 μl) of the lysate were incubated at room temperature for 60 min with 1 ng of the indicated monoclonal antibody (Dupont Co., Wilmington, DE) and then for an additional 60 min with rabbit anti-mouse immunoglobulin coupled to Sepharose beads. (The beads were washed with PBS containing 0.001 *M* EDTA, 0.5% NP-40 and 5 mg/ml bovine serum albumin and then resuspended in the same buffer containing 1 mg/ml of bovine serum albumin before use.) These beads were then washed three times with PBS containing 0.5% NP-40 and 0.4% SDS, resuspended in Laemmli sample buffer, and boiled for 5 min; the proteins eluted from the beads were loaded onto the gel. After electrophoresis, the gel was fixed and treated with an autoradiography enhancer (EN^{3}HANCE; New England Nuclear Co., Boston, MA), dried, and exposed to X-ray film in the presence of an intensifying screen. Uninf.: uninfected cells; αp24, αp17: monoclonal antibodies to the 24-kDa *gag* protein and the 17-kDa *gag* protein of HTLV-IIIb, respectively; αHTLV-1 p24: antibody to the 24-kDa *gag* protein of HTLV-1. Molecular mass markers in kilodaltons are shown to the *left* of the radioautograph and the positions of the 55-kDa (pr55) and 41-kDa (pr41) viral protein bands are indicated to the *right.*

Some lytic virus infections, such as those of adenovirus or poliovirus, actively inhibit as well as compete for host protein synthesis.[18,19] To test whether HTLV-IIIb might actively inhibit host protein synthesis, the apparent rates of protein synthesis were compared at various times after infection in infected and mock-infected C8166 cells; both cultures were maintained in the presence of leu3a monoclonal antibody (TABLE 4). The results of this experiment revealed that at 48 hr after infection, the apparent rate of protein synthesis in the infected culture was only 50% of that in the uninfected culture. By 72 hr after infection, the rates of synthesis in both cultures were similar. However, by this time, at least 40% of the protein synthesized by the infected culture was viral *gag* protein. This experiment raises the possibility that HIV-1 infections inhibit as well as compete for the protein synthesizing capacity of their host cell.

In summary, we have developed a culture system in which we are able to study a synchronous, active HIV-1 infection. Our initial work with this system has revealed that HTLV-IIIb infections produce unexpectedly high levels of viral RNA and proteins (TABLE 3, FIG. 3). Our studies have also raised the possibility that active HIV-1 infections can interfere with host protein synthesis (TABLE 4).

What might be the molecular basis for high levels of viral RNA and protein synthesis by a retrovirus? Our initial studies on HTLV-IIIb DNA synthesis indicate that virus-expressing cells contain 100 to 1000 copies of unintegrated DNA. This DNA is linear and in the nucleus. Our hypothesis is that active HIV-1 infections efficiently express unintegrated DNA and that this expression of unintegrated DNA results in the production of high levels of viral RNA and protein. We also think that the ability of HIV-1 to produce high levels of viral RNA and protein contributes to HIV-1-induced cell killing. Thus, we suggest that HIV-1 infections can kill cells by taking over the synthetic machinery of their host.

REFERENCES

1. SODROSKI, J., W. C. GOH, C. ROSEN, K. CAMPBELL & W. A. HASELTINE. 1986. Nature **322:** 470-474.
2. LIFSON, J. D., M. B. FEINBERG, G. R. REYES, L. RABIN, B. BANAPOUR, S. CHAKRABARTI, B. MOLL, F. WONG-STAAL, K. S. STEIMER & E. G. ENGLEMAN. 1986. Nature **323:** 726-728.
3. LIFSON, J. D., G. R. REYES, M. S. MCGRATH, B. S. STEIN & E. G. ENGLEMAN. 1986. Science **232:** 1123-1127.
4. SOMASUNDARAN, M. & H. L. ROBINSON. 1987. J. Virol. **61:** 3114-3119.
5. FOLKS, T., S. BENN, A. RABSON, T. THEODORE, M. D. HOGAN, M. MARTIN, M. LIGHTFOOTE & K. SELL. 1985. Proc. Natl. Acad. Sci. USA **82:** 4539-4543.
6. POPOVIC, M., M. G. SARNGADHARAN, E. READ & R. C. GALLO. 1984. Science **224:** 497-500.
7. ROSEN, C. A., J. C. SODROSKI, K. CAMPBELL & W. A. HASELTINE. 1986. J. Virol. **57:** 379-384.
8. MADDON, P. J., A. G. DALGLEISH, J. S. MCDOUGAL, P. R. CLAPHAM, R. A. WEISS & R. AXEL. 1986. Cell **47:** 333-348.
9. HARADA, S., Y. KOYANAGI & N. YAMAMOTO. 1985. Science **229:** 563-566.
10. SALAHUDDIN, S. Z., D. V. ABLASHI, P. D. MARKHAM, S. F. JOSEPHS, S. STURZENEGGER, M. KAPLAN, G. HALLIGAN, P. BIBERFIELD, F. WONG-STAAL, B. KRAMARSKY & R. C. GALLO. 1983. Virology **129:** 51-64.
11. DALGLIESH, A. G., P. C. L. BEVERLY, P. R. CLAPHAM, D. H. CRAWFORD, M. R. GREAVES & R. A. WEISS. 1984. Nature **312:** 763-767.
12. KLATZMAN, D., E. CHAMPAGNE, S. CHAMARET, J. GRUEST, D. GUEFAND, T. HERCEND, J.-C. GLUCKMAN & L. MONTAGNIER. 1984. Nature **312:** 767-768.
13. LIFSON, J. D., G. R. REYES, M. S. MCGRATH, B. S. STEIN & E. G. ENGLEMAN. 1986. Science **232:** 1123-1127.
14. SATTENTAU, Q. J., A. G. DALGLIESH, R. A. WEISS & P. C. L. BEVERLEY. 1987. Science **234:** 1120-1124.
15. VARMUS, H. & R. SWANSTROM. 1984. *In* RNA Tumor Viruses, 2nd ed. R. Weiss, N. Teich, H. Varmus & J. Coffin, Eds.: 450-453. Cold Spring Harbor Laboratory. Cold Spring Harbor, NY.
16. DICKSON, C., R. EISENMAN, H. FAN, E. HUNTER & N. TEICH. 1984. *In* RNA Tumor Viruses, 2nd ed. R. Weiss, N. Teich, H. Varmus & J. Coffin, Eds.: 518-519. Cold Spring Harbor Laboratory. Cold Spring Harbor, NY.
17. WHITE, B. A. & F. C. BANCROFT. 1982. J. Biol. Chem. **257:** 8569-8572.
18. R. J. SCHNEIDER & T. SHENK. 1987. Annu. Rev. Biochem. **56:** 317-332.
19. FRAENKEL-CONRAT, H. & R. R. WAGNER, EDS. 1987. Comprehensive Virology. Vol. 19. Plenum Press. New York.

Pathogenesis of Human Immunodeficiency Virus Infection

JAY A. LEVY

Cancer Research Institute
Department of Medicine
University of California, School of Medicine
San Francisco, California 94143

INTRODUCTION

When the acquired immunodeficiency syndrome (AIDS) was first recognized in 1981, the cause of this new disease complex was a mystery. While a variety of potential etiologies were considered, the most likely was a new human pathogen. Since hemophiliacs receiving filtered blood products developed the disease, a virus was strongly suspected. Work with animal model systems had indicated a variety of viruses that can suppress the immune system, notably parvoviruses and retroviruses.[1] In particular, it was timely that many studies on retroviruses in animal model systems, especially in the mouse, had progressed rapidly in the ten years preceding the recognition of AIDS.[2] Thus, the groundwork was laid for the initial studies leading to the identification and characterization of the human immunodeficiency virus (HIV).

The pioneer work of Ludwik Gross on the discovery of the first mammalian leukemia virus, followed by that of Charlotte Friend, John Moloney and Frank Rauscher, greatly encouraged the scientific community to conduct research on RNA tumor viruses, particularly in the mouse.[3] Many of the st·.dies on HIV are based on observations made between 1960 and 1980 on these and other viruses that were found to contain the enzyme reverse transcriptase. Research in our laboratory on murine type C viruses certainly provided a basis for our work on HIV; many similarities could be found between the two (TABLE 1). The wide host range of mouse xenotropic viruses demonstrated that human cells could be infected by retroviruses and that a heterogeneity among these viruses existed.[4] And, most importantly, the work with animal lentiviruses (visna, equine infectious anemia)[2] presaged the problems we face with their human counterpart.

THE HUMAN IMMUNODEFICIENCY VIRUSES

In 1983, Barre-Sinoussi and colleagues at the Pasteur Institute reported the isolation of a retrovirus from the lymph node of an individual with lymphadenopathy syndrome, a clinical state associated with AIDS.[5] They first considered this virus a human T

TABLE 1. Similarities between HIV and Mouse Type C Retroviruses[a]

1. Infection of hematopoietic cells
2. Infection of human cells
3. Cytopathic properties
4. Ability to enter latent state
5. Heterogeneity of virus strains
6. Association with sperm
7. Low neutralization titers

[a] For review of properties of mouse retroviruses, see Ref. 4.

cell lymphotropic virus because of its growth in helper T lymphocytes. They soon recognized its difference from the human T cell leukemia viruses, types I and II (HTLV-I and HTLV-II), and named it lymphadenopathy-associated virus (LAV). Subsequent work from laboratories at the National Institutes of Health and our own group confirmed the observations of the Pasteur Institute group and described similar viruses in AIDS patients in the United States.[6,7] These agents were initially called human T cell lymphotropic virus, type III (HTLV-III) and AIDS-associated retrovirus (ARV). The rapid success in cloning and sequencing these prototype AIDS viruses led to their recognition as related members of the human lentivirinae subfamily of retroviruses.[8] They were quite distinct from the oncovirinae and spumavirinae subfamilies, and thus their designation as human immunodeficiency viruses (HIV) became the accepted distinguishing name.[9]

The ongoing investigations on HIV have provided several observations that revised the initial conclusions about their biological properties. First, their presumed preference to grow in T lymphocytes was found to be too limiting a definition, since their replication has been reported in macrophages, promyelocytes and—more recently—in a variety of different susceptible human cells, including those of the bowel, skin, and connective tissue (TABLE 2).[10] With results similar to those from work with the mouse xenotropic viruses,[4] the HIV were found to be heterogenous; some isolates preferentially grew in one cell type over another. In the host, this cell tropism appeared to correlate with certain clinical conditions and may indeed be an important aspect of viral pathogenesis. As will be discussed below, in comparison to viruses that replicated best in T lymphocytes, those that replicated well in macrophages appeared to be more readily recoverable from the cerebrospinal fluid and the brain, where they were present in individuals with AIDS showing neurological symptoms. The isolates which grew preferentially in T lymphocytes were primarily found in patients with immune deficiency and opportunistic infections.

Two years after the discovery of HIV-1, studies of West African AIDS patients hospitalized in Portugal showed that they had no substantial serologic reaction to the AIDS virus. This observation led to the eventual isolation of a virus with properties distinct from the initially studied HIV.[11] Cloning and sequence analyses of this new virus demonstrated that the West African isolate was 55% different from HIV-1 and thus merited consideration as a distinct HIV subtype: HIV-2.[12] Primarily found in West Africa, HIV-2, like HIV-1, is expected to spread in the world. Four isolates of HIV-2 have now been well-characterized; like HIV-1, they show a heterogeneity of biological properties. One particular feature that thus far is unique to the HIV-2 subtype is the existence of completely non-cytopathic isolates; these do not form syncytia and multinucleated cells in culture and do not kill the lymphocytes they infect.[13,14] This identification of non-cytopathic HIV-2 has lent support to the conclusion of some investigators that infection with HIV-2 may be less pathogenic than that

TABLE 2. Cells Susceptible to HIV[a]

Hematopoietic
T lymphocytes
B lymphocytes
Macrophages
Promyelocytes
Megakaryocytes
Dendritic cells
Brain
Macrophages (microglia)
Astrocytes
Capillary endothelial cells
Oligodendrocytes
Skin
Langerhans cells
Fibroblasts
Bowel
Crypt cells
Enterochromaffin cells
Colon carcinoma cells
Macrophages
Lymphocytes

[a] Results from studies of infected tissues and cell culture experiments.

with HIV-1.[15] Nevertheless, at least in one case, the individual infected with a non-cytopathic HIV-2 had AIDS, characterized by neurological findings and diarrhea, despite a near normal lymphocyte count.[13] The mechanism of disease induction by HIV-2 is not known, and further longitudinal studies of individuals infected with HIV-2 are required to evaluate its relative pathogenic role.

Biological Features of HIV

The ability of HIV to infect cells, particularly helper T lymphocytes, appears to be mediated primarily by the CD4 antigen present on susceptible cells.[16] Most recent work defining the mechanism of viral entry into cells has indicated that a particular epitope on the CD4 molecule is responsible and that the external, not the cytoplasmic, regions of this molecule mediate the process.[17] Attachment of the viral 120-kDa glycoprotein (gp120) to CD4 is involved, but unless other steps for viral penetration are possible, infection does not take place. For instance, mouse cells expressing the CD4 antigen after transfection with the gene for the CD4 molecule bind HIV but are not infected by the virus.[18] These observations have suggested that attachment and subsequent fusion are key steps in the infectious cycle. Once the CD4-gp120 interaction has taken place, a fusion domain on the 41-kDa envelope glycoprotein (gp41) that has homology to a region on the fusing paramyxoviruses[19] interacts with a portion of the cell membrane to permit entry of the virion core. Some recent work with monoclonal antibodies has indicated the potential presence of such a fusion domain on human but not animal cells.[20] This observation combined with the fact that viral entry is pH-independent[21] has taken emphasis away from receptor-mediated endocytosis as the major mechanism for virus infection of cells. In addition, work in several laboratories is now indicating that CD4 may not be the only means of viral entry. Cells lacking CD4 expression can be infected by the virus. These cells include brain-derived cell lines and human fibroblasts.[22] Determination of whether virus-cell fusion mediates virus entry into these cell types requires further study.

Most of the characterization of the AIDS retroviruses has been with the HIV-1 subtype; it is expected that similar observations will be obtained with variants of the HIV-2 subtype when they have been isolated and studied. Clearly this human lentivirus subfamily is heterogenous. As noted above, one of the first differences seen among HIV-1 isolates was their relative ability to infect and replicate in various cell lines. The list of cells susceptible to HIV-1 now includes those from the hematopoietic, gastrointestinal and neurological systems, and from the skin (TABLE 2). The presence of HIV in the bowel epithelium, particularly in enterochromaffin cells that have endocrine function, suggests a direct role of the virus in the chronic diarrhea and malabsorption observed in some AIDS patients.[23]

When various isolates of HIV are examined for their relative ability to replicate in representative cells of these susceptible tissues, other observations can be made. Some viruses readily infect and grow in the cells, some infect cells but replicate to a low level, and some show no evidence of productive infection in the cells. Thus, two distinct characteristics defining the heterogeneity of HIV are their host range and their relative replicative properties in certain cell types.

Another biological feature that varies among HIV is the ability of the virus to induce syncytia formation in infected cells, produce balloon degeneration, and cause cell death. Isolates can be found that produce all three of these cytopathic effects (CPE), but others kill cells without any morphological evidence of a pathological process.[22] The fusion causing formation of multinucleated cells appears to be mediated by an interaction of the viral envelope gp120 with the CD4 antigen expressed on the surface of helper T cells and other cells in the hematopoietic system.[24] This syncytia formation may also be mediated by a post-attachment fusion process, described above for HIV entry, that involves the gp41 transmembrane envelope protein. A binding of CD4 with gp120 has been implicated in induction of CPE, since virus replication in cells with low or no expression of CD4 is not associated with CPE.[25] One noteworthy possibility is that the level of HIV replication influences the cytopathology. Viruses that replicate to high titer in lymphocytes are generally most cytopathic.[25,26] This observation has suggested that large quantities of certain viral proteins themselves, particularly the envelope proteins, may be responsible for the pathogenic process. For instance, the envelope proteins might disrupt the permeability of the cell membrane, creating an influx of ions (Na^+, K^+) which cause enlargement, ballooning, and eventual death of the infected cells.[27] Such observations have been made with other fusing viruses, such as the paramyxovirus.[28]

Serological Properties of HIV

One of the early observations made on HIV isolates concerned their diverse susceptibility to neutralization by antisera. At first, only low-level neutralization was detected,[29] but with improvements in these assays, substantial neutralization of some isolates could be demonstrated and presumed HIV serotypes identified.[30] These studies have suggested that if envelope proteins are important for induction of immune

TABLE 3. Potential Characteristics of a Neurotropic HIV[a]

Characteristic	HIV Isolate from	
	Blood	Brain
Neutralization	+++	+
Growth in T cell lines	+++	−
Growth in macrophages	+	+++
Plaque in MT-4 cells[b]	++	−

[a] From Levy.[36]
[b] The plaque assay indicates highly cytopathic strains of HIV.

responses to HIV, then polyvalent vaccines will need to be developed. However, an infinite number of HIV serotypes may not exist, since several HIV share epitopes sensitive to neutralization. Similar serological differences among HIV-2 isolates have been found, but a notable observation is that antibodies to HIV-2 can cross-react to neutralize HIV-1 isolates.[31] This finding has suggested that, in vaccines, envelope proteins from HIV-2 may be more effective than those from HIV-1.

Biological and Serological Properties Can Identify HIV with Distinct Cell Tropisms and Enhanced Virulence in the Host

Based on data from the studies of various HIV described above, an analysis of viruses obtained from the brain and the blood shows differences in their biological and serological properties. HIV isolated from the cerebrospinal fluid (CSF) or brain preferentially grow in macrophages, produce little cytopathic effect in T lymphocytes, and are not very neutralizable in comparison to HIV isolates from the blood of individuals with immune deficiency [22,32] (TABLE 3). These *in vitro* findings on HIV can reflect clinical observations in the infected individual. Some patients have nearly normal T lymphocyte counts and no opportunistic infections, but severe dementia and other neurologic symptoms. Their viruses grow well in macrophages but not in T lymphocytes.

In our laboratory, studies on the biological properties among viruses sequentially isolated from the same individuals over time have provided other noteworthy information. As disease progresses in an infected host, the HIV recovered are variants of the initial isolate, as demonstrated by restriction enzyme analysis, but have properties increasingly more characteristic of virulent strains.[26] These properties include a wide cellular host range, rapid replication, and enhanced cell killing of lymphocytes (TABLE 4). These findings with HIV are the first indication for any virus that it undergoes changes, either by selection or mutation, to become more pathogenic after infection of a host. They suggest an important role for this evolution of the HIV in disease induction and progression. Molecular studies looking at recombination between viruses of low and high cytopathicity should give some indication of which region of the virion is responsible for the properties of virulence.

Studies of deletion mutants of HIV strongly suggest that the *orf*-B region of the genome is involved in virus replication.[33] Viruses that lack expression of this gene product replicate to 5-10 times higher levels than does the standard HIV-1. Varying degrees of production of the 27-kDa *orf*-B protein (p27) may therefore induce a continuum of expression, from low virus titers to latency.[22] In the latter state, no infectious progeny is produced. Molecular analysis of sequential isolates should provide insight into how an HIV undergoes changes in the infected host over time; variability in the *orf*-B region is expected to be involved.

IMMUNOLOGICAL RESPONSE TO HIV

Equally important in the pathogenesis of AIDS is the host's response to the virus. As with many other viral infections, the effect of HIV on the immune system can result in immune enhancement or immune suppression. In the former case, polyclonal activation of B cells, which in some cases leads to B cell lymphomas, can be observed. Conceivably, the proliferation of endothelial cells, leading to Kaposi's sarcoma, also results from HIV infection. The virus may induce, directly or indirectly, angiogenesis-promoting factors that cause unlimited replication of these endothelial cells, eventually leading to transformation.[34]

Autoimmunity

Autoantibody production, probably resulting from B cell proliferation, can frequently be observed with viral infections. A variety of clinical conditions reflecting autoimmune syndromes have been observed in AIDS patients, and antibodies to specific proteins of platelets, lymphocytes, and nerves have been described (TABLE 5).[10] For example, the reaction of autoantibodies to a protein of M_r 18,000 (p18) on activated helper T cells or virus-infected helper T cells has led to the suggestion that this autoantibody plays a role in depletion of $CD4^+$ lymphocytes.[35] In support of this hypothesis is the finding that anti-p18 autoantibodies are at higher prevalence in individuals with disease than in those who are asymptomatic. The mechanism involved could be the carrier-hapten model suggested for induction of immune responses to tumor antigens following viral infection: the host produces antibodies to normal cellular proteins that have been made more immunogenic by their association with the viral proteins expressed on the cells.[36] Interventions aimed at decreasing the level of anti-lymphocyte antibodies could help to prolong the asymptomatic stage of the disease.

TABLE 4. Features of HIV Correlating with Virulence in the Host

1. Wide cellular host range
2. Rapid kinetics of replication
3. High levels of virus production
4. High cytopathicity
5. Formation of plaques in MT-4 cells

TABLE 5. Autoantibodies in HIV Infection[a]

Target	Clinical Sign
Platelet	ITP[b]
Red blood cell	Anemia
Neutrophil	Neutropenia
Peripheral nerve	Neuropathy
Lymphocyte	Immune deficiency
Lupus anticoagulant (phospholipid)	Thrombosis; neurological disease (?)
Nucleus	Autoimmunity (ANA)[c]

[a] From Levy.[36]
[b] ITP, immune thrombocytopenic purpura.
[c] ANA, anti-nuclear antibody.

Humoral Immune Response to HIV

We have discussed above the HIV-neutralizing capability of some sera that has provided information on proposed HIV serotypes. This response can be beneficial in the host, particularly early in infection, to prevent spread of HIV to many tissues of the body. Unfortunately, most individuals do not have high neutralizing titers against their own isolates of HIV.[29,36]

Another immune response involving antibodies that could provide protection in the infected host is antibody-dependent cellular cytotoxicity (ADCC). By this process, effector cells of the host respond against antibodies attached to envelope proteins expressed on the surface of infected cells.[37] The viral proteins gp120 and gp41 both appear to be involved.[38] This cytopathic activity could be especially helpful early in infection. However, the same mechanism, ADCC, has been implicated in the reduction of uninfected $CD4^+$ lymphocytes in infected individuals.[39] The viral envelope proteins shed into the blood can attach to the CD4 molecule on the surface of uninfected cells, which then could become targets for anti-envelope antibodies and destruction by the ADCC process. Obviously, the relative effects of the beneficial and compromising aspects of this ADCC response need to be evaluated.

One recent observation on humoral responses to HIV with relevance for vaccine development is that enhancing antibodies for HIV infection are present. These antibodies can be found in immunized animals, infected chimpanzees, and infected humans.[40,41] The antibodies appear to bind to the virion and, instead of neutralizing the virus, enhance its infection of both macrophages and lymphocytes. In some sera, this enhancement is only observed when complement is present; in others, heated serum has the same effect on certain viruses. In several cases the titer of enhancing antibodies far exceeds that of neutralizing antibodies, but in undiluted blood neutralization may be dominant.[41] Thus, the *in vitro* observations on enhancement may not have clinical relevance. Nevertheless, in our laboratory several sera have been found which have purely enhancing effects on the individual's own virus and no neutralizing antibody.[41] Moreover, with some sera, one HIV isolate can be enhanced in infection and another neutralized.[41] Obviously, different epitopes on these viruses are recognized by the immune response of the infected host. Finally, an increase in the enhancing antibody titer has been noted as an infected individual progresses in the disease state (E. Robinson, personal communication).

The mechanism of enhancement appears to involve both complement and Fc receptors, but definitive data on the process are not yet available. Whether the CD4 antigen plays a role in this enhancement is also not known. Most importantly, since HIV-immunized guinea pigs show high levels of virus-enhancing antibodies, any vaccination approach in humans must involve caution concerning the epitopes on the viral surface that participate in this process. Clearly, the possibility of eliciting both autoantibodies and enhancing antibodies should be considered in any trials involving vaccination of humans with the envelope proteins of HIV.

Cellular Immune Responses

In assessing cellular immune response to HIV infection, both cytotoxic and suppressing activities have been detected. The presence of cytotoxic effector cells in ADCC has been cited above. In addition, $CD8^+$ cells from lung exudates as well as from peripheral blood have been found to kill infected cells expressing viral proteins encoded by the core (*gag*), envelope, and even the polymerase regions of the viral genome.[42–44] Whether this activity is clinically important in infected individuals is not yet known.

Another response of $CD8^+$ cells to HIV infection has been under study in our laboratory. These T lymphocytes have been found to have strong activity in suppressing HIV replication.[45] The mechanism involved in this response does not appear to be cell killing, but rather production by $CD8^+$ cells of a diffusible substance that inhibits virus replication.[22] Continual release of this inhibitory factor is required, since virus-releasing cells removed from the presence of $CD8^+$ cells quickly resume virus replication. Studies of several HIV-infected individuals at different stages of infection have revealed that this activity of $CD8^+$ cells reflects the clinical state. Individuals early after infection have strong $CD8^+$cell antiviral activity, whereas those with frank AIDS often show very little control of HIV replication by their suppressor T lymphocytes. Since the total number of $CD8^+$ cells does not decrease notably over time in infected individuals, this diminution in the antiviral activity of $CD8^+$ cells most likely reflects a loss of some intrinsic property of these cells, or of a specific population of this lymphocyte subset. Approaches toward enhancing the $CD8^+$cell response, providing the $CD8^+$cell factor, or replacing the suppressor subset through procedures similar to those for lymphocyte activated killer (LAK) cell therapy merit attention.

PATHOGENESIS OF HIV

Studies of HIV have distinguished isolates of this human lentivirus by their host range, their replicating properties, and their relative ability to infect and kill a wide variety of human cells. Serological differences have also been appreciated. All these characteristics are mirrored in the heterogeneity observed by molecular analysis.[26,46] Using the differences in biological and serological properties as distinguishing characteristics, one can identify specific HIV types that infect the brain, the immune system, and possibly the bowel and other tissues of the body. These laboratory investigations have also revealed the evolution of HIV strains in the infected host to become more virulent viruses associated with progression of the disease.

While the events in pathogenesis are not well-defined, they can be summarized by the following proposed steps: The virus enters many individuals through contact with infected seminal fluid. Free viruses, but most likely virus-infected cells,[47] directly infect the bowel mucosa (crypt cells of the epithelium), with subsequent spread throughout the body. Alternatively, the virus-infected cells enter the circulation through lesions and abrasions in the bowel mucosa. Individuals infected through intravenous needles or blood transfusions gain the virus through direct interaction of virus-infected cells or, less likely, free virus, with lymphocytes or macrophages in the body. Recent results suggest that any cell in the body coming in contact with virus-infected cells could be a target for HIV infection (TABLE 2). Differences in virus replication in a specific cell type, however, would determine how easily this infection spreads. This heterogeneity also influences how soon the virus is recognized by the host (e.g., immune responses) and is detected by presently available laboratory techniques. Helper T lymphocytes give rise to the most productive HIV infection, macrophages to somewhat less, and low-level HIV replication is observed with other cells of the body, including fibroblasts.[48] The macrophage is a cell now suspected of maintaining an efficient latent infection.

The virus enters the brain either via migrating macrophages or through an as yet unexplained passage of free virus through the blood-brain barrier to susceptible cells.[36] Conceivably, entry into the brain is first via infection of endothelial cells.[49] While the HIV infection of microglia is easily detected by *in situ* hybridization and electron microscopic studies, glial cells and even neurons may also be infected directly with HIV; however, this infection may elude detection because of the low level of virus replication in these cells. Nevertheless, HIV infection of glial cells may participate in the pathogenic process by compromising the function of these brain cells. Effects of HIV on the growth cycle of nerve-derived cells in culture have been demonstrated.[51] Similar conclusions can be made for other cells that are infected by HIV but show limited production of infectious virions. In the case of the brain, pathogenic events not causing immune destruction may directly produce disease since, as noted above, individuals with normal lymphocyte numbers have died solely with neurological symptoms. Moreover, because many patients with neurological symptoms also have gastrointestinal problems, we have suggested that infection of enterochromaffin cells in the bowel may involve the same HIV that infects the brain.[22] During embryogenesis, enterochromaffin cells migrate from the neural crest to the gastrointestinal tract and thus could have cell counterparts in the brain.

Once infection has been established, progression to disease depends on the extent of virus replication, virus spread, and the host response that either eliminates the virus-infected cells (cytotoxic response) or suppresses virus replication ($CD8^+$ suppressor cells). Data from epidemiological and laboratory studies suggest that the infection follows a progressive course with episodic release of HIV and, in many individuals, a relentless destruction of the immune or the neurological system. This slow, indolent course can take 5-10 years to give rise to symptoms and disease. Clearly, the balance between virus spread, emergence of virulent strains, and efficient host immune response determines the ultimate outcome of the infection.

Recent studies suggest that the progression to disease is associated with the appearance of high levels of replicating HIV in the circulation. Detection of the viral 25-kDa (p25) core antigen in the serum is a poor prognostic sign and has been found to be linked to a sudden enhanced reduction in the number of $CD4^+$ cells.[22] This observation suggests that high levels of HIV replication lead to increased destruction of $CD4^+$ cells and, thus, further compromise of the immune system. Why the virus emerges is not clear but may be related to the inability of $CD8^+$ cells to limit virus replication. If indeed the inherent antiviral capability of the $CD8^+$ cells diminishes, the virus present in the blood would be "free" to undergo multiple replication cycles and evolve (mutate) into a more pathogenic strain. Alternatively, episodic releases of virus in the host over time could lead to a more pathogenic type that further compromises the antiviral activity of the immune system.[22] The ultimate outcome by either mechanism is a further decrease in the immune response, viremia, increased destruction of white cells by HIV, and the eventual development of infections, malignancies, and death.

CONCLUSIONS

I commented in the INTRODUCTION on how work with animal retroviruses, particularly those in the mouse, provided the fundamental observations that helped research progress rapidly in identifying and understanding many basic features of HIV. The studies involving HIV have so far defined the parameters and variables involved in infection and progression to disease. A further understanding of the heterogeneity of HIV, of what governs the emergence of different serotypes and pathogenic subtypes, and of the ability of the host to recognize these viruses and respond to them offers the key to the control and elimination of this new human disease. Strategies of antiviral therapy and vaccination must consider each of the properties of the virus and of the host response, including the compromising events of autoimmunity and enhancing antibodies, so that correct approaches can be developed. For HIV-infected individuals, the promise should at least be offered that the observed ability of a human host to control other viral infections that may be carried in the body for a lifetime, such as herpes and measles, can equally well be expected to apply for the human lentivirus. The avenues needed to achieve this objective are being defined and should provide directions for achieving this goal in the future.

REFERENCES

1. NOTKINS, A., S. MERGENHAGEN & R. HOWARD. 1970. Annu. Rev. Microbiol. **24:** 525-537.
2. LEVY, J. A. 1986. Cancer Res **68:** 2253-2257.
3. GROSS, L. 1980. Oncogenic Viruses. Pergamon Press. New York.
4. LEVY, J. A. 1978. Curr. Top. Microbiol. Immunol. **79:** 111-213.
5. BARRE-SINOUSSI, F., M. NUGEYRE, C. DAUGUET, *et al.* 1983. Science **220:** 868-871.
6. GALLO, R. C., V. S. KALYANARAMAN, M. G. SARNGADHARAN, *et al.* 1984. Science **224:** 550-502.
7. LEVY, J. A., A. D. HOFFMAN, S. M. KRAMER, *et al.* 1984. Science **225:** 840-842.
8. RABSON, A. & M. MARTIN. 1985. Cell **40:** 477-480.
9. COFFIN, J., A. HAASE, J. A. LEVY, *et al.* 1986. Science **232:** 697.
10. LEVY, J. A. 1988. *In* Infectious Diseases Clinics of North America. M. Sande & P. Volberding, Eds. Vol. 2: 285-297. W. B. Saunders. Philadelphia.
11. CLAVEL, F., D. GUETARD, F. BRUN-VEZINET, *et al.* 1986. Science **233:** 343-346.
12. GUYADER M., M. EMERMAN, P. SONIGO, *et al.* 1987. Nature **326:** 662-669.
13. EVANS, L. A., J. MOREAU, K. ODEHOURI, *et al.* 1988. Science **240:** 1522-1525.
14. KONG, L. I., S.-W. LEE, J. C. KAPPES, *et al.* 1988. Science **240:** 1522-1525.
15. KANKI, P. J. 1987. AIDS **1:** 141-145.
16. FAUCI, A. S. 1988. Science **239:** 617-622.
17. BEDINGER, P., A. MORIARTY, R. C. VON BORSTEL, II, *et al.* 1988. Nature **334:** 162-164.

18. Maddon, P. J., A. G. Dalgleish, J. S. McDougal, *et al.* 1986. Cell **47:** 333-348.
19. Gallaher, W. R. 1987. Cell **50:** 327-328.
20. Weiner, D. B., W. V. Williams, J. A. Hoxie, *et al.* 1988. *In* Vaccines 1988. Cold Spring Harbor Laboratory Press. Cold Spring Harbor, NY. In press.
21. Stein, B. S., S. D. Gowda, J. F. Lifson, *et al.* 1987. Cell **49:** 659-668.
22. Levy, J. A. 1988. Nature **33:** 519-522.
23. Nelson, J. A., C. A. Wiley, C. Reynolds-Kohler, *et al.* 1988. Lancet **1:** 259-262.
24. Lifson, J. D., G. R. Reyes, M. S. McGrath, *et al.* 1986. Science **232:** 1123-1127.
25. Stevenson, M., C. Meier, A. M. Mann, *et al.* 1988. Cell **53:** 483-496.
26. Cheng-Mayer, C., D. Seto, M. Tateno & J. A. Levy. 1988. Science **240:** 80-82.
27. Garry, R. F., A. A. Gottlieb, K. P. Zuckerman, *et al.* 1988. Biosci. Rep. **8:** 35-48.
28. Ulug, E. T., R. F. Garry, M. R. F. Waite & H. R. Bose, Jr. 1984. Virology **132:** 118-130.
29. Weiss, R. A., P. R. Clapham, R. Cheingson-Popov, *et al.* 1985. Nature **316:** 69-72.
30. Cheng-Mayer, C., J. Homsy, L. A. Evans & J. A. Levy. 1988. Proc. Natl. Acad. Sci. USA **85:** 2815-2819.
31. Weiss, R. A., P. R. Clapham, J. N. Weber, *et al.* 1988. AIDS **2:** 95-100.
32. Cheng-Mayer, C. & J. A. Levy. 1988. Ann. Neurol. **23:** s58-s61.
33. Luciw, P. A., C. Cheng-Mayer & J. A. Levy. 1987. Proc. Natl. Acad. Sci. USA **84:** 1434-1438.
34. Levy, J. A. & J. L. Ziegler. 1983. Lancet **2:** 78-81.
35. Stricker, R. B., T. M. McHugh, D. J. Moody, *et al.* 1987. Nature **327:** 710-713.
36. Levy, J. A. 1989. AIDS: Pathogenesis and Treatment. Marcel Dekker, Inc. New York. pp. 159-229.
37. Rook, A. H., H. L. Clifford, T. Folks, *et al.* 1978. J. Immunol. **138:** 1064-1067.
38. Evans, L. A., G. Thomson-Honnebier, K. Steimer, *et al.* 1989. AIDS. In press.
39. Weinhold K. J., H. K. Lyerly, T. J. Matthews, *et al.* 1988. Lancet **1:** 902-905.
40. Robinson, W. E., Jr., D. C. Montefiori & W. M. Mitchell. 1988. Lancet **1:** 790-794.
41. Homsy, J., M. Tateno & J. A. Levy. 1988. Lancet **1:** 1285-1286.
42. Walker, B., S. Chakrabarti, B. Moss, *et al.* 1987. Nature **328:** 348-351.
43. Plata, F., B. Autran, L. P. Martins, *et al.* 1987. Nature **328:** 348-351.
44. Walker, B. D., C. Flexner, T. J. Paradis, *et al.* 1988. Science **240:** 64-66.
45. Walker, C. M., D. J. Moody, D. P. Stites & J. A. Levy. 1986. Science **234:** 1563-1566.
46. Hahn, B. H., G. M. Shaw, M. E. Taylor, *et al.* 1986. Science **232:** 1548-1553.
47. Levy, J. A. 1988. J. Am. Med. Assoc. **259:** 3037-3038.
48. Tateno, M., F. Gonzalez-Scarano & J. A. Levy. 1989. Proc. Natl. Acad. Sci. USA. In press.
49. Wiley, C. A., R. D. Schrier, J. A. Nelson, *et al.* 1986. Proc. Natl. Acad. Sci. USA **83:** 7089-7093.
50. Lee, M. R., D. D. Ho & M. E. Gurney. 1987. Science **237:** 1047-1051.
51. Dewhurst, S., K. Sakai, J. Bresser, *et al.* 1987. J. Virol. **61:** 3774-3782.

Immunobiology of the HIV Envelope

DANI P. BOLOGNESI

Departments of Surgery and
Microbiology and Immunology
Duke University Medical Center
Durham, North Carolina 27710

INTRODUCTION

The envelope of the human immunodeficiency virus (HIV) is not only an essential building block of the virus, it also plays a major role in its life cycle, particularly during the early stages of infection. It very likely determines, at least in part, the host range and tissue specificity of HIV, and it participates in pathogenic processes mediated by the virus. Because of its strategic location on the outer surface of the virion and the infected cell, it represents an optimal target for immune attack and thus a prime candidate for consideration in the development of vaccine and therapeutic strategies. Efforts to better understand its structural, functional, and antigenic properties will thus be well worthwhile.

IMMUNODOMINANT SITES ON THE HIV ENVELOPE FOR ANTIBODIES OF UNKNOWN BIOLOGICAL FUNCTIONS

There are two major regions of the envelope which elicit antibodies of unknown biological function. One is situated on the 120-kDa envelope glycoprotein, gp120, (amino acids 572 to 591)[1] and the other on the 41-kDa envelope glycoprotein, gp41, (amino acids 504 to 518).[2] Because of the nearly universal response by HIV infected individuals to these highly conserved regions, they have considerable value for development of diagnostic tests. Indeed, the successes in identifying the actual epitopes and reproducing these as recombinant molecules or synthetic peptides has launched second generation screening and diagnostic assays.[3-5] One of these molecules was even able to encompass both antigenic activities in a single bacterial recombinant fragment.[3] At the present time, it remains to be determined if these regions are involved in essential functions of the envelope that might be targeted for vaccine or therapeutic strategies.

FUNCTIONS OF THE HIV ENVELOPE DURING INFECTION

The early phases of HIV infection, as studied in T4 lymphocytes, involve the processes of (1) binding to the CD4 receptor, (2) anchoring of the viral membrane to that of the target cell, and (3) fusion of the viral and cell membranes, followed by penetration of the viral contents into the cell (FIG. 1).

Of these steps, the binding of the virus to its receptor is the best studied. It occurs between the exterior envelope glycoprotein (gp120) and a portion of the CD4 receptor molecule. The regions of the ligand[5a] and of the receptor[6–8] involved in binding have been identified. Monoclonal antibodies to the receptor are quite effective in blocking virus infection,[9] as are soluble forms of the receptor[10–14] or gp120 itself.[15]

An essential process for virus infectivity and pathogenicity is the phenomenon of fusion. With HIV, this occurs after the binding of the virus to the CD4 receptor, through a complex process thought to involve both gp120 and the transmembrane envelope glycoprotein, gp41.[16] The fusogenic domain is thought to reside within the amino-terminal portion of gp41.[17,18] Fusion can also occur between virus-infected cells exhibiting gp120 and gp41 on their surface and uninfected cells bearing the CD4 receptor.[19–21] This latter process eventually results in multinucleated giant cell formation and represents a form of virus cytopathicity.

REGIONS OF THE ENVELOPE WHICH ELICIT ANTIBODIES NEUTRALIZING VIRUS INFECTIVITY

On the basis of experience with other viruses, it is not surprising that the HIV envelope represents a major target for antibodies that can interfere with infection. A number of studies have been done to define the epitopes which serve as targets for immune attack. Two of these epitopes stand out and will be the focus of this discussion.

When experimental animals are immunized with the full-length HTLV-III$_B$ 160-kDa envelope glycoprotein (gp160), or with certain recombinant fragments thereof,[22] one notes the production of high-titered, isolate-restricted, virus-neutralizing and cell-fusion-blocking antibodies. A large fraction of the anti-HIV activity in these sera appears to be directed against an immunodominant portion of gp120 which can be replaced by a synthetic peptide consisting of 24 amino acids of the gp120 sequence.[23] Following independent approaches, two other laboratories have identified synthetic peptides representative of this segment of gp120 which induce neutralizing antibodies.[24,25] One of these studies predicted this outcome because this region has characteristics of a B cell epitope.[24] Similarly, monoclonal neutralizing antibodies have also been found to bind this same region of the envelope glycoprotein.[26–28] Thus, the portion of gp120 lying between residues 307 and 330 is apparently an important epitope for the development of high-titered, type-specific neutralizing antibodies against HIV-1. It is situated within a hypervariable region of the virus envelope,[29] and it is thought to exist as a loop formed by two disulfide-linked cysteine residues (L. A. Lasky, personal communication). The two cysteines, residues 303 and 337, are themselves highly conserved within the viral envelope glycoprotein. Thus, although the amino acid sequence within this loop is variable, the loop itself i present in the gp120 from different strains of the virus.

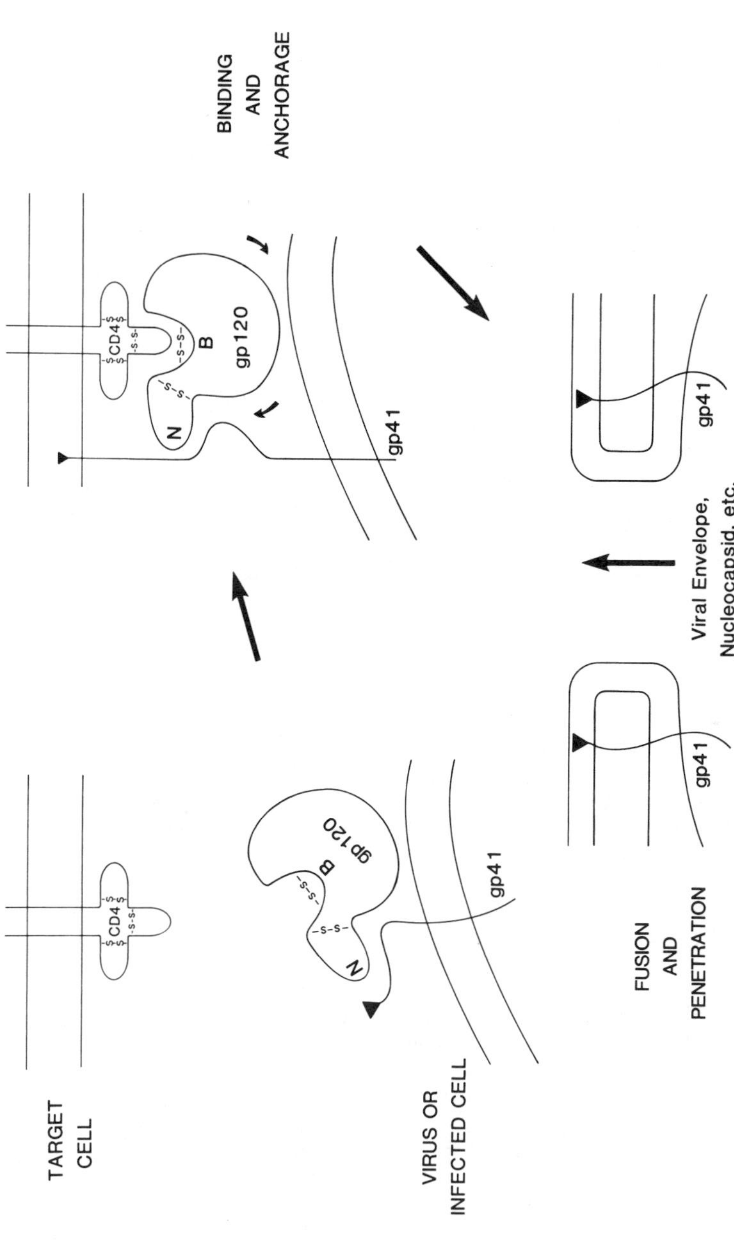

FIGURE 1. Selected steps during the early stages of HIV infection. After binding of the exterior viral envelope glycoprotein (gp120) to the CD4 receptor of the target cell, the membranes of the virus (or of a virus-infected cell) are anchored to the target cell by the transmembrane viral glycoprotein (gp41). The membranes then fuse, allowing the contents of the virus (or of the virus-infected cell) to spill into the target cell. **N**, dominant neutralizing epitope; **B**, binding site to CD4; ▼, putative fusogenic domain of gp41.

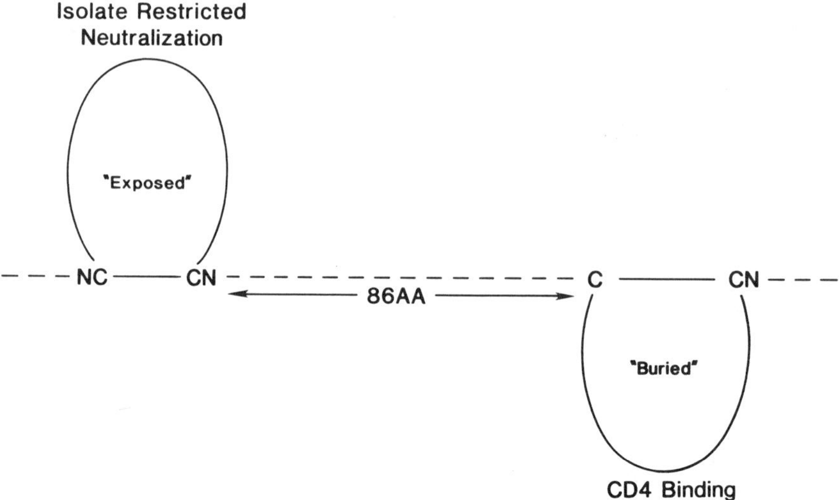

FIGURE 2. Schematic of two disulfide-bridged loop structures in HIV gp120 involved in infectivity of the virus. The exposed hypervariable loop between cysteine residues 302 and 337 (*left*) contains the epitope which elicits viral isolate-restricted neutralizing antibodies. The conserved loop between cysteines 424 and 451 (*right*), which is hypothesized to be inaccessible ("buried") in the native protein, may include the binding site for the CD4 receptor. This epitope elicits antibodies that block binding of gp120 to CD4, but it remains to be determined if antibodies can be made to this region which have broad neutralizing activity. 86AA, 86 amino acids.

On the other hand, in contrast to the studies on immunization of experimental animals, sera taken from HIV-infected humans generally exhibit broad (rather than isolate-restricted) neutralizing activity and contain a high titer of antibodies which block gp120 binding to the CD4 receptor. Presumably, such antibodies are directed at more conserved structures within gp120, possibly including those involved in CD4 binding.[5a] Thus, these antibodies may be related to the group-specific neutralizing activity often noted in human sera. One line of circumstantial evidence in support of this idea is the fact that the aforementioned activities generally correlate with the gp120-CD4 blocking titer in such sera.[30]

Whatever the nature of the broader neutralizing activity of the human sera and of the gp120-CD4 blocking antibodies recovered from them in the natural infection, studies to date indicate that it has been difficult to duplicate this response in animals immunized with viral envelope subunits or even to reproduce this blocking effect *in vitro* by using monoclonal antibodies to the gp120 region that is the binding site for CD4. It is not clear if the monoclonal antibodies generated to this region of gp120 are of insufficient affinity or whether they fail to interact effectively with the binding site on the native molecule because it is somehow inaccessible. Such inaccessibility could occur because gp120 is extensively glycosylated[15] and/or because the binding domains may exist as a cleft in the molecule, as seen with picornaviruses.[31]

In summary, if the two epitopes of gp120 discussed here are viewed in terms of the biological activity against the virus of the antibodies they elicit, several sharp contrasts between them can be seen (FIG. 2). One epitope elicits neutralizing antibodies which are isolate-restricted and primarily directed to a hypervariable loop structure of gp120 that is not involved in CD4 binding. This site is immunodominant and the immunoreactive epitope can be reproduced with synthetic peptides. The class of neutralizing antibodies reactive with the second epitope is apparently directed at a more conserved region, which may be related to the CD4 binding site of gp120. However, the immunoreactivity of this domain is conformation-dependent, and the epitope appears to be less immunogenic.

In addition to these two sites, other regions of the envelope have been reported to represent targets for neutralizing antibodies. These observations have been obtained by using synthetic peptides from gp41, gp120, and a peptide that spans both molecules[32] (see also, Ref. 39). In general the titers of neutralizing antibodies to peptides representing these regions have been relatively low ($\frac{1}{16}$-$\frac{1}{128}$) in comparison to those which have been achieved against the dominant hypervariable loop (> $\frac{1}{1000}$). One of these regions,[33] however, merits particular attention because it is coincident with a site reported to be involved in virus entry after binding to the receptor.[34] This viral entry step also appears to involve the dominant neutralizing epitope.[30]

ANTIBODIES WHICH INHIBIT FUSOGENIC ACTIVITIES

There are two types of assays that measure fusion: (1) assays that score syncytia occurring subsequent to virus infection and (2) assays that employ already infected cells admixed with uninfected partners exhibiting CD4. In a sense these assays are analogous mechanistically (see FIG. 1), but one feature distinguishes them when their behavior is viewed in terms of the effects of anti-envelope antibodies. Whereas all antibodies which prevent infection by free virus also, consequently, prevent the occurrence of syncytia of the cells used as targets for the infection, the same need not be true when such antibodies are tested in the assay employing already infected cells, where infection is not essential. Stated otherwise, while the molecules involved for fusion (gp120, gp41 and CD4) are the same for each type of assay, the difference between the dynamics of fusion of a CD4-bearing target cell to a small particle such as the virus and those for fusion to an infected cell which bears viral envelope proteins across extended regions of its membrane may well dictate different requirements for inhibition by antibodies. Indeed, not all antibodies which neutralize virus infectivity inhibit cell-cell fusion, or at least they do not when compared on a molar basis. One class of antibodies, both polyclonal and monoclonal, that does achieve reasonable parity in the two assays represents those directed at the immunodominant neutralizing site. As noted above, these antibodies inhibit a post-binding step in virus infection which is probably linked to the fusion process.[30] Antibodies present in HIV-infected chimpanzees and humans also block fusion, but neither their target epitopes nor their mechanisms of action have been conclusively identified. Finally, certain monoclonal antibodies prepared against gp41 have been reported to strongly inhibit fusion, but their target on this molecule has not been mapped (R. Weiss, personal communication). It will be of interest to learn if the latter epitope represents the putative fusogenic sequence at the amino terminus of gp41.

EPITOPES ASSOCIATED WITH IMMUNITY AGAINST INFECTED CELLS

Three distinct regions of the envelope, all in gp120, are recognized by T cells, according to evidence based primarily on studies in mice (FIG. 3). These are situated (1) in a conserved region near the amino terminus of gp120,[35] (2) within the hypervariable neutralization loop,[36] and (3) within the conserved region for binding of gp120 to CD4.[35] The one within the neutralization epitope can also be a target for cytotoxic T lymphocytes (CTL).[36] Evidence that human sera can recognize the region within the CD4 binding site on gp120[37] and also the other regions of gp120 and gp41[38,39] has recently been reported. Whether studies in mice are generally predictive for recognition of epitopes by humans remains to be established, but it is a likely possibility, judging from the results of studies with other pathogens.[40]

A distinct but related issue is the identity of regions that are targets for antibodies that mediate cellular cytotoxicity (antibody-dependent cellular cytotoxicity, ADCC). Although fine mapping studies have not been done, it appears that conserved regions of the envelope, situated mainly on gp120, may be the primary targets.[41] One such region (FIG. 3) appears to coincide with the carboxyl terminus of gp120.[42] It should be stressed that variable regions should not be excluded from consideration as potential targets for ADCC, particularly in relation to specific reactivities with virus isolates from a given patient (E. Fenyo, personal communication).

To date, no solid evidence has been obtained that antibodies to the HIV envelope are able to direct complement-dependent lysis of virus-infected cells. In fact, evidence to the contrary has been reported.[41,43] On the other hand, antibodies which associate with complement have been reported to facilitate infection of target cells bearing high levels of complement receptors[44] but not of other target cells for HIV (unpublished observations).

EPITOPES WHICH MIMIC PRODUCTS OF NORMAL CELLULAR GENES

Molecular mimicry is increasingly being recognized as an important process in pathogenesis and immune suppression accompanying virus infections.[45] Viruses bearing structures analogous to those present on the surface of normal cells could present such regions to the immune system in such a manner that they are recognized as foreign antigens, thereby eliciting immune responses which attack normal cells. Alternatively these regions could represent growth factor-like elements which could influence a variety of normal cellular functions. HIV displays examples of each of these types of mimicry, as well as other mechanisms by which it can cause the destruction or impairment of normal cells.

The first report of molecular mimicry in HIV concerned a homology to interleukin-2 (IL-2) in the carboxyl-terminal region of gp41.[46] Subsequently, homology to HLA-DR (histocompatibility leukocyte antigen DR), also within gp41, was documented, and the anti-DR activities present in HIV-infected individuals were reported to be able to impair normal immune function. Finally, homology to neuroleukin, a nerve-cell growth factor, has been reported to involve a region of gp120 coinciding with a putative neutralizing epitope.[48] However, the homology to neuroleukin could not be

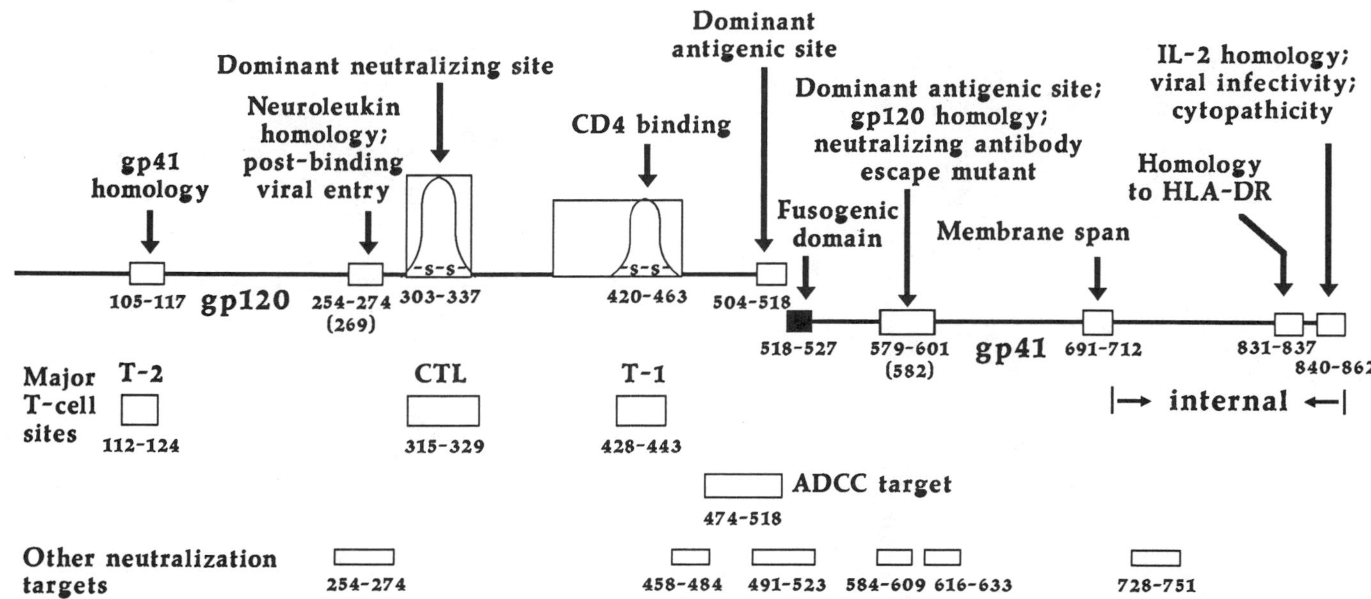

FIGURE 3. Summary of the functional and immunogenic sites on the HIV envelope discussed in this report. HLA-DR, histocompatibility leukocyte antigen DR; IL-2, interleukin-2; CTL, cytotoxic T lymphocyte; ADCC, antibody-dependent cellular cytotoxicity.

substantiated, and the nature of the epitope-related normal cellular sequence remains to be established.

Various data, primarily from *in vitro* studies, indicate that HIV has some other unique ways to impair the immune system. Release of its exterior envelope glycoprotein, an event which apparently occurs readily from the virus or from infected cells,[49] generates a molecule which actively binds to CD4-bearing normal lymphocytes. This binding of the released envelope protein to the CD4 receptor targets these cells for immune attack both by antibodies which mediate ADCC[41] and by cytotoxic T cells which recognize processed forms of gp120 after its internalization by CD4-bearing lymphocytes.[50,51] Both events can result in the destruction of normal CD4-positive T cells without the necessity for their infection by HIV. To what extent this process occurs *in vivo* depends on the levels of gp120 synthesis, secretion, and shedding. To date, free gp120 has not been detected in the circulation, but this result is not surprising, given its powerful affinity for CD4. Adding another twist, it has been suggested that gp120-CD4 complexes might expose new epitopes on CD4 which then elicit anti-CD4 antibodies in some HIV-infected patients (J. Sodroski and W. Haseltine, personal communication). Such antibodies could also impair the function of CD4-bearing cells.

Finally, immunosuppressive sequences may exist in the envelope itself. Regions homologous to those present in the transmembrane glycoprotein of type C retroviruses and known to be highly suppressive for macrophage function[52] are also present in HIV gp41.[53] In addition, it was recently reported that disappearance of antibodies to this region correlated with progression of the disease.[54]

CONCLUDING REMARKS

This discussion serves to emphasize the importance of defining functional and immunogenic regions of the HIV envelope. A summary of those studied and documented to date is depicted in FIGURE 3. More are certain to be added to this list, particularly as information becomes available on precisely how gp120 and gp41 interact with one another and with the target cell during the process of infection, as well as on other phases of the infectious cycle. For instance, there may be regions in one molecule that can affect the configuration of a functional epitope in the other. Such an example may relate to a mutation in gp41 which allows the virus to escape neutralization,[55] even though the site of this mutation is not a target for neutralization. It is likely that gp120 and gp41 interact at multiple sites and their dynamic interaction during the early phases of infection may represent a well-orchestrated process (FIG. 1) whose perturbation could be lethal for the virus, on the one hand, or could negate the function of protective antibodies on the other. One such contact region between the two molecules has been described.[55a]

Upon examination of this map of the HIV envelope, one is also struck by the alignment of regions involved in essential virus functions (e.g., binding, gp120-gp41 contact regions, etc.) with those independently identified as capable of eliciting anti-envelope immune responses that are biologically important. Also of note is a proximity of T and B cell epitopes, the most outstanding example being that the dominant neutralizing site also serves as a target for CTL. This correspondence of sites raises the question of whether antibodies to this region might impair CTL activity and thus serve as blocking antibodies which promote rather than retard infection.

Along these lines, it is also becoming increasingly likely, on the basis of results from recent preliminary studies, that HIV can infect cells by mechanisms that do not involve CD4. These include the use of other receptors, as suggested for cells of neuroectodermal origin (R. Weiss and J. Levy, personal communication), as well as antibody-mediated pathways of virus entry which may apply to target cells with Fc receptors (i.e., macrophages) or receptors for complement. Thus, one must consider such possibilities in any vaccine strategy in order to exclude unwanted reactivities (i.e., enhancing antibodies), and one must identify those unknown elements that are responsible for viral entry into secondary target cells.

Also of note is the possibility that the envelope itself is toxic for the infected cell through several possible mechanisms beginning with its ability to complex to CD4. Formation of this complex can occur both within the cell and at the cell surface, thereby creating havoc with functions for which CD4 is essential to the well-being of the particular cell.[55b] Another possible mechanism relates to a carboxyl-terminal region of gp41 which appears to be critical to HIV cytopathocity.[5b] This region includes that of IL-2 homology.[46] Because this segment is situated within the intracellular domain of gp41, it could impair normal signal transduction processes required for cell growth and differentiation.

Furthermore, the issue of envelope variability deserves some attention. Is this merely a mechanism to evade immune recognition and response or is this a fundamental property of the virus that allows it to overtake the organism irrespective of protective immunity? Both may be features of HIV, and how to overcome them is central to development of successful preventive and interventive approaches.

In closing, it should be emphasized that while the envelope of HIV may well be a primary target of immune attack, other viral components may be equally important. The phenomenon of antigen processing and presentation on the cell surface in association with MHC (major histocompatibility complex) products makes any HIV gene product (structural or regulatory) a potential target for immune attack, as has been amply documented for other viral systems.[57]

ACKNOWLEDGMENTS

A number of colleagues have contributed to the work described in this report: Drs. Thomas J. Matthews, Kent J. Weinhold, Alphonse Langlois, Barton F. Haynes, Thomas Palker, Micheal Skinner, Kim Lyerly, Douglas Tyler, and Chet Nastala (Duke University Medical Center); Drs. James Rusche, Kashi Javaherian, and Scott Putney (Repligen Corporation); Drs. R. C. Gallo, Flossie Wong-Staal, and William Blattner (National Cancer Institute); Dr. Alfred Prince (New York Blood Center); and Dr. Jorg Eichberg (Southwest Research Foundation).

REFERENCES

1. Palker, T. J., T. J. Matthews, M. E. Clark. G. J. Cianciolo, R. R. Randall, A. J. Langlois, G. C. White, B. Safai, R. Snyderman, D. P. Bolognesi & B. F. Haynes. 1987. A conserved region at the COOH terminus of human immunodeficiency virus gp120 envelope protein contains an immunodominant eptiope. Proc. Natl. Acad. Sci. USA **84:** 2479-2483.

2. WANG, J. J. G., S. STEEL, R. WISNIEWOLSKI & C. YI WANG. 1986. Detection of antibodies to human T-lymphotropic virus type III by using a synthetic peptide of 21 amino acid residues corresponding to a highly antigenic segment of gp41 envelope protein. Proc. Natl. Acad. Sci. USA **83:** 6159-6163.
3. KENEALY, W., D. REED, R. CYBULSKI, D. TRIBE, P. TAYLOR, C. STEVENS, T. MATTHEWS & S. PETTEWAY. 1987. Analysis of human serum antibodies to human immunodeficiency virus (HIV) using recombinant ENV and GAG antigens. AIDS Res Hum. Retroviruses **3**(1): 95-105.
4. GNANN, JR., J. W., J. B. MCCORNICK, S. MITCHELL, J. A. NELSON & M. B. A. OLDSTONE. 1987. Synthetic peptide immunoassay distinguishes HIV type 1 and HIV type 2 infections. Science **237:** 1346-1349.
5. KEMP, B. E., D. B. RYLATT, P. G. BUNDESEN, R. R. DOHERTY, D. A. MCPHEE, D. STAPLETON, L. E. COTTIS, K. WILSON, M. A. JOHN, J. M. KHAN, D. P. DINH, S. MILES & C. J. HILLYARD. 1988. Autologous red cell agglutination assay for HIV-1 antibodies: Simplified test with whole blood. Science **241:** 1352-1354.
5a. LASKY, L. A., G. NAKAMURA, D. H. SMITH, C. FENNIE, C. SHIMASAKI, E. PATZER, P. BERMAN, T. GREGORY & D. J. CAPON. 1987. Delineation of a region of the human immunodeficiency virus type 1 gp120 glycoprotein critical for interaction with the CD4 receptor. Cell **50:** 975-985.
6. JAMESON, B. A., P. E. RAO, L. I. KONG, B. H. HAHN, G. M. SHAW, L. E. HOOD & S. B. H. KENT. 1988. Location and chemical synthesis of a binding site for HIV-1 on the CD4 protein. Science **240:** 1335-1339.
7. LANDAU, N. R., M. WARTON & D. R. LITTMAN. 1988. The envelope glycoprotein of the human immunodeficiency virus binds to the immunoglobulin-like domain of CD4. Nature **334:** 159-162.
8. LIFSON, J. D., K. M. HWANG, P. L. NARA, B. FRASER, M. PADGETT, N. M. DUNLOP & L. E. EIDEN. 1988. Synthetic CD4 peptide derivatives that inhibit HIV infection and cytopathicity. Science **241:** 712-716.
9. SATTENTAU, Q. J., A. G. DALGLEISH, R. A. WEISS & P. C. L. BEVERLEY. 1986. Epitopes of the CD4 antigen and HIV infection. Science **234:** 1120-1123.
10. SMITH, D. H., R. A. BYAN, S. A. MARSTERS, T. GREGORY, J. E. GROOPMAN & D. J. CAPON. 1988. Blocking of HIV-1 infectivity by a soluble, secreted form of the CD4 antigen. Science **238:** 1704.
11. FISHER, R. A., J. M. BERTONIS, W. MEIER, V. A. JOHNSON, D. S. COSTOPOULOS, T. LIU, R. TIZARD, B. D. WALKER, M. S. HIRSCH, R. T. SCHOOLEY & R. A. FLAVELL. 1988. HIV infection is blocked in vitro by recombinant soluble CD4. Nature **331:** 76-77.
12. HUSSEY, R. E., N. E. RICHARDSON, M. KOWALSKI, N. R. BROWN, H. C. CHANG, R. F. SILICIANO, T. DORFMAN, B. WALKER, J. SODROSKI & E. L. REINHERZ. 1988. A soluble CD4 protein selectively inhibits HIV replication and syncytium formation. Nature **331:** 78-81.
13. DEEN, K. C., J. S. MCDOUGAL, R. INACKER, G. FOLENA-WASSERMAN, J. ARTHOS, J. ROSENBERG, P. J. MEDDON, R. AXEL & R. W. SWEET. 1988. A soluble form of CD4 (T4) protein inhibits AIDS virus infection. Nature **331:** 82-83.
14. TRAUNECKER, A., W. LUKE & K. KARJALAINEN. 1988. Soluble CD4 molecules neutralize human immunodeficiency virus type 1. Nature **331:** 84-86.
15. MATTHEWS, T. J., K. J. WEINHOLD, H. K. LYERLY, A. J. LANGLOIS, H. WIGZELL & D. P. BOLOGNESI. 1987. Interaction between the human T-cell lymphotropic virus type III_B envelope glycoprotein gp120 and the surface antigen CD4: Role of carbohydrate in binding and cell fusion. Proc. Natl. Acad. Sci. USA **84:** 5424-5428.
16. KOWALSKI, M., J. POTZ, L. BASIRIPOUR, T. DORFMAN, W. C. GOH, E. TERWILLIGER, A. DAYTON, C. ROSEN, W. HASELTINE & J. SODROSKI. 1987. Functional regions of the envelope glycoprotein of human immunodeficiency virus type 1. Science **237:** 1351-1355.
17. GALLAHER, W. R. 1987. Detection of a fusion peptide sequence in the transmembrane protein of human immunodeficiency virus. Cell **50:** 327-328.
18. GONZALEZ-SCARANO, F., M. N. WAXHAM, A. M. ROSS & J. A. HOXIE. 1987. Sequence similarities between human immunodeficiency virus gp41 and paramyxovirus fusion proteins. AIDS Res. Hum. Retroviruses **3**(3): 245-252.

19. LIFSON, J. D., G. R. REYES, M. S. MCGRATH, B. S. STEIN & E. G. ENGLEMAN. 1986. AIDS retrovirus induced cytopathology: Giant cell formation and involvement of CD4 antigen. Science **232:** 1123-1127.
20. SODROSKI, J., W. C. GOH, C. ROSEN, K. CAMPBELL & W. A. HASELTINE. 1986. Role of the HTLV-III/LAV envelope in syncytium formation and cytopathicity. Nature **322:** 470-474.
21. LIFSON, J. D., J. E. FEINBERG, W. C. SMALL, G. R. REYES, L. RABIN, B. BANAPOUR, S. CHAKRABARTI, B. MOSS, F. WONG-STAAL, K. S. STEIMER & E. G. ENGLEMAN. 1986. Induction of CD4-dependent cell fusion by the HTLV-III/LAV envelope glycoprotein. Nature **323:** 725-728.
22. RUSCHE, J. R., D. L. LYNN, M. ROBERT-GUROFF, A. J. LANGLOIS, H. K. LYERLY, H. CARSON, K. KROHN, A. RANKI, R. C. GALLO, D. P. BOLOGNESI, S. D. PUTNEY & T. J. MATTHEWS. 1987. Humoral immune response to the entire human immunodeficiency virus envelope glycoprotein made in insect cells. Proc. Natl. Acad. Sci. USA **84:** 6924-6928.
23. RUSCHE, J. R., K. JAVAHERIAN, C. MCDANAL, J. PETRO, D. L. LYNN, R. GRIMAILI, A. J. LANGLOIS, R. C. GALLO, L. O. ARTHUR, P. J. FISCHINGER, D. P. BOLOGNESI, S. D. PUTNEY & T. J. MATTHEWS. 1988. Antibodies that inhibit fusion of human immunodeficiency virus-infected cells bind a 24-amino acid sequence of the viral envelope, gp120. Proc. Natl. Acad. Sci. USA **85:** 3198-3202.
24. PALKER, T. J., M. E. CLARK, A. J. LANGLOIS, T. J. MATTHEWS, K. J. WEINHOLD, R. R. RANDALL, D. P. BOLOGNESI & B. F. HAYNES. 1988. Type-specific neutralization of the human immunodeficiency virus with antibodies to *env*-encoded synthetic peptides. Proc. Natl. Acad. Sci. USA **85:** 1-5.
25. KENEALY, W. H., T. J. MATTHEWS, M. C. GANFIELD, A. J. LANGLOIS, D. M. WASELEFSKY, D. P. BOLOGNESI S. R. Petteway. 1989. Antibodies from human immunodeficiency virus (HIV-1) infected individuals bind to a short amino acid sequence which elicits neutralizing antibodies in animals. AIDS Res. Hum. Retroviruses **5**(2). In press.
26. SKINNER, M. A., R. TING, A. J. LANGLOIS, K. J. WEINHOLD, H. K. LYERLY, K. JAVAHERIAN & T. J. MATTHEWS. 1988. Characteristics of a neutralizing monoclonal antibody to the HTLV-III_B envelope glycoprotein. AIDS Res. Hum. Retroviruses **4:** 187-197.
27. MATSUSHITA, S., M. ROBERT-GUROFF, J. RUSCHE, A. KOITO, T. HATTORI, H. HOSHINO, K. JAVAHERIAN, K. TAKATSUKI & S. PUTNEY. 1988. Characterization of a human immunodeficiency virus neutralizing monoclonal antibody and mapping of the neutralizing epitope. J. Virol. **62:** 2107-2114.
28. THOMAS, E. K., J. N. WEBER, J. MCCLURE, M. C. CLAPHAM, M. C. SINGHAL, M. K. SHRIVER & R. A. WEISS. 1988. Neutralizing monoclonal antibodies to the AIDS virus. AIDS **2:** 25-29.
29. STARCICH, B. R., B. H. HAHN, G. M. SHAW, P. D. MCNEELY, S. MODROW, H. WOLF, E. S. PARKS, W. P. PARKS, S. F. JOSEPHS, R. C. GALLO & F. WONG-STAAL 1986. Identification and characterization of conserved and variable regions in the envelope gene of HTLV-III/LAV, the retrovirus of AIDS. Cell **45:** 637-648.
30. SKINNER, M. A., A. J. LANGLOIS, C. B. MCDANAL, D. P. BOLOGNESI & T. J. MATTHEWS. 1988. Serum from HIV infected humans prevents gp120 binding to CD4 and this activity is not elicited in animals immunized with envelope protein components. J. Virol. **62:** 4195-4200.
31. COLONNO, R. J., J. H. CONDRA, S. MIZUTANI, P. L. CALLAHAN, M. E. DAVIES & M. A. MURCKO. 1988. Evidence for the direct involvement of the rhinovirus canyon in receptor binding. Proc. Natl. Acad. Sci. USA **85:** 5449-5452.
32. CHAHN, T. L., G. R. DREESMAN, & P. KANDA. 1986. Induction of anti-HIV neutralizing antibodies by synthetic peptides. EMBO **5:** 3065-3071.
33. HO, D. D., J. C. KAPLAN, I. E. RACKAUSKAS & M. E. FURNEY. 1988. Second conserved domain of gp120 is important for HIV infectivity and antibody neutralization. Science **239:** 1021-1023.
34. WILLEY, R. L., D. H. SMITH, L. A. LASKY, T. S. THEODORE, P. L. EARL, B. MOSS, D. J. CAPON & M. A. MARTIN. 1988. In vitro mutagenesis identifies a region within the

envelope gene of the human immunodeficiency virus that is critical for infectivity. J. Virol. **62:** 139-147.

35. CEASE, K. B., H. MARGALIT, J. L. CORNETTE, S. D. PUTNEY, W. G. ROBEY, C. OUYANG, H. Z. STREICHER, P. J. FISCHINGER, R. C. GALLO, C. DELISI & J. A. BERZOFSKY. 1987. Helper T-cell antigenic site identification in the acquired immunodeficiency syndrome virus gp120 envelope protein and induction of immunity in mice to the native protein using a 16-residue synthetic peptide. Proc. Natl. Acad. Sci. USA **84:** 4249-4253.
36. TAKAHASHI, H., J. COHEN, A. HOSMALIN, K. B. CEASE, R. HOUGHTEN, J. L. CORNETTE, C. DELISI, B. MOSS, R. N. GERMAIN & J. A. BERZOFSKY. 1988. An immunodominant epitope of the human immunodeficiency virus envelope glycoprotein gp160 recognized by class I major histocompatibility complex molecule-restricted murine cytotoxic T lymphocytes. Proc. Natl. Acad. Sci. USA **85:** 3105-3109.
37. BERZOFSKY, J. A., A. BENSUSSAN, K. B. CEASE, J. F. BOURGE, R. CHEYNIER, Z. LURHUMA, J. J. SALAUN, R. C. GALLO, G. M. SHEARER & D. ZAGURY. 1988. Antigenic peptides recognized by T-lymphocytes from AIDS viral envelope-immune humans. Nature **334:** 706-708.
38. AHEARNE, P. M., T. J. MATTHEWS, H. K. LYERLY, G. C. WHITE, D. P. BOLOGNESI & K. J. WEINHOLD. 1988. Cellular immune response to viral peptides in patients exposed to HIV. AIDS Res. Hum. Retroviruses **4:** 259-267.
39. SCHRIER, R. D., J. W. GNANN, A. J. LANGLOIS, K. SHRIVER, J. A. NELSON & M. B. A. OLDSTONE. 1988. B and T lymphocyte responses to an immunodominant epitope of human immunodeficiency virus. J. Virol. **62:** 2531-2536.
40. GOOD, M. F., W. L. MALOY, M. N. LUNDE, H. MARGALIT, J. L. CORNETTE, G. L. SMITH, B. MOSS, L. H. MILLER & J. A. BERZOFSKY. 1987. Construction of synthetic immunogen: Use of new T-helper epitope on Malaria circumsporozoite protein. Science **235:** 1059-1062.
41. LYERLY, H. K., T. J. MATTHEWS, A. J. LANGLOIS, D. P. BOLOGNESI & K. J. WEINHOLD. 1987. Human T-cell lymphotropic virus III_B glycoprotein (gp120) bound to CD4 determinants on normal lymphocytes and expressed by infected cells serves as target for immune attack. Proc. Natl. Acad. Sci. USA **84:** 4601-4605.
42. LYERLY, H. K., D. L. REED, T. J. MATTHEWS, A. J. LANGLOIS, P. M. AHEARNE, S. R. PETTEWAY, D. P. BOLOGNESI & K. J. WEINHOLD. 1988. Anti-gp120 antibodies form HIV seropositive individuals mediate broadly reactive anti-HIV ADCC. AIDS Res. Hum. Retroviruses **3**(4): 409-422.
43. NARA, P. L., W. G. ROBEY, M. A. GONDA, S. G. CATER & P. J. FISCHINGER. 1987. Absence of cytotoxic antibody to human immunodeficiency virus-infected cells in humans and its induction in animals after infection or immunization with purified envelope glycoprotein gp120. Proc. Natl. Acad. Sci. USA **84:** 3797-3801.
44. ROBINSON, JR., W. E., D. C. MONTEFIORI & W. M. MITCHELL. 1988. Antibody-dependent enhancement of human immunodeficiency virus type 1 infection. Lancet **1**(April): 790-794.
45. OLDSTONE, M. B. A. 1987. Molecular mimicry and autoimmune disease. Cell **50:** 819-820.
46. REIHER, W. E., J. E. BLALOCK & T. K. BRUNCK. 1986. Sequence homology between acquired immunodeficiency syndrome virus envelope protein and interleukin 2. Proc. Natl. Acad. Sci. **83:** 9188-9192.
47. GOLDING, H., F. A. ROBEY, F. T. GATES, W. LINDER, P. R. BEINING, T. HOFFMAN & B. GOLDING. 1988. Identification of homologous regions in human immunodeficiency virus I gp41 and human MHC class II domain. J. Exp. Med. **167:** 914-923.
48. LEE, M. R., D. D. HO & M. E. GURNEY. 1987. Functional interaction and partial homology between human immunodeficiency virus and neuroleukin. Science **237:** 1047-1051.
49. GELDERBLOM, H. R., H. REUPKE & G. PAULI. 1985. Loss of envelope antigens of HTLV-III/LAV, a factor in AIDS pathogenesis? Lancet (November): 1016-1017.
50. SILICIANO, R. F., T. LAWTON, C. KNALL, R. W. KARR, P. BERMAN, T. GREGORY & E. L. REINHERZ. 1988. Analysis of host-virus interactions in AIDS with anti-gp120 T cell clones: Effect of HIV sequence variation and a mechanism for $CD4^+$ cell depletion. Cell **54:** 561-575.

51. LANZAVECCHIA, A., E. ROOSNEK, T. GREGORY, P. BERMAN & S. ABRIGNANI. 1988. T cells can present antigens such as HIV gp120 targeted to their own surface molecules. Nature **334:** 530-532.
52. CIANCIOLO, G. J., T. J. MATTHEWS, D. P. BOLOGNESI & R. SNYDERMAN. 1980. Macrophage accumulation in mice is inhibited by low molecular weight products from murine leukemia viruses. J. Immunol. **124:** 2900-2905.
53. CIANCIOLO, G. J., T. D. COPELAND, S. OROSZLAN & R. SYNDERMAN. 1985. Inhibition of lymphocyte proliferation by a synthetic peptide homologous to retroviral envelope proteins. Proc. Acad. Natl. Sci. USA **230:** 453-455.
54. KLASSE, P. J., R. PIPKORN & J. BLOMBERG. 1988. Presence of antibodies to a putatively immunosuppressive part of human immunodeficiency virus (HIV) envelope glycoprotein gp41 is strongly associated with health among HIV-positive subjects. Proc. Acad. Natl. Sci. USA **85:** 5225-5229.
55. REITZ, JR., M. S., C. WILSON, C. NAUGLE, R. C. GALLO & M. ROBERT-GUROFF 1988. Generation of a neutralization-resistant variant of HIV-1 is due to selection for a point mutation in the envelope gene. Cell **54:** 57-63.
55a. MCPHEE, D. A., D. L. STAPLETON, S. A. CUMMING, N. C. PAVUK, R. R. DOHERTY & B. E. KEMP. Putative contact region between HIV-envelope proteins gp120 and gp41: Antiviral action of synthetic peptide analogs. Manuscript submitted.
55b. HOXIE, J. A., J. D. ALPERS, J. L. RACKOWSKI, K. HUEBNER, B. S. HAGGARTY, A. J. CEDARBAUM & J. C. REED. 1986. Alterations in T4 (CD4) protein and mRNA synthesis in cells infected with HIV. Science **234:** 1123-1127.
56. FISHER, A. G., K. RATNER, H. MITSUYA, L. MARSELLE, M. E. HARPER, S. BRODER, R. C. GALLO & F. WONG-STAAL. 1986. Infectious mutants of HTLV-III with changes in the 3′ region and markedly reduced cytopathic effects. Science **233:** 655-659.
57. TOWNSEND, A. R. M., F. M. GOTCH & J. DAVEY. 1985. Cytotoxic T-cells recognize fragments of influenza nucleoprotein. Cell **42:** 457-467.

Human Retroviruses: Their Role in Neoplasia and Immunodeficiency

ROBERT C. GALLO AND LATA S. NERURKAR

Laboratory of Tumor Cell Biology
Division of Cancer Etiology
National Cancer Institute
National Institutes of Health
Bethesda, Maryland 20892

The task of implicating viruses in human cancers has always been more difficult than that of associating them with animal cancers, given the fact that their involvement in cancer is far less frequent than their involvement in characteristic viral illnesses. It would be ideal if an infectious etiology of cancer could satisfy Koch's postulates, one of which requires infectious agents to induce the disease in the normal host; but this is, of course, not possible. However, fulfilling more realistic, modified criteria, *viz., in vitro* cell transformations, detection of virus/viral genomes in infected cells obtained from patients or in cells infected *in vitro,* host immune response (e.g., appearance of specific antibodies following natural virus infections), epidemiological studies showing a relatively high incidence of disease in risk groups, have all provided increasing evidence that viruses are indeed involved in the pathogenesis of several forms of human cancer. This report will provide a brief summary of our current understanding of the mode of action of certain human viruses, particularly the retroviruses, and their interactions with the cells of the immune system to cause cancer and immune deficiency.

VIRUS-INDUCED TRANSFORMATIONS

Both direct and indirect mechanisms are evident in virus-induced transformations (FIG. 1). The direct mechanism involves, as a primary step, virus infection of the progenitor cell which ultimately gives rise to a tumor cell. In the indirect mechanism, the target cell of virus infection is not the progenitor of a tumor cell but in some manner is responsible for the development of a tumor which originates from a different kind of cell. The examples of direct transformation are seen in a retrovirus group, e.g., human T lymphotropic virus type-I (HTLV-I) causing adult T cell leukemia/lymphoma (ATL), or in a DNA virus group, e.g., papilloma virus causing cancer of the cervix or Epstein-Barr virus (EBV) causing Burkitt's lymphoma (BL). However, some of these viruses, particularly the DNA viruses (EBV and papilloma), in themselves are not sufficient; other events are needed before complete malignant transformations can take place. In the case of EBV, malaria is one likely factor by which chronic antigenic stimulation provides mitotic stimuli to B cells; when coupled with

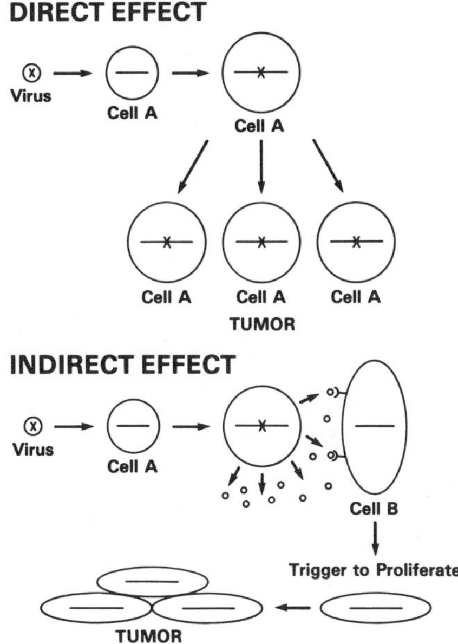

FIGURE 1. Virus-induced tumor formation by direct and indirect mechanisms. Whereas in the direct mechanism (**upper panel**) the virus-infected cell (Cell A) is the progenitor of the tumor cells, in the indirect mechanism (**lower panel**) the target cell (Cell A) of the virus infection is responsible for the development of a tumor which originates from a different kind of cell (Cell B).

its immunosuppressive effects, it may lead to an increased number of EBV-immortalized B cells. Ultimately, this appears to lead to c-*myc* gene translocation. Some studies suggest still additional factors may be involved. The role of HTLV-I in ATL appears similar, but there are important differences. HTLV-I infects T cells, particularly CD4-positive helper T cells, which ultimately become the tumor cells. Although every infected cell does not become a tumor cell, and every infected individual does not develop cancer, there is a notable difference between the efficiency with which HTLV-I leads to leukemia and the efficiency with which EBV leads to B cell lymphoma, e.g., a much greater disease association (higher ratio of incidence of neoplasia to the incidence of infection) is evident in the case of HTLV-I than of EBV. This suggests that HTLV-I not only immortalizes, but also introduces into the infected cells additional mechanisms which may facilitate the process of tumorigenesis.

Some recent results provide evidence for indirect effects of a virus in tumor formation. For instance, HTLV-I is associated with some cases of B cell leukemia; human immunodeficiency virus type-1 (HIV-1) is associated with a wide range of malignancies, most frequently Kaposi's sarcoma (KS) in homosexual men and B cell lymphoma. Inconsistent detection of virus or viral genomes in the tumor cells, despite exhaustive search for them, implies an indirect role for these viruses in these malignancies, and recent results in our laboratory support this conclusion (see below).

Patients with HTLV-I and, of course, especially those with HIV-1 infections show impaired immune function. Impairment in immune surveillance mechanisms may be important in determining which infected individuals will develop cancer. However, no data are available to support or discredit such a possibility. In order to obtain the necessary data, one would have to conduct periodic tests of immune functions in a large number of infected people and to correlate the outcome of such tests with the appearance of cancer.

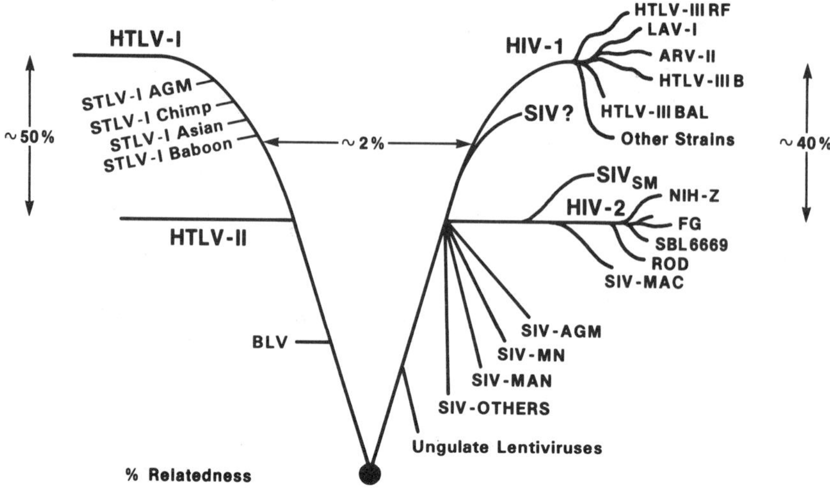

FIGURE 2. The known human retroviruses and pertinent simian retroviruses. Schematic illustration of relatedness among various retroviruses of humans, monkeys, and other animals is indicated.

INDUCTION OF NEOPLASIA BY RETROVIRUSES

Retroviruses induce neoplasia by many different and often unrelated mechanisms:

1. Some animal retroviruses (acutely transforming viruses) transduce a cellular gene (c-*onc* gene) which gives the resultant progeny the capacity to subsequently induce malignancy. These viruses are usually replication-defective and require replication-competent helper viruses for their infection.
2. Another mechanism which is seen in some animal retroviruses, e.g., Friend mouse leukemia virus, involves interaction of the virus envelope with the cell. The details of this mechanism are not well understood.
3. A third mechanism, called insertional mutagenesis, appears to be one of the most common methods used by retroviruses, particularly those belonging to the chronic tumor virus group. The provirus is integrated near a specific cellular gene, which is then activated by the viral long terminal repeat (LTR) sequences (*cis* activation). The best representative example of a virus employing this mechanism is the avian leukosis virus (ALV), which causes chicken B cell leukemia when the c-*myc* gene is activated. Since the integration is highly selective, this mechanism requires extensive viral replication.
4. With the discovery of human retroviruses, a new mechanism, called *trans* activation, was revealed only a few years ago. HTLV-I and HTLV-II have additional genes for *trans* activation of transcription, *tax*-1 and *tax*-2, respectively. It is generally believed that the *tax* genes of HTLVs, and their counterparts in simian and bovine systems, play an important role in cell transformation and immortalization, thus causing leukemias and lymphomas in infected animals. Uniquely, the process is very slow and requires a long latency period before the manifestation of the disease.

HUMAN RETROVIRUSES

As of now, four human retroviruses have been isolated and molecularly characterized. They belong to two distinct groups (FIG. 2): the leukemia viruses (HTLV-I and HTLV-II)[1] and the immunodeficiency viruses (HIV-1 and HIV-2).[2,3] The diseases caused by or associated with these viruses are listed in TABLE 1. The HTLVs and HIVs are approximately 90-100 nm in diameter; they display different morphological and biological characteristics, which have been the main reasons for classifying them in different subfamilies. The HTLVs belong to the type C retrovirus group and the Oncoviridae subfamily, and the HIVs belong to the Lentiviridae subfamily. Mature virions of the latter have a cylindrical or rod-shaped nucleoid/core compared to the more round and less compact cores of the Oncoviridae subfamily. The viruses within each group show close homology (50-60%), whereas the homology between the two groups is ca. 2%, with only slight immunological cross-reactivity.[1,2] A major difference between these groups is the difference in their mutation rates. The HIVs have much higher transmission and replication rates than the HTLVs, which may be responsible for the high mutation rates of the HIVs. Different HIV-1 isolates differ from each other by up to even 10-20%, with major variations in the envelope region;[4,5] HIV-2 follows a similar pattern.[6] On the other hand, the majority of HTLV isolates obtained from most diverse geographical locations are almost identical.[7] Both viruses have similar counterparts in the simian systems (FIG. 2). Simian T lymphotropic virus type-I (STLV-I) has over 95% homology with HTLV-I and can cause lymphomas in infected animals.[8] Simian immunodeficiency virus (SIV) produces AIDS-like syndrome in macaques and has 75% homology with HIV-2.[9,10] Viruses of both the HTLV and HIV groups have tropism toward the CD4-positive helper T cell subset, infect cells of myeloid lineage, e.g., monocyte/macrophages, and cause neurological disorders.

TABLE 1. Diseases Caused by or Associated with Human Retroviruses

Virus	Diseases
HTLV-I	Acute T cell leukemia (ATL) and sometimes other more chronic forms of T4 cell malignancies Tropical spastic paraparesis (TSP) or HTLV-I-associated myelopathy (HAM) B cell leukemia (indirect) Minor immune deficiency
HTLV-II	Hairy cell leukemia (small % of cases in the U.S.A. and in Europe) Chronic T4 cell lymphoma (small % of cases in the U.S.A. and in Europe) T cell chronic lymphocytic leukemia (TCLL) (small % of cases in the U.S.A. and in Europe) Dermatopathic lymphadenopathy(?)[a]
HIV-1	Acquired immune deficiency syndrome (AIDS) Central nervous system (CNS) disease (dementia, acute psychosis) Enhancement of B cell lymphoma (indirect) Kaposi's sarcoma (indirect)
HIV-2	Some immune deficiency

[a] Suggestive evidence implicates HTLV-II.

The common features of HTLVs and HIVs are depicted in TABLE 2. The most remarkable similarity between these viruses is the presence of several extra genes (FIG. 3). Typical animal retroviruses have only three major structural genes, i.e., *gag, pol,* and *env.* HTLVs have at least three extra genes, two of which, *tax* and *rex,* are required for virus replication[11] and may be required for cell transformation. HIVs have at least six extra genes, two of which, *tat* and *rev,* have remarkable functional similarity with the *tax* and the *rex* gene, respectively, of HTLVs. In fact, recent data show that *rex* can substitute for *rev* in *rev*-negative HIV-1 mutants in the absence of any apparent sequence homology with *rev.*[12] Other accessory genes of HIV have regulatory functions. They are important in determining virus infectivity and latency.[13] The presence of these extra genes in HTLVs and HIVs suggests the existence of fine control mechanisms for virus replication and expression and, hence, a higher degree of evolution compared to the animal retroviruses. In fact, not all ungulate lentiviruses, which often are discussed as close models for HIV, have all these extra genes (or at least, they are not yet recognized), and they do not infect helper T cells. But all lentiviruses, including HIV, do have some features in common, e.g., they are tropic to cells of monocyte/macrophage lineage and cause neurological disorders.

THE HTLV-I AND LEUKEMOGENESIS

Adult T Cell Leukemias-Lymphomas (Direct)

Usually, an aggressive form of adult T cell leukemia (ATL) is associated with HTLV-I infection.[14,15] In about one-third of the cases, the cells show abnormally lobulated nuclei. On rare occasions, the malignancy does not exhibit a leukemic phase and typical ATL cells may not be obvious. However, all forms of HTLV-I-induced T cell leukemias have common underlying features:

1. The leukemia appears in a small fraction, i.e., 0.5-2.0% of the infected people.
2. The virus produces leukemia after a long latent period subsequent to seroconversion.
3. The virus has preference for CD4-positive T cells and has a unique ability to immortalize them.
4. The leukemic cells are interleukin-2 receptor- (IL-2R-) positive and HTLV-I-infected.
5. The virus (provirus) integration is random, and no specific integration site within the host genome is observed. The integration site varies in tumors from different patients but appears to be identical in all leukemic cells in a given patient, confirming that the virus infection occurs before the clonal expansion.
6. The virus has *trans*-acting genes. It appears that direct or indirect action (via cellular genes) of these genes is important in the process of leukemogenesis.

It is believed that, during the long latency period, HTLV-I continuously replicates and infects the CD4-positive T cells. In fact, both these events may even be required for leukemogenesis. For the purpose of understanding what mechanism(s) are involved in the development of leukemia, it becomes important to study regulation of HTLV-I replication. DNA sequence analysis of the HTLV-I provirus has revealed a region in addition to the three viral structural genes. This region, call pX, is located near

TABLE 2. Common Features of All Human Retroviruses (HTLVs and HIVs)

Have common modes of transmission
Use $CD4^+$ cells as a major target
Exhibit latency in $CD4^+$ cells until immune stimulation
Cause CNS and immune cell disorders
Cause immunodeficiency: modest-mild-rare in HTLV-I and severe in HIV-1 infections
Cause increased B cell malignancies by apparently indirect mechanisms
Have very closely related counterparts present in Old World primates
Have ungulate virus as second closest relative: ungulate retrovirus, bovine leukemia virus (BLV) for HTLVs and ungulate lentiretroviruses for HIVs
Have three or more extra genes present with regulatory roles in viral replication and expression
Have regulatory gene products encoded by doubly spliced mRNA (unique among the retroviruses)
Have functionally similar genes able to cause increased proliferation (hyperplasia) of epidermal cells: HTLV-I *tax* gene and HIV-1 *tat* gene
Have functionally similar *rex* gene (HTLV-I) and *rev* gene (HIV-1); *rex* gene can substitute for *rev* gene in *rev*-negative HIV-1 mutants despite lack of apparent sequence homology to *rev*
Have no sequence homology with DNA of uninfected human cells (unlike relationship between most animal retroviruses and their hosts)
Have cell-related sequences with a specific regulatory role: NFκB-responsive sequence in the LTR of HIVs and a *tax*-responsive cellular sequence in the HTLVs

the 3′ end of the viral genome and has no sequences homologous to human chromosomal DNA; thus, it is not an oncogene derived from a cellular homolog. At least three open reading frames are revealed to be present in this region. One of them, called *tax,* encodes a product of 40 kDa (previously called $p40^x$, *tat*-1, or p40) and enhances viral transcription by activating 21-base pair (bp) repeats in the viral LTR.[16] The *tax* gene has several additional effects on the cellular genes and their expression, directly or indirectly:

1. *Tax* protein activates the expression of the human *fos* proto-oncogene promoter, both in tissue culture and in *tax*-expressing transgenic mice.[17] (Pavlakis *et al.,* personal communication).
2. *Tax* protein may utilize or partially share the cAMP-mediated pathway for transcriptional activation, and bind to the transcriptional factors which then activate the cellular genes. The cell sequences which respond to these transcriptional activators are closely related to the sequences within the 21-bp repeats of HTLV-I LTR.[16,17]
3. *Tax* protein activates sequences to which nuclear factor κB (NFκB) binds and then in turn activates several cellular genes, like the IL-2R gene.[18-20]
4. HTLV-I infection is associated with IL-2R activation and IL-2 production.[21,22] The IL-2R activation initially depends upon *tax* expression, but constitutive expression of IL-2R in fully transformed primary leukemic cells does not require expression of any viral proteins.[23] The events governing the initiation of IL-2R activation are also associated with immortalization of T cells, and the possible involvement of proteins expressed by the pX region is suggested (W. Haseltine, personal communication).

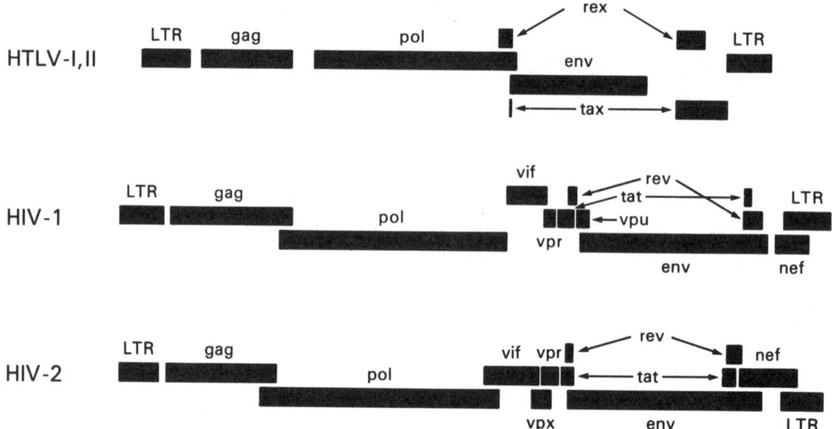

FIGURE 3. Schematic illustration of genomic structure of human retroviruses: HTLV-I and HTLV-II (**top panel**), HIV-1 (**middle panel**), and HIV-2 (**bottom panel**).

Considering these facts, that the site of proviral integration varies in different tumors, that fully transformed leukemic cells need no expression of viral proteins, and that cellular gene alterations are not consistently noted, we speculate that some unknown second event must occur to account for the expression of cellular genes in the leukemic phase (FIG. 4).

The regulatory role of the *rex* gene appears to be solely on the viral genes. The *rex* gene encodes a 27-kDa protein, which localizes in the nucleus. The function of the *rex* gene is in virus self-regulation. Its presence increases stabilization, transport, and translation of mRNA for viral structural proteins and decreases the level of the doubly spliced mRNAs, which code for small regulatory proteins, including *tax* and *rex,* thus negatively controlling virus replication.[24,25] Its role in virus replication is analogous to that of the *rev* gene of HIV.

B Cell Leukemia (Indirect)

In HTLV-I-endemic areas, the prevalence of HTLV-I antibodies in patients with malignancies other than ATL has been shown to be high compared to that in the general population from those areas. Some of this effect can be explained by the large number of blood transfusions these patients receive. But the observations of a high prevalence of HTLV-I antibodies in untransfused cases of chronic lymphocytic leukemia (CLL) in Jamaica or of Hodgkin's disease in endemic areas in Japan suggest that HTLV-I may play some role in the etiology of these malignancies, probably through indirect mechanisms. Blattner and co-workers[26] studied one CLL patient in detail to understand the nature of the disease and its relationship with HTLV-I. Peripheral blood cell surface marker analysis showed that the leukemia was of B cell type. However, we did not find any integrated HTLV-I provirus in the malignant B cells when we tested using a cloned HTLV-I probe. T cell lines established from this patient showed integrated proviral DNA and expression of p19 (the *gag* gene product).

The T cells apparently remained normal, but functional impairment could not be ruled out. Mann and co-workers[27] further studied leukemic B cells of two HTLV-I-seropositive CLL patients. Hybridoma cell lines were generated by fusion of these leukemic cells with a human lymphoblastoid line. Hybridoma clones secreting immunoglobulins with reactivity to p24 *gag* protein from one patient and to gp61 envelope protein from the other patient were observed. The CLL cells thus appear to be the result of a malignant transformation of B cells antigen-committed towards the HTLV-I infection, suggesting an indirect role for this retrovirus in leukemogenesis. Chronic antigenic stimulation, altered immune function, or release of growth factors or lymphokines by HTLV-I-infected cells appear to be possible explanations. The finding that NFκB (a κ gene transcription factor active in mature B cells) activity can be enhanced by the HTLV-I *tax* gene product suggests that the B cell hyperactivity may in some manner be in response to HTLV-I infection.

THE HIV: DIRECT ROLE IN ACQUIRED IMMUNE DEFICIENCY

HIV also is, of course, a $CD4^+$ T cell-tropic virus and efficiently infects fresh cells from cord blood, peripheral blood, and bone marrow. Both the fresh cells and permanent cell lines of T lymphocytic and monocytic origin are good target cells. The HIV infection of mitogenically stimulated primary T cells *in vitro* is followed by a burst of virus replication, formation of multinucleated giant cells, and cell death.[28] Such cytopathic effect leads to depletion of T cells from *in vitro* cultures; *in vivo,* such depletion causes profound functional impairment leading to the state of immunodeficiency in the host. The *in vitro* cytopathic effect of HIV is thus a direct mimicry of

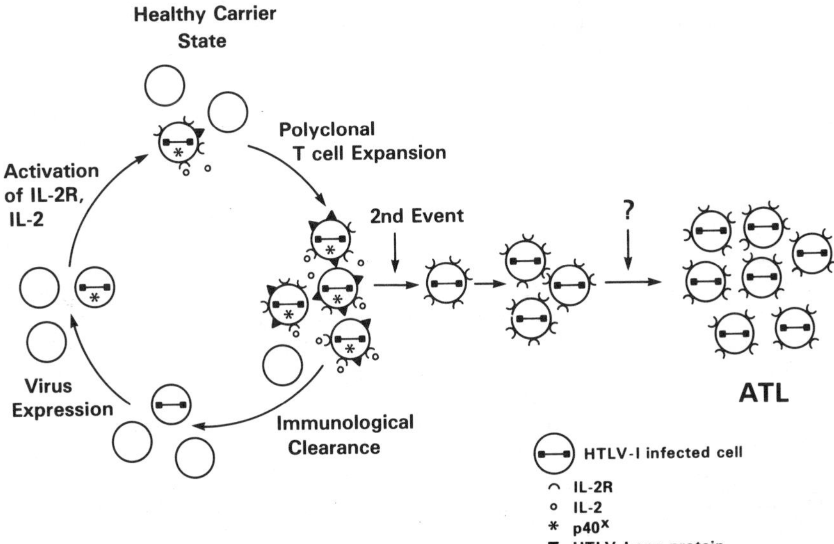

FIGURE 4. Model for development of adult T cell leukemia/lymphoma (ATL). $p40^x$, *tax* protein; IL-2R, interleukin-2 receptor. (Adapted from M. Yoshida, 1988).

TABLE 3. Mechanisms for Depletion of CD4$^+$ T Cells after HIV Infection

Direct killing by HIV following immune stimulation and virus expression
Decreased IL-2 production
Cell-mediated cytotoxicity against uninfected CD4$^+$ cells targeted by the binding of free gp120 to the CD4 and the binding of antibodies against this CD4-gp120 complex
Inhibition of T cell proliferation by some viral protein products
CD4$^+$ T cell lytic effect of another virus, HHV-6, upon replication (HHV-6 is common in HIV-infected people and may replicate more in them; also, HHV-6 activates HIV-1[40])
Defective antigen presentation leading to lower CD4$^+$ T cell proliferation[47]
Lysis of activated (Ia$^+$), autologous, uninfected CD4$^+$ T lymphocytes by gp120-specific class II-restricted cytotoxic lymphocytes (CD4 receptor-mediated uptake of gp120 is a critical event for this lytic process; this mechanism could allow destruction of a large number of activated lymphocytes responding to many pathogens[48])

the *in vivo* phenomenon. HIV selectively replicates in CD4-positive lymphocytes[29] and CD4 antigen on the cell surface acts as a virus receptor or a critical component of this receptor.[30,31] HIV infection of these cells can be blocked by monoclonal antibodies (OKT4A, Leu3A) directed against the portion of the CD4 molecule that is involved in binding to the virus.[30-32]

By direct measurement, the affinity constant of binding of the HIV envelope glycoprotein gp120 and CD4 has been shown[33] to be 4×10^9, which is exceptionally high compared to values seen in other viral systems. Introduction of CD4 into a variety of human cells renders them susceptible to HIV infection,[30] but nonhuman cells expressing the human CD4 gene can only bind to the virus; they do not get infected. This suggests that infectivity is determined by more events than just the virus-CD4 interactions.[34] Although low levels of CD4 expression suffice for virus infection, a high concentration of CD4 is essential for generation of cytopathic effects.[35] Cells expressing low levels of CD4, e.g., monocytes, some B or T cell lines and some endothelial cells, can be easily infected but are resistant to the cytopathic effect. *In vivo,* such resistant cells might act as a virus storehouse and continuously infect susceptible T cells.

The cytopathic effect of the virus can be completely mimicked by use of the cloned virus genome, showing that the HIV-1 genome alone contains all the essential information,[36] and envelope gene products are closely associated with cytopathic properties of the virus. The CD4 antigen is down-regulated on the surface of infected cells but continues to be expressed intracellularly, where it complexes with gp120. The CD4-gp120 interaction at the time of virus release rather than at the time of virus entry seems to play a role in the viral cytopathic effect. In addition, the transmembrane part of the envelope protein, gp41, is also critical for the viral cytopathic effect. Mutants modified in the carboxyl terminus of gp41 show dramatically reduced cytopathic potential but full capability to infect and replicate in CD4-positive cells.[37]

Some of the other mechanisms which may be involved in the overall cytopathic effect of the virus and in cell killing are listed in TABLE 3. Among these, autoimmune mechanisms, as well as immune clearance of CD4-positive cells, are speculated to play a role. CD4-positive cells expressing gp120 on the cell surface or uninfected CD4-positive cells bound to free gp120 may undergo immune clearance.[38] Effector cells capable of antibody-dependent cellular cytotoxicity (ADCC) activity[38] and MHC-restricted cellular cytotoxic activity[39] are observed in peripheral blood of HIV-1-infected patients. Augmentation of the cytopathic effect of HIV may occur in the presence of other viruses, e.g., HTLV-I, human herpesvirus-6 (HHV-6),[40] cytomegalovirus (L. Nerurkar, unpublished observations), and herpes simplex virus. These viruses have *trans*-activating genes which enhance HIV-1 replication and accelerate cell death. Notably, the frequency of infection by these viruses in AIDS patients is quite high. Cellular determinants, e.g., cytokines and nuclear binding factors like NFκB, are involved in further activation of the HIV-1 LTR and hence of HIV-1 replication.[18,41,42]

HIV: INDIRECT ROLE IN NEOPLASIA

HIV infection is associated with an increased incidence of neoplasia, and, notably, B cell lymphoma and Kaposi's sarcoma appear to occur in high frequency. Immune dysfunction as a consequence of T cell loss in HIV infection may be speculated to be the primary cause of increased neoplastic activity. However, inappropriate activation of certain genes and uncontrolled target cell growth could as well be likely mechanisms.

B-CELL LYMPHOMA

According to Dalla Favera and co-workers,[43] about 50 to 60% of all B cell lymphomas in HIV-infected people are EBV-positive and have c-*myc* translocations resembling those seen in BL. This group of lymphomas may develop by following the same mechanistic steps as those involved in BL. The EBV-mediated immortalization may occur with high frequency in response to high B cell activity (a response to chronic antigenic stimulation, e.g., by malaria in BL, by HIV and other opportunistic infections in AIDS). The combination of increased numbers of immortalized cells and long-term enhanced mitosis may increase the chances for c-*myc* translocations to occur.

Those B cell lymphomas in AIDS which are EBV-negative and (as occurs less frequently) lack c-*myc* rearrangements are difficult to explain.[43] Mechanisms involving other viruses need to be looked at. Only a few cases of AIDS-associated lymphomas with sequences specific for other known viruses, e.g., HHV-6, have been found, but these do not suffice to explain all EBV-negative cases of AIDS-associated lymphoma. The ability of the cellular factor NFκB to bind to the κ gene promoter in B cell genes and to similar sequences in the HIV LTR suggests that factors affecting NFκB activation may lead to enhanced B cell activity as well as to HIV-1 replication. Polyclonal hyperactivity of B cells is seen in AIDS patients.[44]

KAPOSI'S SARCOMA

The fact that Kaposi's sarcoma (KS) appears in some patients much before the clinical and laboratory signs of the immune dysfunction of AIDS suggests that failure of immune surveillance may not be the primary cause of KS. Furthermore, KS is

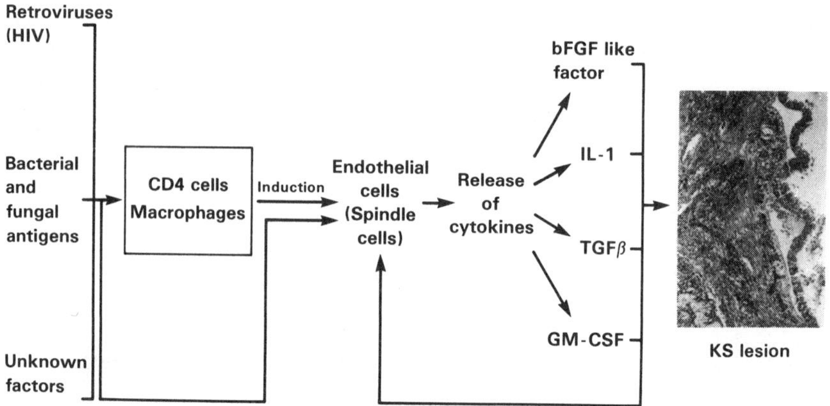

FIGURE 5. Factor-mediated mechanism for the development of the AIDS Kaposi's sarcoma (KS) lesion. bFGF, basic fibroblast growth factor; IL-1, interleukin-1; TGFβ, transforming growth factor β; GM-CSF, granulocyte/monocyte colony-stimulating factor. (Figure prepared by S. Nakamura and Z. Salahuddin.)

seen to occur in epidemic proportions in promiscuous males, and HIV proviral sequences are not found in KS tumor DNA. All these facts noted together lead one to suspect the involvement of another virus. Testing for sequences of known oncogenic viruses, e.g., papilloma viruses, papovaviruses, HTLVs, has not given any positive leads. In an effort to search for a possible new human virus, we grew the KS cells in our laboratory in continuous culture, but with great difficulty. None of the commercially available growth factors could support long-term growth of these cells. A novel growth factor for these cells was found to be released by human CD4-positive lymphocytes after infection with human retroviruses (either HTLV-I, HTLV-II, HIV-1, or HIV-2).[45] This growth factor, when applied to the mixed population of cells present in the KS tumor, led to the growth of cells which appear similar to the so-called spindle cells of KS. These cells showed many, but not all, properties of normal activated endothelial cells. No virus of any kind has been identified in these cultured cells, which in some cases have now been growing for over one year in our laboratory. We found that such *in vitro* cultivated cells themselves produce several biologically active molecules,[45,46] including basic fibroblast growth factor, granulocyte/monocyte colony-stimulating factor, interleukin-1, tumor necrosis factor, tumor growth factor (TGFβ), platelet-derived growth factor, chemotactic factor(s) and chemoinvasive factor(s); and they have the ability to induce growth of new blood vessels (angiogenesis), as shown by the chick chorioallantoic membrane assay.[46] In addition, either fixed or metabolically active cells inoculated into nude mice produced within 10 days lesions that histologically showed resemblance to the early human KS lesions. Chromosomal analysis of these tumors distinctly revealed their mouse origin.[46] Based on all these findings, our hypothesis is summarized as follows (FIG. 5). Upon infecting CD4-positive lymphocytes and macrophages, HIV and, sometimes, other agents may cause release of cytokines by inappropriate activation. Included among these cytokines is the newly found growth factor which promotes activation and growth of cells of possible endothelial origin. Eventually, the endothelial cells are converted into ones with spindle-shaped morphology, which in turn at a certain point release their own growth factors and other cytokines which can have autocrine and paracrine effects.

The reason for the greater incidence of KS in homosexual males, particularly those who are HIV infected, remains a mystery.

SUMMARY

Human retroviruses (HTLVs and HIVs) infect the cells of the immune system and cause mild-to-severe immune dysfunction. They are directly or indirectly responsible for associated neoplasia and central nervous system disorders. The study of these viruses is of great importance, not only because they cause grave illnesses like AIDS, neoplasias, and CNS disease, but also because they have the ability to exert such fine levels of gene regulatory control in their replication and expression. These studies will ultimately shed light on fundamental mechanisms of genetic control in human cells in their normal state and the alterations of these controls in neoplastic or immunologically aberrant states.

REFERENCES

1. GALLO, R. C. 1986. Sci. Am. **255:** 88-98.
2. GALLO, R. C. 1987. Sci. Am **256:** 47-56.
3. SCIENTIFIC AMERICAN. 1988. **259:** 1-128.
4. WONG-STAAL, F., G. M. SHAW, B. H. HAHN, *et. al.* 1985. Science **229:** 759-762.
5. STARCICH, B. R., B. H. HAHN, G. M. SHAW, *et al.* 1986. **Cell** 45: 637-648.
6. ZAGURY, J. F., G. FRANCHINI, M. S. REITZ, *et al.* 1988. Proc. Natl. Acad. Sci. USA **85:** 5941-5945.
7. REITZ, M. S., JR., M. POPOVIC, B. F. HAYNES, *et al.* 1983. Virology **126:** 688-692.
8. HOMMA, T., P. J. KANKI, N. W. KING, *et al.* 1984. Science **225:** 716-718.
9. FRANCHINI, G., C. GURGO, H.-G. GUO, *et al.* 1987. Nature **328:** 539-543.
10. CHAKRABARTI, L., M. GUYADER, M. ALIZON, *et al.* 1987. Nature **328:** 543-547.
11. INOUE, J., M. YOSHIDA & M. SEIKI. 1987. Proc. Natl. Acad. Sci. USA **84:** 3653-3657.
12. RIMSKY, L., J. HAUBER, M. DUKOVICH, *et al.* 1988. Nature **355:** 738-740.
13. HASELTINE, W. A. & F. WONG-STAAL. 1988. Sci. Am. **259:** 34-42.
14. GALLO, R. C. 1984. *In* Cancer Surveys. J. Wyke & R. Weiss, Eds. Vol. 3: 113-159. Oxford University Press. Oxford.
15. WONG-STAAL, F. & R. C. GALLO. 1985. Nature **317:** 395-403.
16. BRADY, J., K.-T. JEANG, J. DUVALL & G. KHOURY. 1987. J. Virol. **61:** 2175-2181.
17. PAVLAKIS, G. N., B. K. FELBER, G. KAPLIN, *et al.* 1988. *In* The Control of Human Retrovirus Gene Expression. B. R. Franza, B. R. Cullen & F. Wong-Staal, Eds.: 281-289. Cold Spring Harbor Laboratory. Cold Spring Harbor, NY.
18. BAEUERLE, P. A. & D. BALTIMORE. 1988. *In* The Control of Human Retrovirus Gene Expression. B. R. Franza, B. R. Cullen & F. Wong-Staal, Eds.: 217-226. Cold Spring Harbor Laboratory. Cold Spring Harbor, NY.
19. INOUE, J., M. SEIKE, T. TANIGUCHI, *et al.* 1986. EMBO J. **5:** 2883-2888.
20. LEUNG, K. & G. J. NABEL. 1988. Nature **333:** 776-778.
21. CROSS, S. L., M. B. FEINBERG, J. B. WOLF, *et al.* 1987. Cell **49:** 47-56.
22. SIEKEVITZ, M., M. B. FEINBERG, N. HOLBROOK, *et al.* 1987. Proc. Natl. Acad. Sci. USA **84:** 5389-5393.
23. ARYA, S. K., F. WONG-STAAL & R. C. GALLO. 1984. Science **223:** 703-707.
24. FEINBERG, M. B., R. F. JARRETT, A. ALDOVINI, *et al.* 1986. Cell **46:** 807-817.
25. FELBER, B. K., M. HADZOPOULOUS-CLADARAS, C. CLADARAS, *et al.* 1989. Proc. Natl. Acad. Sci. USA **86:** 1495-1499.

26. CLARK, J. W., B. H. HAHN, D. L. MANN, *et al.* 1985. Cancer **56:** 495-499.
27. MANN, D. L., P. DE SANTIS, G. MARK, *et al.* 1987. Science **236:** 1103-1106.
28. ZAGURY, D., J. BERNARD, R. LEONARD, *et al.* 1986. Science **231:** 850-853.
29. KLATZMANN, D., F. BARRE-SINOUSSI, M. T. NUGEYRE, *et al.* 1984. Science **225:** 59-63.
30. DALGLEISH, A. G., P. C. L. BEVERLEY, P. R. CLAPHAM, *et al.* 1984. Nature **312:** 763-767.
31. KLATZMANN, D., E. CHAMPAGNE, S. CHAMARET, *et al.* 1984. Nature **312:** 767-768.
32. MCDOUGAL, J. S., A. MAWLE, S. P. CORT, *et al.* 1985. J. Immunol. **135:** 3151-3162.
33. LASKY, L. A., G. NAKAMURA, D. H. SMITH, *et al.* 1987. Cell **50:** 975-985.
34. MADDON, P. J., A. G. DALGLEISH, J. S. MCDOUGAL, *et al.* 1986. Cell **47:** 333-348.
35. DE ROSSI, A., G. FRANCHINI, A. ALDOVINI, *et al.* 1986. Proc. Natl. Acad. Sci. USA **83:** 4297-4301.
36. FISHER, A. G., E. COLLALTI, L. RATNER, *et al.* 1985. Nature **316:** 262-265.
37. FISHER, A. G., L. RATNER, H. MITSUYA, *et al.* 1986. Science **233:** 655-659.
38. LYERLY, H. K., T. I. MATHEWS, A. J. LANGLOIS, *et al.* 1987. Proc. Natl. Acad. Sci. USA **84:** 4601-4605.
39. WALKER, B. D., S. CHAKRABARTI, B. MOSS, *et al.* 1987. Nature **328:** 345-348.
40. LUSSO, P., B. ENSOLI, P. D. MARKHAM, *et al.* 1989. Nature **337:** 370-373.
41. NABEL, G. & D. BALTIMORE. 1987. Nature **326:** 711-713.
42. ROSENBERG, Z. F. & A. S. FAUCI. 1989. AIDS Res. Hum. Retroviruses **5:** 1-4.
43. SUBAR, M., A. NERI, G. INGHIRAMI, *et al.* 1988. Blood **72:** 667-671.
44. LANE, H., C. H. MASUR, L. C. EDGAR, *et al.* 1983. N. Engl. J. Med. **309:** 453-458.
45. NAKAMURA, S., S. Z. SALAHUDDIN, P. BIBERFELD, *et al.* 1988. Science **242:** 426-430.
46. SALAHUDDIN, S. Z., S. NAKAMURA, P. BIBERFELD, *et al.* 1988. Science **242:** 430-433.
47. WIGZELL, H. 1988. J. AIDS **1:** 559-565.
48. SILICIANO, R. F., T. LAWTON, C. KNALL, *et al.* 1988. Cell **54:** 561-575.

Expression and Activation of the K-*fgf* Oncogene[a]

CLAUDIO BASILICO,[b] KAREN M. NEWMAN,[b,c] ANNA MARIA CURATOLA,[b] DANIELA TALARICO,[b,d] ALKA MANSUKHANI,[b] ANNA VELCICH,[e] AND PASQUALE DELLI-BOVI[b]

Departments of [b]Pathology and [e]Biochemistry, New York University School of Medicine New York, New York 10016

The K-*fgf/hst* oncogene has recently emerged as a very interesting representative of the family of growth factor-related oncogenes. This oncogene was originally isolated by transfection assay of human stomach cancer DNA[1,2] and, independently, by assay of Kaposi's sarcoma DNA[3,4] in our laboratory. More recently, it has also been isolated in three other laboratories by transfection of DNA from different tumors (Refs. 5 and 6 and M. Goldfarb, personal communication). It should be mentioned that both in these latter cases and in the two original isolations, evidence for the activation of this oncogene in the tumor types which were the source of the transfecting DNA is still lacking, however.

The K-*fgf* oncogene encodes a novel growth factor with significant homology to the basic and the acidic fibroblast growth factor (FGF),[4] two broad-spectrum mitogens which can stimulate the proliferation of a variety of cells and are thought to play a role in angiogenesis.[7,8] The genes encoding these growth factors are part of a gene family, which, as will be discussed later, is so far known to include five members. The growth factor encoded in the K-*fgf* oncogene had never been previously isolated or purified from human or animal tissues; thus, the investigators in this field were first faced with the problem of accomplishing its characterization. We will summarize in this paper the main properties of the growth factor K-FGF, its similarities to basic and acidic FGFs, and the mechanism by which this oncogene transforms cells. Finally, we will discuss what is known about the mechanism of activation of the K-*fgf* oncogene and the possible role that K-FGF and other members of this growth factor family play in the regulation of growth and development.

[a]This investigation was supported by PHS Grant CA42568 from the National Cancer Institute.

[c]Supported by NIH Training Grant 5-T32-CA09161.

[d]Recipient of a fellowship from the Associazione Italiana Ricerca Cancro.

PROPERTIES OF THE K-FGF PROTEIN

The K-*fgf* oncogene encodes a protein of 206 amino acids with a potential glycosylation site and a hydrophobic amino-terminal sequence that could constitute a signal peptide, like those present in most secretory proteins.[4] To study whether the K-FGF protein was processed and secreted, a cDNA molecule corresponding to the 1.2-kilobase (kb) mRNA of K-*fgf* was inserted into the mammalian expression vector 91023B[9] and transfected into COS cells,[10] which constitutively produce SV40 large T-antigen, as well as into DHFR$^-$ CHO cells. Transfection into COS cells leads to plasmid replication, since the 91023B vector contains the SV40 origin of replication, and transient expression of high levels of the K-FGF protein.[4] In CHO cells, the integrated p9KS3A plasmid was amplified by taking advantage of the DHFR cDNA also present in the plasmid,[9] resulting in an elevated and constitutive production of the K-FGF protein.

Both in the COS transient expression system and in the CHO cells stably expressing K-FGF, we could demonstrate that, following cleavage of the signal peptide at residue 30 or 31 and processing of the polypeptide through the endoplasmic reticulum and Golgi apparatus, K-FGF is efficiently secreted into the culture medium as a glycosylated protein of 175 or 176 amino acids[11] (FIG. 1). It should be pointed out that both basic and acidic FGFs lack a signal peptide,[12,13] are inefficiently secreted, and are released from the producing cells by a mechanism which is not understood.[7,8] Thus, in this respect, K-FGF is quite different from the two classical FGFs.

The biological activity of K-FGF was tested on a variety of cell lines and primary cultures and was compared to that of basic FGF (bFGF), perhaps the best studied member of this growth factor family. K-FGF is a potent mitogen for all fibroblastic lines tested and for endothelial cells derived either from capillaries or umbilical cord vein, as well as for primary melanocytes.[11,14] Although we have not yet compared the potency of the two growth factors because of the unavailability of pure K-FGF, it appears that all cell types that respond to bFGF also respond to K-FGF. Conversely, CHO cells, which to not respond to K-FGF, also do not respond to bFGF, suggesting that the two growth factors may act by binding to the same cellular receptor(s). To further investigate this possibility, we compared the ability of K-FGF and bFGF to stimulate tyrosine phosphorylation in NIH/3T3 cells, as it is known that many receptors possess a tyrosine-specific protein kinase whose activity is stimulated by growth factor binding.[15] As shown in FIGURE 2, anti-phosphotyrosine antibodies detected two phosphotyrosine-bearing proteins of ca. 150 and 90 kDa, respectively, in cells exposed to bFGF or K-FGF; these were not observed in unstimulated cells or cells exposed to platelet-derived growth factor (PDGF). It is likely that the band of higher apparent molecular mass (ca. 150 kDa) represents the FGF receptor,[16] while the 90-kDa band is probably a phosphoprotein which is part of the FGF signal transduction cascade.[17] The observation that K-FGF and bFGF stimulate the same pattern of protein phosphorylation is in agreement with the hypothesis that these growth factors bind to the same receptor(s).

MECHANISM OF ACTIVATION OF THE K-*fgf* ONCOGENE

Proto-oncogenes are normal components of the genetic material of every cell, and, thus, their physiological expression does not induce cell transformation. However,

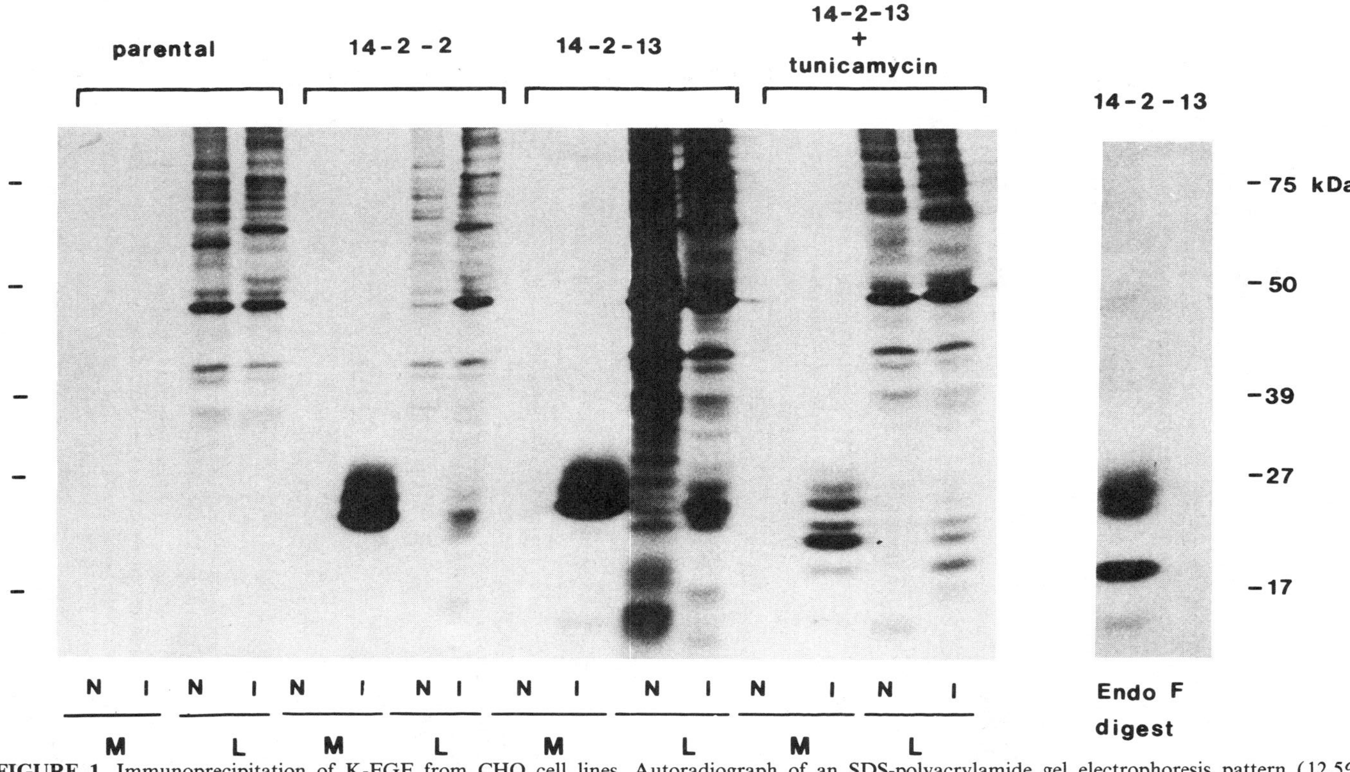

FIGURE 1. Immunoprecipitation of K-FGF from CHO cell lines. Autoradiograph of an SDS-polyacrylamide gel electrophoresis pattern (12.5% acrylamide) of immunoprecipitates of conditioned medium (**M**) and lysates (**L**) from [^{35}S]methionine-labeled CHO cell lines stably expressing the K-*fgf* cDNA (14-2-2 and 14-2-13), the parental cell line, and cell line 14-2-13 incubated in the presence of tunicamycin. For cell line 14-2-13, the electrophoretic pattern of the labeled conditioned medium digested with endoglycosidase F and then immunoprecipitated is also shown (**Endo F digest**). Portions of each sample were immunoprecipitated with (**N**) non-immune rabbit serum or (**I**) immune rabbit serum, as indicated. The molecular masses of protein markers in kilodaltons (kDa) are indicated on the *right* and, by the corresponding *bars* (*left*).

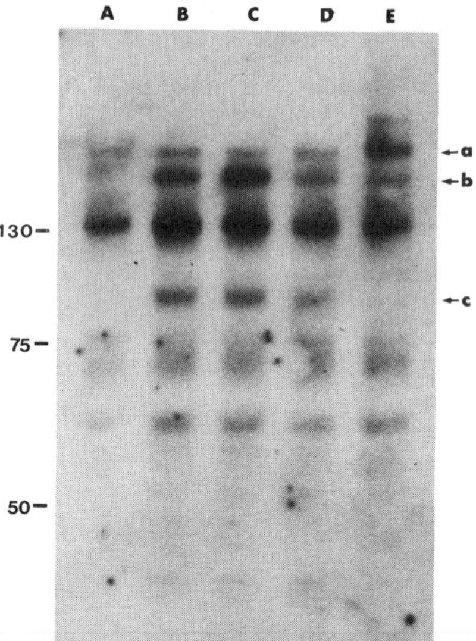

FIGURE 2. Immunoblot analysis of tyrosine phosphorylation. NIH/3T3 cell cultures were exposed to conditioned medium from a CHO cell line secreting K-FGF (1:50 dilution; **Lane B**) or to culture medium with 40 ng/ml of bFGF from D. Rifkin (**Lane C**), with 200 ng/ml of partially purified bFGF from Collaborative Research (**Lane D**), with 1 unit/ml of platelet-derived growth factor (PDGF) from A. J. Pledger (**Lane E**), or with no additions (**Lane A**) for 10 min at 37°C. The samples were processed for immunoblot using affinity-purified anti-phosphotyrosine rabbit serum (a gift from H. Hanafusa). *Arrow a* indicates a protein of ca. 180 kDa in Lane E., *arrow b* a ca. 150-kDa protein in Lanes B and C, and *arrow c* a ca. 90-kDa protein in Lanes B, C, and D. The molecular masses of protein markers in kilodaltons are indicated on the *left.*

proto-oncogenes can become activated to oncogenes, basically through two mechanisms: they can become altered and produce aberrant proteins or their expression can become unregulated. Mutations of a proto-oncogene can alter the substrate specificity, stability, or protein-protein binding properties, etc., of the protein it encodes, while unregulated expression (which can result from gene amplification, changes in transcriptional regulatory sequences, etc.) essentially results in the synthesis of the protein under conditions in which it is normally suppressed. To study which of these two mechanisms was responsible for the activation of the K-*fgf* oncogene, we have cloned its normal human and mouse homologs and determined their DNA sequence, transforming ability, and pattern of expression.

The K-*fgf* oncogene as originally isolated contained two DNA rearrangements, one upstream and one downstream of the coding region[3] (FIG. 3). Cloning of the human normal homolog and comparison of its sequence with that of the oncogene showed that there was no detectable alteration of the oncogene in the DNA fragment contained between these two rearrangements. Sequencing of the K-*fgf* proto-oncogene showed that both the oncogene and the proto-oncogene encoded the same protein,[18] and, indeed, expression of the K-*fgf* proto-oncogene in COS cells produced a protein indistinguishable from K-FGF in its physical properties and biological activity.[11] Thus, the activation of the K-*fgf* oncogene does not result from mutations in its coding sequences.

We then turned our attention to the pattern of K-FGF expression in tissues or cell lines. Northern blot analysis of the mRNA produced by a variety of normal cell lines, as well as by primary mouse embryo cultures, did not detect any evidence of K-*fgf* transcription (unpublished observations). Similarly, most mouse adult tissues tested did not contain detectable K-*fgf* transcripts, and the same was observed for developing mouse embryos from the tenth day of gestation up to birth (G. Martin, personal communication). Thus, it appears that the expression of the K-*fgf* gene is tightly controlled and probably restricted to specific cells or definite stages of development (see below).

When the cloned K-*fgf* proto-oncogene was transfected into NIH/3T3 cells, it was found to have significant transforming activity, only slightly lower than that of the rearranged K-*fgf* oncogene, either in the presence or absence of an SV40 enhancer[18] (unpublished observations). We examined the transformed cells for the expression of K-*fgf* and found that the transfected proto-oncogene was actively transcribed and translated in all of the cell clones tested (data not shown). This somewhat paradoxical result—since in principle proto-oncogenes should not have transforming activity—seems to indicate the following: (1) the transfected K-*fgf* proto-oncogene can be transcriptionally active in cells which do not express the endogenous gene, because the transfected gene is either activated by the SV40 enhancer attached to it or, possibly, by insertion near a cellular transcriptional element; (2) the mechanism of activation of the K-*fgf* proto-oncogene is unregulated expression, rather than the production of an abnormal protein; (3) a gene encoding a growth factor can behave as an oncogene in any cell type which does not tightly regulate its expression and which carries the receptor for that growth factor.

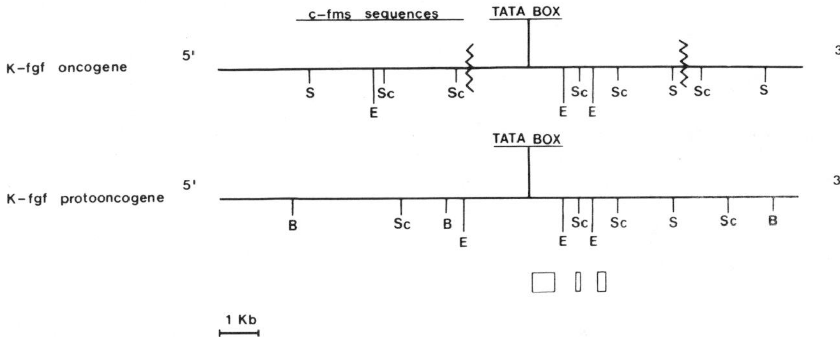

FIGURE 3. Comparison of the restriction map of the K-*fgf* oncogene with that of its normal human homolog (K-*fgf* proto-oncogene). *Squiggles* indicate the position of the rearrangements at the 5′ and the 3′ end of the K-*fgf* oncogene. Presence of c-*fms* sequences at the 5′ end of the K-*fgf* oncogene and the location of the TATA box preceding the coding region (indicated by *open boxes, below*) in each sequence are shown. Restriction sites shown are B, *Bam*H I; Sc, *Sac* I; E, *Eco*R I; S, *Sal* I. Kb, kilobase.

Since the activation of the K-*fgf* oncogene seems to result from overexpression, it is likely that the rearrangements upstream and downstream of the coding sequences present in the original isolate of the K-*fgf* oncogene play a role in its activation. The downstream rearrangement could remove RNA-destabilizing sequences and thus increase the stability of K-*fgf* mRNA, or it could juxtapose new enhancer sequences 3′ of the coding sequences. While some evidence indicates that the K-*fgf* mRNA is somewhat stabilized by the downstream rearrangement, deletion of the downstream sequences in either the rearranged or the unrearranged K-*fgf* gene does not alter transforming ability (unpublished observations). Thus, it is more likely that the upstream rearrangement is responsible for K-*fgf* activation, either because it removes a specific silencer sequence, or because it causes sequences having generalized enhancer activity to be positioned near the K-*fgf* promoter. We are currently involved in determining which of these hypotheses is correct.

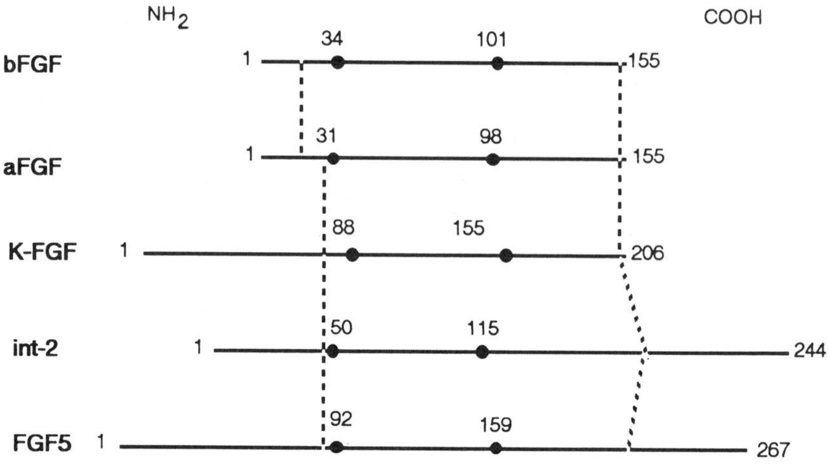

FIGURE 4. Conserved regions within the FGF protein family. Representation of the primary structure of the five FGF polypeptides aligned over their regions of homology (regions included between *broken lines*). Dots (●) indicate two cysteine residues which are conserved in each member of the family. Numbering of amino acid (a. a.) residues, starting with the initiator methionine, is indicated for each polypeptide. bFGF, aFGF: basic and acidic fibroblast growth factors, respectively.

THE FGF FAMILY OF GROWTH FACTORS

In the past year, three new genes have been identified that encode growth factors with significant homology to basic and acidic FGF. The K-*fgf* gene has been discussed above. FGF-5 has also been isolated by transfection of human tumor DNA.[19] In addition, the protein encoded in *int*-2, a putative oncogene identified as a preferred site of integration of mammary tumor virus in mouse breast carcinomas,[20] also bears significant homology to basic and acidic FGFs.[21] While K-FGF and FGF-5 have been shown to have growth factor activity,[4,11,19] this demonstration is still lacking for the gene product of *int*-2, because of problems inherent to its expression in heterologous systems and of its restricted range of transcription in normal tissues. FIGURE 4 shows a comparison of these five proteins of the FGF family. The highest degree of homology exists between basic and acidic FGF (ca. 60% identity), and it extends throughout the length of the two molecules. K-FGF has an amino-terminal portion of about 80 amino acids in length which is unique, followed by a carboxyl-terminal portion which is about 40% homologous to bFGF. In general, all five proteins share a central core of homology corresponding to almost the entire basic FGF molecule. K-FGF, FGF-5 and the gene product of *int*-2 each have unique amino- and carboxyl-terminal portions. The unique amino-terminal portion contains a hydrophobic region, which in the case of K-FGF has been shown to constitute a signal peptide.[11] In the "core" homology regions, two cysteine residues are strikingly conserved in all five molecules, and they bracket a region of higher homology. If the hypothesis that all these growth factors utilize the same receptor is correct, it is tempting to speculate that key elements of the receptor binding site involve these two cysteines and the region between them, and that the site requires an intramolecular disulfide bridge.

If all these factors utilize the same cellular receptor, and therefore presumably are able to affect growth or differentiation of the same target cells, how does the organism regulate their action? What is the evolutionary advantage of producing five growth factors with a similar mode of action? It is possible that there may be subtle differences between the biological activity of each member of this growth factor family which have not yet been determined. Nevertheless, the intriguing pattern of expression of these genes itself provides some potential insights into their physiological role.

Basic and acidic FGF are rather ubiquitously expressed but, as previously mentioned, are not efficiently secreted.[7,8] Paradoxically, they are found in several tissues in considerable amounts, particularly in the brain.[7,8] Neither their function in these locations nor their postulated role in angiogenesis has been clearly demonstrated. While quite little is known about FGF-5 expression, the expression of K-*fgf* and *int*-2 is known to be tightly regulated. Most adult tissues do not express K-*fgf* or *int*-2 mRNA,[22,23] and in developing embryos, *int*-2 transcripts are only found at the peri-implantation stage.[22] An interesting observation has been made in teratocarcinoma cells: K-*fgf* transcription (and production of the growth factor) is easily detected in F9 cells before differentiation is induced, but differentiation shuts off the expression of the gene.[23] Conversely, *int*-2 transcripts are only detected in F9 cells after differentiation is induced.[22] Together with the observation that basic FGF and K-FGF can induce mesodermal differentiation in the early *Xenopus* embryo,[24] (J. Heath, personal communication), this pattern of transcription strongly suggests a role for these genes in early development.

It has to be remembered that basic FGF and K-FGF, at least, are probably among the most potent and generalized mitogens known. It appears that evolution has led the organism to control the action of these growth factors, not by refining their target specificity, but by tightly controlling their expression or release. Thus, while basic and acidic FGF are produced in many tissues, they are not efficiently secreted, and their release is perhaps limited to specific circumstances. The expression of K-FGF, which is efficiently secreted, is highly restricted during development, and *int*-2 follows a similar pattern. Not surprisingly, then, constitutive expression of these latter genes is oncogenic. Study of the elements regulating their transcription should provide important clues about the regulation of gene expression during development.

CONCLUSIONS

The recent discovery of three new oncogenes which encode proteins homologous to FGF has raised a number of important questions about the role of this gene family in normal and neoplastic growth. While the involvement of these oncogenes in human tumors is only beginning to be investigated and has not been discussed in this paper, it is clear that at least one of them, K-*fgf*, encodes a potent growth factor with a broad spectrum of action, whose expression is tightly regulated during growth and development. K-*fgf*-transformed cells constitutively express and secrete a growth factor that creates an autocrine mechanism of growth stimulation. The regulation of transcription of these genes, the nature of their receptor, and their physiological role in growth and development should provide a fertile ground for investigation in the coming years.

REFERENCES

1. SAKAMOTO, H., M. MORI, M. TAIRA, T. YOSHIDA, S. MATSUKAWA, K. SHIMIZU, M. SEKIGUCHI, M. TERADA & T. SUGIMURA. 1986. Transforming gene from human stomach cancers and a noncancerous portion of stomach mucosa. Proc. Natl. Acad. Sci. USA **83:** 3997-4001.
2. TAIRA, M., T. YOSHIDA, K. MIYAGAWA, H. SAKAMOTO, M. TERADA & T. SUGIMURA. 1987. cDNA sequence of human transforming gene *hst* and identification of the coding sequence required for transforming activity. Proc. Natl. Acad. Sci. USA **84:** 2980-2984.
3. DELLI BOVI, P. & C. BASILICO. 1987. Isolation of a rearranged human transforming gene following transfection of Kaposi sarcoma DNA. Proc. Natl. Acad. Sci. USA **84:** 5660-5664.
4. DELLI BOVI, P., A. M. CURATOLA, F. G. KERN, A. GRECO, M. ITTMANN & C. BASILICO. 1987. An oncogene isolated by transfection of Kaposi's sarcoma DNA encodes a growth factor that is a member of the FGF family. Cell **50:** 729-737.
5. ADELAIDE, J., M.-G. MATTEI, I. MARICS, F. RAYBAUD, J. PLANCHE, O. DE LAPEYRIERE & D. BIRNBAUM. 1988. Chromosomal localization of the *hst* oncogene and its coamplification with *int*-2 in a human melanoma. Oncogene **2:** 413-416.
6. KODA, T., A. SASAKI, S. MATSUSHIMA & M. KAKINIMA. 1987. A transforming gene, *hst,* found in NIH 3T3 cells transformed with DNA from three stomach cancers and a colon cancer. Jpn. J. Cancer Res. (GANN) **78:** 325-328.
7. FOLKMAN, J. & M. KLAGSBRUN. 1987. Angiogenic factors. Science **235:** 442-447.
8. GOSPODAROWICZ, D., G. NEUFELD & L. SCHWEIGERER. 1987. Fibroblast growth factor: Structural and biological properties. J. Cell. Physiol. Suppl. **5:** 15-26.
9. WONG, G. G., J. S. WITEK, P. A. TEMPLE, K. M. WILKENS, A. C. LEARY, D. P. LEXENBERG, S. S. JONES, E. L. BROWN, R. M. KAY, E. C. ORR, C. S. SHOEMAKER, D. W. GOLDE, R. J. KAUFMAN, R. M. HEWICK, E. A. WANG & S. C. CLARK. 1985. Human GM-CSF: Molecular cloning of the complementary DNA and purification of the natural and recombinant proteins. Science **228:** 810-815.
10. GLUZMAN, Y. 1981. SV40-transformed simian cells support the replication of early SV40 mutants. Cell **23:** 175-182.
11. DELLI-BOVI, P., A. M. CURATOLA, K. M. NEWMAN, Y. SATO, D. MOSCATELLI, R. M. HEWICK, D. B. RIFKIN & C. BASILICO. 1988. Processing, secretion and biological properties of a novel growth factor of the FGF family with oncogenic potential. Mol. Cell. Biol. **8:** 2933-2941.
12. ABRAHAM, J. A., J. L. WHANG, A. TUMOLO, A. MERGIA, J. FRIEDMAN, D. GOSPODAROWICZ & J. C. FIDDES. 1986. Human basic fibroblast growth factor: Nucleotide sequence and genomic organization. EMBO J. **5:** 2523-2528.
13. JAYE, M., R. HOWK, W. BURGESS, G. A. RICCA, I. M. CHIU, M. W. RAVERA, S. J. O'BRIEN, W. S. MODI, T. MACIAG & W. N. DROHAN. 1986. Human endothelial cell growth factor: Cloning, nucleotide sequence, and chromosome localization. Science **233:** 541-545.
14. HALABAN, R., B. S. KWON, S. GHOSH, P. DELLI-BOVI & A. BAIRD. 1988. bFGF as an autocrine growth factor for human melanomas. Oncogene Res. **3:** 177-186.
15. HUNTER, T. 1986. Phosphorylation in signal transmission and transformation. *In* Oncogenes and Growth Control. P. Kahn & T. Graf, Eds.: 138. Springer-Verlag. Berlin Heidelberg.
16. NEUFELD, G. & D. GOSPODAROWICZ. 1986. Basic and acidic fibroblast growth factors interact with the same cell surface receptors. J. Biol. Chem. **261:** 5631-5637.
17. COUGHLIN, S. R., P. J. BARR, L. S. COUSENS, L. J. FRETTO & L. T. WILLIAMS. 1988. Acidic and basic fibroblast growth factors stimulate tyrosine kinase activity *in vivo.* J. Biol. Chem. **263:** 988-993.
18. YOSHIDA, T., K. MIYAGAWA, H. ODAGIRI, H. SAKAMOTO, P. F. R. LITTLE, M. TERADA & T. SUGIMURA. 1987. Genomic sequence of *hst,* a transforming gene encoding a protein homologous to fibroblast growth factors and the *int*-2 encoded protein. Proc. Natl. Acad. Sci. USA **84:** 7305-7309.
19. ZHAN, X., B. BATES, X. HU & M. GOLDFARB. 1988. The human FGF-5 oncogene encodes a novel protein related to fibroblast growth factor. Mol. Cell. Biol. **8:** 3487-3495.

20. MOORE, R., G. CASEY, S. BROOKES, M. DIXON, G. PETERS & C. DICKSON. 1986. Sequence, topography and protein coding potential of mouse *int*-2: A putative oncogene activated by mouse mammary tumour virus. EMBO J. **5:** 919-924.
21. DICKSON, C. & G. PETERS. 1987. Potential oncogene product related to growth factors. Nature **326:** 833.
22. JAKOBOVITS, A., G. M. SHACKLEFORD, H. E. VARMUS & G. R. MARTIN. 1986. Two protooncogenes implicated in mammary carcinogenesis, *int*-1 and *int*-2, are independently regulated during mouse development. Proc. Natl. Acad. Sci. USA. **83:** 7806-7810.
23. VELCICH, A., P. DELLI-BOVI, A. MANSUKHANI, E. B. ZIFF & C. BASILICO. 1989. Expression of the K-*fgf* protooncogene is repressed during differentiation of F9 cells. Oncogene Res. In press.
24. SLACK, J. M. W., B. G. DARLINGTON, J. K. HEATH & S. F. GODSAVE. 1987. Mesoderm induction in early Xenopus embryos by heparin-binding growth factors. Nature **326:** 197-200.

SV40 T-Antigen as a Dual Oncogene: Structure and Function of the Plasma Membrane-Associated Population[a]

JANET S. BUTEL,[b] DONALD L. JARVIS,[c] AND STEVE A. MAXWELL

Division of Molecular Virology
Baylor College of Medicine
Houston, Texas 77030

AN INTRODUCTION TO SV40 LARGE T-ANTIGEN

SV40 encodes an early protein, large T-antigen (T-ag), which not only mediates replicative functions essential for lytic infection of permissive cells but also single-handedly transforms cells of a non-permissive host.[1–4] A variety of different activities has been ascribed to T-ag (TABLE 1). Some of the activities are directly involved in viral DNA replication, whereas others affect the host cell. A key feature of SV40 infection is that the cell is stimulated to enter S phase, so that the necessary enzymes are available for viral replication. This reproductive strategy probably underlies the oncogenic potential of the virus, an unfortunate side-effect of functions that have evolved to maximize virus replication *in vivo.* The ability of this single viral protein to mediate such a myriad of biological effects is astonishing. The challenge is to determine how T-ag accomplishes these various effects. The answers will have an impact on our understanding of basic processes in both normal and transformed cells.

The multitude of biological responses attributed to T-ag may be due in part to various post-translational modifications of the polypeptide[2–4] and to the ability of T-ag to form homo-oligomers with itself, as well as hetero-oligomers with the 53-kDa cellular protein (p53) and with the retinoblastoma (Rb) susceptibility gene product.[2,3,5–8] Structural variation can generate multiple forms of T-ag, and each form might be capable of providing a separate function. This possibility is supported directly by the observation that different supramolecular forms of T-ag exhibit distinct DNA-binding and ATPase activities[5,9] and, indirectly, by the finding that palmitylation is restricted to the plasma membrane-associated subpopulation of T-ag.[10]

[a]Work in the authors' laboratory was supported in part by Public Health Service Grants CA22555 and CA09197 from the National Cancer Institute.

[b]Address correspondence to Dr. Janet S. Butel, Division of Molecular Virology, Baylor College of Medicine, One Baylor Plaza, Houston, TX 77030.

[c]Current address: Department of Entomology and Texas Agricultural Experiment Station, Texas A&M University, College Station, TX 77843.

TABLE 1. Properties and Functions of SV40 Large T-Antigen[a]

Structural properties
Size
708 amino acids
81,632 daltons
M_r 90,000-100,000
Modifications
Phosphorylation
O-glycosylation
Palmitylation
Poly-ADP-ribosylation
Amino-terminal acetylation
Adenylation
Supramolecular structure
Monomers, dimers, higher homo-oligomers
Hetero-oligomers with p53 or DNA polymerase
Hetero-oligomers with p73 (hsp70)[b]
Hetero-oligomers with Rb gene product[c]
Subcellular distribution
Nucleus
Nucleoplasmic
Chromatin-bound
Nuclear matrix-associated
Plasma membrane
NP-40-soluble
NP-40-insoluble (plasma membrane lamina)
Butanol-soluble
Functions
Specific DNA binding (at viral origin of replication)
Initiation of viral DNA replication
Autoregulation of viral early transcription
Induction of viral late transcription
ATPase activity
Helicase activity
Tight association with protein kinase
Non-specific DNA binding (cellular DNA)
Initiation of cellular DNA replication
Induction of cellular enzyme synthesis
Reactivation of ribosomal RNA genes
Determination of host range
Adenovirus helper function
Complex formation with cellular protein p53
Complex formation with DNA polymerase alpha
Complex formation with hsp70[b]
Complex formation with Rb gene product[c]
Initiation and maintenance of cellular transformation
Induction of immunity to SV40 tumor cells
Target for cytotoxic T cells (tumor-specific transplantation antigen)

[a] See refs. 2, 3, 4, 6, and 60 for original references on which this table is based.
[b] hsp70, 70-kDa heat-shock protein.
[c] Rb, retinoblastoma susceptibility.

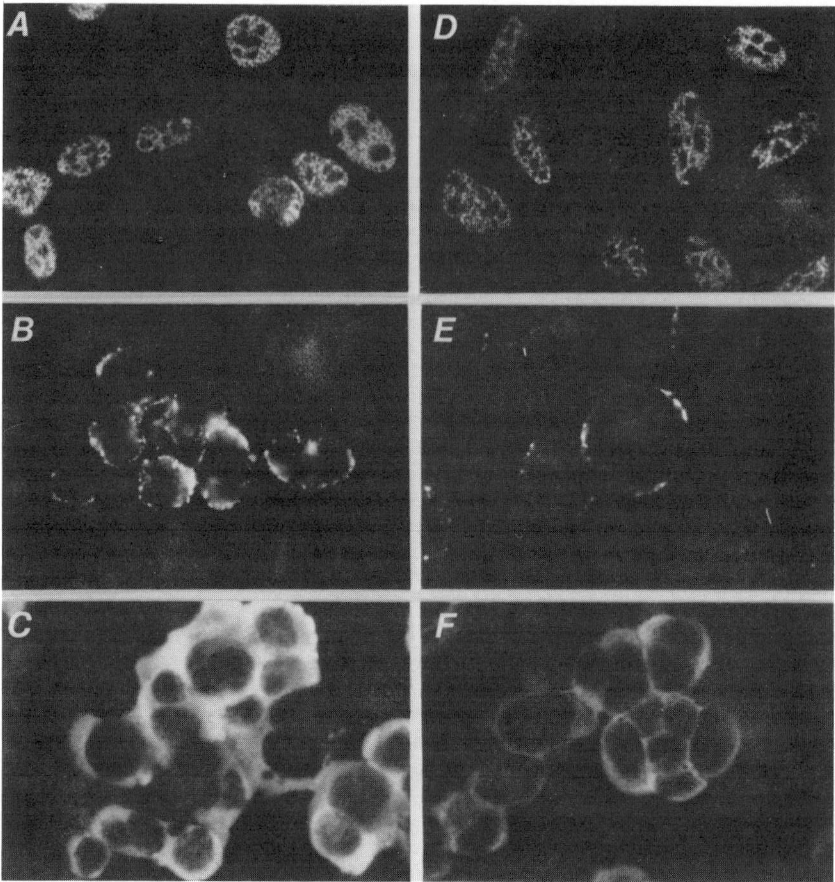

FIGURE 1. Intracellular distribution of tumor antigens in SV40-transformed mouse cells revealed by immunofluorescence. **Panels A-C:** SV40 large T-ag. **Panels D-F:** cellular protein p53. Cells (**A, B, D, E**) were transformed by wild-type SV40 or (**C, F**) by the cT mutant defective for nuclear transport of T-ag and (**A, C, D, F**) were grown on coverslips and fixed in acetone before staining or (**B, E**) were viable and tested in suspension. Note the normal distribution of T-ag in the nucleus (**A**) and plasma membrane (**B**) of transformed cells and the inability of the cytoplasmic T-ag to be transported to the nucleus in the cT-transformed cells (**C**). The distribution of p53 (**D-F**) parallels that of T-ag (**A-C**). Magnification: 365 × (**A-D, F**); 815 × (**E**). (From Butel.[1] Reprinted with permission from *Cancer Surveys.*)

The diverse subcellular localization of T-ag may contribute an essential role in the multifunctionality of the protein.[1,2] Although the majority of the T-ag is localized within the nucleus of the cell, a small amount is found in association with the plasma membrane and is partially exposed on the cell surface (FIG. 1). The nuclear (nT-ag) and the plasma membrane-associated (pmT-ag) forms of T-ag might provide separate functions, based upon putative structural differences, the influence of local microenvironments, or their interactions with different subcellular targets. The remainder of this paper will focus on the structural and functional features of pmT-ag.

PROPERTIES OF MEMBRANE-ASSOCIATED SV40 T-ANTIGEN

The majority ($\geq 95\%$) of total cellular T-ag is localized within the cell nucleus, whereas a small fraction ($\leq 5\%$) is associated with the plasma membrane (TABLE 2).[1,2] It is not known how newly synthesized T-ag molecules are recognized, sorted, and transported to their ultimate subcellular destinations. To determine if these events depend upon structural differences between nT-ag and pmT-ag, we compared the structures of nT-ag and pmT-ag from SV40-infected cells. No differences between the two forms of T-ag were detected by electrophoretic mobility in polyacrylamide gels, by partial proteolytic mapping of methionine- or proline-containing peptides, or by two-dimensional tryptic peptide mapping of methionine-containing peptides. The carboxyl-terminal, methionine-containing tryptic peptide was identified in the two-dimensional maps and was shown to be identical in nT-ag and pmT-ag. Thus, a structural basis for the recognition and differential localization of T-ags could not be demonstrated. We also examined the possibility that pmT-ag was composed of T*-ag, the

TABLE 2. Features of Association of SV40 T-Antigen with the Plasma Membrane of Cells[a]

Structure of pmT-ag
Alternate open reading frame in T-ag gene encoding more hydrophobic carboxyl-terminal 70 amino acids (T*-ag) does not account for pmT-ag:
SDS-PAGE[b] migration: pmT-ag = nT-ag; T*-ag faster
Antibody to T*-ag carboxyl-terminal peptide: no reaction with nT-ag or pmT-ag
Peptide mapping: pmT-ag = nT-ag ≠ T*-ag
Fraction of pmT-ag is palmitylated; nT-ag is not
Both nT-ag and pmT-ag are phosphorylated and O-glycosylated
Disposition of pmT-ag in membrane
Both amino and carboxyl termini of T-ag are exposed on cell surface; internal segment is inaccessible:
Antibody binding
CTL (cytotoxic T lymphocyte) recognition
Slight differences present between orientation of pmT-ag in infected and in transformed cells
Interactions of pmT-ag with cellular proteins
Complex formation with cellular proto-oncogene protein p53 stabilizes p53
Butanol-soluble complex (60K, 56K, 50K, 45K, 35K M_r proteins) is associated with pmT-ag at cell surface
Solubility and stability of pmT-ag
Four solubility subclasses are observed:
High-salt soluble
Non-ionic detergent (NP-40) soluble
Zwitterionic detergent (Empigen BB) soluble: palmitylated pmT-ag
Butanol soluble
Half-life in membrane is relatively short (<30 min)
Some pmT-ag is shed into medium
Transport of pmT-ag to cell surface
Rate of transport is rapid ($\leq$15 min)
Secretory pathway is not involved

[a] See Butel & Jarvis[2] for original references on which this table is based.

[b] SDS-PAGE, SDS-polyacrylamide gel electrophoresis.

theoretical early gene product containing a more hydrophobic carboxyl-terminal sequence of 70 amino acids which would be generated by an alternate open reading frame in the T-ag gene. We used a mutant construct in which the carboxyl terminus of the T-ag was derived from this alternate open reading frame of the SV40 early region, in analogy with T*-ag, to identify peptides unique to T*-ag. None of those peptides was detected in maps of pmT-ag; only wild-type (WT) T-ag-specific peptides were found. These findings indicated that T*-ag does not represent the membrane-associated form of T-ag, but that pmT-ag is encoded within the same reading frame used for nT-ag.[11]

The interaction between T-ag and the plasma membrane positions pmT-ag in a specific and rather unusual way. Antibodies prepared against a synthetic peptide corresponding to the carboxyl-terminal 11 amino acids of T-ag reacted with the surface of SV40-transformed cells.[12] Monoclonal antibodies specific for antigenic determinants on the amino- or carboxyl-terminal portions of T-ag also reacted with the surface of SV40-transformed cells, but some monoclonals that recognized more internal sequences did not.[13–16] A number of individual SV40-specific cytotoxic T lymphocyte (CTL) clones have been isolated and characterized; some recognize amino-terminal sequences, others recognize carboxyl-terminal sequences, but none requires the expression of sequences derived from the internal one-third of the T-ag polypeptide.[17–19] These results indicate that both the amino and carboxyl termini of T-ag are exposed on the cell surface, while an internal region, encompassing about one-third of the molecule, is inaccessible. The reason these internal sequences are unavailable for antibody binding or CTL recognition is not known. They may be buried within the lipid bilayer or localized on the cytoplasmic side of the membrane. They may be exposed on the surface, but masked either by chemical modifications or by the conformational or supramolecular structure of the native protein. In any case, the reproducibly specific orientation assumed by pmT-ag argues that it does not simply stick to the membrane in a random fashion and, therefore, that it probably has a functional role at the cell surface.

At least two populations of T-ag exist at the plasma membrane, and the expression of each is influenced by conditions of cell growth. One population of pmT-ag can be solubilized with the nonionic detergent Nonidet P-40 (NP-40),[10,20] whereas the other is released only with the zwitterionic detergent Empigen BB.[10,21] The latter subclass of pmT-ag was shown to be chemically modified by fatty acid acylation, with covalently bound palmitic acid as the acyl group. Palmitylation is the only known structural difference between pmT-ag and nT-ag; none of the nT-ag populations is modified in this way.[10] Cells grown in suspension have a relatively higher level of NP-40-resistant pmT-ag than do cells grown on a substratum; the latter exhibit predominantly the NP-40-soluble pool of pmT-ag.[21] Actively dividing SV40-transformed cells express higher amounts of pmT-ag,[22] suggesting the involvement of a surface-associated T-ag population in a growth-regulatory pathway initiated at the plasma membrane.

Experiments using radioiodination of the cell surface to trace pmT-ag demonstrated that pmT-ag is unstable; the labeled pmT-ag disappears from the cell surface during a 2-hr chase period at 37°C,[21,23–25] and the half-life of iodinated surface T-ag appears to be less than 1 hr.[25] A portion of the iodinated pmT-ag is shed into the culture medium and can be recovered by immunoprecipitation, but quantitative recovery has never been achieved.[23,24] The pmT-ag lost from the cell surface is rapidly replenished with newly synthesized T-ag molecules that can be iodinated on the "chased" cells.[23–25] These observations suggest that the association of pmT-ag with the plasma membrane is highly dynamic. Others[21] have noted pmT-ag to be more stable, with no detectable change during a chase period of 4 hr. These discrepant results may indicate that the precise interaction of pmT-ag with the plasma membrane depends upon culture conditions that influence the shape of the transformed cells.

Non-karyophilic SV40 mutants have demonstrated that pmT-ag plays a role in SV40-mediated transformation which is distinct from that of nT-ag. A primary sequence near the amino terminus of T-ag contains a nuclear transport signal which, upon mutagenesis of lysine-128 within the signal sequence, prevents nuclear transport of T-ag.[26–29] SV40 mutants constructed to be defective for nuclear transport of T-ag have the ability to transform established cells but are defective in transforming primary baby rat kidney cells, suggesting that pmT-ag complements function(s) provided by nT-ag.[30,31] Recent studies have shown that such non-karyophilic SV40 mutants can transform primary rat fibroblasts when co-transfected with genes for cytoplasmic-

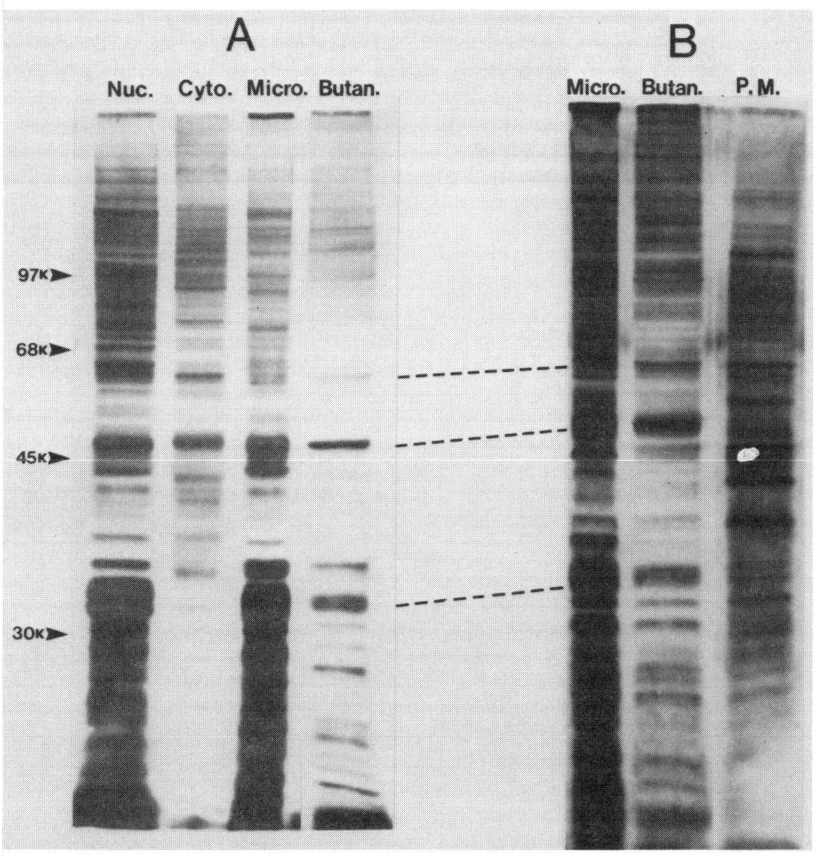

FIGURE 2. Comparison of total cellular proteins extracted from SV40-transformed mouse cells (cell line mKSA) into 2.5% butanol (**Butan.**) at 37°C by a non-cytolytic technique with proteins recovered from subcellular fractions of these cells: nuclei (**Nuc.**), crude cytosol (**Cyto.**), microsomes (**Micro.**), and purified plasma membranes (**P.M.**). Subcellular fractionation was performed by the method of Schmidt-Ullrich *et al.*[61] Proteins were solubilized in an SDS disruption buffer, separated by SDS-polyacrylamide gel electrophoresis, and then visualized by silver staining. Panels *A* and *B* represent results of two different experiments. Note that butanol selectively removes a subset of membrane-associated proteins. Positions of M_r markers (K, $\times$ 10^3) are indicated by *arrowheads.*

localized oncogene proteins such as the polyoma virus middle T-ag or the protein encoded by the Harvey *ras* gene,[32,33] substantiating proposals for a significant role for pmT-ag in SV40-mediated transformation.

Identification of cellular targets for pmT-ag is necessary in order to address its mechanism of action at the cell surface. A cellular proto-oncogene protein, designated p53, has been demonstrated to be a direct substrate of T-ag; its binding to T-ag appears to be intimately involved in SV40-mediated transformation.[6,34,35] The p53 protein in normal, uninfected cells is expressed only transiently at low levels,[36–38] but complex formation with T-ag stabilizes p53, resulting in its accumulation to high levels throughout the cell cycle (FIG. 1). A complex consisting of T-ag and p53 exists on the surface of SV40-transformed cells;[20,25,39–42] the observation that it is not detectable on non-transformed cells initially infected with SV40 suggests a possible role for such a complex in SV40-mediated transformation.[13]

BUTANOL EXTRACTION OF SV40 T-ANTIGEN IN NOVEL PROTEIN COMPLEXES FROM THE SURFACE OF TRANSFORMED CELLS

To study the possible interaction of T-ag with membrane proteins, we applied a non-cytolytic protein extraction technique[43] to SV40-transformed cells. The procedure, which utilizes single-phase concentrations of 1-butanol, has been used in other tumor systems to solubilize extrinsic, peripheral, tumor-specific and tumor-associated transplantation antigens with minimal contamination by cytoplasmic components. Of particular significance is that single-phase concentrations of 1-butanol appear to be less denaturing to surface tumor antigen components than either high-salt solutions or detergent. This technique has also been successful in recovering membrane protein complexes from the surfaces of sea urchin blastula cells; the proteins so isolated were able to efficiently reconstitute cells rendered reaggregation-incompetent by non-cytolytic extraction with butanol. These recovered complexes are believed to be important in position-dependent cell-cell interactions during embryogenesis.[44,45]

The proteins we recovered by butanol extraction of SV40-transformed mouse cells were compared with the protein species found in subcellular fractions of the SV40-transformed cells. The patterns obtained by silver staining of proteins separated by electrophoresis on polyacrylamide gels confirmed that butanol extraction was selective and removed a subset of membrane-associated proteins (FIG. 2).[46]

Extraction of [^{35}S]methionine-labeled proteins from an established SV40-transformed BALB/c mouse cell line (designated mKSA)[20,22,47] was performed using a standard detergent-containing buffer solution (RIPA) at 0°C or a phosphate-buffered saline solution containing either 1 or 2.5% 1-butanol at 0, 22, or 37°C. Solubilized proteins were then immunoprecipitated from each extract using either HAF (polyclonal hamster ascites fluid from SV40 tumor-bearing hamsters[48]) or the p53-specific monoclonal antibodies 200.47 or PAb421. The immunoprecipitates were analyzed by SDS-polyacrylamide gel electrophoresis.[42,49]

Lysis of mKSA cells with detergent-containing buffer released T-ag that was specifically immunoprecipitated with HAF and migrated at 94,000 (94K) M_r (FIG. 3, lane 2). The cellular protein p53 was also solubilized in detergent buffer lysates of mKSA cells and was immunoprecipitated with the p53-specific monoclonal antibodies 200.47[50] (FIG. 3, lane 3) and PAb421[51] (FIG. 3, lane 4). T-ag can be observed to be co-precipitated by 200.47 and PAb421 due to complex formation with p53 (FIG. 3, lanes 3,4).

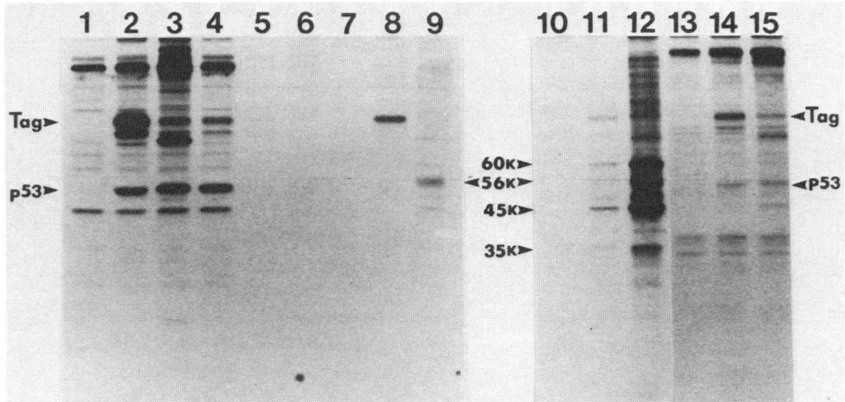

FIGURE 3. Influence of butanol concentration and temperature on solubilization of cell surface T-ag and T-ag/p53 complexes. mKSA cells were metabolically labeled with [^{35}S]methionine and were then disrupted in RIPA detergent-containing buffer with SDS and deoxycholate (DOC) at 0°C (**lanes 1-4**) or were then treated with either 1% (**lanes 13-15**) or 2.5% (**lanes 5-12**) butanol at 0°C (**lanes 5, 6**), 22°C (**lanes 7-9**), or 37°C (**lanes 10-15**). Solubilized ^{35}S-labeled proteins were then immunoprecipitated with normal hamster serum (**lanes 1, 5, 7, 10, 13**), polyclonal anti-T-ag antiserum HAF (**lanes 2, 8, 11, 14**), anti-p53 monoclonal antibody 200.47 (**lanes 3, 6, 9, 12, 15**), or anti-p53 monoclonal antibody PAb421 (**lane 4**). Immunoprecipitates were analyzed by SDS-polyacrylamide gel electrophoresis, and the patterns were visualized by fluorography for 18 hr (**lanes 1-12**) or for 1 week (**lanes 13-15**) on Kodak XAR-5 film at −70°C. *Arrowheads* indicate positions of T-ag (Tag), p53, and M_r 60K, 56K, 45K, and 35K proteins.

Treatment of mKSA cells with single-phase concentrations of 1 or 2.5% 1-butanol at different temperatures yielded a much different spectrum of proteins that were precipitable with HAF and 200.47 (FIG. 3, lanes 5-15).[46] No proteins which could be immunoprecipitated with 200.47 were solubilized from mKSA cells at 0°C with 2.5% butanol (lane 6). However, 2.5% butanol at 22°C solubilized essentially free T-ag, as detected with HAF (lane 8), and a protein (56K M_r) migrating more slowly than p53, which was specifically immunoprecipitated with 200.47 (lane 9). Increasing the extraction temperature to 37°C resulted in the recovery of less T-ag than at 22°C, but additional proteins of 35-60K M_r were recovered and immunoprecipitated with HAF (lane 11). The 200.47 monoclonal antibody co-precipitated not only T-ag but also abundant amounts of the 56K M_r protein as well as the 35-60K M_r proteins (lane 12) that were observed in the parallel HAF immunoprecipitate (lane 11). None of the 35-60K M_r proteins were detectably solubilized either in detergent (lanes 2-4) or in 1% butanol at 37°C (lanes 14,15), suggesting that release of these proteins was dependent upon the butanol concentration. Proteins migrating at 60K, 56K, 50K, 45K, and 35K M_r were reproducibly recovered.

Partial peptide mapping using V8 protease[52] suggested that the 35-60K M_r proteins were not structurally related to each other; each appeared to be a unique protein (data not shown). Thus, treatment of mKSA cells with 2.5% butanol solubilized not only T-ag and T-ag/p53 complexes, but also additional unrelated proteins of 35-60K M_r that could be precipitated with a polyclonal T-ag-specific antiserum and with a p53-specific monoclonal antibody, 200.47. The extraction of these cell surface proteins was critically dependent on temperature, suggesting that the fluidity of the membrane may play an important role in solubilization of cell surface proteins by butanol.

The appearance of the same 35-60K M_r proteins in both the HAF and the 200.47 immunoprecipitates from butanol extracts of mKSA cells suggested that these proteins may be present in a complex with T-ag or p53 or both. To investigate this possibility, other monoclonal antibodies against T-ag or p53 were employed in immunoprecipitation analyses of ^{35}S-labeled proteins from either detergent or butanol extracts of mKSA cells (FIG. 4A, B).[46] Proteins immunoprecipitated from detergent or butanol extracts by monoclonal antibodies were subsequently examined by immunoblotting[53,54] using a rabbit polyclonal anti-T-ag serum[48] (FIG. 4C, D).

Analyses of detergent extracts indicated that T-ag was specifically precipitated by the T-ag-specific monoclonal antibodies (FIG. 4A, C, lanes 4-9) and that it was co-precipitated by the p53-specific monoclonal antibodies 200.47, PAb421, and PAb246 due to complex formation with p53 (FIG. 4A, C, lanes 10-12). Although p53 was present in each of the monoclonal antibody precipitates from detergent extracts (FIG. 4A), only T-ag was reactive with the polyclonal anti-T-ag serum in immunoblot tests (FIG. 4C), confirming that p53 does not share antigenic similarity with T-ag but rather is recovered in immunoprecipitates generated by T-ag-specific serum because of a direct interaction with T-ag.

Similar analyses were performed on the butanol extracts from mKSA cells using both T-ag-specific and p53-specific monoclonal antibodies (FIG. 4B, D). Immunoblotting with polyclonal anti-T-ag serum of proteins precipitated by each of the T-ag-specific monoclonal antibodies revealed that T-ag was, indeed, released into butanol extracts and was recognized by each of the employed monoclonal antibodies (FIG. 4D, lanes 4-11). Differences in the extent of reactivity between butanol-extracted T-ag and several of the monoclonal antibodies were apparent, reflected in the variable amounts of T-ag precipitated (FIG. 4D, lanes 4-11), in contrast to the relatively uniform levels of T-ag recovered from detergent extracts (FIG. 4C, lanes 4-9). This same phenomenon was evident with the anti-p53 monoclonal antibodies 200.47, PAb421, and PAb246 (compare lanes 12-14 of FIG. 4D with lanes 10-12 of FIG. 4C). The 200.47 and PAb421 monoclonal antibodies reacted well with butanol-extracted proteins, but PAb246 reacted only poorly.

Further analyses of the proteins recovered from butanol extracts of mKSA cells yielded additional evidence for protein complexes associated with T-ag (FIG. 4B, D). Monoclonal antibodies directed against either the T-ag amino-terminal sequence of amino acid residues 1-200 (PAb430,[51,55] PAb602[15]) or the carboxyl-terminal sequence of residues 525-698 (PAb101,[56] PAb423[51,55]) were able to co-precipitate the 35-60K M_r proteins (FIG. 4B, lanes 4, 5, 10, and 11). Monoclonal antibodies that recognized epitopes within the internal sequence of T-ag (PAb204,[55,57] PAb414,[51,55] PAb402[51,55]) did not precipitate the 35-60K M_r proteins (FIG. 4B, lanes 7-9), although uncomplexed T-ag was recovered in significant amounts, especially with PAb414, as detectable by immunoblotting (FIG. 4D, lane 8).

Immunoblotting of proteins precipitated from butanol extracts by T-ag-specific monoclonal antibodies showed that only T-ag reacted specifically with the polyclonal anti-T-ag serum (FIG. 4D). No reactivity was evident toward any of the 35-60K M_r proteins, thus establishing that the lower-molecular-weight proteins were not degradation products of T-ag and that they were not precipitated due to fortuitous antigenic cross-reactivities. Rather, they most likely were co-precipitated due to complex formation with T-ag. The amount of [^{35}S]methionine incorporated by metabolic labeling (3 hr) into the uncomplexed T-ag species recognized by PAb204 and PAb402 was considerably less (FIG. 4B, lanes 7 and 9) than the amount of label in the complexed T-ag precipitated by the amino- or carboxyl-terminal-specific monoclonal antibodies (FIG. 4B, lanes 4, 5, 10, and 11), although significant amounts of unlabeled T-ag were precipitated by the former reagents (FIG. 4D). This relationship suggests that older

(≥ 3 hr) T-ag molecules at the membrane may be dissociated from complexes with the 35-60K M_r proteins.

Large amounts of the 35-60K M_r proteins were also recovered with anti-p53 immunoprecipitations from butanol (FIG. 4B, lanes 12, 13), suggesting that these proteins are associated not only with T-ag but also with a p53-related protein.

GROWTH-DEPENDENT EXPRESSION AND RAPID TURNOVER OF SURFACE PROTEIN COMPLEXES

SV40-transformed cells growing in an active state express more surface T-ag than quiescent cultures,[22] and cells growing in suspension express elevated amounts of NP-40-resistant pmT-ag.[21] The effect of growth conditions on the expression of surface protein complexes containing T-ag was examined. The mKSA cell line grown as a suspension culture exhibited higher levels of pmT-ag and T-ag-containing protein complexes, detected by metabolic labeling with [^{35}S]methionine (≤ 3 hr) and extraction with butanol (FIG. 5A, lane 4), than did mKSA cells established to grow as a monolayer culture (FIG. 5A, lane 2).[46] Suspension cultures plated on a substratum yielded considerably less pmT-ag and associated proteins than did the original suspension cultures (FIG. 5A, compare lane 6 with lane 4). In addition, fewer [^{35}S]methionine-labeled, T-ag-containing surface complexes were detected in confluent monolayer mKSA cells (FIG. 5B, lanes 1-4) than in cultures analyzed at either 40% (FIG. 5B, lanes 5-8) or 20% (FIG. 5B, lanes 9-12) confluency. Cells grown to confluency (stationary cultures) incorporated only half the amount of [^{3}H]thymidine incorporated by the subconfluent (growing) cell cultures. The level of [^{35}S]methionine incorporation into butanol-extracted T-ag complexes was 7.9-fold greater for sparsely seeded cultures (20% confluency) than for the confluent cultures. Thus, expression of the surface T-ag-containing protein complexes was influenced dramatically by conditions of cell growth, with higher levels of complexes detected in cells in an active growth state.

A pulse-chase experiment was performed to examine the rate of turnover of surface T-ag-containing complexes (FIG. 6).[46] At the end of a 15-min period of pulse-labeling with [^{35}S]methionine, labeled T-ag and associated complexes could be extracted with butanol and immunoprecipitated with rabbit antiserum directed against T-ag (FIG. 6, lane 1), with the anti-T-ag monoclonal antibody PAb430 (lane 2), or with anti-p53 monoclonal antibody 200.47 (lane 4). As observed previously with longer labeling times, anti-T-ag monoclonal antibody PAb414 failed to co-precipitate any detectable [^{35}S]methionine-labeled protein complexes from butanol extracts (lane 3) under the conditions employed. Incubation of the ^{35}S-labeled cells in unlabeled medium for various chase periods revealed several informative observations about the protein complexes. First, 90% of the protein complexes had become inaccessible to butanol extraction after a 30-min chase period (FIG. 6, compare lanes 6-9 with lanes 11-14). Second, the stoichiometry of the 45K M_r component of the complex changed dramatically, from a 2- to 3-fold excess over the level of each of the other complex components at the end of the 15-min pulse-labeling period to an amount equivalent to the others after a 30-min chase period (compare lanes 1 and 2 with lanes 11 and 12). Third, approximately 10% of the initially labeled complexes were still detectable at the cell surface after even 9 hr (lanes 16-19). Thus, although the majority of the T-ag-containing surface complex exhibits a highly dynamic association with the cell surface, a subpopulation is very stable and remains associated with the cell surface for up to 9 hr.

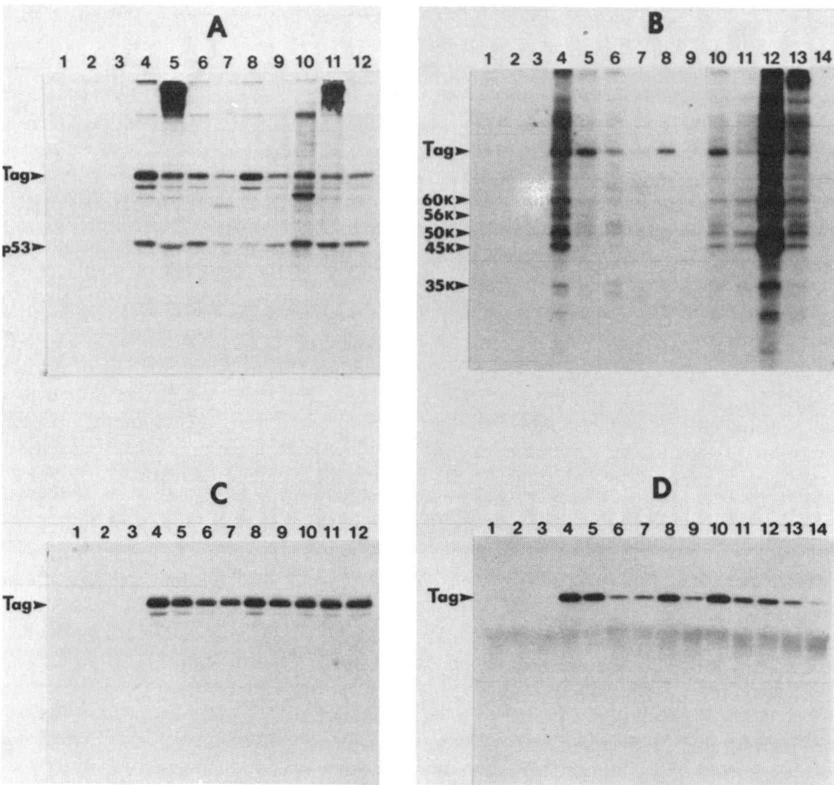

FIGURE 4. Immunoreactivity of detergent- or butanol-soluble proteins with T-ag- and p53-specific monoclonal antibodies. ^{35}S-labeled proteins of mKSA cells were extracted with RIPA detergent-containing buffer without SDS and DOC (**panel A**) or with 2.5% butanol (**panel B**) and were immunoprecipitated with various anti-T-ag and anti-p53 monoclonal antibodies; patterns for immunoprecipitates resolved on SDS-polyacrylamide gels are shown. **Panels C and D** show the results of immunoblotting, using a rabbit polyclonal anti-T-ag serum, of such patterns for the proteins precipitated by the various monoclonal antibodies from the detergent (**C**) and the butanol (**D**) extracts, respectively. Sera used for immunoprecipitation in **panels A and C** were rabbit anti-goat (**lane 1**); irrelevant monoclonal antibodies against rotavirus VP7 (**lane 2**) and adenovirus E1A protein (anti-serum M73) (**lane 3**); the anti-T-ag monoclonal antibodies PAb430 (**lane 4**), PAb441 (**lane 5**), PAb100 (**lane 6**), PAb204 (**lane 7**), PAb414 (**lane 8**), and PAb423 (**lane 9**); and the anti-p53 monoclonals 200.47 (**lane 10**), PAb421 (**lane 11**), and PAb246 (**lane 12**). In **panels B and D,** antisera employed in immunoprecipitation of extracts were rabbit anti-goat (**lane 1**); the two irrelevant monoclonal antibodies used in lanes 2 and 3 of panels A and C (**lanes 2, 3**); the anti-T-ag monoclonals PAb430 (**lane 4**), PAb602 (**lane 5**), PAb100 (**lane 6**), PAb204 (**lane 7**), PAb414 (**lane 8**), PAb402 (**lane 9**), PAb101 (**lane 10**), and PAb423 (**lane 11**); and the anti-p53 monoclonal antibodies 200.47 (**lane 12**), PAb421 (**lane 13**), and PAb246 (**lane 14**). Fluorography (**panels A, B**) was performed on Kodak XAR-5 film for 8 hr at −70°C. Immunoblots (**panels C, D**) were subjected to autoradiography for 2.5 hr. *Arrowheads* indicate positions of T-ag (Tag), p53, and M_r 60K, 56K, 50K, 45K, and 35K proteins.

SIGNIFICANCE OF BUTANOL-EXTRACTABLE PLASMA MEMBRANE-ASSOCIATED T-ANTIGEN PROTEIN COMPLEXES

A role for the pmT-ag/p53-related protein complexes is not yet known, although their fast rate of transport to the surface (≤ 15 min) and rapid turnover at the plasma membrane ($t_{1/2} < 30$ min) suggest an important biological function, such as signal transduction. The cellular proteins of 35-60K M_r that associate with pmT-ag and the p53-related protein remain to be identified, but they may function in some aspect of growth regulation, such as communication between the cell surface and the nucleus. Interaction of pmT-ag with one of the components of the complex or displacement of a member of the normal complex by T-ag may result in an aberrant activity, thereby contributing to the transformed phenotype.

Another possibility to be considered is that one or more of the cellular proteins may be involved in the rapid transport of T-ag to the plasma membrane. Transport

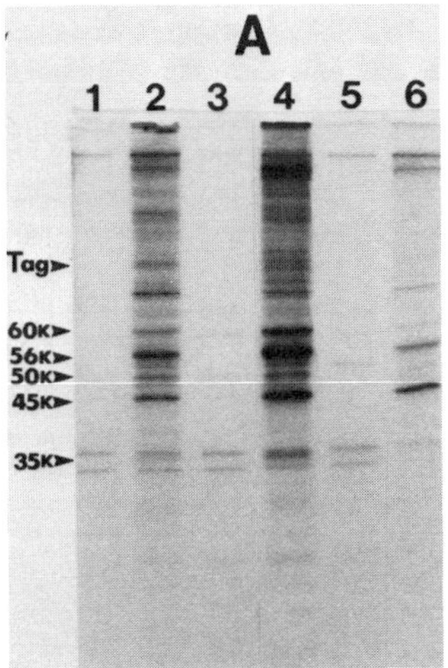

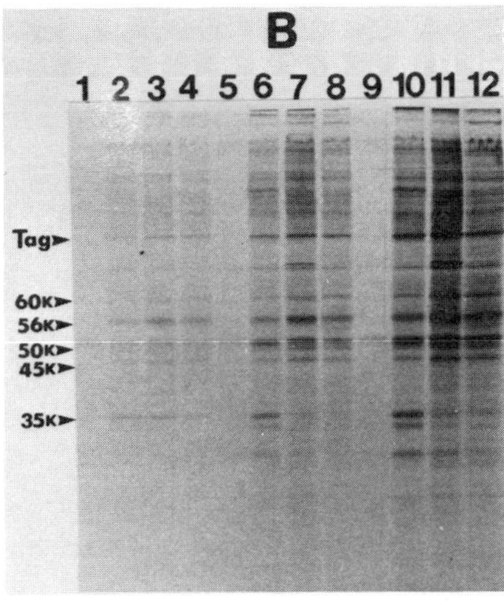

FIGURE 5. Influence of cell growth conditions on the expression of surface protein complexes containing T-ag and p53-related proteins. (**Panel A**) Amounts of protein complexes associated with p53-related protein extracted from mKSA cells grown on a substratum as compared with cells growing in suspension. Butanol extracts were prepared from ^{35}S-labeled mKSA cells (10^7) established to grow as a monolayer (**lanes 1, 2**), from labeled cells grown in suspension (**lanes 3, 4**), and from labeled cells usually grown in suspension but plated back onto a substratum before the metabolic labeling (**lanes 5, 6**). Extracts were immunoprecipitated with either normal hamster serum (**lanes 1, 3, 5**) or anti-p53 monoclonal antibody 200.47 (**lanes 2, 4, 6**). (**Panel B**) Expression of T-ag and associated cellular proteins in quiescent and actively dividing SV40-transformed cells. Monolayer cultures of mKSA cells were seeded at different cell densities and analyzed at different degrees of confluency. Butanol extracts were prepared from ^{35}S-labeled cells at 20% (**lanes 9-12**), 40% (**lanes 5-8**), or 100% (**lanes 1-4**) confluency and immunoprecipitated with monoclonal antibody M73, specific for the adenovirus E1A protein (**lanes 1, 5, 9**); PAb430, specific for T-ag (**lanes 2, 6, 10**); or 200.47 (**lanes 3, 7, 11**) or PAb421 (**lanes 4, 8, 12**), specific for p53. Fluorography was performed for 2 days on Kodak XAR-5 film at −70°C. *Arrowheads* indicate positions of T-ag (Tag) and M_r 60K, 56K, 50K, 45K, and 35K proteins.

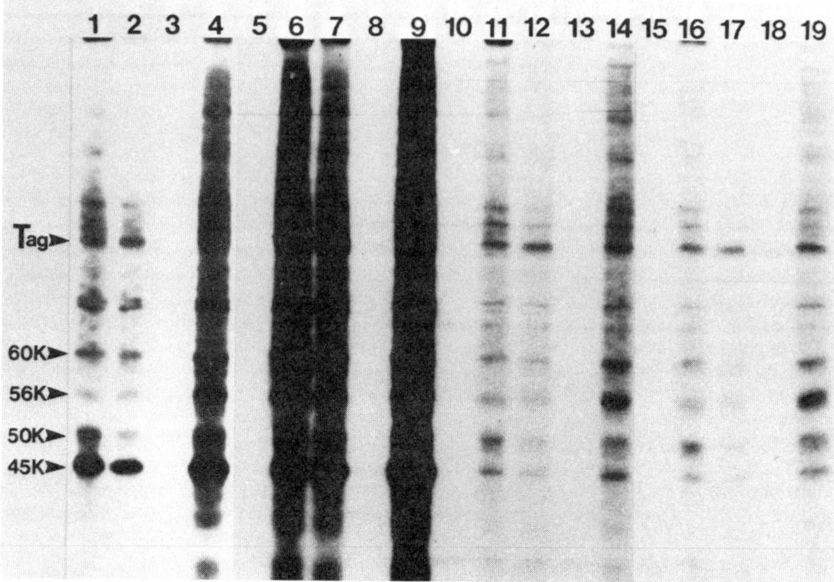

FIGURE 6. Dynamic association of complexes containing T-ag, p53-related protein, and associated cellular proteins with the cell surface. Turnover of protein complexes extracted with 2.5% butanol at 37°C from suspension cultures of mKSA cells was examined by a pulse-chase analysis. After a 15-min pulse-labeling period with [^{35}S]methionine, suspension cells were extracted with butanol (**lanes 5-9**) or were pelleted and suspended in unlabeled medium, returned to 37°C, and extracted with butanol after a chase period of either 30 min (**lanes 10-14**) or 9 hr (**lanes 15-19**). Immunoprecipitated proteins from the butanol extracts were analyzed by SDS-polyacrylamide gel electrophoresis and the patterns were visualized by fluorography. **Lanes 1-4** are shorter exposures of **lanes 6-9** to allow visualization of individual proteins. Proteins were immunoprecipitated from butanol extracts using anti-adenovirus E1A protein monoclonal antibody M73 (**lanes 5, 10, 15**), rabbit anti-T-ag serum (**lanes 6, 11, 16**), the anti-T-ag monoclonal antibodies PAb430 (**lanes 7, 12, 17**) or PAb414 (**lanes 8, 13, 18**), or anti-p53 monoclonal antibody 200.47 (**lanes 9, 14, 19**). **Lanes 1-5** were fluorographed for 8 hr, and **lanes 6-19** were exposed for 2 days on Kodak XAR-5 film at −70°C. *Arrowheads* indicate positions of T-ag (Tag) and M_r 60K, 56K, 50K, and 45K proteins.

of T-ag to the cell surface does not proceed through the secretory pathway via the Golgi apparatus.[58,59] Association of one or more of the 35-60K M_r proteins with T-ag might direct it to a receptor in the plasma membrane that assists in positioning T-ag into an appropriate conformation and topology in the membrane.

MODEL OF CELL TRANSFORMATION BY SV40

Carcinogenesis is believed to be a multi-step phenomenon. In the SV40 system, the steps leading to complete transformation occur concurrently, blurring individual contributions to the process. Experimental evidence is mounting, however, that both nuclear and membrane-associated forms of T-ag are functionally important in mediating phenotypic transformation. A model of how these two forms of T-ag might cooperate is presented in FIGURE 7.

In this model, SV40 DNA sequences are integrated in the cellular chromosome and give rise to transcripts encoding T-ag (FIG. 7, step 1). Transcripts are transported to the cytoplasm (step 2), where T-ag is synthesized (step 3). The majority of newly synthesized T-ag is rapidly directed into the nucleus (step 4) because of the nuclear transport signal contained in its primary sequence. Nuclear T-ag has a long half-life and accumulates to high levels. Some of the T-ag forms complexes with host protein p53. Free T-ag and/or T-ag/p53 complexes bind to chromatin and the nuclear matrix (step 5), causing the expression of cellular genes to be activated (step 6). The effect on cellular transcription, and perhaps also on DNA replication, probably constitutes the T-ag immortalization function; it is essential if the transformation of primary cells is to occur. Although the T-ag function involved in gene activation presumably involves normal cell regulatory protein(s), normal regulation of activity is lost and the cell remains continually activated under the influence of T-ag. The possible role of complex formation between T-ag and the Rb gene product[8] remains to be determined.

A minor fraction of T-ag is transported to the plasma membrane by an unknown pathway (FIG. 7, step 7). Some of this pmT-ag population is complexed with p53. The pmT-ag interacts with other cellular proteins (35-60K) in the membrane (not shown). It is postulated that the complex, or free pmT-ag, generates a growth signal that gets transmitted to the nucleus by an unknown mechanism (step 8). The conformation of pmT-ag might mimic an activated growth factor receptor or the inter-

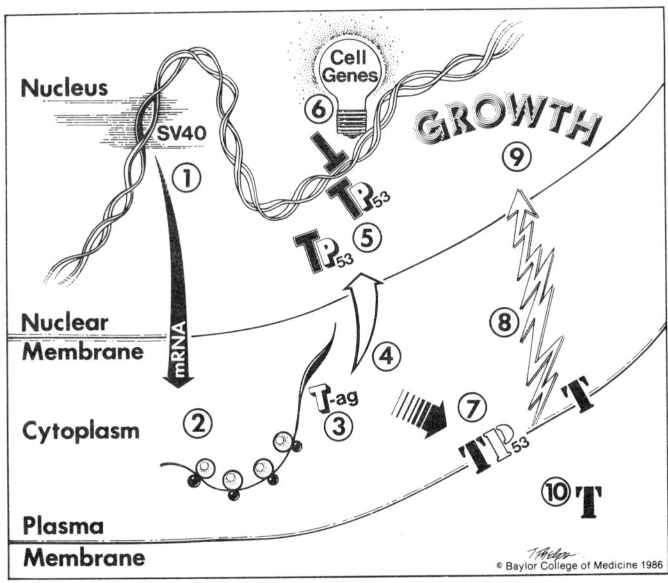

FIGURE 7. Model of mechanism of transformation by SV40. This model proposes that the nuclear and plasma membrane forms of T-ag provide separate and cooperative functions necessary to mediate phenotypic transformation. See text for details. (From Butel.[1] Reprinted with permission from *Cancer Surveys.)*

action of pmT-ag with cellular components might stimulate outbursts of growth-signaling second messenger type molecules. Nuclear proteins, including nT-ag, respond to the growth signal and promote functions culminating in cell division (step 9). The pmT-ag would presumably not be responsive to control measures that regulate normal cell growth, so signaling from the cell surface would occur without interruption. This might result in the phenotypic changes characteristic of complete transformation. The signals generated by pmT-ag apparently can also function in the absence of nT-ag if the cell has been immortalized in some other way.

The pmT-ag with its termini exposed on the extracellular face of the cell (or fragments thereof) would be recognized as foreign by host CTL; this may explain the involvement of T-ag in SV40 tumor-specific transplantation antigen. Some of the pmT-ag is shed (FIG. 7, step 10), with unknown effects on the immune response of the host.

SV40 is unique among known tumor viruses in combining multiple transforming functions into a single protein. If the basic features of this model prove correct, T-ag should be considered a "dual oncogene" protein.[1,2]

SUMMARY

SV40 T-antigen (T-ag) is localized in both the nucleus (nT-ag) and plasma membrane (pmT-ag) of cells and provides multiple functions necessary for cell transformation. The pmT-ag population is structurally very similar to the nT-ag. Transport to the cell surface is by an unknown mechanism that does not involve the secretory pathway. The disposition of T-ag in the membrane exposes both the amino and the carboxyl terminus on the exterior of the cell. Nuclear-transport-defective mutants of T-ag can transform established cells in culture, but not primary cells, suggesting that non-nuclear forms of T-ag may mediate some transformation-related process(es). A non-cytolytic protein extraction technique utilizing 1-butanol solubilized from SV40-transformed cells a multimeric complex composed of pmT-ag and at least five cellular proteins ranging in size from 35,000 (35K) to 60K M_r. Both amino- and carboxyl-terminal T-ag-specific monoclonal antibodies co-precipitated T-ag and the 35-60K M_r proteins, but antibodies against the internal portion of T-ag precipitated only uncomplexed T-ag. The growth state of the cells markedly influenced the expression of the T-ag-containing surface complexes; more complexes were recovered from actively dividing cells than from confluent cell cultures, and suspension cells yielded more complexes than cells on a substratum. The complex exhibited a highly dynamic association with the cell membrane, as demonstrated by pulse-chase analysis. The characteristics of growth-dependent expression and rapid turnover rate suggest a functional role for the membrane complex. The identities of the cellular proteins in the complex with pmT-ag are unknown, although one member (56K) is recognized by p53-specific monoclonal antibodies.

REFERENCES

1. BUTEL, J. S. 1986. SV40 large T-antigen: Dual oncogene. Cancer Surv. **5:** 343-365.
2. BUTEL, J. S. & D. L. JARVIS. 1986. The plasma-membrane-associated form of SV40 large tumor antigen: Biochemical and biological properties. Biochim. Biophys. Acta **865:** 171-195.

3. RIGBY, P. W. J. & D. P. LANE. 1983. Structure and function of simian virus 40 large T-antigen. *In* Advances in Viral Oncology. G. Klein, Ed. Vol. 3: 31-57. Raven Press. New York.
4. STAHL, H. & R. KNIPPERS. 1987. The simian virus 40 large tumor antigen. Biochim. Biophys. Acta **910:** 1-10.
5. BRADLEY, M. K., J. D. GRIFFIN & D. M. LIVINGSTON. 1982. Relationship of oligomerization to enzymatic and DNA-binding properties of the SV40 large T-antigen. Cell **28:** 125-134.
6. CRAWFORD, L. 1983. The 53,000 dalton cellular protein and its role in transformation. *In* International Review of Experimental Pathology. G. W. Richter & M. A. Epstein, Eds. Vol. 25: 1-50. Academic Press. New York.
7. LANE, D. P. & L. V. CRAWFORD. 1979. T antigen is bound to a host protein in SV40-transformed cells. Nature **278:** 261-263.
8. DECAPRIO, J. A., J. W. LUDLOW, J. FIGGE, J.-Y. SHEW, C.-M. HUANG, W.-H. LEE, E. MARSILIO, E. PAUCHA & D. M. LIVINGSTON. 1988. SV40 large tumor antigen forms a specific complex with the product of the retinoblastoma susceptibility gene. Cell **54:** 275-283.
9. GIDONI, D., A. SCHELLER, B. BARNET, P. HANTZOPOULOS, M. OREN & C. PRIVES. 1982. Different forms of simian virus 40 large tumor antigen varying in their affinities for DNA. J. Virol. **42:** 456-466.
10. KLOCKMANN, U. & W. DEPPERT. 1983. Acylated simian virus 40 large T-antigen: A new subclass associated with a detergent-resistant lamina of the plasma membrane. EMBO J. **2:** 1151-1157.
11. JARVIS, D. L., C. N. COLE & J. S. BUTEL. 1986. Absence of a structural basis for intracellular recognition and differential localization of nuclear and plasma membrane-associated forms of simian virus 40 large tumor antigen. Mol. Cell. Biol. **6:** 758-767.
12. DEPPERT, W. & G. WALTER. 1982. Domains of simian virus 40 large T-antigen exposed on the cell surface. Virology **122:** 56-70.
13. SANTOS, M. & J. S. BUTEL. 1984. Antigenic structure of simian virus 40 large tumor antigen and association with cellular protein p53 on the surfaces of simian virus 40-infected and -transformed cells. J. Virol. **51:** 376-383.
14. BALL, R. K., B. SIEGL, S. QUELLHORST, G. BRANDNER & D. G. BRAUN. 1984. Monoclonal antibodies against simian virus 40 nuclear large T tumour antigen: Epitope mapping, papova virus cross-reaction and cell surface staining. EMBO J. **3:** 1485-1491.
15. GOODING, L. R., R. W. GELB, K. A. O'CONNELL & E. HARLOW. 1984. Antibody and cellular detection of SV40 T-antigenic determinants on the surfaces of transformed cells. *In* Cancer Cells: The Transformed Phenotype. A. J. Levine, G. F. van de Woude, T. C. Topp & J. D. Watson, Eds.: 263-269. Cold Spring Harbor Laboratory. Cold Spring Harbor, NY.
16. WHITTAKER, L., A. FUKS & R. HAND. 1985. Plasma membrane orientation of simian virus 40 T antigen in three transformed cell lines mapped with monoclonal antibodies. J. Virol. **53:** 366-373.
17. O'CONNELL, K. A. & L. R. GOODING. 1984. Cloned cytotoxic T lymphocytes recognize cells expressing discrete fragments of the SV40 tumor antigen. J. Immunol. **132:** 953-958.
18. TEVETHIA, S. S., A. J. LEWIS, A. E. CAMPBELL, M. J. TEVETHIA & P. W. J. RIGBY. 1984. Simian virus 40 specific cytotoxic lymphocyte clones localize two distinct TSTA sites on cells synthesizing a 48 kD SV40 T antigen. Virology **133:** 443-447.
19. TANAKA, Y., M. J. TEVETHIA, D. KALDERON, A. E. SMITH & S. S. TEVETHIA. 1988. Clustering of antigenic sites recognized by cytotoxic T lymphocyte clones in the amino terminal half of SV40 T antigen. Virology **162:** 427-436.
20. SANTOS, M. & J. S. BUTEL. 1982. Association of SV40 large tumor antigen and cellular proteins on the surface of SV40-transformed mouse cells. Virology **120:** 1-17.
21. KLOCKMANN, U. & W. DEPPERT. 1985. Evidence for transmembrane orientation of acylated simian virus 40 large T-antigen. J. Virol. **56:** 541-548.
22. SANTOS, M. & J. S. BUTEL. 1985. Surface T-antigen expression in simian virus 40-transformed mouse cells: Correlation with cell growth. Mol. Cell. Biol. **5:** 1051-1057.
23. SOULE, H. R., R. E. LANFORD & J. S. BUTEL. 1982. Detection of simian virus 40 surface-associated large tumor antigen by enzyme-catalyzed radioiodination. Int. J. Cancer **29:** 337-344.

24. LANFORD, R. E. & J. S. BUTEL. 1982. Intracellular transport of SV40 large tumor antigen: A mutation which abolishes migration to the nucleus does not prevent association with the cell surface. Virology **119:** 169-184.
25. SANTOS, M. & J. S. BUTEL. 1984. Dynamic nature of the association of large tumor antigen and p53 cellular protein with the surfaces of simian virus 40-transformed cells. J. Virol. **49:** 50-56.
26. KALDERON, D., W. D. RICHARDSON, A. F. MARKHAM & A. E. SMITH. 1984. Sequence requirements for nuclear location of simian virus 40 large T-antigen. Nature **311:** 33-38.
27. KALDERON, D., B. L. ROBERTS, W. D. RICHARDSON & A. E. SMITH. 1984. A short amino acid sequence able to specify nuclear location. Cell **39:** 499-509.
28. LANFORD, R. E. & J. S. BUTEL. 1984. Construction and characterization of an SV40 mutant defective in nuclear transport of T antigen. Cell **37:** 801-813.
29. LANFORD, R. E., P. KANDA & R. C. KENNEDY. 1986. Induction of nuclear transport with a synthetic peptide homologous to the SV40 T-antigen transport signal. Cell **46:** 575-582.
30. FISCHER-FANTUZZI, L. & C. VESCO. 1985. Deletion of 43 amino acids in the NH_2-terminal half of the large tumor antigen of simian virus 40 results in a nonkaryophilic protein capable of transforming established cells. Proc. Natl. Acad. Sci. USA **82:** 1891-1895.
31. LANFORD, R. E., C. WONG & J. S. BUTEL. 1985. Differential ability of a T-antigen transport-defective mutant of simian virus 40 to transform primary and established rodent cells. Mol. Cell. Biol. **5:** 1043-1050.
32. MICHALOVITZ, D., L. FISCHER-FANTUZZI, C. VESCO, J. M. PIPAS & M. OREN. 1987. Activated Ha-*ras* can cooperate with defective simian virus 40 in the transformation of nonestablished rat embryo fibroblasts. J. Virol. **61:** 2648-2654.
33. VASS-MARENGO, J., A. RATIARSON, C. ASSELIN & M. BASTIN. 1986. Ability of a T-antigen transport-defective mutant of simian virus 40 to immortalize primary cells and to complement polyoma middle T in tumorigenesis. J. Virol. **59:** 655-659.
34. MICHALOVITZ, D., D. ELIYAHU & M. OREN. 1986. Overproduction of protein p53 contributes to simian virus 40-mediated transformation. Mol. Cell. Biol. **6:** 3531-3536.
35. MONTENARH, M., M. KOHLER, G. AGGELER & R. HENNING. 1985. Structural prerequisites of simian virus 40 large T-antigen for the maintenance of cell transformation. EMBO J. **4:** 2941-2947.
36. MERCER, W. E., C. AVIGNOLO & R. BASERGA. 1984. Role of the p53 protein in cell proliferation as studied by microinjection of monoclonal antibodies. Mol. Cell. Biol. **4:** 276-281.
37. MILNER, J. & S. MILNER. 1981. SV40-53K antigen: A possible role for 53K in normal cells. Virology **112:** 785-788.
38. REICH, N. C. & A. J. LEVINE. 1984. Growth regulation of a cellular tumor antigen, p53, in nontransformed cells. Nature **308:** 199-201.
39. CHANDRASEKARAN, K., D. J. WINTERBOURNE, S. W. LUBORSKY & P. T. MORA. 1981. Surface proteins of simian virus 40-transformed cells. Int. J. Cancer **27:** 397-407.
40. LUBORSKY, S. W. & K. CHANDRASEKARAN. 1980. Subcellular distribution of simian virus 40 T antigen species in various cell lines: The 56K protein. Int. J. Cancer **25:** 517-527.
41. SCHMIDT-ULLRICH, R., W. S. THOMPSON, S. J. KAHN, M. T. MONROE & D. F. H. WALLACH. 1982. Simian virus 40 (SV40)-specific isoelectric point-4.7—94,000 M_r membrane glycoprotein: Major peptide homology exhibited with the nuclear and membrane-associated 94,000 M_r SV40 T-antigen in hamsters. J. Natl. Cancer Inst. **69:** 839-849.
42. SOULE, H. R. & J. S. BUTEL. 1979. Subcellular localization of simian virus 40 large tumor antigen. J. Virol. **30:** 523-532.
43. LEGRUE, S. J. 1985. Noncytolytic extraction of cell surface antigens using butanol. Cancer Metast. Rev. **4:** 209-219.
44. NOLL, H., V. MATRANGA, D. CASCINO & L. VITTORELLI. 1979. Reconstitution of membranes and embryonic development in dissociated blastula cells of the sea urchin by reinsertion of aggregation-promoting membrane proteins extracted with butanol. Proc. Natl. Acad. Sci. USA **76:** 288-292.
45. NOLL, H., V. MATRANGA, M. CERVELLO, T. HUMPHREYS, B. KUWASAKI & D. ADELSON. 1985. Characterization of toposomes from sea urchin blastula cells: A cell organelle mediating cell adhesion and expressing positional information. Proc. Natl. Acad. Sci. USA **82:** 8062-8066.

46. Maxwell, S. A. & J. S. Butel. 1988. Unpublished observations.
47. Kit, S., T. Kurimura & D. R. Dubbs. 1969. Transplantable mouse tumor line induced by injection of SV40-transformed mouse kidney cells. Int. J. Cancer **4:** 384-392.
48. Lanford, R. E. & J. S. Butel. 1979. Antigenic relationship of SV40 early proteins to purified large T polypeptide. Virology **97:** 295-306.
49. Jarvis, D. L., R. E. Lanford & J. S. Butel. 1984. Structural comparisons of wild-type and nuclear transport-defective simian virus 40 large tumor antigens. Virology **134:** 168-176.
50. Dippold, W. G., G. Jay, A. B. DeLeo, G. Khoury & L. J. Old. 1981. p53 transformation-related protein: Detection by monoclonal antibody in mouse and human cells. Proc. Natl. Acad. Sci. USA **78:** 1695-1699.
51. Harlow, E., L. V. Crawford, D. C. Pim & N. M. Williamson. 1981. Monoclonal antibodies specific for simian virus 40 tumor antigens. J. Virol. **39:** 861-869.
52. Cleveland, D. W., S. G. Fischer, M. W. Kirschner & U. K. Laemmli 1977. Peptide mapping by limited proteolysis in sodium dodecyl sulfate and analysis by gel electrophoresis. J. Biol. Chem. **252:** 1102-1106.
53. Slagle, B. L., R. E. Lanford, D. Medina & J. S. Butel. 1984. Expression of mammary tumor virus protein in preneoplastic outgrowth lines and mammary tumors of BALB/cV mice. Cancer Res. **44:** 2155-2162.
54. Towbin, H., T. Staehelin & J. Gordon. 1979. Electrophoretic transfer of proteins from polyacrylamide gels to nitrocellulose sheets: Procedure and some applications. Proc. Natl. Acad. Sci. USA **76:** 4350-4354.
55. Mole, S. E., J. V. Gannon, M. J. Ford & D. P. Lane. 1987. Structure and function of SV40 large T-antigen. Philos. Trans. R. Soc. London Ser. B **317:** 455-469.
56. Gurney, E. G., S. Tamowski & W. Deppert. 1986. Antigenic binding sites of monoclonal antibodies specific for simian virus 40 large T-antigen. J. Virol. **57:** 1168-1172.
57. Clark, R., D. P. Lane & R. Tjian. 1981. Use of monoclonal antibodies as probes of simian virus 40 T antigen ATPase activity. J. Biol. Chem. **56:** 11854-11858.
58. Jarvis, D. L., W.-K. Chan, M. D. Estes & J. S. Butel. 1987. The cellular secretory pathway is not utilized for biosynthesis, modification, or intracellular transport of the simian virus 40 large tumor antigen. J. Virol. **61:** 3950-3959.
59. Sharma, S., L. Rodgers, J. Brandsma, M. J. Gething & J. Sambrook. 1985. SV40 T-antigen and the exocytic pathway. EMBO J. **4:** 1479-1489.
60. Tevethia, S. S. & J. S. Butel. 1987. SV40 tumor antigen: Importance of cell surface localization in transformation and immunological control of neoplasia. *In* Development and Recognition of the Transformed Cell. M. I. Greene & T. Hamaoka, Eds.: 231-242. Plenum Press. New York.
61. Schmidt-Ullrich, R., D. F. H. Wallach & F. D. G. Davis. 1976. Membranes of normal hamster lymphocytes and lymphoid cells neoplastically transformed by simian virus 40. I. High-yield purification of plasma membrane fragments. J. Natl. Cancer Inst. **57:** 1107-1116.

Pathways in Which Growth Factors and Oncogenes Interact in Epithelial Cell Mitogenic Signal Transduction

STUART A. AARONSON, JOSEPH P. FALCO, WILLIAM G. TAYLOR, ALEX C. CECH,[a] CINZIA MARCHESE,[b] PAUL W. FINCH, JEFFREY RUBIN, BERNARD E. WEISSMAN, AND PIER PAOLO DI FIORE

Laboratory of Cellular and Molecular Biology
National Cancer Institute
Building 37, Room 1E24
Bethesda, Maryland 20892

INTRODUCTION

Proto-oncogenes, genes which give rise to oncogenes, are critically involved in pathways of mitogenic signal transduction at the receptor and post-receptor level. Of the four proto-oncogenes whose products have been identified, one, c-*sis,* codes for a known growth factor[1,2] while the other three, c-*erb*B, c-*fms,* and c-*erb*A, encode growth factor receptors and a hormone.[3–7] At the post-receptor level, dramatic alterations in levels of expression of two nuclear proto-oncogenes, c-*fos* and c-*myc,* represent early transcriptional events following ligand binding to growth factor receptors.[8–10] As G-proteins, the *ras* proto-oncogene products have a potential role in the transduction of mitogenic signals.[11–14]

One approach towards elucidating the effects of proto-oncogenes or their activated oncogenic counterparts on specific signal transduction pathways has come from studying the ability of such genes to abrogate specific growth factor requirements of different target cells in tissue culture. In serum-containing medium, members of the *ras* and the tyrosine kinase oncogene families have been shown to relieve the epidermal growth factor (EGF) requirement of keratinocytes.[15,16] Specific growth factor requirements of hematopoietic cells also can be abrograted by certain oncogenes.[17,18] Generally, such studies have been performed in serum-containing medium, making it difficult to determine whether other growth factor requirements were abrogated as well as to determine the precise mechanisms involved.

Efforts to develop defined media for cultured cells have led to chemically-defined medium for certain cell types.[19,20] These media generally contain an enriched basal

[a] Howard Hughes Medical Institute/NIH Research Scholar.

[b] Department of General Pathology, University of Catania, Catania, Italy.

medium supplemented with specific growth factors. Epithelial cells are important targets of the neoplastic process. This review describes the development of a defined medium for the clonal BALB/MK keratinocyte line,[15] which requires EGF for growth in serum-containing medium and terminally differentiates when exposed to high calcium concentration,[16] and the use of this system to dissect major pathways of growth factor signal transduction and the ability of oncogenes to interact with these pathways.

SERUM-FREE CULTURE SYSTEM FOR BALB/MK EPIDERMAL KERATINOCYTES

Our efforts to devise a chemically defined medium for BALB/MK cells took advantage of previous reports on serum-free growth of other cell types.[21,22] As shown in FIGURE 1, EGF, insulin, and ethanolamine were essential for cell growth; and the addition of a poly-D-lysine/fibronectin precoating, to facilitate cell attachment and spreading, significantly enhanced cell proliferation. In the optimal serum-free condition, the sustained growth of BALB/MK cells was comparable to that in serum-containing medium supplemented with EGF.[23]

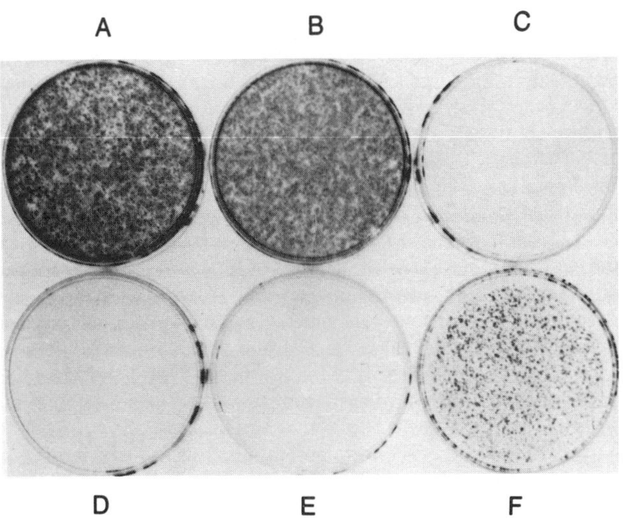

FIGURE 1. Growth of BALB/MK cells in serum-containing and chemically defined medium. Cells were plated at a density of 3×10^4/60-mm petri dish in a 1:1 mixture of Eagle's minimal essential medium and Ham's F12 medium containing 0.05 m*M* calcium and supplemented with different additives (specified below). After 11 days of growth, plates were fixed and stained. Plates **A** thru **E** were precoated with polylysine (20 μg/cm^2) and fibronectin (1 μg/cm^2). Media contained (**A**) 8% dialyzed fetal bovine serum plus 5 ng/ml EGF (serum-plus medium); (**B**) 5 μg/ml of transferrin, 10 n*M* Na_2SeO_3, 0.2 m*M* ethanolamine, 5 μg/ml of insulin, and 5 ng/ml EGF (chemically defined medium); (**C-E**) all defined medium components except (**C**) insulin, (**D**) EGF, or (**E**) ethanolamine. (**F**) cells plated in chemically defined medium in dishes without precoating.

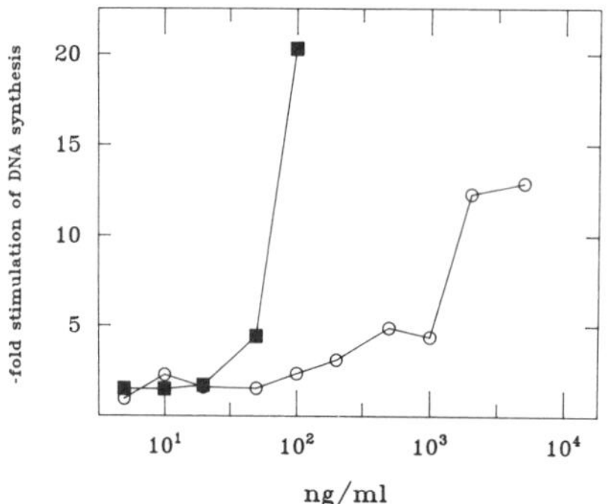

FIGURE 2. Comparison of insulin and IGF-1 stimulation of DNA synthesis in BALB/MK cells. Confluent cultures of BALB/MK cells were incubated in chemically defined medium (see FIG. 1B) for 24 hr and, subsequently, in fresh medium containing graded concentrations of insulin (○) or recombinant IGF-1 (■) and 4 μCi/ml of [^{3}H]thymidine. Data points represent the mean incorporation in duplicate cultures. Results are expressed as stimulation of DNA synthesis relative to [^{3}H]thymidine incorporation by unstimulated cells under identical conditions but without addition of insulin or IGF-1.

RESPONSE OF BALB/MK CELLS TO DIFFERENT GROWTH FACTORS

The mitogenic effects of superphysiological concentrations of insulin in some cell systems are mediated by activation of the IGF-1 (insulin-like growth factor 1) receptor.[24,25] As shown in FIGURE 2, IGF-1 stimulated a significantly greater mitogenic response in BALB/MK cells than did superphysiological levels of insulin. Moreover, in a 10-day growth assay, 50 ng/ml of IGF-1 in combination with EGF and other defined medium components sustained BALB/MK proliferation, whereas insulin at the same concentration did not (J. P. Falco, unpublished data). Thus, IGF-1 not only induced DNA synthesis more efficiently, but was also sufficient in conjunction with EGF to stimulate continued mitotic activity of BALB/MK cells. The fact that IGF-1 was effective at much lower concentrations than insulin supports the conclusion that the effect of insulin was mediated by its activation of the IGF-1 signal transduction pathway. In contrast, IGF-2 induced little, if any, DNA synthesis either on its own or when used to complement EGF or insulin.[23]

Acidic and basic fibroblast growth factors (FGFs) are mitogenic for a wide variety of cell types, including fibroblasts and endothelial cells, as well as other cells of mesodermal derivation.[26,27] There are also a few reports indicating that they are mitogenic for certain epithelial cell types.[28-30] The development of chemically defined medium for BALB/MK cells made it possible to assess the ability of acidic and basic FGFs to induce DNA synthesis and sustain proliferation of keratinocytes either alone or in conjunction with a complementing growth factor. As shown in TABLE 1, both recombinant acidic and basic FGFs were potent inducers of DNA synthesis in BALB/MK cells. Insulin demonstrated synergy with either acidic or basic FGF in promoting DNA synthesis.

In a parallel 8-day growth assay, neither acidic nor basic FGF could alone support the sustained growth of BALB/MK cells. Similarly, either of the FGFs in combination with EGF supported little or no growth. However, each of the FGFs acted in concert with insulin to stimulate growth approaching that achieved with the combination of insulin and EGF. Thus, although acidic and basic FGF act through receptors distinct from those of EGF, they were also able to complement IGF-1 signal transduction to support the growth of BALB/MK. These results demonstrate that the defined growth medium system for BALB/MK cells provides a sensitive assay for factors that can complement either of the major signal transduction pathways required for epithelial cell proliferation.

DETECTION OF NEW EPITHELIAL GROWTH FACTOR ACTIVITIES

We employed the BALB/MK assay as a sensitive means of screening for potential new human mitogens with epithelial cell specificity. Preliminary screening of conditioned medium from various human cell sources has revealed the release by human fibroblast lines of mitogenic activities capable of inducing DNA synthesis in both BALB/MK keratinocytes and NIH/3T3 fibroblasts. Whereas boiling destroyed the mitogenic activity for BALB/MK, the activity for NIH/3T3 cells remained intact. Since growth factors such as TGF-α (transforming growth factor-α) and EGF are heat stable under these conditions, the evidence suggests that the epithelial cell activity may be due to some other agent(s). Efforts to purify and characterize such growth factors are currently in progress.

PATTERNS FOR ABROGATION OF GROWTH FACTOR REQUIREMENTS BY RETROVIRAL ONCOGENES

Previous studies have shown that *ras* oncogenes as well as certain members of the tyrosine kinase oncogene family can abrogate the EGF requirement of BALB/MK cells in serum-containing medium.[15,16] The development of chemically defined medium made it possible to study more precisely the growth factor requirements involved. Individual BALB/MK cultures were infected with retroviruses representing a number of subgroups. BALB-MSV[31] and Ki-MSV[32] retroviruses contained H-*ras* and K-*ras* oncogenes,[33,34] respectively. SM-FeSV[35] and MuLV/*erb*B[36] contained constitutively activated forms of the genes for the CSF-1 (colony-stimulating factor-1: c-*fms* gene)

TABLE 1. Ability of Acidic or Basic Fibroblast Growth Factor (FGF) to Induce DNA Synthesis and Sustain Proliferation of BALB/MK Cells

		Stimulation of DNA Synthesis (-fold)[a]			Increase in Cell Number (-fold)[b]		
Factor	Concentration	Alone	+I	+EGF	Alone	+I	+EGF
None		1.0	6.6	71	<1	<1	<1
Acidic FGF	100 ng/ml	42	170	110	<1	7.7	<1
Basic FGF	100 ng/ml	30	160	90	<1	6.4	<1
EGF	20 ng/ml	71	500	—	11	11	—

[a] Stimulation of DNA synthesis over background was assayed by [^{3}H]thymidine incorporation following growth factor addition. The indicated growth factors were added in the absence of other growth factors (Alone) or in the presence of 10 μg/ml of insulin (+I) or 20 ng/ml of EGF (+EGF).

[b] Increase in cell number calculated from day 1 and day 9 cell counts in a growth assay of BALB/MK cells plated into and maintained in defined medium containing the indicated growth factors. Data represent the mean values for duplicate 2-cm^2 wells seeded with 5000 cells/well.

and the EGF receptor,[4,3] respectively, while GR-FeSV contained *fgr,* a representative of the *src* family of tyrosine kinases.[37] Finally, Moloney-MSV[38] contained the *mos* oncogene,[39] which is structurally related to the tyrosine kinases but appears to encode a protein with serine/threonine kinase activity.[40,41]

Following virus infection, each cell line chronically producing virus was analyzed for release of high-titered transforming virus and, by infectious center assay, for expression of the respective transforming gene by a large fraction of the infected cell population. In most cases, the virus-infected cell lines were preselected by growth in serum-containing medium in the absence of EGF. To ensure that preselection did not appreciably affect the results of analysis in defined medium, we also analyzed cultures of K-*ras*- and *erb*B-infected BALB/MK cells that were not preselected. Similar results were observed with independently derived cultures for any given transforming gene.

When the growth factor requirements of each stably infected cell line were compared to those of uninfected BALB/MK parental cells or BALB/MK cells infected with helper virus alone, two different patterns for the abrogation of growth factor requirements were observed (FIG. 3). The majority, including the H-*ras,* K-*ras, erb*B, *fms,* and *mos* transformants, retained a strict insulin requirement but had lost the requirement for EGF. The *ras* family members grew well in the absence or presence of EGF, while other transformants showed somewhat reduced growth in the absence of EGF. The most striking abrogation of growth factor requirements was observed with the *fgr* transformant, which grew with equal efficiency in the absence of either insulin or EGF and even grew well in the absence of added growth factors. These results argued that *fgr* was able to abrogate both EGF and IGF-1 requirements.

IMPLICATIONS

By use of a chemically defined medium for sustained proliferation of a continuous mouse keratinocyte line,[15] we showed that EGF and insulin were together sufficient to allow growth comparable to that achieved in serum-containing medium.[23] We demonstrated that IGF-1 was able to substitute for insulin at 100-fold lower concentration. It is well documented that insulin is a partial agonist for the IGF-1 receptor.[24,25] Thus, it is likely that insulin interacts with the IGF-1 receptor to promote BALB/MK growth. Among other growth factors analyzed, both recombinant acidic and basic FGFs were able to substitute for EGF but not insulin to support BALB/MK cell proliferation. FGF action is believed to be mediated through binding to a specific receptor.[27] Thus, our evidence indicates that BALB/MK cells contain several independent receptor-mediated pathways which can complement the IGF-1 pathway in stimulating BALB/MK proliferation.

The exquisite dependence of BALB/MK cells on two complementing growth factors was associated with a low background of DNA synthesis in the absence of either factor. Using the defined medium for BALB/MK cells as an assay to detect and eventually purify novel growth factors, we have developed preliminary evidence for epithelial cell-specific growth factors released by human stromal fibroblasts. The purification and characterization of these factors might shed important light on processes involved in normal epithelial cell growth and development.

We also investigated the ability of various oncogenes to complement normal growth factor-activated pathways. V-*erb*B, which encodes a constitutively activated form of the EGF receptor, allowed BALB/MK cells to grow in the absence of EGF in chemically defined medium. V-*fms* encodes an activated form of the CSF-1 receptor, a receptor believed to be specific for cells of the mononuclear phagocyte lineage.[42]

The v-*fms* oncogene, like v-*erb*B, caused BALB/MK cells to grow in the absence of EGF but not of insulin. Thus, if the protein encoded by v-*fms* acts like a constitutively stimulated CSF-1 receptor,[4] it must be able to couple with a signaling pathway in BALB/MK cells that complements the IGF-1 receptor pathway. Previous studies have shown that *ras* and *mos* oncogenes abrograte the EGF requirement of BALB/MK cells in serum-containing medium.[15,16] We confirmed these results in assays utilizing defined medium. In addition, we demonstrated that this abrogation was

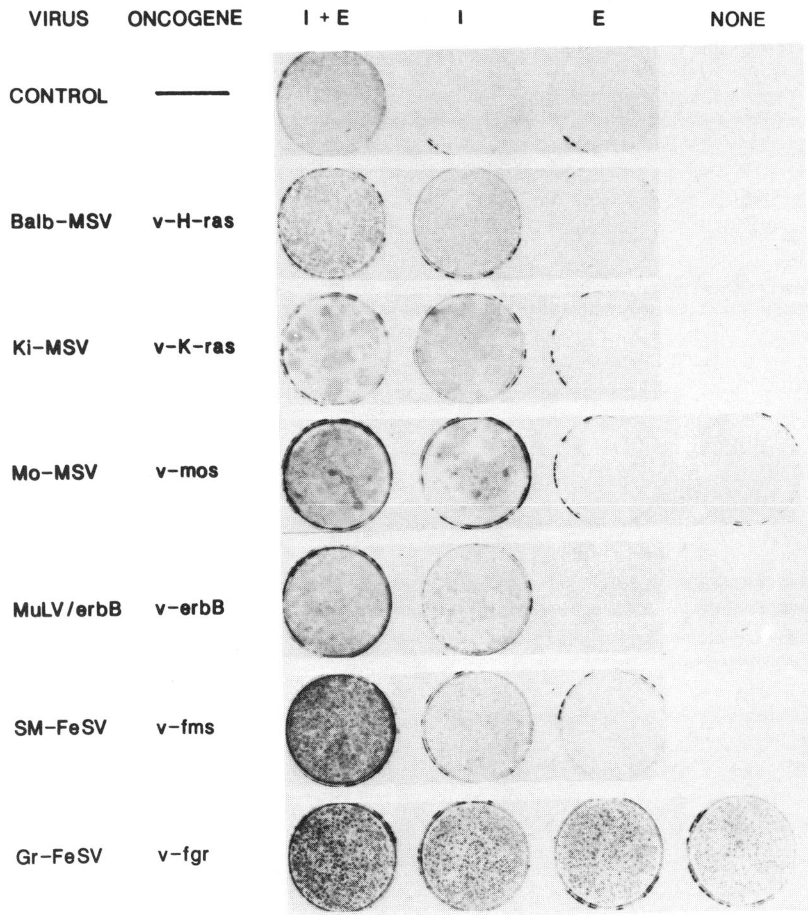

FIGURE 3. Growth factor requirements for growth of BALB/MK cells and retroviral-infected BALB/MK cells in chemically defined media. Uninfected BALB/MK cells and BALB/MK cells stably infected with the indicated viruses (containing the indicated oncogenes) were plated at a density of 3×10^4/dish on poly-D-lysine/fibronectin-precoated 60-mm dishes in chemically defined medium (see FIG. 1B) supplemented with the indicated growth factors. Plates were fixed and stained between 2 and 3 weeks. The conditions utilized for culture were (**I** + **E**) chemically defined medium containing insulin and EGF, (**I**) chemically defined medium containing insulin alone, (**E**) chemically defined medium containing EGF alone, and (**NONE**) unsupplemented chemically defined medium.

specific for the EGF pathway. Thus, the activities of *ras* and *mos* oncogenes, like those of v-*erb*B and v-*fms,* are within the major growth factor pathway complemented by IGF-1 action.[23]

The v-*fgr* oncogene conferred a new phenotype of growth factor-requirement abrogation to infected BALB/MK cells. This oncogene, a member of the *src* family, encodes a unique gene product, p70*gag*-actin-*fgr* protein, a fusion protein with a tyrosine kinase domain and a region of homology to the structural protein γ-actin.[37] V-*fgr*-transformed cells uniquely demonstrated growth in the absence of both insulin and EGF. Thus, v-*fgr,* acting through its tyrosine kinase product, appeared able to subvert both the insulin/IGF-1 and EGF signal transduction pathways. Conceivably, v-*fgr* may act at a point of convergence between the two complementary signal transduction pathways. Alternatively, its tyrosine kinase may activate both pathways at early steps in a promiscuous manner.

The reduction of growth factor requirements observed following introduction of viral oncogenes probably has relevance to the process of malignant transformation, which involves an escape from normal growth constraints. Previous studies have shown that malignant transformation is accompanied by a reduction of serum requirements[43] and by a loss of specific growth factor requirements.[15,17,44] Our present analysis of the ability of different oncogenes to complement EGF or insulin pathways is not comprehensive. Nonetheless, the emerging pattern is that abrogation of the EGF signal transduction pathway is more common than that for IGF-1. Recent studies have shown that genes within the insulin/IGF-1 pathway can be transforming. *In vitro* manipulation of the insulin receptor has been shown to activate its transforming ability.[45] Thus, the much higher frequency of EGF requirement-abrogating oncogenes transduced by retroviruses may reflect a greater number and/or higher potency of such genes. It is also possible that because IGF-1 is in plentiful supply *in vivo,*[46] genetic alterations in IGF-1 signal transduction may not be commonly selected by cells acquiring malignant properties.

REFERENCES

1. Doolittle, R. F., M. W. Hunkapiller, L. E. Hood, S. G. Devare, K. L. Robbins, S. A. Aaronson & H. N. Antoniades. 1983. Science **221:** 275-277.
2. Waterfield, M. D., G. T. Scrace, N. Whittle, P. Stroobant, A. Johnsson, A. Wasteson, B. Westermark, C. H. Heldin, J. S. Huang & T. F. Devel. 1983. Nature, **304:** 35-39.
3. Downward, J., Y. Yarden, E. Mayes, G. Scrace, N. Totty, P. Stockwell, A. Ullrich, J. Schlessinger & M. D. Waterfield. 1984. Nature **307:** 521-527.
4. Sherr, C. J., C. W. Rettenmier, R. Sacco, M. F. Roussel, A. T. Look & E. R. Stanley. 1985. Cell **41:** 665-676.
5. Coussens, L., C. VanBeueren, D. Smith, E. Chen, R. L. Mitchell, C. H. Isacke, I. M. Verma & A. Ullrich. 1986. Nature **320:** 277-280.
6. Sap, J., A. Munoz, K. Damm, Y. Golberg, J. Ghysdael, A. Leutz, H. Berg, & B. Vernstrom. 1981. Nature **324:** 635-640.
7. Weinberger, C., C. C. Thompson, E. S. Ong, R. Lebo, D. J. Gruol & R. M. Evans. 1986. Nature **324:** 641-646.
8. Kelly, K., B. H. Cochran, C. D. Stiles & P. Leder. 1983. Cell **35:** 603-610.
9. Muller, R., R. Bravo, J. Burckhardt & T. Curran. 1984. Nature **312:** 716-720.
10. Di Fiore, P. P., J. Falco, B. E. Weissman & S. A. Aaronson. 1988. Mol. Cell. Biol. **8:** 557-563.
11. Shih, T. Y., A. G. Papageorge, P. E. Stokes, M. O. Weeks & E. M. Scolnick. 1980. Nature **287:** 686-692.

12. MULCAHY, L. S., M. R. SMITH & D. W. STACEY. 1985. Nature **313:** 241-243.
13. WOLFMAN, A. & I. D. MACARA. 1987. Nature **325:** 359-361.
14. LACAL, J. C., J. MOSCAT & S. A. AARONSON. 1987. Nature **330:** 269-272.
15. WEISSMAN, B. E. & S. A. AARONSON. 1983. Cell **32:** 599-606.
16. WEISSMAN, B. E. & S. A. AARONSON. 1985. Mol. Cell. Biol. **5:** 3386-3396.
17. PIERCE, J. H., P. P. DI FIORE, S. A. AARONSON, M. POTTER, J. PUMPHREY, A. SCOTT & J. N. IHLE. 1985. Cell **41:** 685-693.
18. ROVERA, G., M. VALTIERI, F. MAVILIO & E. P. REDDY. 1987. Oncogene **1:** 29-35.
19. BARNS, D. W. & G. H. SATO. 1980. Cell **22:** 649-655.
20. PLEDGER, W. J., J. E. ESTES, T. H. HOWE & E. B. LEAF. 1984. *In* Mammalian Cell Culture: The Use of Serum-free, Hormone Supplemented Media. J. P. Mather, Ed.: 1-15. Plenum Press. New York.
21. BOTTENSTEIN, J. & G. SATO. 1980. Exp. Cell Res. **129:** 361-366.
22. BERTOLERO, F., M. E. KAIGHN, M. A. GONDA & U. SAFFIOTTI. 1984. Exp. Cell Res. **155:** 64-80.
23. FALCO, J. P., W. G. TAYLOR, P. P. DI FIORE, B. E. WEISSMAN & S. A. AARONSON. 1988. Oncogene **2:** 573-578.
24. HILL, D. J. & R. D. MILNER. 1985. Pediatr. Res. **19:** 879-886.
25. KOHN, C. R. 1985. Annu. Rev. Med. **36:** 429-451.
26. ZHAN, X. & M. GOLDFARB. 1986. Mol. Cell. Biol. **6:** 3541-3544.
27. GOSPODAROWICZ, D., G. NEUFELD & L. SCHNEIGERER. 1986. Endocrinology **46:** 187-204.
28. UHLRICH, S., O. LAGENTE, M. LENFANT & Y. COURTOIS. 1986. Biochem. Biophys. Res. Commun. **137:** 1205-1213.
29. RISS, T. L. & D. A. SIRBASKU. 1987. Cancer Res. **47:** 3776-3782.
30. HALABAN, R., S. GHOSH & A. BAIRD. 1987. In Vitro Cell. Dev. Biol. **23:** 47-52.
31. AARONSON, S. A. & M. BARBACID. 1978. J. Virol. **27:** 366-373.
32. KIRSTEN, W. H. & L. A. MAYER. 1967. J. Natl. Cancer Inst. **39:** 311-319.
33. ANDERSEN, P. E., S. G. DEVARE, S. R. TRONICK, R. W. ELLIS, S. A. AARONSON, & E. SCOLNICK. 1981. Cell **26:** 129-134.
34. ELLIS, R. W., D. DEFEO, T. Y. SHIH, M. A. GONDA, M. A. YOUNG, N. TSUCHIDA, D. R. LOWRY & E. M. SCOLNICK. 1981. Nature **292:** 506-511.
35. PORZIG, K. J., M. BARBACID & S. A. AARONSON. 1979. Virology **92:** 91-107.
36. GAZIT, A., J. H. PIERCE, M. H. KRAUS, P. P. DIFIORE, C. Y. PENNINGTON & S. A. AARONSON. 1986. J. Virol. **60:** 19-28.
37. NAHARRO, G., K. C. ROBBINS & E. P. REDDY. 1984. Science **223:** 63-66.
38. AARONSON, S. A. & W. P. ROWE. 1970. Virology **42:** 9-19.
39. OSKARSSON, M., W. L. MCCLEMENTS, D. G. BLAIR, J. V. MAIZEL & G. F. VANDE WOUDE, 1980. Science **207:** 1222.
40. MOELLING, K., B. MEIMAN, P. BEIMLING, U. R. RAPP & T. SANDER. 1984. Nature **312:** 558-561.
41. MAXWELL, S. A. & R. B. ARLINGHAUS. 1985. Virology **143:** 321-333.
42. STANLEY, E. R., L. J. GUILBERT, R. J. TUSHINSKI, & S. H. BARTELEMER. 1983. J. Cell. Biochem. **21:** 151-159.
43. TEMIN, H. M. 1967. Wistar Inst. Symp. Monogr. **7:** 103-116.
44. ETHIER, S. P. & K. C. CUNDIFF. 1987. Cancer Res. **47:** 5316-5322.
45. WANG, L. H., B. LIN, S. J. JONG, D. DIXON, L. ELLIS, R. A. ROTH & W. J. RUTTER. 1987. Proc. Natl. Acad. Sci. USA **84:** 5725-5729.
46. UNDERWOOD, L. E., A. J. D'ERCOLE, D. R. CLEMMONS & J. VANWYK. 1986. Clin. Endocrinol. Metabol. **1:** 59-77.

Cytogenetic and Molecular Analysis of Therapy-Related Leukemia[a]

JANET D. ROWLEY[b] AND MICHELLE M. LE BEAU[c]

Joint Section of Hematology/Oncology
Department of Medicine
The University of Chicago
Chicago, Illinois 60637

It has become apparent over the last fifteen years that one of the costs of medical progress in the successful treatment of lymphoma and solid tumors is the development of acute nonlymphocytic leukemia (ANLL), referred to here as therapy-related ANLL or t-ANLL. The incidence of leukemia is related to the types of therapy used, and it is greatest in patients who receive high doses of alkylating agents with radiotherapy.[1-3]

CYTOGENETIC STUDIES

Of particular interest from the cytogenetic view is that certain chromosome abnormalities are especially common in the leukemic cells of these t-ANLL patients. This pattern of abnormalities, first reported in 1977, has been confirmed by many laboratories.[4-7] The specific abnormalities involve the loss of chromosome 5 or part of its long arm, and/or the loss of chromosome 7 or part of its long arm. The long arm of a chromosome is represented by the letter "q", loss of a whole chromosome is indicated by a minus sign in front of the chromosome, and a deletion of part of the long arm is indicated by a minus sign after the chromosome; therefore, the shorthand for the patients just described would be −5, 5q−, −7, and 7q−, respectively.

We analyzed 63 patients with ANLL who had a history of previous treatment with radiation and/or chemotherapy, including three patients who had received a renal allograft.[8] Many of these patients were diagnosed on the basis of anemia or decreased white blood cell or platelet count; they were usually found to have a

[a]Supported in part by U.S. Department of Energy Contract No. DE-FG02-86ER60408, by USPHS Grant CA42557, by the G. Harold and Leila Y. Mathers Charitable Foundation, by the Zimulus Foundation, and by the University of Chicago Cancer Research Foundation.

[b]Address correspondence to Dr. Janet D. Rowley, The University of Chicago, 5841 S. Maryland, Box 420, Chicago, IL 60637

[c]Scholar of the Leukemia Society of America.

preleukemic or myelodysplastic state (MDS). The MDS patients often develop acute leukemia within a year if they do not die first from the consequences of their impaired bone marrow function. Of these 63 cases with therapy-related ANLL or MDS, 61 had a detectable clonal chromosome abnormality and 55 (87%) had loss of all or part of the long arm of chromosomes 5 and/or 7.[8] In comparison, only 56% of our 140 patients with ANLL *de novo* who were studied during the same period of time had an abnormal karyotype.[9] When the specific chromosomal changes in the t-ANLL patients were examined, 14 patients had a −5, 17 had a 5q−, 34 had a −7, and 7 had a 7q− chromosome. Abnormalities of both chromosomes 5 and 7 were seen in 17 patients. By contrast, only 22 of 140 patients (16%) with ANLL *de novo* had similar aberrations of one or both of these chromosomes. Only 5 of these 140 patients (4%) had abnormalities involving both chromosomes. More recent data on the frequency of abnormalities of chromosomes 5 and 7 in various subtypes of patients are summarized in TABLE 1.

The observations about the unusual chromosome pattern in therapy-related ANLL may have broad applicability. First, it is presumed that the acute leukemia is the result of exposure to known mutagenic agents. One can then turn the question around and ask, Can the karyotype of the leukemic cell be used to identify patients with ANLL *de novo* whose leukemia is related to occupational or environmental exposure to mutagens? Circumstantial evidence suggests that this answer may be yes. Our data at the University of Chicago, plus that of investigators in Sweden and Italy and data from the Fourth International Workshop on Chromosomes in Leukemia, indicate that leukemia patients who have worked in industries where they are exposed to chemicals, solvents, pesticides, and petroleum products have a higher frequency of loss of chromosomes 5 and/or 7 than do patients—such as students, housewives, and white collar workers—who are not exposed.[10–12]

Additional support for the idea that certain chromosome changes are indicators of mutagenic exposure comes from an analysis of the chromosome pattern of leukemic cells in patients of different ages. Several years ago it was noted that loss of chromosome 5 did not occur in children under 20 years of age, and loss of chromosome 7 was relatively rare.[13] The data from the Fourth Workshop support this observation.[12] Given the social implications of these observations, a study of a larger number of leukemia

TABLE 1. Frequency of Abnormalities of Chromosomes 5 and/or 7 in Disease Subtypes[a]

		Patients with Chromosome Abnormality									
		−5		5q−		−7		7q−		Both 5 & 7[c]	
Disease[b]	Total Patients	*n*	%	*n*	%	*n*	%	*n*	%	*n*	%
t-ANLL/t-MDS	57	7	12.3	7	12.3	20	35.1	7	12.3	16	28.1
ANLL *de novo*	96	8	8.3	27	28.1	19	19.8	20	20.8	22	22.9
MDS	34	0	0	18	52.9	6	17.6	4	11.8	6	17.6
Total, all diseases	187	15	8.0	52	27.8	45	24.1	31	16.6	44	23.5

[a] Published and unpublished data from the University of Chicago (Rowley & Le Beau).

[b] t-ANLL, therapy-related acute nonlymphocytic leukemia; t-MDS, therapy-related myelodysplastic state.

[c] Majority of abnormalities of chromosome 5 are 5q−.

patients with the inclusion of a more accurate and detailed history of occupation, hobbies, and the pattern of familial diseases is required to confirm these preliminary data.

When the entire chromosome is missing, one cannot determine whether some specific region is more important than another in the development of leukemia. But in the patients we have who have lost only part of one of these two chromosomes, analysis of the karyotype of the leukemic cells can be used to determine whether a certain specific region is consistently missing. We have evidence for both chromosomes 5 and 7 that such a pattern occurs. In a study in 1982, analysis of the region of chromosome 5 that was deleted in 17 different patients with t-ANLL showed that bands 5q23 and 5q31 were consistently deleted in all of them.[14] This was called the critical region, and it was proposed that it contained the genes whose loss was important in the leukemic transformation observed in these patients. Our more recent analysis of 80 patients showed that all patients who had lost only part of chromosome 5 had a loss of 5q31. FIGURE 1 illustrates the data on 5q deletions for patients with different hematological diseases.

MOLECULAR STUDIES

The observation that 5q31 alone appears to be the critical chromosome band is very important, because it allows us to concentrate on a single chromosome band. Since one band contains more than 5 megabases (5×10^6 nucleotide pairs), analysis of even this limited region is a major undertaking.

One of the major scientific benefits of cytogenetic analysis of tumor tissue is that it provides critical clues about the location of genes that are fundamentally involved in the malignant process. During the past five years, our attention has been focused on mapping genes on chromosome 5. We have done this in order to identify the gene(s) involved in mutagen-induced leukemia. Although it seemed unlikely that we would be fortunate enough to find that one of these genes was involved in the transformation process, collectively they provided us with genetic probes to use in searching for DNA rearrangements or deletions.

Molecular approaches have recently been applied to the study of various kinds of tumors in attempts to identify specific DNA sequences that might be involved in the transformed phenotype. Alterations in the structure and/or expression of cellular oncogenes (proto-oncogenes) are now known to be involved in the development of numerous types of human cancer.[15] Many of the mutational changes involved in the conversion of proto-oncogenes into functional oncogenes appear to be dominant, since the malignant phenotype can be expressed in non-malignant host cells after transfection with the mutated oncogene; these investigations have identified primarily a family of cellular *RAS* genes[d] that have experienced point mutations.

Some tumors apparently involve genetic changes that are recessive at the cellular level. These include cancers that have hereditary forms, such as retinoblastoma and Wilms' tumor. It has been proposed that in hereditary cases, an individual inherits one copy of a recessive mutation from a parent and that this mutation must become

[d] Throughout this paper, human genes are symbolized by capital letters in italics, as recommended by the guidelines approved at the Ninth International Workshop on Human Gene Mapping (Paris, 1987); see Ref. 39.

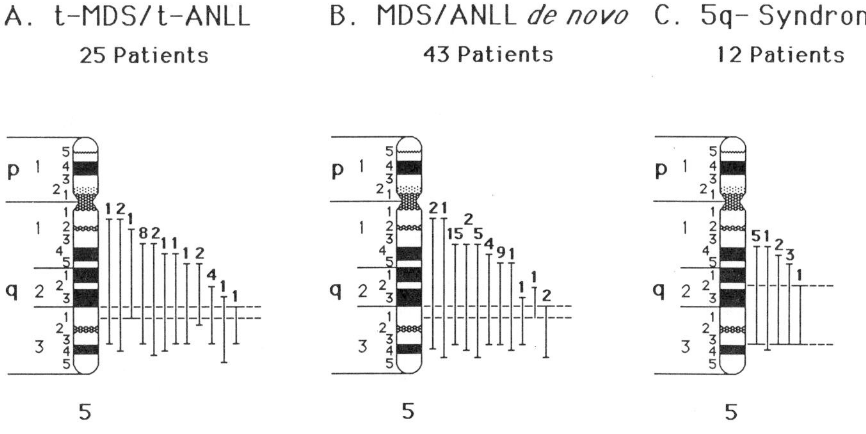

FIGURE 1. Critical region on chromosome 5. The region of the deletion of 5q in patients with (**A**) t-MDS/t-ANLL, (**B**) MDS/ANLL *de novo*, and (**C**) 5q− syndrome. *Vertical bars* indicate the location of the deleted segments observed in various patients; *numbers above bars* are the number of patients with the same deletion. *Dashed horizontal lines* show location of the smallest overlapping region that is deleted in every patient: the critical region. We propose that the critical region 5q31 (**A,B**) is the location of one or more genes involved in leukemogenesis. t-MDS, therapy-related myelodysplastic state; t-ANLL, therapy-related acute nonlymphocytic leukemia.

homozygous in the appropriate somatic cell for a tumor to develop.[16] Specific deletions as a constitutional abnormality, 13q− and 11p−, respectively, have been observed in some patients with retinoblastoma and Wilms' tumor.[17,18] The presence of these deletions led to the hypothesis that the retinoblastoma (*RB*) locus was located in chromosome band 13q14, and that the Wilms' tumor (*WT*) gene was located in 11p13. Another line of evidence is derived from recent molecular studies of retinoblastomas, which have demonstrated that homozygosity may result from mechanisms other than a chromosomal deletion. Specifically, analysis of restriction fragment length polymorphisms (RFLPs) in the genomic DNA from normal cells and tumor cells of the same individuals showed that several retinoblastomas had become homozygous at one or more loci on chromosome 13 for which heterozygosity was observed in the normal cells of the same patient.[19] This change in genotype resulted from either deletion, chromosomal nondisjunction (chromosome loss with or without reduplication of the remaining homolog), or mitotic recombination.

Friend *et al.* have recently described a cDNA clone, which was isolated on the basis of its chromosomal location, that has the properties of a gene which when altered or absent predisposes to retinoblastoma.[20,21] This work was extended by Lee *et al.*, whose analysis of the *RB* gene revealed that this gene contains at least 12 exons distributed over a region of 100 kb (kilobases).[22] Features of the predicted amino acid sequence include a potential metal-binding domain similar to that found in nucleic acid-binding proteins.

There are few data currently available indicating that similar mechanisms may be operating in acute leukemia; however, the high frequency of chromosome loss or deletion in leukemic cells, which may lead to loss of heterozygosity and hemizygosity, suggests that a role for such mechanisms in the pathogenesis of leukemia should be considered. In fact, in collaboration with Dr. Diaz in our research group, we have shown that the alpha-beta interferon gene cluster on the short arm of chromosome 9 is frequently deleted in hematopoietic cell lines, particularly those derived from lymphoid leukemia.[23]

Some very intriguing results of DNA analysis are also providing support for the hypothesis that development of some myeloid leukemias may be related to loss of heterozygosity. A comparison of DNA obtained from paired samples of leukemic and normal cells has shown that the leukemic cells of one patient with t-ANLL whom we have studied at the University of Chicago have become homozygous for at least one marker (D7S372, detected by the probe pYNB3.1R) located on chromosome 7, band 7q32 to 7qter.[24] Whether this is due to crossing over or to loss of one chromosome 7 and reduplication of the other has not been determined at present. This patient had normal chromosome 7s in his leukemic cells. Moreover, Shannon *et al.* have studied DNA from two siblings with ANLL and monosomy 7 in their leukemic cells. The retained chromosome 7 in one child was inherited from the mother.[25] The other child had a chromosome 7 that appeared to have undergone somatic crossing over. Markers on the proximal long arm (band 7q22) were maternal, whereas one on the distal long arm (band 7q31) was paternal; therefore, crossing over occurred somewhere in the midportion of the long arm. Our data provide clear evidence that some proportion of patients who appear to have two normal 7s may have had chromosome rearrangements that lead to homozygous loss of a cancer-suppressor gene. The pattern for the family reported by Shannon *et al.* suggests that there was a chromosome change that leads to loss of one chromosome 7, presumably containing the normal suppressor gene, with the presence of a complementary defect in the other chromosome 7. Careful mapping of the region of crossing over on chromosome 7 in a number of patients should lead to a more precise identification of the location of this gene. Presumably, similar studies regarding chromosome 5 will reveal comparable DNA changes.

MAPPING GENES ON CHROMOSOME 5

We have made remarkable progress in mapping genes to the region of chromosome 5 that is deleted in leukemia *de novo* and in leukemia that is secondary to treatment. The major surprise has been the number of genes related to regulation of cell proliferation that are located on chromosome 5, bands 5q23 to 5q33. The genes for granulocyte-macrophage colony-stimulating factor (*GMCSF*)[e] and macrophage colony-stimulating factor (*MCSF* or *CSF1*), and the proto-oncogene *FMS*—the gene encoding the receptor for the *MCSF* or *CSF1* protein—have been mapped to bands 5q23 to 5q33.[26] All three genes were frequently missing in patients with large deletions of 5q and *GMCSF* was consistently deleted in all patients.

The *IL3* (interleukin-3)[e] gene encodes a hematopoietic colony-stimulating factor that is capable of supporting the proliferation of a broad range of hematopoietic cell types.[27] By using somatic cell hybrids and *in situ* chromosomal hybridization, this gene has been localized to human chromosome 5 at bands q23-31. By *in situ* hybridization, the *IL3* gene was found to be deleted in the 5q− chromosome of four patients with ANLL or MDS.

[e] For nomenclature of genes for colony-stimulating factors and interleukins, see Ref. 39.

More recently, we have localized the genes encoding other hematopoietic growth factors, namely, *IL4* (interleukin-4; B cell stimulatory factor-1) and *IL5* (interleukin-5; eosinophil-differentiation factor), to chromosome 5, at bands q23-31.[28] *In situ* hybridization of the *IL4* and *IL5* probes to normal metaphase chromosomes resulted in specific labeling only of chromosome 5. Of 100 metaphase cells examined from the hybridization assay with the *IL4* probe, 31 (31%) were labeled on region q2 or q3 of one or both chromosome 5 homologs (FIG. 2A). Of 224 labeled sites observed, 54 (24.1%) were located on this chromosome. These sites were clustered at bands q23-32, and this cluster represented 17.4% (39/224) of all labeled sites ($p < 0.0005$). The largest cluster of grains was observed at 5q23-31.

Off 100 metaphase cells examined from the hybridization assay with the *IL5* probe, 36 (36%) were labeled on region q2 or q3 of one or both chromosome 5 homologs (FIG. 2B). Fifty-nine of 237 labeled sites (24.9%) were located on this chromosome; of these, 47 sites were clustered at bands q22-33, and this cluster represented 19.8% (47/237) of all labeled sites ($p < 0.0005$). The largest cluster of grains was observed at 5q23-31. Hybridizations with the *IL4* and *IL5* probes were repeated three times and gave similar results in each experiment.

To determine the relationship of *IL4* and *IL5* to the critical region of chromosome 5, we hybridized these probes to metaphase cells obtained from bone marrow aspirates of a total of four patients with the refractory anemia (RA) 5q− syndrome, with MDS (RA), or with t-ANLL characterized by a deletion of 5q [del(5q)]. In all four cases, specific labeling was observed on the normal chromosome 5 homologs, but not on the rearranged homologs. Thus, these results indicate that the leukemic cells from these patients were hemizygous for the *IL4* and *IL5* loci as a result of an interstitial deletion of 5q. Our data confirm the localization of the *IL5* locus reported by Sutherland *et al.*[29]

Other genes of potential importance that also map to 5q are *CD14* and *EGR1*. The *CD14* gene encodes a myeloid-specific transmembrane protein which is expressed

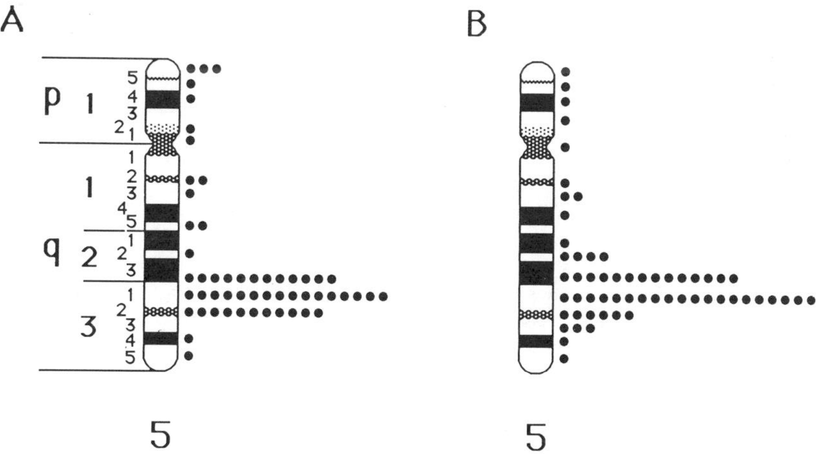

FIGURE 2. Distribution of labeled sites on chromosome 5 in 100 normal metaphase cells from phytohemagglutinin-stimulated peripheral blood lymphocytes that were hybridized with a ^{3}H-labeled *IL4*-specific (**A**) or *IL5*-specific (**B**) probe. Each *dot* indicates one labeled site observed in the corresponding band. Hybridization of these probes resulted in specific labeling of the distal long arm of chromosome 5; the largest cluster of grains was located at 5q23-31.

on the surface of mature granulocytes and monocytes, but not on other hematopoietic cells.[30] The *CD14* protein is recognized by the monoclonal antibodies Mo2, My4, LeuM3, UCHM1, and MoS39. Analysis of the structure of the *CD14* genes and the encoded protein suggests that the protein may be a cellular receptor. By using *in situ* chromosome hybridization, the gene has been localized to bands 5q23-31, the same bands to which the *GMCSF* and *IL3* genes were localized. Analysis of metaphase cells from 5 leukemia patients with a del(5q) after hybridization with a *CD14* probe revealed that the *CD14* gene was deleted from these patients.

EGR1 is an early growth response gene that displays *FOS*-like induction kinetics in fibroblasts, epithelial cells, and lymphocytes following mitogenic stimulation. Sequence analysis of murine *Egr1* cDNA predicts a protein with DNA-binding zinc fingers. The human *EGR1* gene maps to chromosome 5 (bands 5q23-31).[31] *EGR1* mRNA increases dramatically during cardiac and neural cell differentiation or following membrane depolarization *in vitro* and *in vivo,* and it is developmentally regulated during differentiation of F9 teratocarcinoma cells. These results in conjunction with the information concerning the primary structure of the predicted *Egr1*-encoded protein suggest that *EGR1* may function as a nuclear second messenger in diverse biological processes.

We have shown that the genes for a number of growth factor receptors are within the segment of chromosome 5 deleted in the refractory anemia 5q− syndrome and in ANLL (FIG. 3). Our results suggest that genes, especially those directed toward regulating growth and differentiation of hematopoietic cells, may play some role in the pathogenesis of these disorders. The relative variability of the breakpoints in the del(5q) suggests that malignant transformation results from the loss of a critical DNA sequence rather than from the consistent juxtaposition of two genes, as in the case of *ABL* and *BCR* in chronic myelogenous leukemia. The identification of a consistently deleted critical region which we have narrowed to include only band 5q31 further supports this hypothesis. A chromosome deletion may result in a reduction in the level of a corresponding gene product or in the loss of a wild type gene, thereby either allowing the expression of a recessive mutant allele on the homologous chromosome or causing the loss of function of "suppressor" alleles. The latter mechanism has recently been demonstrated in retinoblastoma. It should be noted that no evidence for homozygous deletion of any probe was obtained with *in situ* hybridization. That is, the probes described above hybridized to the normal chromosome 5 in all the patients studied. This is, of course, no measure of the function of these genes. It is quite possible, however, that the genes important in leukemogenesis may be unrelated to any of the specific genes that we have mapped.

With respect to the *CSF* genes, recent data suggest that in some cases of ANLL, constitutive (autocrine) expression of the *GMCSF* gene results in autonomous proliferation *in vitro* of colony-forming leukemia cells.[32] Other experimental data indicate that expression of *CSF* genes is important in malignant transformation. Specifically, GMCSF or IL3 protein production induced by a retroviral expression vector resulted in CSF protein-independence in formerly factor-dependent murine hematopoietic cell lines; these cells were tumorigenic (leukemogenic) when inoculated into nude mice, whereas the parental cell line was not.[33,34] Thus, in these examples, the *CSF* genes appear to act as "dominant" oncogenes.

Autocrine growth as a result of aberrant expression of a growth factor gene located on chromosome 5 has not yet been documented for myeloid leukemia cells with a del(5q). However, loss of genes for the CSF protein receptor may be the relevant genetic alteration in these leukemia cells. For example, an altered level of expression of CSF protein receptor(s) or the production of an altered receptor may affect the proliferation of myeloid cells. In this regard, the v-*fms* product, which differs from the cellular FMS glycoprotein at the final residues of the carboxyl terminus, appears to be an unregulated kinase that provides growth stimulatory signals in the absence of ligand.[35] Moreover, introduction of the v-*fms* gene into simian virus-40-immortalized, CSF1 protein-dependent macrophages resulted in factor-independence and tumorigenicity in nude mice. These results raise the possibility that critical alterations in the kinase domain of FMS might contribute to the pathogenesis of hematological malignancies.

However, the properties of the *EGR1* gene suggest that it may be a more suitable candidate than those encoding growth factors or receptors for playing a role in the malignant transformation of 5q− myeloid cells. Since EGR1 protein binds to DNA and has transcriptional regulatory activity, it may function as a tumor suppressor locus whose absence or loss of function could lead to deregulated cell growth.[31,36]

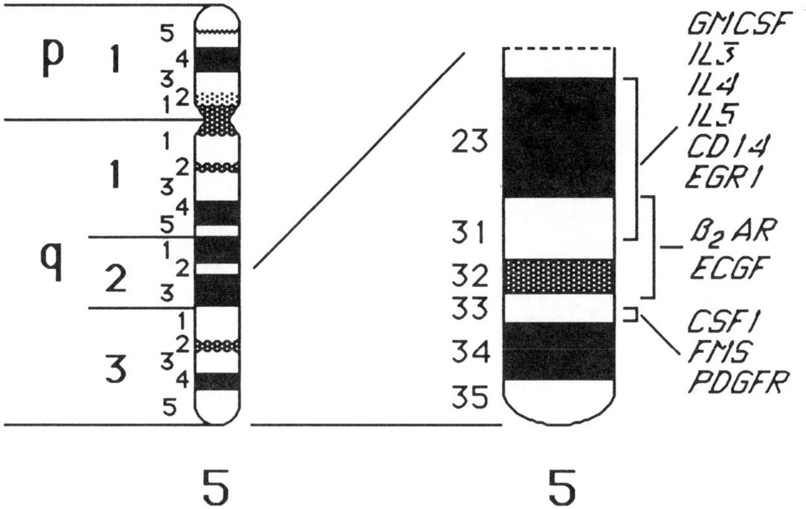

FIGURE 3. Map of the genes located in the distal region of the long arm of chromosome 5. Genes for many of the hematopoietic growth factors and growth factor receptors are located in or near band 5q31, which our data show is the critical region of 5q. PDGFR, platelet-derived growth factor receptor; ECGF, endothelial cell growth factor; β_2AR, β_2 adrenergic receptor.

At the very least, use of these DNA probes is critical for the process of beginning to assemble a map of 5q. It has been shown that *GMCSF* and *IL3* are only 9 kb apart.[37] The mapping data of Dr. Carol Westbrook and colleagues, using pulsed-field gel electrophoresis, suggest that *IL4* and *IL5* are contained within the same 315 kb *Bss*H II fragment.[38] Their data also suggest that the minimum distance between these two linkage groups is at least 120 kb. It is possible that these two groups of genes are relatively close but are separated by a G-C rich region such as an HTF island that contains a clustering of enzyme cleavage sites. We have not yet identified rearrangements of any of the genes located on 5q with standard or pulsed field gel electrophoresis using DNA isolated from leukemic cells with a 5q− chromosome.

CONCLUSION

The studies presented here represent a historical overview of an analysis of a particularly challenging form of acute leukemia. In the last decade we have progressed from identifying two recurring chromosome abnormalities in therapy-related leukemia to refining the localization of the segment of each chromosome that may contain the critical genes. In parallel, we began to map genes related to regulation of hematopoiesis and found that many of them were located on chromosome 5 within or adjacent to this critical region. Moreover, most of these genes were contained within the segment of DNA that was lost in the deletions of 5q. We are continuing the mapping of new genes to chromosome 5. At the same time, we are using the newer techniques of long-range DNA mapping with various forms of pulsed-field gel electrophoresis. It is clear that with perseverance, this combined approach of identifying new genes and anonymous DNA segments located in band 5q31 and using partial DNA digests and pulsed-field gel electrophoresis to link these probes will provide us with a detailed map of 5q31. With this map we should be able to identify very small deletions or rearrangements of genes on the normal chromosome 5. This information will allow us to clone the genes in this segment and to identify which gene(s) contribute to the leukemic phenotype of the myeloid cells.

Identification of such genes will open up a new era in our understanding of the process of leukemogenesis. It will provide us with the probes to examine leukemic cells that appear to have normal chromosomes 5 and 7 by cytogenetic criteria and to determine whether genetic changes have occurred that cannot be detected cytogenetically.

Of most importance to physicians caring for these patients, they can begin to approach the treatment of patients with losses of chromosome 5 and/or 7 with more insight. These leukemic patients are among the most refractory to therapy and a large proportion die relatively soon after the diagnosis of the leukemia is made. Finally, knowledge of even one step in the series of changes leading to leukemogenesis will permit a rational study to determine whether some patients may be more prone to develop leukemia because of abnormalities present in the critical gene. This could lead to different approaches to therapy of primary malignant diseases in these susceptible patients. Thus, the search for the critical genes on these two chromosomes is an undertaking that has very high potential benefit.

REFERENCES

1. Rosner, F. & H. Grunwald. 1975. Hodgkin's disease and acute leukemia: Report of eight cases and review of the literature. Am. J. Med. **58:** 339-353.
2. Coleman, C. N., C. J. Williams, A. Flint, E. J. Glatstein, S. A. Rosenberg & H. S. Kaplan. 1977. Hematologic neoplasia in patients treated for Hodgkin's disease. N. Engl. J. Med. **297:** 1249-1252.
3. Greene, M. H., J. D. Boice, Jr., B. E. Greer, J. A. Blessing & A. J. Dembo. 1982. Acute nonlymphocytic leukemia after therapy with alkylating agents for ovarian cancer. N. Engl. J. Med. **307:** 1416-1421.
4. Rowley, J. D., H. M. Golomb & J. Vardiman. 1977. Non-random chromosomal abnormalities in acute non-lymphocytic leukemia in patients treated for Hodgkin disease and non-Hodgkin lymphomas. Blood **50:** 759-770.
5. Pedersen-Bjergaard, J., P. Philip, N. T. Pedersen, K. Hou-Jensen, A. Svejgaard, G. Jensen & N. I. Nissen. 1984. Acute nonlymphocytic leukemia, preleukemia and

acute myeloproliferative syndrome secondary to treatment of other malignant diseases. Cancer **54:** 452-462.

6. ARTHUR, D. C. & C. D. BLOOMFIELD. 1984. Banded chromosome analysis in patients with treatment-associated acute nonlymphocytic leukemia. Cancer Genet. Cytogenet. **12:** 189-199.
7. GROUPE FRANCAIS DE CYTOGENETIQUE HEMATOLOGIQUE. 1984. Chromosome analysis of 63 cases of secondary nonlymphoid blood disorders: A cooperative study. Cancer Genet. Cytogenet. **12:** 95-104.
8. LE BEAU, M. M., K. A. ALBAIN, J. W. VARDIMAN, R. A. LARSON, R. BLOUGH, E. M. DAVIS, H. M. GOLOMB & J. D. ROWLEY. 1986. Clinical and cytogenetic correlations in 63 patients with therapy-related myelodysplastic syndromes and acute nonlymphocytic leukemia: Further evidence for characteristic abnormalities of chromosomes Nos. 5 and 7. J. Clin. Oncol. **4:** 325-345.
9. LARSON, R. A., M. M. LE BEAU, J. W. VARDIMAN, J. R. TESTA, H. M. GOLOMB & J. D. ROWLEY. 1983. The predictive value of initial cytogenetic studies in 148 adults with acute nonlymphocytic leukemia: A 12 year study (1970-1982). Cancer Genet. Cytogenet. **10:** 219-236.
10. GOLOMB, H. M., G. ALIMENA, J. D. ROWLEY, J. W. VARDIMAN, J. R. TESTA & C. SOVIK. 1982. Correlation of occupation and karyotype in adults with acute nonlymphocytic leukemia. Blood **60:** 404-411.
11. MITELMAN, F., P. G. NILSSON & L. BRANDT. 1981. Chromosome pattern, occupation, and clinical features in patients with acute nonlymphocytic leukemia. Cancer Genet. Cytogenet. **4:** 197-214.
12. Fourth International Workshop on Chromosomes in Leukemia, 1982. 1984. Cancer Genet. Cytogenet. **11:** 249-360.
13. ROWLEY, J. D., G. ALIMENA, O. M. GARSON, A. HAGEMEIJER, F. MITELMAN & E. L. PRIGOGINA. 1982. A collaborative study of the relationship of the morphologic type of acute nonlymphocytic leukemia with patient age and karyotype. Blood **59:** 1013-1022.
14. ROWLEY, J. D. 1983. Chromosome changes in leukemic cells as indicators of mutagenic exposure. *In* Chromosomes and Cancer: Bristol-Myers Symposia Series. J. D. Rowley & J. E. Ultmann, Eds. Vol. 5: 140-159. Academic Press. New York.
15. BISHOP, J. M. 1987. The molecular genetics of cancer. Science **235:** 305-311.
16. KNUDSON, A. G. 1977. Genetics and etiology of human cancer. Adv. Hum. Genet. **8:** 1-66.
17. YUNIS, J. J. & N. RAMSAY. 1978. Retinoblastoma and subband deletion of chromosome 13. Am. J. Dis. Child. **132:** 161-163.
18. RICCARDI, V. M., E. SUJANSKY, A. C. SMITH & U. FRANCKE. 1978. Chromosomal imbalance in the aniridia-Wilms' tumor association: 11p interstitial deletion. Pediatrics **61:** 604-610.
19. CAVENEE, W. K., T. P. DRYJA, R. A. PHILLIPS, W. F. BENEDICT, R. GODBOUT, B. L. GALLIE, A. L. MURPHREE, L. C. STRONG & R. L. WHITE. 1983. Expression of recessive alleles by chromosomal mechanisms in retinoblastoma. Nature **305:** 779-784.
20. DRYJA, T. P., W. CAVENEE, R. WHITE, J. M. RAPAPORT, R. PETERSON, D. M. ALBERT & G. A. BRUNS. 1984. Homozygosity of chromosome 13 in retinoblastoma. N. Engl. J. Med. **310:** 550-553.
21. FRIEND, S. H., R. BERNARDS, S. ROGELJ, R. A. WEINBERG, J. M. RAPAPORT, D. M. ALBERT & T. P. DRYJA. 1986. A human DNA segment with properties of the gene that predisposes to retinoblastoma and osteosarcoma. Nature **323:** 643-646.
22. LEE, W. H., R. BOOKSTEIN, F. HONG, L. J. YOUNG, J. Y. SHEW & E. Y. LEE. 1987. Human retinoblastoma susceptibility gene: Cloning, identification, and sequence. Science **235:** 1394-1399.
23. DIAZ, M. O., S. ZIEMIN, M. M. LE BEAU, P. PITHA, S. D. SMITH, R. R. CHILCOTE & J. D. ROWLEY. 1988. Homozygous deletion of the α and β_1-interferon genes in human leukemia and derived cell lines. Proc. Natl. Acad. Sci. USA **85:** 5259-5263.
24. NEUMAN, W. L., R. A. LARSON, M. M. LE BEAU, J. L. SCHWARTZ, J. D. ROWLEY & R. A. FARBER. 1988. Loss of heterozygosity in secondary acute nonlymphocytic leukemia. Am. J. Hum. Genet. **43:** A29.

25. SHANNON, K. M., A. G. TURHAN, S. S. Y. CHANG, A. M. BOWCOCK, P. C. G. ROGERS, W. L. CARROLL, M. J. COWAN, B. E. GLADER, C. J. EAVES, A. C. EAVES & Y. W. KAN. 1989. Familial bone marrow monosomy 7: Evidence that the predisposing locus is not on the long arm of chromosome 7. J. Clin. Inv. In press.
26. LE BEAU, M. M. 1987. Cytogenetic and molecular analysis of the del(5q) in myeloid disorders: Evidence for the involvement of colony-stimulating factor and *FMS* genes. *In* Recent Advances in Leukemia and Lymphoma. R. P. Gale & D. W. Golde, Eds. Vol. 61: 71-81. Alan R. Liss, Inc. New York.
27. LE BEAU, M. M., N. D. EPSTEIN, A. W. NIENHUIS, Y-C. YANG, S. C. CLARK & J. D. ROWLEY. 1987. *IL-3* maps to human chromosome 5 and is deleted in myeloid leukemias with a del(5q). Proc. Natl. Acad. Sci. USA **84:** 5913-5917.
28. LE BEAU, M. M., R. S. LEMONS, R. ESPINOSA, R. A. LARSON, N. ARZI & J. D. ROWLEY. 1989. *IL-4* and *IL-5* map to human chromosome 5 in a region encoding growth factors and receptors and are deleted in myeloid leukemias with a del(5q). Blood. **73:** 647-650.
29. SUTHERLAND, G. R., E. BAKER, D. F. CALLEN, H. D. CAMPBELL, I. G. YOUNG, C. J. SANDERSON, O. M. GARSON, A. F. LOPEZ & M. A. VODAS. 1988. Interleukin 5 is at 5q31 and is deleted in the 5q− syndrome. Blood **71:** 1150-1152.
30. GOYERT, S. M., E. FERRERO, W. J. RETTIG, A. K. YENAMANDRA, F. OBATA & M. M. LE BEAU. 1988. The CD14 monocyte differentiation antigen maps to a region encoding growth factors and receptors. Science **239:** 497-500.
31. SUKHATME, V. P., X. CAO, L. C. CHANG, C. H. TSAI-MORRIS, D. STAMENKOVICH, P. C. P. FERREIRA, D. R. COHEN, S. A. EDWARDS, T. B. SHOWS, T. CURRAN, M. M. LE BEAU & E. D. ADAMSON. 1988. A zinc finger-encoding gene coregulated with c-*fos* during growth and differentiation and after cellular depolarization. Cell **53:** 37-43.
32. YOUNG, D. C. & J. D. GRIFFIN. 1986. Autocrine secretion of GM-CSF in acute myeloblastic leukemia. Blood **68:** 1178-1181.
33. LANG, R. A., D. METCALF, N. M. GOUGH, A. R. DUNN & T. J. GONDA. 1985. Expression of a hemapoietic growth factor cDNA in a factor-dependent cell line results in autonomous growth and tumorigenicity. Cell **43:** 531-542.
34. WONG, P. M., S. W. CHUNG & A. W. NIENHUIS. 1987. Retroviral transfer and expression of the interleukin-3 gene in hemopoietic cells. Genes Dev. **1:** 358-365.
35. WHEELER, E. F., C. W. RETTENMIER, A. T. LOOK & C. J. SHERR. 1986. The v-fms oncogene induces factor independence and tumorigenicity in CSF-1 dependent macrophage cell line. Nature **324:** 377-380.
36. KLEIN, G. 1988. The approaching era of the tumor suppressor genes. Science **238:** 1539-1545.
37. YANG, Y-C., S. KOVACIC, R. KRIZ, S. WOLF, S. C. CLARK, T. E. WELLEMS, A. NIENHUIS & N. EPSTEIN. 1988. The human genes for GM-CSF and IL3 are closely linked in tandem on chromosome 5. Blood **71:** 958-961.
38. LE BEAU, M. M., S. CHANDRASEKHARRAPA, R. S. LEMONS, J. L. SCHWARTZ, R. A. LARSON & C. A. WESTBROOK. 1989. Molecular and Cytogenetic Analysis of Abnormalities of Chromosome 5 in Myeloid Disorders: Chromosomal Localization and Physical Mapping of *IL-4* and *IL-5*. Cold Spr. Harb. Symp. Quant. Biol.: Cancer Cells, Vol. 7. In press.
39. Ninth International Workshop on Human Gene Mapping, Paris Conference, 1987. 1987. Cytogenet. Cell Genet. **46:** 11–27.

The Molecular Control of Normal and Leukemic Hematopoiesis: Myeloid Cells as a Model System[a]

LEO SACHS

Department of Genetics
Weizmann Institute of Science
Rehovot 76100, Israel

Charlotte Friend was always optimistic and had a wide range of interests in different subjects. Her death is a tragedy for all of us. It is a loss to the wider scientific community, but even more so for those with whom she was most closely associated. Our meetings will not be the same without her. She and I often agreed in discussions, and I trust that what I have to say today would have met with her approval.

INTRODUCTION

The multiplication and differentiation of normal cells are controlled by different regulatory molecules. These regulators have to interact to achieve the correct balance between cell multiplication and differentiation during embryogenesis and the normal functioning of the adult individual. The origin and progression of malignancy result from genetic changes that uncouple the normal balance between multiplication and differentiation so that there are too many growing cells. This uncoupling can occur in various ways.[1,2] When cells have become malignant, how can malignancy be suppressed so that malignant cells revert back to non-malignant? Malignant cells can have different abnormalities in the controls for multiplication and differentiation. Do all the abnormalities have to be corrected, or can they be by-passed in order to suppress malignancy? In this paper, I will mainly discuss results with normal and leukemic myeloid hematopoietic cells that have been used as a model system to answer these questions.

[a] This research is supported by the Ebner Foundation for Leukemia Research; the National Foundation for Cancer Research, Bethesda; and the Jerome A. and Estelle R. Newman Assistance Fund.

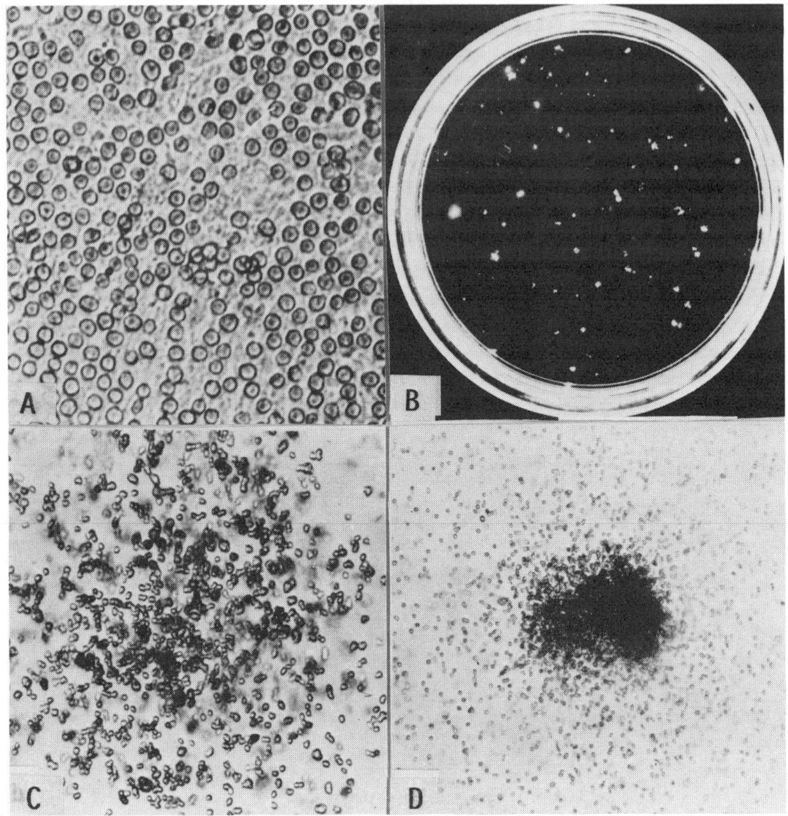

FIGURE 1. (**A**) Culture of mouse mast cells that have multiplied and differentiated on a feeder layer of mouse embryo cells.[3] (**B**-**D**) Clones of macrophages and granulocytes in cultures of normal blood cell precursors incubated with the appropriate myeloid cell regulatory protein: (**B**) Petri dish with clones,[4] (**C**) macrophage clone,[7] and (**D**) granulocyte clone.[7]

NORMAL GROWTH- AND DIFFERENTIATION-INDUCING PROTEINS

An understanding of the mechanisms that control multiplication (growth) and differentiation of normal cells would seem to be an essential requirement to elucidate the origin and suppression of malignancy. The establishment of a cell culture system for the clonal development of normal hematopoietic cells in liquid and semi-solid medium (FIG. 1)[3-5] and the discovery in cell culture supernatants of the regulators of this clonal development[6,7] has led to the identification of a family of different myeloid cell growth- and differentiation-inducing proteins. These include four different myeloid cell growth-inducing proteins called macrophage and granulocyte inducers-type 1 (MGI-1), or colony-stimulating factors (CSF), including interleukin-3 (IL-

3) (TABLE 1).[8–11] Cloning of the mouse and human genes for these four growth inducers has shown that these four genes are unrelated in nucleotide sequence.[12]

How do normal myeloid precursor cells induced to multiply by these growth inducers develop into clones that contain mature differentiated cells that stop multiplying when they terminally differentiate? It appears unlikely that a growth inducer which triggers cell multiplication is also a differentiation inducer whose action includes the stopping of cell multiplication in mature cells. Indeed, proteins that induce myeloid cell differentiation but not growth have been identified and have been called macrophage and granulocyte inducers-type 2 (MGI-2), or differentiation factors.[1,8,13–15] Studies on the amino acid sequence, neutralization by monoclonal antibody,[16] and myeloid cell differentiation-inducing activity of recombinant MGI-2 protein have shown that MGI-2 is interleukin-6 (IL-6).[17,18] Each of the myeloid growth- and differentiation-inducing proteins has a different cell surface receptor.[19,20]

Experiments with normal myeloid precursor cells have shown that in these cells any one of the four growth-inducing proteins enhances cell viability and induces cell multiplication and production of differentiation-inducing protein (FIGS. 2, 3).[1,8,10] The myeloid differentiation inducer MGI-2/IL-6 activates differentiation directly, whereas the myeloid growth inducers activate differentiation indirectly by inducing the production of differentiation inducer (TABLE 1, FIG. 3). This induction of the differentiation inducer by the growth inducer is thus an effective mechanism to couple normal growth with differentiation, a coupling mechanism that may also apply to other cell types. Differences in the time of the switch-on of the differentiation inducer would produce differences in the amount of cell multiplication before differentiation. A differentiation inducer can also switch on production of a growth inducer in myeloid cells.[19] The studies on myeloid cells have thus shown that there are different proteins that participate in the developmental program, growth inducers and differentiation inducers, and that there is a cascade of interactions between growth inducers and differentiation inducers in development.

TABLE 1. Normal Myeloid Hematopoietic Growth- and Differentiation-Inducing Proteins

Nomenclature[a]	Differentiated Cell Type	Induction of Differentiation: Direct	Induction of Differentiation: Indirect[b]
Growth inducers			
MGI-1M = M-CSF = CSF-1	Macrophages	−	+
MGI-1G = G-CFS	Granulocytes	−	+
MGI-1GM = GM-CSF	Macrophages and granulocytes	−	+
IL-3	Macrophages, granulocytes, and others	−	+
Differentiation inducer			
MGI-2 = IL-6	Macrophages and granulocytes	+	−

[a] MGI-1, MGI-2: macrophage and granulocyte inducers, type 1 and type 2; CSF: colony-stimulating factor; M: macrophage; G: granulocyte; IL-3, IL-6: interleukins 3 and 6.

[b] Growth-inducing protein activates production of differentiation-inducing protein.

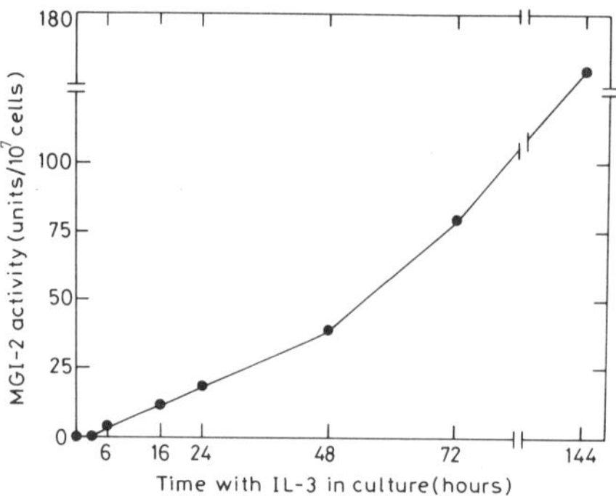

FIGURE 2. Induction of differentiation-inducing protein MGI-2 by growth-inducing protein IL-3 in normal myeloid precursors.[47] We have shown that the protein we called MGI-2 is IL-6.[17,18]

GROWTH-INDUCING PROTEINS AND LEUKEMIA

The normal myeloid growth inducers can be produced by various cell types.[21] However, these growth inducers are not made by the normal myeloid cell precursors, so that the normal precursors require for cell viability and growth the production of growth-inducing protein by other cell types. When cells become malignant, they have escaped some normal control; this state can be associated with changes from an induced to a constitutive expression of certain genes.[1,8,9] In myeloid leukemic cells different clones of leukemic cells have been identified which have shown the various types of changes that can occur in the normal response to growth inducers. There are different leukemic clones that (*a*) need less of or have become independent of normal growth inducer for growth, (*b*) constitutively produce their own growth inducer, or (*c*) are blocked in the ability of growth inducer to induce production of differentiation inducer.[1,8,9,22] Thus, one way in which leukemia can originate is if the production of or response to a normal growth inducer changes, giving a growth advantage to the leukemic over the normal cells.

Growth-inducing proteins enhance cell viability and induce cell multiplication.[10] Independence from normal growth inducer or constitutive production of their own growth inducer can also explain the survival and growth of metastasizing malignant cells in places in the body where the growth inducer required for the survival of normal cells is not present. For cells that are malignant but still need some growth inducer, the organ preference of metastasis could be due to production of the required growth inducer in the organ where the metastasis occurs.

INDUCTION OF DIFFERENTIATION IN LEUKEMIC CELLS

The different types of myeloid leukemic cells include clones that have changed their normal requirement for growth inducer and no longer switch on production of differentiation inducer in response to growth inducer but can still be induced to differentiate to mature non-dividing cells by a normal differentiation-inducing protein (FIG. 4). By incubating these clones, which are called D^+ clones ("D" for differentiation),[23] with normal myeloid differentiation-inducing protein the cells can be induced to differentiate normally to mature macrophages or granulocytes via the normal sequence of gene expression that occurs during differentiation.[1,8,9,21,22] The mature cells, which can be generated from all the cells of a leukemic clone, then stop multiplying like normal mature cells and are no longer malignant *in vivo.*[8,9,10,24] Studies in animals have shown that normal differentiation of D^+ leukemic cells to mature non-dividing cells can be induced not only in culture but also *in vivo.*[8–10,22] These leukemias, therefore, grow progressively when there are too many leukemic cells for the normal amount of differentiation inducer in the body. The development of leukemia can be inhibited in mice with these D^+ leukemic cells by increasing the normal amount of differentiation-inducing protein, either by injecting it or by injecting a compound that increases its production by cells in the body.[8,9,24,25] These myeloid leukemic cells injected into fetuses can participate in hematopoietic cell differentiation in apparently healthy adult animals.[26]

In addition to the D^+ leukemic clones that can be induced to differentiate by a normal myeloid differentiation-inducing protein, there are other D^+ clones that can be induced to differentiate by incubation with a normal myeloid growth-inducing protein (TABLE 2). In these leukemic clones, the growth inducers still seem to induce production of an appropriate differentiation inducer. Not all clones respond to the same protein, even though they may have the appropriate receptors. The results show that most, and probably all, the physiological regulatory proteins of normal myeloid hematopoietic cell development can regulate differentiation of D^+ myeloid leukemic cell clones (TABLE 2).[27] In one of these clones (TABLE 2: WEHI-3B), the genetic

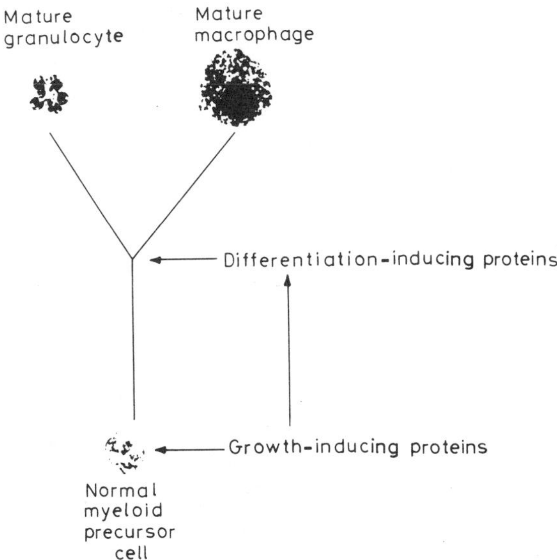

FIGURE 3. Growth of normal myeloid blood cell precursors and their differentiation to macrophages or granulocytes are induced by different proteins, growth-inducing proteins and differentiation-inducing proteins. The growth-inducing proteins enhance cell viability and induce multiplication of normal precursors and production in these cells of differentiation-inducing proteins. Induction of the differentiation inducer by the growth inducer provides a mechanism to couple the multiplication of normal precursor cells with their differentiation.[9]

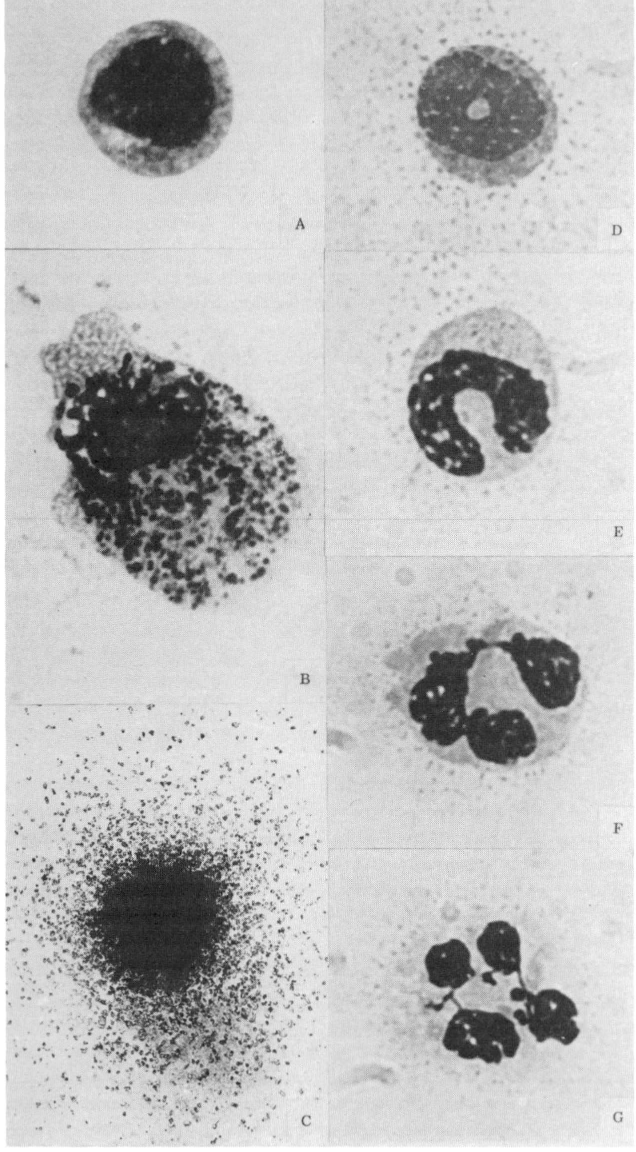

FIGURE 4. Differentiation of myeloid leukemic cells to non-malignant mature macrophages and granulocytes induced by addition of the normal differentiation-inducing protein: (**A**) leukemic cell, (**B**) macrophage, (**C**) colony of cells with macrophages, (**D**-**G**) stages in differentiation to granulocytes.[48]

TABLE 2. Differentiation of Normal and Leukemic Myeloid Cells after Culturing with Various Normal Myeloid Regulatory Proteins

	Differentiation after Culturing with Regulatory Protein[a]				
Cell Type	MGI-2 (IL-6)	IL-3	MGI-1GM (GM-CSF)	MGI-1G (G-CSF)	MGI-1M (M-CSF, CSF-1)
Normal precursor cells	+	+	+	+	+
Leukemic clone 11	+	−	−	±	−
Leukemic clone 7-M12	−	+	+	−	−
Leukemic clone WEHI-3B	−	−	−	+	−

[a] MGI-2 (IL-6) induces differentiation directly, whereas the other proteins induce differentiation indirectly.

abnormalities present include rearrangement of the homeobox gene Hox 2.4[28,29]; and there is a deletion of one copy of the Hox 4.1 homeobox gene[30] in mouse myeloid leukemias which frequently show a deletion in one copy of chromosome 2.[31]

The study of different clones of myeloid leukemic cells has also shown that in addition to D^+ clones, there are differentiation-defective clones: D^- clones[23] (FIG. 5). Some D^- clones can be induced by a normal myeloid regulatory protein to differentiate to an intermediate stage of differentiation which then slows down the growth of the cells, and others cannot be induced to differentiate even to this intermediate stage.[8-10,21,22,32] Since normal differentiation inducer can induce the D^+ clones to differentiate to mature non-dividing cells, it has been suggested that D^+ clones represent the early stages of leukemia and that the formation of various types of D^-

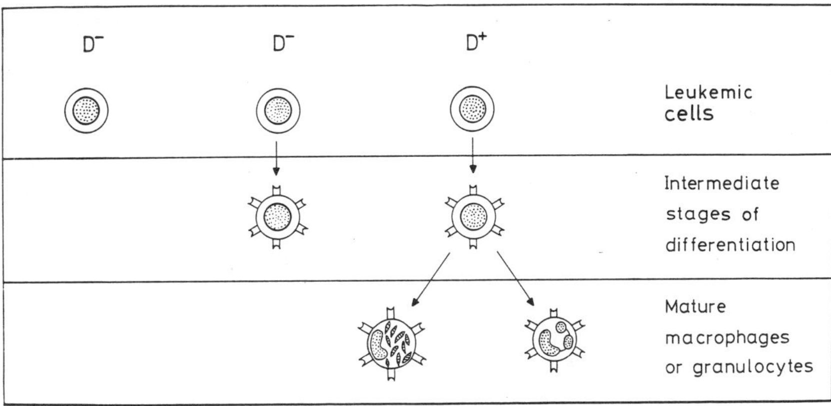

FIGURE 5. Classification of different types of clones of myeloid leukemic cells according to their ability to be induced to differentiate by normal myeloid differentiation-inducing protein. Some differentiation-defective (**D**$^-$) clones can be induced by normal differentiation-inducing protein to differentiate to intermediate stages (*center panel*), whereas other D^- clones (*left*) are not induced to differentiate even to an intermediate stage.[9] **D**$^+$ clones (*right*) are induced to differentiate to mature non-dividing cells by the normal differentiation-inducing protein.

clones may represent later stages in the further progression of leukemia.[22] Studies on changes in the synthesis of cellular proteins in normal myeloid precursors and in D^+ and D^- myeloid leukemic cells have shown that changes from inducible to constitutive gene expression have occurred in the leukemic cells and that the most differentiation-defective D^- clones showed the highest amount of constitutive gene expression.[1,9] The protein changes during differentiation of normal myeloid precursors are induced as a series of parallel multiple pathways of gene expression. It can be assumed that normal differentiation requires synchronous initiation and progression of these multiple parallel pathways. The presence of constitutive instead of induced gene expression for some pathways can be expected to produce asynchrony in the coordination required for differentiation. Depending on the pathways involved, this asynchrony can then produce blocks in the induction and termination of the differentiation program.[1,2,9]

DIFFERENT PATHWAYS FOR INDUCING DIFFERENTIATION

Studies with a variety of chemicals other than normal hematopoietic regulatory proteins have shown that many compounds can induce differentiation in D^+ clones of myeloid leukemic cells. These include certain steroid hormones, chemicals such as cytosine arabinoside, adriamycin, methotrexate and other chemicals that are used today in cancer chemotherapy, and also X-irradiation. At high doses X-irradiation and these compounds used in cancer chemotherapy kill cells, whereas at low doses they can induce differentiation. Not all these compounds are equally active on the same leukemic clone.[8,22] A variety of chemicals can also induce differentiation in clones that are not induced to differentiate by a normal hematopoietic regulatory protein, and in some clones induction of development requires combined treatment with different compounds.[8] These results show that although the response to induction of differentiation by a normal myeloid regulatory protein has been altered in the D^- clones, they have not lost all the genes for differentiation. In addition to certain steroids and chemicals used today in chemotherapy and irradiation, other compounds that can induce differentiation in myeloid leukemic cells include insulin, retinoic acid, bacterial lipopolysaccharide, and certain plant lectins and phorbol esters.[8,9,22] In addition to the normal myeloid protein regulators, insulin, retinoic acid, and the steroid hormones that can induce differentiation are physiological compounds. It is probable that all myeloid leukemic cells no longer susceptible to the normal regulatory proteins by themselves could be induced to differentiate by the appropriate combination of compounds.

The ability of a variety of compounds to induce differentiation in malignant cells is not restricted to myeloid leukemic cells. Erythroleukemic cells can be induced to differentiate by various chemicals.[33,34] Erythropoietin, a normal protein that induces the production of hemoglobin in normal erythrocytes, does not induce hemoglobin in these erythroleukemias. Thus, these erythroleukemias are like the D^- myeloid leukemias that are not induced to differentiate by a normal myeloid regulatory protein. It has also been shown that some of the compounds that induce differentiation in leukemic cells can induce differentiation in tumors derived from other types of cells.[35]

Not only do different compounds induce differentiation, but there are different ways of inducing differentiation. In myeloid leukemic cells, some compounds induce differentiation by inducing the production of a normal differentiation-inducing protein in the D^+ leukemic cells, whereas other compounds, such as the steroid hormones, induce differentiation without inducing this protein.[9] Different compounds can induce different parts of the differentiation program. When combined treatment with several compounds is required, this combined treatment then produces by complementation the appropriate gene expression necessary for differentiation. The complementation of gene expression can occur at the level of mRNA production and mRNA translation.[9] Studies on different mutants of myeloid leukemic cells have also shown that the changes in constitutive protein synthesis which inhibit differentiation by the steroid hormone dexamethasone are different from those that inhibit differentiation by a normal differentiation-inducing protein.[9] These experiments have identified different pathways of gene expression for inducing differentiation and have also shown that genetic changes which inhibit differentiation by one compound need not affect differentiation by another compound that uses alternative pathways.

CHROMOSOME CHANGES, CELL DIFFERENTIATION, AND BYPASSING OF GENETIC DEFECTS IN THE SUPPRESSION OF MALIGNANCY

Evidence has been obtained with various types of tumors, including sarcomas[21] and teratocarcinomas[35] in addition to myeloid leukemias,[21,22] that malignant cells have not lost all the genes that control normal growth. This was first shown in sarcomas by the finding that it was possible to reverse the malignant phenotype to non-malignant phenotype with a high frequency in cloned sarcoma cells whose malignancy had been induced by chemical carcinogens, X-irradiation, or a tumor-inducing virus.[36–38] In sarcomas induced after transformation by chemical carcinogens[39] or X-irradiation[40] of normal fibroblasts in culture, this reversal of malignancy included reversion to the limited life-span found in normal fibroblasts.[38] Chromosome studies on normal fibroblasts, sarcomas, revertants from sarcomas which had regained a non-malignant phenotype, and re-revertants showed that the difference between these malignant and non-malignant cells is controlled by the balance between genes located on specific chromosomes; these genes were at that time called genes for expression (E) and genes for suppression (S) of malignancy.[21,36,41,42] When there is enough S to neutralize E malignancy is suppressed, and when the amount of S is not sufficient to neutralize E malignancy is expressed. These early experiments showed[2,21] that in addition to genes (E) for expression of malignancy (now called oncogenes), there are other genes on specific chromosomes, S genes, that can suppress the action of oncogenes.

The suppression of malignancy in sarcomas[21] was obtained by chromosome segregation, resulting in a change in gene dosage due to a change in the balance of specific chromosomes. This suppression of malignancy by chromosome segregation, with a return to the gene balance required for suppression of the malignant phenotype, occurred without hybridization between different types of cells. The non-malignant cells were thus derived from the malignant ones by genetic segregation. Suppression of malignancy associated with chromosome changes including changes in gene balance has also been found after hybridization between different types of cells.[43–46] These studies on cell hybrids have led to conclusions similar to those obtained from the studies on reversal of malignancy in sarcomas without hybridization between different cell types.

The D^+ myeloid leukemic cells also have an abnormal chromosome composition.[31] But suppression of malignancy in these cells, which also occurred in certain clones with a high frequency, was not associated with chromosome changes. Suppression of malignancy in these D^+ leukemic cells was obtained by induction of the normal sequence of cell differentiation by addition of a normal myeloid regulatory protein. In this approach to suppression of the malignant phenotype, the stopping of cell multiplication by the induction of differentiation to mature cells bypasses the genetic changes that produced the malignant phenotype, i.e., the changes in the requirement for the normal growth inducer and the block in the ability of the growth inducer to trigger production of the differentiation inducer. Genetic changes which make cells defective in their ability to be induced to differentiate by the normal differentiation inducer occur in the evolution of myeloid leukemia. But even these D^- cells can be induced to differentiate by other compounds, either singly or in combination, that can induce the differentiation program by alternative pathways. In these cases the stopping of cell multiplication by inducing differentiation along alternative pathways also bypasses the genetic changes that inhibit response to the normal differentiation inducer. This bypassing of genetic defects is presumably also the mechanism in erythroleukemias for the suppression of malignancy by the induction of differentiation.

Studies on the chromosomes of myeloid leukemic cells have also shown that the change from D^- to D^+ and *vice versa,* i.e., changes in the ability to be induced to differentiate to mature non-dividing cells by a normal myeloid regulatory protein, is controlled by the balance between genes that allow induction of differentiation and genes that suppress differentiation.[31] It was then also shown in hybrids between different cell types that certain chromosome changes can suppress malignancy by restoring the ability of the cells to be induced to differentiate to non-dividing cells *in vivo* in a location in the body where the cells are exposed to what is presumably the normal differentiation inducer.[44,46] These particular chromosome changes also change hybrid cells from D^- to D^+. The same mechanism may possibly apply to the suppression of malignancy in sarcomas that was obtained without hybridization between different cell types. Chromosome changes can thus change malignant cells from D^- to D^+, so that the cells can then be induced to differentiate when exposed to normal differentiation inducer.

It can, therefore, be concluded from studies on the molecular regulators of growth and differentiation in normal development, on changes in the normal developmental program in tumor cells, and on the suppression of malignancy that (*a*) malignancy can be suppressed by inducing differentiation either with or without genetic changes in the malignant cells (FIG. 6), (*b*) this suppression does not have to restore all the normal controls, and (*c*) genetic defects that give rise to malignancy can be bypassed and their effects nullified by inducing differentiation which stops cells from multiplying. This suppression of malignancy by inducing differentiation and the bypassing of genetic defects can also be of value in cancer therapy.[8–10,22,24,25]

SUMMARY

The establishment of a cell culture system for the clonal development of hematopoietic cells has made it possible to identify the proteins that control growth and differentiation of different hematopoietic cell lineages and to discover the molecular basis of normal and abnormal cell development in blood-forming tissues. A model system with myeloid cells has shown that normal hematopoietic cells require different proteins to induce cell multiplication and cell differentiation and that a cascade of interactions between proteins determines the correct balance between immature and mature cells in normal development. Gene cloning has shown that there is a family of different genes for these proteins. Normal protein regulators of hematopoiesis can control the abnormal growth of certain types of leukemic cells and suppress malignancy by inducing differentiation to mature non-dividing cells, and there are different pathways of inducing differentiation. Results from studies on the molecular control of growth and differentiation in normal myeloid hematopoietic cells, on changes in the normal developmental program, and on the suppression of malignancy in myeloid

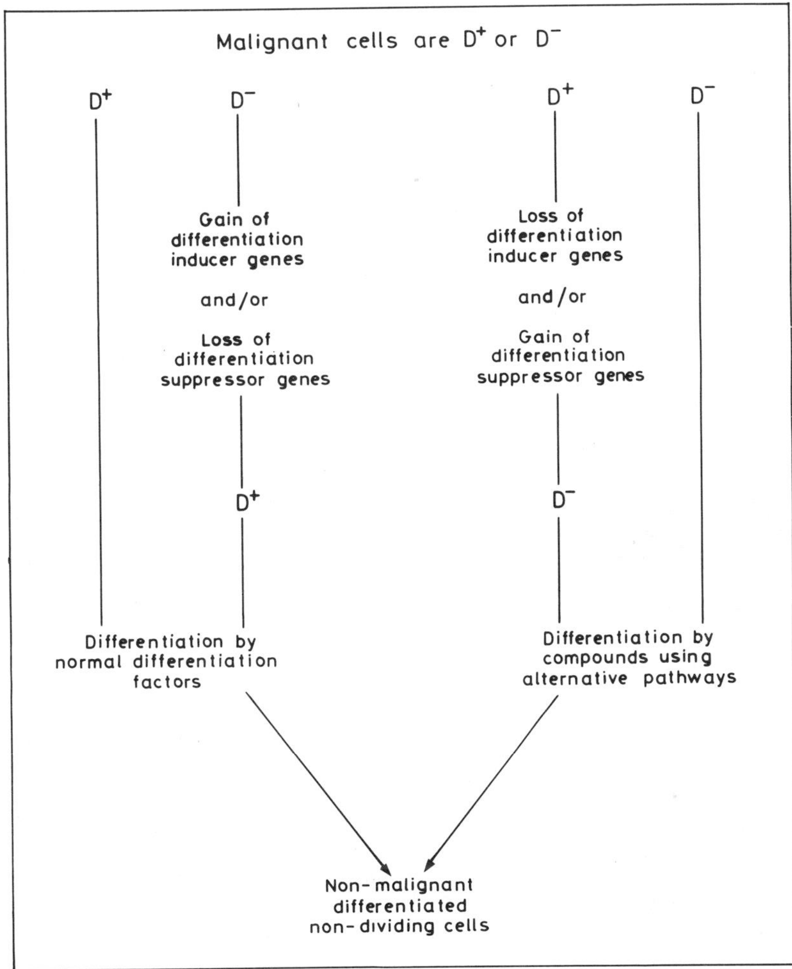

FIGURE 6. Cell differentiation and malignancy. Suppression of malignancy by inducing differentiation can be achieved in different ways. Malignant cells can (**D**$^+$) or cannot (**D**$^-$) be induced to differentiate to mature non-dividing cells by normal regulatory proteins. The D$^-$ cells can, however, be induced to differentiate by other compounds that induce differentiation by alternative pathways. Chromosome changes that change the balance between genes for induction and genes for suppression of differentiation can change cells from D$^-$ to D$^+$ and *vice versa.*[2]

leukemia have shown that (*a*) malignancy can be suppressed by inducing differentiation either with or without genetic changes in the malignant cells, (*b*) this suppression of malignancy does not have to restore all the normal controls, and (*c*) genetic abnormalities that give rise to malignancy, which include changes in homeobox genes, can be bypassed and their effects nullified by inducing differentiation that stops cells from multiplying.

REFERENCES

1. SACHS, L. 1980. Constitutive uncoupling of pathways of gene expression that control growth and differentiation in myeloid leukemia: A model for the origin and progression of malignancy. Proc. Natl. Acad. Sci. USA **77:** 6153-6156.
2. SACHS, L. 1987. Cell differentiation and bypassing of genetic defects in the suppression of malignancy. Cancer Res. **47:** 1981-1986.
3. GINSBURG, H. & L. SACHS. 1963. Formation of pure suspension of mast cells in tissue culture by differentiation of lymphoid cells from the mouse thymus. J. Natl. Cancer Inst. **31:** 1-40.
4. PLUZNIK, D. H. & L. SACHS. 1965. The cloning of normal "mast" cells in tissue culture. J. Cell. Comp. Physiol. **66:** 319-324.
5. BRADLEY, T. R. & D. METCALF. 1966. The growth of mouse bone marrow cells in vitro. Aust. J. Exp. Biol. Med. Sci. **44:** 287-300.
6. PLUZNIK, D. H. & L. SACHS. 1966. The induction of clones of normal "mast" cells by a substance from conditioned medium. Exp. Cell Res. **43:** 553-563.
7. ICHIKAWA, Y., D. H. PLUZNIK & L. SACHS. 1966. In vitro control of the development of macrophage and granulocytes colonies. Proc. Natl. Acad. Sci. USA **56:** 488-495.
8. SACHS, L. 1982. Normal developmental programmes in myeloid leukaemia: Regulatory proteins in the control of growth and differentiation. Cancer Surv. **1:** 321-342.
9. SACHS, L. 1987. The molecular regulators of normal and leukaemic blood cells. The Wellcome Foundation Lecture 1986. Proc. R. Soc. London Ser. B **231:** 289-312.
10. SACHS, L. 1987. The molecular control of blood cell development. Science **238:** 1374-1379.
11. METCALF, D. 1985. The granulocyte-macrophage colony-stimulating factors. Science **299:** 16-22.
12. CLARK, S. C. & R. KAMEN. 1987. The human hematopoietic colony-stimulating factors. Science **236:** 1129-1237.
13. SACHS, L. 1986. Growth, differentiation and the reversal of malignancy. Sci. Am. **254:** 40-47.
14. TOMIDA, M, Y. YAMAMOTO-YAMAGUCHI & M. HOZUMI. 1984. Purification of a factor inducing differentiation of mouse myeloid leukemic M1 cells from conditioned medium from mouse fibroblast L929 cells. J. Biol. Chem. **259:** 10978-10982.
15. OLSSON, I., M. G. SARNGADHARAN, T. R. BREITMAN & R. C. GALLO. 1984. Isolation and characterization of a T lymphocyte-derived differentiation inducing factor for the myeloid leukemic cell line HL-60. Blood **63:** 510-517.
16. SHABO, Y. & L. SACHS. 1988. Inhibition of differentiation and affinity purification with a monoclonal antibody to a myeloid cell differentiation-inducing protein. Blood **72:** 1543-1549.
17. SHABO, Y., J. LOTEM, M. RUBINSTEIN, M. REVEL, S. C. CLARK, S. F. WOLF & L. SACHS. 1988. The myeloid blood cell differentiation-inducing protein MGI-2A is interleukin 6. Blood **72:** 2070-2073.
18. SACHS, L., J. LOTEM & Y. SHABO. 1989. The molecular regulators of macrophage and granulocyte development: Role of MGI-2/IL-6. *In* Regulation of the Acute Phase and Immune Responses: Interleukin-6. Ann. N.Y. Acad. Sci. **557:** 417-437.
19. LOTEM, J. & L. SACHS. 1986. Regulation of cell surface receptors for different hematopoietic growth factors on myeloid leukemic cells. EMBO J. **5:** 2163-2170.
20. LOTEM, J. & L. SACHS. 1987. Regulation of cell surface receptors for hematopoietic differentiation-inducing protein MGI-2 on normal and leukemic myeloid cells. Int. J. Cancer **40:** 532-539.
21. SACHS, L. 1974. Regulation of membrane changes, differentiation and malignancy in carcinogenesis. Harvey Lect. **68:** 1-35. Academic Press. New York.
22. SACHS, L. 1978. Control of normal cell differentiation and the phenotypic reversion of malignancy in myeloid leukemia. Nature **274:** 535-539.
23. FIBACH, E., M. HAYASHI & L. SACHS. 1973. Control of normal differentiation of myeloid leukemic cells to macrophages and granulocytes. Proc. Natl. Acad. Sci. USA **70:** 343-346.
24. LOTEM, J. & L. SACHS. 1981. In vivo inhibition of the development of myeloid leukemia by injection of macrophage and granulocyte inducing protein. Int. J. Cancer **28:** 375-386.

25. LOTEM, J. & L. SACHS. 1984. Control of *in vivo* differentiation of myeloid leukemic cells. IV. Inhibition of leukemia development by myeloid differentiation-inducing protein. Int. J. Cancer **33:** 147-154.
26. GOOTWINE, E., C. G. WEBB & L. SACHS. 1982. Participation of myeloid leukemic cells injected into embryos in hematopoietic differentiation in adult mice. Nature **299:** 63-65.
27. LOTEM, J. & L. SACHS. 1988. In vivo control of differentiation of myeloid leukemic cells by recombinant granulocyte-macrophage colony stimulating factor and interleukin 3. Blood **71:** 375-382.
28. BLATT, C., R. GOLDBERG, D. ABERDAM & L. SACHS. 1987. Homeobox gene rearrangement in myeloid leukemic cells. *In* Third Annual Meeting on Oncogenes, Fredrick, MD: 364.
29. BLATT, C., D. ABERDAM, R. SCHWARTZ & L. SACHS. 1988. DNA rearrangement of a homeobox gene in myeloid leukemic cells. EMBO J. **7:** 4283-4290.
30. BLATT, C. & L. SACHS. 1988. Deletion of a homeobox gene in myeloid leukemias with a deletion in chromosome 2. Biochem. Biophys. Res. Commun. **156:** 1265-1270.
31. AZUMI, J. & L. SACHS. 1977. Chromosome mapping of the genes that control differentiation and malignancy in myeloid leukemic cells. Proc. Natl. Acad. Sci. USA **74:** 253-257.
32. ICHIKAWA, Y., N. MAEDA & M. HORIUCHI. 1976. In vitro differentiation of Rauscher virus induced myeloid leukemic cells. Int. J. Cancer **17:** 789-796.
33. FRIEND, C. 1978. The phenomenon of differentiation in murine erythroleukemic cells. Harvey Lect. **68:** 1-35. Academic Press. New York.
34. MARKS, P. & R. A. RIFKIND. 1978. Erythroleukemia differentiation. Annu. Rev. Biochem. **47:** 419-448.
35. GARDNER, R. L. 1983. Teratomas in prespective. Cancer Surv. **2:** 1-19.
36. RABINOWITZ, Z. & L. SACHS. 1968. Reversion of properties in cells transformed by polyoma virus. Nature **220:** 1203-1206.
37. RABINOWITZ, Z. & L. SACHS. 1970. Control of the reversion of properties in transformed cells. Nature **225:** 136-139.
38. RABINOWITZ, Z. & L. SACHS. 1970. The formation of variants with a reversion of properties of transformed cells. V. Reversion to a limited life span. Int. J. Cancer **6:** 388-398.
39. BERWALD, Y. & L. SACHS. 1963. In vitro cell transformation with chemical carcinogens. Nature **200:** 1182-1184.
40. BOREK, C. & L. SACHS. 1966. In vitro cell transformation by x-irradiation. Nature **210:** 276-278.
41. HITOTSUMACHI, S., Z. RABINOWITZ & L. SACHS. 1971. Chromosomal control of reversion in transformed cells. Nature **231:** 511-514.
42. YAMAMOTO, T., Z. RABINOWITZ & L. SACHS. 1973. Identification of the chromosomes that control malignancy. Nature New Biol. **243:** 247-250.
43. KLEIN, G. 1981. The role of gene dosage and genetic transposition in carcinogenesis. Nature **194:** 313-318.
44. STANBRIDGE, E. J. 1984. Genetics analysis of tumorogenicity in human cell hybrids. Cancer Surv. **3:** 335-350.
45. BENEDICT, W. F., B. E. WEISMANN, C. MARK & E. J. STANBRIDGE. 1984. Tumorigenicity of human HT1080 fibrosarcoma × normal fibroblast hybrids: Chromosome dosage dependency. Cancer Res **44:** 3471-3479.
46. HARRIS, H. 1985. The suppression of malignancy in hybrid cells: The mechanism. J. Cell Sci. **79:** 83-94.
47. LOTEM, J. & L. SACHS. 1983. Coupling of growth and differentiation in normal myeloid precursors and the breakdown of this coupling in leukemia. Int. J. Cancer **32:** 127-134.
48. FIBACH, E., T. LANDAU & L. SACHS. 1972. Normal differentiation of myeloid leukemic cells induced by a differentiation-inducing protein. Nature New Biol. **237:** 276-278.

Alteration of the Program of Terminal Differentiation Caused by Oncogenes in the Hemopoietic Progenitor Cell Line 32D Cl3 (G)[a]

GIOVANNI ROVERA, BRENT KREIDER,[b]
NEELAM SHIRSAT, DONATELLA VENTURELLI,[c]
GIUSEPPE NASO, AND FULVIO MAVILIO[d]

The Wistar Institute of Anatomy and Biology
Thirty-sixth Street at Spruce
Philadelphia, Pennsylvania 19104-4268

INTRODUCTION

Terminal differentiation of adult tissues is regulated by the presence in the microenvironment of growth and differentiation factors.[1] It is also controlled by intracellular mechanisms, which include the sequential expression of high-affinity receptors for such growth factors on the cell surface,[2] the coupling of growth factor receptors to specific signal transduction pathways,[3] and the presence in the nucleus of tissue-specific, diffusible products of *trans*-acting genes that act on well-defined DNA sequences, which constitute the *cis*-acting transcriptional control elements.[4] Finally, it has been postulated that hierarchies of regulatory genes exist which, once expressed, assure the appropriately sequential execution of the program of differentiation for a specific cell lineage.[5,6] Interference with any of these mechanisms may lead to impaired differentiation and, in some cases, to malignant transformation.[7]

The maturation of hemopoietic progenitor cells into granulocytes and macrophages is one of many models to study the mechanisms regulating terminal differentiation.[8,9] It has several advantages: early identifiable morphological changes in the nucleus and cytoplasm of the differentiating cells, the availability of recombinant growth factors—growth factors are known to influence the differentiation process[10–12] (TABLE 1)—a variety of specific markers (immunological, functional, molecular) that allow the evaluation of the orderly progression of the differentiation program, and the

[a]This work was supported by grants from the National Cancer Institute and the American Cancer Society.

[b]Predoctoral fellow supported by NIH Training Grant number 5T32CA09171-13.

[c]Fellow of Associazione Italiana Per La Ricerca Sul Cancro.

[d]Supported from grant 87.01553.44 from the Italian National Research Council (Progetto Finalizzato Oncologia).

TABLE 1. Growth and Differentiation Factors (Cytokines) for the Myelomonocytic Lineage

Cytokine[a]	Molecular Mass (kDa)[b]	Secreted Form (amino acid residues)	mRNA (kb)[c]	Cellular Sources	Species Specifity
IL-3	gp28	140	0.95	T cell	Yes
IL-4	gp15	129	0.65	T cell Mast cell	Yes
IL-5	gp20[d]	123	0.9	T cell	No
IL-6	gp26	184	1.3	Macrophage T cell Fibroblast	No
GM-CSF	gp35	127	0.9	T cell Endothelial cell Fibroblast	Yes
G-CSF	gp20	177	1.2	Macrophage Neutrophil Endothelial cell	No
M-CSF	gp35[d]	189	1.5-4.0	Macrophage Neutrophil Endothelial cell Fibroblast	No

flexibility of the differentiation pathways, which include production of monocytes/macrophages and neutrophilic, basophilic and eosinophilic granulocytes (FIG. 1). The study of granulocyte/macrophagic differentiation has, however, the disadvantage that hemopoietic progenitor cells are difficult to obtain in large amounts and in pure form from bone marrow cells. Since they require cumbersome multiple purification steps with relatively low yields, a large number of starting cells is needed.[13,14]

Alternative *in vitro* models to study at least some aspects of granulocytic-monocytic differentiation have become available in the past several years. However, the classical clonogenic assays[15] are usually not amenable to detailed molecular studies, and often the interpretation of the results is made difficult by the presence of accessory cells that can influence and modify the response to specific growth factors. Murine and human leukemic cell lines[16–18] do not usually respond to physiological stimuli; their differentiation program is impaired by the molecular events leading to malignancy.

In the past several years, non-malignant murine hemopoietic progenitor cell lines that require interleukin-3 (IL-3) for continuous growth have been established.[19–21] We have examined in detail a clone of a murine cell line (32D Cl3) which we received in 1986 from J. Greenberger. This clone responds to granulocyte colony-stimulating factor (G-CSF) by readily differentiating into neutrophilic granulocytes.[22] Since comparison with other 32D Cl3 lines obtained from other laboratories indicated that the ability to survive and differentiate in G-CSF was unique to the subclone received by us (our observations and personal communication from J. Greenberger), we now designate cells of this subclone 32D Cl3 (G) to avoid confusion.

The salient features of 32D Cl3 (G) cells are listed in Table 2: they include dependency on IL-3 for growth,[21] presence of a diploid karyotype,[22] inability to re-

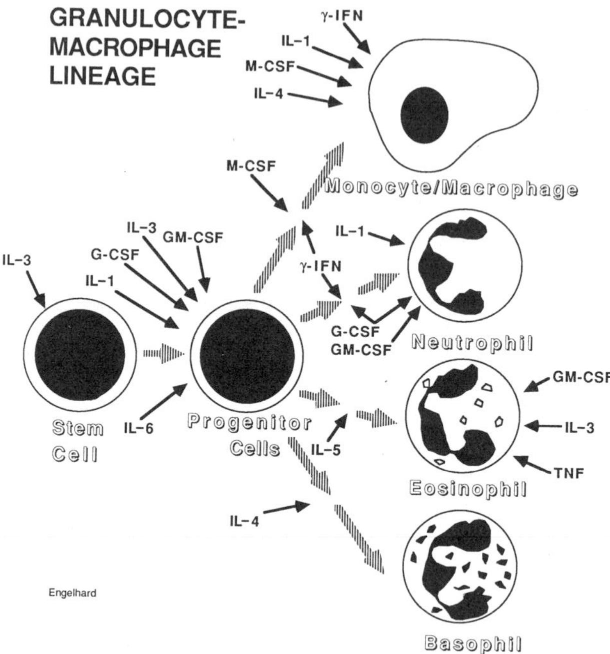

FIGURE 1. Granulocyte-macrophage lineage. The differentiation pathways for maturation of hemopoietic progenitor cells include production of monocytes/macrophages and neutrophilic, basophilic and eosinophilic granulocytes. A variety of growth factors are known to influence the differentiation process: granulocyte, granulocyte-macrophage, and macrophage colony-stimulating factors (**G-CSF; GM-CSF, M-CSF**); interleukins 1, 3, 4, 5, 6 (**IL-1, IL-3, IL-4, IL-5, IL-6**); γ-interferon (γ-**IFN**); and tumor necrosis factor (**TNF**).

populate the marrow of irradiated syngeneic recipients,[21] lack of tumorigenicity, ability to generate rare progeny cells that require IL-2, erythropoietin, and granulocyte-macrophage colony-stimulating factor (GM-CSF) for growth.[31]

ANTAGONISM, PRIMING AND MEMORY TO RESPOND TO GROWTH FACTORS

32D Cl3 (G) cells require murine IL-3 (mIL-3) for growth in chemically defined medium (HB 102, Hana Biologicals) and rapidly die in medium without mIL-3 or in media supplemented with a variety of other hemopoietic factors.[21,23] However, in the absence of mIL-3 but in the presence of G-CSF, the great majority of the cells transiently proliferate for two weeks, increasing approximately 4-5-fold in number.[22]

The recombinant human G-CSF (rhG-CSF) used in these experiments is a glycosylated form of rhG-CSF (rhG-CSF is not species-specific)[24,25] expressed in mammalian cells in our laboratory by use of an SV40-based expression vector containing an rhG-CSF cDNA cloned from the human glioblastoma multiform cell line U87MG.[26]

After addition of rhG-CSF (1-50 U/ml), sequential morphological changes occur leading to the formation in about 3 days of promyelocytes and, a few days later, of myelocytes and metamyelocytes. At approximately 12 days, the great majority of cells are neutrophilic granulocytes.[22] Using a cDNA probe specific for myeloperoxidase,[27,28] a marker of the primary azurophilic granules first appearing at the early promyelocytic stage, and a cDNA probe specific for lactoferrin,[29] a marker of the neutrophilic granules appearing at the late myelocytic stage,[30] we found it possible to demonstrate that the mRNAs for these two markers accumulate in the cells in an orderly and predictable fashion at different times during induction of differentiation.

Although in the presence of rhG-CSF alone the whole population of 32D Cl3 (G) cells differentiates *in vitro,* the simultaneous presence of mIL-3 inhibits this process; the inhibition of differentiation is directly proportional to the relative concentration of mIL-3 compared to that of rhG-CSF present in the medium.[22] In the presence of 200 U/ml of mIL-3, 32D Cl3 (G) cells cannot be stimulated to differentiate by even 500 U/ml of rhG-CSF. In the presence of lower concentrations of mIL-3, the culture of cells becomes an asynchronously differentiating population of myeloid cells reminiscent of the heterogenous myeloid population present in a steady-state bone marrow.[22]

Over the course of a 12-day treatment with rhG-CSF, 32D Cl3 (G) cells progressively lose their ability to form colonies in semi-solid media in the presence of mIL-3. After 12 days of continuous rhG-CSF treatment, the pool of cells able to self-maintain in IL-3 becomes exhausted,[22] although rare clones able to grow continuously in rhG-CSF without mIL-3 can be isolated by maintaining the total population for several weeks in rhG-CSF.[31]

32D Cl3 (G) cells do not readily proliferate in the presence of recombinant murine GM-CSF (rmGM-CSF, a gift from Dr. M. Prystowsky, University of Pennsylvania), although rare clones able to grow in rmGM-CSF can be isolated.[31] However, when 32D Cl3 (G) cells are treated with rhG-CSF for a minimum of 3 days, the cell population becomes competent to proliferate in the presence of rmGM-CSF. The population of rhG-CSF-primed cells can massively expand in rmGM-CSF, and the population of cells thus obtained contains elements of both the neutrophilic granulocyte and the monocytic lineages. Concomitant with acquisition of the ability to grow in rmGM-CSF is the appearance on the cell surface of the 32D Cl3 (G) cells of high-affinity rmGM-CSF receptors.[32] Such 32D Cl3 (G) cells primed with rhG-CSF [32D Cl3 (GM) cells] remain competent to respond to rmGM-CSF for a long time (at least 1 year) even if the cells are returned to mIL-3 containing medium and are never exposed to rmGM-CSF.

TABLE 2. Properties of 32D Cl3 (G) Cells, a Model of Normal Granulocytic Differentiation *in Vitro*

IL-3 dependent
Diploid karyotype
Ability to grow in chemically defined medium
Possibly pluripotent progenitor (rare generation of clones dependent on IL-2, erythropoietin, and GM-CSF)
H_2K haplotype
Non-tumorigenic in irradiated syngeneic host

GROWTH FACTOR RECEPTORS AND TRANSDUCTION SIGNALS

It is well known that structural alterations of the ligand-binding domains and of the intracytoplasmic domains of the EGF receptor and of the CSF-1 (macrophage colony-stimulating factor: M-CSF) receptor lead to an altered transduction signal and to growth factor-independent growth.[33,34] The hemopoietic growth factor receptors for GM-CSF, rhG-CSF, and mIL-3 have not yet been molecularly cloned. It is, therefore, impossible at the present time to analyze the alterations at the level of gene expression or the genetic mutations of these receptors that could interfere with the programs of proliferation and of terminal differentiation of myeloid progenitor cells.

By use of a retroviral vector with a selectable Eco *gpt* marker, the cDNA coding for the EGF receptor[35] (EGF-R) has been introduced into and expressed on the surface of 32D Cl3 (G) cells, although these receptors are not normally expressed on the surface of normal hemopoietic cells. When the normal EGF-R is thereby expressed on the surface of such cells as a 170-kDa glycosylated peptide, the cells become able to grow in the presence of a physiological concentration (10 ng/ml) of EGF, indicating that the cells can utilize this EGF-R for the transduction of mitogenic signals. When the cDNA for a gene encoding a truncated form of EGF-R (v-*erbB*) is introduced into the cells, their requirement for growth factors is abrogated and such cells (32D-*erbB* cells) are able to generate tumors when transplanted into syngeneic hosts. These results show that a naive hematopoietic cell expresses all of the intracellular components of the EGF signaling pathway necessary to evoke a mitogenic response and sustain continuous proliferation. Apparently, the signaling pathway utilized by EGF is different from that utilized by mIL-3, since exposure to EGF led to a rapid stimulation of phosphoinositide metabolism, while mIL-3 had no effect on phosphoinositide turnover.

Whether other growth factor receptors not usually expressed in hemopoietic cells can function in transducing signals in the hemopoietic environment is at present not known. Using retroviral vectors, we have expressed the nerve growth factor receptor (NGF-R) on the surface of 32D Cl3 (G) cells, but we have not detected any effect of the NGF-R on proliferation or differentiation of these cells.[36] The *erbB2* oncogene is also unable to abrogate the growth factor dependency of such cells (Pierce and Aaronson, personal communication).

In order to investigate which alterations of the transduction signal affect the differentiative program of 32D Cl3 (G) cells, we have introduced into these cells v-*abl,* v-Ha-*ras* or v-Ki-*ras,* three oncogenes known to interfere with the signal transduction pathway.[37] Abelson murine leukemia virus (A-MuLV) containing the *abl* oncogene was used to infect 32D Cl3 (G) cells; it abrogated the requirement for mIL-3,[38] similar to the effect reported for other mIL-3 dependent cell lines.[47] However, these 32D-*abl* cells were also unable to differentiate in the presence of rhG-CSF, even at high concentrations.[38] When the parental 32D Cl3 (G) cells were exposed to rhG-CSF, even for a short time, they became resistant to the transforming effect of A-MuLV, as judged by the failure of A-MuLV to promote the appearance of mIL-3-independent clones. These findings suggest that the ability of Abelson virus to transform myeloid progenitor cells is due to the interference of the v-*abl* gene product with the mechanism that controls the commitment of the cells to differentiation.

A different phenotypic response was obtained when 32D Cl3 (G) cells were infected with Harvey or Kirsten viruses containing an activated v-Ha-*ras* or v-Ki-*ras* gene. In both cases, it was not possible to obtain retroviral-transformed cells which showed abrogation of the mIL-3 requirement. It was, however, possible to rescue clones that would grow continuously in rhG-CSF, with an apparent differentiation block at the level of promyelocytes.[39] 32D-Ki-*ras* cells showed a heterogeneous morphology, in-

TABLE 3. Phenotypic Response of 32D Cl3 (G) Cell-derived Clones to Growth Factors and Chemical Inducers of Differentiation

Cell Clone	Transforming Gene	IL-3 Dependency	Growth Factor-Induced Responses		Chemically Induced Differentiation	Tumorigenicity (Nude Mice)	Reference
			G-CSF[a]	Others[b]			
32D Cl3 (G)	none	+	D[c]	–	–	–	22
32D Cl3 (GM)	none	+	D[c]	GM-CSF[d]	–	–	32
32D-EGF-R	EGF-R	+	D[e]	EGF[f]	–	–	35
32D-*erbB*	v-*erbB*	–	–	–	–	+	35
32D-*abl*	v-*abl*	–	–	–	–	+	38
32D-Ki-*ras*	v-Ki-*ras*	+	PD[g]	GM-CSF,IL-4	+	–	39
32D-Ha-*ras*	v-Ha-*ras*	+	PD[g]	GM-CSF,IL-4	+	–	39

[a] D, differentiation; PD, proliferation and differentiation.
[b] Clone showed response to growth factor(s) listed.
[c] Differentiation to neutrophilic granulocyte.
[d] Long-term proliferation and differentiation along granulocytic and monocytic lineages.
[e] Differentiation to neutrophilic granulocyte and massive cell death.
[f] Proliferation with partial differentiation along granulocytic and monocytic lineages.
[g] Long-term proliferation and differentiation to promyelocyte.

cluded a limited number of myelocytes and metamyelocytes, and expressed high levels of both the myeloperoxidase and lactoferrin mRNAs. 32D-Ha-*ras* cells showed a more immature phenotype and expressed myeloperoxidase but not lactoferrin (LF) mRNA.[39]

The apparent differentiation block of both 32D-Ki-*ras* and 32D-Ha-*ras* cells can be reversed with chemical inducers of differentiation, like retinoic acid, sodium butyrate or dimethylsulfoxide, leading to differentiation into granulocytes. These inducers of differentiation were found to be ineffective on the parental 32D Cl3 (G) cells or on such cells transformed by the *abl* or *erbB* genes.[39] TABLE 3 summarizes the effect of growth factors and chemical inducers of differentiation on the different clones derived from 32D Cl3 (G) cells.

DISCUSSION

The 32D Cl3 (G) hemopoietic progenitor cell line is a highly suitable model to study *in vitro* the extracellular and intracellular mechanisms controlling differentiation of the neutrophilic and the monocytic lineage from an early progenitor cell. It should be kept in mind, however, that the 32D Cl3 (G) cell line, despite its diploid karyotype and lack of tumorigenicity in a recipient syngeneic host, is an immortal line. Therefore, it contains genetic alterations that prevent us from predicting with certainty that the phenomenon observed with this cell line can be extrapolated to the normal hematopoietic counterpart. The ability to respond to physiologically acting growth factors and the ability to differentiate make this line uniquely valuable to investigate the mode of action of growth factors and their receptors in controlling the choice of differentiation pathways and the relationship between proliferative and differentiative pathways.

The phenomena of antagonism between IL-3 and G-CSF, of G-CSF priming of these cells to respond to GM-CSF, and of the memory for responsiveness to GM-CSF once the cells are primed by pretreatment with G-CSF could represent mechanisms that are active in normal marrow progenitor cells or could be artifacts secondary to the immortalization process of the IL-3-dependent lines. It is well known, for example, that in marrow clonogenic assays IL-3 not only supports proliferation but also causes terminal differentiation of the cells along multiple lineages.[40,41] It has been argued, however, that the phenomenon of terminal differentiation observed in IL-3-treated cells is secondary to the production by accessory cells or by the same progenitor cells of a series of other factors (G-CSF, M-CSF, IL-4, IL-6, LIF) that are themselves responsible for the terminal differentiation.

G-CSF has been generally believed to act only on late progenitor cells of the neutrophilic granulocytic lineage and, therefore, it is surprising to find out that G-CSF can prime 32D Cl3 (G) cells to become responsive to GM-CSF. However, G-CSF was purified and cloned by two independent groups[25,42] who observed evidence that it was a pluripotent factor, and recent work by Ikebuchi and co-workers[43] indicated that G-CSF is synergistic with IL-3 in clonogenic assays to generate colonies of multiple lineages. These observations suggest that G-CSF is not just a lineage-specific differentiation factor but also acts on pluripotent cells, therefore apparently in agreement with our findings indicating that G-CSF makes the cells competent to respond to GM-CSF.

As originally proposed by Walker *et al.*[48] using marrow progenitor cells, the antagonism exerted by IL-3 on the G-CSF response of 32D Cl3 (G) cells could be explained by a hierarchical control of the expression of the growth factor receptors.

Preliminary data indicate that IL-3 causes a down-regulation of the G-CSF and the GM-CSF receptors in 32D Cl3 (G) cells. Our findings are, however, in apparent contrast with the hypothesis of Walker *et al.*,[48] which suggested that down-regulation of growth factor receptors *per se* causes terminal differentiation of the cells. We rather suggest that the down-regulation of several types of receptors from the cell surface simply leaves only one option to the cells, that is, to appropriately respond to the most dominant growth factor available in the environment.

The memory that the hemopoietic cells develop to respond to GM-CSF after a short priming by G-CSF is a phenomenon that has never been reported in hemopoietic cells. This phenomenon is probably due to demethylation of the GM-CSF receptor gene, since there is ample evidence that methylated and demethylated DNA are stably inherited and that demethylation is usually associated with activation of gene expression.[44] More direct experiments to confirm this hypothesis await the molecular cloning of this gene. The involvement of inheritable activated genes coding for specialized functions has been postulated for every differentiation system in which multiple cell divisions occur, as in the various hemopoietic lineages. The permanent expression of receptors for a specific growth and differentiation factor explains how a stem cell eventually will proceed through the terminal differentiation pathway in an irreversible way.

The finding for 32D Cl3 (G) cells that the EGF receptor, a molecule normally not present on the surface of hematopoietic cells, is able to transduce proliferative signals when its expression on the surface of such cells is brought about by introduction of the appropriate cDNA has recently been confirmed for another IL-3-dependent cell line, $FDCP_1$. However, it has also been reported that if the EGF-R was expressed on the surface of normal myeloid cells, EGF was able to potentiate their response to IL-3 but did not, alone, support their proliferation.[45] This suggests that, indeed, the IL-3-dependent cell lines have features that are different from those of myeloid progenitor cells.

The 32D Cl3 (G) cells can be utilized to study *in vitro* the ability of oncogenes to interfere not only with growth factor-dependent proliferation but also with terminal differentiation. Our studies indicate that *abl* and *erbB* block the differentiative response to G-CSF and that *ras* interferes with the process of terminal differentiation induced by G-CSF, favoring proliferation over differentiation. It is important to point out, however, that the block of terminal differentiation at the level of the promyelocyte/myelocyte obtained by introducing into the cells an activated *ras* oncogene is a rare phenomenon. Only approximately one *ras*-transformed clone for every 10^7 transformed cells can be selected in G-CSF-containing medium, suggesting that other genetic alterations in a small number of the cells in the target population co-operate with the activated *ras* oncogene to elicit that particular phenotype.

Charlotte Friend,[46] with her demonstration that a chemical agent like DMSO could cause terminal differentiation of leukemic cells transformed by the Friend leukemia virus, gave an enormous impetus to the efforts to determine whether these and similar agents could help to overcome leukemic transformation. Using 32D Cl3 (G) cells containing well-defined transforming oncogenes (*erbB, abl, ras*), we have shown that differentiation in response to these chemical agents occurs only for those cells that have an activated *ras* oncogene, not for cells that are transformed by v-*abl* or v-*erbB* oncogenes, and not even for the parental cell population. It seems that these chemical agents, the mode of action of most of which is still not clearly understood, act only on target cells that are already on the brink of terminal differentiation and have alterations of their signal transduction pathway. It will be worthwhile in the future to determine whether ability of cells in freshly obtained cases of acute leukemias to respond to chemical inducers of differentiation is strictly correlated to the presence in the cells of an activated *ras* oncogene.

In summary, 32D Cl3 (G) cells appear to represent a unique model to study *in vitro* terminal differentiation of hemopoietic cells. It will be worthwhile to investigate whether in addition to the neutrophilic granulocytic and macrophagic lineages the cells can also be directed toward the eosinophilic and basophilic lineages and to the erythroid lineage by use of appropriate growth factors and to determine the mechanisms for making the cells competent to respond to such growth factors. The availability in the future of cloned genes for the receptors for all the hemopoietic growth factors should allow detailed investigation of the phenomena of priming and of memory for the expression of such receptors. Finally, the use of 32D Cl3 (G) cells should facilitate those molecular studies leading to an understanding of the role of regulatory genes on the process of terminal differentiation.

ACKNOWLEDGMENT

We thank Janice Papaleo for typing this manuscript.

REFERENCES

1. FERAMISCO, J., B. OZANNE & C. STILES. 1985. Growth factors and transformation. *In* Cancer Cells 3. Cold Spring Harbor Laboratory. Cold Spring Harbor, New York.
2. YARDEN, Y. & A. ULLRICH. 1988. Growth factor receptor tyrosine kinases. Annu. Rev. Biochem. **57:** 443.
3. BERRIDGE, M. J. 1986. Inositol lipids and cell proliferation. *In* Oncogenes and Growth Control. P. Kahn & T. Graf, Eds. Springer-Verlag. Berlin-Heidelberg.
4. MANIATIS, T., S. GOODBOURN & J. A. FISCHER. 1987. Regulation of inducible and tissue specific gene expression. Science **236:** 1237.
5. BLAU, H. M. 1988. Hierarchies of regulatory genes may specify mammalian development. Cell **53:** 673.
6. BLAU, H. M., G. K. PAVLATH, E. C. HARDEMAN, C. P. CHIU, L. SILBERSTEIN, S. G. WEBSTER, S. C. MILLER & C. WEBSTER. 1985. Plasticity of the differentiated state. Science **230:** 758.
7. KAHN, R. & T. GRAF, Eds. 1986. Oncogenes and growth control. Springer-Verlag. Berlin-Heidelberg.
8. METCALF, D. 1985. The granulocyte-macrophage colony-stimulating factors. Science **229:** 16.
9. SACHS, L. 1987. The molecular control of blood cell development. Science **238:** 1374.
10. CLARK, S. C. & R. KAMEN. 1987. The human hematopoietic colony-stimulating factors. Science **236:** 1229.
11. SIEFF, C. A. Hematopoietic growth factors. 1987. J. Clin. Invest. **79:** 1549.
12. MIYAJIMA, A., S. MIYATAKE, J. SCHREURS, J. DEVRIES, N. ARAI, T. YOKOTA & K. ARAI. 1988. Coordinate regulation of immune and inflammatory responses by T cell-derived lymphokines. FASEB J. **2:** 2462.
13. SPANGRUDE, G. J., S. HEIMFELD & I. L. WEISSMAN. 1988. Purification and characterization of mouse hematopoietic stem cells. Science **241:** 58.
14. JAFFE, B. D., D. E. LABATH, G. D. JOHNSON, L. MOSCINSKI, K. R. JOHNSON, G. ROVERA, W. N. NAUSEEF & M. B. PRYSTOWSKY. 1988. Myeloperoxidase and protooncogene expression in GM-CSF-induced bone marrow differentiation. Oncogene **2:** 167.
15. METCALF, D. 1984. Clonal Culture of Hemopoietic Cells: Techniques and Applications. Elsevier. Amsterdam.

16. FIBACH, E., M. HAYASHI & L. SACHS. 1973. Control of normal differentiation of myeloid leukemic cells to macrophages and granulocytes. Proc. Natl. Acad. Sci. USA **70:** 343.
17. COLLINS, S. J. 1987. The HL-60 promyelocytic leukemia cell line: Proliferation, differentiation and cellular oncogene expression. Blood **70:** 1233.
18. FERRERO, D. & G. ROVERA. 1984. Human leukaemic cell lines. *In* Clinics in Hematology. E. A. McCulloch, Ed. Vol. 13(2): 4461.
19. DEXTER, T. J., J. GARLAND, D. SCOTT, E. SCOLNICK & D. METCALF. 1980. Growth of factor dependent hematopoietic precursor cell lines. J. Exp. Med. **152:** 1036.
20. MOORE, M. A. S. 1978. Regulation of granulopoiesis in vitro. *In* Hematopoietic Cell Differentiation. D. W. Golde, M. J. Cline, D. Metcalf & C. F. Fox, Eds.: 445. Academic Press. New York.
21. GREENBERGER, J. S., M. A. SAKAKEENY, R. K. HUMPHRIES, C. J. EAVES & R. J. ECKNER. 1983. Demonstration of permanent factor-dependent multipotential (erythroid/neutrophil/basophil) hematopoietic progenitor cell lines. Proc. Natl. Acad. Sci. USA **80:** 2931.
22. VALTIERI, M., D. J. TWEARDY, D. CARACCIOLO, K. JOHNSON, F. MAVILIO, S. D. ALTMANN, D. SANTOLI & G. ROVERA. 1987. Cytokine-dependent granulocytic differentiation: Regulation of proliferative and differentiative responses in a murine progenitor cell line. J. Immunol. **138:** 3829-3825.
23. METCALF, D. 1985. Multi-CSF-dependent colony formation by cells of a murine hematopoietic cell line: Specificity and action of multi-CSF. Blood **63:** 357.
24. SOUZA, L. M., T. C. BOONE, J. GABRILOVE, P. H. LAI, K. M. ZSEBO, D. C. MURDOCK, CHAZIN, J. BRUSZEWSKI, H. LU, K. K. CHEN, J. BARENDT, E. PLATZER, M. A. S. MOORE, R. MERTELSMANN & K. WELTE. 1986. Recombinant human granulocyte colony stimulating factor: Effects on normal and leukemic myeloid cells. Science **232:** 61.
25. NAGATA, S., M. TSUCHIYA, S. ASANO, Y. KAZIRO, T. YAMAZAKI, I. YAMAMOTO, Y. HIRA, N. KUBOTA, M. OHEDA, H. NOMURA & M. ONO. 1986. Molecular cloning and expression of cDNA for human granulocyte colony-stimulating factor. Nature **319:** 415.
26. TWEARDY, D. J., L. A. CANNIZZARO, P. A. PALUMBO, S. SHANE, K. HUEBNER, P. VAN TUINEN, D. H. LEDBETTER, J. B. FINAN, JKP. C. NOWELL & G. ROVERA. 1987. Molecular cloning and characterization of a cDNA for human granulocyte colony-stimulating factor (G-CSF) from a glioblastoma multiform cell line and localization of the G-CSF gene to chromosome 17q21. Oncogene Res. **1:** 209.
27. JOHNSON, K. R., W. M. NAUSEEF, A. CARE, M. J. WHEELOCK, H. P. KOEFFLER, S. SHANE, S. HUDSON, M. SELSTED, C. MILLER & G. ROVERA. 1987. Characterization of cDNA clones for human myeloperoxidase: Predicted amino acid sequence and evidence for multiple mRNA species. Nucleic Acids Res. **15:** 2013.
28. VENTURELLI, D., I. GEMPERLEIN, N. SHIRSAT, S. HUDSON, S. BITTENBENDER & G. ROVERA. Comparative analysis of the human and murine myeloperoxidase genes: Coding and regulatory sequences. Manuscript in preparation.
29. SHIRSAT, N. *et al.* The structure of the murine lactorferrin gene. Manuscript in preparation.
30. RADO, T. A., J. BALLEKENS, G. ST. LAURENT, L. PARKER & E. J. BENZ, JR. 1984. Lactoferrin biosynthesis during granulocytopoiesis. Blood **64:** 1103.
31. MIGLIACCIO, G., A. R. MIGLIACCIO, B. KREIDER, G. ROVERA & J. W. ADAMSON. Selection of lineage restricted cell lines immortalized at different stages of hematopoietic differentiation from the murine cell line 32D. Manuscript submitted.
32. KREIDER, B., P. PHILLIPS, M. PRYSTOWSKY & G. ROVERA. G-CSF induced competence and memory to respond to GM-CSF in an IL3 dependent murine hemopoietic precursor cell line. Manuscript in preparation.
33. VENNSTROM, B. & K. KAMM. 1988. The erbA and erbB oncogenes. *In* The Oncogene Handbook. E. P. Reddy, A. M. Skalka & T. Curran, Eds.: 25. Elsevier Science Publishers. Amsterdam.
34. RETTENMIER, C. W. & C. J. SHERR. 1988. The fms oncogene. *In* The Oncogene Handbook. E. P. Reddy, A. M. Skalka & T. Curran, Eds.: 73. Elsevier Science Publishers. Amsterdam.
35. PIERCE, J. H., M. RUGGIERO, T. P. P. FLEMING, P. DIFIORE, J. S. GREENBERGER, J. SCHLESSINGER, G. ROVERA & S. A. AARONSON. 1988. Signal transduction through the EGF receptor transfected into interleukin-3-dependent hemopoietic cells. Science **239:** 628.
36. MAVILIO, F., A. ROSS, B. KREIDER & G. ROVERA. Unpublished observations.

37. REDDY, E. P., A. M. SKALKA & T. CURRAN, Eds. 1988. The Oncogene Handbook. Elsevier. Amsterdam.
38. ROVERA, G., M. VALTIERI, F. MAVILIO & P. REDDY. 1987. Effect of Abelson murine leukemia virus on granulocytic differentiation and interleukin-3 dependence of a murine progenitor cell line. Oncogene **1:** 29.
39. MAVILIO, F., B. KREIDER, M. VALTIERI, G. NASO, N. SHIRSAT, D. VENTURELLI, P. REDDY & G. ROVERA. 1988. Alteration of growth and differentiation factors response by Kirsten and Harvey sarcoma viruses in the IL-3-dependent murine hematopoietic cell line 32D Cl3(G). Oncogene **4:** 301-308.
40. PRYSTOWSKI, M. D., G. OTTEN, M. F. NAUYOKAS, J. VARDIMAN, J. N. IHLE, E. GOLDWASSER & F. W. FITCH. 1984. Multiple hemopoietic lineages are found after stimulation of mouse bone marrow precursor cells with IL-3. Am. J. Pathol. **117:** 171.
41. RENNICK, D. M., F. D. LEE, T. YOKOTA, K. I. ARAI, H. CANTOR & G. J. NABEL. 1985. A cloned cDNA induces a multilineage growth factor: Multiple activities of interleukin 3. J. Immunol. **134:** 910.
42. WELTE, K., E. PLATZER, L. LU, J. L. GABRILOVE, E. LEVI, R. MERTELSMANN & M. A. S. MOORE. 1985. Purification and biochemical characterization of human pluripotent hematopoietic colony-stimulating factor. Proc. Natl. Acad. Sci. USA **82:** 1526.
43. IKEBUCHI, K., S. C. CLARK, J. IHLE, L. SOUZA & M. OGAWA. 1988. Granulocyte colony-stimulating factor enhances interleukin 3-dependent proliferation of miltipotential hemopoietic progenitors. Proc. Natl. Acad. Sci. USA **85:** 3445.
44. CEDAR, H. 1988. DNA methylation and gene activity. Cell **53:** 3.
45. VON RUDEN, T. & E. F. WAGNER. 1988. Expression of functional human EGF receptor on murine marrow cells. EMBO J. **7:** 2749.
46. FRIEND, C., W. SCHER, J. G. HOLLAND & T. SATO. 1971. Hemoglobulin synthesis in murine virus-induced leukemia cells: In vitro stimulation of erythroid differentiation by dimethylsulfoxide. Proc. Natl. Acad. Sci. USA **68:** 378.
47. IHLE, J. N., J. KELLER, A. REIN, J. CLEVELAND & U. RAPP. 1985. *In* Cancer Cells: Growth Factors and Transformation 3: 211. Cold Spring Harbor Laboratory. Cold Spring Harbor, New York.
48. WALKER, F., N. A. NICOLA, D. METCALF & A. W. BURGESS. 1985. Hierarchical downmodulation of hemopoietic growth factor receptors. Cell **43:** 269.

Friend Virus-Induced Erythroleukemia: A Multistage Malignancy[a]

YAACOV BEN DAVID[b] AND ALAN BERNSTEIN[c]

Division of Molecular and Developmental Biology
Mount Sinai Hospital Research Institute
Toronto, Ontario M5G 1X5
Canada

INTRODUCTION

The erythroleukemia induced by Friend leukemia virus in susceptible adult mice is a multistage malignancy that can be induced by either of two strains of Friend virus[1,2] (FV-A and FV-P). These two strains are complexes of a replication-defective spleen focus-forming virus (SFFV-A and SFFV-P, respectively) and a replication-competent Friend murine leukemia virus (F-MuLV). The early stage of the disease commences virtually immediately after inoculation of virus and is characterized by massive splenic proliferation of non-tumorigenic erythroid cells with limited self-renewal capability that are still capable of terminal differentiation to mature red blood cells. The late stage of Friend leukemia occurs 3-8 weeks after virus inoculation and is associated with the appearance of cells that are both tumorigenic *in vivo*[3] and capable of forming spleen colonies in genetically anemic *Sl/Sl*^{d} mice[4] and stable cell lines *in vitro.* Permanent cell lines can be established from colonies grown in semi-solid methylcellulose medium from individual spleens of Friend virus-infected mice.[5]

Over the past decade, a major effort in our laboratory and others has centered around characterizing the molecular events that underlie the preleukemic and leukemic stages of Friend disease. From these studies it appears that the *env* gene-related glycoprotein (gp55) encoded by the SFFV genome is responsible for the proliferation of infected erythroblasts during the preleukemic stage of Friend disease.[6,7] Although the role of the SFFV genome in the subsequent events of the leukemic progression is not clear, we have previously shown that preparations of helper-free SFFV can induce a transient erythroblastosis without the appearance of malignant cells in the spleens of infected mice.[8] This observation, together with the length of the time required to

[a] Work from the authors' laboratory is supported by grants from the National Cancer Institute of Canada and the Medical Research Council of Canada.

[b] Y. B. D. is a Fellow of the Leukemia Research Fund.

[c] Address correspondence to Dr. Alan Bernstein, Division of Molecular and Developmental Biology, Mt. Sinai Hospital Research Institute, 600 University Avenue, Toronto, Ontario M5G 1X5, Canada.

generate malignant cell clones, suggests that additional molecular events are necessary for malignant transformation. Thus, the transition from the early polyclonal stage of Friend disease to the appearance of monoclonal malignant erythroleukemic cells[9,10] may be associated with additional molecular events that confer a selective growth advantage on emerging leukemic clones.

THE p53 ONCOGENE IN FRIEND LEUKEMIA

In an attempt to understand the molecular events that underlie the progression from the early to the late stages of Friend leukemia, we have examined the structure and expression of a number of cellular proto-oncogenes in malignant cell clones derived from Friend virus-infected mice. These studies have demonstrated that the cellular p53 gene seems to be involved in the evolution of Friend leukemia.

p53 is a cellularly encoded protein first detected in SV40-transformed cells due to its physical association with SV40 large T-antigen[11,12] and its activity as a transplantation antigen in chemically induced sarcomas.[13] p53 is also found at elevated levels in cells transformed by other biological or physical agents.[14,15] In addition, p53 levels are frequently high in tumor cell lines and in a wide variety of primary human tumors.[16]

Several *in vitro* studies have suggested that the p53 gene is a *myc*-like, dominant-acting oncogene. p53 can immortalize early primary rodent cells[17,18] and co-operate with *ras* to transform primary cells in culture.[19] Despite these *in vitro* data, direct evidence that over-expression of the p53 gene or activation of the gene by mutation can contribute to the oncogenic process is lacking. The p53 gene has neither been detected as part of a naturally occurring acutely transforming retrovirus nor been shown to be consistently involved in chromosomal translocations or gene amplification in naturally occurring tumors. Hence, aside from the high levels of p53 protein in various tumors, little is known about the role of p53 protein in either human or experimentally induced malignancies.

In an attempt to understand the role of p53 in oncogenesis and to determine whether changes in the structure or expression of the p53 gene play a causative role in the late, tumorigenic stages of Friend erythroleukemia, we have analyzed the structure and expression of this gene in newly isolated erythroleukemic cell clones induced by the various isolates of Friend leukemia virus. These studies have shown that the majority of such cell lines express very high steady-state levels of p53 protein, as determined by Western blotting. However, a significant proportion (20-40%) of these Friend cell lines do not express detectable levels of p53 protein. Southern gel analysis has shown that the failure to express p53 protein in these cell lines is associated with major genomic rearrangements of the p53 gene in these cells.[20] These rearrangements are associated either with complete loss of p53 synthesis or with the expression of a truncated polypeptide antigenically related to p53. Furthermore, these rearrangements appear to take place *in vivo* during the evolution of Friend leukemia, prior to the isolation of malignant cell clones in culture.[20]

By cloning the altered p53 genes from various Friend erythroleukemic cell lines, it was possible to show that there are two general categories of rearrangements responsible for the loss of p53 synthesis in these cells (FIG. 1). First, internal deletions occur that result in the loss of p53 coding sequences and either the generation of truncated polypeptides[21,22] (cell lines DA22-1 and DP15-2 in FIG. 1) or the complete inactivation of the gene[23] (cell line CB3 in FIG. 1). Second, our initial analyses of the cell line DP20-1 revealed that the p53 rearrangement in these cells is the result of

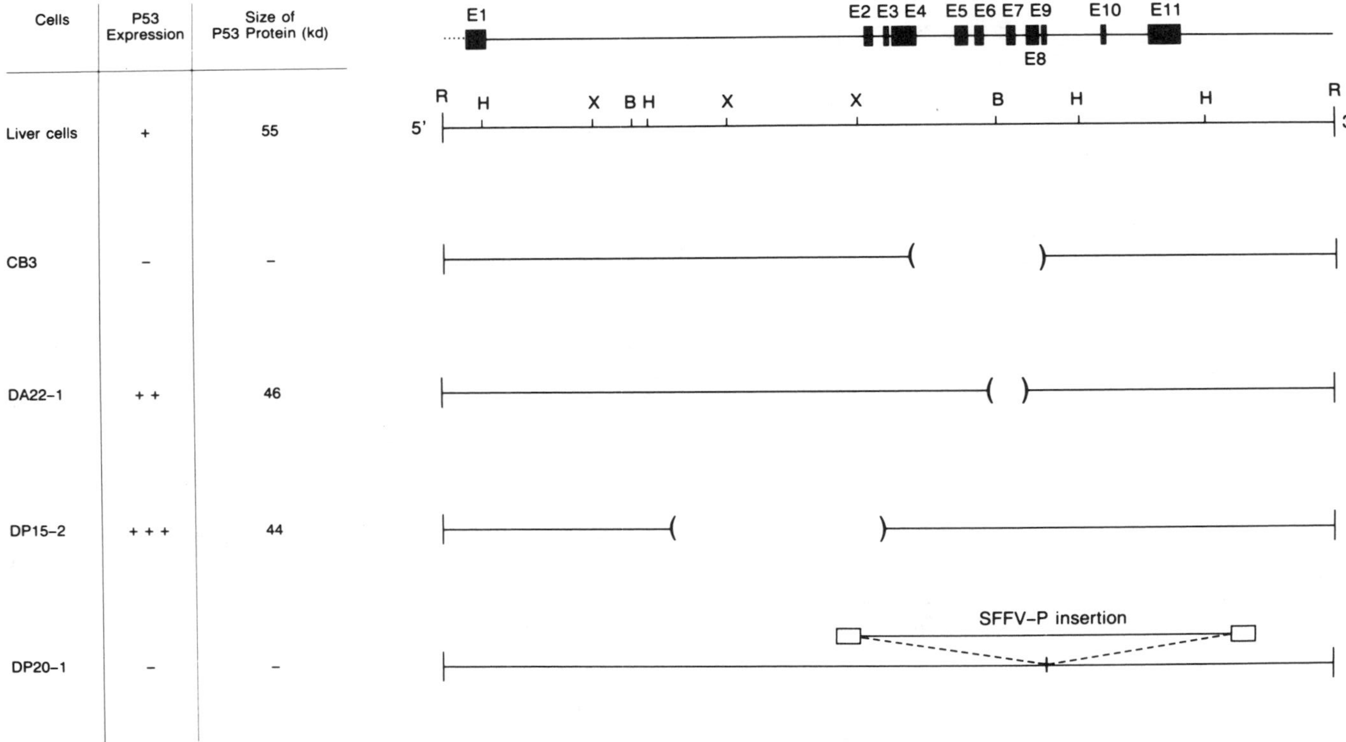

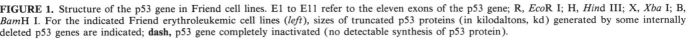

FIGURE 1. Structure of the p53 gene in Friend cell lines. E1 to E11 refer to the eleven exons of the p53 gene; R, *Eco*R I; H, *Hin*d III; X, *Xba* I; B, *Bam*H I. For the indicated Friend erythroleukemic cell lines (*left*), sizes of truncated p53 proteins (in kilodaltons, kd) generated by some internally deleted p53 genes are indicated; **dash,** p53 gene completely inactivated (no detectable synthesis of p53 protein).

the insertion of SFFV in an intron towards the 3′ end of the gene (FIG. 1). Southern gel analysis of a large number of independently isolated Friend cell lines induced by either the anemia- or polycythemia-inducing strains of Friend virus (FV-A or FV-P) revealed that approximately 20-30% of these cells have an inactivated p53 gene as the result of an insertional mutagenic event by SFFV. These observations extend previous studies showing the insertion of a murine retrovirus within the p53 gene in a single cell line derived from a mouse infected with Abelson murine leukemia virus.[24]

The high frequency of rearrangement of the p53 gene in Friend erythroleukemic cells suggests either that such alterations confer a selective growth advantage on these cells or that the p53 gene is structurally labile. Two observations argue against the latter possibility. First, the molecular characterization of the rearranged p53 alleles in a number of independent Friend cell lines suggests that distinct molecular events, including a variety of deletions and retroviral insertions, are responsible for the alterations in the p53 gene in these cells. Second, almost all of the Friend cell lines with one unrearranged p53 gene have undergone a reduction to homozygosity similar to that observed in the tumors of patients with retinoblastoma. This observation suggests that at least two events involving the p53 gene have taken place in these cells. These observations thus argue against any simple model involving hot-spots for genomic rearrangements within the p53 gene.

A further observation in favor of the mechanism of *in vivo* selection for inactivation of the p53 gene comes from studies on the clonal origin of Friend tumor cells.[10] It is possible to isolate, from the same mouse, malignant clones that either have normal p53 genes or contain a rearranged p53 gene. This result, together with observations suggesting that the late stages of Friend leukemia are clonal, raises the possibility that the clones with rearrangements in their p53 genes are derived from the clones with unrearranged p53 genes by tumor progression *in vivo.* Alternatively, these two populations of tumor cells in Friend leukemia, distinguishable on the basis of the status of their p53 gene, might arise as the result of two (or more) unrelated transformation events. To decide between these two hypotheses, we examined the clonal origins of the tumor cells in Friend spleens by using the integration sites of F-MuLV as a unique clonal marker. Southern gel analysis of DNA from individual Friend cell clones indicated that, from the same mouse, all of the clones with a normal p53 gene were clonally related, but they were unrelated to the Friend cell lines with a rearranged p53 gene.[10] These observations demonstrate that Friend tumor cells with rearrangements in their p53 gene arise as the result of a unique transformation event and provide further evidence that such p53 rearrangements confer a selective growth advantage to these cells *in vivo.*

p53: A DOMINANT OR RECESSIVE ONCOGENE?

The conclusion that inactivation of the p53 gene confers a positive growth advantage on preleukemic erythroid cells suggests that p53 should more properly be considered a recessive rather than a dominant oncogene. However, this conclusion does not account for the majority of Friend tumor clones that express very high levels of p53 protein or for earlier studies suggesting that over-expression of p53 protein is associated with the transformation, immortalization, and co-operation with *ras* of cells in culture.

One way of resolving this paradox is to suggest that p53 is indeed a recessive oncogene and that activation of its transforming potential can be obtained either by complete inactivation of the gene (e.g., by deletion or retroviral insertions) or by more subtle mutations which functionally inactivate the protein. Three observations are consistent with this hypothesis. First, epitope and RNase mapping studies on the p53 protein and mRNA present in Friend cell lines that express high levels of p53 protein suggest that small mutations have occurred in the p53 gene in at least some of these Friend cell lines. Second, recently published experiments have demonstrated that mutation in the p53 coding region is required to activate the p53 protein for co-operativity assays with the *ras* oncogene and that mutations in a surprisingly large number of sites throughout the protein can activate its transforming potential. Third, we have generated transgenic mice expressing high levels of p53 protein encoded by one of two mutant p53 alleles. These mice have a greatly elevated tumor incidence, with a particularly high susceptibility to lung adenocarcinomas, osteogenic sarcomas, and lymphomas.[25]

Taken together, the experiments summarized above suggest that activation of the transforming potential of the p53 gene can result either from its complete inactivation or from more subtle (point) mutations that functionally inactivate the p53 protein. According to this dominant-negative model of p53 action, p53 mutants that encode a functionally inactive protein would contribute to the transformed phenotype by inhibiting the normal activities of any wild-type p53 protein expressed in these cells.

CONCLUDING REMARKS

Studies on the leukemia induced by the various Friend virus isolates have contributed, in a major way, to our understanding of the viral, cellular, and host genetic controls of leukemogenesis. Molecular analysis of the late stages of Friend leukemia has also provided new insights into carcinogenesis, including the identification of a possible new oncogene (*Spi*-1)[26] and recognition of the possibility that the p53 oncogene is a negative, not a positive, regulator of cell growth.

ACKNOWLEDGMENT

This paper is dedicated to the memory of Charlotte Friend, a superb scientist and a good friend.

REFERENCES

1. TEICH, N., J. WYKE, T. MAK, A. BERNSTEIN & W. HARDY. 1984. Pathogenesis of retrovirus-induced disease. *In* RNA tumor viruses, 2nd Ed. R. Weiss, N. Teich, H. Varmus & J. Coffin, Eds.: 857-880. Cold Spring Harbor Laboratory. Cold Spring Harbor, NY.
2. SCHIFF, R. D. & A. OLIFF. 1986. The pathophysiology of murine retrovirus-induced leukemias. Crit. Rev. Oncol. Hematol. **5:** 257-323.
3. WENDLING, F., F. MOREAU-GACHELIN & P. TAMBOURIN. 1981. Emergence of tumorigenic cells during the course of Friend virus leukemia. Proc. Natl. Acad. Sci. USA **78:** 3614-3618.
4. MAGER, D., T. W. MAK & A. BERNSTEIN. 1980. Friend leukemia virus-transformed cells, unlike normal stem cells, form spleen colonies in *Sl/Sl*^{d} mice. Nature **288:** 592-594.

5. MAGER, D., T. W. MAK & A. BERNSTEIN. 1981. Quantitative colony method for tumorigenic cells transformed by two distinct strains of Friend leukemia virus. Proc. Natl. Acad. Sci. USA **78:** 1703-1707.
6. MAGER, D. & A. BERNSTEIN. 1985. Induction of clonogenic and erythroleukemic cells by different helper virus pseudotypes of Friend spleen focus-forming virus. Virology **141:** 337-341.
7. RUSCETTI, S. & L. WOLFF. 1984. Spleen focus-forming virus: Relationship of an altered envelope gene to the development of a rapid erythroleukemia. Curr. Top. Microbiol. Immunol. **122:** 21-44.
8. BERGER, S. A., N. SANDERSON, A. BERNSTEIN & W. D. HANKINS. 1985. Induction of the early stages of Friend erythroleukemia with helper-free Friend spleen focus-forming virus. Proc. Natl. Acad. Sci. USA **82:** 6913-6917.
9. MOREAU-GACHELIN, F., J. ROBERT-LEZENES, F. WENDLING, A. TAVITIAN & P. TAMBOURIN. 1985. Integration of spleen focus-forming virus proviruses in Friend tumor cells. J. Virol. **53:** 292-295.
10. CHOW, V., Y. BEN-DAVID, A. BERNSTEIN, S. BENCHIMOL & M. MOWAT. 1987. Multistage friend erythroleukemia: Independent origin of tumor clones with normal or rearranged p53 cellular oncogenes. J. Virol. **61:** 2777-2781.
11. LANE, D. P. & L. V. CRAWFORD. 1979. T antigen is bound to a host protein in SV40 transformed cells. Nature **278:** 261-263.
12. LINZER, D. I. H. & A. J. LEVINE. 1979. Characterization of a 54k dalton cellular SV40 tumor antigen present in SV40-transformed cells and uninfected embryonal carcinoma cells. Cell **17:** 43-52.
13. DELEO, A. B., G. JAY, E. APPELLA, G. C. DUBOIS, L. W. LAW & L. J. OLD. 1979. Detection of a transformation-related antigen in chemically induced sarcomas and other transformed cells of the mouse. Proc. Natl. Acad. Sci. USA **76:** 2420-2424.
14. CRAWFORD, L. 1983. The 53000-dalton cellular protein and its role in transformation. Int. Rev. Exp. Pathol. **25:** 1-50.
15. CRAWFORD, L. V., D. C. PIM, E. G. GURNEY, P. GOODFELLOW & J. TAYLOR-PAPADIMITRIOU. 1981. Detection of a common feature in several human tumor cell lines—A 53,000 dalton protein. Proc. Natl. Acad. Sci. USA **78:** 41-45.
16. CRAWFORD, L. V., D. C. PIM & P. LAMB. 1984. The cellular protein p53 in human tumors. Mol. Biol. Med. **2:** 261-272.
17. JENKINS, J. R., K. RUDGE & G. A. CURRIE. 1984. Cellular immortalization by a cDNA clone encoding the transformation-associated phosphoprotein p53. Nature **312:** 651-654.
18. ROVINSKI, B. & S. BENCHIMOL. 1988. Immortalization of rat embryo fibroblasts by the cellular p53 oncogene. Oncogene **2:** 445-452.
19. ELIYAHU, D., A. RAZ, P. GRUSS, D. GIVOL & M. OREN. 1984. Participation of p53 tumor antigen in transformation of normal embryonic cells. Nature **312:** 646-649.
20. MOWAT, M. A., A. CHENG, N. KIMURA, A. BERNSTEIN & S. BENCHIMOL. 1985. Rearrangements of the cellular p53 gene in erythroleukemic cells transformed by Friend virus. Nature **314:** 633-636.
21. ROVINSKI, B., D. MUNROE, J. PEACOCK, M. MOWAT, A. BERNSTEIN & S. BENCHIMOL. 1987. Deletion of 5′-coding sequences of the cellular p53 gene in mouse erythroleukemia: A novel mechanism of oncogene regulation. Mol. Cell. Biol. **7:** 847-853.
22. MUNROE, D. G., B. ROVINSKI, A. BERNSTEIN & S. BENCHIMOL. 1988. Loss of a highly conserved domain on p53 as a result of gene deletion during Friend virus-induced erythroleukemia. Oncogene **2:** 621-624.
23. BEN-DAVID, Y., V. R. PRIDEAUX, V. CHOW, S. BENCHIMOL & A. BERNSTEIN. 1988. Inactivation of the p53 oncogene by internal deletion or retroviral integration in erythroleukemic cell lines induced by Friend leukemia virus. Oncogene **3:** 179-185.
24. WOLF, D. & V. ROTTER. 1984. Inactivation of p53 gene expression by an insertion of Moloney murine leukemia virus-like DNA sequences. Mol. Cell. Biol. **4:** 1402-1410.
25. LAVIGUEUR, A., V. MALTBY, D. MOCK, J. ROSSANT, T. PAWSON & A. BERNSTEIN. 1989. High incidence of lung, bone and lymphoid tumors in transgenic mice overexpressing mutant alleles of the p53 oncogene. Manuscript submitted.
26. MOREAU-GACHELIN, F., A. TAVITIAN & P. TAMBOURIN. 1988. *Spi*-1 is a putative oncogene in virally induced murine erythroleukaemias. Nature **331:** 277-280.

Interactions between Hematopoietic Growth Factors in Normal and Leukemic Stem Cell Differentiation[a]

MALCOLM A. S. MOORE

James Ewing Laboratory of Developmental Hematopoiesis
Memorial Sloan-Kettering Cancer Center
New York, New York 10021

INTRODUCTION

"Reversal of malignancy" in leukemia is a goal that is attractive but rarely attainable. Biological manipulation of myeloid leukemic cells *in vitro* and *in vivo* has permitted manipulation of the self-renewal and differentiation probabilities of leukemic cells to an extent that the selective advantage of the leukemic clone can be overcome. Clonogenic assays have revealed that the majority of human acute non-lymphocytic leukemias (ANLL) retain the capacity for a proliferative response to hematopoietic growth factors such as G-CSF, M-CSF, GM-CSF[b] and interleukin-3 (IL-3).[1–6] Myeloid leukemic cells may also produce autocrine factors (IL-1, G-CSF, GM-CSF) that drive proliferation of the transformed cells.[7–11] The significance of this autocrine phenomenon as an underlying cause of leukemic transformation has been questioned.[12] While intellectually attractive, the hypothesis that autocrine phenomena play a significant role in leukemogenesis is at variance with the body of data demonstrating dependence upon exogenous growth factors for leukemic cell proliferation *in vitro.*[1–6] Expression of the GM-CSF gene has been reported in approximately 50% of patients with ANLL, as assessed by Northern blot analysis of RNA prepared from leukemic cells depleted of T cells and monocytes.[10,11] While depletion of cell populations that normally produce CSFs and interleukins would appear to be an important control for determination of the source of potential autocrine growth factors in samples of leukemic blast cells, the cell separation procedure itself is probably responsible for induction of growth factor gene transcription; GM-CSF gene expression was detected in 5 of 10 cases after *in vitro* T cell- and monocyte-depletion steps.[12]

The synergistic or concatenate interactions between hematopoietic growth factors in reconstitution of marrow function following irradiation or chemotherapy[13–15] prompted us to assess the role of these agents in stimulating leukemic cell differentiation and recovery of normal hematopoiesis.

[a]Supported by Grants CA20194, CA32156 and CA31780 from the National Cancer Institute, American Cancer Society Grant CH-3K, and the Gar Reichman Fund of the Cancer Research Institute.

[b]G-CSF, M-CSF, GM-CSF: granulocyte-, macrophage-, granulocyte-macrophage-colony-stimulating factor, respectively.

TABLE 1. Cytokines Inducing Leukemic Cell Differentiation

Cytokine[a]	Leukemic Target	References
G-CSF	M1 (murine)	16,20
	WEHI-3 (murine)	17-19,23,25
	HL-60 (human)	18,19,21,25
	U-937 (human)	22,25
	Primary leukemia (human)	19,23,24,25
LIF/HILDA/DIF/D-Factor[b]	M1 (murine)	26-29
IL-6/IFN-β_2/MGI-2A[c]	M1 (murine)	30,31
	WEHI-3 (murine)	31
	AML-193 (human)	32
	U-937 (human)	34
IL-6 + IFN-γ	U-937 (human)	34
IL-1	M1 (murine [*in vivo*])	35
IL-1 + IFN-β_1	M1 (murine)	36
IL-1 + TNF	M1 (murine)	37
TNF	M1 (murine)	37

[a] G-CSF, granulocyte colony-stimulating factor; LIF, leukemia inhibitory factor; HILDA, human interleukin-DA; DIF, differentiation-inducing factor; D-Factor, differentiation factor; IL, interleukin; IFN, interferon; MGI-2A, macrophage-granulocyte inducer-type 2A; TNF, tumor necrosis factor.

[b] LIF and HILDA are identical and probably are also identical to DIF and D-Factor.

[c] MGI-2A is very similar, if not identical, to IL-6, which is identical to IFN-β_2.

G-CSF has proved effective in inducing terminal differentiation of primary human leukemic cells, as well as human and murine leukemic cell lines (TABLE 1). *In vivo,* increased survival was observed following continuous treatment with recombinant human G-CSF in mice bearing a differentiation-inducible variant of the murine myelomonocytic leukemic cell line WEHI-3.[25] Leukemic myeloid cells characteristically exhibit an uncoupling of proliferation and differentiation, so that immature progenitors accumulate. G-CSF promotes neutrophil differentiation in both normal and leukemic cells. In contrast, a cytokine termed HILDA (human interleukin-DA) was isolated from human T cell lines[26] and from a variety of human tumor cell lines,[27] based upon its ability to induce proliferation, but not differentiation, of a murine IL-3-dependent cell line (DA1a). HILDA proved identical to a leukemia inhibitory factor (LIF) cloned from a T lymphocyte DNA library and capable of inducing macrophage differentiation in M1 murine myeloid leukemic cells.[28] HILDA/LIF does not stimulate proliferation of normal progenitor cells and is apparently distinct from the known colony-stimulating factors.[26,28] In contrast to G-CSF, LIF/HILDA does not induce differentiation of WEHI-3 and HL-60 myeloid leukemic cells. From its biochemical properties and biological actions, LIF appears to be the same factor as D-Factor purified from L cell-conditioned medium by Tomida *et al.*[29]

A differentiation-inducing protein termed macrophage-granulocyte inducer, type 2A (MGI-2A) induces differentiation, but not proliferation, of normal myeloid progenitor cells and some clones of myeloid leukemic cells.[30] Purification and amino acid sequencing indicated that MGI-2A was very similar, if not identical, to IL-6 (also called interferon-β_2 or B cell differentiation factor).[30,31] IL-6 is a differentiation factor for normal and transformed B cells, inducing the secretion of immunoglobulin. It also induces the differentiation of cytotoxic T cells from thymocytes in the presence of IL-2.[31] IL-6 produces rapid inhibition of proliferation of the murine M1 myeloid leukemic cell line with induction of phagocytic activity and morphological changes characteristic of mature macrophages.[31,34] IL-6 also enhanced the expression of the Fc gamma receptor (FcγR) and c-*fms* in differentiation-responsive but not in unresponsive sub-lines of the murine WEHI-3 leukemia. In an analysis of three growth factor-dependent human leukemic cell lines that respond with continuous proliferation in the presence of GM-CSF and IL-3 in culture, one myeloid leukemic line exhibited terminal basophilic-granulocytic differentiation in the presence of IL-6, but a synergistic proliferative response was seen when the same cell line was treated with both GM-CSF and IL-6.[32] While IL-6 had little effect by itself on ANLL blast-cell colony formation, it synergized with GM-CSF and IL-3 in stimulating proliferation of myeloid blast progenitors, both leukemic and normal.[33] IL-6 induced partial differentiation of human histiocytic lymphoma U-937 cells.[34] The effect of IL-6 was synergized by IFN-γ (TABLE 1).

In vivo, administration of IL-1 has been shown to induce terminal differentiation of IL-1 sensitive, but not IL-1 resistant, clones of murine myeloid leukemic cells, and IL-1 and GM-CSF acted synergistically to induce differentiation of a GM-CSF responsive, IL-1 non-responsive clone of leukemic cells.[35] The *in vivo* action of IL-1 was associated with the rapid induction into the circulation of the differentiation-inducing protein MGI-2A, now identified as IL-6.[30]

Synergistic interactions between IL-1, tumor necrosis factor (TNF), and interferon-beta (IFN-β) can also be seen *in vitro* in the induction of differentiation of M1 cells.[36] All three cytokines are antiproliferative for M1 cells, and treatment of cells with a mixture of any two of the three cytokines results in at least additive growth inhibition. The differentiation-inducing factor for M1 cells which is found in lipopolysaccharide-stimulated peritoneal macrophage-conditioned medium was also identified as TNF, and part of the differentiation-inducing capacity was shown to be the result of a cooperative effect between TNF and IL-1.[37]

METHODS

Tissue Culture Media and Reagents

Iscove's modified Dulbecco's medium (IMDM) was prepared from Dulbecco's modified Eagle's medium as described previously.[13] Twenty percent fetal calf serum (KC Biologicals, Lenasca, KS) was used as the serum supplement. Recombinant human (rh) interleukin-1 alpha and beta (rhIL-1α and rhIL-1β) were kindly provided by Dr. D. Webb (Syntex Inc, Palo Alto, CA); rhG-CSF by Dr. L. Souza (Amgen, Thousand Oaks, CA); rhG-CSF-1 by Dr. P. Ralph, (Cetus Corp. Emeryville, CA); and recombinant murine (rm) GM-CSF (rmGM-CSF), rhIL-6, and rmIL-6 by Dr. S. Gillis (Immunex Inc, Seattle, WA).

Leukemic Cell Lines

Differentiation-inducible variants of the murine WEHI-3 B myelomonocytic leukemic cell line (W-3B-D$^+$) and a non-inducible variant (W-3B-D$^-$) were used as

TABLE 2. Differentiation of HL-60 Human Myeloid Leukemic Cells in Clonogenic Assay

Stimulus	Colonies[a] % Differentiated	% of Control
Medium (control)	2 ± 1	100
Retinoic acid 10^{-7} *M*	100 ± 10	43
rhIL-1β		
1000 U/ml	70 ± 6	60
100 U/ml	34 ± 8	80
10 U/ml	21 ± 4	86
1 U/ml	18 ± 8	75

[a] 600 cells per ml were plated and scored (% Differentiated) for diffuse (differentiated) versus compact (undifferentiated) colonies at 14 days. Total number of colonies versus number in control (% of Control) indicates relative cloning efficiency.

targets for the cytokine differentiation assay. Both the D^+ and D^- cells cloned with a 20-50% efficiency in agarose culture. Differentiation was assessed as the conversion of compact, undifferentiated colonies to partially diffuse (pd) or fully diffuse (d) colonies, reflecting the differentiation of leukemic blast cells to granulocytes and macrophages with enhanced migratory properties. HL-60 human promyelocytic leukemic cells in both a differentiation-inducible (D^+) and in non-inducible (D^-) variants were also used as targets in differentiation assays using diffuse-differentiated colonies as an end point.

RESULTS

The differentiation-inducing ability of rhIL-1β was tested on sublines of the HL-60 promyelocytic leukemia in clonal assay. In a highly differentiation-inducible subline of HL-60, where 10^{-7} *M* 13-*cis*-retinoic acid produced conversion of 100 % of the colonies from compact-undifferentiated to diffuse-differentiated, IL-1 was also capable of inducing granulocyte-macrophage differentiation (TABLE 2). A second subline of HL-60 was only weakly inducible with retinoic acid, and no significant differentiation was evident with IL-1β alone, except at the highest concentration used (100 U/ml) (TABLE 3). rhG-CSF at concentrations of 1000 U/ml or greater was as effective as retinoic acid in inducing granulocytic differentiation of this subline of HL-60 but had no significant effect on cloning efficiency. No synergism was seen when IL-1 and G-CSF were combined, although a significant additive effect on differentiation was seen with 100 U/ml of rhIL-1β in combination with lower concentrations (10 or and 100 U/ml) of rhG-CSF.

The murine myelomonocytic leukemia cell line WEHI-3 B exists in granulocyte-macrophage differentiation-inducible (D^+) and non-inducible (D^-) forms. As in HL-60, the induction of differentiation in WEHI-3B was associated with conversion of compact colonies to partially or fully diffuse, differentiated colonies by seven days of culture. Between 63% and 100% of D^+ colonies were induced to differentiate in the presence of 2.5% of serum from mice treated with *Corynebacterium parvum* and endotoxin. This type of serum is the most potent source of differentiation stimuli for WEHI-3 and is a rich source of IL-1, G-CSF, GM-CSF, TNF, IL-6 and interferon, all agents with demonstrable differentiation-inducing ability (TABLE 1). While no single factor was as effective as *C. parvum* sera, rhG-CSF at 10,000 U/ml induced a third of the colonies to differentiate (TABLE 4), and the effect was seen with as little as 10 U/ml of rhG-CSF (TABLE 5). rmGM-CSF, even at high concentrations, was not an effective differentiation-inducing factor (TABLE 4). rhIL-1β was as effective as G-CSF in inducing differentiation (TABLE 4) with significant activity at 0.1 U/ml (TABLE 5).

rmIL-6 has been reported to induce WEHI-3 differentiation[31] and may be a component of *C. parvum* serum synergizing with G-CSF in a manner similar to that observed between IL-1 and G-CSF. Neither IL-6 nor combinations of IL-6 plus G-CSF were as effective as *C. parvum* serum in inducing differentiation (TABLE 6). Partial differentiation of up to 28% of the leukemic colonies was observed with IL-6 alone, but the combination of IL-6 and G-CSF was not significantly more effective than G-CSF alone.

The time needed to irreversibly alter the self-renewal versus differentiation probability of leukemic blast cells upon exposure to cytokines was investigated by incubating WEHI-3 D^+ cells for 72 hr in suspension culture with rhG-CSF, rhIL-1α, or a combination of the two. After this exposure, cells were washed extensively and plated in clonal assay for seven days in the presence or absence of rhG-CSF (TABLE 7). rhG-CSF induced differentiation of 25% of the WEHI-3 leukemic colonies (a lower value than observed in earlier experiments, reflecting the propensity of the D^+ variant

TABLE 3. Differentiation of HL-60 Promyelocytic Leukemic Cells in Clonal Assay in Response to rhIL-1β and rhG-CSF

	Colonies[a]	
Stimulus	% Differentiated	% of Control
Medium (control)	2 ± 1	100
Retinoic acid 10^{-7} *M*	23 ± 17	103
rhG-CSF		
10,000 U/ml	27 ± 6	93
1,000 U/ml	22 ± 4	96
100 U/ml	13 ± 9	103
10 U/ml	4 ± 3	91
rhIL-1β		
100 U/ml	8 ± 3	111
10 U/ml	6 ± 4	96
1 U/ml	4 ± 4	101
0.1 U/ml	1 ± 1	107
rhIL-1β (100 U/ml) + rhG-CSF[b]		
10,000 U/ml	25 ± 6	98
1,000 U/ml	24 ± 4	94
100 U/ml	18 ± 6	102
10 U/ml	13 ± 9	94

[a] 600 cells per ml were plated and scored (% Differentiation) for diffuse (differentiated) versus compact (undifferentiated) colonies at 14 days. Total number of colonies versus number in control (% of Control) indicates relative cloning efficiency.

[b] Combined treatment with 100 U/ml of rhIL-1β and indicated concentrations of rhG-CSF.

to convert to a D^- state). Nevertheless, pre-incubation with IL-1 for 72 hr sensitized 40% of the clonogenic cells to undergo differentiation in a subsequent seven-day assay in the absence of exogenous factors and promoted 53% colony differentiation when rhG-CSF was added to the clonogenic assay. Pre-incubation with rG-CSF was as effective in promoting subsequent leukemic colony differentiation as was the presence of G-CSF during the clonogenic assay. However, pre-incubation with G-CSF plus addition of G-CSF to the clonal assay nearly doubled the differentiation response over pre- or post-cloning treatment alone. Pre-incubation with IL-1 and G-CSF was significantly more effective than either agent alone in promoting subsequent colony differentiation (TABLE 7). The greatest degree of differentiation (72%) resulted from pre-incubation of cells in suspension culture with IL-1 and G-CSF followed by cloning in the presence of G-CSF.

TABLE 4. Differentiation of Murine Myelomonocytic Leukemic Cells (WEHI-3B-D^+) in Clonogenic Assay

	Colonies[a]	
Stimulus	% Differentiated	% of Control
Medium (control)	5 ± 3	100
C. parvum sera (2.5%)[b]	100 ± 7	56
rhG-CSF 10,000 U/ml	31 ± 8	102
rmGM-CSF 10,000 U/ml	9 ± 2	101
rhIL-1β		
1,000 U/ml	33 ± 7	108
100 U/ml	43 ± 11	100
10 U/ml	33 ± 10	100
1 U/ml	35 ± 8	97

[a] 300 cells per ml were plated and scored (% Differentiation) for diffuse (differentiated) versus compact (undifferentiated) colonies at 7 days. Total number of colonies versus number in control (% of Control) indicates relative cloning efficiency.

[b] Sera from mice treated with *C. parvum* and endotoxin.

DISCUSSION

Postdeterministic differentiation of normal hematopoietic cells requires the presence of appropriate factors with variable degrees of lineage specificity. Sequential interactions between various cytokines are involved in the differentiation pathway, with IL-1 and IL-6 in particular identified as agents acting upon early stem cells, "priming" them to respond to differentiation factors such as G-CSF, GM-CSF, M-CSF and IL-5. Our studies using murine and human myeloid leukemic cell lines confirm and extend earlier observations that G-CSF, but not GM-CSF, can directly facilitate granulocytic differentiation of myeloid leukemic blast cells. In addition, we show that IL-1 is directly effective as a differentiation-inducing agent, and, as in normal hematopoiesis, it may act additively or synergistically with other factors. The observation that IL-1 can "prime" leukemic cells to subsequent G-CSF treatment has implications for possible modes of leukemia therapy to be explored in the future.

TABLE 5. IL-1 and G-CSF Induction of Differentiation of a D$^+$ Variant of the WEHI-3 Myelomonocytic Leukemia Cell Line in Clonal Assay

	Colonies[a]	
Stimulus	% Differentiated	% of Control
Medium (control)	4 ± 4	100
C. parvum sera (2.5%)[b]	63 ± 7	100
rhIL-1β		
10 U/ml	56 ± 7	92
1 U/ml	27 ± 15	106
0.1 U/ml	19 ± 9	103
rhG-CSF		
10 U/ml	20 ± 17	101
1 U/ml	9 ± 5	109
0.1 U/ml	10 ± 1	119

[a] 300 cells per ml were plated and scored (% Differentiation) for diffuse (differentiated) versus compact (undifferentiated) colonies at 7 days. Total number of colonies versus number in control (% of Control) indicates relative cloning efficiency.

[b] Sera from mice treated with *C. parvum* and endotoxin.

TABLE 6. IL-6 and G-CSF Induction of Differentiation of a D$^+$ Variant of the WEHI-3 Myelomonocytic Leukemia Cell Line in Clonal Assay

	Colonies[a]		
	% Differentiated		
Stimulus	Partial	Complete	% of Control
Medium (control)	8 ± 2	3 ± 3	100
C. parvum sera (2.5)[b]	41 ± 18	54 ± 9	72
rmIL-6			
10,000 U/ml	28 ± 12	3 ± 1	94
1,000 U/ml	24 ± 14	4 ± 4	117
100 U/ml	15 ± 5	2 ± 2	114
rhG-CSF 100 U/ml	39 ± 3	3 ± 2	124
rhG-CSF (100 U/ml) + IL-6[c]			
10,000 U/ml	48 ± 29	6 ± 2	152
1,000 U/ml	43 ± 20	5 ± 2	97
100 U/ml	49 ± 37	9 ± 4	104

[a] 300 cells per ml were plated and scored (% Differentiation) for fully diffuse (completely differentiated), partially diffuse (partially differentiated), or compact (undifferentiated) colonies at 7 days. Total number of colonies versus number in control (% of Control) indicates relative cloning efficiency.

[b] Sera from mice treated with *C. parvum* and endotoxin.

[c] Combined treatment with rhG-CSF (100 U/ml) and indicated concentrations of IL-6.

TABLE 7. Influence of Pre-incubation of Murine Myelomonocytic Leukemic Cells (WEHI-3B-D$^+$) with IL-1 or G-CSF on Subsequent Differentiation in Clonogenic Assay

72-hr Pre-incubation Stimulus[a]	% Differentiated Colonies[b]	
	Medium	G-CSF (10,000 U/ml)
Medium (control)	0.3 ± 0.6	24 ± 15
rhIL-1α 100 U/ml	40.0 ± 8	53 ± 3
rhG-CSF 10,000 U/ml	24.0 ± 11	47 ± 7
IL-1α + G-CSF	57.0 ± 5	72 ± 9

[a] WEHI-3 cells were incubated at 2 × 10^4 cells/ml for 72 hr in medium in the absence (control) or in the presence of IL-1α, or G-CSF, or a combination of rhIL-1α (100 U/ml) plus rhG-CSF (10,000 U/ml) prior to clonogenic assay in the presence or absence of rhG-CSF.
[b] % of colonies with diffuse morphology.

Extrapolation from studies on leukemic cell lines to the design of maturation therapy applicable to patients with leukemia or preleukemic disorders should be undertaken with caution. Certain cell lines (e.g., M1, HL-60), or variants thereof, may be universal responders to differentiation stimuli and in this regard be atypical. IL-6, for example, was identified as a macrophage-granulocyte inducer (MGI-2A) for M1 cells and is a potent inducer of macrophage differentiation of this cell line.[35] Phenotypic changes during differentiation involved inhibition of proliferation, induction of phagocytic activity, and, at a molecular level, a decrease in the accumulation of proto-oncogene c-*myc* mRNA and increases in the expression of mRNAs for FcγR and proto-oncogenes c-*fos* and c-*fms* (CSF-1R). In contrast, IL-6 was only weakly active as a differentiation-inducer on WEHI-3B D$^+$ cells in this study and enhanced the expression of FcγR and c-*fms* genes in D$^+$ but not in D$^-$ cells in the study of Chiu and Lee.[31]

Leukemia inhibitory factor is also not a leukemia-specific agent, since it stimulates proliferation of early hematopoietic progenitor cells.[26,27] Furthermore, it induces differentiation of the murine M1 myeloid leukemic cell line but not the murine WEHI-3 myelomonocytic leukemia cells.

Treatment modalities for leukemia involve chemotherapy and/or radiotherapy, resulting in severe depression of hematopoiesis and immune function. Administration of cytokines such as IL-1 and G-CSF has proved effective *in vivo* in counteracting myelotoxicity in both preclinical and clinical studies.[13–15,38,39] Cytokines that possess the potential for inducing leukemic blast cells to differentiate to functionally normal, non-dividing end cells and, at the same time, promote recovery of normal hematopoietic stem cells clearly have a role in leukemia therapy.

REFERENCES

1. MOORE, M. A. S., G. SPITZER, N. WILLIAMS & D. METCALF. 1974. Agar Culture studies in 127 cases of untreated acute leukemia: The prognostic value of reclassification of leukemia according to in vitro growth characteristics. Blood **44:** 1-6.

2. Delwel, R., L. Dorssers, I. Touw, G. Wagemaker & B. Lowenberg. 1987. Human recombinant multilineage colony stimulating factor (interleukin-3): Stimulator of acute myelocytic leukemia progenitor cells in vitro. Blood **70:** 333-336.
3. Lowenberg, B., M. Salem & R. Delwel. 1988. Effects of recombinant multi-CSF, GM-CSF, G-CSF and M-CSF on the proliferation and maturation of human AML in vitro. Blood Cells **14:** 539-549.
4. Miyauchi, J., C. A. Kelleher, G. G. Wong, Y.-C. Yang, S. C. Clark, S. Minkin, M. D. Minden & E. A. McCulloch. 1988. The effects of combinations of the recombinant growth factors GM-CSF, G-CSF, IL-3, and CSF-1 on leukemic blast cells in suspension culture. Leukemia **2:** 382-387.
5. Miyauchi, J., C. A. Kelleher, Y. C. Yang, G. G. Wong, S. C. Clark, M. D. Minden, S. Minkin & E. A. McCulloch. 1987. The effects of three recombinant growth factors, IL-3, GM-CSF, and G-CSF, on the blast cells of acute myeloblastic leukemia maintained in short-term suspension culture. Blood **70:** 657-663.
6. Suzuki, T., K. Nagata, I. Murohashi & N. Nara. 1988. Effect of recombinant human M-CSF on the proliferation of leukemic blast progenitors in AML patients. Leukemia **2:** 358-362.
7. Cozzolino, F., A. Rubartelli & D. Aldinucci. Interleukin 1 as an autocrine growth factor for acute myeloid leukemia cells. Proc. Natl. Acad. Sci. USA. Manuscript submitted.
8. Furukawa, Y., M. Ohta, Y. Miura & M. Saito. 1987. Interleukin-1 derived from human monocytic leukemia cell line JOSK-I acts as an autocrine growth factor. Biochem. Biophys. Res. Commun. **147:** 39-46.
9. Russell, N. H. & I. A. G. Reilly. 1989. Role of autocrine growth factors in the leukemic transformation of the myelodysplastic syndromes. Leukemia **3:** 83-84.
10. Young, D. C., K. Wagner & J. D. Griffin. 1987. Constitutive expression of the granulocyte-macrophage colony-stimulating factor gene in acute myeloblastic leukemia. J. Clin. Invest. **79:** 100-106.
11. Young, D. C., G. D. Demetri, T. J. Ernst, S. A. Cannistra & J. D. Griffin. 1988. In vitro expression of colony-stimulating factor genes by human acute myeloblastic leukemia cells. Exp. Hematol. **16:** 378-382.
12. Kaufman, D. C., M. R. Baer, X. Z. Gao, Z. Wang & H. D. Preisler. 1988. Enhanced expression of the granulocyte-macrophage colony stimulating factor gene in acute myelocytic leukemia cells following in vitro blast cell enrichment. Blood **72:** 1329-1332.
13. Moore, M. A. S. & D. J. Warren. 1987. Interleukin-1 and G-CSF synergism: *In vivo* stimulation of stem cell recovery and hematopoietic regeneration following 5-fluorouracil treatment in mice. Proc. Natl. Acad. Sci. USA **84:** 7134-7138.
14. Neta, R., J. J. Oppenheim & S. D. Douches. 1988. Interdependence of the radioprotective effects of human recombinant interleukin 1α, tumor necrosis factor a, granulocyte colony-stimulating factor, and murine recombinant granulocyte-macrophage colony-stimulating factor. J. Immunol. **140:** 108-111.
15. Benjamin, W. R., N. S. Tare & T. J. Hayes. 1988. Regulation of hemopoiesis in myelosuppressed mice by human recombinant IL-1α. J. Immunol. **142:** 792-799.
16. Tomida, M., Y. Y. Yamaguchi, M. Hozumi, T. Okabe & F. Takaku. 1986. Induction by recombinant human granulocyte colony-stimulating factor of differentiation of mouse myeloid leukemic M1 cells. FEBS Lett. **207:** 271-275.
17. Nicola, N. A. & D. Metcalf. 1981. Biochemical properties of differentiation factors for murine myelomonocytic leukemic cells in organ conditioned media—separation from colony-stimulating factors. J. Cell. Physiol. **109:** 253-264.
18. Welte, K. W., E. Platzer, L. Lu, P. Harris, E. Levi, R. Mertelsmann & M. A. S. Moore. 1985. Purification and biochemical characterization of human pluripotent hematopoietic colony-stimulating factor. Proc. Natl. Acad. Sci. USA **82:** 1526-1530.
19. Souza, L. M., T. C. Boone, J. L. Gabrilove, P. H. Lai, K. M. Zsebo, D. C. Murdock, V. R. Chazin, J. Bruszewski, H. Lu, K. K. Chen, J. Barendt, E. Platzer, M. A. S. Moore, R. Mertelsmann & K. Welte. 1986. Recombinant human granulocyte colony-stimulating factor: Effects on normal and leukemic myeloid cells. Science **232:** 61-65.

20. TSUDA, H., L. M. NECKERS & D. H. PLUZNIK. 1986. Colony stimulating factor-induced differentiation of murine M1 myeloid leukemia cells is permissive in early G_1 phase. Proc. Natl. Acad. Sci. USA **83:** 4317-4321.

21. HARRIS, P. E., P. RALPH, J. GABRILOVE, K. WELTE, R. KARMALI & M. A. S. MOORE. 1985. Distinct differentiation-inducing activities of y (gamma)-interferon and cytokine factors acting on the human promyelocytic leukemia cell line HL-60. Cancer Res. **45:** 3090-3095.

22. HARRIS, P. E., P. RALPH, P. LITCOFSKY & M. A. S. MOORE. 1985. Distinct activities of interferon-y (gamma), lymphokine and cytokine differentiation inducing factors acting on the human monoblastic leukemia cell line U937. Cancer Res. **45:** 9-13.

23. YUO, A., S. KITAGAWA, T. OKABE, A. URABE, Y. KOMATSU, S. ITOH & F. TAKAKU. 1987. Recombinant human granulocyte colony-stimulating factor repairs the abnormalities of neutrophils in patients with myelodysplastic syndromes and chronic myelogenous leukemia. Blood **70:** 404-411.

24. PEBUSQUE, M. J., M. LAFAGE, M. LOPEZ & P. MANNONI. 1988. Preferential response of acute myeloid leukemias with translocation involving chromosome 17 to human recombinant granulocyte colony-stimulating factor. Blood **72:** 257-265.

25. MOORE, M. A. S. 1987. Growth and maturation factors in leukemia. *In* Principles of Cancer Biotherapy. R. K. Oldham, Ed.: 399-446. Raven Press. New York.

26. MOREAU, J.-F., M. BONNEVILLE, A. GODARD, H. GASCAN, V. BRUART, M. A. S. MOORE & J. P. SOULILLOU. 1987. Characterization of a factor produced by human T cell clones exhibiting eosinophil-activating and burst-promoting activities. J. Immunol. **138:** 3844-3849.

27. GASCAN, H., A. GODARD, V. PRALORAN, J. NAULET, J.-F. MOREAU, Y. JACQUES & J.-P. SOULILLOU. Characterization of HILDA/leukemia inhibitory factor secreted by human tumor cell lines. J. Immunol. In press.

28. GEARING, D. P., N. M. GOUGH, J. A. KING, D. J. HILTON, N. A. NICOLA, R. J. SIMPSON, E. C. NICE, A. KELSO & D. METCALF. 1987. Molecular cloning and expression of cDNA encoding a murine myeloid leukemia inhibitory factor (LIF). EMBO J. **6:** 3995-4002.

29. TOMIDA, M., Y. YAMAMOTO-YAMAGUCHI & M. HOZUMI. 1984. Purification of a factor inducing differentiation of mouse myeloid leukemic M1 cells from conditioned medium of mouse fibroblast L929 cells. J. Biol. Chem. **259:** 10978-10982.

30. SHABO, Y., J. LOTEM, M. RUBINSTEIN, M. REVEL, S. C. CLARK, S. F. WOLF, R. KAMEN & L. SACHS. 1988. The myeloid blood cell differentiation-inducing protein MGI-2A is interleukin-6. Blood **72:** 2070-2073.

31. CHIU, C.-P. & F. LEE. 1989. IL-6 is a differentiation factor for M1 and WEHI-3B myeloid leukemic cells. J. Immunol. **142:** 1909-1915.

32. CARACCIOLO, D., S. C. CLARK & G. ROVERA. 1989. Human interleukin-6 supports granulocytic differentiation of hematopoietic progenitor cells and acts synergistically with GM-CSF. Blood **73:** 666-670.

33. HOANG, T., A. HAMAN, O. GONCALVES, G. G. WONG & S. C. CLARK. 1988. Interleukin-6 enhances growth factor-dependent proliferation of the blast cells of acute myeloblastic leukemia. Blood **72:** 823-826.

34. CHEN, L., D. NOVICK, M. RUBINSTEIN & M. REVEL. 1988. Recombinant interferon-β2 (interleukin-6) induces myeloid differentiation. FEBS Lett. **239:** 299-304.

35. LOTEM, J. & L. SACHS. 1988. In vivo control of differentiation of myeloid leukemic cells by cyclosporine A and recombinant interleukin-1α. Blood **72:** 1595-1601.

36. ONOZAKI, K., H. URAWA, T. TAMATANI, Y. IWAMURA, T. HASHIMOTO, T. BABA, H. SUZUKI, M. YAMADA, S. YAMAMOTO, J. J. OPPENHEIM & K. MATSUSHIMA. 1988. Synergistic interactions of interleukin 1, interferon-β, and tumor necrosis factor in terminally differentiating a mouse myeloid leukemic cell line (M1). Evidence that interferon-β is an autocrine differentiating factor. J. Immunol. **140:** 112-119.

37. TAMATANI, T., H. URAWA, T, HASHIMOTO & K. ONOZAKI. 1987. Tumor necrosis factor as an interleukin 1-dependent differentiation inducing factor (D-Factor) for mouse myeloid leukemic cells. Biochem. Biophys. Res. Commun. **143:** 390-397.

38. GABRILOVE, J. L., A. JAKUBOWSKI, H. SCHER, C. STERNBERG, G. WONG, J. GROUS, A. YAGODA, K. FAIN, M. A. S. MOORE, B. CLARKSON, H. F. OETTGEN, K. ALTON, K. WELTE & L. SOUZA. 1988. Effect of granulocyte colony-stimulating factor on neutropenia

and associated morbidity due to chemotherapy for transitional-cell carcinoma of the urothelium. New Engl. J. Med. **318:** 1414-1422.

39. BRONCHUD, M. H., J. H. SCARFFE, N. THATCHER, D. CROWTHER, L. M. SOUZA, N. K. ALTON, N. G. TESTA & T. M. DEXTER. 1987. Phase I/II study of recombinant human granulocyte colony-stimulating factor in patients receiving intensive chemotherapy for small cell lung cancer. Br. J. Cancer **56:** 809-813.

Programmed Cell Death in the Blastocyst[a]

G. BARRY PIERCE, ROBERT A. GRAMZINSKI, AND RALPH E. PARCHMENT

Department of Pathology
University of Colorado School of Medicine
4200 East Ninth Avenue
Denver, Colorado 80262

Embryonal carcinoma cells injected into blastocysts are normalized, incorporate into the inner cell mass (ICM), which will form the embryo proper, and, with the embryonic cells, participate in embryonic development and sometimes even eventuate chimeric mice.[1-3] Ideally, these chimeric animals have cancer-derived normal cells in each tissue, but the ideal is not always attained. The phenomenon appears to be strain-specific: certain strains of embryonal carcinoma do not form chimeras when injected into blastocysts, some form chimeras with tumors, and some form chimeras in which certain tissues are usually chimeric but others lack cancer-derived cells.[4-7] Irrespective, it seemed reasonable to conclude that the blastocyst can abrogate the malignancy of at least some strains of embryonal carcinoma and normalize the cells so that they then behave as normal ICM cells. We decided to study the mechanism of blastocyst regulation of embryonal carcinoma to learn not only about regulatory events in the blastocyst, but also about the possibility of developing non-toxic therapy for embryonal carcinoma.

To this end, two embryonal carcinomas, ECa 247[8] and P19,[9] were selected for study. Tumor and colony formation of ECa 247 are abrogated by the blastocyst.[10,11] However, this strain will not make chimeras when injected into blastocysts, because it preferentially localizes in the trophectoderm, which forms extraembryonic tissues.[4] P19 does not make viable full-term chimeras, but about 60% of the midterm embryos derived from blastocysts injected with these cells are chimeric.[12] Thus, study of these strains of embryonal carcinoma in the blastocyst provides an opportunity to compare and contrast regulation of cells with extraembryonic and embryonic potentials.

Initial studies were performed with ECa 247. The first experiments demonstrated blastocyst abrogation of tumor formation when single embryonal carcinoma cells were placed in blastocysts and the injected blastocysts were put in the testes of compatible strains. Eighty percent fewer tumors developed from the ECa 247 cells in the blastocyst than from single embryonal carcinoma ECa 247 cells injected directly into the testis.[10]

[a] This work was supported in part by a gift from RJR Nabisco, Inc., and NIH Grants CA47369 and CA35367.

This effect was due to regulation inside the blastocyst, since ECa 247 cells in the perivitelline space were not regulated. Abrogation of tumor formation appeared to be tumor-specific, because leukemia, melanoma, and sarcoma cells were not regulated by the blastocyst.[13] The non-embryonal carcinoma cell lines also served as a necessary control to demonstrate that the results obtained with embryonal carcinoma cells were not due to technical artifacts such as mechanical injury to cells or loss of cells. Blastocysts injected with ECa 247 cells and then cultured *in vitro* abrogated colony formation as well.[11]

Colony formation of ECa 247 was not abrogated by culturing the cells in apposition to trophectoderm or ICM in Eagle's minimal essential media with 10% fetal calf serum, nor by culturing the cells directly in blastocoel fluid.[14] At the time these experiments were performed, our attention was focused on regulation of differentiation by the blastocyst, and we attributed any dead embryonal carcinoma cells to mechanical trauma rather than to the effects of a toxic factor in blastocoel fluid. Analysis of blastocoel fluid presented a formidable logistical task because of the small size of the embryo. The blastocyst is a hollow cellular sphere composed of about 64 cells at 3½ days of gestation. It measures about 80 μm in diameter. The shell, the zona pellucida, is a porous, putty-like membrane lined by 52 trophectodermal cells. These cells, which will form extraembryonic tissues, have tight junctions and form the wall of the blastocoel. The blastocoel contains 1×10^{-3} μl of fluid. Attached to the blastocoel surface of the trophectoderm and bathed by blastocoel fluid is a mass of 12 cells, the ICM. These will form the embryo proper. Because of the paucity of cells and fluid, indirect means were required to test their effects on the regulation of embryonal carcinoma. To this end, ECa 247 was cocultured with individual components of the blastocyst in standard tissue culture media: none of the components was able to alter the malignancy of the cancer cells, and it appeared that a combination of cells and blastocoel fluid would be required.[14] As with ECa 247, colony formation of P19 cells was abrogated by the blastocyst; and colony formation of both strains was abrogated when the cells were incorporated in trophectodermal vesicles.[14,15] It was concluded that both a soluble activity in blastocoel fluid and contact with trophectoderm were required for regulation.

For analysis of the effect of blastocoel fluid on embryonal carcinoma cells in the presence of ICM, giant blastocysts about eight times larger in volume than normal blastocysts were made by fusing eight 8-cell eggs according to the method of Pedersen and Spindle.[16] Then the blastomeres were evacuated from the zonae pellucidae of normal blastocysts by use of a small pipet. The washed zonae pellucidae were used as carriers of the cellular preparations to be tested in the giant blastocoel fluid.[16] For example, ICMs and embryonal carcinoma cells were injected into the zonae pellucidae, which in turn were placed in the blastocoels of the giant blastocyst. This created a situation in which the normal and neoplastic cells were in contact with each other and were bathed by giant blastocoel fluid but could not contact the cells of the giant blastocyst. After 24 hr of incubation, the zona pellucida carriers with their cells were rescued from the giant blastocysts, and the ability of the cancer cells to form colonies of neoplastic cells was determined by culturing the preparations in normal media. In the control situation, washed zonae pellucidae containing ICMs with attached cancer cells were incubated in tissue culture media alone, and the number of neoplastic colonies formed was compared to that for the experimental cells. Abrogation of colony formation was observed for ECa 247, but this incubation in blastocoel fluid in contact with ICM had no effect on colony formation of P19.[16] In addition, during these studies evidence was obtained suggesting that blastocoel fluid might contain toxic molecules.[14] The toxic activity was less tumor-specific than was the regulation of differentiation of embryonal carcinoma. For example, although there was no regulation of L1210 leukemia cells, there was abrogation of colony formation for Chinese hamster ovary (CHO) cells injected into blastocysts and cultured *in vitro.* This effect could be abolished by placing a conduit across the trophectoderm, allowing outflow of fluid from the blastocoel. CHO cells were not regulated under these conditions, and it was concluded that the toxic factor(s) killed CHO cells.[14] At that time, this toxicity was considered unimportant for regulation of embryonal carcinoma by the blastocyst, since the formation of chimeras by definition requires viable embryonal carcinoma cells. Thus, the presence of dead cells was attributed to mechanical trauma and ignored. In light of the observations made with ICMs in giant blastocysts, we can now hypothesize that there is in blastocoel fluid an activity toxic for CHO cells which also kills some normal ICM cells and the embryonal carcinoma with trophectodermal potential.

To test this hypothesis, zonae pellucidae, each containing only a single embryonal carcinoma cell, were incubated in giant blastocysts for 24 hr and rescued; then, the number of dead and viable cells was compared to controls in which the zonae pellucidae containing a single cell were cultured continuously in standard media. Forty-four percent of ECa 247 cells died in blastocoel fluid, which, interestingly, did not kill any P19 cells.[16] The idea that a toxin existed in blastocoel fluid that was lethal for one population of embryonal carcinoma cells (trophectodermal potential) but spared another (embryonic potential) could clearly have important implications for the development of the blastocyst.

The ICM of the early blastocyst, like ECa 247, has the potential to differentiate into trophectoderm,[17–22] a potential which is lost with time so that ICMs of late blastocysts, like P19, only differentiate into embryonic structures.[18,20,22–24] During the transition from early to late blastocyst, dead cells appear in the ICMs,[25,26] after which the ICMs cannot differentiate into trophectoderm.[22–24] Although other explanations for these phenomena can be considered, we favor the idea that there are subpopulations of ICM cells, caricatured by ECa 247 and P19, with trophectoderm and embryonic potential, respectively, and that the toxic factor in blastocoel fluid is responsible for initiating programmed cell death of pretrophectodermal cells in the ICM.

This idea is further strengthened by data from studies using C44,[27] a line of embryonal carcinoma cells derived from OTT6050.[28] Like other tumors, this one makes embryoid bodies when converted to the ascites. These embryoid bodies bear a strong resemblance morphologically, immunohistochemically, and functionally to normal blastocysts.[29] They even contain dead ICM cells and neoplastic blastocoel fluid. Enough neoplastic cell blastocoel fluid can be acquired for biochemical analysis. We have data which suggest that it contains a toxic factor similar to that described in normal blastocoel fluid. This factor preferentially kills ICM cells with trophectodermal potential, and, similarly, embryonal carcinoma cells with trophectodermal potential. This is the first demonstration that programmed cell death, conventionally viewed as "death from within," is in fact mediated by external factors. The end result is murder—not suicide. Irrespective, the net result would appear to be elimination of redundant cells at the time of induction so that the new phenotype is uncontaminated by unneeded cells. This mechanism would ensure the separation of embryonic and extraembryonic lineages. Purification of the toxic factor is nearing completion, and there are plans to subject the purified material to structural analysis by mass spectrometry.

ACKNOWLEDGMENTS

The authors gratefully acknowledge Andrea Lewellyn for her technical work and Vicky Starbuck for editorial assistance.

REFERENCES

1. BRINSTER, R. L. 1974. Effect of cells transferred into the mouse blastocyst on subsequent development. J. Exp. Med. **140:** 1049-1056.
2. PAPAIOANNOU, V. E., M. W. MCBURNEY, R. L. GARDNER & R. L. EVANS. 1975. Fate of teratocarcinoma cells injected into early mouse embryos. Nature **258:** 70-73.
3. MINTZ, B. & K. ILLMENSEE. 1975. Normal genetically mosaic mice produced from malignant teratocarcinoma cells. Proc. Natl. Acad. Sci. USA **72:** 3585-3589.
4. PIERCE, G. B., J. ARECHEGA, A. JONES, A. LEWELLYN & R. S. WELLS. 1987. The fate of embryonal carcinoma cells in mouse blastocysts. Differentiation **33:** 247-253.
5. PAPAIOANNOU, V. E., E. P. EVANS, R. L. GARDNER & C. F. GRAHAM. 1979. Growth and differentiation of an embryonal carcinoma cell line (C145). J. Embryol. Exp. Morphol. **54:** 277-295.
6. ILLMENSEE, K. 1978. Reversion of malignancy and normalized differentiation of teratocarcinoma cells in chimeric mice. *In* Genetic Mosaics and Chimeras in Mammals. L. B. Russell, Ed.: 3-25. Plenum. New York.
7. HANAOKA, K., Y. KATO & T. NOGUCHI. 1986. Comparative study on the ability of various teratocarcinomas to form chimeric mouse embryos. Dev. Growth Differ. **28:** 223-231.
8. LEHMAN, J. M., W. C. SPEERS, D. E. SWARTZENDRUBER & G. B. PIERCE. 1974. Neoplastic differentiation: Characteristics of cell lines derived from a murine teratocarcinoma. J. Cell. Physiol. **84:** 13-28.
9. MCBURNEY, M. W. & B. J. ROGERS. 1982. Isolation of male embryonal carcinoma cell lines and their chromosomal replication patterns. Dev. Biol. **89:** 503-508.
10. PIERCE, G. B., S. H. LEWIS, G. MILLER, E. MORITZ & P. MILLER. 1979. Tumorigenicity of embryonal carcinoma as an assay to study control of malignancy by the murine blastocyst. Proc. Natl. Acad. Sci. USA **76:** 6649-6651.
11. WELLS, R. S. 1982. An *in vitro* assay for growth regulation of embryonal carcinoma by the blastocyst. Cancer Res. **42:** 2736-2741.
12. ROSSANT, J. & M. W. MCBURNEY. 1983. Diploid teratocarcinoma cell lines differ in their ability to differentiate normally after blastocyst injection. *In* Cold Spring Harbor Conferences on Cell Proliferation: Teratocarcinoma Stem Cells. L. Silver, S. Strickland & G. Martin, Eds. Vol. 10: 625-633. Cold Spring Harbor Laboratory. Cold Spring Harbor, NY.
13. PIERCE, G. B., C. G. PANTAZIS, J. E. CALDWELL & R. S. WELLS. 1982. Specificity of control of tumor formation by the blastocyst. Cancer Res. **42:** 1082-1087.
14. PIERCE, G. B., D. AGUILAR, G. HOOD & R. S. WELLS. 1984. Trophectoderm in control of murine embryonal carcinoma. Cancer Res. **44:** 3987-3996.
15. PIERCE, G. B., A. LEWELLYN & R. PARCHMENT. 1989. Mechanism of programmed cell death in the blastocyst. Proc. Natl. Acad. Sci. USA **86:** 3654–3658.
16. PEDERSEN, R. A. & A. I. SPINDLE. 1980. Role of the blastocele microenvironment in early mouse differentiation. Nature **284:** 550-552.
17. HOGAN, B. & R. TILLY. 1978. In vitro development of inner cell masses isolated immunosurgically from mouse blastocysts. II. Inner cell masses from 3.5 to 4.0 day p.c. blastocysts. J. Embryol. Exp. Morphol. **45:** 107-121.
18. HANDYSIDE, A. H. 1978. Time of commitment of inside cells isolated from preimplantation mouse embryos. J. Embryol. Exp. Morphol. **45:** 37-53.
19. SPINDLE, A. I. 1978. Trophoblast regeneration by inner cell masses isolated from cultured mouse embryos. J. Exp. Zool. **203:** 483-489.

20. FLEMING, T. P., P. D. WARREN, J. C. CHISHOLM & M. H. JOHNSON. 1984. Trophectodermal processes regulate the expression of totipotency within the inner cell mass of the mouse expanding blastocyst. J. Embryol. Exp. Morphol. **84:** 63-90.
21. NICHOLS, J. & R. L. GARDNER. 1984. Heterogeneous differentiation of external cells in individual isolated early inner cell masses in culture. J. Embryol. Exp. Morphol. **80:** 225-240.
22. ROSSANT, J. & W. J. LIS. 1979. Potential of isolated mouse inner cell masses to form trophectoderm derivatives *in vivo.* Dev. Biol. **70:** 255-261.
23. GARDNER, R. L. & M. H. JOHNSON. 1972. An investigation of inner cell mass and trophoblast tissues following their isolation from the mouse blastocyst. J. Embryol. Exp. Morphol. **28:** 279-312.
24. GARDNER, R. L. & V. E. PAPAIOANNOU. 1975. Differentiation in the trophectoderm and inner cell mass. *In* The Early Development of Mammals. M. Balls & A. E. Wild, Eds.: 107-132. Cambridge University Press. London.
25. EL-SCHERSHABY, A. M. & J. R. HINCHLIFFE. 1974. Cell redundancy in the zona-intact preimplantation mouse blastocyst: A light and electron microscopic study of dead cells and their fate. J. Embryol. Exp. Morphol. **31:** 643-654.
26. HANDYSIDE, A. H. & S. HUNTER. 1986. Cell division and death in the mouse blastocyst before implantation. Roux's Arch. Dev. Biol. **195:** 519-526.
27. MONZO, M., X. ANDRES & D. RUANO-GIL. 1983. Etude morphologique d'une population homogene de cellules de terato-carcinome. Bull. Assoc. Anat. **67:** 91-98.
28. STEVENS, L. C. 1970. The development of transplantable teratocarcinomas from intratesticular grafts of pre- and post-implantation mouse embryos. Dev. Biol. **21:** 364-382.
29. PARCHMENT, R. E., A. DAMJANOV, I. DAMJANOV, R. A. GRAMZINSKI & G. B. PIERCE. Neoplastic embryoid bodies of embryonal carcinoma as a source of blastocele fluid. Manuscript in preparation.

Proto-oncogenes and Differentiation versus Transformation of Striated Muscle Cells[a]

J. HAREL, M. P. LEIBOVITCH, M. GUILLIER, A. G. BORYCKI, AND S. A. LEIBOVITCH

Laboratoire d'Oncologie Moléculaire
UA 1158 du CNRS
Institut Gustave-Roussy
Rue Camille Desmoulins
94805 Villejuif, France

INTRODUCTION

It would be a truism to recall that unrestricted cell proliferation is a necessary but not sufficient condition for malignant transformation. Besides the crucial role of host factors, a multitude of observations demonstrate that cancer cells display variable neoplastic properties and are generally more-or-less dedifferentiated, whereas they often express anachronistic or ectopic gene products (see Refs. 1 and 2 for review). The concept that misprogramming of genetic information is operational in carcinogenesis[1-4] is indeed an old one, but it remained essentially speculative until the late sixties. In 1971 a successful approach to verify this concept was opened by the pioneer work of Charlotte Friend and her colleagues, who showed that erythroid differentiation of Friend erythroleukemia cells was induced by addition of dimethyl sulfoxide.[5] Further advances were rendered possible by the rapid development of research on proto-oncogenes (or c-onc genes) initially characterized as the cellular counterparts of the transforming (viral) genes (v-onc) of oncogenic retroviruses (see Ref. 6 for review).

Over the last few years, a growing body of evidence suggests that many of the proto-oncogenes identified thus far (possibly all of them) are normally involved in cell proliferation, development, and differentiation. For example, the proteins encoded by the c-*sis,* c-*fms,* c-*erB* and c-*erbA* genes are related, respectively, to platelet-derived growth factor (PDGF),[7,8] the cell surface receptor for the macrophage growth factor CSF-1,[9] the cell surface receptor for epithelial growth factor (EGF),[10] and the nuclear receptor for thyroid hormone.[11,12] Expression of the c-*myc*[13-15] and c-Ki-*ras*[14,16] genes is enhanced when quiescent cells in culture are induced to proliferate or when liver is regenerating.[17] A rapid but transient expression of the c-*fos* proto-oncogene precedes

[a] These studies were performed with the financial support of Institut Gustave-Roussy, CNRS, INSERM, and Association pour la Recherche sur le Cancer (ARC).

that of c-*myc* when fibroblasts or lymphocytes are treated with growth factors.[18–21] In line with this pattern, the levels of both c-*myb* and c-*myc* RNAs strongly decline during the differentiation of human myelocytic leukemia cells,[21] and the same is true, at least for c-*myc* transcripts, in other lines of murine[22] or human[23] hematopoietic cells.

Contrasting with the brief and transient expression of c-*fos* gene products in stimulated fibroblasts or lymphocytes, c-*fos* transcripts accumulate to a stable, maximal level in terminally differentiated macrophages,[21] and the same is true for c-*fms* transcripts.[24] The case of c-*fos* is exemplar, because it appears to have a pivotal role during the growth, differentiation, and development of various cell lineages or tissues.[25]

Transfer of a recombinant c-*fos* gene into mouse embryonal carcinoma (EC) F9 stem cells induced the expression of specific endodermal tissue markers.[26,27] However, less pronounced or no differentiation-promoting effects were observed in other EC cell lines.[27] Other recent data argue for a role of the *fos* gene in the regulation of bone formation[28] and in functional activities of neuronal tissues.[29,30] A physiological role for other proto-oncogenes in the nervous system is very probable, in view of recent reports showing that the transfer of an oncogenic *ras* gene[31] or inoculation of p21 *ras* protein,[32] as well as the transfection of a v-*src* oncogene,[33] into PC12 mouse cells triggers their neuronal differentiation—the latter result is consistent with the demonstration that pp60^{src} proteins accumulate in differentiated neuronal cells.[34] Although less documented, the case of the c-*mos* gene is nonetheless interesting. It was reported to be expressed at a very low level or not at all in a variety of mouse tissues, with the exception that its expression is elevated in testes, ovaries, and embryos.[35] It was further demonstrated that c-*mos* gene products are localized in the male and female germ lines, where their level is developmentally regulated.[36–38] However, the comparison of mouse and rat testes revealed striking species-specific variations in c-*mos* as well as in c-*abl* gene expression.[38]

These examples and some of the data presented in this paper illustrate the existence of large variations in expression of proto-oncogenes from one cell lineage or tissue to another and, within a lineage, from periods of cell proliferation to development or differentiation. Furthermore, at least some of the best-known proto-oncogenes appear to serve different functions depending on the cell type in which they are located, or its developmental stage, or even the animal species investigated. Therefore, in order to explore the role of proto-oncogenes in relation to normal cell growth, differentiation, neoplastic transformation and tumor progression, it appears necessary to have at one's disposal model *in vitro* systems consisting of cultured cells of well-defined origin capable of undergoing a well-characterized differentiation program and, for comparison, transformed derivatives of differing malignant potentials. As far as possible, it is also important to confirm *in vivo* the data obtained *in vitro*. During the last few years, we have established and studied in our laboratory such model systems, consisting of clonal lines of rat myoblasts. This paper reviews some of our previous data and presents new observations.

DIFFERENTIAL CHARACTERISTICS OF THE MYOGENIC L6a1 CELL AND ITS NON-FUSING TRANSFORMANTS

The origin and characteristics of the L6a1 cell line and its tumorigenic M4 and RMS4 derivatives established in our laboratory have been described.[39–44] In brief, the L6a1 line was obtained by subcloning the L6 cell of Yaffe,[45] derived from rat skeletal

TABLE 1. Differential Characteristics of the L6a1 Cell, the L6a1-Derived M4 Cell, and the M4-Derived RMS4 Cell

	Cell[a]		
Characteristics	L6a1	M4	RMS4
Doubling time (hr)			
In 10% FCS	22.3	21.7	20.8
In 2% FCS	65	25.6	24.2
Detachment time[b] (min)	25	15	10
% Colony-forming cells (in soft agar)	0.01	11-12	48-50
Tumorigenicity assay			
No. of cells inoculated	5×10^6	5×10^6	2×10^6
No. of tumor-bearing rats	0/10	8/10	10/10
Time of latency[c] (days)	—	25-30	4-6
Myogenic capacity	Yes	No	No

[a] The culture conditions and characterization methods for the three cell lines were as previously described.[39,41] Recent analyses confirmed that the L6a1 cell is euploid, the M4 nearly euploid, and the RMS4 hyperploid.

[b] Time required for the detachment (in 0.25% trypsin) of nearly all cells from semiconfluent monolayers.

[c] Time of appearance of palpable tumors after subcutaneous inoculation into suckling rats.

muscle of the fetal type. M4 is one of the subclones derived from the minor fraction of L6a1 cells that remained mononuclear after several cycles of differentiation, and RMS4 is one of the subclones derived from the tumors which developed in baby rats inoculated with M4 cells.

Typical properties of the three cell types that have remained stable to the present time are summarized in TABLE 1. These and other characteristics (cytological abnormalities, morphological aspects of the cell cultures, and the occurrence of rhabdomyosarcomas in animals) allowed us to conclude that L6a1 cells are essentially non-malignant, whereas M4 and RMS4 cells may be considered of low and high malignancy, respectively. When plated in the usual growth medium containing 10% fetal calf serum (FCS), the three cell types exhibit equivalent growth rates for 60-65 hr, until reaching confluency. Thereafter L6a1 cells are contact-inhibited, and this condition triggers the differentiation process characterized by the appearance of muscle-specific mRNAs, such as those coding for actin, myosin heavy chain (MHC), myosin light chain 2 (MLC2), troponin T (TnT), etc. However, this process remains abortive if the cells are maintained in the high-serum (i.e., 10% FCS) medium. Its continuation requires the transfer of the cell cultures to a low-serum medium (1-2% FCS), and it is completed 4-5 days later when the great majority of cells have fused to form myotubes. Throughout this process, muscle-specific transcripts and proteins accumulate at increasing levels while other gene products, like the cytoskeletal actins, are eliminated. In contrast, the tumorigenic M4 and RMS4 sublines, which have lost contact inhibition, continue to proliferate when transferred to the low-serum medium, and they express no detectable amount of muscle-specific gene products.

The fact that under optimal growth conditions the three cell types display comparable doubling times (see TABLE 1) and superimposable growth curves[41] for at least three cell generations was fundamental for comparative studies in order to ascertain that the eventual changes in gene activity observed in the transformed cells were not simply the result of changes in normal growth parameters. In a previous study (which may now appear a little old-fashioned) we used extracts from L6a1, M4 and RMS4 cells collected during the period of exponential growth for cDNA-mRNA hybridizations in liquid medium to compare poly(A)-rich mRNA populations from each cell type. By rough estimation, 28,000-30,000 distinct mRNA species, arbitrarily defined as 1.8 kilobases (kb) long and mostly belonging to the low-abundance class of mRNAs, appeared to be expressed in proliferating L6a1 cells, whereas (as indicated by recycling experiments) 10-12% of these mRNA species were seemingly absent from RMS4 cells. Conversely, 700-800 of the mRNA species expressed in RMS4 cells were seemingly absent from proliferating L6a1 cells. Moreover, changes of the same sort but of less pronounced amplitude were found in M4 cells. This suggested that a subset of genes normally expressed during the growth of myogenic cells is inactivated in relation to, or as a result of, neoplastic conversion, while a smaller set is activated, and that the number of genes involved correlates with cancer progression.[40]

DIFFERENTIAL EXPRESSION OF PROTO-ONCOGENES IN NEOPLASTIC TRANSFORMANTS COMPARED TO PROLIFERATING L6a1 MYOBLASTS

Consideration of these results in light of recent developments in oncogene research led us to suppose that in L6a1 cell transformants the tumor-activated set of genes was more likely to include proto-oncogenes than was the tumor-inactivated set and that the number of activated proto-oncogenes and (or) their level of expression were presumably greater in the highly malignant transformant than in the less malignant ones.

TABLE 2. Comparative Quantification of Proto-oncogene Transcripts in Proliferating L6a1 Cells and Transformants M4 and RMS4

	Cell[a]		
Proto-oncogene	L6a1	M4	RMS4
c-*myc*, c-*fms*	+++	+++	+++
c-*abl*, c-*myb*, c-*mos* c-*fgr*, c-Ha-*ras*	+	+	+
c-Ki-*ras*	+++	++	++++
c-N-*ras*	++	+++	+++
c-*fes*	+++	++	+
c-*erbB*	+++	+++	0
c-*fos*	+++	0	0
c-*src*, c-*sis*	+	+	0
c-*erbA*	+	0	0

[a] All cells were collected during their phase of exponential growth and processed for dot-blot hybridization with the ^{32}P-labeled proto-oncogene probes (6-8 $\times$ 10^5 cpm/ng, 10^6 cpm/ml). Rough quantitative comparisons based on densitometric measurement were performed as previously described,[41] except that total cellular RNA (30 μg per dot) was used.

In order to test this hypothesis, we used various recombinant DNA clones kindly provided by other laboratories to investigate c-onc transcripts in the three cell types and to search for obvious c-onc alterations in the genome of the neoplastic transformants. In the first series of these assays published,[41] the poly(A)-rich fraction of the cellular RNA was analyzed by the Northern blot and dot-blot hybridization procedures. It was found that all 15 proto-oncogenes assayed (listed in TABLE 2), with the apparent exception of one (c-*mos*), expressed detectable levels of transcripts during the growth of L6a1 cells. Surprisingly, in addition to c-*mos,* two other proto-oncogenes (c-*fos,* c-*erbA*) expressed no detectable polyadenylated mRNA in M4 and RMS4 cells, whereas three additional ones (c-*erbB,* c-*sis,* c-*src*) appeared to be expressed in M4 and absent from RMS4. Furthermore, c-*fes* transcripts appeared to be markedly less abundant in the highly malignant cells than in the less malignant and non-malignant ones. It should be stressed that this step-wise inactivation of certain proto-oncogenes in tumor cells may be considered as very significant in the case of c-*fos,* c-*erbB* and c-*fes,* which display relatively high levels of transcripts during the growth of L6a1 cells.

By contrast, only two proto-oncogenes appeared to be more-or-less overexpressed in the neoplastic transformants: the c-N-*ras* gene in both M4 and RMS4 cells and the c-Ki-*ras* gene in the RMS4 cell, in the form of an abnormal transcript of 3.8 kb which is also present but barely detectable in M4 cells and is absent from L6a1 cells. This suggested an oncogenic activation of either one or both *ras* genes. Transfection experiments, which will be reported elsewhere, have shown that in the transformed cells, the c-Ki-*ras* acts as an oncogene, although it bears no known transforming mutation characteristic of the *ras* oncogenes. Finally, it was observed that the six other proto-oncogenes expressed similar levels of transcripts in the three types of proliferating cells, levels markedly higher for c-*myc* and c-*fms* than for c-*abl,* c-*myb,* c-*fgr* and c-Ha-*ras.*

Most of these published data were confirmed in separate experiments using Northern blot (see FIG. 1) or dot-blot hybridization (see TABLE 2) or S_1-nuclease mapping analyses (not shown). In the experiments illustrated by FIGURE 1, we used as an internal control a recombinant DNA probe which cross-reacts with the muscle-specific α actin mRNAs of 1.65 kb as well as with the cytoskeletal β and γ actin mRNAs of 2.2 kb. The same probe is also a differentiation marker, since β and γ actin transcripts are progressively replaced by α actin transcripts during the formation of myotubes. In FIGURE 1 it may be seen that the three lines of proliferating myoblasts display similar levels of β and γ actin mRNAs as well as similar levels of c-*fms,* c-*myc,* and c-Ha-*ras* transcripts. By contrast, the level of c-N-*ras* mRNA is comparatively increased in both M4 and RMS4 cells, with an abnormal 3.8-kb c-Ki-*ras* transcript obviously abundant in RMS4 cells, while c-*fes* transcripts are decreased in M4 cells and absent from RMS4 cells, and c-*fos* transcripts are absent from both transformants.

In other assays using total cellular RNA instead of the poly(A)-rich fraction, essentially similar results were obtained, with one notable exception. All the rat myoblasts investigated were found to express low levels of c-*mos* transcripts 3.6 kb long. These were hardly if at all detectable in the poly(A)-containing RNA, probably because c-*mos* mRNAs have no poly(A) chains or only very short ones, as reported for other cell systems.[35] Our previous Northern blot analyses (as discussed above) had been confirmed by rough quantitative comparisons based on densitometric measurements of dot-blot hybridization signals between c-onc probes and poly(A)-rich cellular RNAs.[41] Aside from a few experimental variations, these previous results have now been confirmed using total cellular RNA (except, of course, for the discrepancy concerning the c-*mos* transcripts). The results of the assays of total cellular RNA are summarized in TABLE 2.

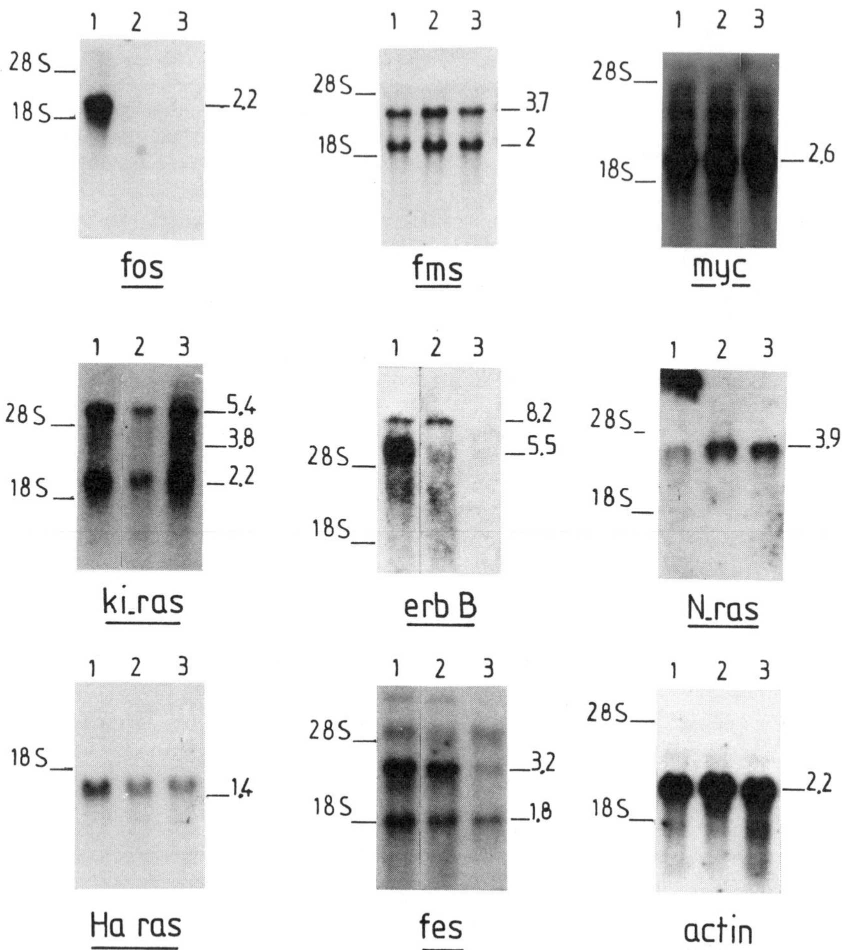

FIGURE 1. Northern blot analysis of proto-oncogene and cytoskeletal actin gene transcripts in L6a1 myoblasts (**lanes 1**) compared to low-malignancy M4 (**lanes 2**) and high-malignancy RMS4 (**lanes 3**) transformants. All cells were collected during periods of similar growth rates after 48 hr of culture in 10% FCS. The poly(A)-containing fraction of total cellular RNA was purified, and aliquots of 3 μg were processed for Northern blot hybridizations with ^{32}P-labeled probes (6-8 $\times$ 10^5 cpm/ng, 10^6 cpm/ml) as previously described.[41] Exposure time was 48 hr for radioautograms of patterns probed for proto-oncogene transcripts and 6 hr for patterns showing actin transcripts, used as an internal control. Positions of ribosomal RNAs (18S, 28S) are indicated to *left* of each panel, and sizes of transcripts (kilobases, kb) are indicated to *right* of individual panels.

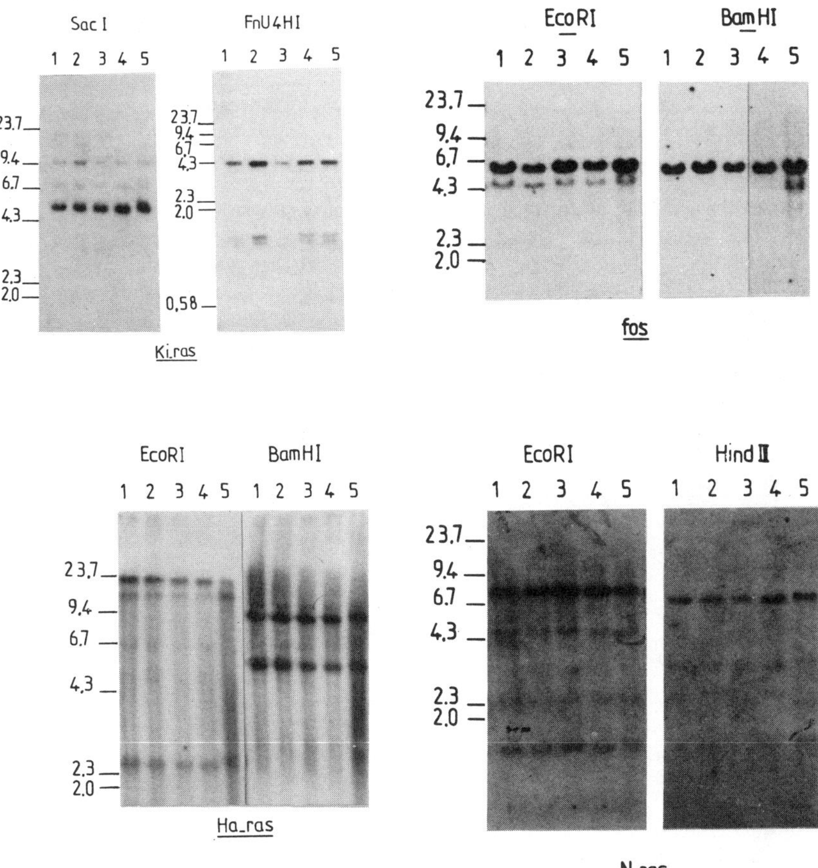

FIGURE 2. Southern blot analysis of c-*fos* and c-*ras* genomic sequences. Aliquots of 10 ng of high-molecular-weight DNA from proliferating L6a1 myoblasts (**lanes 1**), L6a1 myotubes (**lanes 2**), M4 cells (**lanes 3**), RMS4 cells (**lanes 4**), and normal rat spleen (**lanes 5**) were digested with the indicated restriction enzymes and analyzed with *fos* and *ras* probes as previously described.[41] Exposure time for the radioautograms shown was 18 hr. Positions of size markers for restriction fragments (kilobases, kb) are indicated to the *left* of each panel.

In our former studies, analyses of cellular DNAs by the Southern technique failed to detect any obvious alteration, such as amplification, rearrangement or deletion, which could account for the change in activity of certain proto-oncogenes observed in the neoplastic transformants. These data have been confirmed and completed, and analysis of the c-*fos,* c-Ha-*ras,* c-Ki-*ras,* and c-N-*ras* genes is shown in FIGURE 2. It may be seen that in DNAs from the three cell lines and from normal rat spleen each of these proto-oncogenes exhibits the same pattern of restriction fragments as well as hybridization signals of comparable intensities. However, these analyses did not address the possible occurrence of subtle alterations such as point mutations or discrete sequence rearrangements.

CHANGES IN PROTO-ONCOGENE EXPRESSION AFTER L6a1 CELL DIFFERENTIATION

In our previous studies, the poly(A)-containing c-onc transcripts were analyzed comparatively in L6a1 myoblasts and terminally differentiated myotubes.[41] It was found that the completion of the differentiation process caused no obvious change in the levels of c-*abl,* c-*myb,* and c-Ha-*ras* RNAs but resulted in a significant rise in the level of c-N-*ras* transcripts and in a marked reduction or disappearance of all other c-onc RNAs.[41,43] These results were confirmed by further assays using total cellular RNAs, and, in addition (for the reasons discussed above), low levels of c-*mos* transcripts were demonstrated in L6a1 myoblasts, levels that were found to be somewhat increased after the formation of myotubes (manuscript in preparation). These changes in accumulation of c-onc transcripts in myotubes compared to myoblasts are summarized in TABLE 3.

EXPRESSION OF c-*fos,* c-*fms,* AND *ras* FAMILY GENES: IMPLICATIONS

Three features of these results appeared to be of particular interest. First, the relatively high abundance of c-*fos* mRNA in L6a1 myoblasts, contrasting with its absence from both lines of non-differentiating transformants, despite the similar growth rates of all three cell lines, suggested a possible relationship between the inactivation of c-*fos* and the loss of myogenic capacity. It was therefore interesting to analyze more precisely the changes in c-*fos* expression at various stages during L6a1 cell growth and differentiation and to investigate other lines of non-fusing myoblasts for c-*fos* expression.

Second, the accumulation of two c-*fms*-related transcripts, (3.7 and 2.0 kb) in the three lines of proliferating myoblasts was surprising because it has so far been assumed that expression of the c-*fms* gene, in the form of a single mRNA species 3.7

TABLE 3. Levels of Proto-oncogene Transcripts in L6a1 Myotubes Compared to Proliferating Myoblasts

Proto-oncogene	Level in Myotubes vs. Myoblasts[a]
c-*abl,* c-*myb,* c-Ha-*ras*	Unchanged
c-*mos,* c-N-*ras*	Augmented
c-*src,* c-*fes,* c-*fgr,* c-Ki-*ras*; c-*fos,* c-*myc,* c-*sis,* c-*fms*; c-*erbA,* c-*erbB*	Markedly reduced[b]

[a] L6a1 myoblasts were collected at semiconfluency and myotubes at 96 hr after the transfer of confluent monolayers of L6a1 cell to the low-serum medium. Total cellular RNA was extracted and processed for Northern blot and dot-blot hybridizations.

[b] For some transcripts, levels were undetectable in the myotubes.

kb long, is normally restricted to mononuclear phagocytic cells, macrophage-containing tissues and the placenta (see Ref. 44 for a review). Moreover, this view was further supported by the demonstration that the mature translation product of the c-*fms* proto-oncogene is a surface glycoprotein with tyrosine kinase activity, and that it is closely related or identical to the receptor for the macrophage colony-stimulating factor called mCSF or CSF-1.[48,50] This led us to search for c-*fms* transcripts in other types of myoblasts and to analyze the corresponding proteins.

Third, the finding that L6a1 cell differentiation does not affect the expression of c-Ha-*ras* transcripts but results in an increased expression of c-N-*ras*, contrasting with the repression of c-Ki-*ras*, suggested that the three c-*ras* genes serve different functions at different stages of myogenesis. A first step in exploring this question was to complete the analyses of c-*ras* genes at various stages of the myogenic process *in vitro* and during critical periods of muscular development *in vivo*.

Some of the results obtained in investigating these three points have been published recently. They are summarized here, along with confirming data and additional observations not previously reported.

UNIQUE PATTERN OF c-*fos* EXPRESSION IN GROWTH-ARRESTED MYOBLASTS: c-*fos* INACTIVATION CORRELATES WITH LOSS OF MYOGENIC CAPACITY

Time-course analyses of c-*fos* transcripts compared to other c-onc transcripts and to mRNAs that encode muscular and extracellular matrix proteins and the β and γ actins of the cytoskeleton were carried out throughout the growth and differentiation periods of L6a1 cells, using the Northern blot and dot-blot techniques. It was found that during their exponential growth phase, L6a1 cells express stable levels of c-*fos* and β and γ actin mRNAs as well as stable levels of α1(I) collagen, α2(I) collagen and fibronectin mRNAs, as previously demonstrated,[41] but they display no detectable muscle-specific transcripts.[41–43] When the cells start forming confluent monolayers, the level of c-*fos* mRNA sharply rises by up to 3-4-fold, peaks, and rapidly declines in parallel with the arrest of DNA synthesis, which precedes the appearance of muscle-specific transcripts. Following the transfer of confluent cultures to the low-serum medium, c-*fos* transcripts become rapidly undetectable. In contrast, muscle-specific transcripts, such as those encoding actin, myosin heavy chain (MHC), myosin light chain 2 (MLC_2), and troponin T (TnT), accumulate increasingly, while c-*myc* mRNA, β and γ actin mRNAs, and fibronectin mRNA are progressively eliminated.[43] It was also demonstrated that this up- and down-regulation of c-*fos* RNAs, seemingly unique, correlates with the arrest of L6a1 cell growth and (or) early events of the differentiation process and does not simply result from changes in the concentration of exogenous growth factors in the culture medium.[43]

On the other hand, we analyzed for c-onc-gene expression various other lines of rat myoblasts, in particular, four sublines of non-fusing transformants obtained in the laboratory by transfecting L6a1 cells with the v-*fos* oncogene included in a recombinant FBJ provirus. Analysis of the cellular DNAs by the Southern technique showed that the v-*fos* gene is stably integrated in all these transformants but revealed no obvious alteration of the endogenous c-*fos* gene.[43] However, Northern blot analyses demonstrated a complete or nearly complete extinction of the expression of the c-*fos* gene in all these transformants (FIG. 3), as well as in the other types of non-fusing rat myoblasts investigated.

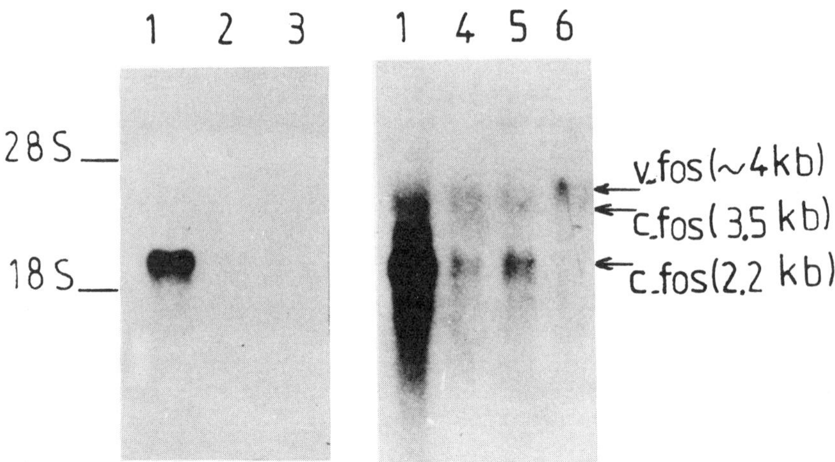

FIGURE 3. Northern blot analysis of c-*fos* transcripts in L6a1 myoblasts compared to various non-differentiating transformants. **Lanes 1:** L6a1 myoblasts (2 days in 10% FCS); **Lane 2:** M4 cells; **Lane 3:** RMS4 cells; **Lanes 4-6:** three distinct lines of v-*fos*-induced transformants.[43] In order to detect low levels of v-*fos* transcripts in the latter transformants, exposure time for the radioautograms was increased from 2 days (*left panel*) to 10 days (*right panel*). Positions of 28S and 18S ribosomal RNAs are indicated to *left* and sizes of transcripts (kb, kilobases) to *right* of panels.

THE c-*fms* GENE IS EXPRESSED IN A VARIETY OF PROLIFERATING MYOBLASTS AND CODES FOR CSF-1 RECEPTOR-RELATED PROTEINS

In a recent report,[44] we presented data showing that expression of both c-*fms* transcripts (2.0 and 3.7 kb) is cell-cycle dependent in L6a1 myoblasts and that both are expressed at more-or-less elevated levels in the other lines of cultured myoblasts analyzed. We further demonstrated that the 3.7-kb transcript includes the three domains (intracellular, transmembrane and extracellular) of the putative c-*fms* gene product while the 2.0-kb transcript corresponds to the intracellular domain. Moreover, we performed cell-free translation assays which showed that the poly(A)-rich RNAs isolated from myoblasts directed the synthesis of two c-*fms*-related proteins of 69 and 115-116 kilodaltons (kDa). In this paper, we will present results confirming these published data and a summary of more detailed analyses of the proteins.[46]

The time-course analysis shown in FIGURE 4 confirms that both c-*fms* transcripts are progressively eliminated during the process of L6a1 cell differentiation monitored by the increasing accumulation of muscle-specific transcripts, measured in this case by the level of the 0.88-kb mRNAs which encode MLC_2.

In order to verify that expression of either one or both c-*fms* transcripts is not an abnormal feature of certain lines of myoblastic cells, a variety of other lines of rat and mouse myoblasts were investigated. Thus far, all these lines were found to express more-or-less elevated levels of both c-*fms*-related transcripts, the 2.0 and the 3.7 kb form, and, occasionally, varying amounts of another transcript (4.5 kb long) which may represent a premessenger RNA. FIGURE 5 shows Northern blot analyses of seven clonal cell lines derived from nickel-induced rhabdomyosarcomas in the laboratory of M. F. Poupon.[47] These lines markedly differ from each other in terms of neoplastic properties and/or myogenic capability. Interestingly, the clone 8 line, which is weakly tumorigenic and retains the capacity to differentiate, appears to express a barely detectable level of transcripts when cultivated in the usual growth medium, but addition of epithelial growth factor (EGF) causes a marked increase of this level, while addition of fibroblast growth factor (FGF) has no effect (see FIG. 5). Furthermore, both c-*fms* transcripts were detected in all the rat muscle tumors analyzed and also, at low levels, in striated muscles from fetuses and newborn animals. As expected from previous studies (cited in Ref. 44), only the 3.7-kb transcript was observed in normal spleen and also—but unexpectedly—in baby rat thymus; whereas no c-*fms* transcript was detected in a variety of other adult tissues, including muscle.[44]

The functional capacity of c-*fms* transcripts was verified by cell-free translation assays[44] using RNA from L6a1 myoblasts which was size-fractionated in a sucrose gradient. The [^{35}S]methionine-labeled proteins were immunoprecipitated with a polyclonal rabbit antiserum that cross-reacts with all c-*fms*-encoded proteins (kindly provided by Dr. Rohrschneider)[50] and analyzed by polyacrylamide gel electrophoresis. It may be seen in FIGURE 6 that those fractions of the sucrose gradient that contained a mixture of both 2.0- and 3.7-kb transcripts coded for two labeled c-*fms*-related antigens with apparent molecular masses of about 69 kDa and 116 kDa, whereas slower moving fractions coded only for the 69-kDa species and faster moving ones only for the 116-kDa species.

The 116-kDa species was reminiscent of previous reports showing that a polypeptide of this size in mononuclear phagocytes is the short-lived precursor to immature and mature glycoproteins of 130 and 165-170 kDa associated with tyrosine kinase activities.[48-50] That precursor is normally undetectable, but it accumulates in macrophages treated with tunicamycin, a well-known inhibitor of glycosylation.[51] In order to determine whether similar proteins are expressed in muscle stem cells, extracts from L6a1 myoblasts and myotubes and various rat tissues were immunoprecipitated with the *fms* protein-specific antiserum; the immune complexes were subjected to cell-free kinase assays and analyzed by polyacrylamide gel electrophoresis. As shown in

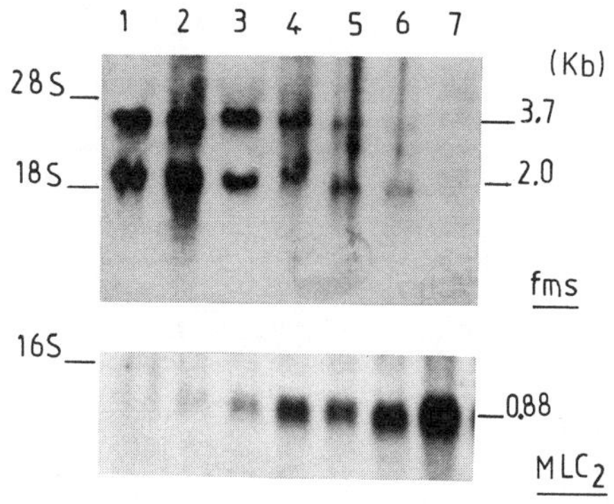

FIGURE 4. Time-course analysis of c-*fms* transcripts during L6a1 cell differentiation. Aliquots of 25 μg of total cellular RNA were first analyzed for c-*fms* transcripts (*upper panel*). After exposure to X-ray film for 18 hr, the blots were dehybridized and then rehybridized with the muscle-specific probe MLC_2 (myosin light chain 2; *lower panel*) as described.[44] **Lanes 1, 2:** cells cultured 48 hr and 72 hr, respectively, in 10% FCS; **Lanes 3-7:** 72 hr in 10% FCS followed by incubation in 2% FCS for 3 hr, 19 hr, 25 hr, 48 hr, and 96 hr, respectively. Positions of RNA markers are indicated to the *left* and sizes of transcripts (kb, kilobases) are indicated to the *right* of each panel.

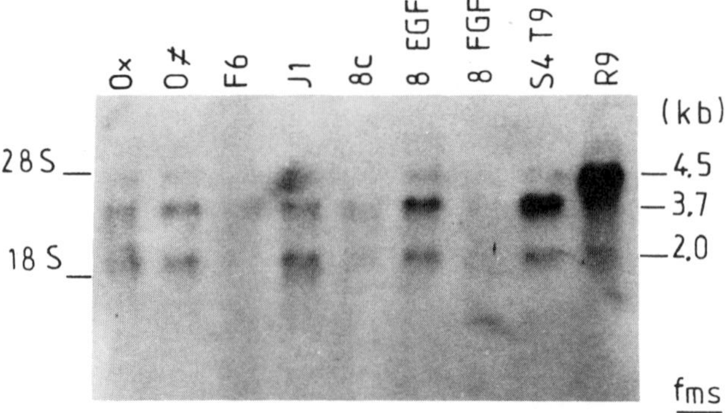

FIGURE 5. Northern blot analysis of c-*fms* transcripts in various clonal lines of rat myoblasts unrelated to L6a1 cells. Total cellular RNA was prepared from cultures of cell lines 0x, 0≠, F6, J1, 8, S4 T9, and R9 (obtained from M. F. Poupon) after cells were cultured for 48 hr in 10% FCS. Lanes contain RNA from indicated cell lines, except for 8c, which indicates the clone 8 cells grown in 10% FCS (c, control) and 8 EGF and 8 FGF, which indicate clone 8 cells incubated for 48 hr in 10% FCS, followed by a 6-hr incubation in fresh medium supplemented with epithelial (100 ng/ml) or fibroblast (200 ng/ml) growth factor, respectively, before isolation of RNA. See Ref. 44 for details. Positions of ribosomal RNA markers are indicated to the *left* and sizes of c-*fms* transcripts (kb, kilobases) are indicated to the *right* of the radioautogram.

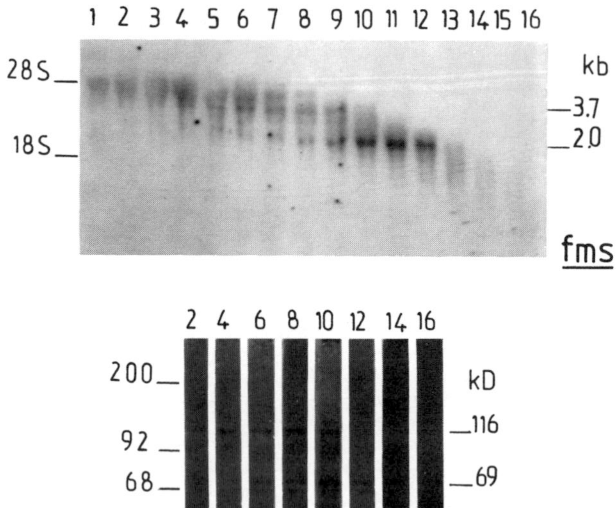

FIGURE 6. Cell-free synthesis of c-*fms*-related proteins. **Top panel:** total RNA from L6a1 myoblasts was size-fractionated by centrifugation in a sucrose gradient and aliquots of 16 fractions were analyzed for c-*fms* transcripts; radioautogram of Northern blot is shown. **Bottom panel:** the remaining portions of pairs of adjacent fractions (fractions 1 + 2, 3 + 4, etc.) were pooled and their RNA was used to prime cell-free translations in a rabbit reticulocyte lysate system. After precipitation with rabbit antiserum against *fms*-encoded proteins,[50] the [^{35}S]methionine-labeled antigens were separated by gel electrophoresis (see Ref. 44 for details); an autoradiogram of the gel pattern is shown. Positions of ribosomal RNAs and c-*fms* transcripts (kb, kilobases) are indicated at *left* and *right*, respectively, of **top panel,** and of marker proteins and c-*fms*-related antigens (kD, kilodaltons) at *left* and *right*, respectively, of **bottom panel.**

FIGURE 7, extracts from L6a1 myoblasts exhibited two ^{32}P-labeled bands of about 130 and 170 kDa, and phosphoamino acid analysis[46] demonstrated that both antigens were exclusively phosphorylated on tyrosine. Notably, both were recognized by the polyclonal rabbit antibody as well as by a monoclonal rat antibody (purchased from Oncogene Sciences, Inc). In some experiments, the former but not the latter antibody revealed a third antigen of 69 kDa, which is probably the translation product of the 2.0-kb transcript; it is currently under investigation. As expected, the 130- and the 170-kDa species were found to be abundant in placenta and spleen extracts but were undetectable in various other adult tissues and in L6a1 myotubes.

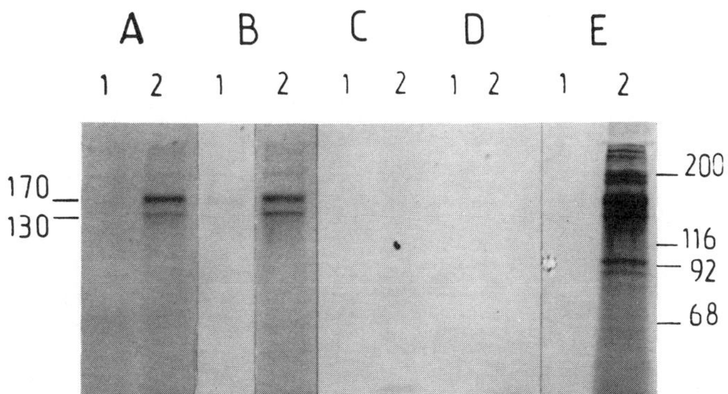

FIGURE 7. Analysis of c-*fms*-related proteins synthesized *in vivo.* (**A**) L6a1 myoblasts, (**B**) M4 transformants, (**C**) L6a1 myotubes, (**D**) adult rat hind-limb muscle, (**E**) placenta. Cell and tissue lysates were treated with normal rabbit serum (*lanes 1*), or with the anti-*fms* antiserum (*lanes 2*), and the precipitates were processed for cell-free kinase assays[48–50] in the presence of [^{32}P]ATP, followed by polyacrylamide gel electrophoresis. Positions of protein markers and c-*fms*-related proteins (kilodaltons) are indicated to *right* and *left* of radioautogram, respectively.

In other assays,[46] cultivated myoblasts were metabolically labeled with [^{35}S]methionine in the presence or absence of tunicamycin, and immune complexes were analyzed by polyacrylamide gel electrophoresis. Extracts of untreated cells displayed two radioactive bands of about 130 and 170 kDa, while extracts of tunicamycin-treated cells showed a major band of 115-116 kDa. Pulse-chase labeling experiments demonstrated that the 130-kDa species was entirely replaced by the 170-kDa species within the first 4 hr of the chase. Digestion with glycosidic enzymes of immune complexes from myoblasts showed that these two proteins differ in their composition of *N*-linked carbohydrate chains, like the c-*fms*-encoded glycoproteins expressed in macrophages. Finally c-*fms* antigens were found to be abundant at the surface of myoblasts, which is also true for the surface of mononuclear phagocytic cells.

DIFFERENTIAL EXPRESSION OF THE THREE c-*ras* GENES DURING MYOGENESIS *IN VITRO*

The graph in FIGURE 8, which confirms and completes previous data,[43] illustrates a time-course analysis of various c-*ras* family transcripts at various stages of L6a1 cell growth and differentiation. Analysis of mRNAs for three extracellular matrix proteins previously shown to be divergently regulated during L6a1 cell differentiation[41] and for two muscle-specific proteins served as controls. It may be seen that during their growth period, L6a1 myoblasts express stable levels of c-Ha-*ras*, c-Ki-*ras*, and c-N-*ras* mRNAs, as well as stable levels of α1(I) collagen and fibronectin mRNAs, but no detectable muscle-specific transcripts. During the differentiation period, marked by the increasing accumulation of MLC_2 mRNA followed by TnT mRNA, the level of c-Ha-*ras* mRNA remains practically unchanged, like that of α1(I) collagen mRNA and in contrast with the progressive rise in the level of c-N-*ras* mRNA and the strong decline in the level of c-Ki-*ras* mRNA, which precedes the diminution of fibronectin and α2(I) collagen mRNAs.

In order to determine whether these contrasting regulation patterns of c-*ras* genes actually correlate with differentiation events or simply result from changes in the concentration of growth factors, two series of assays were carried out.

First, confluent L6a1 cell cultures were transferred to fresh high-serum medium, and cell extracts prepared from the cultures at different times were used for a time-course analysis of c-*ras* transcripts compared to those for cytoskeletal β and γ actins, muscle-specific α actin, and TnT. Under those conditions, the cells do not fuse; the differentiation process is none-the-less triggered (as shown by the appearance of muscle-specific transcripts), but it remains abortive, as indicated by the persistence of abundant β and γ actin mRNAs and the low levels of α actin and TnT RNAs. Unfortunately, the analysis could not be prolonged much longer than 25 hr, because after this time most L6a1 cells detach from the substrate if maintained in the high-serum medium. It may, however, be seen in FIGURE 9A that the level of c-N-*ras* mRNA increases significantly as muscle-specific transcripts become detectable, whereas the level of c-Ha-*ras* mRNA stays apparently stable and that of c-Ki-*ras* starts declining.

Second, confluent L6a1 cell cultures (in 10% FCS) were incubated either in 1% FCS, 20% FCS, or 1% FCS supplemented with purified growth factors at concentrations (indicated in the legend to FIG. 9B) several times higher than those known to induce the expression of the c-*fos* and c-*myc* proto-oncogenes, the β and γ actin genes, and the lactate dehydrogenase (LDH) genes in other cell systems.[47] As shown

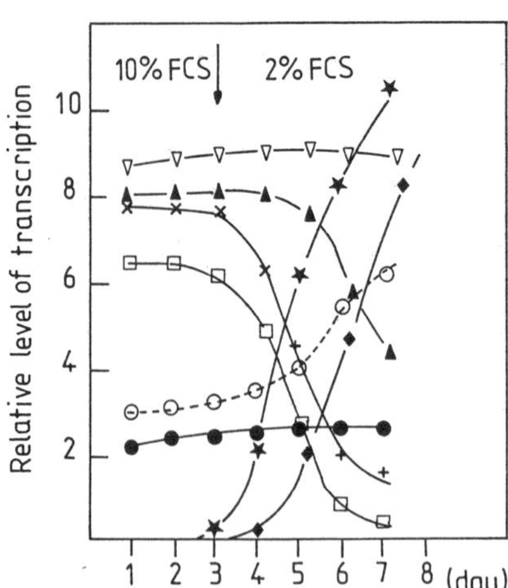

FIGURE 8 Differential time-course for the regulation of the 3 c-*ras* genes during myogenesis *in vitro*. L6a1 cells were collected after the indicated time of culture, and total cellular RNA samples were processed for dot-blot hybridization with the indicated ^{32}P-labeled probes. Hybridization signals, quantified by densitometric measurements, are expressed in arbitrary units. Transcripts: (●), c-Ha-*ras*; (○), c-N-*ras*; (□), c-Ki-*ras*; (▽), α1(I) collagen; (▲), α2(I) collagen; (★), myosin light chain 2 (MLC_2); (◆), troponin T (TnT); (x), fibronectin. *Arrow* indicates substitution of 2% FCS for 10% FCS in medium.

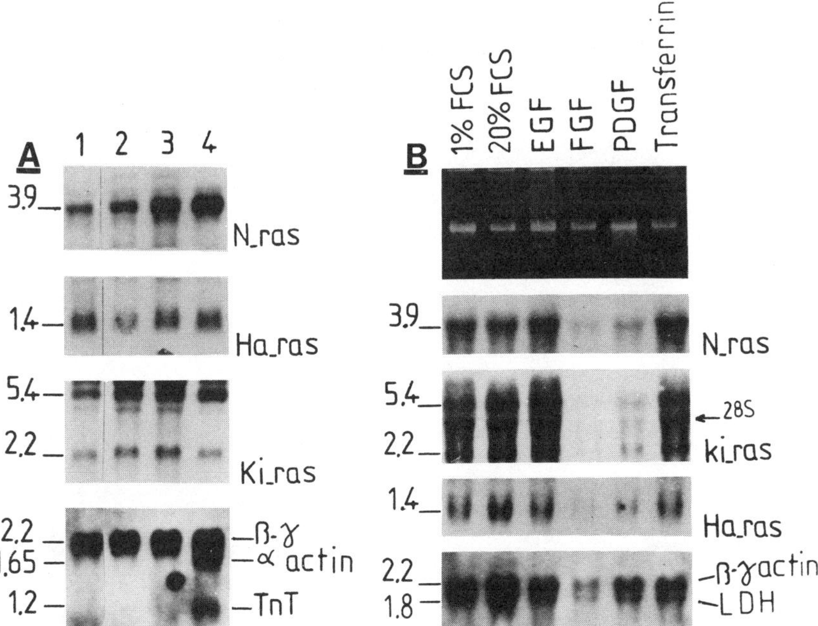

FIGURE 9. Effects of serum and purified peptide growth factors on the accumulation of c-*ras* transcripts in growth-arrested myoblasts. (**A**) L6a1 cells reaching confluency after 72 hr of culture in 10% FCS were collected immediately (*lanes 1*) or incubated in 20% FCS (instead of 1-2% FCS) and collected 3 hr (*lanes 2*), 5 hr (*lanes 3*) or 25 hr (*lanes* 3) later. Samples of total cellular RNA were prepared from each culture and used for Northern blotting with the indicated probes. The Northern blots first hybridized to the c-Ki-*ras* probe were dehybridized and then rehybridized to the actin and TnT probes. (**B**) Confluent L6a1 cells were incubated for 24 hr with 20% FCS, 1% FCS alone, or 1% FCS supplemented with either EGF (100 ng/ml), FGF (200 ng/ml), PDGF (platelet-derived growth factor, 5 units/ml), or transferrin before cells were collected and samples of total cellular RNA were prepared for Northern blotting. Radioautograms of Northern blots are shown in all panels of **A** and **B**, except for the *top* panel of **B**, which is a photograph of the ethidium bromide-stained gel used for the blots shown in **B**, demonstrating the presence of equivalent amounts of total cellular RNA in each lane. Probes used are indicated to the *right* of each panel, as is the position of 28S ribosomal RNA (**B**); transcript sizes (kilobases, kb) are indicated to the *left*. TnT, Troponin T; LDH, lactate dehydrogenase.

in FIGURE 9B, addition of transferrin or EGF caused no noticeable change in the levels of the three c-*ras* gene transcripts or in the levels of the β and γ actin and LDH mRNAs. Incubation in 20% FCS induced a slight and doubtful increase in the level of c-Ha-*ras*, LDH and β and γ actin mRNAs but did not affect the levels of c-Ki-*ras* and c-N-*ras* transcripts. In contrast, addition of fibroblast growth factor (FGF) strongly reduced the levels of all these transcripts (although it caused no obvious cytotoxic action), whereas addition of platelet-derived growth factor (PDGF) had less pronounced inhibitory effects.

DIFFERENTIAL EXPRESSION OF THE THREE c-*ras* GENES DURING MUSCLE DEVELOPMENT *IN VIVO*

It has been shown in the last few years that the multigenic families which encode certain muscle proteins are developmentally regulated *in vivo* and that extracellular matrix constituents as well as the trophic influence of the nerves play important roles in this development. In rodent species, for example, a double transition between fetal and adult isoforms of myosin heavy and light chains is correlated with the age of the animals during the perinatal and postnatal development of cardiac[52] and skeletal muscles,[53,54] and great changes in neuronal and sympathetic innervation of muscle fibers occur during the first 2-3 weeks after birth.[55]

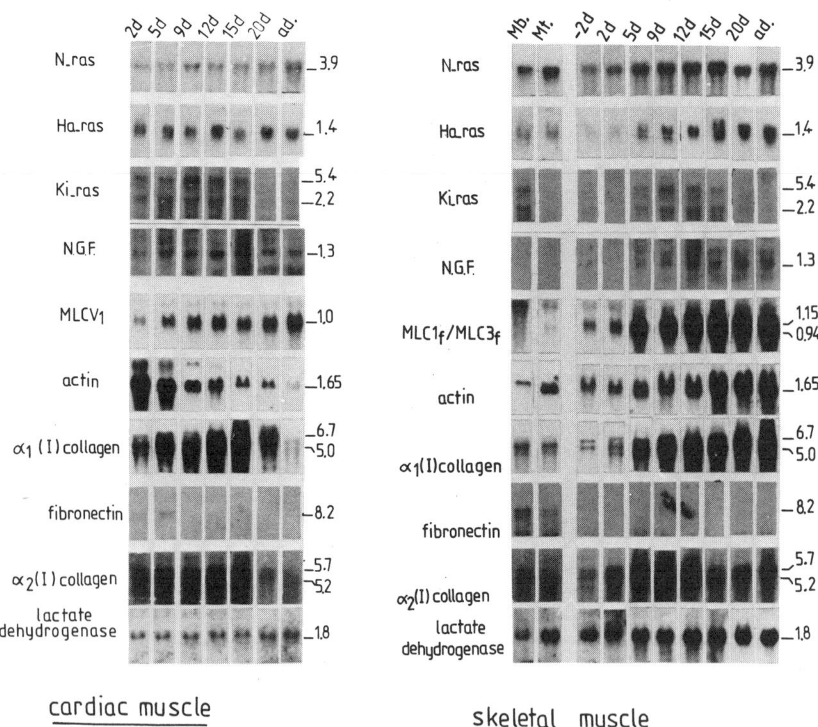

FIGURE 10. Differential regulation of the three c-*ras* genes during cardiac and skeletal muscle development *in vivo.* Aliquots of 30 μg of total RNA from heart tissue (*left panel*) or hind-limb skeletal muscles (*right panel*), freshly excised from fetal or neonatal Wistar rats at the indicated time (in days) preceding (**−2d**) or following birth and from adult (**ad.**) animals, were processed for Northern blot hybridizations with the indicated probes. Total cellular RNA from L6a1 myoblasts (**Mb**) and myotubes (**Mt**) was similarly processed. The recombinant DNA probes utilized as differentiation markers have been described: the fast myosin light chains 1 or 3 of adult skeletal muscles ($MLC1_f/MLC3_f$),[58] the V1 isoform of adult cardiac ventricular myosin light chain ($MLCV_1$).[57] N.G.F., nerve growth factor; actin, adult α actin: skeletal isoform. Sizes of transcripts (kilobases, kb) are indicated to the *right* of each panel and probes used to the *left.*

It was therefore of interest to complement our time-course studies *in vitro* by similar studies *in vivo,* especially in view of preliminary data showing expression of c-N-*ras* mRNA in fetal and adult muscles.[43] In the experiment whose results are illustrated in FIGURE 10, cardiac and hind-limb muscles were analyzed for c-onc transcripts compared to $\alpha 1$(I) collagen, $\alpha 2$(I) collagen, fibronectin and nerve growth factor (NGF) mRNAs, using lactate dehydrogenase (LDH) mRNA as a stable internal control and mRNAs from L6a1 myoblasts and L6a1 myotubes as external controls. As developmental markers, we used a molecularly cloned recombinant DNA specific for the V1 isoform of the adult ventricular myosin light chain (MLC-V_1) of cardiac muscle[57] and one specific for the fast myosin light chains 1 and 3 (MLC1_f, MLC3_f) of skeletal muscle.[58] We also used another marker for both types of striated muscles, namely, the adult α actin isoform of the skeletal type, because it is expressed in fetal and neonatal heart, where it is down-regulated at later stages, while it is up-regulated in skeletal tissues.

The data in FIGURE 10 (also confirmed in replicate experiments using either total tissue RNA, as in FIG. 10, or poly(A)-rich fractions) show the expected time-course for the regulatory patterns of all these markers and demonstrate that the three c-*ras* genes more-or-less markedly differ from each other in their pattern of expression. In skeletal muscle between the second and the fifteenth day after birth, the amount of c-Ha-*ras* mRNA increases from barely detectable levels to the consistently detectable ones found in adult animals, whereas these levels appear to be similarly elevated at all ages in cardiac muscle, perhaps in relation to the more precocious functional maturation of the latter tissue compared to the former. During the same period, the level of c-N-*ras* rises in a fairly similar manner in both types of muscle. By contrast, in both tissues, the level of c-Ki-*ras* transcripts increases up to 9-12 days after birth and declines thereafter to negligible values. Finally, similar time-course analyses of c-*mos* transcripts were performed. Preliminary results showed that in the rat species, at least, c-*mos* RNA accumulates at increasing levels during the postnatal development of skeletal muscle, whereas it is successively up- and then down-regulated in heart muscle (data not shown).

CONCLUDING DISCUSSION

One interesting aspect of our studies is the demonstration that all the 15 proto-oncogenes analyzed are more-or-less transcriptionally active during the growth of L6a1 myogenic cells. With due caution because of the possibility for idiosyncrasies in established cell lines, we conclude that this finding suggests that a balance in the expression of many, if not all, c-onc genes is instrumental in the proliferation of myoblasts and possibly also in their commitment to differentiation. At least, this hypothesis of coordinated cell-growth-related functions is pertinent for the 10 c-onc genes whose transcripts disappear or sharply decline in level following the arrest of cell multiplication. Furthermore, this hypothesis is consistent with an increasing body of evidence, recently reviewed and interpreted by Sporn and Roberts,[59] showing that many peptide growth factors are in fact multifunctional, with actions that include both stimulation and inhibition of cell proliferation, as well as effects unrelated to proliferation. Moreover, these factors form part of a complex signaling language, and their action appears to depend on a network of other substances and signals, which varies from one cell type to another and, for a given cell type, from one developmental stage to another.

Two examples of the latter concepts are given here. One concerns the inhibiting effects of certain peptide growth factors upon expression of c-*ras* and other genes in myoblasts. The other one is our demonstration that the c-*fms* gene, whose expression had been considered to be restricted to mononuclear phagocytes and macrophage-containing tissues, is highly expressed in all the proliferating myoblasts, either normal or transformed, investigated by us. We further demonstrated that its major translation product undergoes the same glycosylation steps as the CSF-1 receptor of macrophages and that this protein is located at the cell surface. It remains to be determined whether CSF-1 itself or some other inducer plays a role in the proliferation of myoblasts. We have begun investigating this question in cooperation with another group of investigators. Obviously, the answer may have important implications concerning the interplay between muscle stem cells and macrophages in various physiological and pathological conditions, including in tumors.

Another aspect of our studies which is worth discussing is the finding that following neoplastic transformation, the activation of a c-Ki-*ras* oncogene coincides with the apparent inactivation of other proto-oncogenes normally expressed during the proliferation of the parental myogenic cells. Furthermore, the degree of inactivation seemingly correlates with the degree of neoplastic conversion. This suggests that in the process of tumor progression, a step-wise inactivation of proto-oncogenes may be as important as the expression of oncogenes. Another hypothesis, more amenable to experimental approaches at the moment, is that proto-oncogenes like c-*fos* and c-*erbA* (both are shut off in L6a1-derived non-fusing transformants) are involved in the commitment to myogenic differentiation. In the case of the c-*erbA* gene, this hypothesis is rendered likely by recent data showing that certain isoforms of the c-*erbA*-encoded nuclear receptor for the thyroid hormone T_3 activate the transcription of the genes that code for sarcomeric myosin heavy chains.[60] In the case of the c-*fos* gene, the v-*fos* oncoprotein has been shown to be a *trans* activator of the mouse (I) collagen promoter,[61] and we had previously found that some (I) collagen transcripts highly expressed in the normal myogenic cells are greatly decreased in the non-fusing transformants.[42] Moreover, we have also demonstrated that the c-*fos* gene is repressed in a variety of non-fusing transformants.[43]

A final interesting aspect is the demonstration that the three individual c-*ras* genes displayed contrasting patterns of developmental regulation during the myogenic process *in vitro* and during postnatal development of striated muscles *in vivo.* Of course, in interpreting the latter data the heterogeneity of muscle tissues should be kept in mind and the contribution of non-muscle cells to these observations has not been ruled out. However, there is a rough correlation between the results obtained *in vivo* and *in vitro.* Furthermore, the differences observed could be expected, considering that the L6a1 line is of fetal type and that the *in vitro* models cannot perfectly mimic the developments occurring *in vivo.* It is generally admitted that c-*ras* proteins are instrumental in the transduction of mitotic signals from the cell surface to the nucleus. However, recent data indicate that this transduction pathway also involves transcription factors[62] that may regulate other gene functions. Besides, the role of individual c-*ras* proteins has not been elucidated. Our data strongly suggest that expression of the c-Ki-*ras* gene has a role at the proliferative stage of myogenesis, whereas the c-Ha-*ras* and c-N-*ras* genes serve physiological functions at later stages, including in fully developed muscles. It is probable that these functions concern cellular responses to various signals, especially hormones and nerve impulses. In this respect it is notable that the level of c-N-*ras,* like that of nerve growth factor (NGF) mRNA, increases during the postnatal period of development and that both remain elevated in adulthood. In effect, during this period, the density of sympathetic innervation increases very markedly in parallel with the accumulation of NGF. Finally, similar time-course analyses of c-*mos* products have been undertaken. The results obtained thus far tend to confirm preliminary data[43] that strongly suggested an involvement of this proto-oncogene in muscle development.

ACKNOWLEDGMENTS

The contributions of the many researchers who provided the recombinant DNA clones and other reagents used in our previously published studies and listed in those publications are gratefully acknowledged. We heartily thank Dr. M. Buckingham for her gift of the new recombinant DNA clones utilized as developmental markers of cardiac and skeletal muscles, Dr. Y. Courtois for his gift of purified peptide growth factors, Ms. B. Solhonne for her technical assistance, and Mrs. J. Auffret for her fast and skillful handling of the manuscript.

REFERENCES

1. URIEL, J. 1979. Adv. Cancer Res. **29:** 127-173.
2. SCHAPIRA, F. 1981. Curr. Top. Biol. Med. Res. **5:** 27-75.
3. WEINHOUSE, S. 1972. Cancer Res. **32:** 2007-2016.
4. SHIELDS, R. 1977. Nature **269:** 752-753.
5. FRIEND, C., W. SCHER, J. G. HOLLAND & T. SATO. 1971. Proc. Natl. Acad. Sci. USA **68:** 378-381.
6. BISHOP, J. M. 1987. Science **235:** 305-311.
7. WATERFIELD, M. D., G. T. SCRACE, N. WHITTLE, R. STROOBANT, A. JOHNSON, A. WATERSON, K. B. WESTERMARK, C. H. HELDIN, J. S. HUANG & J. DEVEL. 1983. Nature **304:** 35-39.
8. CHIU, I. M., E. P. REDDY, D. GIVOL, K. C. ROBBINS, S. R. TRONICK & S. A. AARONSON. 1984. Cell **37:** 923-929.
9. SHERR, C. J., C. W. RETTENMIER, R. SACCA, M. F. ROUSSEL, A. T. LOOK & R. STANLEY. 1985. Cell **41:** 665-676.
10. DOWNWARD, Z., Y. YARDIN, F. MAGES, G. T. SCRACE, G. TOTHY, P. STOCKWELL, A. ULLRICH, F. SCLESSINGER & M. D. WATERFIELD. 1984. Nature **307:** 324-327.
11. SAP, J., A. MUNOZ, K. DAMM, Y. GOLDBERG, J. GHYSDAEL, A. LEUTSZ, H. BEUG & B. VENNSTROM. 1986. Nature **324:** 635-640.
12. WEINBERGER, C., E. C. THOMSON, E. S. ONG, R. LEBO, D. I. GRUOL & R. M. EVANS. 1986. Nature **324:** 641-645.
13. KELLY, K., B. H. COCHRAN, C. D. STILES & P. LEDER. 1983. Cell **35:** 603-610.
14. CAMPISI, J., E. H. GRAY, A. B. PARDEE, M. DEAN & G. E. SONNENSHEIM. 1983. Cell **36:** 241-247.
15. MULLER, R., R. BRAVO, J. BURCKHARDT & T. CURRAN. 1984. Nature **313:** 241-247.
16. MULCAHY, L. S., M. R. SMITH & D. W. STACEY. 1984. Nature **313:** 241-243.
17. GOYETTE, M., C. J. PETROPOULOS, P. SHAND & N. FAUSTO. 1983. Science **219:** 510-512.
18. GREENBERG, M. E. & E. B. ZIFF. 1984. Nature **311:** 433-437.
19. KRUIJER, W. A., J. A. COOPER, T. HUNTER & I. M. VERMA. 1984. Nature **312:** 711-716.
20. MÜLLER, R., T. CURRAN, D. MÜLLER & L. GUILBERT. 1985. Nature **314:** 546-548.
21. GONDA, T. J. & D. METCALF. 1983. Nature **310:** 249-251.
22. LACHMAN, H. M. & A. I. SKOULTCHI. 1983. Nature **310:** 592-594.
23. WESTIN, E. H., F. WONG-STAAL, E. P. GELMANN, R. DALLA-FAVERA, T. S. PAPPAS, J. A. LAUTENBERG, E. ALESSANDRA, E. P. REDDY, S. R. TRONICK, S. A. AARONSON & R. C. GALLO. 1984. Proc. Natl. Acad. Sci. USA **79:** 2490-2494.

24. SARIDAN, E., T. MITCHELL & D. KUFE. 1985. Nature **316:** 64-66.
25. VERMA, I. M. & W. R. GRAHAM. 1987. Adv. Cancer Res. **49:** 29-52.
26. MÜLLER, R. & E. F. WAGNER. 1984. Nature **311:** 438-442.
27. RÜTHER, U., E. F. WAGNER & R. MÜLLER. 1985. EMBO J. **4:** 1775-1762.
28. RÜTHER, V., C. GARBER, D. KOMITOWSKI, R. MÜLLER & F. WAGNER. 1987. Nature **325:** 412-416.
29. MORGAN, J. I., D. R. COHEN, J. L. HEMPSTEAD & T. CURRAN. 1987. Science **237:** 192-197.
30. DRAGUMOW, M. & H. A. ROBERTSON. 1987. Nature **329:** 341-342.
31. NODA, M., M. KO, A. OGURA, D.-G. LIU, T. TAMANO, T. TAKANO & Y. IKAWA. 1985. Nature **318:** 73-75.
32. BAR-SAGI, D. & F. R. FERAMISCO. 1985. Cell **42:** 841-848.
33. ALEMA, S., P. CASABLORE, E. AGOSTINI & G. TATO. 1985. Nature **316:** 557-559.
34. BRUGGE, J. S., P. C. COTTON, A. L. QUERAL, J. N. BARRETT, D. DONNER & R. W. KEANE. 1985. Nature **316:** 554-557.
35. PROPST, F. & G. F. VANDE WOUDE. 1985. Nature **315:** 516-518.
36. PROPST, F., M. P. ROSENBERG, A. IYER, K. KAUL & G. F. VANDE WOUDE. 1987. Mol. Cell. Biol. **7:** 1629-1637.
37. MÜTTER, G. L. & D. J. WOLGEMUTH. 1987. Proc. Natl. Acad. Sci. USA **84:** 5301-5305.
38. PROPST, F., M. P. ROSENBERG, M. K. OSKARSSON, L. B. RUSSELL, M. C. NGUYEN-HUU, J. NADEAU, N. A. JENKINS, N. G. COPELAND & G. VANDE WOUDE. 1988. Oncogene **2:** 227-233.
39. HILLION, J., M. P. LEIBOVITCH, S. A. LEIBOVITCH & J. HAREL. 1982. Bull. Cancer (Paris) **69:** 413-419.
40. HILLION, J., S. A. LEIBOVITCH, M. P. LEIBOVITCH, M. RAYMONDJEAN, J. KRUK & J. HAREL. 1984. Cancer Res. **44:** 2959-2965.
41. LEIBOVITCH, S. A., M. P. LEIBOVITCH, M. GUILLIER, J. HILLION & J. HAREL. 1986. Cancer Res. **46:** 4097-4103.
42. LEIBOVITCH, S. A., J. HILLION, M. P. LEIBOVITCH, M. GUILLIER, A. SCHMITZ & J. HAREL. 1986. Exp. Cell Res. **166:** 526-534.
43. LEIBOVITCH, M. P., S. A. LEIBOVITCH, J. HILLION, M. GUILLIER, A. SCHMITZ & J. HAREL. 1987. Exp. Cell Res. **170:** 80-92.
44. LEIBOVITCH, S. A., M. P. LEIBOVITCH, M. GUILLIER & J. HAREL. 1988. Oncogene Res. **2:** 293-298.
45. YAFFE, D. 1986. Proc. Natl. Acad. Sci. USA **61:** 477-483.
46. LEIBOVITCH, S. A., M. P. LEIBOVITCH, A. G. BORYCKI & J. HAREL. 1989. Expression of CSF1-receptor-related proteins in muscular stem cells. Oncogene Res. In press.
47. BECKER, M., M. F. POUPON & Y. COURTOIS. 1986. *In* Coordinated Regulation of Gene Expression. R. M. Clayton & D. E. S. Truman, Eds.: 227-246. Plenum Press. London, New York.
48. MANGER, R., N. NAJITA, E. J. NICHOLS, S. HAKAMORI & L. ROHRSCHNEIDER. 1984. Cell **39:** 227-237.
49. RETTENMIER, C. W., J. H. CHEN, M. F. ROUSSEL & C. J. SHERR. 1985. Science **228:** 320-322.
50. WOOLFORD, J., V. ROTHWELL & L. ROHRSCHNEIDER. 1985. Mol. Cell. Biol. **5:** 345-346.
51. KUO, S. O. & J. O. LAMPEN. 1974. Biochem. Biophys. Res. Commun. **58:** 287-295.
52. LOMPRÉ, A. M., B. NADAL-GINARD & V. MAHDAVII. 1984. J. Biol. Chem. **259:** 6437-6446.
53. WHALEN, R. G., S. M. SELL, G. S. BUTLER-BROWNE, K. SCWARTZ, P. BOUVERET & I. PINSET-HÄRSTRÖM. 1981. Nature **292:** 805-809.
54. PERISAMY, M., D. F. WIERORCK & B. NADAL-GINARD. 1984. J. Biol. Chem. **259:** 13573-13578.
55. MAYER, Y. H., H. CZOSNEK, P. E. ZEELON, D. YAFFE & G. NUDEL. 1984. Nucleic Acids Res. **12:** 1087-1099.
56. SHELTON, D. L. & L. F. REICHHARDT. 1984. Proc. Natl. Acad. Sci. USA **81:** 7951-7955.
57. BARTON, P. J. R., A. COHEN, B. ROBERT, Y. FISZMAN, F. BONHOMME, J.-L. GUÉNET, D. P. LEADER & M. BUCKINGHAM. 1985. J. Biol. Chem. **260:** 8578-8584.
58. ROBERT, B., P. DAUBAS, M. A. AKIMENKO, A. COHEN, I. GARNER, J. L. GUÉNET & M. BUCKINGHAM. 1984. Cell **39:** 129-148.
59. SPORN, M. B. & A. B. ROBERTS. 1988. Nature **332:** 217-219.

60. IZUMO, S. & V. MAHDAVI. 1988. Nature **334:** 539-542.
61. SETOYAMA, C., R. FRUNZIS, G. LIAN, M. MUDYI & B. DE COMBRUGGHE. 1986. Proc. Natl. Acad. Sci. USA **83:** 3213-3217.
62. IMBER, J. L., C. SCHATZ, C. WAZYLYCK, B. CHATTON & B. WAZYLYCK. 1988. Nature **332:** 275-278.

Sperm Maturation: Membrane Domain Boundaries

DANIEL S. FRIEND

Department of Pathology
University of California
San Francisco, California 94143

INTRODUCTION

Spermatogenesis begins with the division of a stem cell (spermatogonian type A), which mitotically replaces itself while giving rise to several further generations, the last of which (spermatogonia B) produces the spermatocyte. After two meiotic divisions reduce the chromosome number by half, the resulting spermatid extensively remodels its cytoplasm before it is released into the epididymis as a morphologically mature cell.[1] However, this epididymal sperm continues to experience major modifications in its plasma membrane before carrying out its destiny—the delivery of the sperm genome to the egg—thus restoring the diploid number of chromosomes. In the epididymis, the composition of the sperm membrane alters and the cell gains motility; in the female genital tract it undergoes capacitation, and in the neighborhood of the egg in the fallopian tube it undergoes the acrosome reaction.[2–4] Capacitation is a term that includes all the functional changes the sperm experiences before it can undergo an acrosome reaction and fertilize an egg.[2] A major feature, and one which marks the end point of the process, is the ability of the plasma membrane to transport calcium ions through a voltage-sensitive channel.[5] After the membrane gains that ability, an appropriate stimulus can initiate release of the acrosomal content by multiple fusions between the acrosome and the plasma membrane.[2,6,7] This exocytotic event is called the acrosome reaction. The zymogens thus released assist the sperm in burrowing through the investments of the egg.[2]

Don Fawcett introduced the use of the guinea pig sperm (FIG. 1), with its large acrosome, as an attractive model for studying cell differentiation and maturation.[8,9] Highly polarized, the sperm cell provides advantages for correlating structural with functional changes in its membrane, because the alterations occur at fixed times, while the cell is in a specific anatomical compartment, and they occur in recognizable domains of the membrane.

In this paper I'd like to call your attention to several specific features of guinea pig sperm structure that relate to maturation and that may help in gaining an understanding of events in less polarized somatic cells:

1. Near the end of maturation, there are boundaries to free diffusion of proteins, lipids,[9,10] and glycoconjugates in the plane of the sperm membrane, and each boundary is demarcated by a defined cytoskeletal undercoat (FIGS. 1 and 2).[8–11]
2. These boundaries in the sperm membrane differentially modulate the flow of

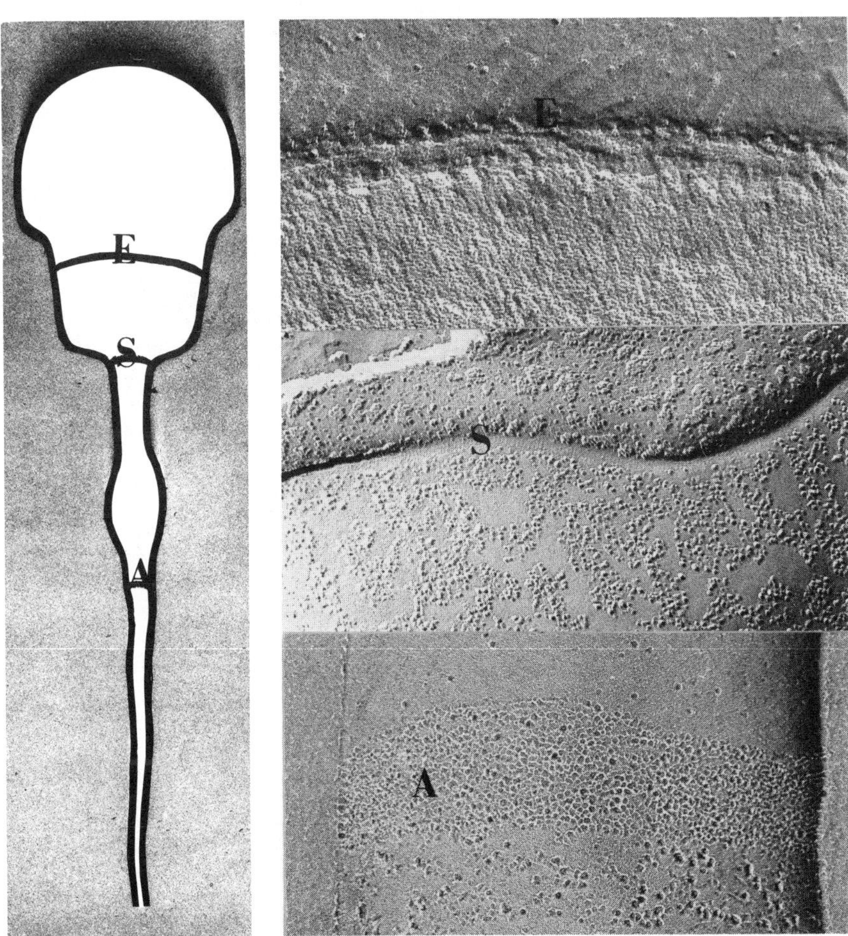

FIGURE 1. (left) Diagram of a guinea pig sperm. Barriers to the free diffusion of molecules in the plane of the plasma membrane occur at the equatorial segment (**E**), at the striated ring (**S**) by the junction of the head and tail, and at the annulus (**A**) separating the tail's midpiece and principal piece.

FIGURE 2. (right) Freeze-fracture images of modifications seen beneath the membrane (*top panel*), and in the hydrophobic interior of the membrane in the equatorial region (**E**), the striated ring (**S**), and the annulus (**A**), located as shown in FIGURE 1. Magnifications: (*top panel*) 90,000×; (*middle panel*) 88,000×; (*bottom panel*) 105,000×, all reproduced at 69%.

molecules in the plane of the membrane when the cells are in different physiological states.[7,12–20]

3. In the guinea pig sperm, there is a close association of one cytoskeletal protein, vimentin, with both the plasma membrane and the nuclear envelope.[21]

SPERM STRUCTURE

The anterior part of the sperm head is involved in the acrosome reaction, the secretory process by which enzymes are released for penetration of the investments of the egg. The post-acrosomal segment of the sperm head is involved in fusion with the egg, and the tail or flagellum propels the cell to its final destination. Each of these functional zones (acrosomal cap, or anterior head; post-acrosomal segment, or posterior head, and tail) has a morphological boundary coincident with barriers to the free diffusion of molecules in the plane of the membrane.[18]

The first boundary underlies the equatorial segment. The acrosomal cap portion of the guinea pig sperm plasma membrane has a glycocalyx that contains antigenic determinants, including the anterior head (AH) antigen of Primakoff and Myles, that do not cross into the post-acrosomal segment (FIG. 3).[22] A freeze-fracture preparation of the acrosomal cap area has a distinctive paracrystalline pattern. During the process of capacitation, when the sperm membrane is becoming competent to transport extracellular calcium, there is a loss of the paracrystalline freeze-fracture pattern of the plasma membrane overlying the acrosome, and free sterols become increasingly demonstrable in the membrane, as shown by the perturbability of the membrane with the polyene filipin.[7,23,24] But, just as the demarcation for reactivity with the anti-anterior head antibody is sharply defined at the equatorial segment, so is the difference in perturbability of the membrane with the polyene. These observations reflect (1) a difference in the sterol concentration in the fusogenic versus the non-fusogenic part of the membrane, with a barrier to sterol diffusion at the site of the equatorial segments, and (2) membrane/cytoskeletal associations in the post-acrosomal region which restrain deformation of the membrane.[23] At the conclusion of capacitation, some filaments appear at this equatorial segment; these will mark the posterior margin of the ensuing vesiculation during the acrosome reaction (FIG. 4, left).[6,25] In the equatorial region of the guinea pig sperm, one cytoskeletal element that has been demonstrated is vimentin (FIG. 4, right), as first shown by Virtanen *et al.*[21] This narrow band of intermediate filament protein attached to the membrane at the boundary between these two functionally and compositionally distinct membrane domains may participate in controlling diffusion in the plane of that membrane (FIG. 5).

Similar diffusion barriers associated with cytoskeletal differentiations also appear at the junction of the head and tail and in the tail, between the energy-transducing midpiece and the flagellar wave-propagating principal piece (FIG. 1). The head/tail demarcation is seen as the posterior striated ring (FIG. 2) that overlies a bundle of elements with the diameter of intermediate filaments in the basal plate of the implantation fossa; this plate connects the tail to the head via its insertion into the nuclear envelope (FIG. 6).[1,8,24,25] Like the equatorial region, this basal plate also immunostains for filaments, with antibodies (provided by W. Sullivan, Department of Biochemistry, University of California, San Francisco) raised against the insoluble carcasses of *Drosophila* embryos (FIG. 6), and for actin.[10] This region acts as the final barrier to the anterior flow of the antigen recognized by the posterior tail (PT-1) antibody of Myles and Primakoff (FIG. 7).[20] It migrates from the principal piece only during capacitation, and only up to the striated ring separating the tail and head.

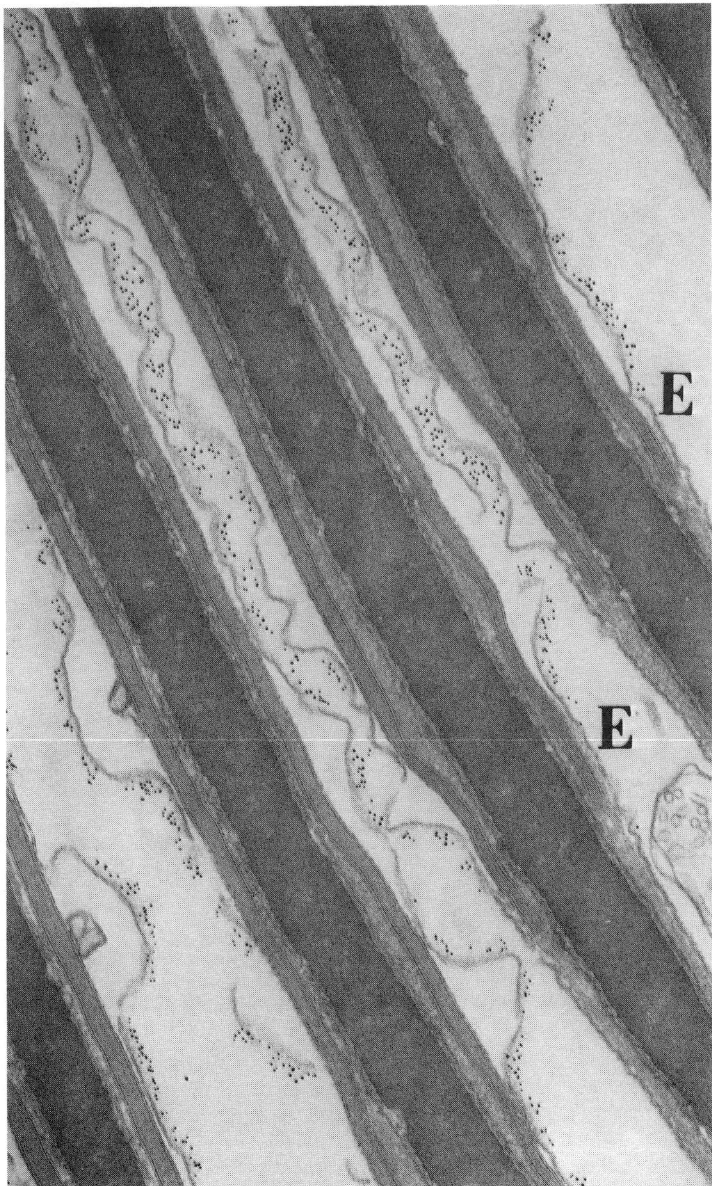

FIGURE 3. Immunogold labeling with mouse monoclonal antibody specific for the guinea pig sperm anterior head antigen of Myles and Primakoff. In epididymal sperm, the labeling abruptly ends at the equatorial segment (**E**). Magnification 50,000×.

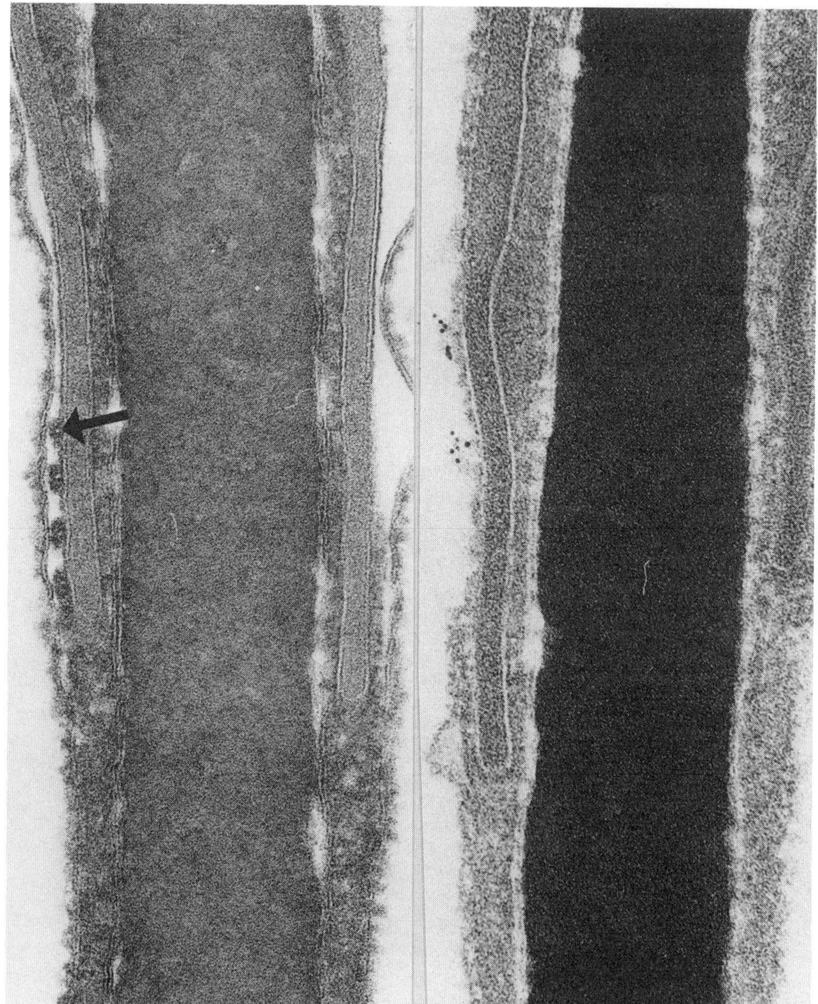

FIGURE 4. Filaments in the equatorial segment. **Left:** At the end of capacitation, immediately preceding the acrosome reaction, filaments (*arrow*) appear between the plasma membrane and the acrosome. Magnification: 116,000×, reproduced at 96%. **Right:** In a Triton-permeabilized preparation, immunogold labeling with anti-vimentin antibody reacts with the intermediate filament protein vimentin. Magnification: 120,000×, reproduced at 96%.

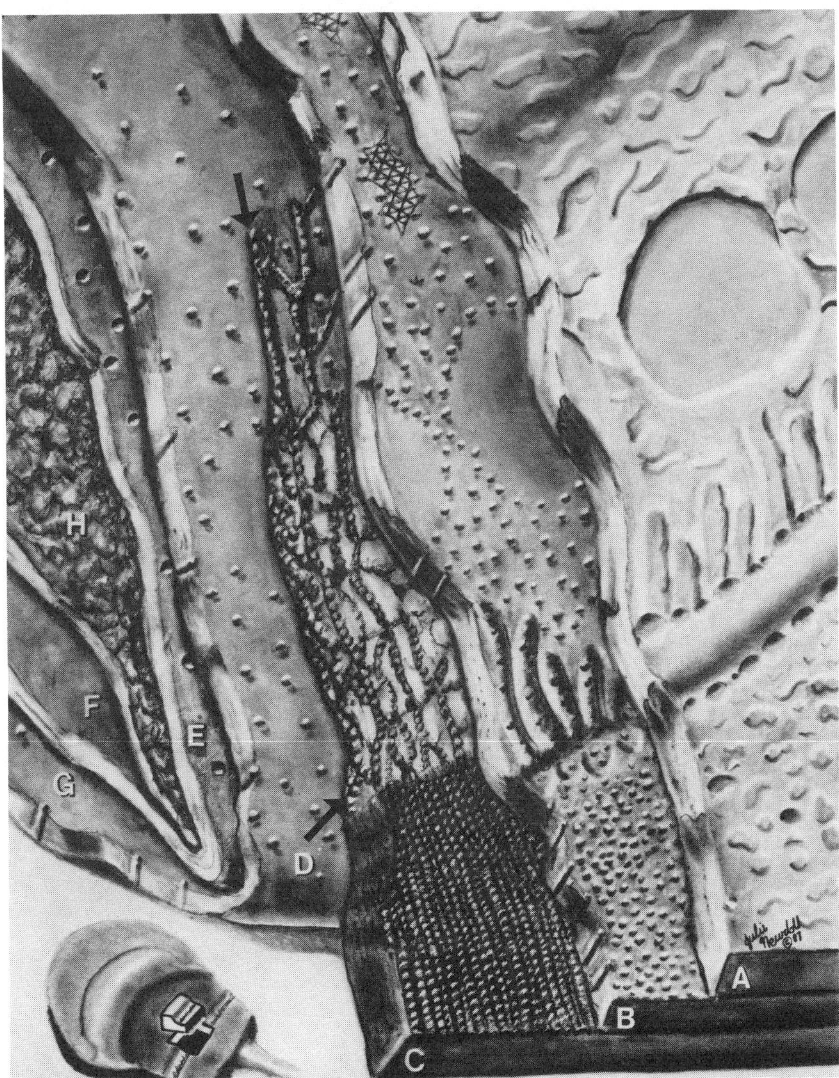

FIGURE 5. Diagram of the sperm equatorial segment dramatizing surface, intramembranous, and cytoplasmic modifications in a fully capacitated sperm. *Arrows* demarcate the cytoskeletal zone that marks the posterior margin of vesiculation during the acrosome reaction and the limits to free diffusion of antigens characterized by their reaction with the anterior head (AH) and posterior head (PH 20, PH 30) antibodies of Myles and Primakoff. **A:** outer leaflet, plasma membrane; **B:** inner leaflet, plasma membrane; **C:** cytoskeletal filaments; **D, G:** outer leaflet, acrosomal membrane; **E, F:** inner leaflet, acrosomal membrane; **H:** acrosomal content.

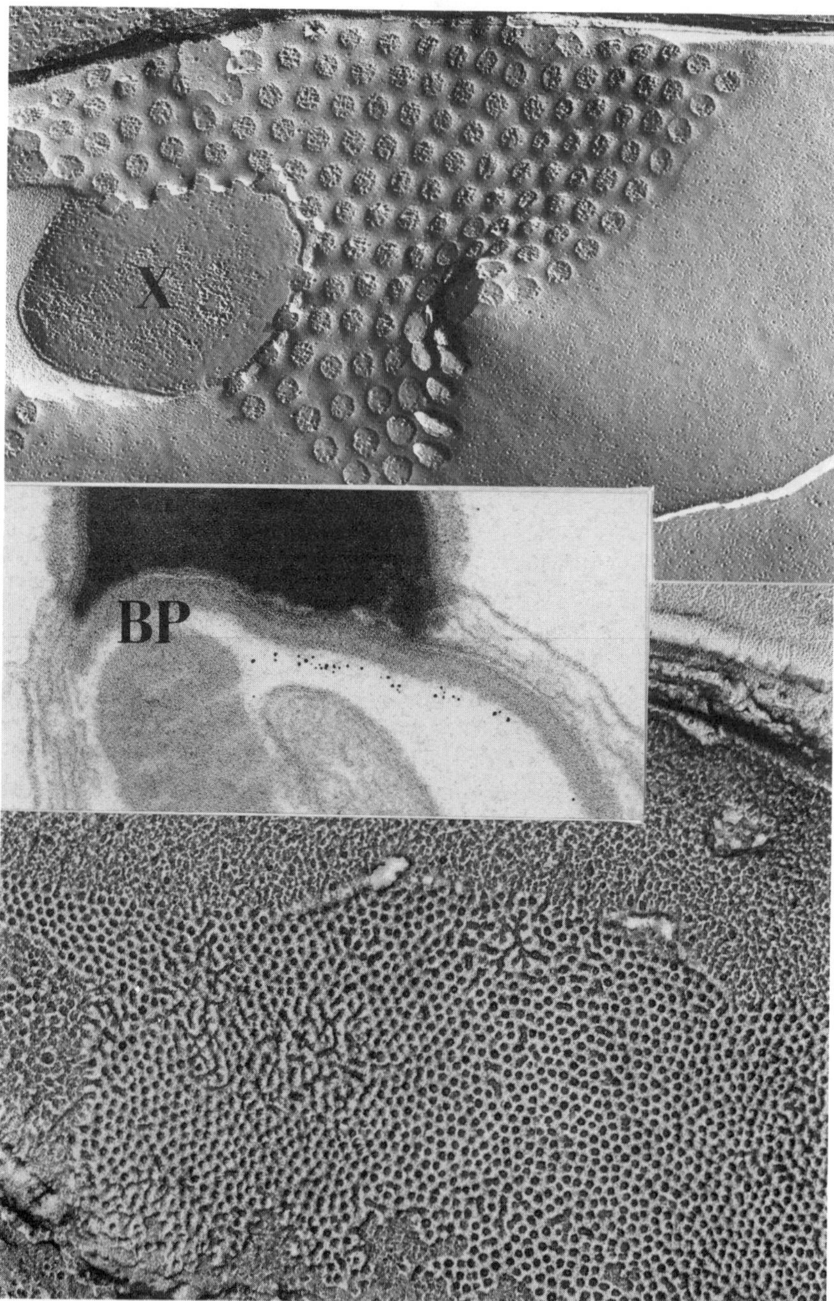

FIGURE 6. The striated ring. Underlying the striated ring and surrounded by nuclear pores (visible in the freeze-fracture preparation, *upper panel*) is the basal plate (**BP**), which attaches the tail to the implantation fossa in the nuclear envelope. Portions of the basal plate react with gold-labeled anti-cytoskeletal antibodies, including those specific for intermediate filaments (*inset*). Freeze-etching of the surface of the basal plate (*lower panel*) reveals intermediate filament-size elements. Magnifications: (*upper panel*) 40,000×; (*inset*) 80,000×; (*lower panel*) 116,000×.

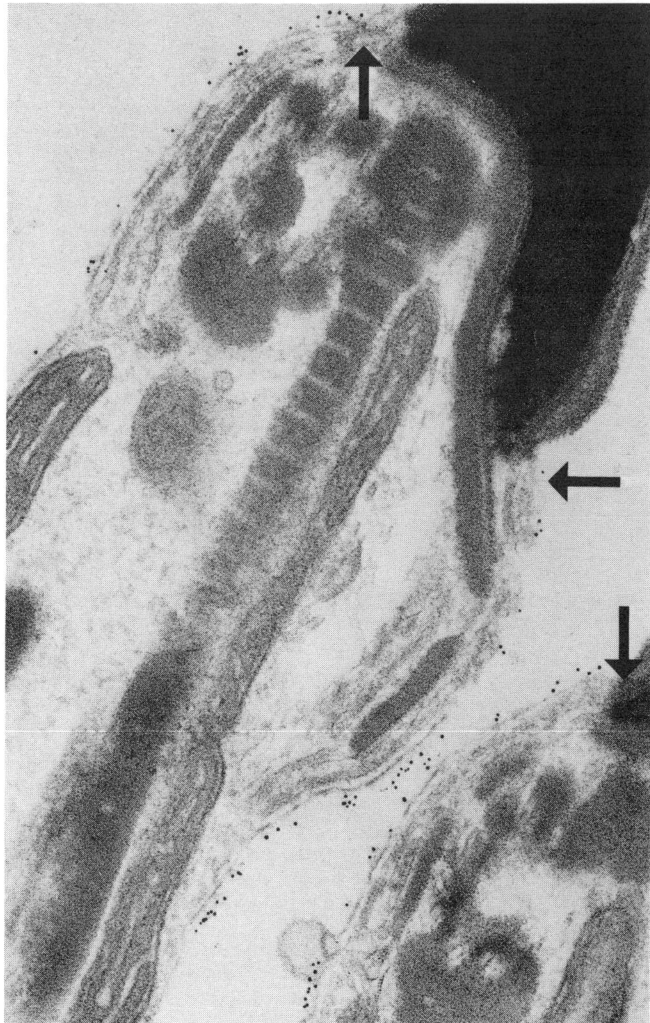

FIGURE 7. Barrier to flow of molecules in the plane of the membrane at the striated ring. In capacitated sperm, the antigen recognized by the PT-1 antibody migrates rostrally to the striated ring (*arrows*) but never crosses onto the head. Immunogold staining. Magnification: 73,000×.

The third barrier, the annulus, is at the juncture of the mitochondrial-rich midpiece and the principal piece of the tail (FIG. 8, upper figure). It, too, has a dense cytoskeleton (its composition has not yet been defined) closely attached to the membrane. The PT-1 antigen crosses this barrier only during capacitation.[18] Occasionally, midpiece intramembranous particles flow in the opposite direction across this barrier at the same time.

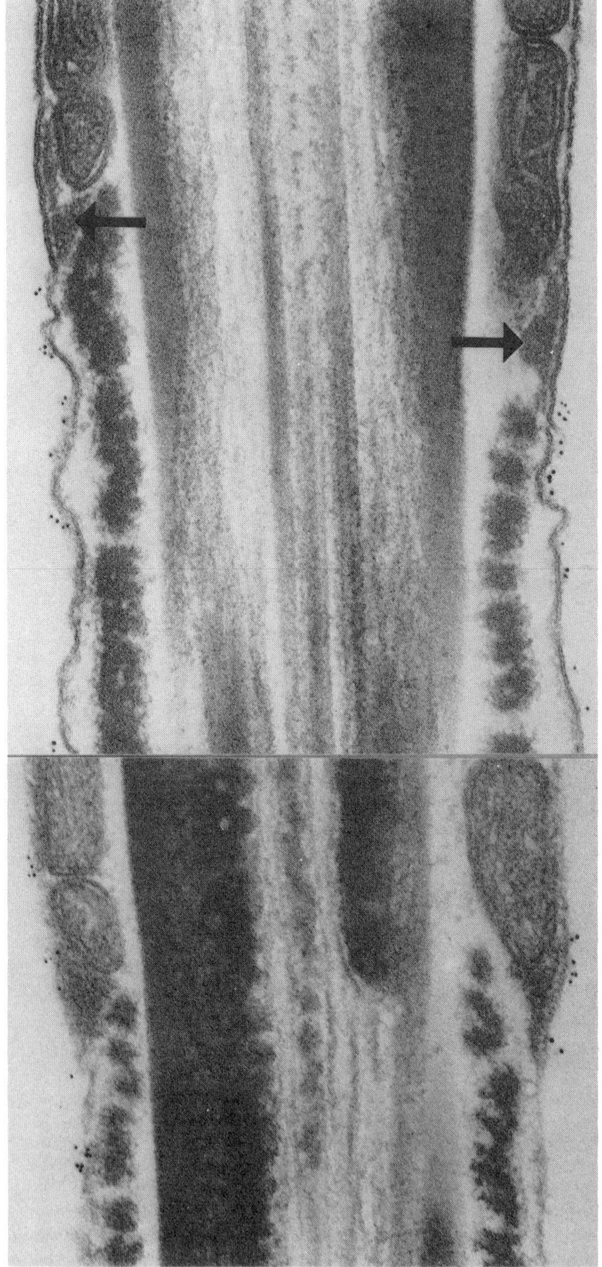

FIGURE 8. Barrier at the annulus is modulated by capacitation. **Upper panel:** In epididymal sperm, the antigen recognized by the PT-1 antibody remains restricted to the plasma membrane of the principal piece; the annulus excludes it. Immunogold staining. Magnification: 100,000×. **Lower panel:** During sperm capacitation, the antigen recognized by the PT-1 antibody crosses the membrane overlying the cytoskeletal component of the annulus. Immunogold staining. Magnification: 94,000×.

Applying the anti-PT-1 antibody conjugated with gold and performing the label-fracture procedure of Pinto da Silva,[26] we see the immunogold label on the outer half membrane of the principal piece of the tail. The gold doesn't correspond to the intramembranous particles of this leaflet, implying that the antigen recognized by the anti-PT-1 antibody partitioned with the inner leaflet. In this section, the label is exclusively confined to the principal piece of the tail. However, during the process of capacitation, the gold and the antigenic determinants move across the annulus (FIG. 8, lower figure), toward the head, and all the way to the striated ring.

At this point, I would like to remind you that the composite morphology of the membrane consists of the cytoskeleton just underneath the bilayer, the freeze-fracture particles in the plane of the membrane, and the antigenic determinant portion of membrane molecules on the cell surface. The zipper is a good model for this relationship (FIG. 9).[9,11] Immunogold labels applied to whole cells only bind to molecules which reside on the surface, and, thus, do not detect the underlying structures.

My general point about sperm development, maturation, and morphology is that cytoskeletal substructures line boundaries that prevent and then modulate the flow of proteins, lipids, and glycoconjugates within the plane of the membrane.[27,28] During development of the sperm cell—spermatogenesis—before such boundaries are established, molecules are generally disposed at random in the plane of the membrane. When the cytoskeleton becomes fully fixed in its position, an event which occurs at a time-point coincident with the migration of nuclear pores around the implantation fossa, boundary function appears and the membrane is segregated into domains. Subsequent physiological changes are associated with planar movement across the boundaries.

SOMATIC CELLS

Do the somatic cells have membrane-associated filaments that can influence the flow of molecules within the plane of the membrane?[29–34] Based on observations in the guinea pig sperm, I would like to speculate about somatic cells with respect to three anecdotal observations:

1. The seemingly homogeneous plasma membrane of a non-polarized cell is composed of microdomains of differing composition.
2. The properties of the microdomains in the plane of the membrane are influenced by its underlying cytoskeleton.[22]
3. Infection by some DNA viruses, e.g., baculovirus, affects the nuclear envelope, the nuclear pores, and the anchorage of cytoskeletal proteins, as well as the plasmalemma.

One example of structural and functional microdomains in the plasma membrane of somatic cells is provided by comparing filipin perturbability (sterol concentration) in the apical versus the basolateral portions of the membrane of ciliated or microvillar epithelium. Respiratory epithelial cells have about eight times the amount of sterol, i.e., filipin perturbations, in the apical portion of the plasma membrane as they have in lateral portions. During viral infection, the viruses enter the apical portion of the cell and, in some instances, then slide down the microvillar core of actin filaments into the cytoplasm. When such cells are dissociated, they lose their tight junctions and undergo randomization of proteins and lipids in the plane of the membrane. If

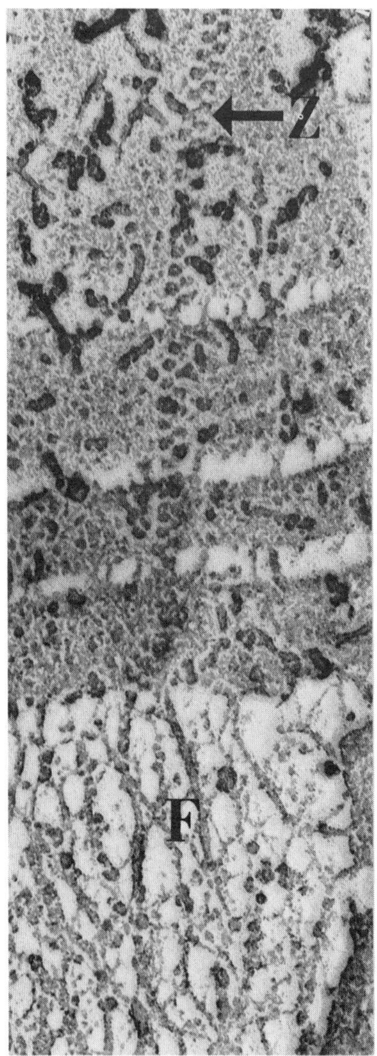

FIGURE 9. The zipper-like structure of the principal piece of the tail has a cytoplasmic filament (**F**), intramembranous particles, and a surface structural representation (**Z**). In general, antibodies bind only to molecules exposed on the membrane surface, but, like a zipper, the many membrane surface structures have intra- and submembranous components. Magnification: 150,000×.

one examines either such dissociated cells or seemingly non-polarized mouse erythroleukemia cells[35] after viral infection, one sees that, in areas of budding viruses, the virus-membrane interactions do not really occur at random locations, but only in patches of filipin-perturbable (i.e., free sterol-containing) membrane, presumably where cytoskeletal elements have become detached. Thus, compositional and biophysical microdomains seem to exist in these cell populations.

Another point about hematopoietic cells is that the spectrin-based cytoskeletal undercoat of the red blood cell (RBC), even of the fully mature cell, influences the behavior of molecules in the plane of the overlying membrane. Seen from inside the cell, the spectrin undercoating is contiguous. While the cytoskeleton is attached, exposure of the red cells to the polyene filipin brings about only a very few, random membrane perturbations by the polyene:sterol interaction. But if one cross-links the spectrin with diamide, or heat-denatures it, or if the same filipin procedure is applied to spectrin-deficient RBC, one gets a 5.5-fold increase in the filipin-perturbability of the membrane, characteristically in microdomains or patches of that membrane.[23] The implication is that the cytoskeleton has an influence on the penetrability of the polyene into the membrane, or that generation of areas of membrane bare of cytoskeleton permits expression of the cytochemical reaction of filipin with sterol or generally renders those areas of the membrane malleable. Whatever the cause, affecting spectrin alters the properties seen in the plane of the overlying membrane.

A final point I want to speculate about, based on studies of sperm maturation, concerns nuclear pores. In early stages of spermiogenesis, pores form in the nuclear envelope in the anterior portion of the head and appear along with or after clusters of particles which resemble communicating or gap junction-type particles in the membrane. During the acrosomal cap phase of spermatid maturation, the clusters of particles and the nuclear pores migrate posteriorly. In the morphologically mature sperm cell, all the nuclear pores are exclusively in a redundant part of the nuclear envelope in the tail of the sperm, shrouding the intermediate filament and other cytoskeletal proteins of the basal plate. Baculovirus- and other DNA virus-infected somatic cells have nuclear pores obliterated by a dense material, and cytoskeletal filament (actin) immunoreactivity is then found in the nucleus (personal communication, Loy Volkman, University of California, Berkeley). My guess is that virus infection affects cytoskeletal:nuclear pore interaction; such an alteration may confer some pathological characteristics to the virus-infected cell.[33,34] I have not observed obvious cytoskeleton:nuclear pore derangements in retrovirus-infected cells.

CONCLUSIONS

The highly polarized sperm cell has distinct diffusion-regulating boundaries within the plane of its continuous membrane. The borders of the membrane domains are underlain by immuno-identifiable or structurally distinct attachments of cytoskeletal elements; two of these boundaries, the equatorial segment and the basal plate, contain vimentin. Certain proteins and lipids may cross these barriers only during specific maturational states of the cell, e.g., after sperm capacitation. Similar controls may be exerted in seemingly non-polarized somatic cells, and these controls may be affected by viral infection. One can speculate that the filament:nuclear pore association is susceptible to alteration during infection by DNA containing viruses.

REFERENCES

1. Fawcett, D. W. 1975. The mammalian spermatozoon. Dev. Biol. **44:** 394-436.
2. Yanagimachi, R. 1988. Mammalian fertilization. *In* The Physiology of Reproduction. E. Knobil & J. Neill *et al.,* Eds.: 135-185. Raven Press. New York.
3. Suzuki, F. & R. Yanagimachi. 1986. Membrane changes in Chinese hamster spermatozoa during epididymal maturation. J. Ultrastruct. Mol. Struct. Res. **96:** 91-104.
4. Olson, G. E. & M.-C. Orgebin-Crist. 1982. Sperm surface changes during epididymal maturation. Ann. N. Y. Acad. Sci. **383:** 372-391.

5. KAZAZOGLOU, T., R. W. SCHACKMANN, M. FOSSET & B. M. SHAPIRO. 1985. Calcium channel antagonists inhibit the acrosome reaction and bind to plasma membranes of sea urchin sperm. Proc. Natl. Acad. Sci. USA **82:** 1460-1464.
6. FRIEND, D. S., L. ORCI, A. PERRELET & R. YANAGIMACHI. 1977. Membrane particle changes attending the acrosome reaction in guinea pig spermatozoa. J. Cell Biol. **74:** 561-577.
7. FRIEND, D. S. 1980. Freeze-fracture alterations in guinea pig sperm membranes preceding gamete fusion. *In* Membrane-Membrane Interactions. N. B. Gilula, Ed.: 153-165. Raven Press. New York.
8. FAWCETT, D. W. 1965. The anatomy of the mammalian spermatozoon with particular reference to the guinea pig. Z. Zellforsch. Mikrosk. Anat. **67:** 279-296.
9. FRIEND, D. S. & D. W. FAWCETT. 1974. Membrane differentiations in freeze-fractured mammalian sperm. J. Cell Biol. **63:** 641-664.
10. OLSON, G. E., V. P. WINFREY & S. P. FLAHERTY. 1987. Cytoskeletal assemblies of mammalian spermatozoa. Ann. N. Y. Acad. Sci. **513:** 222-246.
11. FRIEND, D. S. & J. E. HEUSER. 1981. Orderly particle arrays on the mitochondrial outer membrane in rapidly frozen sperm. Anat. Rec. **199:** 159-175.
12. WOLF, D. E. 1987. Diffusion and the control of membrane regionalization. Ann. N. Y. Acad. Sci. **513:** 247-261.
13. O'RAND, M. G. 1982. Modification of the sperm membrane during capacitation. Ann. N. Y. Acad. Sci. **383:** 392-404.
14. COWAN, A. E., D. G. MYLES & D. E. KOPPEL. 1987. Lateral diffusion of the PH-20 protein on guinea pig sperm: Evidence that barriers to diffusion maintain plasma membrane domains in mammalian sperm. J. Cell Biol. **104:** 917-923.
15. KAN, F. W. F. & P. PINTO DA SILVA. 1987. Molecular demarcation of surface domains as established by label-fracture cytochemistry of boar spermatozoa. J. Histochem. Cytochem. **35:** 1069-1078.
16. AGUAS, A. P. & P. PINTO DA SILVA. 1983. Regionalization of transmembrane glycoproteins in the plasma membrane of boar sperm head is revealed by fracture-label. J. Cell Biol. **97:** 1356-1364.
17. BEARER, E. L. & D. S. FRIEND. 1982. Modification of anionic-lipid domains preceding membrane fusion in guinea pig sperm. J. Cell Biol. **92:** 604-615.
18. MYLES, D. G., D. E. KOPPEL, A. E. COWAN, B. M. PHELPS & P. PRIMAKOFF. 1987. Rearrangement of sperm surface antigens prior to fertilization. Ann. N. Y. Acad. Sci. **513:** 262-273.
19. WOLF, D. E., S. HAGOPIAN, R. LEWIS, J. K. VOGLMAYR & G. FAIRBANKS. 1986. Lateral regionalization and diffusion of a maturation-dependent antigen in the ram sperm plasma membrane. J. Cell Biol. **102:** 1826-1831.
20. MYLES, D. G., P. PRIMAKOFF & A. R. BELLVÉ. 1981. Surface domains of the guinea pig sperm defined with monoclonal antibodies. Cell **23:** 433-439.
21. VIRTANEN, I., R. A. BADLEY, R. PAASIVUO & V.-P. LEHTO. 1984. Distinct cytoskeletal domains revealed in sperm cells. J. Cell Biol. **99:** 1083-1091.
22. PRIMAKOFF, P. & D. G. MYLES. 1983. A map of the guinea pig sperm surface constructed with monoclonal antibodies. Dev. Biol. **98:** 417-428.
23. CLARK, M. R., S. MEL, F. LUPU & D. S. FRIEND. 1987. Influence of the membrane undercoat or filipin perturbation of the red blood cell membrane. Expt. Cell Res. **171:** 321-330.
24. FRIEND, D. S. 1982. Plasma membrane diversity in a highly polarized cell. J. Cell Biol. **93:** 243-249.
25. HOLT, W. V. 1984. Membrane heterogeneity in the mammalian spermatozoon. Int. Rev. Cytol. **87:** 159-172.
26. PINTO DA SILVA, P. & F. W. KAN. 1984. Label fracture: A method for high resolution labeling of cell surface. J. Cell Biol. **99:** 1156-1161.
27. WOLF, D. E. 1987. Overcoming random diffusion in polarized cells—Corralling the drunken beggar. Bio Essays **61:** 116-121.
28. PHELPS, B. & D. G. MYLES. 1987. The guinea pig sperm surface protein, PH-20, reaches the surface via two transport pathways and becomes localized to a domain after an initial uniform distribution. Dev. Biol. **123:** 63-72.

29. PERIDES, G., C. HARTER & P. TRAUB. 1987. Electrostatic and hydrophobic interactions of the intermediate filament protein vimentin and its amino terminus with lipid bilayers. J. Biol. Chem. **262:** 13742-13749.
30. EVANS, R. M. 1988. Cyclic AMP-dependent protein kinase-induced vimentin filament disassembly involves modification of the N-terminal domain of intermediate filament subunits. FEBS Lett. **234:** 73-78.
31. ZIEVE, G. W. & E. J. ROEMER. 1988. Cordycepin rapidly collapses the intermediate filament networks into juxtanuclear caps in fibroblasts and epidermal cells. Exp. Cell Res. **177:** 19-26.
32. EVANS, R. M. 1988. The intermediate-filament proteins vimentin and desmin are phosphorylated in specific domains. Eur. J. Cell Biol. **46:** 152-160.
33. CARMO-FONSECA, M., A. J. CIDADÃO & J. F. DAVID-FERREIRA. 1987. Filamentous cross-bridges link intermediate filaments to the nuclear pore complexes. Eur. J. Cell Biol. **45:** 282-290.
34. BLOBEL, G. 1985. Gene gating: A hypothesis. Proc. Natl. Acad. Sci. USA **82:** 8527-8529.
35. PREISLER, H. D., D. HOUSEMAN, W. SCHER & C. FRIEND. 1973. Effects of 5-Bromo-2′-dioxyuridine on production of globin messenger RNA in dimethyl sulfoxide-stimulated Friend leukemia cells. Proc. Natl. Acad. Sci. USA **70:** 2956-2959.

Shope Fibroma: A Model System to Study Tumorigenesis by Poxviruses[a]

B. G.-T. POGO,[b] K. M. OBOM, J. HADDAD, AND J. G. HOLLAND

Center for Experimental Cell Biology and
Department of Microbiology
Mount Sinai School of Medicine
City University of New York
New York, New York 10029

Many of you have spoken about Charlotte's numerous attributes as a friend, human being, scientist, and supporter of women's causes and about her great achievements with better words than I can use. I was fortunate to meet her many years ago in 1959 and to become her friend for life. It was not until 20 years later that I had the opportunity to join her at Mount Sinai. Then we spent a great deal of time together sharing the daily routine of scientific life. Charlotte enriched the life of the many people she came close to; she certainly enriched mine. I miss her.

When I told Charlotte that I was planning to work on tumorigenic poxviruses, she was very enthusiastic and immediately recalled Duran Reynals' experiments. She said—and I quote—"Poxviruses are in the twilight zone of carcinogenesis; they are not like the classic oncogenic viruses, but still they cause hyperplasia: it is worthwhile studying them." She certainly had a knack for words, a great imagination and intuition. Poxviruses still are in the twilight zone, in spite of the fact that she was so supportive and enthusiastic. In the last months of her life, I used to visit her every day and tell her about the happenings in the laboratory. When I mentioned the first results with nude mice, she said, as she always used to tell us, "Repeat it three times." Well, we repeated it three times, Charlotte!

INTRODUCTION

Although nowadays completely forgotten as oncogenic viruses, the poxviruses were recognized as tumorigenic agents as early as 1898, when Sanarelli[1] demonstrated that rabbit myxoma was an infectious disease. As summarized in TABLE 1,[1-10] poxviruses can cause benign or malignant tumors either by themselves or by interacting with other agents, such as chemical carcinogens or immunosuppressants.

[a] Supported by Grants CA-29262 and CA-10000 from the National Institutes of Health and by the Chemotherapy Foundation.

[b] Address correspondence to Beatriz G.-T. Pogo, M.D., Center for Experimental Cell Biology, Mount Sinai School of Medicine, One Gustave Levy Place, New York, N.Y. 10029.

TABLE 1. Oncogenic Poxviruses

In Vivo
Self-limiting neoplasia
Shope fibroma virus (SFV)
Squirrel fibroma
Hare fibroma
Molluscum contagiosum
Yaba monkey tumor
Malignant growth
Myxoma[1]
SFV plus coal tar[2]
SFV in newborn[3] and immunosuppressed animals[4]
Vaccinia virus plus methylcholanthrene[5]
Malignant fibroma[6]
In Vitro
Transformation
Vaccinia virus in mouse embryo cells[7]
Molluscum contagiosum in human embryonic fibroblasts[8]
Yaba monkey tumor virus in JINET cells[9]
Shope fibroma virus in SIRC cells[10]

Studies on *in vitro* transformation of primary mouse fibroblast cultures by vaccinia virus were reported some years ago.[7] *Molluscum contagiosum* has also been shown to transform human embryo fibroblasts morphologically, although it failed to replicate in these cells.[8] The most comprehensive work to date to show *in vitro* cell transformation has been on the Yaba monkey virus by Rouhandeh's group.[9] We have recently shown transformation by Shope fibroma virus (SFV).[10] The potential of poxviruses as oncogenic agents can no longer be ignored, since a gene for a growth factor, similar to epidermal growth factor (EGF) and transforming growth factor α (TFG-α), has been identified in vaccinia,[11] and EGF-like DNA sequences have been shown in Shope fibroma,[12] myxoma,[13] and *Molluscum contagiosum.*[14] Growth factors and growth factor receptors have been associated with certain oncogenes and may play a role in deregulation of cell growth.

Shope fibroma virus induces benign tumors (fibromas) in adult rabbits that regress spontaneously, as first observed by Shope.[15] The regression seems to be mediated by an immunological response, since in newborns or in immunosuppressed animals the tumors continue growing and invade other tissues locally.[2–4] Recently, the genome of SFV has been cloned,[16] and the sequences for two viral proteins have been identified by McFadden and collaborators.[12,17]

Our laboratory has been interested in the mechanism of oncogenesis by poxviruses. To assess the oncogenic potential of SFV, two experimental approaches were explored. First, a spontaneously immortalized rabbit cornea fibroblast cell line (SIRC cells) was infected with ultraviolet-(UV-) inactivated SFV, and the establishment of cell lines with a transformed phenotype was investigated. This approach has been successfully used to demonstrate the oncogenic potential of herpesvirus types 1 and 2[19,20] and Yaba monkey tumor virus.[9] Second, transfection of NIH/3T3 cells with SFV DNA was performed to obtain transformed cell lines that were characterized for their tumorigenic ability. This transformation assay has been widely used to demonstrate the presence of oncogenes in human tumors. Results from the first approach suggest that UV-inactivated SFV can elicit the second step of transformation *in vitro,* malignant transformation of immortalized rabbit fibroblasts, but in a transient manner. From the second line of work, results indicated that SFV DNA can transform NIH/3T3 cells and convert them to a tumorigenic phenotype. The molecular mechanisms which the two types of transformation evoke are not completely understood at the moment.

MATERIALS AND METHODS

Rabbit cornea fibroblasts (SIRC) cells from the American Type Culture Collection were cultured as monolayers in minimal essential medium (MEM, Flow Laboratories) supplemented with 5% fetal bovine serum and were dissociated with trypsin:EDTA (GIBCO). NIH/3T3 cells obtained from Dr. Charlotte Friend, derived from cultures originally obtained from Dr. G. M. Cooper (Harvard Medical School), were maintained in Dulbecco's modified Eagle's medium (Flow) with 5% fetal bovine serum, following the protocol used in Dr. Cooper's laboratory.

The Patuxent strain of Shope fibroma virus was obtained from Dr. H. Hinze (University of Wisconsin), and propagated, assayed, and purified as previously described.[20,21] Extraction of viral and cellular DNAs, restriction analysis, agarose gel electrophoresis, Southern blotting, and nick-translation hybridization procedures were performed as previously reported.[10] Efficiency of cloning of normal and transformed cells was assayed using the soft-agar cloning method of Rhim.[22]

Transfection experiments were carried out as previously described.[10] *Focus-derived* lines were established by picking foci from NIH/3T3 cell cultures transfected with DNA from SFV or rabbit fibroma, from transformed 3T3 cells, or from spontaneously arising transformants.

Expression of the SFV genome was investigated by dot-blot hybridization of total RNA isolated by the guanidium isothiocyanate/cesium chloride procedure[23] to [^{35}S]deoxyadenosine 5′-(α-thio)triphosphate- (^{35}S-dATP-) labeled SFV DNA.

RESULTS AND DISCUSSION

Rabbit Cells Transformed by UV-Inactivated SFV

SIRC cells infected with SFV UV-inactivated by three logarithmic units readily became transformed. After the second passage, the cells piled up, forming distinctive foci. Cell lines were easily established from an individual focus. The biological and molecular properties of these cell lines were studied after serial passage *in vitro.* Virus was detected until the tenth passage, after which no infectivity was recorded. The presence of viral antigens was investigated by immunoprecipitation of labeled cell extracts, followed by electrophoresis. Several polypeptides with M_r similar to those of polypeptides produced in productively infected cells were detected as late as passage 49, after which the results were negative.

The presence of viral DNA sequences was investigated in cell transformants that no longer produced infectious particles. Viral sequences were detected in nuclear DNA in one cell line between passages 10 and 42 but were no longer present at passage 47. No evidence for integration of the viral DNA was found.

The biological properties of the cell transformants were investigated by studying cell growth, serum dependence, and tumorigenicity. The rate of growth and the serum dependence of the transformants and the parental line were compared. The transformants grew faster and were able to grow at a lower serum concentration than the control (parental) cells. When inoculated into rabbits, the transformants produced tumors that regressed spontaneously, whereas the parental line did not induce tumors.

The results obtained with the cells transformed by UV-inactivated virus are summarized in TABLE 2. They indicated that SFV was able to change the properties of the SIRC cells to a transformed phenotype in a transient manner. The loss of the transformed phenotype occurred in all the cell lines studied around the 50th passage. Several explanations can account for the loss of the malignant phenotype after serial passage: (1) the number of transformed cells was small, and the non-transformed cells overgrew them; (2) transformed cells reverted to the non-transformed state; (3) SFV has a weak oncogenic potential that results in an unstable type of transformation, or (4) rabbit cells, like human cells, express suppressor genes.[24] Experiments using cell lines which were each derived from a single focus, in which all cells may be transformed, gave the same pattern of transformation, thus eliminating the first possibility. Reversion to the non-transformed state, although unlikely, cannot be ruled out. It is probable that the constant expression of certain genes is necessary to maintain the transformed phenotype. Whether these genes are lost because of instability of the viral sequences or because of the expression of cellular suppressor genes is not clear at the moment.[10]

Transfection of NIH/3T3 Cells with SFV DNA

To investigate further the oncogenic potential of SFV, transfection of NIH/3T3 cells with SFV DNA was performed. This transformation assay has been widely used to demonstrate the presence of oncogenes in many tumors. Although NIH/3T3 cells are already immortalized, they have a low degree of spontaneous transformation and provide favorable conditions for the expression of weak oncogenes. Several lines of NIH/3T3 cells were used, but only those obtained from Dr. C. Friend (and originally from G. Cooper, Harvard University) gave reproducible results. The average number

TABLE 2. Characteristics of the Malignant Phenotype in SIRC Cells Transformed with UV-Inactivated Shope Fibroma Virus (SFV)[a]

Lack of infectious particles
Resistance to superinfection with SFV
Presence of viral DNA sequences in the nucleus
Expression of viral proteins
Low serum-dependence
High cloning efficiency in agar
Induction of tumors in rabbits

[a] This transformation was not stable, since in all cell lines studied a loss of the malignant phenotype was observed at around the 50th passage.

TABLE 3. Transformation of NIH/3T3 Cells by DNA from Primary Transfectants or by Viral or Oncogene DNA

DNA[a]	Exp. No.	μg DNA Tested	Foci/μg DNA	Foci/Plate (ave.)
Primary Transfectant				
F2p3	1	20	0.50	1.1
	2	15	0.07	
F3p5	1	20	0.45	1.2
	2	15	0.20	
F4p5	1	15	0.40	0.4
Fc-Ha-*ras*	1	2	14.50	5.8
NIH/3T3 (control)	1	20	0.60	
	2	15	0.40	0.4
	3	15	0.30	
Virus or Oncogene				
SFV	1	10	2.40	2.3
c-Ha-*ras*	1	2	8.00	3.0
Calf thymus (control)	1	20	0.10	0.4

[a] NIH/3T3 cells were transfected with DNA from purified shope fibroma virus (SFV), cloned c-Ha-*ras*, calf thymus, or the primary transfectant cell lines at the concentrations indicated, under the conditions described in MATERIALS AND METHODS. F2, F3, F4: cell lines obtained by primary transfection of NIH/3T3 cells with SFV (p, passage); Fc-Ha-*ras:* cell line obtained by primary transfection of NIH/3T3 cells with c-Ha-*ras*.

of foci obtained per microgram of viral DNA was around 2.4, whereas it was 8.0 with the c-Ha-*ras* oncogene. DNA from calf thymus induced approximately 0.1 foci per microgram of DNA (TABLE 3). The efficiency of transfection using the neomycin-resistance (pSV2*neo*) gene in the presence of geneticin was calculated to be 0.1%. The foci induced by SFV DNA are type II according to the classification of Perucho *et al.*,[25] in contrast to those induced by the c-Ha-*ras* oncogene, which are type I. A comparison of the foci obtained after transfection of NIH/3T3 monolayers with the different DNAs is shown in FIGURE 1. Foci remained smaller and less discrete in plates transfected with SFV DNA compared with those transfected with c-Ha-*ras* or pSV2*neo* DNAs. The degree of foci induction by SFV DNA was always lower than that obtained with the c-Ha-*ras* oncogene or the pSV2*neo* gene. This could be due, in part, to the fact that poxvirus DNA lacks the promoter sequences recognized by the cell polymerases and may not be correctly or efficiently transcribed. Addition of DMSO to the cultures slightly increased the efficiency of transfection with SFV DNA but not with c-Ha-*ras*. Furthermore, transfection experiments using DNA from primary transfectants did not show any increase in the number of foci induced over the number of transformants obtained with SFV DNA; on the contrary, the number of foci per microgram of DNA was lower in the latter case, as shown in TABLE 3. As expected for an oncogene, an increase was observed in the number of foci obtained by transfection with DNA from lines transfected with c-Ha-*ras* compared to the number originally induced by the c-Ha-*ras* DNA. The lack of increase in the number of foci induced by the DNA of the SFV primary transfectants may be explained by the fact that the viral sequences responsible for the induction of foci may be present in lesser amounts in these cells than in the viral DNA.

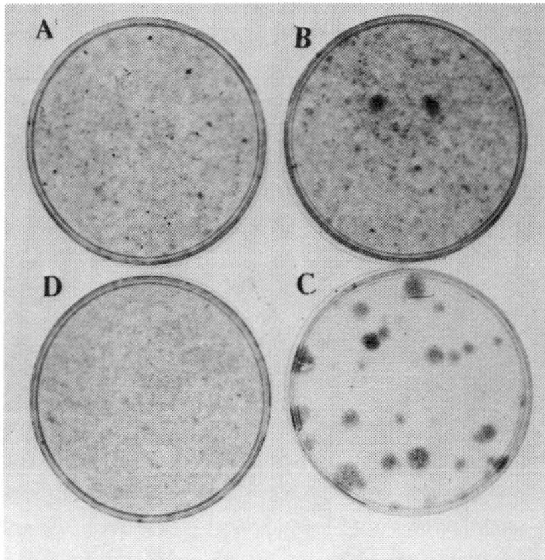

FIGURE 1. Focus assay after transfection of NIH/3T3 cells with different DNAs. NIH/3T3 cells were transfected with 1 μg of test DNA and 20 μg of carrier calf thymus DNA by the calcium phosphate precipitation technique. Cultures were grown in the presence of Dulbecco's medium supplemented with 5% fetal bovine serum. After three weeks, the cells were fixed with methanol and stained with Giemsa. Plates were transfected with (**A**) SFV DNA, (**B**) c-Ha-*ras*/plasmid DNA, (**C**) pSV2*neo* plasmid (culture grown in the presence of 400 μg per ml of geneticin), (**D**) calf thymus DNA alone.

Characterization of Cell Lines Derived from Isolated Foci

Cell lines were established from individual foci resulting from transfection of NIH/3T3 cells with SFV DNA (lines F) and from spontaneous foci (lines C). They were assayed for two phenotypic changes associated with complete transformation: anchorage independence and induction of tumors. The results of these experiments indicated that, of six focus-derived lines, four were anchorage independent and five induced tumors in nude mice between two and five weeks after inoculation. All contained SFV DNA sequences at early passages. None of the lines derived from spontaneous foci were either anchorage independent or induced tumors in nude mice (Obom and Pogo, manuscript submitted). The expression of viral DNA was also detected at early passages, as shown by hybridization of RNA from the F lines to nick-translated SFV DNA (FIGURE 2). For comparison, RNA from SFV-infected SIRC cells taken at different times after infection was also used for hybridization. Of the three lines tested, only two (F2 and F3: dot-blots A and B in FIG. 2) contain RNA sequences that hybridized to SFV DNA. Three more lines tested (F5, F6 and F7) also gave a positive signal (data not shown). It is surprising that line F4 (dot-blot C in FIG. 2), which does not express SFV DNA sequences, did not induce tumors in mice, although it was anchorage independent. FIGURE 3 shows one of the mice inoculated with cells from line F5 that developed tumors at both sites of inoculation. Histological examination of these tumors revealed that they were fibrosarcomas, some with a great abundance of small vessels. However, no evidence for metastasis was found when the mice were examined after they were sacrificed.

Experiments are now under way to determine which sequences of the SFV DNA are responsible for transformation. Cloned *Bam*H I fragments of SFV DNA (kindly provided by Dr. Grant McFadden, University of Edmonton, Alberta) are being used in transfection experiments.

Transfection of NIH/3T3 Cells with DNA from Rabbit Fibroma

Tumors can be easily induced in rabbits by subcutaneous inoculation of 10^6 focus-forming units (FFU) of SFV. These tumors (fibromas), which are formed of loosely

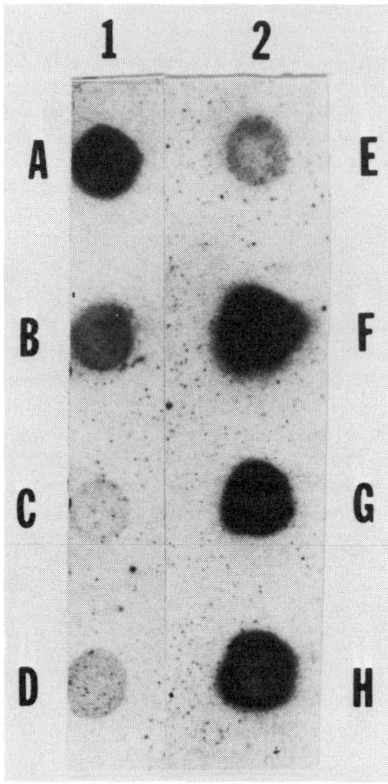

FIGURE 2. Dot-blot of RNA extracted from focus-derived cell lines (*column 1*) and SIRC cells infected with SFV (*column 2*). Aliquots containing 20 μg of total RNA were dotted onto nitrocellulose and hybridized to ^{35}S-dATP-labeled SFV DNA. RNA from focus-derived cell lines (p8, passage 8): (**A**) F2p8, (**B**) F3p8, (**C**) F4p7, (**D**) control p8. RNA from SIRC cells infected with SFV for (**E**) 8 hr, (**F**) 24 hr, (**G**) 32 hr, (**H**) 48 hr.

proliferating, non-infiltrating fibroblasts, regress after reaching 4 cm in size, approximately two weeks after inoculation. DNA extracted from one of these tumors was transfected into NIH/3T3 cells. The results are summarized in TABLE 4. The number of foci obtained with the DNA from rabbit fibroma was low compared to the number obtained with SFV DNA. However, it should be emphasized that only 0.05% of the total tumor DNA was SFV DNA, as determined by hybridization with nick-translated SFV DNA. Whether the SFV DNA or a modified cell DNA is responsible for transformation is not clear at the moment. Cell lines were derived from the foci and tested for tumorigenic conversion and anchorage dependence. One of the three cell lines tested was able to induce tumors in nude mice and showed slightly higher efficiency of cloning in agar than the parental NIH/3T3 cells.

Characterization of Cell Lines Derived from Nude Mice Tumors

Pieces of the tumors induced by F lines in nude mice were placed on sterile stainless steel grids in petri dishes and covered with tissue culture medium. Cells growing from these explants were collected in the medium and cell lines were established, which

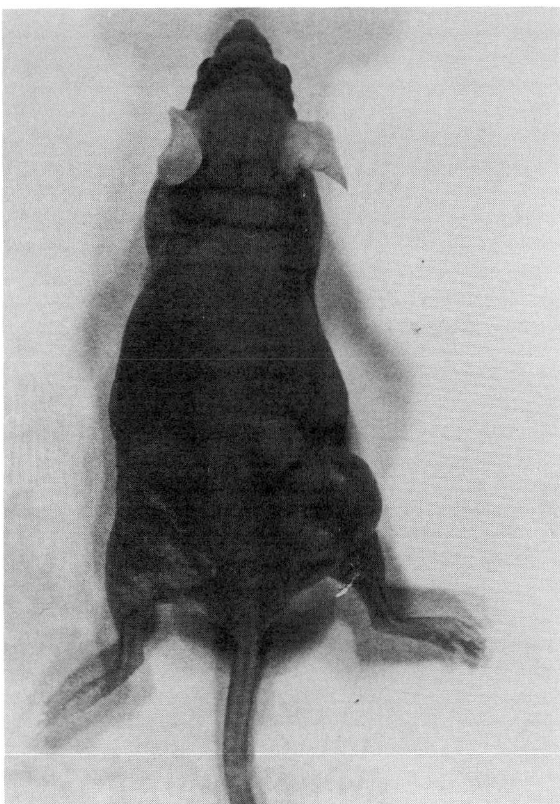

FIGURE 3. Nude mouse showing tumors induced by a focus-derived cell line.

TABLE 4. Transfection of NIH/3T3 Cells with DNA Extracted from Rabbit Fibroma

DNA[a]	Foci/μg DNA[b]
Rabbit fibroma[c]	0.30
SFV	2.80
Salmon sperm	0.15
None	0

[a] NIH/3T3 cells were transfected with 20 μg of DNA from rabbit fibroma or salmon sperm or with 10 μg of Shope fibroma virus (SFV) DNA and monitored for the presence of foci for three weeks.

[b] Results are the average of 3 independent experiments.

[c] Only 0.05% of the total tumor DNA from rabbit fibroma used for transfection consists of SFV DNA.

TABLE 5. Transformation of NIH/3T3 Cells by Tumor-derived Cell-Line DNA

DNA[a]	Exp. No.	Foci/μg DNA	Foci/Plate (ave.)
T2	1	3.2	12.4
	2	3.0	
T3	1	3.8	11.8
	2	2.1	
NIH/3T3	1	1.4	5.6

[a] NIH/3T3 cells were transfected with 20 μg of DNA extracted from tumor-derived cell lines (T2, T3) or from non-transformed NIH/3T3 cells and monitored for the presence of foci. After 3 weeks, the cells were fixed and stained, and the number of foci determined.

were designated T lines. Two of these lines were further characterized. DNA extracted from lines T2 and T3 also transformed NIH/3T3 cells, as shown in TABLE 5. When inoculated into nude mice, T2 and T3 cells induced tumors with a shorter latency period than did the F lines (TABLE 6).

Histological examination of these tumors stained with hematoxylin-eosin (FIG. 4) revealed that they were very invasive and highly vascularized sarcomas. The tumor cells stained red with the trichrome stain, indicating their muscle nature. Moreover, immunohistochemical staining for muscle common antigen was also positive, confirming the diagnosis of leiomyosarcoma, probably angioleiomyosarcoma. This finding, observed in all the tumor cell lines studied, suggested that the viral DNA was able to promote the growth of fibroblasts and of smooth muscle cells from vessels, thus implicating the participation of a fibroblastic growth factor. Experiments are now under way to investigate this possibility.

CONCLUSIONS

From the results discussed here, three main observations should be emphasized: (1) UV-inactivated SFV can trigger the second step of carcinogenesis *in vitro,* malignant transformation, when inoculated into an already immortalized cell line. This trans-

TABLE 6. Induction of Tumors in Female Nude Mice by Tumor-derived Cell Lines

Cell Line[a]	No. Tumors/No. Sites	Latency
T2	12/12	1 week
T3	6/10	2 weeks
C3	0/10	—

[a] Tumor cell lines (T2, T3) were derived from tumors induced in nude mice by focus-derived cell lines as described in MATERIALS AND METHODS. To test for tumorigenesis, 1-2 $\times 10^6$ cells were inoculated subcutaneously into 4-6-week-old female nude mice at two hind-limb sites. Development of tumors was monitored in the mice inoculated with the C line (derived from spontaneous foci) for 8 weeks.

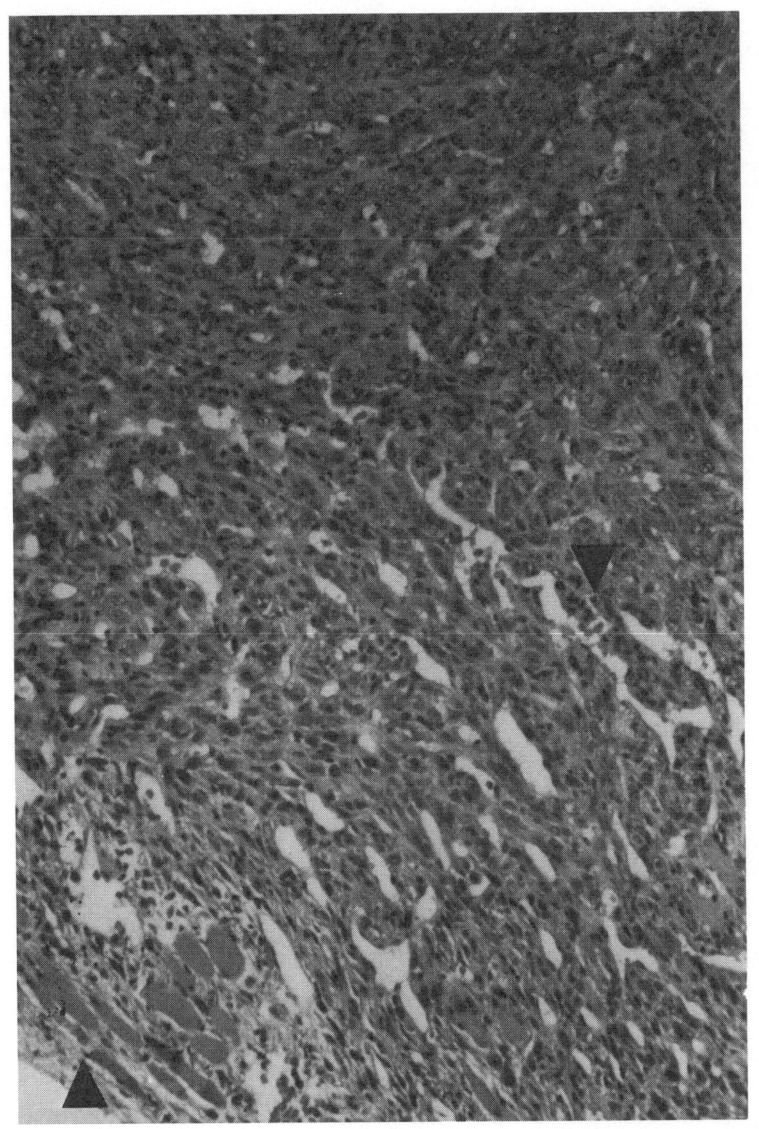

FIGURE 4. Microscopic section of a tumor induced in a nude mouse by cells of a T line, hematoxylin-eosin stain. Note the tumor cells invading the adjacent skeletal muscle (*upper left arrowhead*) and forming the walls of vascular spaces (*lower arrowhead*), indicating angiogenesis.

formation, however, is not stable, since a loss of the malignant phenotype occurred at about the 50th passage in all cell lines studied. (2) SFV DNA can induce the formation of foci in certain NIH/3T3 cells. Cells derived from these foci are able to induce tumors in nude mice and some are anchorage independent. Viral sequences and their expression can be detected only in early cell passages. This may be attributed to the lack of sensitivity of the hybridization procedure or to the loss of the viral sequences from the cells. Since the cells remain tumorigenic, a hit-and-run mechanism, as postulated for herpesvirus,[26] may be involved. (3) Cell lines derived from the tumors developed in the nude mice caused a special type of tumor of smooth muscle, angioleiomyosarcoma, when inoculated back into the animals, suggesting the involvement of a fibroblastic growth factor.

The molecular mechanism by which Shope fibroma virus causes neoplasia is still not well understood. The participation of the putative growth factor resembling EGF and TGF-α, mentioned above, cannot be ruled out, although preliminary experiments in our laboratory indicated that DNA fragments containing this gene transformed NIH/3T3 cells but did not make them tumorigenic (Obom and Pogo, unpublished experiments). Whether the expression of the growth factor and other factors is necessary for tumorigenic conversion is under investigation. It should be borne in mind that the mechanism of transformation by cytoplasmic DNA viruses may be different from any known mechanism of viral oncogenesis.

ACKNOWLEDGMENTS

We are indebted to Dr. Steven Hajdu, from Memorial Sloan-Kettering Cancer Center, New York, for performing cytochemistry reactions and to Ms. Dolores Klaft for excellent secretarial help.

REFERENCES

1. Sanarelli, G. 1898. Zentrabl. Bakteriol. Parasitenkd Abt. 1: Orig. **23:** 865-873.
2. Andrewes, C. H. & C. G. Ahlstrom. 1938. J. Pathol. Bact. **47:** 87-99.
3. Duran-Reynals, F. 1940. Yale J. Biol. Med. **13:** 99-110.
4. Harel, J. & T. Constantin. 1954. Bull. Assoc. Fr. Etude Cancer **41:** 482-497.
5. Duran-Reynals, F. & E. Bryan. 1952. Ann. N. Y. Acad. Sci. **54:** 977-991.
6. Strayer, D. S., E. Skaletsky, G. F. Cabirac, P. A. Sharp, L. B. Corbeil, S. Sell & J. L. Leibowitz. 1983. J. Immunol. **130:** 399-404.
7. Koziorowska, J., K. Wlodarski & M. Mazurowa. 1971. J. Natl. Cancer Inst. **46:** 225-241.
8. Barbanti-Brodani, G., A. Mannini-Palenzona, O. Vardi, M. Portolani & M. LaPlaca. 1974. J. Gen. Virol. **24:** 237-246.
9. Rouhandeh, H. & A. Vafai. 1982. Virology **120:** 77-92.
10. Obom, K. M. & B. G. T. Pogo. 1988. Virus Res. **9:** 33-48.
11. Blomquist, M. C., L. T. Hunt & W. C. Baker. 1984. Proc. Natl. Acad. Sci. USA **81:** 7363-7367.
12. Chang, W., C. Upton, S. Hu, A. F. Purchio & G. McFadden. 1986. Mol. Cell Biol. **7:** 535-540.
13. Upton, C., J. L. Macen & G. McFadden. 1987. J. Virol. **61:** 1271-1275.

14. PORTER, C. D. & L. C. ARCHARD. 1987. J. Gen. Virol. **68:** 673-682.
15. SHOPE, R. E. 1932. J. Exp. Med. **56:** 793-802.
16. DELANGE, A. M., C. MACAULAY, W. BLOCK, T. MUELLER & G. MCFADDEN. 1984. J. Virol. **50:** 408-416.
17. UPTON, C. & G. MCFADDEN. 1986. J. Virol. **60:** 920-927.
18. DUFF, R. & F. RAPP. 1971. J. Virol. **8:** 496-477.
19. DUFF, R. & F. RAPP. 1973. J. Virol. **12:** 209-217.
20. POGO, B. G. T., P. FREIMUTH & A. STEIN. 1982. J. Virol. **41:** 97-105.
21. BERKOWITZ, E. M. & B. G. T. POGO. 1985. Virology **142:** 437-440.
22. RHIM, J. S. 1977. Virology **82:** 100-110.
23. MANIATIS, T., E. F. FRITSCH & J. SAMBROOK. 1982. Molecular Cloning, A Laboratory Manual. Cold Spring Harbor Laboratory. Cold Spring Harbor, N. Y.
24. CRAIG, R. W. & R. SAGER. 1985. Proc. Natl. Acad. Sci. USA **82:** 2062-2066.
25. PERUCHO, M., M. GOLDFARB, K. SHIMIZU, C. LAMA, J. FOGH & M. WIGLER. 1981. Cell **27:** 467-476.
26. GALLOWAY, D. A. & J. K. MCDOUGALL. 1983. Nature **302:** 21-23.

Host-Mediated Induction of Tumor Heterogeneity[a]

G. H. HEPPNER, Y.-C. CHONG, AND A. M. FULTON

E. Walter Albachten Department of Immunology
Michigan Cancer Foundation
Detroit, Michigan 48201

Tumor heterogeneity, that is, the existence within single neoplasms of clonal tumor cell subpopulations of diverse phenotype, has been the subject of intense investigation over the past 10-15 years. It has been demonstrated, repeatedly, that one can isolate tumor subpopulations that differ in behavioral characteristics, such as growth rate, sensitivity to treatment, immunogenicity and ability to metastasize, as well as subpopulations that differ in molecular, genetic, and biochemical characteristics, such as karyotype, production of various growth factors or other mediators, and expression of marker antigens or receptors.[1,2] Depending upon the phenotype, it has also been possible to demonstrate heterogeneous tumor populations within tissue pieces or suspensions of whole tumors. These evidences of tumor cell diversity, as well as the generally accepted tenet that most cancers are clonal in origin,[3] have raised the question of the source of tumor cell divergence.

Nowell has proposed that tumor heterogeneity and the related phenomenon of tumor progression are due to an instability in the genome of tumor cells.[4] Much attention has been given to the basis of that instability, particularly as it relates to inherent alterations in tumor cell gene structure or regulation. Data have been presented to show that tumor cells may differ from their normal counterparts in having higher rates of mutation, structural changes,[4] or altered regulatory capacities, as in their mechanisms for DNA methylation,[5] and that these alterations underlie the genetic instability which is manifested as tumor heterogeneity. These studies, which have given variable and contradictory results,[6,7] have focused on the tumor cell itself as the origin of this diversity. Our own research, by contrast, has concentrated on the host as a potential source. The reasons for this emphasis, and our results to date, are described below.

GENETIC INSTABILITY OF MAMMARY TUMOR SUBPOPULATIONS

In 1981, Cifone and Fidler[7] reported that highly metastatic clones of a variety of murine tumors had a higher spontaneous rate of mutation than did non-metastatic

[a]Supported by NIH Grant CA27437 and by the Concern Foundation.

or poorly metastatic clones. These results suggested an extension of the Nowell hypothesis, namely, that genetic instability increases with increasing tumor progression. We attempted to reproduce these findings in another model system, a series of tumor subpopulation lines derived from a single BALB/cfC_3H mouse mammary tumor.[8,9] These lines differ in regard to many properties, including their ability to metastasize.[10] In contrast to the results of Cifone and Fidler, we found that, although the spontaneous mutation rate (mutation to 6-thioguanine or ouabain resistance) varied among the lines, this variation did not correlate with the variation in their ability to metastasize.[11] Results similar to ours have also been published by others.[12] We did, however, find that susceptibility to induction of drug-resistant variants by the mutagen ethyl methanesulfonate (EMS) did correlate with metastasis.[11] The highest frequencies of mutation were seen in the metastatic lines. It should be mentioned that Frost and associates[13] could not reproduce these findings on sensitivity to induced mutation in a variety of cell types, including ours. However, the study by Frost *et al.* was done with a different mutagen (*N*-methyl-nitro-*N*-nitrosoguanidine, MNNG), and the cloning efficiency they reported for our cells was only a fraction of the value we usually see. Furthermore, although Frost *et al.* did reproduce our findings for the early time points, they found that after 10 days the values for the frequency of mutations in cell types of low and high metastatic potential converged. It is difficult to assess the meaning of this finding. The conditions under which one would expect observations about induced mutation to be applicable *in vivo* are very different from those of the *in vitro* mutagenicity assays but, at least, would probably involve chronic or repeated exposure to an endogenous mutagen (see below). Under such circumstances, the meaning of delayed convergence following a single exposure to a mutagen is uncertain. Regardless of the ultimate interpretation of any of the above studies, our results led us to focus, not on the tumor cell itself, but on an outside source as the origin of diversity.

TUMOR-ASSOCIATED MACROPHAGES OF MAMMARY TUMOR SUBPOPULATIONS

One of our long-standing interests is the nature of tumor-infiltrating inflammatory cells.[14] As part of this work, we isolated and characterized tumor-associated macrophages (TAM) from tumors produced by the same series of lines used in the genetic instability studies. We found that the type and function of TAM correlated with the metastatic ability of these lines, but that, to our surprise, the TAM from the metastatic tumors were enriched for phenotypically activated macrophages[15] and were more often tumoricidal[16] than were the non-activated TAM from the non-metastatic tumors. We also found that the tumor cells themselves were differentially sensitive to the growth-inhibitory effects of macrophages; metastatic cells were more resistant to macrophage-mediated cytostasis *in vitro* than were non-metastatic cells.[17] (This resistance could be abrogated by fully activating the macrophages and by inhibiting the production of immunosuppressive PGE_2 by the metastatic cells.[17]) These results suggested that the *in vitro* tumoricidal activity of TAM from metastatic tumors might not be the function of most relevance to metastasis in our system; rather, another characteristic of activated macrophages might be of greater significance. It was at this time that our attention was drawn to the work of Weitzman, Stossel and colleagues[18–21] on the ability of human phagocytic cells to cause DNA alterations, as measured by a variety of assays.

PHAGOCYTE "MUTAGENICITY" AND CANCER DEVELOPMENT

Evidence for the role of macrophages and polymorphonuclear cells in cancer development and progression has recently been reviewed.[22] Suffice it to say here that there is a growing body of literature suggesting that phagocytes can be involved causally in early stages of tumor initiation and promotion through production of a variety of inducers of genetic damage. These inducers are likely to be active oxygen metabolites, which in macrophages are associated with the activation stage. Phagocytic mutagenicity has been detected using both bacterial assay systems[18,23] and tests for induction of drug resistance in mammalian cells.[21] Other assays of phagocyte-induced DNA damage in mammalian cells include examination for sister chromatid exchange[20] and for induction of 5,6-saturated thymidine bases.[24] Weitzman and co-workers have even reported *in vitro* transformation and induction of tumorigenicity in 10T1/2 cells exposed to human peripheral monocytes.[25] Such reports led us to combine our observations on the differential sensitivities of metastatic versus non-metastatic tumor cells to an external mutagen and to macrophage cytostasis with our observations on the differential distribution of activated TAM within metastatic versus non-metastatic tumors into the following hypothesis: Tumor-associated macrophages (TAM) contribute to tumor progression by releasing endogeneous mutagens which fuel the genetic instability of tumor cells, leading to the induction of tumor heterogeneity.

MUTAGENIC TUMOR-ASSOCIATED MACROPHAGES

Metastasis is a complex, multistage process that probably involves genetic (and epigenetic) alterations at numerous loci. In order to explore the validity of our hypothesis, it was necessary to select a less complex phenotype in which to detect genetic change. Our first assay system was the Ames assay, using *Salmonella typhimurium* tester strains TA 98 (a frame-shift detector) and TA 100 (a detector of base-pair substitutions). As reported by Fulton *et al.*,[26] whole-cell suspensions of tumors from some of our mammary tumor lines were mutagenic in the Ames assay; the mutagenic activity was associated with the TAM fraction. Among the tumor lines tested, there were some differences in activity against the two tester strains, although these differences could not be associated with known differences in the tumor or TAM populations. TAM from all the metastatic tumors tested were mutagenic; TAM from some non-metastatic tumors were active, whereas others of these were not. Thus, the presence of mutagenic TAM was not absolutely associated with the metastatic phenotype.

Further demonstration of mutagenic activity in TAM from metastatic mammary tumors was reported by Yamashina *et al.*[27] in our laboratory, using the induction of 6-thioguanine- (6-TG-) resistant (6-TG^r) variants in mouse mammary tumor line 66 as the assay system. TAM isolated from line 66 tumors, which are metastatic tumors, were co-cultured for 7 to 9 days with line 66 tumor cells, after which these tumor cells were plated in 6-TG-containing medium. Resistant variants grew out at a mean frequency (for the six tumors examined) of $6.5/10^5$ surviving tumor cells, as compared to 0.6 in controls not co-cultured with TAM. (The number of tumor cells surviving after the 7-9 days in co-culture with macrophages was not different from that for controls not exposed to macrophages.) Detailed studies on the ability of macrophages to induce 6-TG^r variants were carried out with adherent cells from peritoneal exudates.

This ability was dependent upon the degree of activation (MVE-2[b]-elicited macrophages > thioglycollate-elicited; resident macrophages had no activity) and the ratio of macrophages to tumor cells in the culture flasks (at least 50:1 required for consistent results). The activity was inhibited by the presence of oxygen radical scavengers during the culture period. The mutagenic activity could not be attributed to any particular oxygen metabolite, since superoxide dismutase (SOD), catalase, mannitol, and SOD plus catalase were all able to inhibit the induction of 6-TG^r variants, albeit with relative activities that varied somewhat from experiment to experiment. That the induction of 6-TG resistance was due to a genetic change was indicated by a significant decrease in the enzyme whose deficiency establishes the resistant state (hypoxanthine-guanine phosphoribosyl transferase, HGPRT) and by extremely low reversion frequencies to wild-type (1.3×10^{-6} to 3×10^{-7}). In these characteristics, macrophage-induced variants were essentially identical to a 6-TG^r variant induced by EMS. Furthermore, 6-TG^r variants were not less sensitive to macrophage toxicity than were wild-type cells, indicating that the occurrence of selection for (pre-existing) 6-TG-resistant variants during co-culture with the macrophages was unlikely.

Thus, the mutagenic activity of TAM and other activated macrophage populations has been demonstrated in two different assay systems—one bacterial and the other mammalian. For further studies of the mechanism of this mutagenic activity, it was necessary to scale-down the size required for the assay samples in order to be able to examine multiple replicates of different inhibitors and utilize fewer numbers of macrophages. Therefore, we have turned to another test of genetic damage, namely, DNA strand-break assays.

MACROPHAGE-INDUCED DNA STRAND-BREAKS IN MAMMARY TUMOR CELLS

Our earlier studies implicated reactive oxygen intermediates as the agents responsible for macrophage-induced genetic change. Since radiobiologists have established that a principal consequence of the generation of hydroxyl radicals by X-irradiation is their induction of DNA strand-breaks, we decided to use this endpoint for further study of macrophage-tumor cell interactions. For most studies, we have employed the fluorometric analysis of DNA unwinding under alkaline conditions as described by Birnboim and Jevcak[28] to assay for DNA strand-breaks (FIG. 1). This assay detects the amount of double-stranded DNA (DS-DNA) remaining after partial unwinding induced by high pH. Unwinding commences at every break point. Thus, the more DS-DNA detected, the fewer breaks (double and single) in the original sample. Dose-response curves obtained for DNA strand-breaks induced by irradiation or enzyme-generated reactive oxygen intermediates show a linear relationship for dose versus change in the level of DS-DNA (data not shown).

For our initial studies, we co-incubated MVE-2-elicited mouse peritoneal macrophages with line 66 tumor cells for 1 hr at a 1:1 ratio. Tumor cells were then immediately analyzed for DNA strand breaks. As shown in a representative experiment in FIGURE 2, MVE-2-elicited macrophages induced a significant number of strand-breaks, evidenced by the large decrease in DS-DNA relative to the untreated samples. This degree of damage is roughly equivalent to 600-1000 rads of irradiation. In this

[b]MVE-2, a fraction of pyran copolymer.

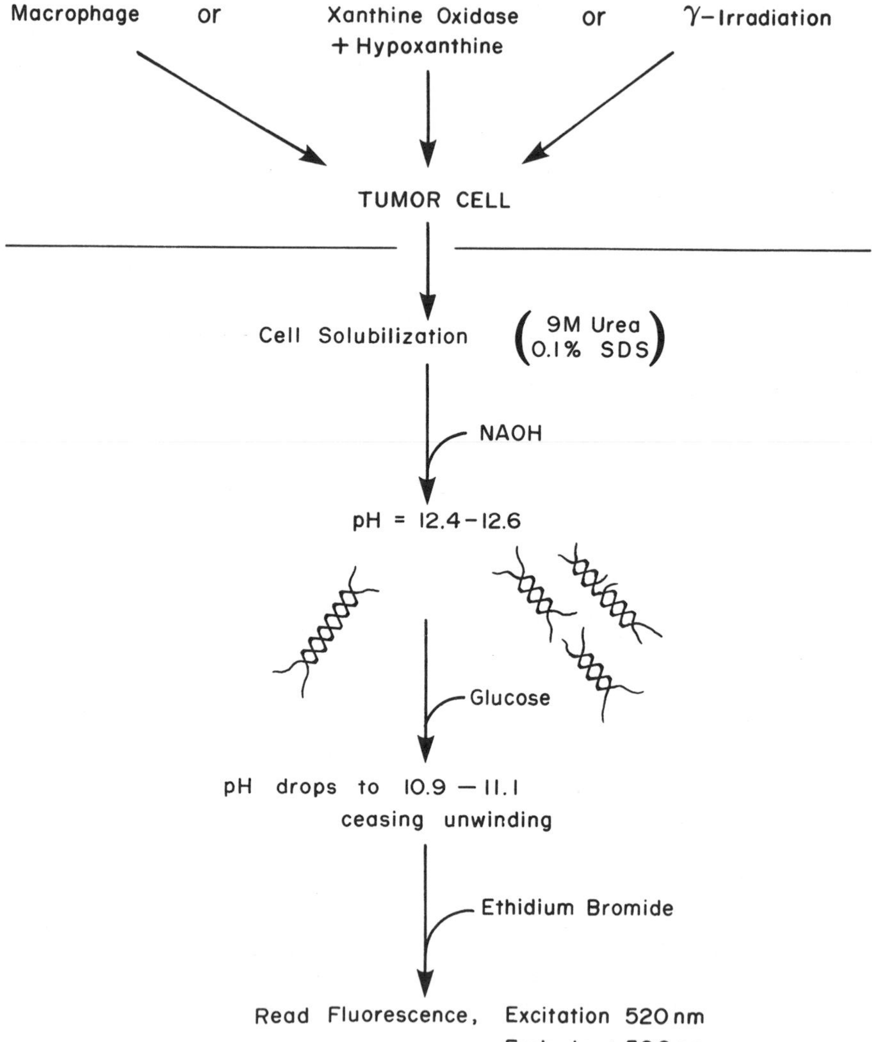

FIGURE 1. Fluorometric analysis of DNA unwinding (FADU) under alkaline conditions as described by Birnboim and Jevcak.[28] DNA strand-breaks, induced by macrophages, enzyme-generated reactive oxygen species, or irradiation create sites for DNA unwinding under alkaline conditions. The level of double-stranded DNA remaining in the sample is thus inversely related to the number of strand-breaks.

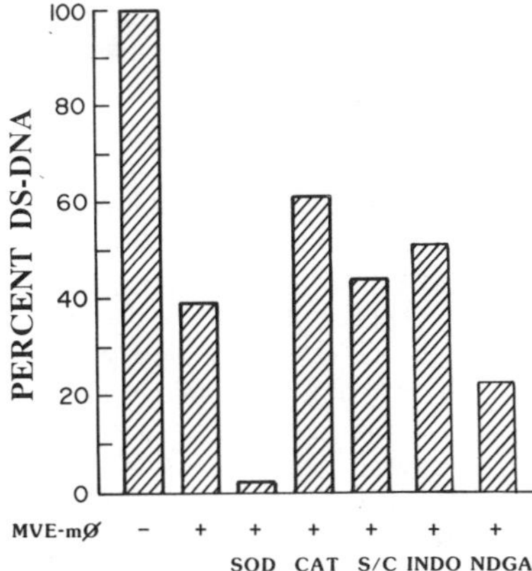

FIGURE 2. Induction of DNA strand-breaks in line 66 tumor cells by MVE-2-elicited macrophages (MVE-mϕ). MVE-2-elicited macrophages and line 66 murine mammary tumor cells were co-incubated for 1 hr at 1:1 ratios (+); or tumor cells were incubated alone (−); or the macrophages and tumor cells were co-incubated (+) in the presence of superoxide dismutase (SOD, 300 U/ml), catalase (CAT, 300 U/ml), SOD plus CAT (S/C), indomethacin (INDO, 1 μM), or nordihydroguaretic acid (NDGA, 3 μM). Tumor cell DNA was then analyzed by FADU assay (see FIG. 1). The amount of double-stranded DNA (DS-DNA) detected is reported as the percentage remaining in comparison to the level in untreated samples, i.e., those not subjected to alkaline conditions.

experiment, addition of SOD resulted in more strand-breaks than were seen for incubation of the tumor cells with macrophages alone, whereas catalase was protective. In some other experiments, SOD had no effect. Taken together, these data implicate H_2O_2 as the damaging agent. Activated macrophages have a high respiratory rate; addition of SOD would be expected to generate H_2O_2 from superoxide and hydrogen, and catalase would deplete the H_2O_2. The inhibitor of the cyclo-oxygenase pathway of arachidonate metabolism, indomethacin, was also protective, in contrast to the lipoxygenase inhibitor nordihydroguaretic acid (NDGA). Similar results have been obtained with elicited macrophages treated with the "complete" activator, LPS (lipopolysaccharides).

Knowing that resident peritoneal macrophages express lower levels of oxidative metabolism than do MVE-2-elicited macrophages, we expected that they would induce fewer DNA strand-breaks. Therefore, we were at first surprised to find, as shown in FIGURE 3 and in numerous other experiments, that resident macrophages consistently induced more strand-breaks than did MVE-2-elicited macrophages. However, the inhibitor profiles for these two macrophage populations are different. For resident

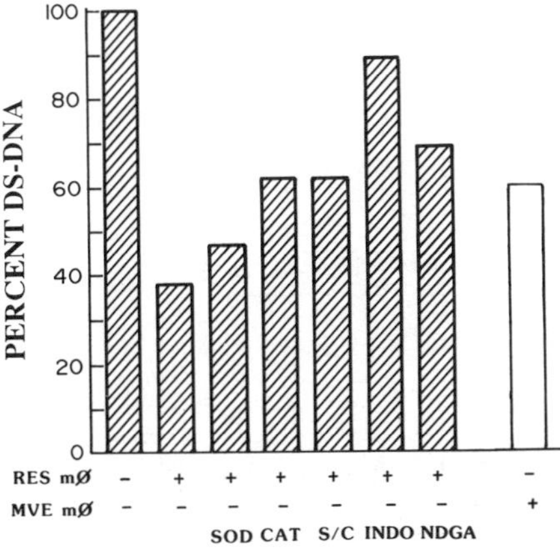

FIGURE 3. Induction of DNA strand-breaks in line 66 tumor cells by resident macrophages. Resident peritoneal (RES mϕ) or MVE-2-elicited macrophages (MVE mϕ) were incubated with murine mammary tumor line 66 cells, and DNA analysis for strand-breaks was carried out as described in the legend for FIGURE 2. *Hatched bars* are co-incubations of resident macrophages plus tumor cells (+), or tumor cells alone (−), or resident macrophages and tumor cells co-incubated (+) in the presence of the indicated inhibitors (see legend for FIG. 2); *open bar* (+) is MVE-2-elicited macrophages plus tumor cells analyzed on the same day.

macrophages, SOD and NDGA are both protective, implicating arachidonate metabolism as an important source of the oxygen metabolites. The differences in strand-breaking activity between MVE-2-elicited and resident macrophages are summarized in FIGURE 4. On the basis of these findings and the additional knowledge that resident macrophages have more active arachidonate metabolism (leading to both cyclo-oxygenase and lipoxygenase products) than do MVE-2-elicited macrophages, we have tentatively concluded that resident macrophages induce strand-breaks both by respiratory oxygen intermediates which are removed with SOD and catalase and by arachidonate metabolites. This is not without precedent, as there is evidence that other DNA-clastogenic factors produced in response to phorbol esters are lipoxygenase metabolites.[29] The observation, shown above, that NDGA is not protective against MVE-2-elicited macrophages is explained by the fact that these cells have little lipoxygenase activity. Indomethacin is protective, however, either because even low levels of cyclo-oxygenase products are important for strand-breaking activity, or, more likely, because indomethacin can directly scavenge reactive oxygen species, as has been reported in other systems.[30] Thus, although both resident and activated populations can induce DNA strand-breaks, the effectors implicated depend on the metabolic state of the macrophage.

The data obtained with the strand-break assay must, however, be compared with that from our previous studies with mutation assays, in which macrophage mutagenicity was shown to be a function of activated macrophages; resident macrophages did not induce 6-TG^r variants in line 66 cells. The strand-break data thus raise the issue of the relevance of DNA strand-break assays to mutagenicity. Mutagenicity involves a wider spectrum of activity than just strand-breakage. For example, there may be differences in the ability of line 66 cells to rejoin breaks induced by resident versus MVE-2-elicited macrophages. DNA strand-break assays may also measure cytostatic or cytotoxic outcomes of macrophage-tumor cell interactions, whereas detection of mutagenicity is restricted to those target tumor cells still able to proliferate after interaction with the macrophages. Furthermore, it may be that the source of active oxygen metabolites is of importance to mutagenicity: DNA strand-breakage by MVE-2-elicited macrophages is less susceptible to inhibition by arachidonate inhibitors than is that by resident macrophages; and, as already discussed, it is the MVE-2-elicited macrophages, not the resident populations, which are mutagenic.

	RES mØ	*MVE-2 mØ*
Strand Break Activity	+++	++
SOD	↓	↑ →
CAT	↓	↓
INDO	↓	↓
NDGA	↓	→

FIGURE 4. A comparison of the relative strand-breakage activity and inhibitory profiles for resident (RES mϕ) and MVE-2-elicited macrophages (MVE-2 mϕ). *Downward arrow* indicates that there is less damage in the presence of the agent (i.e., more double-stranded DNA was detected), *upward arrow* indicates an increased level of strand-breaks, and *horizontal arrow* indicates no detectable effect by agent. The *boxes* indicate differences in the inhibitory profiles of the two types of macrophages. Agents: SOD, superoxide dismutase (300 U/ml); CAT, catalase (300 U/ml); INDO, indomethacin (1 μM); NDGA, nordihydroguaretic acid (3 μM).

Another factor, which we have just begun to investigate, is the role of target cell sensitivity in the outcome of the macrophage-mediated strand-break assay.

Ultimately, of course, it must be shown that macrophage-induced genetic damage has relevance to the natural history of tumors *in vivo.* Showing this will not be an easy task. Furthermore, we do not know whether our results with mouse mammary tumors are applicable to any other system. An intriguing preliminary report has just appeared[31] showing that TAM isolated from 3LL tumors selected for resistance to macrophage inhibition are, as in our system, more tumoricidal *in vitro* and more able to produce large amounts of reactive oxygen metabolites than are TAM isolated from tumors produced by macrophage-sensitive 3LL cells. Again, as in our system, the macrophage-resistant tumors are more metastatic than are the sensitive tumors. Although mutagenicity studies have not yet been reported in the 3LL system, these findings, along with our own studies, and coupled with the large body of literature implicating inflammatory cells in tumor promotion, encourage us to think that such cells may also play a contributory role in tumor progression.

ACKNOWLEDGMENTS

The authors thank Mrs. Leslie Dorcey Paul for helpful discussions and Mrs. Margaret Peterson for expert secretarial assistance.

REFERENCES

1. Fidler, I. J. & M. L. Kripke. 1977. Metastasis results from preexisting variant cells within a malignant tumor. Science **197:** 893-897.
2. Heppner, G. H. 1984. Tumor heterogeneity. Cancer Res. **44:** 2259-2265.
3. Fialkow, P. J. 1979. Clonal origin of human tumors. Annu. Rev. Med. **30:** 135-143.
4. Nowell, P. C. 1976. The clonal evolution of tumor cell populations. Science **194:** 23-28.
5. Frost, P. & R. S. Kerbel. 1984. On the possible epigenetic mechanism(s) of tumor cell heterogeneity. Cancer Metastasis Rev. **2:** 375-278.
6. Elmore, E., T. Kakumaga & J. C. Barrett. 1983. Comparison of spontaneous mutation rates of normal and chemically transformed human skin fibroblasts. Cancer Res. **43:** 1650-1655.
7. Cifone, M. A. & I. J. Fidler. 1981. Increasing metastatic potential is associated with increasing genetic instability of clones isolated from murine neoplasms. Proc. Natl. Acad. Sci. USA **78:** 6949-6952.
8. Dexter, D. L., H. M. Kowalski, B. A. Blazar, Z. Fligiel, R. Vogel & G. H. Heppner. 1978. Heterogeneity of tumor cells from a single mouse mammary tumor. Cancer Res. **38:** 3174-3181.
9. Heppner, G. H., D. L. Dexter, T. DeNucci, F. R. Miller & P. Calabresi. 1978. Heterogeneity in drug sensitivity among tumor cell subpopulations of a single mouse mammary tumor. Cancer Res. **38:** 3758-3763.
10. Miller, F. R., B. E. Miller & G. H. Heppner. 1983. Characterization of metastatic heterogeneity among subpopulations of a single mouse mammary tumor: Heterogeneity in phenotypic stability. Invasion Metastasis **3:** 22-31.
11. Yamashina, K. & G. H. Heppner. 1985. Correlation of frequency of induced mutation and metastatic potential in tumor cell lines from a single mouse mammary tumor. Cancer Res. **45:** 4015-4019.

12. KENDAL, W. S. & P. FROST. 1986. Metastatic potential and spontaneous mutation rates: Studies with two murine cell lines and their recently induced metastatic variants. Cancer Res. **46:** 6131-6135.
13. FROST, P., W. KENDAL, B. HUNT & M. ELLIS. 1988. The prevalence of ouabain-resistant variants after mutagen treatment. Invasion Metastasis **8:** 73-86.
14. WEI, W. Z., S. RATNER, A. M. FULTON & G. H. HEPPNER. 1986. Inflammatory infiltrates of experimental mammary cancers. Biochim. Biophys. Acta **865:** 13-26.
15. MAHONEY, K. H., A. M. FULTON & G. H. HEPPNER. 1983. Tumor-associated macrophages of mouse mammary tumors. II. Differential distribution of macrophages from metastatic and nonmetastatic tumors. J. Immunol. **131:** 2079-2085.
16. LOVELESS, S. E. & G. H. HEPPNER. 1983. Tumor-associated macrophages of mouse mammary tumors. I. Differential cytotoxicity of macrophages from metastatic and nonmetastatic tumors. J. Immunol. **131:** 2074-2078.
17. YAMASHINA, K., A. FULTON & G. HEPPNER. 1985. Differential sensitivity of metastatic versus nonmetastatic mammary tumor cells to macrophage-mediated cytostasis. J. Natl. Cancer Inst. **75:** 765-770.
18. WEITZMAN, S. A. & T. P. STOSSEL. 1981. Mutation caused by human phagocytes. Science **212:** 546-547.
19. WEITZMAN, S. A. & T. P. STOSSEL. 1982. Effects of oxygen radical scavengers and antioxidants on phagocyte induced mutagenesis. J. Immunol. **128:** 2770-2772.
20. WEITBERG, A. B., S. A. WEITZMAN, M. DESTREMPES, S. A. LATT & T. P. STOSSEL. 1983. Stimulated human phagocytes produce cytogenetic changes in cultured mammalian cells. N. Engl. J. Med. **308:** 26-30.
21. WEITZMAN, S. A. & T. P. STOSSEL. 1984. Phagocyte-induced mutation in Chinese hamster ovary cells. Cancer Lett. **22:** 337-341.
22. HEPPNER, G. & L. DORCEY. 1988. Macrophages and development of cancer. *In* Macrophages and Cancer. G. Heppner & A. Fulton, Eds.: 197-208. CRC Press, Inc. Boca Raton, FL.
23. BARAK, M., S. ULITZUR & D. MERZBACH. 1983. Phagocytosis-induced mutagenesis in bacteria. Mutat. Res. **121:** 7-16.
24. LEWIS, J. G. & D. O. ADAMS. 1985. Induction of 5,6-ring-saturated thymine bases in NIH-3T3 cells by phorbol ester-stimulated macrophages: Role of reactive oxygen intermediates. Cancer Res. **45:** 1270-1275.
25. WEITZMAN, S. A., A. B. WEITBERG, E. P. CLARK & T. P. STOSSEL. 1985. Phagocytes as carcinogens: Malignant transformation produced by human neutrophils. Science **227:** 1231-1233.
26. FULTON, A. M., S. E. LOVELESS & G. H. HEPPNER. 1984. Mutagenic activity of tumor-associated macrophages in *Salmonella typhimurium* strains TA 98 and TA 100. Cancer Res. **44:** 4308-4311.
27. YAMASHINA, K., B. E. MILLER & G. H. HEPPNER. 1986. Macrophage-mediated induction of drug-resistant variants in a mouse mammary tumor cell line. Cancer Res. **46:** 2396-2401.
28. BIRNBOIM, H. C. & J. J. JEVCAK. 1981. Fluorometric method for rapid detection of DNA strand breaks in human white blood cells produced by low doses of radiation. Cancer Res. **41:** 1889-1892.
29. OCHI, T. & P. A. CERUTTI. 1987. Clastogenic action of hydroperoxy-5,8,11,13-icosatetraenoic acids on the mouse embryo fibroblasts $C_3H/10T1/2$. Proc. Natl. Acad. Sci. USA **84:** 990-994.
30. PEKSE, G., K. VAN DYKE, D. PEDEN, H. MENGOLI & D. ENGLISH. 1983. Antioxidation theory of non-steroidal anti-inflammatory drugs based upon the inhibition of luminal-enhanced chemiluminescence from the myeloperoxidase reaction. Agents Actions **12:** 371-375.
31. REMELS, L., R. LUCAS, L. BOUWENS & P. DE BAETSELIER. 1988. Characterization of tumor-associated macrophages (TAM) isolated from macrophage-resistant and macrophage-sensitive 3LL tumors. Clin. Exp. Metastasis **6**(Suppl. 1): 73.

Organization and Expression of Homeobox Genes in Mouse and Man[a]

CLAUDIA KAPPEN,[b,c,d] KLAUS SCHUGHART,[b,c] AND FRANK H. RUDDLE[b,e]

Departments of [b]Biology and [e]Human Genetics
Yale University
New Haven, Connecticut 06511

INTRODUCTION

The mammalian homeobox genes were originally identified by their sequence similarities to *Drosophila* homeobox genes, such as Ultrabithorax (*Ubx*) and Antennapedia (*Antp*).[1] *Ubx* and *Antp* are homeobox genes fundamentally involved in fly development (for review, see Ref. 2). Most highly conserved in insect and mammalian genes is the homeobox domain. This region consists of 183 nucleotide base-pairs encoding sixty-one amino acids. The average similarities in nucleotide sequences between insects and mammals are approximately 70%. The conservation is even more pronounced at the amino acid level (for review, see Ref. 3). Subdomains of the homeobox are believed to form helix-turn-helix motifs, which have been implicated in DNA binding. Direct experimental evidence shows that homeobox proteins can bind to *cis* flanking regions of homeobox genes in both insects and mammals.[4,5] Evidence from *Drosophila* studies shows that the homeobox protein may bind to the same gene that encodes it or to another homeobox gene or genes. These interactions may serve a regulatory function in that homeobox genes are controlling or coordinating the activity of effector genes which in turn mediate developmental events.[6] This concept is amply supported by observations on mutations in *Drosophila* homeobox genes which dramatically affect epigenesis, thus demonstrating the importance of homeobox genes in the mediation of development. The function of the cognate mammalian genes is not yet clearly understood, but everything we do know is consistent with a developmental control function. Unfortunately, developmental mutations comparable to those in fly genes have not yet been recorded for mammalian homeobox genes.

[a]This work was supported by NIH Grant GM09966.

[c]Supported by postdoctoral fellowships from the Deutsche Forschungsgemeinschaft (FRG).

[d]To whom correspondence should be addressed at the Department of Biology, Yale University, Kline Biology Tower, P.O. Box 6666, New Haven, Connecticut 06511-8112.

STRUCTURE OF MAMMALIAN HOMEOBOX GENES

The typical mammalian homeobox gene is 5-10 kilobases (kb) in size. In comparison, *Drosophila* genes may be eight to ten times larger. The coding regions of the mammalian and insect genes are similar. The mouse *Hox-2.2* gene[7] may be taken as a prototype for mammalian homeobox genes (FIG. 1). The *Hox-2.2* genomic sequence extends over at least 2.6 kb. The deduced cDNA sequence predicts a protein having 225 amino acids. Two exons are known, and it is probable that one or more upstream exons exist. Conserved sequences are present in three separate regions, the homeobox domain, an amino acid hexamer region 5′ of the splice site, and an amino-terminal octamer sequence. The hexameric site has been implicated in subunit interaction, thus suggesting that a functional dimer may be formed.[7] Repeats of acidic amino acids are frequently encoded in the coding portions of these genes, such as the $(Glu)_5$ string in the carboxyl-terminal domain of *Hox-2.2*. Their function is not established, but they may be involved in some aspect of DNA binding and transcriptional regulation. A good match for a polyadenylation signal (AATAAA) is seen in the 3′ non-coding flanking region.

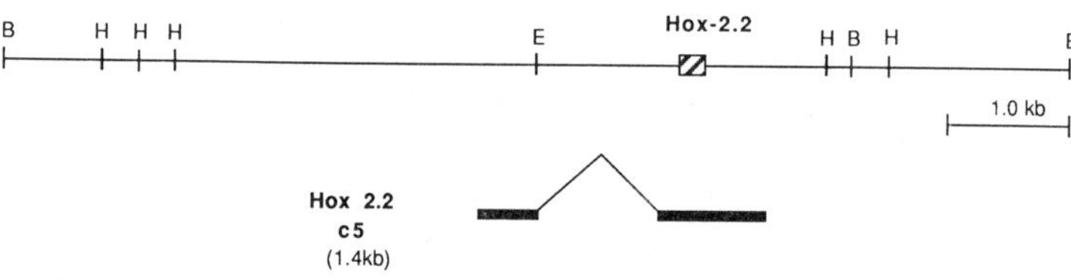

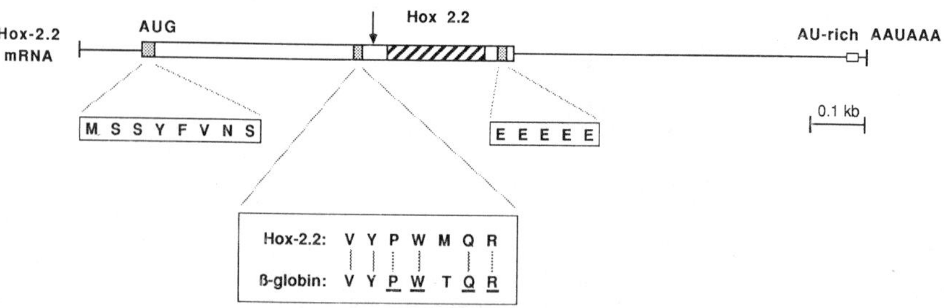

FIGURE 1. Structure of the *Hox-2.2* gene. **Upper panel:** restriction map of the *Hox-2.2* gene (*above*) and structure of the isolated cDNA clone (*below*). Exons are indicated by *thick bars.* **Lower panel:** predicted structure of the *Hox-2.2* mRNA. In the open reading frame (*box*), the three *shaded regions* indicate the regions encoding the conserved amino terminus, the hexapeptide, and the glutamic acid-rich region, respectively. The homeobox is shown as a *striped box.* An AU-rich region and a consensus transcriptional stop signal are present in the predicted 3′ untranslated region of the *Hox-2.2* mRNA. The presumptive splice site is indicated by the *arrow.* Amino acid sequences of the three conserved regions are given in *boxes* below the mRNA structure. The *Hox-2.2* hexapeptide is shown aligned to the corresponding region of β-like globins. The *underlined* amino acid residues in the β-globin sequence are involved in α_1-β_2 subunit interactions.

EXPRESSION OF *Hox* TRANSCRIPTS WITHIN THE CENTRAL NERVOUS SYSTEM

Homeobox genes are expressed both prenatally and in the adult, predominately in ectodermal and mesodermal tissues and their derivatives (for reviews, see Refs. 8-10). A specific expression of transcripts has been described with respect to time and place that does not necessarily follow recognized organ or tissue boundaries. However, all of the homeobox genes studied to date are expressed in the central nervous system (CNS), where their expression pattern can be followed along the entire anterior-posterior axis.

It should be emphasized that homeobox gene expression is a complex subject, which cannot be adequately dealt with here. Each gene encodes a variety of transcripts, and these may differ in expression, depending on the tissue and time of development. A particular transcript may also appear in different tissues at a particular time; or it may be expressed, extinguished, and then reappear. The patterns are also complex and involved in terms of dorsal/ventral, anterior/posterior, and lateral expression. Here, only one aspect of expression will be addressed, namely, the extent of anterior expression pattern in the CNS.

A number of homeobox genes have been studied in regard to their anterior/posterior expression pattern in the CNS in mice, using an *in situ* hybridization technique to detect mRNA in tissue sections with isotopically labeled antisense RNA probes. An example of the technique for *Hox-2.2* is shown in FIGURE 2. An interesting relationship emerges when one compares the anterior boundary of expression of homeobox genes in the CNS in relationship to their location in the homeobox gene clusters. *Hox-1.5* is expressed in the extreme anterior portion of the medulla.[11] The anterior boundaries of *Hox-2.1* and *Hox-2.2* expression are located behind that of *Hox-1.5* in the medulla, with the expression of *Hox-2.1* anterior to that of *Hox-2.2*.[7] *Hox-2.5* expression was located in the spinal cord, with its anterior boundary at the first cervical vertebra.[12] Expression of *Hox-3.1* is also detected in the spinal cord, but more posteriorly, at the level of the third cervical vertebra.[13] Thus, there is an overlapping pattern for the expression of homeobox gene transcripts throughout the medulla and spinal cord. Moreover, the order of anterior limit of expression parallels the order of genes in the homeobox clusters. The functional significance, if any, of this arrangement and colinearity is not apparent. However, it is intriguing that in *Drosophila* similar homeobox genes have similar patterns of arrangement and colinear expression.[14]

HOMEOBOX GENE CLUSTERS

The *Drosophila* homeobox genes are organized in clusters. It was gratifying to see that mammalian homeobox genes are organized similarly. The mouse clusters characterized so far contain as many as seven genes, and it is likely that this is a minimum estimate for the number present. The genes are spaced every 5 to 10 kb, and in all instances examined, they are transcribed in the same direction. All genes appear to be functional with respect to a possible protein product; so far, no pseudogenes have been recognized. Homeobox gene clusters have been mapped to mouse chromosomes

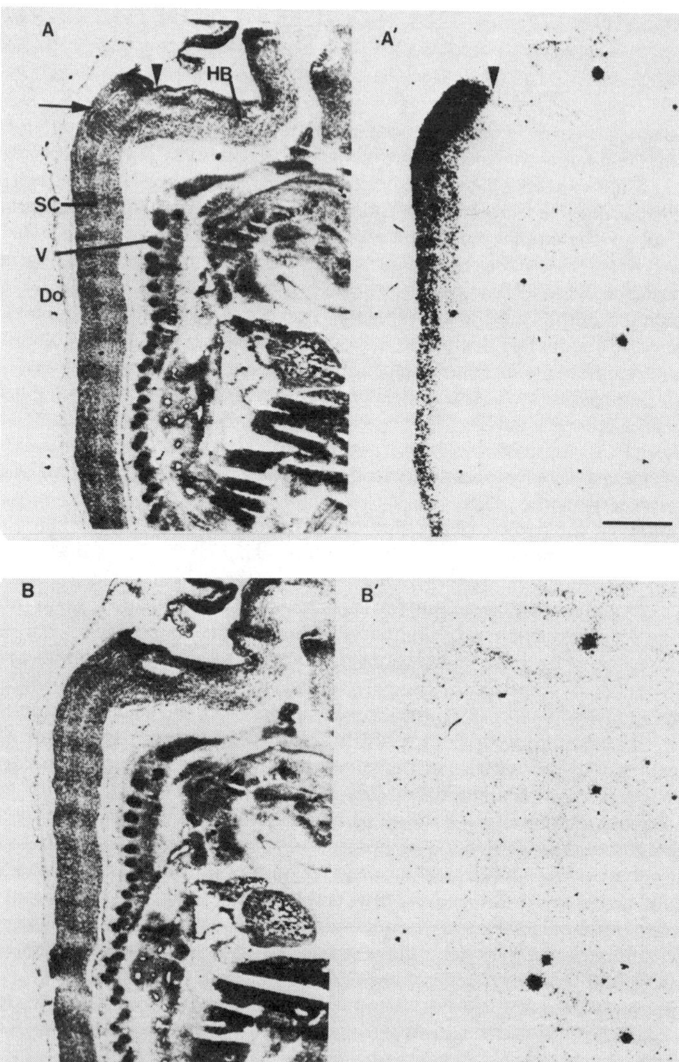

FIGURE 2. Analysis of *Hox-2.2* expression in the central nervous system of 13.5-day mouse embryos with the *in situ* hybridization technique and comparison to *Hox-2.1* expression. (**A**) Sagittal section stained with Giemsa. HB, hindbrain; SC; spinal cord; V, vertebrae; Do, dorsal. *Arrow* indicates the region of cross-section shown in **C, C′**, and **D, D′** (*facing page*). (**A′**) Autoradiograph (10-day exposure of film) of section in **A** hybridized with an isotopically labeled *Hox-2.2* antisense RNA probe. *Arrowheads:* anterior boundary of specific labeling. *Bar*, ca. 1 mm. Giemsa-stained section (**B**) adjacent to the one depicted in **A** and autoradiograph (**B′**) of section shown in **B** hybridized with an isotopically labeled control *Hox-2.2* sense RNA probe.

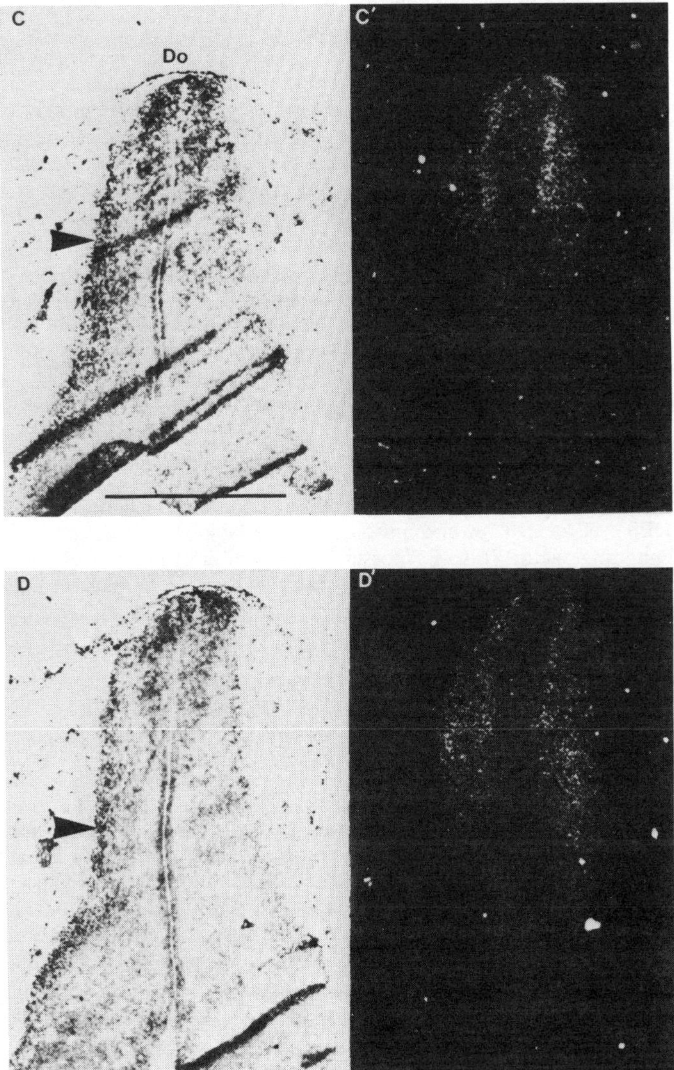

FIGURE 2 C, D. Region of cross-section, as indicated in **A.** Bright field view (**C**) of a cross-section through the hindbrain hybridized with the *Hox-2.2* antisense probe and developed in emulsion for three weeks; dark-field view (**C′**) of this section, showing autoradiographic grains. *Bar* (**C**), ca. 1 mm. (**D**) Section adjacent to **C** hybridized with an isotopically labeled *Hox-2.1* antisense probe; dark-field view (**D′**) of this section, showing autoradiographic grains. *Arrowheads* indicate rostral boundaries of specific labeling (**C, D**).

2, 6, 11, and 15. Human cognate clusters have been mapped to human chromosomes 2, 7, 17, and 12, respectively (reviewed in Ref. 15).

Comparison of the homeobox gene clusters provides evidence for strong paralogous homologies. On the basis of nucleotide and deduced amino acid sequences of homeobox domains, or of cDNA sequences where they are available, it is strikingly clear that the genes most highly related by sequence similarity are arranged in identical order on Hox clusters 1, 2, and 3. Also, the spacing between genes on the *Hox-1* and *Hox-2* clusters is remarkably similar (FIG. 3). Only fragmentary data are so far available for the *Hox-3* and *Hox-4* clusters. However, for all of the known mouse homeobox genes, sequence comparisons show that homeobox genes within a cluster are less similar to each other than they are to those of different clusters (manuscript in preparation). All of these findings are consistent with the view that the homeobox clusters have arisen first by an expansion process along an ancient linkage group, possibly by unequal crossing-over, and then—at least in the Deuterostomia—have increased in number by at least two chromosome duplication events. This proposal is even further supported by comparison of genes syntenic to the homeobox gene loci. Unexpectedly, a strong paralogous homology is also found between the linkage groups in mouse and human (FIG. 4). Thus, for example, in humans, collagen loci (COL) are present on chromosomes 2, 7, 17, and 12. Cytokeratins (CYK) are present on chromosomes 17 and 12, and another member of the intermediate filament family, desmin (DES), is located on chromosome 2. Interleukin 6 (IL6) and granulocyte colony-stimulating factor (GCSF) possess sequence similarities, and they map to chromosomes 7 and 17, respectively. The paralogies between human chromosomes 2, 7, 17, and 12 are consistent with the occurrence of at least two chromosome duplication events in the mammals or their precursors.

EVOLUTION OF THE HOMEOBOX CLUSTER ARRAY

The findings reviewed above are consistent with the evolution of homeobox genes as a process of gene duplication mediated first by expansion within a linkage group, followed in the deuterostomes by chromosomal duplication. One might speculate that these chromosome duplications most probably occurred by genome duplication, since polyploidy would obviate problems associated with genetic imbalance. Some of the homeobox genes discussed here can be considered cognates between mammals and insects. This view is supported by sequence similarities, patterns of gene and gene-complex organization, and the parallelism between the anterior/posterior position of

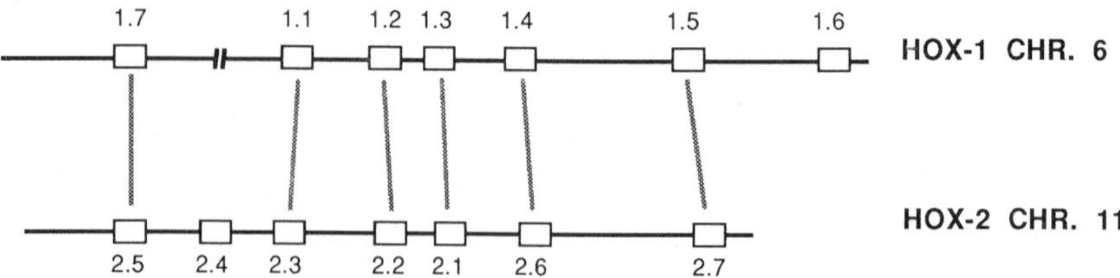

FIGURE 3. Schematic representation of the order of genes in the *Hox-1* and *Hox-2* clusters located on chromosomes 6 and 11, respectively. *Hatched bars* indicate sequence similarities between genes from both clusters.

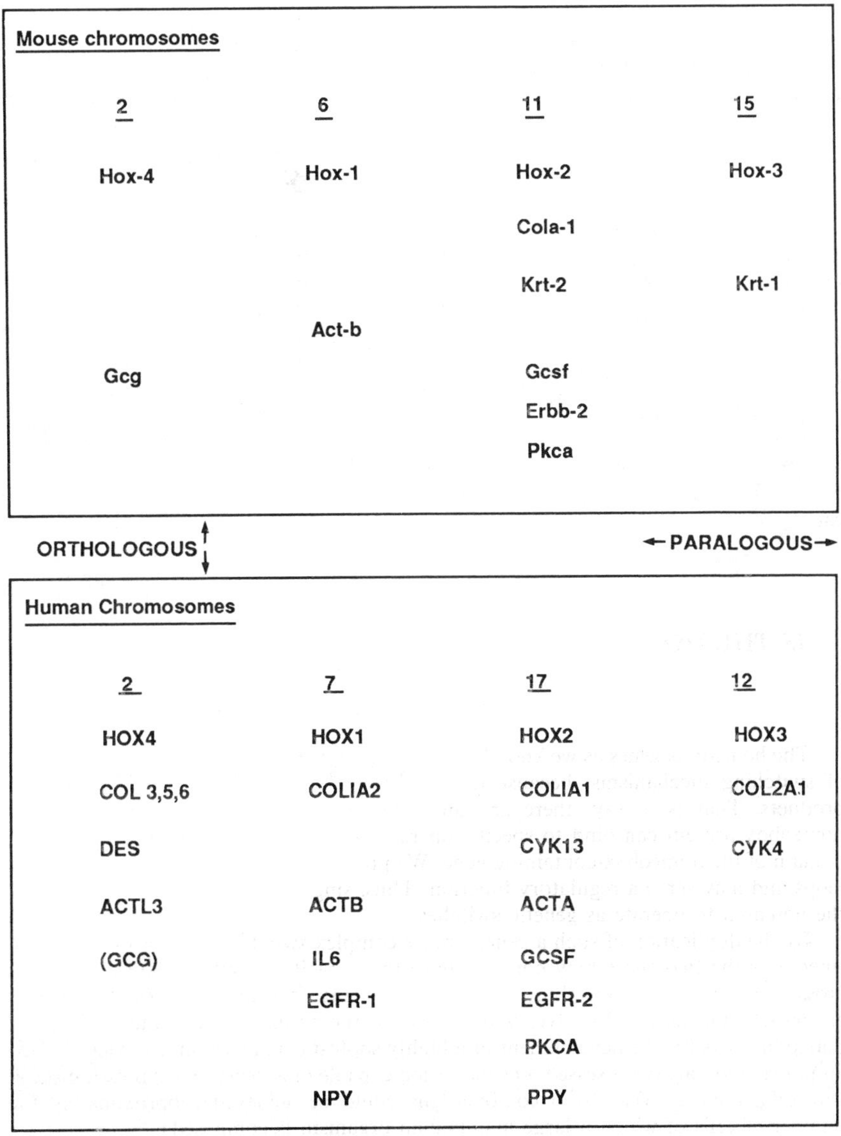

Mouse chromosomes

2	6	11	15
Hox-4	Hox-1	Hox-2	Hox-3
		Cola-1	
		Krt-2	Krt-1
	Act-b		
Gcg		Gcsf	
		Erbb-2	
		Pkca	

ORTHOLOGOUS ↕ ← PARALOGOUS →

Human Chromosomes

2	7	17	12
HOX4	HOX1	HOX2	HOX3
COL 3,5,6	COLIA2	COLIA1	COL2A1
DES		CYK13	CYK4
ACTL3	ACTB	ACTA	
(GCG)	IL6	GCSF	
	EGFR-1	EGFR-2	
		PKCA	
	NPY	PPY	

FIGURE 4. Orthologous and paralogous relationships between human and mouse chromosomes containing homeobox clusters. The genes identified on either human or mouse linkage groups are indicated. Krt, keratins; Act/ACT, actins and actin-like sequences; Gcg/GCG, glucagon; EGFR, epidermal growth factor receptor; Erbb-2, erythroblastic leukemia viral oncogene homolog 2; Pkca/PKCA, protein kinase C alpha peptide; NPY, neuropeptide Y; PPY, pancreatic polypeptide.

gene expression in the CNS and the position of the gene within the gene clusters. If this assumption is correct, then it follows that to some extent the lateral expansion of the genes within a primordial homeobox gene cluster may have occurred before the divergence of protostomes and deuterostomes, an event estimated to have taken place about 500 million years ago. Consistent with this interpretation is the fact that in lower insects, such as *Tribolium,* the Bithorax and Antennapedia complexes are contiguous. At some later time in insect evolution, this cluster separated into two separate gene clusters, but it is still located on the same chromosome arm, 3R, in *Drosophila.*

In the insects, there is no evidence for chromosome duplication to produce more genes. However, the *Drosophila* genes, as pointed out above, are significantly larger in terms of their *cis* flanking domains; this most probably can be considered as a more modern, advanced feature. Also, some of the *Drosophila* homeobox genes are ordered in opposite transcriptional orientation,[16] suggesting a further separate evolution of the gene cluster in insects. To more precisely date the chromosome duplication events in the deuterostomes with respect to the divergence of echinoderms and ancestral protochordates, it will be of considerable interest to survey the gene number and patterns of gene organization in the extant echinoderms and primitive chordates.

In summary, the evidence presented supports a concept of homeobox evolution in deuterostomes comprising two steps, namely the expansion of a homeobox gene cluster along one ancient linkage group, followed by subsequent chromosome duplication event(s).

IS THE HOMEOBOX GENE SYSTEM AN INFORMATIONAL ARRAY?

The homeobox genes as we know them today can be assumed to have the properties of switching mechanisms, because of the DNA-binding properties of the protein products. That is to say, there are several well-documented instances where the homeobox protein can bind to specific operator sites in the *cis* flanking, non-coding domain of the homeobox-containing gene. We presume these circuits may be feedback loops and may serve a regulatory function. Thus, single homeobox genes would have the potential to operate as genetic switches.

By the duplication of such a gene, a more complex switching apparatus is created, since now the two genes may not only have the capacity to self-regulate, but also to cross-regulate each other; thus, a network is being formed.[17] As the gene family expands, duplicates, and evolves with respect to the nature of these interactions, the potential exists for the development of a highly sophisticated switching device. If such an information array possessed 50 genes, each capable of at least two expression states (on/off), then 2^{50} (ca. 10^{15}) combinations could be achieved (approximately the number of cells of which a large mammalian organism is composed).

However, since the number of genes expressed at a given time in particular cells may be limited, and, furthermore, effects may also vary according to the levels of expression of either component, considerably more variability and a high degree of specificity in terms of information can be envisioned. Such a system not only would be cybernetically regulating the expression of its component genes, but also might be responsive to input (environmental) information, and, in turn, function to coordinate the patterns of expression of effector genes. Presumably, effector genes would be those directly involved in growth and morphogenesis, as, for instance, genes encoding growth factors, receptors, structural proteins, etc.[18] We believe this informational array model may be beneficial in itself, since it can be used as a guide to experimental design. We may ask on the basis of theory, how many elements (genes) are optimal in such an informational system, and how that number compares with the number observed in an experimentally defined system. We may ask how many interconnections are optimal for such a system and whether the number expected is generally seen. A modeling approach to understanding this system may, because of the potentially large numbers of genes involved, be more useful than will be a simple descriptive approach, where one attempts to establish all possible interrelationships and their consequences.

ACKNOWLEDGMENT

We thank Mrs. Marie Siniscalchi for her help in the preparation of the manuscript.

REFERENCES

1. McGinnis, W., R. L. Garber, J. Wirz, A. Kuroiwa & W. J. Gehring. 1984. A homologous protein-coding sequence in *Drosophila* homeotic genes and its conservation in other metazoans. Cell **37:** 403-408.
2. Gehring, W. J. & Y. Hiromi. 1986. Homeotic genes and the homeobox. Annu. Rev. Genet. **20:** 147-173.
3. Scott, M. P., J. W. Tamkun & G. W. Hartzell. 1988. The structure and function of the homeodomain. Biochim. Biophys. Acta (Reviews on Cancer). In press.
4. Desplan, C., J. Theis & P. H. O'Farrell. 1985. The *Drosophila* developmental gene, engrailed, encodes a sequence-specific DNA binding activity. Nature **318:** 630-635.
5. Fainsod, A., L. D. Bogarad, T. Ruusala, M. Lubin, D. R. Crothers & F. H. Ruddle. 1986. The homeodomain of a murine protein binds 5′ to its own homeobox. Proc. Natl. Acad. Sci. USA **83:** 9532-9536.
6. Fienberg, A. A., M. F. Utset, L. D. Bogarad, C. P. Hart, A. Awgulewitsch, A. Ferguson-Smith, A. Fainsod, M. Rabin & F. H. Ruddle. 1987. Homeo box genes in murine development. *In* Current Topics in Developmental Biology. A. A. Moscona & A. Monroy, Eds. Vol. 23: 233-256. Academic Press, Inc. New York.
7. Schughart, K., M. F. Utset, A. Awgulewitsch & F. H. Ruddle. 1988. Structure and expression of Hox-2.2, a murine homeobox-containing gene. Proc. Natl. Acad. Sci. USA **85:** 5582-5586.
8. Awgulewitsch, A., M. F. Utset, C. P. Hart, A. Fainsod, W. McGinnis & F. H. Ruddle. 1987. Organization of murine homeo box loci and their spatially restricted expression during development. *In* Molecular Approaches to Developmental Biology. R. A. Firtel & E. H. Davidson, Eds.: 147-165. Alan R. Liss, Inc. New York.
9. Gaunt, S. J., P. T. Sharpe & D. Duboule. 1988. Spatially restricted domains of homeo-gene transcripts in mouse embryos: Relation to a segmented body plan. Development **104**(Suppl.). In press.
10. Holland, P. W. H. & B. L. M. Hogan. 1988. Expression of homeo box genes during mouse development: A review. Genes Dev. **2:** 773-782.
11. Fainsod, A., A. Awgulewitsch & F. H. Ruddle. 1987. Expression of the murine homeo box gene Hox-1.5 during embryogenesis. Dev. Biol. **124:** 125-133.

12. Bogarad, L. D., M. F. Utset, A. Awgulewitsch, T. Miki, C. Hart & F. H. Ruddle. 1989. The developmental expression pattern of a new murine homeo box gene: Hox-2.5. Dev. Biol. In press.
13. Awgulewitsch, A., M. F. Utset, C. P. Hart, W. McGinnis & F. H. Ruddle. 1986. Spatial restriction in expression of a mouse homoeo box locus within the central nervous system. Nature **320:** 328-335.
14. Harding, K., C. Weeden, W. McGinnis & M. Levine. 1985. Spatially regulated expression of homeotic genes in *Drosophila.* Science **233:** 953-959.
15. Ruddle, F. H., C. P. Hart, M. Rabin, A. Ferguson-Smith & D. Pravtcheva. 1987. Comparative genetic analysis of homeo box genes in mouse and man. *In* New Frontiers in the Study of Gene Functions. G. Poste and S. T. Crooke, Eds.: 73-86. Plenum. New York.
16. Regulski, M., K. Harding, R. Kostriken, F. Karch, M. Levine & W. McGinnis. 1985. Homeo box genes of the Antennapedia and Bithorax complexes of *Drosophila.* Cell **43:** 71-80.
17. Frigerio, G., M. Burri, D. Bopp, S. Baumgartner & M. Woll. 1986. Structure of the segmentation gene paired and the *Drosophila* PRD gene set as part of a gene network. Cell **47:** 735-746.
18. Lewis, E. B. 1978. A gene complex controlling segmentation in *Drosophila.* Nature **276:** 565-570.

Interferons and the Differentiation of Friend Cells[a]

G. B. ROSSI,[b,c] R. ALBERTINI,[b] A. BATTISTINI,[b]
E. M. COCCIA,[b] G. ROMEO,[b] G. FIORUCCI,[b]
G. MARZIALI,[b] U. TESTA,[d] AND E. AFFABRIS[e]

Laboratories of [b]Virology and [d]Hematology-Oncology
Istituto Superiore di Sanità
Rome, Italy
and
[e]Institute of Microbiology
University of Messina
Messina, Italy

Interferons (IFNs) (for reviews, see Refs. 1 and 2) are a family of proteins produced, upon induction, by most cell types in a large variety of vertebrates. Each of these molecules is able to confer upon the cells that come in contact with it resistance to viral infection. This happens in a species-specific manner. Human, mouse and rat IFNs are classified into three antigenically distinct types: alpha (> 10 subtypes), beta (1-2 subtypes), and gamma. IFN-α and IFN-β can be induced in a variety of cells by various agents, e.g., certain viruses or bacteria and double-stranded RNA (dsRNA). Production of IFN-γ is induced in lymphoid cells by mitogens and antigens. The type of IFN produced may depend on the nature of the producing cell and/or of the inducer. IFN molecules must interact with the surface of the cell through different receptors to activate cellular response. It is not clear as yet whether IFNs act inside of the cells or send second message signals via the receptor. IFN-α and IFN-β share the same receptor. In addition, they, as well as IFN-γ, induce a set of proteins. Two induced enzymes, which have been well characterized, are induced by all IFN types. They are the 2′,5′-oligoadenylate synthetase (2-5A synthetase) and a protein kinase that phosphorylates serine and threonine residues. Localized activation of these enzymes during viral infection results in the inhibition of viral protein synthesis and a decrease in virus yield. Both activities need dsRNA for their activation *in vitro.* 2-5A synthetase is an oligonucleotide polymerase, which synthesizes from ATP a series of oligonucleotides (indicated as 2-5A) with unusual 2′-5′ phosphodiester bonds. This enzyme has recently been described to exist in multiple forms with different intracellular locations.[3] The 2-5A oligomers bind and activate with high affinity and specificity a latent endoribonuclease (RNase L) that cleaves RNA *in vitro.* Moreover,

[a]This work was supported in part by grants from Consiglio Nazionale delle Ricerche, Rome, Italy: Progetti Finalizzati "Oncologia" N. 8701151.44 and N. 86.02683.44 and from the Associazione Italiana per la Ricerca contro il Cancro, Milan, Italy.

[c]Address correspondence to Prof. Giovanni B. Rossi, Istituto Superiore di Sanità, Laboratory of Virology, Viale Regina Elena, 299, 00161 Roma, Italy.

the 2-5A content inside the cells is regulated by the antagonistic activities of the 2-5A synthetase and of a constitutive phosphodiesterase that catabolizes 2-5A products. The protein kinase induced by IFN (p67K) catalyzes the phosphorylation of the alpha subunit of the initiation factor eIF-2, thus inhibiting protein synthesis initiation. This process is also reversible, and a constitutive phosphatase may remove the phosphate group which was transferred to the alpha subunit of eIF-2. An autophosphorylation of the p67K protein, serving to regulate its own activity, has also been hypothesized to occur.

IFNs, although originally identified for their antiviral activity, do also induce several pleiotropic effects, such as inhibition of tumor cell growth, both *in vitro* and *in vivo,* and modulation of various immunological functions. Finally, indications that IFNs play a role in cell differentiation have come from observations in many differentiating and differentiated cell systems.[4] Most data on the effects of IFNs on cell differentiation have been accumulated in studies of hematopoiesis, affording substantial evidence of the effects of the various IFNs on different aspects of normal and leukemic cell differentiation. In leukemic cell lines, IFNs may either stimulate or inhibit cell growth and differentiation, depending on the dosage and/or the type of IFN employed.[5] In clinical trials carried out with human IFN-α, erythropenia and/or leukopenia have frequently been observed.[6]

Friend erythroleukemia cells (FLC) represent a multivalent system to study biological and biochemical effects of IFNs. They are murine proerythroblasts chronically infected by and producing Friend murine leukemia virus complex. The cells are tumorigenic when injected into syngeneic mice. The addition of dimethyl sulfoxide (DMSO) or of several other compounds to FLC cultures causes a massive shift of the cells towards the normoblast stage of erythroid differentiation. This is a *bona fide* example of terminal differentiation, as a complete cessation of cell division occurs even if the cells are still nucleated.[7]

Treatment with mouse fibroblast (f) IFN (which is a mixture of alpha and beta types) induces the antiviral state in Friend cells, fully but reversibly inhibiting Friend virus release as well as the replication of superinfecting RNA lytic viruses (the most commonly used viruses for this assay are encephalomyocarditis virus and vesicular stomatitis virus). In addition, f-IFN is able to inhibit Friend cell growth *in vitro* and *in vivo* and to modulate erythroid differentiation, i.e., low doses of f-IFN enhance DMSO-induced Friend cell differentiation, whereas high doses inhibit it.[8,9] Recently, the effect of f-IFN on DMSO-induced differentiation of FLC was investigated in more detail, using single IFN types, now available via recombinant DNA technology. In particular, we have analyzed the effect of murine (mu) IFN-α_1, IFN-β, and IFN-γ. As sources of IFNs we have used partially purified mu-IFN-α_1 and mu-IFN-β produced constitutively by Chinese hamster ovary cells transfected with the respective mouse genes (a gift of Dr. M. Von Heuvel, Erasmus University, Rottherdam, The Netherlands), murine recombinant IFN-β (a gift of Dr. Kobayashi, Toray Industries Inc., Japan), and murine recombinant IFN-γ (a gift of Dr. G. R. Adolf, Boehringer Ingelheim, Wien, Austria).

EFFECT OF MURINE INTERFERON-ALPHA$_1$ ON FRIEND CELL DIFFERENTIATION

Dose-response curves of the effect of mu-IFN-α_1 on DMSO-induced erythroid differentiation of FLC show that the administration of IFN-α_1 at doses of up to 1,000

U/ml does not modify the differentiation process. Higher doses lower the percentage of differentiated cells.[10] The effect is specific, since it is abolished both in wild type (w.t.) and f-IFN-resistant FLC when the IFN-α_1 preparations are preincubated with monoclonal antibodies neutralizing the IFN-α_1.[10] The inhibitory effect of IFN-α_1 on differentiation is even more pronounced in a Friend cell clone resistant to the antiviral and antiproliferative effect of f-IFN,[10,11] which has specific, saturable binding sites for f-IFN, as does w.t.[12]

Mutant cells exhibiting resistance to one or more effects of a given effector molecule have been of considerable importance for research in numerous areas of cell biology. A number of human and mouse cell lines have been described which exhibit an IFN-resistant phenotype.[13] The biochemical and genetic analysis of these mutants has been useful to study the molecular basis of the biological and biochemical effects of IFN. In particular, the isolation of mutants defective in some specific pathways may supply a tool for the study of specific activities induced by IFNs. In our f-IFN-resistant mutant clone treated with f-IFN or IFN-α_1, we have never observed induction of the antiviral state, of 2-5A synthetase mRNA or protein, or of protein kinase, either in the absence of DMSO or in the presence of DMSO and ongoing differentiation.[10,14,15] Within the 2-5A synthetase pathway, the constitutive RNase is, however, able to be activated by 2-5A oligonucleotides in the f-IFN-resistant cells (as it is in the w.t. cells).[16] This suggests that the increased expression of 2-5A synthetase genes seen after f-IFN treatment in w.t. cells is completely blocked in these f-IFN-resistant cells. In addition, since inhibition of differentiation is observed after treatment of f-IFN-resistant cells with DMSO and mu-IFN-α_1, it follows that the inhibitory effect of IFN-α_1 is *not* mediated via the 2-5A synthetase or 67K protein kinase pathways.

This observation prompted us to analyze in more detail the inhibitory effect of IFN-α_1 in these f-IFN-resistant cells. Differentiation of DMSO-treated FLC is accompanied by a substantial increase in globin mRNAs, globin chains and heme, eventually leading to hemoglobin (Hb) accumulation inside the cell. After 96 hr of culture in the presence of DMSO (1.5%), 80-90% of the cells become differentiated. Treatment of the IFN-resistant cells with 20,000 U/ml of mu-IFN-α_1 lowers by 90% the percentage of differentiated cells *and* the Hb and heme accumulation induced by DMSO. Interestingly, this inhibition by mu-IFN-α_1 is not accompanied by a comparably severe reduction in the steady-state levels of cytoplasmic alpha and beta globin mRNAs and of the synthesis of globin chains but is antagonized by the simultaneous addition of hemin to the cells treated with DMSO and IFN-α_1 (manuscript submitted for publication). These results suggest that a decrease in heme synthesis is a major limiting step in the synthesis of Hb during mu-IFN-α_1 treatment. To investigate this aspect, we have examined the first step of iron uptake into the cell. Transferrin is the major and perhaps the only source of iron for the heme biosynthesis of erythroid cells.[17] Diferric transferrin binds to specific receptors on the cell surface.[17,18] Such receptors are found on all rapidly dividing cells.[19] The ability of FLC to bind transferrin and take up iron increases substantially as a result of DMSO-stimulated differentiation.[20] Recently, it has been shown[21] that in human lymphoblastoid cells and in mitogen-induced lymphocytes, IFN-α reduces the number of transferrin receptors. This effect has been ascribed to a concurrent inhibition of cell growth. The pattern of ^{125}I-labeled transferrin binding to FLC at different days of culture shows two major phenomena. The first one is the induction of transferrin receptors due to the growth stimulation of fresh medium, which peaks at 48 hr and is followed by a decline to very low values on day 4 of growth, when the cultures are at saturation. This early increase in transferrin binding is more pronounced in control than in DMSO-induced FLC. These results are in agreement with data[21] showing a correlation between the expression of transferrin receptors and cell proliferation. The second phenomenon is related to an effect of DMSO occurring on days 3 and 4 of culture. While the level of transferrin receptors in control FLC peaks at 48 hr of culture and then declines to low levels at day 3-4 of culture, the expression of transferrin receptors in DMSO-induced FLC remains high at days 3 and 4. The addition to DMSO-treated cells of doses of IFN-α_1 that inhibit Hb synthesis induces a drastic decline of binding of ^{125}I-labeled transferrin at a time when the majority of the cells become differentiated. Scatchard analysis of the binding data indicates that mu-IFN-α_1 decreases the number of transferrin receptors without affecting the affinity of the receptor for its ligand. The regulation of transferrin receptors is a very complex phenomenon, and many molecules, such as, heme, iron, and growth factor(s)[22] are involved in this regulation. In our system, inhibition of differentiation by DMSO plus IFN-α_1 is also accompanied by a drastic reduction of heme content. It is not clear whether this reduction is responsible for the reduction of globin mRNA accumulation. Analysis of iron metabolism and of the heme biosynthetic pathway could help to clarify the effect of IFN-α_1 on FLC.

EFFECT OF MURINE INTERFERON-BETA ON FRIEND CELL DIFFERENTIATION

Treatment of DMSO-induced FLC with mu-IFN-β in a wide range of dosages (50 to 50,000 U/ml) inhibits cellular growth but stimulates erythroid differentiation: the number of differentiated cells more than doubles.[10] Mu-IFN-β treatment in the absence of differentiation inducers does not induce any significant increase in the spontaneous level of FLC differentiation, but it accelerates the rate of differentiation after induction. The effect is specific in that it is neutralized by incubation with monoclonal antibodies against mu-IFN-β.[10] FLC resistant to f-IFN are also resistant to this stimulatory effect on erythroid differentiation, as well as to all other effects of mu-IFN-β tested so far (i.e., antiproliferative and antiviral effects, induction of 2-5A synthetase and of 67K protein kinase).[10] The IFN-β-stimulated increase in the percentage of differentiated w.t. cells induced by DMSO is paralleled by an increase of Hb, of globin chains, and of globin mRNA steady-state levels (manuscript submitted for publication). Interestingly, experiments on ^{125}I-labeled transferrin binding indicate that, in spite of a marked inhibitory effect on cell growth, the number of transferrin receptors in cells treated with DMSO plus IFN-β is slightly increased. Previous reports,[21] as noted above, provided evidence that human IFN-α depresses the expression of transferrin receptors with a dose-dependence similar to that observed for its antiproliferative effect. It was, thus, suggested that a decreased number of transferrin receptors may be one of the mechanisms responsible for the antiproliferative action of IFN. This is certainly *not* the case in our system with IFN-β; this IFN exerts a great inhibitory effect on the growth of w.t. FLC, but slightly stimulates ^{125}I-labeled transferrin binding, and simultaneously increases the percentage of differentiated cells and the level of Hb synthesis.

EFFECT OF MURINE INTERFERON-GAMMA ON FRIEND CELL DIFFERENTIATION

To further analyze the response of Friend cells to IFNs, the effect of mu-IFN-γ was also investigated. IFN-γ is produced by lymphoid cells after mitogenic or antigenic stimulation. Treatment of Friend cells with natural or recombinant preparations of IFN-γ inhibits cell proliferation and induces the antiviral state. When the cells are induced to differentiate by DMSO, treatment with mu-IFN-γ (up to 100 U/ml) does not influence differentiation. Inhibitory effects on differentiation are detectable when doses higher than 100 U/ml are used, natural preparations being more effective than the recombinant ones.[10] The inhibitory effect is observed also in the f-IFN-resistant cell clone that is sensitive to IFN-γ[10,23] and it is abolished by neutralization with a monoclonal antibody raised against IFN-γ.[10] Another cell clone obtained from f-IFN-resistant cells[15] and resistant to induction of the antiviral state by IFN-γ, is fully resistant to all the effects induced by IFN-γ in FLC, i.e., the inhibition of cell growth and of cell differentiation, thus supporting the concept that all these effects are induced by IFN-γ.

CONCLUSIONS

In FLC cultures exposed separately to three different murine IFN types (alpha$_1$, beta, and gamma), IFN-β enhances chemically induced erythroid differentiation, whereas IFN-α_1 and IFN-γ do not affect the differentiation process up to a threshold dosage, and then, at higher doses, they inhibit it. The observation that low doses of IFN-β are sufficient to induce the stimulatory effect may suggest a higher susceptibility of erythroid cells to this type of IFN. In regard to this point, it has recently been suggested that the spontaneous production of a beta-like IFN molecule during the late stage of hematopoietic differentiation may play a role in an autocrine mechanism for inhibition of cell growth during terminal differentiation.[24–26]

ACKNOWLEDGMENT

The skillful secretarial assistance of Ms. V. Mazzeo is gratefully acknowledged.

REFERENCES

1. GRESSER, I., Ed. 1980-1988. Interferons Vol. 1-9. Academic Press. New York.
2. REVEL, M. & J. CHEBATH. 1986. Trends Biochem. Sci. **11:** 166-170.
3. CHEBATH, J., P. BENECH, A. HOVANESSIAN, J. GALABRU & M. REVEL. 1987. J. Biol. Chem. **262:** 3852-3857.
4. ROSSI, G. B. 1985. *In* Interferons I. Gresser, Ed. Vol. 6: 31-68. Academic Press. New York.
5. ROSSI, G. B., E. AFFABRIS, G. ROMEO, M. FEDERICO & E. M. COCCIA. 1987. *In* The Interferon System: A Current Review to 1987. F. Dianzani, J. Baron, G. J. Stanton & W. R. Fleischmann, Jr., Eds.: 285-297. University of Texas Press. Austin, Texas.
6. SCOTT, G. M. 1983. *In* Interferons. I. Gresser, Ed. Vol. 5: 84-114. Academic Press. New York.
7. REUBEN, R. C., R. A. RIFKIND & P. A. MARKS. 1980. Biochim. Biophys. Acta (Reviews on Cancer) **605:** 325-346.

8. Rossi, G. B., A. Dolei, M. R. Capobianchi, C. Peschle & E. Affabris. 1980. Ann. N.Y. Acad. Sci. **350:** 279-293.
9. Rossi, G. B., A. Dolei, L. Cioé & C. Peschle. 1982. Tex. Rep. Biol. Med. **41:** 381-387.
10. Affabris, E., M. Federico, G. Romeo, E. M. Coccia & G. B. Rossi. 1988. Virology. **167:** 185-193.
11. Affabris, E., C. Jemma & G. B. Rossi. 1982. Virology **120:** 441-452.
12. Affabris, E., G. Romeo, F. Belardelli, C. Jemma, N. Mechti, I. Gresser & G. B. Rossi. 1983. Virology **125:** 508-512.
13. Lebleu, B. & J. Content. 1983. *In* Interferon. I. Gresser, Ed.: 47-94. Academic Press. New York.
14. Rossi, G. B., E. Affabris, G. Romeo, M. Federico, E. M. Coccia, N. Mechti & B. Lebleu. 1986. *In* The 2-5A System: Molecular and Clinical Aspects of the Interferon-regulated Pathway. B. Williams & R. Silverman, Eds. Vol. 202: 285-296. Plenum Press. Toronto.
15. Coccia, E. M., M. Federico, G. Romeo, E. Affabris, F. Cofano & G. B. Rossi. 1988. J. Interferon Res. **8:** 113-127.
16. Federico, M., G. Romeo, E. Affabris, E. M. Coccia & G. B. Rossi. 1986. J. Interferon Res. **6:** 233-240.
17. Jandl, J. H., J. K. Inman, R. L. Simmons & D. W. Allen. 1959. J. Clin. Invest. **38:** 161-185.
18. Morgen, E. H. 1964. Br. J. Hematol. **10:** 442.
19. Karin, M. & B. Mintz. 1981. J. Biol. Chem. **256:** 3245-3252.
20. Siang-yin, H., H. U. Yang, J. Gardner, P. Aisen & A. Skoultchi. 1977. Science **197:** 559-561.
21. Besancon, F., M. F. Bourgeade & U. Testa. 1985. J. Biol. Chem. **260:** 13074-13080.
22. Testa, U., E. Pelosi-Testa, F. Mavilio, M. Petrini, N. M. Spasi, S. Petti, P. Samoggia, E. Montesoro, G. Giannella, L. Bottero, A. Camagna, G. Salvo, G. Isacchi, D. Habetswallner & C. Peschle. 1987. J. Receptor Res. **7:** 355-375.
23. Romeo, G., E. Affabris, M. Federico, N. Mechti, E. M. Coccia, C. Jemma & G. B. Rossi. 1985. J. Biol. Chem. **260:** 3833-3838.
24. Friedman Einat, M., M. Revel & A. Kimchi. 1982. Mol. Cell. Biol. **2:** 1472-1480.
25. Yarden, A., H. Shure Gottlieb, J. Chebat, M. Revel & A. Kinachi. 1984. EMBO J. **3:** 969-973.
26. Resnitzky, D., A. Yarden, D. Zipori & A. Kimchi. 1986. Cell **46:** 31-40.

Cancer Genes by Illegitimate Recombination[a]

PETER H. DUESBERG,[b] REN-PING ZHOU, AND DAVID GOODRICH

Department of Molecular Biology
University of California, Berkeley
Berkeley, California 94720

INTRODUCTION

The only proven cancer genes to date are the *onc* genes of directly transforming retroviruses.[1-4] These qualify to be classified as autonomous transforming genes because they transform diploid cells in culture with single-hit kinetics and because all susceptible cells become transformed as soon as they are infected. Accordingly, tumors induced by such viruses in animals are all polyclonal. Such viruses have never been found in healthy animals, a statement that cannot be made for retroviruses without *onc* genes or for DNA tumor viruses, both of which are commonly found in animals outside the laboratory and only transform cells indirectly and inefficiently.[5-7]

However, retroviruses with *onc* genes play a very minor role as natural carcinogens.[2] This is because these viruses have an extremely low "birth rate"—less than one hundred have been isolated in over 80 years of tumor virus research[6]—and because the transforming genes of these viruses are very unstable, having half-lives of only a few replicative cycles.[8-10] In fact, spontaneous deletion of the *src* gene of Rous sarcoma virus (RSV) was the original basis for the discovery of *onc* genes.[8,11] The short half-life of retroviral *onc* genes is also the reason that such viruses have never caused epidemics of cancer and, hence, have never played a major role as natural carcinogens.[2] The unstable element of retroviral *onc* genes, a sequence that is not essential for the retrovirus, was originally termed transformation-specific.[12] Although this sequence is not really less stable than the essential retrovirus genes,[9] deletion mutants which lack it remain viable and hence readily detectable.[8,13] By contrast, deletions of essential retrovirus genes are not detectable, because they do not survive unless complemented by a helper virus.[6,13]

Since the transformation-specific sequences of retroviruses have very short half-lives, they must be recent genetic acquisitions. Indeed, the most plausible source of nonessential genetic information for viruses is the host cell, from which viruses can

[a] Another version of this paper was presented by one of the authors (P. D.) at a conference, "The Boundaries between Promotion and Progression during Carcinogenesis," held in Cleveland, Ohio, on September 28-30, 1988.

[b] Supported by Outstanding Investigator Grant #5-R35-CA39915-03 from the National Cancer Institute and Grant #1547AR1 from the Council for Tobacco Research.

transduce genetic information, as was originally demonstrated for the bacterial virus, lambda.[14] The cellular origin of transformation-specific sequences was first confirmed in the 1970s for the transforming *ras* genes of the Harvey and Kirsten sarcoma viruses, using liquid hybridization between viral cDNA sequences and cellular DNA.[15,16] This technique demonstrated that all transformation-specific sequences of retroviral *onc* genes were derived from one or more cellular genes, which have since been termed proto-*onc* genes.[1,2]

Liquid hybridization is adequate to compare sequence homologies, but it is insufficient to compare genetic structures or functional homologies of genes that share homologous sequences. It only became possible to compare the genetic structure of the proto-*onc* genes to that of the viral *onc* genes much later, since at that time molecular cloning and nucleic acid sequencing had not yet been discovered or licensed for work on oncogenic viruses. Nevertheless, the hybrid nature of some viral *onc* genes, those which include retrovirus-derived and proto-*onc* gene-derived coding regions, like the Δ*gag-myc* gene of MC29 virus, provided the first clues that viral *onc* genes and proto-*onc* genes were not isogenic.[17] This was confirmed later when the corresponding proto-*myc* gene had been cloned and sequenced (see below).[18]

THE ONCOGENE CONCEPT: CANCER VIA ACTIVATION OF LATENT CELLULAR ONCOGENES

The Oncogene Concept

On the basis of the homology between the transformation-specific sequences of retroviruses and the sequences of cellular proto-*onc* genes, it was proposed that retroviral *onc* genes are "cellular oncogenes" (c-*onc*) transduced from the cell[6,19–21] and are analogous to the complete bacterial genes transduced by bacterial viruses.[14] Thus, the retroviruses were viewed as the lambda phages of eukaryotes. This proposal, later termed the oncogene concept,[22] predicted that there were latent cancer genes in normal cells, hence these genes were termed "enemies from within."[19] The proponents of the oncogene concept postulate that these cellular oncogenes are not only converted to cancer genes from without the cell by transducing retroviruses, but also from within, either directly by "activation" or indirectly by inactivation of a suppressor gene or an anti-oncogene[23,24] like other latent or inactive cellular genes. According to the oncogene concept, five different mechanisms "activate" latent cellular oncogenes or proto-oncogenes to cancer genes (TABLE 1).[6,22–28]

Three Classes of Cellular Oncogenes

In addition to proto-*onc* genes related to retroviral *onc* genes, two other classes of cellular genes are now also termed cellular proto-*onc* genes or oncogenes and are thought to be subject to activation by the mechanisms listed in TABLE 1. One class consists of genes from tumors; these genes—unlike their counterparts from normal cells—can upon transfection transform the morphology and enhance the tumorigenic-

TABLE 1. Mechanisms that Activate Cellular Oncogenes According to the Oncogene Concept

Amplification
Translocation with or without gene rearrangement
Point mutation
Inactivation of suppressor genes or anti-oncogenes
Promoter or enhancer insertion from an integrating retrovirus

ity of the highly aneuploid mouse NIH/3T3 cell line.[6,21,25–28] The other class consists of cellular genes that serve as preferential integration sites of retroviruses in mammary tumors of certain inbred strains of mice but are not related to viral *onc* genes and do not transform 3T3 cells, or any other cells.[6,21,25,26,29]

Promises and Problems of the Oncogene Concept

At first sight, the oncogene concept was appealing because known derivatives of some cellular oncogenes, namely, the viral *onc* genes, are authentic cancer genes. Above all, it promised access to the long-sought cancer genes of virus-negative cancers—access in the form of hybridization or antibody probes derived either from retroviral *onc* genes,[30–32] from cloned, 3T3 cell-transforming tumor DNAs,[6,25,26] or from specific retrovirus integration sites in tumors of retrovirus-infected animals.[7,29] The idea of activation from within was the key to the enormous popularity of the oncogene concept, because directly oncogenic viruses could only be isolated from a handful of animal cancers and have yet to be found in any human cancer.[2,6,22]

However, a serious problem with the concept was that it postulated the existence in normal cells of latent cancer genes that could be activated by a multiplicity of mechanisms (TABLE 1). But activated cancer genes are the least desirable genes conceivable for multicellular eukaryotes—even a death gene would be preferable. If a single cell dies in a multicellular organism, its place can be taken by another. If a single cell is converted to an autonomous cancer cell, though, it will inevitably kill the organism by authoring a clonal tumor.[34,35]

Predictions of the Oncogene Concept Remain Unconfirmed

The oncogene concept makes five experimentally testable predictions, listed in TABLE 2. Despite numerous efforts in the last 6 to 8 years, these predictions have not been confirmed, with the possible exception of Prediction 3 in some cases (see below).

Prediction 1. Structural comparisons between viral *onc* genes and corresponding proto-*onc* genes have revealed that viral *onc* genes and proto-*onc* genes are not isogenic. Instead, all viral *onc* genes are tripartite hybrids consisting of retroviral promoters and coding regions derived mostly from virus and proto-*onc* genes, or sometimes only from proto-*onc* genes and terminating retroviral control elements (FIG. 1).[1,2] On the

TABLE 2. Predictions Made by the Oncogene Concept

1. Cellular oncogenes and viral *onc*-genes are isogenic.
2. Transcriptional activation of cellular oncogenes leads to cancer.
3. Activated cellular oncogenes transform diploid cells.
4. Diploid cancers exist with activated oncogenes as the only genetic distinction.
5. The probability of oncogene activation is $\leq$ the probability of cancer.

basis of such studies, the hypothesis emerged that substitution of the cellular promoter and as yet poorly defined, non-transcribed regulatory sequences by the strong, constitutive, promoter of a retrovirus, termed the LTR (long terminal repeat), is a structural alteration that is essential to convert a proto-*onc* gene to a viral *onc* gene.[2,36–38]

In the cases of the conversion of proto-*myc* to the *myc* genes of the avian carcinoma/leukemia viruses MC29, MH2, OK10 and CMII[38,39] and of proto-*ras* to the *ras* genes of Harvey, Balb and other murine sarcoma viruses,[36,37] we have demonstrated that promoter substitution is indeed sufficient to convert a proto-*onc* gene to a viral *onc* gene. This was proven with virus constructs in which the native proto-*myc* or proto-*ras* genes were linked to a retroviral LTR promoter in a retroviral vector. These synthetic retroviruses transformed diploid cells as wild type avian and murine tumor viruses with *myc* or *ras* genes did.[36–38]

Prediction 2. Several, but not all, proto-*onc* genes are highly expressed in normal cells, for example, proto-*myc,* indicating that proto-*onc* expression is not sufficient to transform cells.[1,2,6]

Prediction 3. Of the proto-*onc* genes from tumor cells not one "activated" by mechanism(s) of the oncogene concept other than alteration of germline configuration has been shown to transform diploid cells in culture.[1,2,6,25,26,40] On the contrary, point mutated ("activated") proto-*ras* genes like those found in some human cancers[30,31] have been observed in clonal hyperplasias of mice. These hyperplasias subsequently differentiated into normal tissues.[41,42] Likewise, transgenic mice have been generated that are tumor-free, yet carry in every cell recombinant *ras* genes with a point mutation linked to a mammary tumor virus promoter[43] or carry proto-*myc* genes "activated" by rearrangements with globin genes that were derived from murine or human B-cell lymphomas.[44,45] Since some of these mice developed clonal tumors, the "activated" oncogenes were proposed to be necessary for tumorigenesis (see below).

However, proto-*myc* genes isolated from retrovirus-induced chicken leukemias were recently shown to transform diploid avian cells as proviral DNAs from retroviruses with *onc* genes do.[38] The native promoters of these proto-*myc* genes had been substituted in the animal by that of a retrovirus. FIGURE 2 shows two such hybrid genes from chicken lymphomas. These genes are equivalent to viral *myc* genes in that they each have a 5′ retroviral LTR promoter linked to a proto-*myc* coding region which has retained its native 3′ terminus. Upon transfection, these genes transformed primary quail cells as the corresponding proviral DNAs of retroviruses with *myc* genes did. These are as yet the only known cellular genes that, upon transfection, transform diploid cells in culture.[38] Nevertheless, even the host range of viral *onc* genes appears to be restricted to certain species. For example, the autonomous *myc* gene of avian carcinoma virus MH2[61] and the murine proto-*myc* gene appear to be unable to transform murine cells, even in a murine retrovirus vector.[62,63] Moreover, there is no known mammalian retrovirus with a *myc* gene.[1,2] Therefore, there is no evidence to postulate that even an "activated" cellular *myc* gene may be a sufficient or necessary cause of mammalian tumors, as has been done in the case of murine plasmacytoma and human Burkitt's lymphoma.[21,27,43–45,49,50]

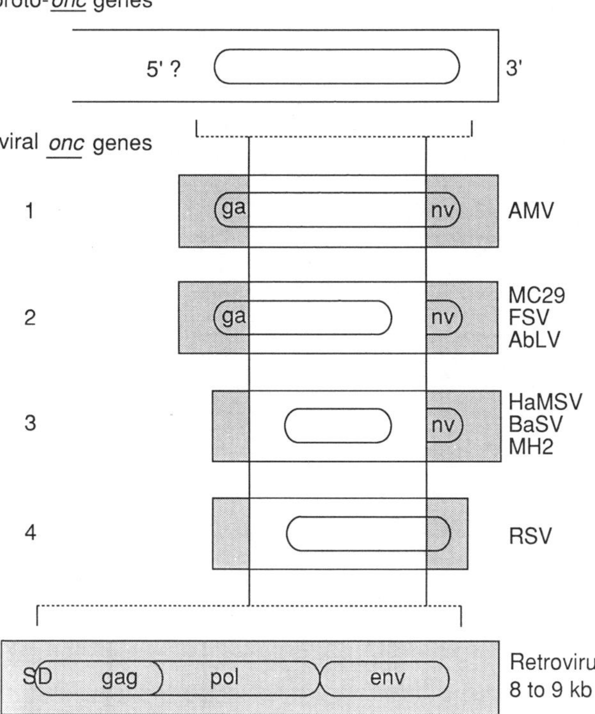

FIGURE 1. The generic, recombinant structures of retroviral *onc* genes and their relationship to viral *onc* genes and cellular proto-*onc* genes. The genes are compared as transcriptional units or mRNAs. All known viral *onc* genes are tripartite hybrids of a central sequence derived from a cellular proto-*onc* gene (*unshaded*) flanked by 5′ and 3′ elements derived from retroviral genes (*stippled*). Actual size differences, ranging from about 2 to 7 kilobases (kb), are not faithfully depicted in this schematic diagram. The map order of the three essential retrovirus genes, *gag, pol,* and *env,* and the splice donor (SD) are indicated (*bottom panel*). Four groups of viral *onc* genes are distinguished on the basis of the origins of their coding sequence. **Group 1:** The coding unit (indicated by *closed loop*) has a tripartite structure of a central proto-*onc*-derived sequence that is initiated and terminated by viral coding sequences. Avian myeloblastosis virus (AMV) is an example.[6] **Group 2:** The coding unit is initiated by a viral sequence and terminated by a proto-*onc* sequence. The Δ*gag-myc* gene of avian carcinoma virus MC29 is an example;[17,18] the hybrid *onc* genes of Fujinami avian sarcoma virus (FSV) and Abelson murine leukemia virus (AbLV) are other examples.[6] **Group 3:** The coding unit of the viral *onc* gene is colinear with a reading frame of a cellular proto-*onc* gene. The *ras* gene of the Harvey and Balb murine sarcoma viruses (HaSV and BaSV)[36,37] and the *myc* gene of the avian carcinoma virus MH2 are examples (see FIG. 2).[38] **Group 4:** The coding unit is initiated by a proto-*onc*-derived domain and terminated by a viral reading frame. The *src* gene of Rous sarcoma virus (RSV) is an example.[2,6] The transcriptional starts and 5′ non-transcribed regulatory sequences of most proto-*onc* genes are as yet not, or not exactly, known.[2,36–38] It is clear, however, that proto-*onc*-specific regulatory elements are always replaced by viral promoters and enhancers and that proto-*onc* coding sequences are frequently recombined with viral coding sequences. This figure is adapted from Ref. 2.

The oncogene concept further proposes that the LTR of an integrated retrovirus could convert a proto-*onc* gene into an element with the transforming ability of a retroviral *onc* gene, not only by promoter substitution as originally postulated,[32] but also by position-independent enhancer effects.[25,26,33] However, neither a proto-*myc* gene with a retrovirus integrated downstream, which was isolated from a chicken lymphoma (FIG. 2), nor similar constructs made *in vitro* were found to transform quail embryo cells upon transfection.[38] Therefore, it was concluded that retrovirus integration can

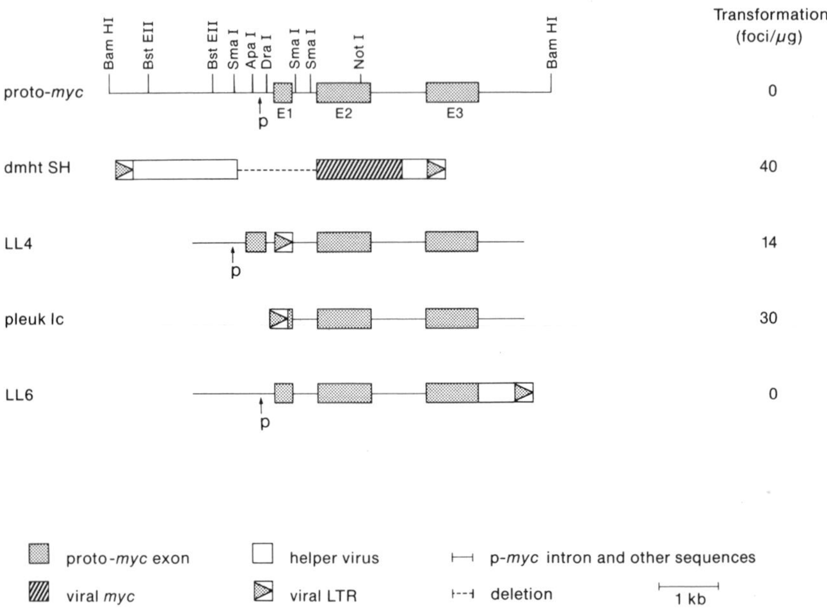

FIGURE 2. Structure of cloned proto-*myc* genes from chicken lymphomas. Three molecularly cloned proto-*myc* genes from retrovirus-positive avian leukemias, LL4, pleuk 1C and LL6, are analyzed. Their structures and transforming functions are compared to native chicken proto-*myc* DNA and to the proviral DNA of MH2 virus (dmht SH) with a deletion (*dotted line*) in the non-transforming *mht*-sequence.[38] The MH2 virus carries a transformation-specific *myc* sequence (*hatched area*). *Open boxes,* viral sequences; *stippled boxes,* proto-*myc* exons 1 to 3; *boxes with (stippled) arrowheads,* retroviral LTRs—in which the arrowheads point in the transcriptional direction; *solid lines,* other sequences. Major restriction enzyme sites of proto-*myc* are indicated. The distance between the two *Bam*H I sites of chicken proto-*myc* is about 9.5 kilobases (kb). p (*arrow*) indicates the position of the proto-*myc* promoter. Transfection of cloned cellular proto-*myc* DNAs into quail embryo cells has been described.[38] The transforming efficiencies shown, measured in focus-forming units per microgram of DNA (foci per μg), are the average of at least two independent assays. This figure is adapted from Ref. 38.

convert a proto-*myc* gene to a transforming gene only if the viral LTR is present in a position which allows it to function as a classical promoter, as it does in viral *myc* genes, but not if its location requires it to function as a position-independent enhancer. Accordingly, it was suggested that the leukemia from which the non-transforming proto-*myc* hybrid gene was isolated may not have been caused by this altered proto-*myc* gene, although it cannot be excluded that a proto-*myc* gene which cannot transform embryo cells *in vitro* may transform lymphocytes *in vivo.*[38]

TABLE 3. Probability of Proto-*ras* Gene Activation by Point Mutation

Net probability of a point mutation in prokaryotic or eukaryotic cells per nucleotide per mitosis, after repairs:[2]	ca. 10^{-9}
At least 50 different mutations are said to "activate" proto-*ras*,[2,25] and eukaryotes are diploid. Thus, the probability of proto-*ras* activation per mitosis:	10^{-7}

Prediction 4. As yet, no diploid tumors have been described that differ from normal cells only by the single change of having a cellular oncogene "activated" by a mechanism like point mutation, amplification or transcriptional activation (TABLE 1)—processes that do not rearrange its genetic structure.[2] The only exceptions are tumors caused by retroviruses with *onc* genes, which are initially diploid.[2] Other possible exceptions may be tumors, like the chicken leukemias, induced by retroviruses that substitute for the promoter of a proto-*onc* gene, although the karyotype of such tumors has yet to be determined.

Indeed, most, if not all, animal and human cancers have chromosome abnormalities.[2,35,46–48] For example, the human bladder carcinoma cell lines from which proto-*ras* with a point mutation was first isolated[30,31] contain over 86 chromosomes, including several abnormal marker chromosomes.[2] In view of such fundamental genetic alterations, the point mutation of proto-*ras* that is said to have caused the tumor[30,31] seems like a very minor event.

Prediction 5. Clearly, if activation of a proto-*onc* gene according to the oncogene concept were directly relevant to cancer, the probability of cancer should be at least as high as the sum of the probabilities of activation of all cellular oncogenes. Since about 50 putative cellular oncogenes have been described,[6,21–28] cancer should occur at least 50 times more often than the activation of a given oncogene by any of the five mechanisms listed above (TABLE 1).

However, there is an astronomical discrepancy between the real probabilities of cancer in man and animals and the probabilities predicted by the oncogene concept. For example, the probability of activating proto-*ras* by a point mutation according to the oncogene concept is about 10^{-7} per mitosis (TABLE 3). Since proto-*ras* with a point mutation is a "dominant oncogene" according to the 3T3 assay,[6,25,28,30,31] one mutation should be sufficient for transformation, although such a mutation may not transform every cell in which it arises, because its transforming host range might be limited.

By contrast, the probability of spontaneous conversion of a human (or animal) cell to the clonal precursor of a malignant cancer is only 2×10^{-17} per mitosis (TABLE 4). Thus, the probability of proto-*ras* activation according to the oncogene

TABLE 4. Probability for a Human Cell to Initiate a Clonal Malignant Cancer

The probability per mitosis of spontaneous malignant transformation of a cell, based on the reality of human cancer, is the product of the following factors:	
Cancers are monoclonal:[2,34,35]	1
1 in 5 humans develop cancer:[2]	2×10^{-1}
Adult humans consist of about 10^{14} cells, which undergo an average of 10^2 mitoses per lifetime:[2]	$10^{-14} \times 10^{-2}$
Thus, the probability per mitosis for a human cell to originate a clonal tumor is	2×10^{-17}

concept is about 10^{10} times higher than the probability of malignant transformation of a human cell to a cancer cell *in vivo.* Moreover, only a small minority of human cancers contain proto-*ras* mutations.[2,25]

Other events that do not affect the genetic structure of genes, such as amplification, translocation, elevated expression, or inactivation or deletion of *trans*-acting suppressor genes, also each occur at probabilities between 10^{-4} and 10^{-9} per mitosis.[2,4] Hence, there is a discrepancy between the probabilities of cancer as predicted by the oncogene concept and as observed in reality of a factor of at least 10^8 or more, depending on how many of the 50 postulated cellular oncogenes—and of the five different mechanisms said to activate them—are included in the estimate and depending on how many cell lineages are assumed to be susceptible to transformation by a given oncogene.

It follows that the oncogene concept has basically failed in predicting the reality of cancer, because the probability of generating cancer genes by most of the postulated mechanisms is much higher than the level of cancer actually observed. Moreover, a gene or combination of genes that transform diploid cells *in vitro* has yet to be isolated from a human tumor. Only one class of such genes, namely the retrovirus-proto-*myc* recombinant genes from chicken lymphomas (FIG. 2), has been isolated from animals.

ARE ACTIVATED PROTO-*ONC* GENES NECESSARY FOR CANCER?

In view of these difficulties with the original oncogene concept that postulated functional equivalence between viral and cellular oncogenes, it has been argued more recently that activated cellular oncogenes are necessary, but not sufficient, for carcinogenesis.[6,26,40,49] For example, it was proposed that activated proto-*myc* would complement activated proto-*myc* would complement activated proto-*ras* for a sufficient double of transforming genes, because these two activated oncogenes were found in the same tumor cell lines.[40] Hence, one "activated" oncogene by itself might occur much more frequently than cancer, and would not be expected to transform diploid cells upon transfection.

This proposal is a critical revision of the original oncogene concept, which held that, upon activation, cellular oncogenes are like viral *onc* genes and that their effects can be observed when they are introduced into non-malignant cells.[20,24–28,30,31] It sets apart "activated" cellular oncogenes from both viral *onc* genes, which are sufficient, and normal proto-*onc* genes, which are not known to be (directly) necessary, for carcinogenesis.

To support this proposal, it would be necessary to demonstrate a consistent correlation between the presence of a particular "activated" proto-*onc* gene and a given cancer. To prove the proposal, it would be necessary to identify genes in spontaneous tumors that complement the allegedly necessary oncogenes, resulting in their functioning as dominant cancer genes in diploid cells. However, to date, no such correlation or complementary gene has been identified. For example, proto-*ras* mutations are found only in a minority of primary tumors but never in all tumors of a given type.[1,25–28] Moreover, transgenic mice have been generated that contain in every cell both *ras* and a reportedly complementary[40] *myc* gene, each "activated" by the promotor of mammary tumor virus.[43] Such mice all develop normally. However, they have a propensity to develop monoclonal tumors later, although some don't develop tumors for 150 days.[43] Accordingly, it was concluded that even a combination of "activated" *ras* and *myc* is not sufficient for carcinogenesis.[43] Further, it has been claimed, based on studies of cultured cell lines, that there are consistent translocations of proto-*myc* from chromosome 8 to either chromosome 2, 14 or 22 in all Burkitt's lymphomas.[49,50] Yet, cytogenetic studies of primary Burkitt's lymphomas have identified normal chromosomes 8, but other clonal chromosome abnormalities instead, in up to 50% of the tumors.[51,52] It has been suggested that the consistent translocations observed in cultured cell lines derived from such tumors are artifacts of selection *in vitro.*[51] Moreover, many proto-*myc* translocations observed in cultured Burkitt's lymphoma cell lines do not alter the germline structure of proto-*myc,* and others eliminate the native promoter but do not provide an alternative promoter.[1,2,49,50] It is unlikely that such promoterless or normal proto-*myc* genes cause cancer. Similarly, it has been claimed that retinoblastomas arise by a consistent deletion or inactivation of the retinoblastoma-suppressor (*Rb*) gene.[24] However, a recent analysis found mutations or deletions of the *Rb* gene in only 22% of 34 tumors analyzed.[53]

Thus, there is neither a consistent correlation in support of, nor functional proof for, the hypothesis that the "activated" oncogenes known to date are even necessary for carcinogenesis. Until there is functional evidence—or at least a consistent correlation—the hypothesis that certain "activated" oncogenes are necessary to initiate or maintain carcinogenesis remains unproven. Instead, aneuploidy and many quantitative changes in chromosomes are consistently found in tumor cells.[2,35,46–48]

CANCER GENES GENERATED *DE NOVO* BY ILLEGITIMATE RECOMBINATION

Based on the fundamental differences between viral *onc* genes and proto-*onc* genes (FIG. 1), it is proposed here that cancer genes do not pre-exist in either retroviruses or cells, but are generated *de novo.* Such genes appear to be generated by rare illegitimate recombinations between cellular proto-*onc* genes and retroviral genes or other cellular genes. This proposal is based on the following:

1. The retroviral *onc* genes are proven recombinant cancer genes (FIG. 1).
2. The recombinant retroviral LTR-proto-*myc* genes of the avian lymphomas (FIG. 2) are potential cancer genes. They function like viral *onc* genes upon transfection into primary embryo cells and are probable *onc* genes in viral lymphomas.
3. The chromosome abnormalities found in nearly all virus-negative tumors are consistent with this proposal. Some of the rearrangements that generated these abnormalities may have generated, by recombination, as yet unidentified cancer genes. The clonality of the chromosome abnormalities of a given tumor, e.g., the marker chromosomes, further support this view.[2,35,46–48] The clonality indicates that the chromosome rearrangement coincided with the origin of the tumor cell and thus, possibly, even caused it. Indeed, the retroviral *onc* genes may be viewed as oncogenic chromosome rearrangements cloned in retrovirus vectors. Hence, tumors induced by such viruses are diploid—at least initially.[2]

Clearly, most rearrangements based on illegitimate recombinations would not generate cancer genes. Instead, they would inactivate genes or have no effect. Very few combinations would be expected to generate "new" genes, such as viral *onc* genes, with new functions (FIG. 1). Again, the origin of retroviral *onc* genes from cellular proto-*onc* genes and retroviruses may serve as a model for how recombinant cancer genes are generated, because retroviruses, once integrated into the chromosome of the host cell, are exactly like other cellular genes. As illustrated in FIGURE 3, two recombinations are necessary to generate a retrovirus with an *onc* gene from a proto-*onc* gene and a retrovirus without an *onc* gene. The probability of generating an oncogene retrovirus by this process based on illegitimate recombination between cellular genes is estimated to be 10^{-28} per mitosis, based on the assumptions listed in TABLE 5. The low probability of such an event is quite consistent with the reality of only 50 to 100 known isolates of such oncogenic recombinant retroviruses in 80 years of retrovirus research.[6,20]

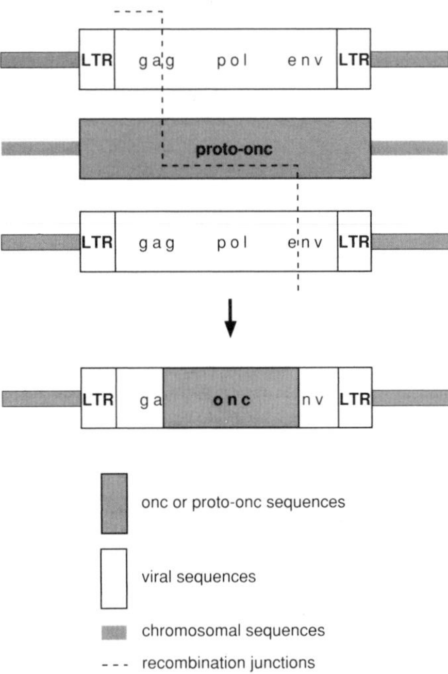

FIGURE 3. Model for spontaneous transduction of oncogenic sequences from proto-*onc* genes by retroviruses via illegitimate recombination. We propose that a transforming retrovirus can be generated by two illegitimate DNA recombinations between an integrated retrovirus about 9 kilobases in length and a cellular proto-*onc* gene (see FIG. 1).

However, it may be argued that the origin of retroviruses is not a model for the origin of cellular cancer genes by illegitimate chromosome recombination, because retroviruses were proposed to recombine with cellular information via RNA-heterodimers.[10,21,54,55] This proposal is based on the fact that all retroviral RNAs are diploid.[56,57] Hence, heterodimers may be formed that may recombine efficiently by copy-choice transcription involving viral reverse transcriptase.[54]

We have recently re-examined this proposal, using as the hypothetical recombination intermediate the same incomplete Harvey sarcoma provirus that was the original basis of the model.[55] In this model system, the incomplete 5′-LTR-*ras* Harvey provirus (FIG. 4) was proposed to recover the missing 3′ LTR from a helper Moloney retrovirus

TABLE 5. Probability of Generating an Oncogenic Retrovirus by Illegitimate Recombination

Probability of a rearrangement per cell division, based on data for live-born babies with chromosome abnormalities:[2,58]	ca. 10^{-4}
Probability that a rearrangement affects a 10-kb proto-*onc* gene in a eukaryotic cell of 10^6 kb:	10^{-5}
Probability that rearrangement affects an integrated provirus 9 kb in length:	10^{-5}
Thus, the probability of generating an LTR-proto-*onc* hybrid gene per mitosis is	10^{-14}
And the probability of generating a virus involving two such recombinations is	10^{-28}

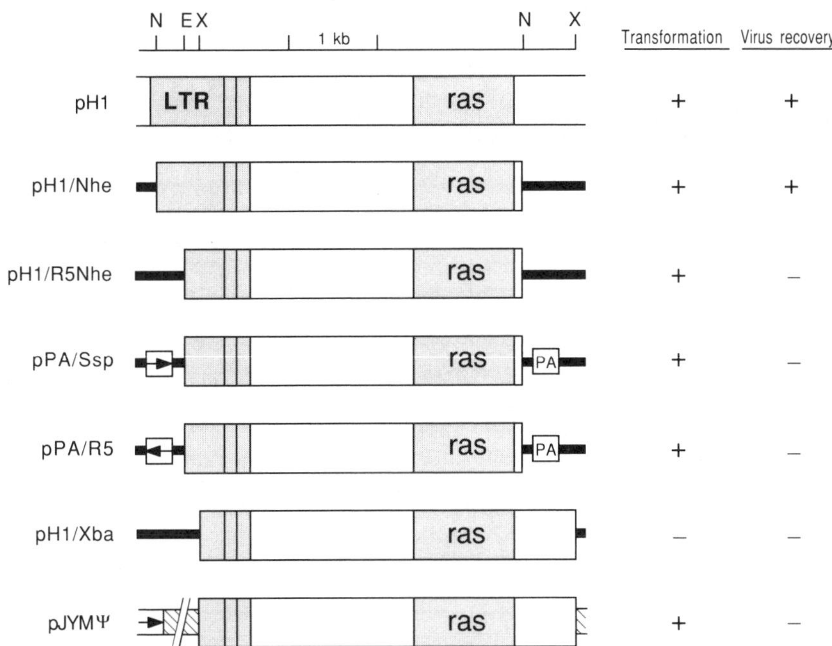

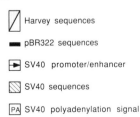

FIGURE 4. Transformation and regeneration of Harvey sarcoma virus in cells transfected by incomplete Harvey proviruses with a single intact or partially deleted LTR. Harvey proviral constructions were transfected into NIH/3T3 cells. Cells were scored for transformation 2 to 3 weeks later. It can be seen that only constructs with one complete (pH1) or nearly complete (pH1/Nhe) LTR regenerated infectious virus. However, nearly all constructs generated sufficient *ras* RNA to transform cells. Restriction enzyme sites (*top panel*) that define the extent of the deletions of the LTR are N, *Nhe* I; E, *Eco*R V; X, *Xba* I. *Large stippled and open boxes,* Harvey viral elements; *solid black line,* pBR322 sequences; *arrows and PA in small boxes,* SV40 promoter/enhancer and poly(A) signal sequences, respectively; *hatched boxes,* SV40 sequences. (From Goodrich & Duesberg.[58] Reprinted with permission from the *Proceedings of the National Academy of Sciences of the United States of America.*)

by recombination between one LTR-*ras* RNA and one complete Moloney virus RNA linked in a heterodimer[55] (just as illustrated for the proposed chromosomal DNA recombinations shown in FIG. 3). However, this RNA model did not exclude as the mechanism of virus regeneration an alternate interpretation that proposes illegitimate DNA recombination between sequences flanking the incomplete LTR-*ras* provirus.[58]

In order to distinguish between RNA and DNA recombination as the mechanism of virus regeneration, we have deleted the U3 element of the only LTR of the incomplete LTR-*ras* provirus and, in some constructs, we have substituted deleted retroviral promoter elements of a heterologous SV40 promoter to enhance transcription for heterodimer formation (FIG. 4). Indeed, the cells transfected with U3-deleted LTR-*ras* DNAs were transformed and the amount of LTR-*ras* RNA packaged by the helper virus was as much—or nearly as much—as that in the wild-type Harvey sarcoma virus infection.[58] However, virus recovery was observed only with LTR-*ras* proviruses that carried one complete LTR (FIG. 4). Since the RNAs transcribed from the intact and deleted provirus templates are identical, heterodimer recombination, if it involves RNA, should have occurred with all constructs capable of expressing RNA (FIG. 4). Because this was not observed, it follows that virus regeneration involved DNA recombination.[58]

The process proposed in this model is consistent with the process involved in the excision of SV40 or lambda viruses from host cells[59] or the spontaneous amplification of chromosomal regions observed in gene amplification.[60] An LTR-*ras* probe with one defective LTR cannot, of course, regenerate a functional virus by this mechanism because an intact LTR is essential for a viable virus. Thus, there is no evidence against the view that the generation of retroviral *onc* genes proceeds via DNA recombination. However, there is independent evidence for DNA recombination, namely, the occurrence of intron sequences in some retroviral *onc* genes[58] or the existence of partial recombinants in cells, like the LTR-proto-*myc* hybrid genes with oncogenic potential in avian lymphomas (FIG. 2).

It would appear then, that comparative analyses of viral *onc* genes and cellular proto-*onc* genes have not identified pre-existing cellular oncogenes. Instead, these analyses have revealed that there are fundamental genetic differences between viral *onc* genes and proto-*onc* genes and that viral *onc* genes are the products of rare illegitimate recombinations. In view of the viral model and the clonal chromosome abnormalities in almost all cancer cells, it is proposed that cancer genes are generated *de novo* by rare illegitimate recombinations. To identify either autonomous cancer genes or combinations of mutually dependent ones, assays must be developed for transformation to malignancy of diploid cells.

SUMMARY

Retroviral *onc* genes are as yet the only proven cancer genes. They are generated by rare illegitimate recombinations between retroviruses and cellular genes, termed proto-*onc* genes. The claims that these proto-*onc* genes cause virus-free cancers upon "activation" by mechanisms that do not alter their germline structure are challenged. Instead, it is proposed that retroviral *onc* genes and cellular cancer genes are generated *de novo* by illegitimate recombinations that alter the germline structure of normal genes.

REFERENCES

1. Duesberg, P. H. 1985. Activated oncogenes: Sufficient or necessary for cancer? Science **228:** 669-677.
2. Duesberg, P. H. 1987. Cancer genes: Rare recombinants instead of activated oncogenes. Proc. Natl. Acad. Sci. USA **84:** 2117-2124.
3. Duesberg, P. H. 1987. Latent cellular oncogenes: The paradox dissolves. J. Cell Sci. Suppl. **7:** 169-187.
4. Duesberg, P. H. 1987. Cancer genes generated by rare chromosomal rearrangements rather than activation of oncogenes. Med. Oncol. Tumor Pharmacother. **4:** 163-175.
5. Tooze, J., Ed. 1973. The Molecular Biology of Tumor Viruses. Cold Spring Harbor Laboratory. Cold Spring Harbor, N.Y.
6. Weiss, R., N. Teich, H. Varmus & J. Coffin, Eds. 1985. RNA Tumor Viruses: Molecular Biology of Tumor Viruses, 2nd ed. Cold Spring Harbor Laboratory. Cold Spring Harbor, N.Y.
7. Duesberg, P. H. 1987. Retroviruses as carcinogens and pathogens: Expectations and reality. Cancer Res. **47:** 1199-1220.
8. Martin, G. S. & P. H. Duesberg. 1972. The α-subunit on the RNA of transforming avian tumor viruses: (I) Occurrence in different virus strains; (II) Spontaneous loss resulting in non-transforming variants. Virology **47:** 494-497.
9. Coffin, J. M., P. N. Tsichlis, C. S. Barker, S. Voynow & H. L. Robinson. 1980. Variation in avian retrovirus genomes. Ann. N. Y. Acad. Sci. **354:** 410-425.
10. Temin, H. M. 1988. Evolution of cancer genes as a mutation-driven process. Cancer Res. **48:** 1697-1701.
11. Duesberg, P. H. & P. K. Vogt. 1970. Differences between the ribonucleic acids of transforming and nontransforming avian tumor viruses. Proc. Natl. Acad. Sci. USA **67:** 1673-1680.
12. Duesberg, P. H. 1979. Transforming genes of retroviruses. Cold Spring Harbor Symp. Quant. Biol. **44:** 13-27.
13. Duesberg, P. H. 1983. Retroviral transforming genes in normal cells? Nature **304:** 219-226.
14. Zinder, N. D. 1953. Infective heredity in bacteria. Cold Spring Harbor Symp. Quant. Biol. **18:** 261-269.
15. Scolnick, E. M., F. Rands, P. Williams & W. P. Parks. 1973. Studies on the nucleic acid sequences of Kirsten sarcoma virus: A model for formation of a mammalian RNA-containing sarcoma virus. J. Virol. **12:** 458-463.
16. Scolnick, E. M. & W. P. Parks. 1974. Harvey sarcoma virus: A second murine type C sarcoma virus with rat genetic information. J. Virol. **13:** 1211-1219.
17. Mellon, P., A. Pawson, K. Bister, G. S. Martin & P. H. Duesberg. 1978. Specific RNA sequences and gene products of MC29 avian acute leukemia virus. Proc. Natl. Acad. Sci. USA **75:** 5874-5878.
18. Watson, D. K., E. P. Reddy, P. H. Duesberg & T. S. Papas. 1983. Nucleotide sequence analysis of the chicken c-*myc* gene reveals homologous and unique regions by comparison with the transforming gene of avian myelocytomatosis virus MC29, Δ*gag-myc*. Proc. Natl. Acad. Sci. USA **80:** 2146-2150.
19. Bishop, J. M. 1981. Enemies within: The genesis of retrovirus oncogenes. Cell **23:** 5-6.
20. Weiss, R., N. Teich, H. Varmus & J. Coffin, Eds. 1982. RNA Tumor Viruses: Molecular Biology of Tumor Viruses. Cold Spring Harbor Laboratory. Cold Spring Harbor, N.Y.
21. Watson, J. D., N. H. Hopkins, J. W. Roberts, J. A. Steitz & A. M. Weiner. 1987. *In* Molecular Biology of the Gene. Vol. II. Benjamin Publishing Co. New York.
22. Weiss, R. A. 1986. The oncogene concept. Cancer Rev. **2:** 1-17.
23. Knudson, A. G., Jr. 1985. Hereditary cancer, oncogenes, and antioncogenes. Cancer Res. **45:** 1437-1443.
24. Friend, S. H., R. Bernards, S. Rogelj, R. A. Weinberg, J. M. Rapaport, D. M. Albert & T. P. Dryja. 1986. A human DNA segment with properties of the gene that predisposes to retinoblastoma and osteosarcoma. Nature **323:** 643-646.
25. Varmus, H. 1984. The molecular genetics of cellular oncogenes. Annu. Rev. Genet. **18:** 553-612.

26. BISHOP, J. M. 1987. The molecular genetics of cancer. Science **235:** 305-311.
27. MARSHALL, C. 1985. Human oncogenes. *In* RNA Tumor Viruses: Molecular Biology of Tumor Viruses, 2nd ed. R. Weiss, N. Teich, H. Varmus & J. Coffin, Eds.: 487-558. Cold Spring Harbor Laboratory. Cold Spring Harbor, N.Y.
28. BARBACID, M. 1986. Mutagens, oncogenes and cancer. Trends Genet. **2:** 188-192.
29. NUSSE, R. 1988. The *int* genes in mammary tumorigenesis and in normal development. Trends Genet. **4:** 291-295.
30. TABIN, C. J., S. M. BRADLEY, C. I. BARGMANN, R. A. WEINBERG, A. G. PAPAGEORGE, E. M. SCOLNICK, R. DHAR, D. R. LOWY & E. H. CHANG. 1982. Mechanism of activation of a human oncogene. Nature **300:** 143-149.
31. REDDY, E. P., R. K. REYNOLDS, E. SANTOS & M. BARACID. 1982. A point mutation is responsible for the acquisition of transforming properties by the T24 human bladder carcinoma oncogene. Nature **300:** 149-152.
32. HAYWARD, W. S., B. G. NEEL & S. M. ASTRIN. 1981. Activation of a cellular *onc* gene by promoter insertion in ALV-induced lymphoid leukosis. Nature **290:** 475-480.
33. PAYNE, G. S., J. M. BISHOP & H. E. VARMUS. 1982. Multiple arrangements of viral DNA and an activated host oncogene in bursal lymphomas. Nature **295:** 209-214.
34. CAIRNS, J. 1978. Cancer: Science and Society. W. H. Freeman and Company. San Francisco.
35. HEIM, S., N. MANDAHL & F. MITELMAN. 1988. Genetic convergence and divergence in tumor progression. Cancer Res. **48:** 5911-5916.
36. CICHUTEK, K. & P. H. DUESBERG. 1986. Harvey *ras* genes transform without mutant codons, apparently activated by truncation of a 5′ exon (exon-1). Proc. Natl. Acad. Sci. USA **83:** 2340-2344.
37. CICHUTEK, K. & P. H. DUESBERG. 1989. Recombinant Balb and Harvey sarcoma viruses with normal proto-*ras* coding regions transform embryo cells in culture and cause tumors in mice. J. Virol. **63:** 1377-1383.
38. ZHOU, R.-P. & P. H. DUESBERG. 1988. *myc* protooncogene linked to retroviral promoter, but not to enhancer, transforms embryo cells. Proc. Natl. Acad. Sci. USA **85:** 2924-2928.
39. PFAFF, S. & P. H. DUESBERG. 1988. Two autonomous *myc* oncogenes in avian carcinoma virus OK10. J. Virol. **62:** 3703-3709.
40. LAND, H., L. F. PARADA & R. A. WEINBERG. 1983. Cellular oncogenes and multistep carcinogenesis. Science **222:** 771-778.
41. BALMAIN, A., M. RAMSDEN, G. T. BOWDEN & J. SMITH. 1984. Activation of the mouse cellular Harvey-*ras* gene in chemically induced benign skin papillomas. Nature **307:** 658-660.
42. REYNOLDS, S. H., S. J. STOWERS, R. R. MARONPOT, M. W. ANDERSON & S. A. AARONSON. 1986. Detection and identification of activated oncogenes in spontaneously occurring benign and malignant hepatocellular tumors of the B6C3F1 mouse. Proc. Natl. Acad. Sci. USA **83:** 33-37.
43. SINN, E., W. MULLER, P. PATTENGALE, I. TEPLER, R. WALLACE & P. LEDER. 1987. Coexpression of MMTV/v-Ha-*ras* and MMTV/c-*myc* genes in transgenic mice: Synergistic action of oncogenes *in vivo.* Cell **49:** 465-475.
44. ADAMS, J. M., A. W. HARRIS, C. A. PINKERT, L. M. CORCORAN, W. S. ALEXANDER, S. CORY, R. D. PALMITER & R. L. BRINSTER. 1985. The c-*myc* oncogene driven by immunoglobulin enhancers induces lymphoid malignancy in transgenic mice. Nature **318:** 533-538.
45. ALEXANDER, W. S., J. W. SCHRADER & J. ADAMS. 1987. Expression of the c-*myc* oncogene under control of an immunoglobulin enhancer in Eμ-*myc* transgenic mice. Mol. Cell Biol. **7:** 1436-1444.
46. WOLMAN, S. R. 1983. Karyotypic progression in human tumors. Cancer Metastasis Rev. **2:** 257-293.
47. TRENT, J. M. 1984. Chromosomal alterations in human solid tumors: Implications of the stem cell model to cancer cytogenetics. Cancer Surv. **3:** 393-422.
48. LEVAN, A. 1956. Chromosomes in cancer tissue. Ann. N. Y. Acad. Sci. **63:** 774-792.
49. LEDER, P., J. BATTEY, G. LENOIR, C. MOULDING, W. MURPHY, M. POTTER, T. STEWART & R. TAUB. 1983. Translocations among antibody genes in human cancer. Science **227:** 765-771.

50. KLEIN, G. 1983. Specific chromosomal translocations and the genesis of B-cell derived tumors in mice and men. Cell **32:** 311-315.
51. BIGGAR, R. J., E. C. LEE, F. K. NKRUMAH & J. WHANG-PENG. 1981. Direct cytogenetic studies by needle stick aspiration of Burkitt's lymphoma in Ghana, West Africa. J. Natl. Cancer Inst. **67:** 769-776.
52. BERGER, R., A. BERNHEIM, F. SIGAUX, F. VALENSI, M.-T. DANIEL & G. FLANDRIN. 1985. Two Burkitt's lymphomas with chromosome 6 long arm deletions. Cancer Genet. Cytogenet. **15:** 159-167.
53. GODDARD, A. D., H. BALAKIER, M. CANTON, J. DUNN, J. SQUIRE, E. REYES, A. BECKER, R. A. PHILLIPS & B. L. GALLIE. 1988. Infrequent genomic rearrangement and normal expression of the putative Rb1 gene in retinoblastoma tumors. Mol. Cell. Biol. **8**(5): 2082-2088.
54. COFFIN, J. M. 1979. Structure, replication, and recombination of retrovirus genomes: Some unifying hypotheses. J. Gen. Virol. **42:** 1-26.
55. GOLDFARB, M. P. & R. A. WEINBERG. 1981. Structure of the proviruses within NIH 3T3 cells transfected with Harvey sarcoma virus DNA. J. Virol. **38:** 125-135.
56. DUESBERG, P. H. 1968. Physical properties of Rous sarcoma RNA. Proc. Natl. Acad. Sci. USA **60:** 1511-1518.
57. MANGEL, W. F., H. DELIUS & P. H. DUESBERG. 1974. Structure and Molecular weight of the 60-70S RNA and the 30-40S RNA of the Rous sarcoma virus. Proc. Natl. Acad. Sci. USA **71:** 4541-4545.
58. GOODRICH, D. W. & P. H. DUESBERG. 1988. Retroviral transduction of oncogenic sequences involves viral DNA instead of RNA. Proc. Natl. Acad. Sci. USA **85:** 3733-3737.
59. HANAHAN, D., D. LANE, L. LIPSICH, M. WIGLER & M. BOTCHAN. 1980. Characteristics of an SV-40 plasmid recombinant and its movement into and out of the genome of a murine cell. Cell. **21:** 127-140.
60. SCHIMKE, R. T., S. W. SHERWOOD, A. B. HILL & R. N. JOHNSTON. 1986. Overreplication and recombination of DNA in higher eukaryotes: Potential consequences and biological implications. Proc. Natl. Acad. Sci. USA **83:** 2157-2161.
61. ZHOU, R.-P., N. KAN, T. PAPAS & P. DUESBERG. 1985. Mutagenesis of avian carcinoma virus MH2: Only one of two potential transforming genes (*gag-myc*) transforms fibroblasts. Proc. Natl. Acad. Sci. USA **82:** 6389-6393.
62. RAPP, U. R., J. L. CLEVELAND, T.N. FREDRICKSON, K. L. HOLMES, H. C. MORSE, III, H. W. JANSEN, T. PATSCHINSKY & K. BISTER. 1985. Rapid induction of hemopoietic neoplasms in newborn mice by a *raf(mil)/myc* recombinant murine retrovirus. J. Virol. **55:** 23-33.
63. ZERLIN, M., M. A. JULIUS, C. CERNI & K. B. MARCU. 1987. Elevated expression of an exogenous c-*myc* gene is insufficient for transformation and turmorigenic conversion of established fibroblasts. Oncogene **1:** 19-27.

CLOSING REMARKS

Leukemia, Viruses, Development, and the Real World

FRANK LILLY

Department of Genetics
Albert Einstein College of Medicine
Bronx, New York 10461

In the one-character play entitled *Dr. Kheal,* by María Irene Fornés, the professor asks his audience how to do a million little things, to which he answers: "One at a time." Next he asks how to do a million *big* things, to which he gives the same answer. Finally, he asks how to do *one* big thing and then chuckles at his own wit and profundity. For an answer, he draws an esoteric shape on the blackboard and begins to fill it from the bottom with little dots.

It is not given to us all to accomplish even one really big thing in our careers, but Charlotte Friend managed to do at least two of them. The first was, of course, her discovery of the murine retrovirus isolate that bears her name, and this accomplishment involved a long battle and a lot of determination on her part. For most of us, it is difficult to place ourselves back in time to the mid-1950s and to register the fact that, in the scientific climate of that time, the concept that some cancers might be caused by viruses was considered to be absurd. A brief review of the history of some "cancer viruses" may help to illustrate the difficulties that necessitated Charlotte's battle.

At the time of Charlotte's discovery of her virus, almost fifty years had elapsed since Peyton Rous's discovery of a virus that caused tumors in chickens. Rous had had his own severe problems in gaining acceptance of his finding. One contemporary has been quoted as saying to him that if those growths in the chickens were cancer, his isolate was not a virus, and if his isolate was a virus, his chickens did not have cancer. Rous himself abandoned the study of his virus after some years, a fact that reflects in part this sort of negative response from his colleagues and in part the primitive state of virology in those early decades of this century.

Another cancer-inducing virus was discovered in the late 1930s and extensively studied in the 1940s by John Bittner. This virus gave rise to breast tumors in mice. If you will go back and review Bittner's numerous papers in this area, you will note that he never once referred in print, as we now do, to the mammary tumor *virus,* but rather he always called it the mammary tumor *agent.* For good or bad reasons, he was under the clear impression that to call his agent a virus in public, which I am told he would do in private, was a politically dangerous action, not good for one's career.

Finally, we come to the crucial studies of Ludwik Gross that resulted in the isolation from high-leukemia AKR mice of a virus that caused lymphoid tumors in some low-leukemia mice. Gross's work preceded Charlotte's by only a small number of years, and at the time she discovered her virus, his findings had still not found acceptance among many researchers in the cancer field. This was in part because Gross's early virus isolates were relatively weak in their leukemogenic activities and also in part because early efforts to replicate his work in other laboratories had not yet proved successful, due to the use of different substrains of mice from those that Gross had used. But another reason for the lack of acceptance of his work was the firm conviction that the leukemias of AKR mice were caused by genetic factors, and no one was prepared at that time for the idea that a virus might become an integral part of the host genome and behave there much as any other genetic factor behaves.

It was in this scientific climate that Charlotte's virus was discovered and in this climate that she submitted her findings to the *Journal of Experimental Medicine.* There it sat on the desk of Peyton Rous, an editor of the journal, for a year of discussions and alterations before it was finally published. During that year, Charlotte presented her work at a meeting of the American Association for Cancer Research, and she never forgot the ferocity of the attacks from the audience to which she was subjected after the presentation.

I never got around to asking Charlotte about a very peculiar phrase in the title of her *Journal of Experimental Medicine* paper; it refers to cell-free transmission of a disease "having the character of a leukemia." What an odd way of saying it! I can't believe that she seriously doubted that the disease *was* a leukemia, and thus I have always wondered if that circumlocution might have been imposed on her, perhaps by Rous himself.

Even after publication of her paper, acceptance of the idea that her virus caused cancer was very far from universal. One factor in this reluctance was the criterion that malignant cells be transplantable in mice of the same strain as the tumor-bearing mouse; several years elapsed before the proper conditions were discovered for obtaining transplantable Friend virus-induced tumors. By this time, Gross's work had been successfully repeated by others, and Gross himself had developed much more potent strains of his leukemogenic virus. These developments together with Charlotte's work had, by the early 1960s, finally imposed the undeniable existence of cancer-inducing viruses on the reluctant field of cancer research and set the stage for the gradual expansion of the study of retroviruses into what has become a vast area for investigation, with importance far beyond the subject of cancer.

Although she was quite rigorous in dealing with her experiments and with her ideas about their interpretation, Charlotte took very personally the attacks on her work and the off-hand dismissal that it frequently elicited. Could her treatment have been related to the fact that she was still a handsome young single woman, with a strong accent from Manhattan's lower East Side, who would have been perfectly acceptable doing routine technical operations but who had no business upsetting the applecart with novel and important discoveries? Well, yes, of course; these were the 1950s, the Eisenhower years, when most women still "knew their place."

Nevertheless, the fact remains that the idea of cancer viruses was indeed a revolutionary one and not easy to swallow, even though it was not exactly a fresh one. It is with some embarrassment that I recall instances when I tended to dismiss at first certain now-classical findings as being unlikely—suppressor T cells, natural killer cells, for example—inconvenient things, they seemed to me, that might just go away if I ignored them. For this reason I can find just a little empathy with those early doubters, as I can with those who cannot quite bring themselves to believe, for example, that a diverse array of mechanisms might conduce one or more of a particular subset of cellular genes to participate in the generation of the malignant phenotype.

Charlotte was in many ways one of the most generous scientists I have ever known. Nowadays, with science being the highly competitive field that it is, many of us find it useful to hang on to the reagents we develop as long as we can. Charlotte, to the contrary, was happy to pass on her virus, along with all of the know-how that she had learned in working with it, to anyone who showed an interest. And she was particularly eager to help out any young scientist who needed information and encouragement.

I recall my first interaction with her. I was at the time a Ph.D. student at the Sloan-Kettering Institute. After a lecture to the students, given by someone else, I asked a question that received a rather muddled answer. Charlotte, who had sat in on the lecture, came over to me, and we discussed the question at some length. Realizing that she also could not give an entirely satisfactory answer, she went away, did some library work, and came back to me later with a well worked-out answer. I've never forgotten that generosity, though I have quite forgotten what the question was.

Charlotte was a sensitive human being. She was sensitive to the feelings and problems of other people and would go out of her way to help solve those problems or, failing that, to console. She was also sensitive to slights and discourtesies that she received from other people. Many years after the incident, she expressed to me her irritation with a scientist who, having managed to adapt her virus to be highly leukemogenic in a mouse strain that Charlotte's early work had shown to be resistant, reported in a paper that, contrary to what Dr. Friend had published, her virus worked very well in those mice!

As we all know now, Friend virus includes both a replication-competent and a replication-defective retrovirus. For reasons that I never really understood, Charlotte resisted this finding for many years. Conceivably, she might have been right that her earliest isolates did not contain a defective virus, but as far as I know all existing sublines of the virus that have been examined do contain it. Charlotte and I used to joke about her reluctance to accept the defective virus. At one point I tried to convince her that she should be proud to have discovered not just one but in fact two viruses that were totally unique in the mouse leukemia virus world. But she would have nothing to do with that idea.

A few years ago, realizing that we were both going to the same meeting in Scotland, we decided to travel together. We rented a car and drove around for a day before the meeting and during a spell of playing hooky from one part of the meeting. I have to say that she was one of the most enjoyable travel companions I have ever had, with a strong feeling for seeing a part of the world new to both of us and with an enthusiasm for trying side roads, eating in unlikely places, and just going wherever our whims took us.

After Charlotte had at last won the battle and imposed the idea that her virus actually caused a kind of leukemia, her next major undertaking was to seek to identify what *kind* of leukemia it was. Here the battle was not so much with other scientists as it was with the problem itself. She was convinced that the tumor cells induced by her virus belonged to the erythrocytic lineage, and the pathological and morphological data, gathered by herself and others, lent considerable support to that idea. However, I recall a presentation by her on this subject at a conference in about 1965; this time her paper was received not with antagonism but rather with considerable indifference. She knew that one of the classical theories about cancer held that malignant cells were blocked in a particular stage of differentiation, and she searched high and low for a means to unblock her cells. In the process she found in the late 1960s a lot more evidence for her idea, such as some benzidine staining that indicated a modest production of hemoglobin in some cells of her tumor lines. But still, she hadn't yet been able to make out of this work her second "big thing."

The real answer finally came in 1970. Finding her virus had not been an accident, since she had done the experiment for precisely that purpose. But this time the finding was in part a stroke of serendipity, though we must remember that serendipitous discoveries generally come only to those who are prepared to recognize them. A close colleague had suggested to her the use of dimethyl sulfoxide for a purpose quite different from that of stimulating erythrocytic maturation. Charlotte noted that, after a brief residence in medium containing this chemical, cells of her tumor lines turned markedly pink. She had done it again, a second big thing, this time with the discovery of a means to unblock tumor cells and allow them to continue further down their destined pathway of differentiation.

There is no need for me to go into the far-ranging developments from this finding except to say that she was well aware of many of its implications. Soon after making her discovery, she was already musing about the possibility of what has come to be called differentiation therapy for cancer.

Charlotte is not forgotten and will not be forgotten for a long time to come. I speak for a host of people in saying simply that she was a dedicated scientist and a dedicated friend, and that we miss her.

Development of a Retrovirus Packaging System to Study *Fv-1* Restriction

LAWRENCE R. BOONE, CYNTHIA L. INNES, AND PAUL L. GLOVER[a]

National Institute of Environmental Health Sciences
Research Triangle Park, North Carolina 27709

Fv-1 restriction is generally observed in cell culture as a 100- to 1000-fold reduction in murine leukemia virus (MuLV) infectivity in cells of the restrictive *Fv-1* genotype. The mechanism of this host-range restriction is not known precisely, but it apparently involves some aspect of reverse transcription and integration.[1,2] Viruses that preferentially replicate in cells of the *Fv-1*^{n} genotype (prototype NIH Swiss) are designated N-tropic, whereas viruses that preferentially replicate in cells of the *Fv-1*^{b} genotype (prototype BALB/c) are designated B-tropic. N-tropic viruses are dominantly restricted by the *Fv-1*^{b} allele and B-tropic viruses are dominantly restricted by the *Fv-1*^{n} allele. The determinant for sensitivity to the *Fv-1* gene resides in *gag* protein p30, the (30 kDa) virion capsid protein.[3,4]

One of the controversial and confounding problems with respect to *Fv-1* is the phenomenon of multi-hit infectivity kinetics.[5] Some investigators argue that this is a fundamental property of the *Fv-1* mechanism and reflects abrogation of *Fv-1* by the initial infecting virus,[6] whereas others suggest that restriction is observed simply as a reduction of infectivity in restrictive hosts, with no requirement for two virus particles in order to initiate a successful infection.[7,8]

In order to carefully examine the kinetics of restriction, we have developed a system sensitive to *Fv-1* restriction in the absence of viral replication. We constructed a packaging mutant of N-tropic MuLV WN1802N by removal of the *cis*-acting packaging site located between the upstream long terminal repeat (LTR) and the start of the *gag* gene region.[9] Transfection of this mutant into mink CCL64 cells results in a cell line capable of packaging retrovirus vectors into ecotropic, *Fv-1* N-tropic virions. The system, designated N-PAC, contains the N-tropic MuLV packaging mutant construct and an antibiotic-selectable retrovirus vector, RSV-linker 1 (generously provided by Elwood Linney, Duke University). The assay involves antibiotic selection of cells which have been successfully infected with this vector. The effects of the *Fv-1* gene product are limited to a single round of reverse transcription and integration. This avoids the assay complications and compounded effects of multiple rounds of infection with replicating virus.

[a]Present address: Burroughs Wellcome Co., Research Triangle Park, North Carolina 27709.

TABLE 1. *Fv-1* Restriction of N-PAC

Virus	G418-Resistant CFU/ml[a]		
	AKR (*FV-1*^{nn})	SIM.R (*FV-1*^{bb})	N/B
RSV linker-1(N-PAC)	8.5×10^5	6.5×10^3	130
RSV linker-1(MoMuLV)	4.5×10^5	2.1×10^5	2.1

[a] 24 hr following infection, cultures were selected with G418 and colonies were stained and counted on day 14.

As shown in TABLE 1, the magnitude of restriction in restrictive SIM.R cells (*Fv-1*^{bb}) is approximately 100-fold compared to permissive AKR cells (*Fv-1*^{nn}). The NB-tropic Moloney MuLV was approximately 2-fold less infectious for SIM.R, possibly due to a previously unrecognized effect of *Fv-1*^{b} on NB-tropic virus but likely to reflect effects not related to *Fv-1*. Single-hit kinetics were observed in permissive and restrictive cells, suggesting that multi-hit kinetics may not be an essential feature of *Fv-1* restriction.

REFERENCES

1. YANG, W. K., J. O. KIGGANS, D.-M. YANG, C.-Y. OU, R. W. TENNANT, A. BROWN & R. H. BASSIN. 1980. Proc. Natl. Acad. Sci. USA **77:** 2994-2998.
2. JOLICOEUR, P. & E. RASSART. 1980. J. Virol. **33:** 183-195.
3. OU, C.-Y., L. R. BOONE, C.-K. KOH, R. W. TENNANT & W. K. YANG. 1983. J. Virol. **48:** 779-784.
4. DESGROSEILLERS, L. & P. JOLICOEUR. 1983. J. Virol. **48:** 685-696.
5. PINCUS, T., J. W. HARTLEY & W. P. ROWE. 1975. Virology **65:** 333-342.
6. DURAN-TROISE, G., R. H. BASSIN, A. REIN & B. I. GERWIN. 1977. Cell **10:** 479-488.
7. JOLICOEUR, P. & D. BALTIMORE. 1975. J. Virol. **16:** 1593-1598.
8. SCHUH, V., M. E. BLACKSTEIN & A. A. AXELRAD. 1976. J. Virol. **18:** 473-480.
9. MANN, R., R. C. MULLIGAN & D. BALTIMORE. 1983. Cell **33:** 153-159.

Differential Expression of *Fv-1* in Fibroblasts Derived from Embryonal Carcinoma Cells

CATHERINE K. HEITMAN, CYNTHIA L. INNES, ANTON M. JETTEN, AND LAWRENCE R. BOONE [a]

National Institute of Environmental Health Sciences Research Triangle Park, North Carolina 27709

The *Fv-1* locus in mice is the major genetic determinant influencing susceptibility to murine leukemia virus (MuLV) infection.[1] With few exceptions, mouse cells in culture exhibit *Fv-1* restriction. Typically, this is observed as a 100- to 1000-fold reduction in titer relative to cells of the permissive genotype.

Little is known about *Fv-1* gene expression is undifferentiated mouse embryonal carcinoma (EC) cell lines. Murine EC cell lines have been established from primary cell cultures of pluripotent teratocarcinomas. EC lines have the capacity to differentiate *in vitro* and have been proposed as models for normal cell differentiation. It has previously not been possible to demonstrate whether EC cells express *Fv-1* restriction, because MuLV replication is blocked at the transcriptional level in these cells. Recently, however, several retrovirus vectors have been constructed which are expressed in EC cells. One of these, designated RSV linker-1 (generously provided by Elwood Linney, Duke University), contains a *neo* resistance gene driven from a Rous sarcoma virus promoter/enhancer region.

RSV linker-1 rescued by N-, B-, and NB-tropic MuLV was used to determine the *Fv-1* phenotype of F9 and PCC4.aza1R. These two clonal, undifferentiated EC lines were derived from the 129 mouse strain, which carries the $Fv\text{-}1^{nr}$ allele. Our results indicate that F9 cells do express *Fv-1*; however, PCC4.aza1R cells are relatively permissive for all viruses tested, suggesting that *Fv-1* is not expressed in this line (TABLE 1).

We additionally determined the *Fv-1* phenotype of cells derived by differentiation of PCC4.aza1R cells by using the same G418-resistant colony assay, except with the MSV-DHFR-*neo* vector.[2] Retinoic acid (RA) is known to promote *in vitro* differentiation of PCC4.aza1R into mesenchymal cell types.[3] Subsequent 5-azacytidine (5-azaC) treatment further induces a preadipocyte phenotype in some cells, which differentiate into either brown or white fat cells when grown to confluence in the presence of insulin and dexamethasone. Three fibroblast cell lines (PCC4D2, PCC4D4, PCC4D7) and one epithelial cell line (Diff 5) derived by RA-induced differentiation of PCC4.aza1R cells were examined for their *Fv-1* phenotype. The quantitative assay for G418 resistance indicated that titers of NB-tropic (Moloney MuLV), N-tropic (Gross passage A and RFM MuLV), B-tropic (WN1802B) and amphotropic (4070A)

[a] To whom correspondence should be addressed at the National Institute of Environmental Health Sciences, P.O. Box 12233, Research Triangle Park, NC 27709.

TABLE 1. Analysis of *Fv-1* Phenotype in EC Cells and in Sublines after *in vitro* Differentiation

Cell Line	Cell Type	*Fv-1* Expression[a]
F9	EC	+
PCC4.aza1R	EC	−
PCC4D1	Preadipocyte	+
PCC4D2	Fibroblast	−
PCC4D4	Fibroblast	−
PCC4D7	Fibroblast	−
Diff 5	Epithelial	−

[a] *Fv-1* phenotype was established by G418-resistant colony assays following infection with an antibiotic-selectable vector rescued by viruses of N-, B-, and NB-tropism.

viruses in PCC4D2, D4, D7 and in Diff 5 were similar to those measured in SC-1 mouse cells, which are phenotypically silent for *Fv-1* (data summarized in TABLE 1). However, a preadipocyte cell line (PCC4D1) derived by simultaneous RA and 5-azaC treatment was found to exhibit a strong restriction of B-tropic MuLV and endogenous N-tropic (RFM) MuLV. This restriction pattern is characteristic of the *Fv-1*^{nr} allele carried by the 129 mouse strain. *Fv-1* expression and the preadipocyte phenotype are probably not linked, since 5-azaC-induced preadipocyte sublines from PCC4D4 and PCC4D7 fibroblasts (which, as reported above, do not express *Fv-1*) also do not express *Fv-1*.

Fv-1 appears to be induced in 1 of 5 lines differentiated from PCC4.aza1R cells. The differential expression of this gene in a closely matched set of cells makes it feasible to clone it by subtractive cDNA cloning techniques. The differentiation of EC cells is being further explored as a model for the control of *Fv-1* gene expression.

REFERENCES

1. JOLICOEUR, P. 1979. Curr. Top. Microbiol. Immunol. **86:** 68-122.
2. WILLIAMS, D. A., I. R. LEMISCHKA, D. G. NATHAN & R. C. MULLIGAN. 1984. Nature **310:** 476-480.
3. JETTEN, A. M., M. E. R. JETTEN & M. SHERMAN. 1979. Exp. Cell Res. **124:** 381-391.

Molecular and Biological Characterization of FLV Produced by Different Cell Lines

M. E. JOESTEN, M. E. ROYSTON, AND B. G.-T. POGO

Center for Experimental Cell Biology
Mount Sinai School of Medicine
New York, New York 10029

The molecular and biological properties of Friend leukemia virus (FLV) produced by different cell lines were investigated.

The SQA cell line, derived from the spleens of mice infected with FLV-A, yields a virus that remains leukemogenic in adult and newborn mice after serial passage *in vitro.*[1] When inoculated into mice, the SQA virus induced ecotropic and xenotropic transcripts in patterns that differed somewhat among the organs involved and between different stages of development (TABLE 1). These may be related to the pathogenicity of the virus. To identify the genomic sequences involved in leukemogenicity, the cDNA of the SQA virus and the activated endogenous viruses have been cloned. These studies are now in progress.

The same virus used to create the SQA cell line was also used to establish the rat cell line 3Y1+A, which lacks endogenous murine sequences.[2] The virus synthesized by this line became attenuated after serial passage *in vitro.* 3Y1+A cells were subcloned and the state of both the provirus and its transcripts were examined after serial passage *in vitro.* Analysis of the provirus revealed that rearrangements and multiple insertions occurred at later passages. Originally, one 9-kilobase insertion was observed; however, analysis of clones derived from this cell line showed the presence of a number of other inserts which varied with the passage number. The viral transcripts also differed when compared to the SQA cell line, which still produces a leukemogenic virus (TABLE 2). Some viral transcripts appeared to differ in size among the various subclones, and polyadenylated forms were undetectable in many of the subclones.

We can conclude that (1) expression of ecotropic and xenotropic sequences in livers and spleens of infected mice varies with the age of the animal and the organs involved; (2) activation of endogenous sequences may play an important role in leukemogenesis in the adult animal; (3) during serial passage of the clones of the 3Y1+A cell line, proviral inserts appear that may represent either rearrangements or multiple insertions of the original infecting virus; (4) there appears to be a correlation between the attenuation of leukemogenicity and the decrease of viral expression below the level of detectability; and (5) no xenotropic sequences are ever found in the infected rat cells.

In this work we attempted to analyze the pattern of FLV-A expression in mice and in a rat cell line that lacks endogenous murine viruses. This viral isolate differs from the molecularly cloned FLV in that it is active in both adult and newborn mice, without the participation of a defective virus. However, it is possible that the activation

TABLE 1. Comparison of Proviral Sequences and Their Expression in SQA Cells and in Tissues from SQA Virus-Infected Animals

	Common Bands[a]		Bands Not in Common[a]	
	Clone 57 (ecotropic)	Clone 56-82 (xenotropic)	Clone 57 (ecotropic)	Clone 56-82 (xenotropic)
DNA				
SQA cells and infected tissues	9, 5.9, 5.4, 4.1, 2.9, 2.0 kb	6.4, 5.1, 3.5 kb		original spleen has 4.5 and 3 kb; other spleens have 3.8 kb
Control tissues	9, 5.9, 2.9, 2.0 kb	6.4, 5.1, 4.5, 3.5 kb	adult spleen has 4.1 kb; adult liver has 5.1 kb	
RNA transcripts				
SQA cells and infected tissues (all but adult liver)	9.5, 6.2, 4.5, 3.2, 1.9 kb (2nd passage spleens and newborn liver lack 6.2 kb)	6.5, 4.8, 3.5, 2.9, 1.9 kb (2nd passage spleens lack 6.5 kb; 2nd passage newborn liver has only 3.5 kb)		
Control tissues	only a faint band visible at 9.5 kb was detected	none detected		

[a] Southern blots of 10 μg of *Kpn* I-digested DNA or Northern blots containing 15 μg of total cellular RNA were hybridized with clone 57, a plasmid containing a full-length FLV with 1 LTR, or with clone 56-82, a xenotropic sequence-specific probe. The values are given in kilobase pairs for DNA and kilobases for RNA.

TABLE 2. Comparison of FLV Expression in Cell Lines of Murine and Rat Origin

Cells Lines	Total RNA[a]		Poly(A)$^+$ RNA[a]	
	Common Species	Unique Species	Common Species	Unique Species
Murine				
SQA	9.4, 4.5, 3.2, 1.9 kb	6.2 kb, 6.8 kb	9.4 kb	6.2 kb, 6.8 kb
5-86[b]				
Rat				
3Y1 + A	9.4, 4.5, 3.5, 1.9 kb		9.4 kb	3.6 kb
clone 24A			none detected	
clone H12			none detected	
clone A5	9.5, 4.8, 3.5, 2.0 kb		none detected	
clone E4			none detected	
H12 subclones				
MB2	9.5, 4.8, 3.5, 2.0 kb		—	—
MC5			—	—
MD1			—	—

[a] Northern blots of 10-50 μg of total cellular RNA or 2 μg of poly(A)$^+$ RNA were hybridized to an ^{35}S-labeled probe, FLV-clone 57. Values given for hybridizing RNA bands are in kilobases (kb). *Dash* indicates assay not done.

[b] Cell line 5-86 is a weakly leukemogenic murine cell line.

of endogenous viruses may play a role in this effect; or, it may simply accompany this disease state. Further work, including analysis of the molecularly cloned viruses and the use of specific oligonucleotide probes, will help us to gain an understanding of the role of endogenous sequences.

REFERENCES

1. Friend, C., B. G.-T. Pogo & J. G. Holland. 1984. Proc. Natl. Acad. Sci. USA **81:** 1831-1834.
2. Brown, E. H., M. Zajak-Kaye, B. G.-T. Pogo & C. Friend. 1985. Proc. Natl. Acad. Sci. USA **82:** 5925-5929.

HIV Infection of Neural Cells

J. M. HAROUSE,[a] M. LAUGHLIN, J. A. HOXIE,
J. Q. TROJANOWSKI, AND F. GONZALEZ-SCARANO

Departments of Neurology, Microbiology, Medicine, and Pathology
University of Pennsylvania Medical Center
Philadelphia, Pennsylvania 19104

The type 1 human immunodeficiency virus (HIV-1), the primary etiologic agent of the acquired immunodeficiency syndrome (AIDS), has been implicated in AIDS-associated encephalopathy.[3,4,7,9] The pathogenesis of this encephalopathy is unclear. Results from *in situ* hybridization with genomic probes suggest that cells of the macrophage/microglial lineage actively produce HIV within the central nervous system.[9,14] However, a number of investigators have also identified glial and endothelial cells as HIV-infected, using both *in situ* hybridization and antigen detection techniques.[13]

Using a cell culture model, we have attempted to define the nature of the HIV neural cell infection in terms of entry pathway, latency, and induction of viral replication. Several cell lines and primary cell cultures representing distinct cell types of central nervous system (CNS) origin, namely, choroid plexus, gliomas, and medulloblastomas (MED) were infected with HIV-1_{IIIB} (TABLE 1). To assess whether a specific cell type or cell surface molecule was associated with infection, we screened cells of different origin that expressed a variety of internal and surface markers. Characteristics including the cell-surface expression of histocompatibility antigens or the expression of lymphoid antigens like CD4 could not be correlated with HIV-1 infectability. Characteristics defining neural cell types, like the presence of glial fibrillary acidic protein or neurofilament proteins, also showed no correlation with infectability.

As TABLE 1 indicates, both "neuronal", and "glial" cells were infectable, and choroid plexus fibroblasts were also capable of harboring virus which could be rescued. All infectable CNS-derived cells used, except MED 341, produced latent viral infections detectable only by cocultivation with an indicator, CD4-positive cell line, SUP-T1.[5,8,11,12] Virus could be rescued by cocultivation months after initial infection; however, with the exception of MED 341, neither infectious virus nor viral antigen could be detected in unstimulated cultures. The MED 341 cell line produced both virus and $p24^{gag}$ protein antigen ($p24^{gag}$) detectable in the medium after infection. This cell line is unusual: in contrast to the others, it may contain a truncated CD4 protein.

We then assessed the ability of serum containing neutralizing activity to inhibit infection of three of these cell lines: MED 217, U373 and DAOY. As shown in TABLE 2, there was no evidence that pretreatment of the viral inoculum with low dilutions of serum containing neutralizing activity had any effect on the recovery of virus after cocultivation. We determined that the serum had neutralizing activity by infecting

[a] Address for correspondence: 209 Johnson Pavilion, 36th and Hamilton Walk, University of Pennsylvania, Philadelphia, PA 19104-6076.

TABLE 1. Infection of CNS-Derived Cells by HIV-1

Cell	Type[a]	p24[b]	Virus[c]	Latent Infection[d]
MED 217	Neuron/glial[e]	−	−	+
U373	Glial	−	−	+
DAOY	Neuronal	−	−	+
Choroid plexus	?Fibroblast	−	−	+
HF-1	Glial	−	−	+
MED 341	Neuron/glial	+	+	+
U251	Glial	−	−	±
HTB138	Glial	−	−	−
MED 283	Neuron	−	−	−

[a] Cell type was determined by the use of a number of cell markers, and, in the case of U373 and choroid plexus cells, by electron microscopy.

[b] Production of p24 *gag* protein antigen: present in medium after infection.

[c] Production of HIV virus: present in medium after infection.

[d] Presence of latent HIV infection: virus could be rescued by cocultivation with an indicator cell line.

[e] Recent data from other laboratories indicates that this cell is of muscle origin.

HeLa T4 cells[10] and assaying for the production of $p24^{gag}$ with an antigen-capture assay on a daily basis for one week. A 1:100 dilution of the serum resulted in a > 10-fold decrease in the production of p24 in the supernatant.

In addition, we attempted to inhibit the infection of U373 and MED 217 cells by pre-incubating the virus inoculum with a preparation of soluble CD4 (sCD4).[1,2] For these experiments, 100 ng/ml of sCD4 was incubated with 2×10^4 tissue-culture infectious doses of HIV-1_{IIIb} for 1 hr at room temperature, then inoculated on the appropriate cell line and incubated for 2 hr at 37°C. Cocultivation with SUP-T1 cells at 7 days resulted in the development of cytopathic effect in treated and untreated cultures 8-9 days later.

These results suggest that HIV-1 infection of CNS-derived tumor cells involves a pathway which is distinct from the lymphoid pathway, since we could not block infection with antibodies against CD4 nor with soluble CD4 preparations. The latent infection of CNS cells *in vivo* may provide a reservoir of virus available to infect circulating lymphoid and monocytic cells.

TABLE 2. Effect of Soluble CD4 (sCD4) or Antibody to HIV on Infection of CNS-derived Cells by HIV-1[a]

		Antibody	
Cell	sCD4	HIV[b]	CD4[c]
U373	+	+	+
DAOY	ND	+	ND
MED 217	+	+	ND

[a] Infection by HIV was assessed as recovery of virus after cocultivation of latently infected cells with an indicator cell line. +, virus recovered; ND, not done.

[b] HIV: human HIV^+ antisera.

[c] CD4: anti-CD4 rabbit polyclonal antibody, AA 187-218[6] (courtesy of Dr. B. Jameson).

REFERENCES

1. DALGLEISH, A. G., P. C. L. BEVERLY, P. R. CLAPHAM, D. H. CRAWFORD, M. F. GREAVES & R. A. WEISS. 1984. The CD4 (T4) antigen is an essential component of the receptor for the AIDS retrovirus. Nature **312:** 763-767.
2. DEEN, K. C., J. S. MCDOUGAL, R. INACKER, G. FOLENA-WASSERMAN, J. ARTHROS, J. ROSENBERG, P. J. MADDON, R. AXEL & R. W. SWEET. 1988. A soluble form of CD4 (T4) protein inhibits AIDS virus infection. Nature **331:** 82-84.
3. GABUZDA, D. H., D. D. HO, S. M. DE LA MONTE, M. S. HIRSCH, T. R. ROTA & R. A. SOBEL. 1986. Immunohistochemical identification of HTLV-III antigen in brains of patients with AIDS. Ann. Neurol. **20:** 289-295.
4. GABUZDA, D. H. & M. S. HIRSCH. 1987. Neurologic manifestations of infection with human immunodeficiency virus. Ann. Intern. Med. **107:** 383-391.
5. HOXIE, J. A., J. D. ALPERS, D. RACKHOWSKY, K. HUEBNER, B. S. HAGGARTY, A. J. CEDARBAUM & J. C. REED. 1986. Alterations in T4 (CD4) protein and mRNA synthesis in cells infected with HIV. Science **234:** 1123-1127.
6. JAMESON, B. A., P. E. RAO, L. I. KONG, B. HAHN, G. SHAW, L. E. HOOD & S. B. KENT. 1988. Location and chemical synthesis of a binding site for HIV-1 on the CD4 protein. Science **240:** 1335-1339.
7. JOHNSON, R. T. & J. C. MCARTHUR. 1986. AIDS and the brain. Trends Neurosci. **9:** 91-94.
8. KLATZMANN, D., E. CHAMPAGNE & S. CHAMARET. 1984. T-lymphocyte T4 molecule behaves as the receptor for human retrovirus LAV. Nature **312:** 767-768.
9. KOENIG, S., H. E. GENDELMAN, J. M. ORENSTEIN, M. C. DEL CONTO, G. H. PEZESHKPUR, M. YUNGBLUTH, F. JANOTTA, A. ASKAMITI & A. S. FAUCI. 1986. Detection of AIDS virus in macrophages in brain tissue from AIDS patients with encephalopathy. Science **233:** 1089-1093.
10. MADDON, P. J., A. G. DALGLEISH, J. S. MCDOUGAL, P. R. CLAPHAM, R. A. WEISS & R. AXEL. 1986. The T4 gene encodes the AIDS virus receptor and is expressed in the immune system and the brain. Cell **47:** 333-348.
11. MADDON, P. J., D. R. LITTMAN, M. GODFREY, D. E. MADDON, L. CHESS & R. AXEL. 1985. The isolation and nucleotide sequence of a cDNA encoding the T cell surface protein T4: A new member of the immunoglobulin gene family. Cell **42:** 93-104.
12. MCDOUGAL, J. S., M. S. KENNEDY, J. N. SLIGH, S. P. CORT, A. MAWLE & J. K. A. NICHOLSON. 1986. Binding of HTLV-III/LAV to $T4^+$ cells by a complex of 110k viral protein and the T4 molecule. Science **231:** 382-385.
13. WILEY, C. A., R. D. SCHRIER, J. A. NELSON, P. W. LAMPERT & M. B. A. OLDSTONE. 1986. Cellular localization of human immunodeficiency virus infection within the brains of acquired immune deficiency syndrome patients. Proc. Natl. Acad. Sci. USA **83:** 7089-7093.
14. WOOD, G. S., N. L. WARNER, R. A. WARNKE. 1983. Anti-leu-3/T4 antibodies react with cells of monocyte/macrophage and Langerhans lineage. J. Immunol. **131:** 212-216.

Identification and Purification of Multiple HTLV-I Tax-Inducible Enhancer Binding Proteins

TSE-HUA TAN AND ROBERT G. ROEDER

Laboratory of Biochemistry and Molecular Biology
The Rockefeller University
1230 York Avenue
New York, New York 10021

Human T cell leukemia virus type I (HTLV-I) has been identified as the etiological agent of adult T cell leukemia/lymphoma (ATL) and appears to be involved in the chronic neurological disease, tropical spastic paraparesis (also called HTLV-I-associated myelopathy). HTLV-I encodes a 40-42 kDa nuclear protein, named tax, that acts in *trans* to increase the rate of transcription from the HTLV-I[1] and the interleukin-2 receptor[2] promoter. The HTLV-I promoter contains three copies of a 21-base pair (bp) repeat (hereafter called tax-responsive element or TRE) that is involved both in basal level expression and in tax-mediated induction.[3] Recent results indicate that tax does not interact directly with the TREs but rather that host-cell proteins mediate the tax response.[2] To study the biochemical mechanism(s) of the transcriptional activation mediated by tax, we have undertaken a systematic study of the nuclear factors that bind to the HTLV-I TRE.

The gel-retardation assay was used to screen HeLa nuclear extract-derived chromatographic fractions for proteins that bind specifically to the HTLV-I TRE. Three specific protein-DNA complexes, named B1, B2 and B3, were detected (FIG. 1a). The nuclear factors responsible for B1, B2, and B3 are designated TREB-1, TREB-2, and TREB-3, respectively. TREB stands for HTLV-I *t*ax *r*esponsive-*e*lement-*b*inding protein. Mutations in the center of the TRE (FIG. 1b) disrupt both the formation of the three protein-DNA complexes *in vitro* (FIGS. 1c and 1d) and expression from this promoter *in vivo* (see accompanying paper by TAN, JIA AND ROEDER, this volume.). TREB-3 bound more avidly to a multimerized TRE than to a single copy TRE (FIG. 1d), while the other two factors, TREB-1 and TREB-2, bound equally well to either of these. The factors responsible for complexes B1, B2, and B3 were totally or partially purified according to the scheme shown in FIGURE 2. TREB-1 has been purified to near homogeneity by affinity chromatography on a TRE-oligonucleotide column, and its binding activity was localized to a protein of 43-35 kDa (data not shown).

We have thus identified and either partially or completely purified three nuclear factors that bind to the TREs within the HTLV-I promoter. The affinity-purified TREB-1 was shown to activate transcription from the HTLV-I promoter *in vitro* (data not shown) and is a good candidate for the factor that mediates either basal activation or the *trans*-activation by tax *in vivo.* However, this does not preclude the possibility that TREB-2 or TREB-3 might also be involved in either basal or tax-induced transcription. A more interesting possibility is that distinct TREBs are involved in basal

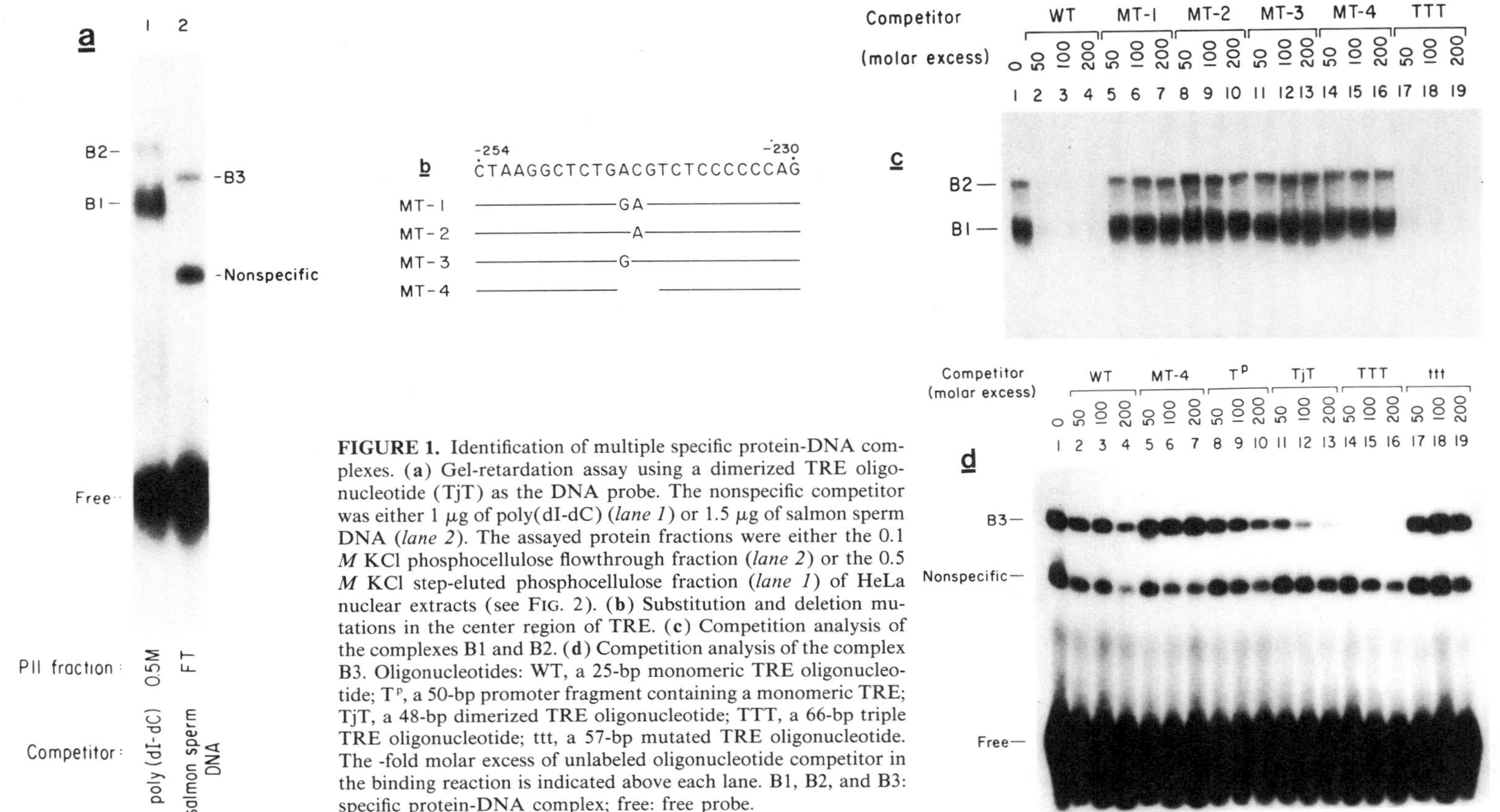

FIGURE 1. Identification of multiple specific protein-DNA complexes. (**a**) Gel-retardation assay using a dimerized TRE oligonucleotide (TjT) as the DNA probe. The nonspecific competitor was either 1 μg of poly(dI-dC) (*lane 1*) or 1.5 μg of salmon sperm DNA (*lane 2*). The assayed protein fractions were either the 0.1 *M* KCl phosphocellulose flowthrough fraction (*lane 2*) or the 0.5 *M* KCl step-eluted phosphocellulose fraction (*lane 1*) of HeLa nuclear extracts (see Fig. 2). (**b**) Substitution and deletion mutations in the center region of TRE. (**c**) Competition analysis of the complexes B1 and B2. (**d**) Competition analysis of the complex B3. Oligonucleotides: WT, a 25-bp monomeric TRE oligonucleotide; T^P, a 50-bp promoter fragment containing a monomeric TRE; TjT, a 48-bp dimerized TRE oligonucleotide; TTT, a 66-bp triple TRE oligonucleotide; ttt, a 57-bp mutated TRE oligonucleotide. The -fold molar excess of unlabeled oligonucleotide competitor in the binding reaction is indicated above each lane. B1, B2, and B3: specific protein-DNA complex; free: free probe.

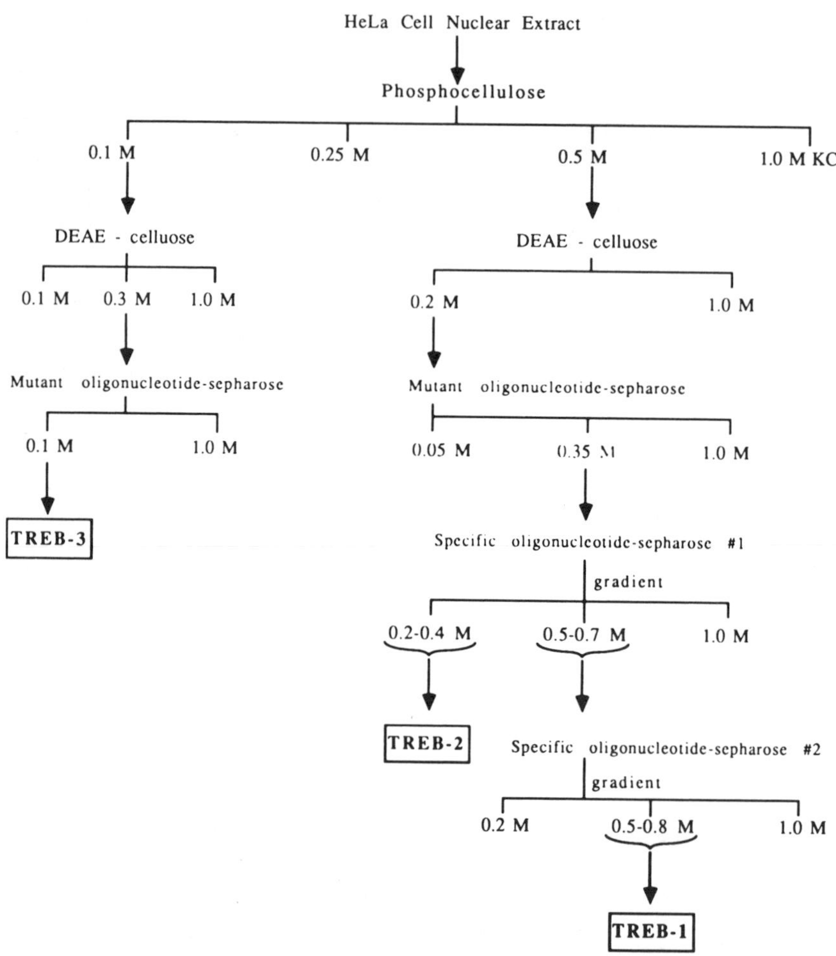

FIGURE 2. Purification scheme for the HTLV-I TRE-binding proteins, TREB-1, TREB-2 and TREB-3.

activity versus the tax-induced response. The observations that at least two copies of the TRE are necessary to act effectively as the tax-inducible enhancer[3] and that TREB-3, in contrast to TREB-1 and TREB-2, binds preferentially to multiple copies of the TRE suggest the interesting possibility that TREB-3 may in fact play a greater role in mediating the tax activation. This study provides an important first step in the definition and mechanistic analysis of the transcription factors that mediate the basal and/or tax-inducible HTLV-I enhancer function.

REFERENCES

1. SODROSKI, J., C. ROSEN & W. HASELTINE. 1985. Science **228:** 1430-1434.
2. BRADY, J., K.-T. JEANG, J. DUVALL & G. KHOURY. 1987. J. Virol. **61:** 2175-2181.
3. RUBEN, S., H. POTEAT, T.-H. TAN, K. KAWAKAMI, R. ROEDER, W. HASELTINE & C. A. ROSEN. 1988. Science **241:** 89-92.

The HTLV-I Tax-Inducible Enhancer Is Responsive to Various Inducing Agents

TSE-HUA TAN,[a] RAN JIA, AND
ROBERT G. ROEDER[b]

Laboratory of Biochemistry and Molecular Biology
The Rockefeller University
New York, New York 10021-6399

Human T cell leukemia virus type I (HTLV-I) is both a T-lymphotropic and a neurotropic human retrovirus. Efficient transcription and replication of the HTLV-I genome requires both the viral LTR (long terminal repeat) and the virus-encoded transcriptional activator tax, which functions through tax-responsive elements (TREs) in the LTR. The TGACG motif found in the center of the 21-base pair TRE is also present in cyclic AMP- (cAMP-) responsive elements (CREs) within the cAMP-inducible gene promoters and in activating transcription factor- (ATF-) binding sites (adenovirus E1a-responsive) within the adenovirus early gene promoters (TABLE 1). Interestingly, the molecular weight (43,000) of the TRE-binding protein TREB-1 is similar to that of CREB[1] (rat somatostatin gene CRE-binding protein) and ATF.[2] It is an intriguing possibility that TREB-1, CREB, and ATF may be identical or similar factors and that the TREs may confer upon heterologous promoters responsiveness to various inducing agents, including tax, cAMP, and E1a.

Gel retardation assays combined with competition experiments were performed to examine whether TRE, CRE and ATF-binding sites are recognized by the same factors that bind to the HTLV-I TRE. Indeed, TREB-1, TREB-2, and TREB-3 also bound to the CREs and ATF-binding sites. Using chloramphenicol acetyltransferase (CAT) assays in a transient expression system, we found that the tax-inducible HTLV-I promoter was responsive to the cAMP analog 8-Br-cAMP, the adenylate cyclase activator forskolin, and to E1a. In addition, the cAMP-inducible c-*fos* promoter was also responsive to tax and E1a (FIG. 1a). Trimerized wild type but not trimerized mutant TRE can confer tax responsiveness upon the heterologous SV40 promoter when tested in the presence of the tax-expressing plasmid, $pHtax_I$ (FIG. 1b). This wild type construct, pT_3CAT, was also responsive to cAMP and E1a, while the mutant construct, pt_3CAT, was not (FIG. 1c). Furthermore, the transcriptional activation of the HTLV-I promoter by tax was inhibited by the protein kinase inhibitor H-7 (FIG. 1d).

[a] Current address: National Cancer Institute, Frederick Cancer Research Facility, Frederick, MD 21701.

[b] To whom correspondence should be addressed at Box 237, The Rockefeller University, 1230 York Avenue, New York, NY 10021-6399.

TABLE 1. Compilation of TRE/CRE/ATF Sequences

Promoter[a]	Sequence[b]	Agreement[c]	Positions
HTLV-I LTR	C G T **T G A C G** A C A A C C	*11*	*−100 to −87*
	C C C **T G A C G** T G T C C C	*12*	*−199 to −186*
	C T C **T G A C G** T C T C C C	*14*	*−248 to −235*
HTLV-II LTR	C T C **T G A C G** A T T A C C	*11*	*−86 to −73*
	C C C **T G A C G** T C C C T C	*12*	*−179 to −166*
	C T C **T G A C G** T C T C C C	*14*	*−219 to −206*
BLV LTR	T G C **T G A C G** G C A G C T	*12*	*−128 to −115*
	A G C **T G A C G** T C T C T G	*13*	*−150 to −163*
Somatostatin	C T C **T G A C G** T C A G C C	*14*	*−38 to −51*
Fibronectin	C C G **T G A C G** T C A C C C	*13*	*−176 to −163*
c-*fos*	C C G **T G A C G** T T T A C A	*10*	*−69 to −52*
	T G C **T G A C G** C A G A T G	*9*	*−300 to −287*
Enkephalin	A G C **T G A C G** C A G G C C	*12*	*−83 to −96*
hCG	C C A **T G A C G** T C A A T T	*11*	*−114 to −127*
	C C A **T G A C G** T C A A T T	*11*	*−132 to −145*
TH	C T T **T G A C G** T C A G C C	*13*	*−36 to −49*
PEPCK	C T C **T G A C G** T A A G G G	*12*	*−80 to −93*
VIP	C T G **T G A C G** T C T T T C	*13*	*−67 to −80*
E1A	T T G **T G A C G** T G G C G C	*10*	*−438 to −425*
	G G G **T G A C G** T A G T A G	*9*	*−406 to −393*
	A A G **T G A C G** T T T T T G	*10*	*−332 to −319*
E2A	A G A **T G A C G** T A G T T T	*11*	*−77 to −64*
E3	C T G **T G A C G** A A A G C C	*13*	*−52 to −65*
E4	A A A **T G A C G** T A A C G G	*10*	*−41 to −54*
	A A G **T G A C G** A T T T G A	*8*	*−147 to −134*
	A A G **T G A C G** T A A C G T	*12*	*−171 to −158*
	G G G **T G A C G** T A G G T T	*12*	*−237 to −224*
	T T G **T G A C G** T G G C G C	*10*	*−269 to −256*

Summary of Sequences

	1	2	3	4	5	6	7	8	9	10	11	12	13	14
Frequency of consensus base(s)	*22*	*18*	*22*	*28*	*28*	*28*	*28*	*28*	*21*	*21*	*20*	*17*	*21*	*20*
Base frequency														
A	*7*	*4*	*4*	*0*	*0*	*28*	*0*	*0*	*4*	*9*	*11*	*6*	*1*	*2*
G	*2*	*8*	*11*	*0*	*28*	*0*	*0*	*28*	*1*	*3*	*7*	*7*	*6*	*6*
C	*15*	*6*	*11*	*0*	*0*	*0*	*28*	*0*	*2*	*12*	*1*	*10*	*12*	*14*
T	*4*	*10*	*2*	*28*	*0*	*0*	*0*	*0*	*21*	*4*	*9*	*5*	*9*	*6*

TRE/CRE/ATF Consensus Sequence[d]

1	2	3	4	5	6	7	8	9	10	11	12	13	14
C A	T G	C G	<u>T</u>	<u>G</u>	<u>A</u>	<u>C</u>	<u>G</u>	T	C A	T A	C G	Y	Y

[a] BLV, bovine leukemia virus; hCG, human chorionic gonadotropin; TH, tyrosine hydroxylase; PEPCK, phosphoenolpyruvate carboxykinase; VIP, human vasoactive intestinal peptide; E1A, E2A, E3, E4: adenovirus early gene promotors.

[b] TGACG motif is indicated in **bold face**.

[c] Number of bases agreeing with those of consensus sequence.

[d] TGACG motif is underlined. Y, pyrimidine.

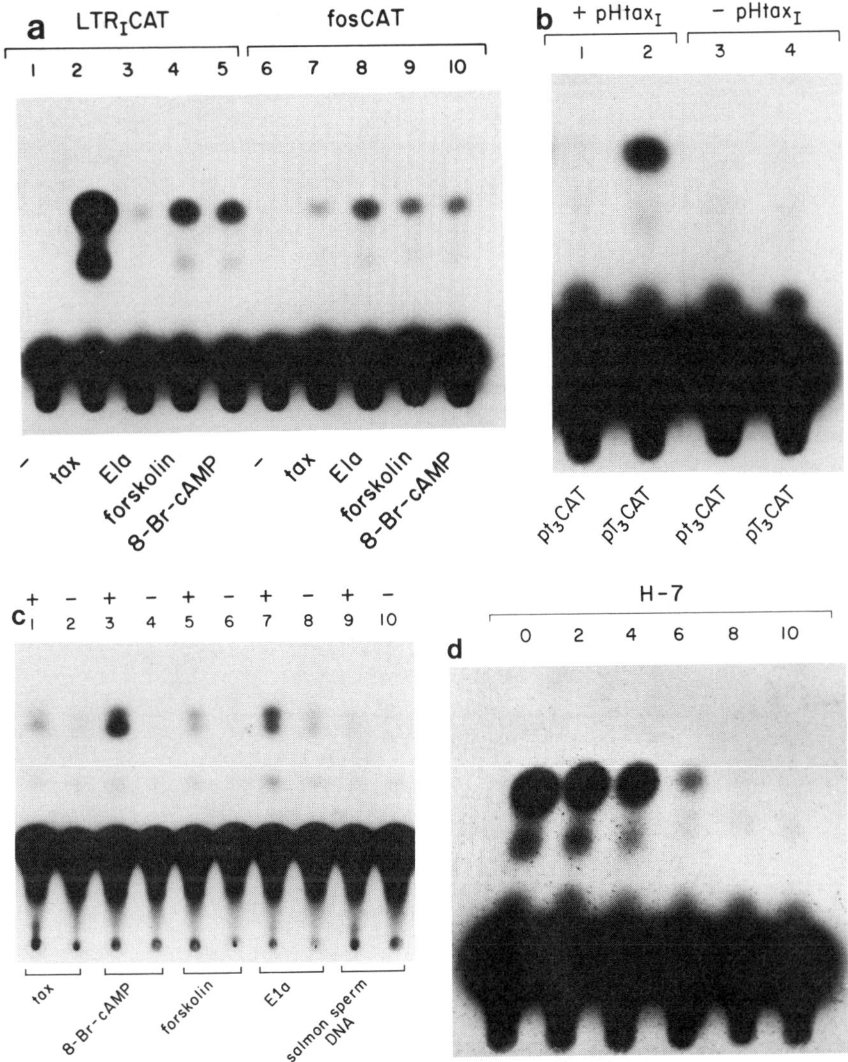

FIGURE 1. CAT assays. (**a**) Induction of HTLV-I and c-*fos* promoter expression by various inducing agents was assessed by CAT assays in a transient expression system. CV-1 cells were transfected with either the HTLV-I promoter-CAT construct, LTR$_I$CAT, or the c-*fos* promoter-CAT construct, *fos*CAT. (**b**) CAT assays of the tax-inducible expression of T$_3$CAT. NIH/3T3 cells were cotransfected with the tax-expressing plasmid, pHtax$_I$, and either pT$_3$CAT or pt$_3$CAT plasmid (+ pHtax$_I$) or with a CAT-containing plasmid alone (− pHtax$_I$). The pT$_3$CAT plasmid contains wild type trimerized TRE oligonucleotide cloned 5′ to the enhancerless SV40 early promoter linked to the reporter CAT gene; pt$_3$CAT is a similar construct containing a mutant trimerized TRE in place of the wild type. (**c**) CAT assays of the induction of T$_3$CAT expression by various inducing agents. K562 cells were transfected with either pT$_3$CAT (+) or pt$_3$CAT (−) plasmid. (**d**) Inhibition of tax-mediated activation by the protein kinase inhibitor, H-7. CV-1 cells were cotransfected with both pLTR$_I$CAT and pHtax$_I$ plasmids in the presence of the protein kinase inhibitor, H-7, at 0, 2, 4, 6, 8, and 10 $\times$ 10^{-5} *M*, as indicated.

This study indicates that TREB-1, CREB, and ATF are one and the same. Besides the TREB-1/CREB/ATF factor, several laboratories have identified two other factors that bind to the CRE[3] and one 72-65 kDa protein that binds to the ATF-binding site.[4] It is possible that TREB-2 and TREB-3 are identical to these recently identified factors. More study is needed in order to delineate the exact role of each of the three identified factors (TREB-1/CREB/ATF, TREB-2, and TREB-3) in the three different signal induction pathways. The observations that HTLV-I TRE can also be induced by cAMP and that the tax-mediated activation was inhibited by a protein kinase inhibitor indicate that a protein kinase is involved in tax-mediated activation. Work to establish a positive identification for the protein kinase which is involved in the tax-mediated *trans* activation is under way. It is an intriguing possibility that the different TREB factors may play distinct roles in HTLV-I gene expression (e.g., basal versus induced expression, activation by different inducing agents, or mediation of T-lymphotropism versus neurotropism). Further studies of the action of these factors from different sources (e.g., T cells and neural cells or cells treated with various inducing agents) and in the context of tax expression should lead to an understanding of their mechanism of action and their role in leukemogenesis and the pathogenesis of HTLV-I.

REFERENCES

1. YAMAMOTO, K. K., G. A. GONZALEZ, W. H. BIGGS & M. R. MONTMINY. 1988. Nature **334:** 494-498.
2. HURST, H. C. & N. C. JONES. 1987. Genes Dev. **1:** 1132-1146.
3. ANDRISANI, O. M., D. POT, Z. ZHU & J. E. DIXON. 1988. Mol. Cell. Biol. **8:** 1947-1956.
4. CORTES, P., *et al.* 1988. Genes Dev. **2:** 975-990.

Rat Embryo Fibroblasts Transformed by p53 Plus *ras* Possess Tumor-specific Transplantation Activity

ALAN B. FREY [a] AND ARNOLD J. LEVINE

Department of Biology
Princeton University
Princeton, New Jersey 08544

Primary rat embryo fibroblasts (REF) are efficiently transformed when cotransfected with an oncogene whose protein product acts in the nucleus (p53, *myc,* or adenovirus E1a) plus *ras,* an oncogene whose protein product is involved in regulation of signal transduction at the level of the plasma membrane. The effect of these two transfected oncogenes upon the metabolism of primary REF likely involves an alteration in expression of selected genes, including those which regulate the expression of other genes and also those involved in the production of the biological signal which normally results from the occupancy of growth factor receptors by their ligand. Transformed cells also produce proteins or glycolipids called tumor-associated antigens (TAA), which have an impact upon host immune recognition of the transformed cell. Since TAA expression is correlated with the expression of the transformed phenotype, an understanding of the function of these molecules will provide insights into the mechanism by which transformed cells escape immune detection.

p53-plus-*ras*-transformed REF demonstrate several hallmark properties of transformed cells, including altered morphology, growth in low-serum media, immortalization, and tumorigenicity in syngeneic animals.[1] Because the absolute level of expression of several oncogenes has been demonstrated to be directly related to the acquisition of the transformed phenotype in other systems, the accumulation of p53 and *ras* proteins in transformed REF was characterized. Extracts of total cellular protein were analyzed by immunoblotting with the appropriate antisera and the relative levels of the accumulated oncogene products examined. As seen in FIGURE 1, the different REF lines express very different levels of p53. The extent of morphological transformation of a given cell line was shown to be unrelated to the levels of oncogene expression. Furthermore, there was no apparent relation between the level of expression of p53 and the tumorigenicity of a given cell line. The level of *ras* protein was likewise examined and found to be related neither to the extent of morphological transformation nor to the tumorigenicity of a given cell line.

p53-plus-*ras*-transformed REF express tumor-specific transplantation antigen (TSTA) activity, as demonstrated using a standard tumor-rejection assay. The TSTA

[a] Current address: Department of Cell Biology, New York University Medical Center, 550 First Avenue, New York, New York 10016.

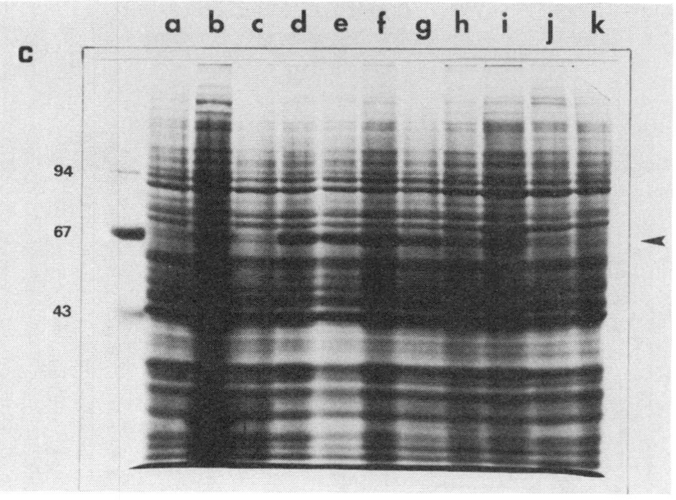

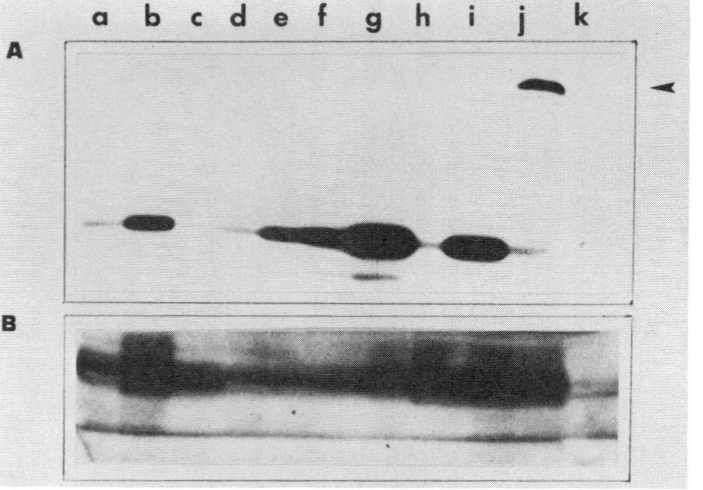

FIGURE 1. Production of p53 and *ras* polypeptides in various transformed REF cell lines. Transformed REF cell lines were harvested from tissue culture by scraping and were washed twice with cold phosphate-buffered saline (PBS) by resuspension and centrifugation. Cells were resuspended for counting, and the cells in sample volumes calculated to contain 1.5×10^6 cells were pelleted by centrifugation and quick-frozen in liquid N_2. Soluble proteins were extracted from thawed cell pellets by vortexing in hypotonic lysis buffer containing a non-ionic detergent. Extracted proteins were then divided into three equal portions, solubilized by addition of SDS-polyacrylamide gel electrophoresis sample buffer, sonicated briefly, and subjected to electrophoresis in gels containing SDS. Immunoblotting of the resultant gels was then done with either mouse monoclonal anti-p53 (**panel A**) or sheep polyclonal anti-human *ras* (**panel B**) antibody. The resultant autoradiographs are shown here. **Panel C** shows the gel pattern of the separated polypeptides following staining with Coomassie blue; positions of molecular weight markers are indicated to *left.* The *arrowhead* in **panel A** indicates the position of a protein of approximately 100 kDa which is exclusively synthesized in p53-plus-*ras*-transformed cell line B1. The nature and identity of this protein is currently being investigated. The *arrowhead* in **panel C** indicates protein(s) of 70 kDa which is synthesized in greater abundance in some p53-plus-*ras*-transformed cell lines. Extracts were prepared from p53-plus-*ras*-transformed REF cells as indicated: (**lane a**) KH215 clone 4, (**lane b**) KH215 clone 3, (**lane c**) KH215 clone 2, (**lane d**) KH215 clone 1, (**lane e**) T36, (**lane f**) A4, (**lane g**) A1, (**lane h**) B3, (**lane i**) B2, (**lane j**) B1, and (**lane k**) E1a clone 1.

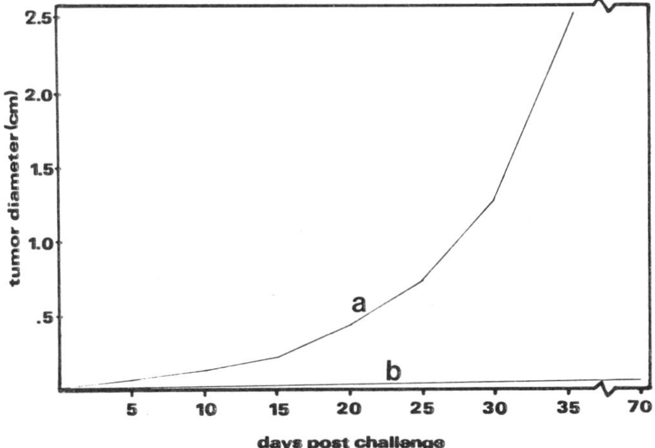

FIGURE 2. Cross-immunization of REF cell lines transformed by transfection with different oncogenes. Pairs of Fisher rats were immunized twice at 7-day intervals with 2-5 $\times$ 10^6 transformed cells which had received 10,000 rad of irradiation. Animals were challenged with 2 $\times$ 10^3 B3 cells 10 days after the last immunization, and tumor production was monitored at 5-day intervals. (This experiment was repeated twice for each cell clone tested, using cells which had been passaged in tissue culture for different lengths of time. Cells used in the first of each pair of experiments were passaged for about 70 doublings; those used in the second were passaged for about 100 doublings.) Control animals received untransformed REF cells as the immunogen. Curves shown are the average results observed for (**A**) animals immunized with untransformed REF cells or transformed cells: p53-plus-*ras* line B4; p53-plus-*ras* KH215 line C4; Rat 1-p53 lines a and b; *myc*-plus-*ras* lines 1, 3, 4, A, C, or X; adenovirus E1a-plus-*ras* lines E1, E2, E3, E4, E5, E6, E7, Ea, or Ec; or REF SV40 T and (**B**) animals immunized with transformed cells: p53-plus-*ras* lines A1, A2, A3, A4, B1, B2, B3, T36; p53-plus-*ras* KH215 lines C1, C2, C3; or *myc*-plus-*ras* lines 2, 5, B, D, E, F, or I; and adenovirus E1a-plus-*ras* line Eb.

activity is shared in common among most of the p53-plus-*ras*-transformed REF cell lines in that, when rendered unable to divide, 11 of the 13 independent cloned lines were able to confer protective immunity to a challenge dose with a highly tumorigenic line, clone B3 (FIG. 2). Additional cell lines created with other oncogenes whose protein products act in the nucleus, *myc,* and, to a lesser extent, E1a, cross-reacted in the tumor rejection assay (54% and 10% for *myc* and *E1a,* respectively). The demonstration of shared cross-reactivity between tumor-producing cells of different origins implies a common mechanism of interaction of the individual transformed cells with the host immune system. The nature of the TSTA activity is currently unknown, but a variety of biochemical evidence suggests that the p53 and *ras* polypeptides themselves are not TSTA molecules. In addition, the TSTA activity is not likely to represent fetal embryonic antigens, since primary REF do not demonstrate any protective immunity at any dose tested. Since the products of the two transfected oncogenes themselves have been shown not to possess TSTA activity, there are three likely possibilities concerning the nature of the TSTA activity: (1) the TSTA activity is not expressed at all in primary REF and is synthesized *de novo* as a consequence of transformation by the exogenous oncogenes; (2) the TSTA molecules pre-exist in primary REF but at levels too low to function in a transplantation rejection assay;

or (3) the TSTA molecules are expressed in REF in a non-immunogenic form which is rendered immunogenic by the process of transformation. After we complete purification of the TSTA activity expressed in B3 cells, we will address these mechanistic questions.

REFERENCE

1. FREY, A. B. & A. J. LEVINE. 1989. p53-Plus-ras transformed rat embryo fibroblasts express tumor specific transplantation antigen activity which is shared by independently transformed cells. Manuscript submitted.

Glucocorticoids Alter Transcription from the Mouse Ha-*ras* Promoter Region in a Transient Gene Expression Assay

JILL C. PELLING, JUDY STRAWHECKER, NATALIE BETZ, AND RENEE NEADES

Eppley Cancer Institute and
The Department of Biochemistry
University of Nebraska Medical Center
Omaha, Nebraska 68105-4090

Activation and expression of the mouse c-Ha-*ras* oncogene has been shown to play a role in epidermal papilloma development during two-stage skin carcinogenesis in SENCAR mice.[1] Previous studies in our laboratory have demonstrated that elevated expression of mouse c-Ha-*ras* mRNA occurs early in the development of mouse skin tumors induced by the two-stage model of initiation and promotion.[2] In order to more fully characterize the factors regulating Ha-*ras* expression, we have begun to sequence the 5′ upstream non-coding region of the mouse c-Ha-*ras* gene, subclones of which were generously provided by Dr. James Ihle, Frederick Cancer Research Facility. In the process of screening the upstream region for known regulatory elements, we have identified two sites containing the hexanucleotide 5′-AGAACA-3′ and one site with 5′-ACAACA-3′. The hexanucleotide sequence AGAACA is the core consensus sequence in the glucocorticoid-responsive element (GRE) of mouse mammary tumor virus (MMTV). The MMTV GREs have been identified as the regulatory elements required for hormonal induction by glucocorticoids, and they are the binding sites for the glucocorticoid-receptor complex.[3] The locations of the putative GREs in the mouse c-Ha-*ras* oncogene are indicated in FIGURE 1. Since glucocorticoids inhibit mouse skin two-stage carcinogenesis when applied topically to initiated mouse skin prior to tumor development,[4] we were interested in investigating the effect of glucocorticoids on expression of the mouse c-Ha-*ras* oncogene. In this report we present our observations on the effect of the glucocorticoid dexamethasone (DEX) on gene expression driven by the mouse c-Ha-*ras* promoter region in a transient gene expression assay.

Three mouse c-Ha-*ras* plasmid vectors were constructed in which 330 base pairs (bp), 410 bp, or 974 bp of the mouse c-Ha-*ras* 5′ upstream region were fused to the chloramphenicol acetyltransferase (CAT) gene. The p330*ras*-CAT and p410*ras*-CAT plasmids contained one putative GRE and the p974*ras*-CAT plasmid contained two potential GREs (FIG. 1). The plasmids were transfected into HeLa cells using the calcium precipitation technique,[5] and 1 μM DEX was added to the culture medium 4 hr later. The cells were harvested after 48 hr, and CAT assays were performed on whole cell extracts according to standard techniques.[5] Our results are summarized in

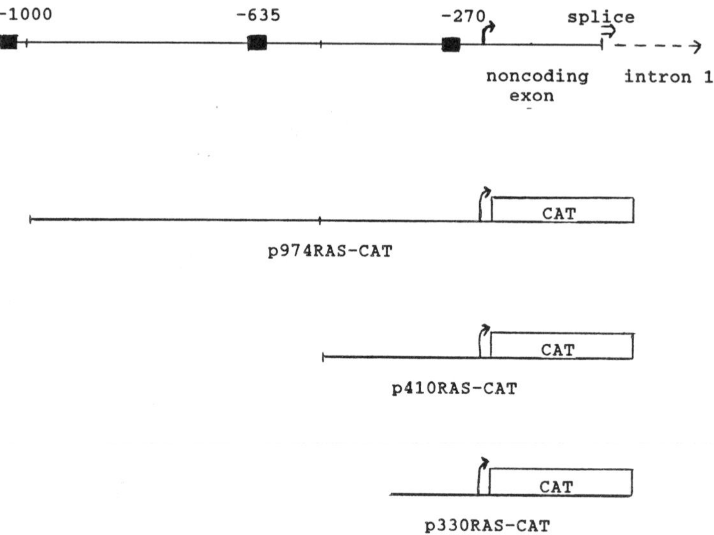

FIGURE 1. The mouse Ha-*ras* 5′ upstream flanking region. Locations of the putative glucocorticoid response elements (5′-AGAACA-3′) at positions 635 and 1000 and of 5′-ACAACA-3′ at position 270 are indicated. DNA fragments of 974 base pairs, 410 base pairs and 330 base pairs in length were fused upstream from the CAT gene to form the three *ras*-CAT plasmids shown; these were used in cell transfection studies.

FIGURE 2. The level of CAT gene expression driven by the p330 plasmid was enhanced approximately 2-fold in the presence of DEX, whereas expression by the p974 plasmid or p974* plasmid was enhanced up to 3.5-fold. Our results suggest that the level of DEX-inducibility correlates with the number of putative GREs present. In addition, we have used Southwestern blot analysis to demonstrate that the 330bp and 974bp DNA fragments of the mouse 5′ upstream region bind the 97-kDa glucocorticoid receptor protein in total cell extracts of both HeLa G cells and primary SENCAR mouse epidermal cells (Strawhecker and Pelling, manuscript in preparation).

In conclusion, our data indicate that the presence of DEX causes a 3- to 4-fold increase in the level of expression from the mouse Ha-*ras* 5′ upstream non-coding region. Our findings argue against the hypothesis that inhibition of mouse skin tumorigenesis by topical DEX treatment is due to direct inhibition of mouse c-Ha-*ras* gene expression.[4] Our results indicate that further experiments are warranted to more fully characterize the regulatory factors influencing expression of the mouse c-Ha-*ras* gene during tumorigenesis.

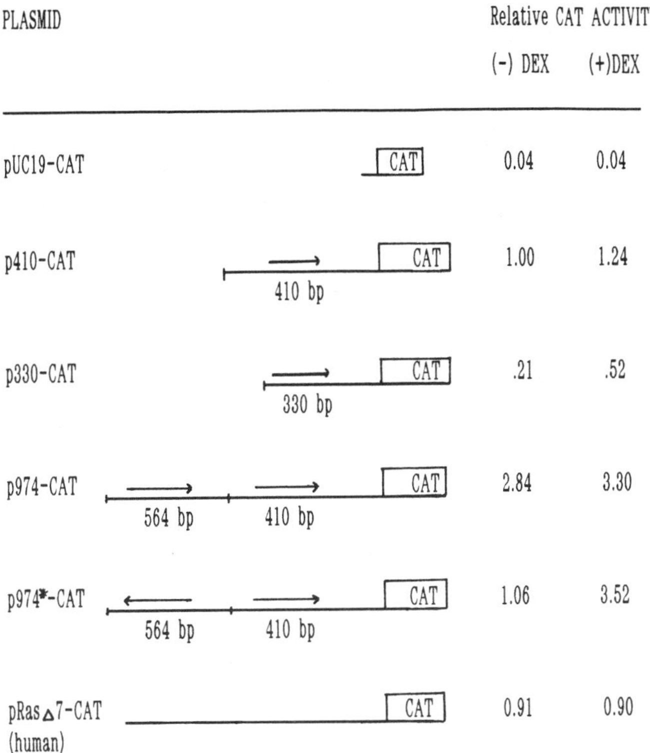

PLASMID
Relative CAT ACTIVITY
(-) DEX
(+)DEX
pUC19-CAT
CAT
0.04
0.04
p410-CAT
CAT
410 bp
1.00
1.24
p330-CAT
CAT
330 bp
.21
.52
p974-CAT
CAT
564 bp
410 bp
2.84
3.30
p974*-CAT
CAT
564 bp
410 bp
1.06
3.52
pRasΔ7-CAT
(human)
CAT
0.91
0.90

FIGURE 2. Effect of dexamethasone on relative CAT activities of Ha-*ras*-CAT hybrid plasmids in HeLa cells. HeLa cells were transfected with the indicated plasmids, whose composition is shown. Dexamethasone (DEX) was added at a concentration of 1 μM [(+) **DEX**] 4 hr later or not added [(−) **DEX**], and cells were harvested for CAT assays after 48 hr. The p974*-CAT plasmid has the 564-bp fragment in an inverse orientation relative to the p974-CAT plasmid.

REFERENCES

1. Balmain, A., M. Ramsden, G. T. Bowden & J. Smith. 1984. Nature **307:** 658-661.
2. Pelling, J. C., S. M. Fischer, R. Neades, J. Strawhecker & L. Schweickert. 1987. Carcinogenesis **8:** 1481-1484.
3. Evans, R. M. 1988. Science **240:** 889-895.
4. Schwarz, J. A., A. Viaje, T. J. Slaga, S. H. Yuspa, H. Hennings & U. Lichti. 1977. Chem. Biol. Interact. **17:** 331-347.
5. Gorman, C. 1985. *In* DNA Cloning, Volume II, A Practical Approach, D. M. Glover, Ed.: 143–190. IRL Press. Oxford; Washington, D.C.

Suppression of the Progression Phenotype by 5-Azacytidine in Rat Embryo Cells Doubly Transformed by Type 5 Adenovirus and the Ha-*ras* Oncogene[a]

GREGORY J. DUIGOU,[b] LEE E. BABISS,[c] AND PAUL B. FISHER [b]

[b]*Departments of Neurological Surgery, Pathology, and Urology*
Cancer Center/Institute of Cancer Research
Columbia University, College of Physicians and Surgeons
New York, New York 10032
and
[c]*Rockefeller University*
New York, New York 10031

Recent studies indicate that different classes of oncogenes, i.e., nuclear and cytoplasmic, can cooperate in the induction of cellular transformation and tumor progression.[1] These observations are compatible with the multifactor and multistep nature of carcinogenesis.[2,3] The precise biochemical and molecular changes which mediate the development of the transformed state as well as the evolution of the transformed phenotype, in which a transformed cell acquires an increased expression of transformation-related phenotypes (a process termed *progression*), have not yet been elucidated. To define the molecular basis of progression of the transformed phenotype, we have developed a model cell culture system which employs type 5 adenovirus-(Ad5) transformed cell lines representing specific stages in the progression lineage.[4] A cloned Ad5- (H5ts125) transformed Sprague-Dawley rat embryo (RE) cell line, E11, can be made to progress to a more aggressive transformed cell phenotype by selection for tumorigenicity in nude mice or by selection of cells capable of enhanced anchorage-independent growth in agar.[4,5] This progression phenotype of the selected cells can be reversed by a single exposure to the demethylating agent 5-azacytidine (AZA), and the revertants can reacquire the progression phenotype by reselection for increased growth in agar suspension.[4] These cells which have progressed grow more efficiently in 0.4% agar medium and demonstrate shorter latent periods for tumor formation in nude mice as compared to E11 cells or AZA-revertants of cells with the progression phenotype. There is no difference, however, in the expression of the integrated Ad5 transforming genes, E1A or E1B, or of several oncogenes, including *ras,* among cells expressing different states of progression.[6]

[a]This research was supported by the National Cancer Institute, Grant CA35675.

a

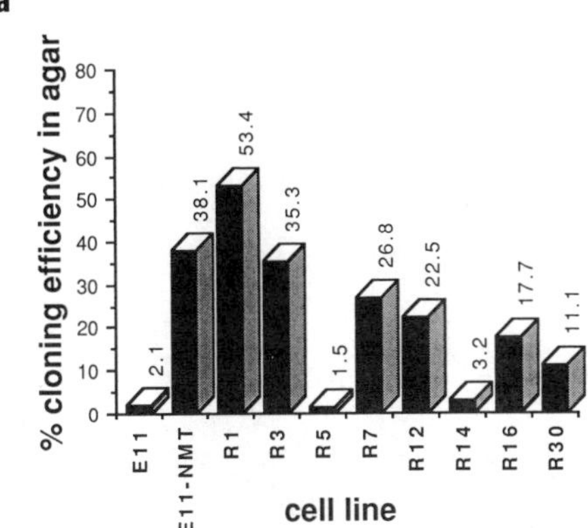

b

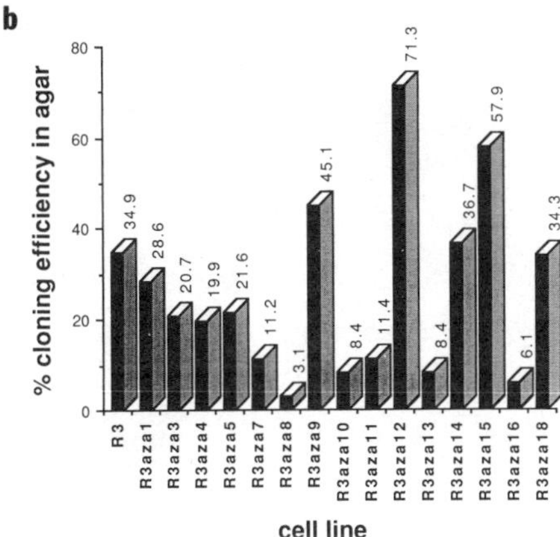

FIGURE 1. Growth of E11, E11-NMT, E11-*ras* and E11-*ras*-AZA cells in agar medium. 4 × 10^3 cells were resuspended in 60-mm plates in 0.4% agar medium containing 7.5% fetal bovine serum, and the number of cells displaying anchorage-independent growth were counted three weeks after plating. **Panel A:** Cloning efficiency of E11, E11-NMT and (R1, R3, R5, R7, R12, R14, R16, R30) G418-resistant E11 cells cotransfected with *ras* and pSV2*neo* DNA. **Panel B:** Cloning efficiency of R3 cells and (R3aza) R3 cells exposed to 10 μM 5-azacytidine for 24 hr.

It is apparent that changes in expression of the *ras* oncogene family may be involved in the development of a variety of cancers of both rodent and human origin.[7,8] A significant proportion of human tumors exhibit changes in *ras* oncogenes, often involving amplification of the *ras* oncogene or point mutations in the *ras* oncogene.[7,8] The cloned T24 human bladder carcinoma c-Ha-*ras (ras)* oncogene can induce transformation of NIH/3T3 cells or transform primary RE fibroblasts in collaboration with genes that can immortalize these cells (i.e., E1A, *myc,* polyoma large T-antigen; reviewed in Ref. 1). To determine if E11 cells could be genetically engineered to display the progression phenotype, E11 cells were cotransfected with the *ras* oncogene plus pSV2-*neo* DNA, at a 3:1 DNA ratio (15 μg: 5 μg), and eight colonies of E11 cells resistant to the neomycin analog G418 were isolated and assayed for their ability to grow in agar. Parental E11 cells grew poorly in agar (ca. 2% cloning efficiency) compared with E11-NMT (nude mouse tumor) cells (ca. 38%) (FIG. 1a). The eight G418-resistant cotransfected E11 cell clones varied in their ability to grow in 0.4% agar medium (FIG. 1a). Clones R1, R3, R7, R12, R16, and R30 exhibited efficient anchorage-independent growth, while clones R5 and R14 displayed the same reduced agar cloning efficiency as parental E11 cells.

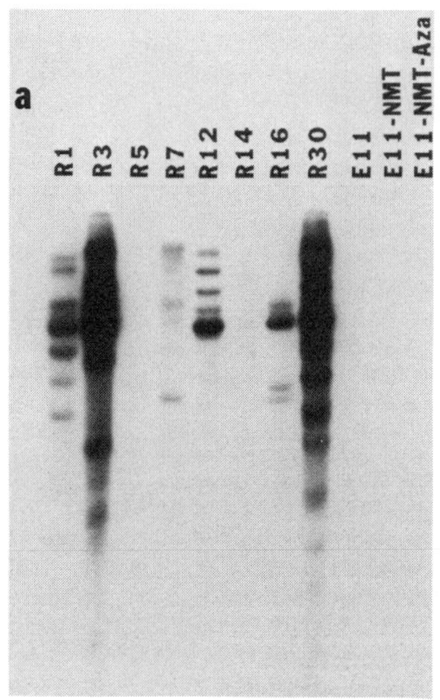
a
R1
R3
R5
R7
R12
R14
R16
R30
E11
E11-NMT
E11-NMT-Aza

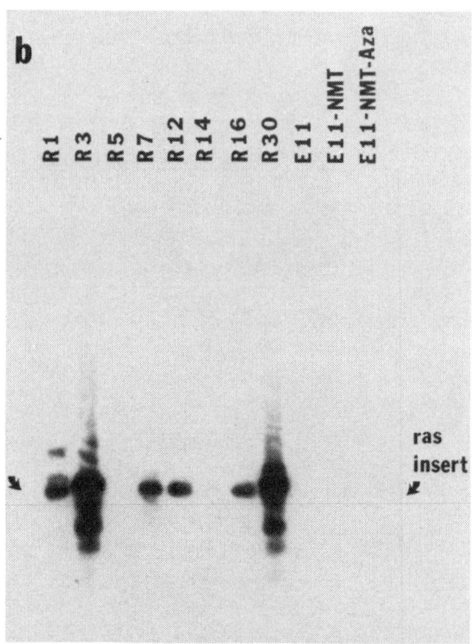
b
R1
R3
R5
R7
R12
R14
R16
R30
E11
E11-NMT
E11-NMT-Aza
ras
insert

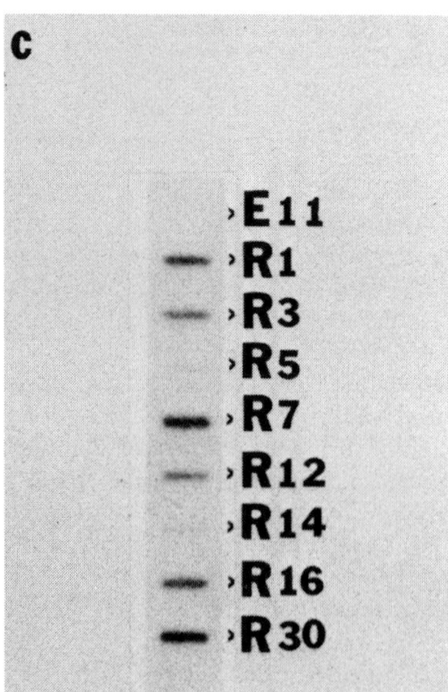
c
E11
R1
R3
R5
R7
R12
R14
R16
R30

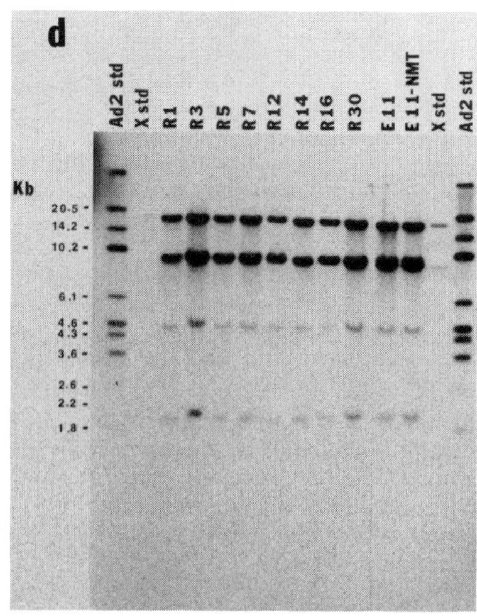
d
Ad2 std
X std
R1
R3
R5
R7
R12
R14
R16
R30
E11
E11-NMT
X std
Ad2 std
Kb
20.5
14.2
10.2
6.1
4.6
4.3
3.6
2.6
2.2
1.8

To determine if the cotransfected E11 clones selected for resistance to G418 contained the *ras* oncogene, cellular DNA was extracted from the eight G418-resistant E11 clones, digested with restriction endonucleases (*Xba* I or *Msp* I), and analyzed by Southern transfer-hybridization using a nick-translated ^{32}P-labeled *ras* DNA probe. There is a single *Xba* I site within the T24 *ras* oncogene, and Southern blot analysis of *Xba* I-digested cellular DNA reveals several *ras* DNA-containing fragments within clones R1, R3, R7, R12, R16, and R30 cells (FIG. 2a). Clones R1, R3, and R30 contained a more complex pattern of *ras* DNA integration than the other clones. In addition, DNA from R3 and R30 hybridized with a larger quantity of *ras* probe than did cellular DNA from the other cell lines, possibly reflecting duplications of integrated *ras* DNA or simply a greater number of sites of intact integrated *ras* DNA. In agreement with their E11-like phenotype for growth in agar, R5 and R14 did not contain detectable human *ras* DNA. *Msp* I cleaves the *ras* oncogene several times and generates a single 1.1-kilobase (kb) DNA fragment containing only *ras* DNA sequences. Southern blot analysis of *Msp* I-digested DNA from R1, R3, R7, R12, R16, and R30 cells yielded a DNA fragment that hybridizes to *ras* DNA, indicating that these cells contain the *Msp* I fragment of the *ras* oncogene. Analysis of DNA from R1, R3, and R30 cells indicated additional *ras* DNA-containing *Msp* I fragments suggestive of disruption or rearrangement of the *ras* gene prior to, during, or after integration into cellular DNA.

To determine if the integrated *ras* DNA was transcriptionally active, total cytoplasmic RNA was analyzed by slot-blotting using a ^{32}P-labeled *ras* DNA probe (FIG. 2c). The R1, R3, R7, R12, R16, and R30 cell lines contained detectable *ras* RNA, whereas E11 parental cells, as well as R5 and R14 cells, did not contain RNA homologous to human *ras* DNA. These observations indicate that insertion and expression of a human *ras* oncogene in Ad5-transformed RE cells, which already express the E1A and E1B Ad5 transforming genes, results in a further elaboration in their expression of the transformed phenotype.

E11 cells were originally generated by transformation of secondary Sprague-Dawley RE cells by a DNA replication mutant of Ad5 (H5ts125).[9] By Southern blot analysis, it appears that the entire Ad5 genome is integrated into E11 cellular DNA without rearrangement.[10] It has been shown that Ad5-transformed cells contain randomly integrated, covalently associated adenoviral DNA which remains stable in its integration during different stages of progression.[5] Since normal rat cells do not contain Ad5 DNA, the presence and arrangement of integrated Ad5 DNA serves as a physical marker of E11 heritage. Southern blot analysis of *Xba* I-digested DNA from parental and cotransfected G418-resistant E11 cells (FIG. 2d) indicates that the amount and arrangement of integrated Ad5 DNA appears to be unaltered in both parental and G418-resistant transfected cell lines. Rearrangement or loss of integrated Ad5 DNA is, therefore, not responsible for the different transformation phenotypes of the transfected cell lines.

FIGURE 2. Analysis of integration and expression of Ha-*ras* DNA and the stability of integrated Ad5 DNA sequences in *ras*-transfected E11 cells. 10 μg of cellular DNA was digested using *Xba* I (**Panel A**) or *Msp* I (**Panel B**), size-fractionated through 0.6% agarose gels, and analyzed by Southern transfer-hybridization[10] using a ^{32}P-labeled nick-translated T24 Ha-*ras* DNA probe purified from pBR322 DNA sequences. Slot-blot analysis of 20 μg of RNA per slot using a ^{32}P-labeled nick-translated *ras* DNA probe is depicted in **panel C.** 10 μg of cellular DNA was digested with *Xba* I and subjected to Southern blot analysis using a ^{32}P-labeled nick-translated Ad5 DNA probe (**Panel D**). In **panel D,** size standards (Kb, kilobases) were generated by adding a 1:1 mixture of independently digested *EcoR* I and *Bam*H I fragments of Ad2 DNA (*Ad2 std*) to the outer lanes of the gel and adding *Xba* I-digested Ad5 DNA to the lanes labeled *X std.*

In previous studies we have demonstrated that reaching a particular stage of progression in the transformed phenotype in Ad5-transformed RE cells is a reversible process which is affected by the state of DNA methylation, presumably involving the expression of cellular genes whose gene products serve as suppressors of the progression phenotype.[4] A single exposure of E11-NMT cells to the demethylating agent AZA results in a high-frequency reversion of these cells to the transformation state of parental E11 cells. Further support for the reversibility of progression of the transformed state has come from studies indicating that the E11-NMT phenotype could be restored in the AZA-revertants by reisolating clones following growth in agar.[4] Based on these observations, we analyzed the effect of AZA on expression of the progression phenotype in E11 cells genetically engineered by insertion of *ras* and expressing an enhanced ability to grow in 0.4% agar (FIG. 1b). Clone R3 cells were seeded at low densities (100, 200, or 400 cells/60-mm petri dish), treated with growth medium or growth medium supplemented with 10 μM AZA for 24 hr, and grown for 10 to 14 days in AZA-free medium. A series of control and AZA-treated subclones was reisolated and tested for their ability to grow in agar. All of the control subclones grew with cloning efficiencies which were similar to the parental R3 clone. In contrast, 6 of 15 AZA-treated subclones displayed a dramatic reduction in agar cloning efficiency to levels equal to or approaching that of the E11 subclone (FIG. 1b). These results suggest that a suppressor gene(s), which is sensitive to states of methylation, when activated in RE cells transformed by multiple oncogenes, i.e., Ad5 E1A plus E1B genes and the *ras* gene, can revert the progression phenotype.

The genetic identity and the mechanism of action of the suppressor gene(s) in transformed RE cells are presently unknown. The ability of the suppressor gene(s) to inhibit expression of the progression phenotype in Ad5-transformed RE cells is not associated with changes in the transcription rates or steady-state mRNA levels of the E1A and E1B transforming genes of Ad5.[6] Preliminary studies also indicate that reversion of the progression phenotype in transformed RE cells containing multiple oncogenes is not correlated with consistent changes in the expression of the *ras* oncogene. These observations suggest that the suppressor gene can prevent expression of the progression phenotype even with expression of Ad5 and *ras* transforming genes. The model system described in this paper should prove valuable in identifying and molecularly cloning the gene(s) which mediate expression of the progression phenotype in virally transformed RE cells.

REFERENCES

1. WEINBERG, R. A. 1985. Science **230:** 770-776.
2. FISHER, P. B. 1984. *In* Tumor Promotion and Cocarcinogenesis: In Vitro Mechanisms of Tumor Promotion. T. J. Slaga, Ed.: 57-123. CRC Press, Inc. Boca Raton, FL.
3. WEINSTEIN, I. B. 1988. Cancer Res. **48:** 4235-4143.
4. BABISS, L. E., S. G. ZIMMER & P. B. FISHER. 1985. Science **228:** 1099-1101.
5. FISHER, P. B., K. DORSCH-HASLER, I. B. WEINSTEIN & H. S. GINSBERG. 1979. Nature **281:** 591-594.
6. DUIGOU, G. J., L. E. BABISS & P. B. FISHER. 1988. Manuscript in preparation.
7. BARBACID, M. 1987. Annu. Rev. Biochem. **56:** 779-827.
8. TAKEO, T., D. J. SLAMON, H. BATTIFORA & M. J. CLINE. 1986. Cancer Res. **46:** 1465-1470.
9. FISHER, P. B., I. B. WEINSTEIN, D. EISENBERG & H. S. GINSBERG. 1978. Proc. Natl. Acad. Sci. USA **75:** 2311-2314.
10. DORSCH-HASLER, K., P. B. FISHER, I. B. WEINSTEIN & H. S. GINSBERG. 1980. J. Virol. **34:** 304-315.

Malignant Transformation of Normal Human Keratinocytes by SV40 Virus

JOHN J. WILLE [a]

Kettering Meyer Laboratories
Southern Research Institute
Birmingham, Alabama 35255

Transformation of normal human epithelial cells has recently been reviewed.[1] In 1979, Steinberg and Defendi[2] reported that human epidermal keratinocytes could be morphologically transformed by infection with Simian virus 40, (SV40). SV40 transformation of normal human keratinocytes brings about many phenotypic changes, including increased life-span of the cultures, alterations in their expression of cytokeratin, fibronectin and cytoskeletal proteins and in their responses to tumor promoters.[3–9] SV40-transformed keratinocytes also share many *in vitro* similarities with keratinocytes derived from human squamous carcinoma cell lines.[10–12] None of these SV40-transformed cell lines, however, was tumorigenic *in vivo* when assayed in athymic nude mice. Recently, it was reported that human fetal keratinocytes transfected with a recombinant plasmid containing an origin-defective SV40 genome were transformed to malignancy after approximately 45 *in vitro* passages.[13] In this paper, we report results on the rapid development of a fully malignant human keratinocyte cell line by direct infection of normal human newborn keratinocytes with whole SV40 virus.

Virus stocks were obtained from the American Type Culture Collection. Additional virus stocks were raised by infecting postconfluent cultures of CV 1 cells and harvesting the medium and cell lysates by high-speed centrifugation. Plaque assays were performed as previously described.[14] Primary and secondary cultures of normal human foreskin keratinocytes were grown in serum-free MCDB 153 medium as previously described.[15] Early passage monolayer cultures were infected with 5×10^6 plaque-forming units of SV40 virus and were refed with fresh medium 90 min after infection. Both untreated and SV40-treated cultures were fed serum-free medium until all growth ceased. Cultures were then refed DMEM:F12 medium (1:1) containing 10% fetal calf serum and 5 μg/ml hydrocortisone.[16]

Fifty percent ($^{12}/_{24}$) of the SV40-treated normal human keratinocyte cultures showed focal areas of transformed keratinocyte growth when arrested cultures were refed serum-containing medium. Eventually, 15 different cell lines were isolated by repeated subculture; all were cryostatically preserved for future study. Four cell lines picked at random stained positive for cytoplasmic keratin (cytokeratin) 10 and for nuclear SV40 large T-antigens when assayed by the technique of indirect immunofluorescence microscopy.

[a] Address correspondence to Dr. John J. Wille, Biochemistry Department, Southern Research Institute, 2000 Ninth Avenue South, Birmingham, AL 35255.

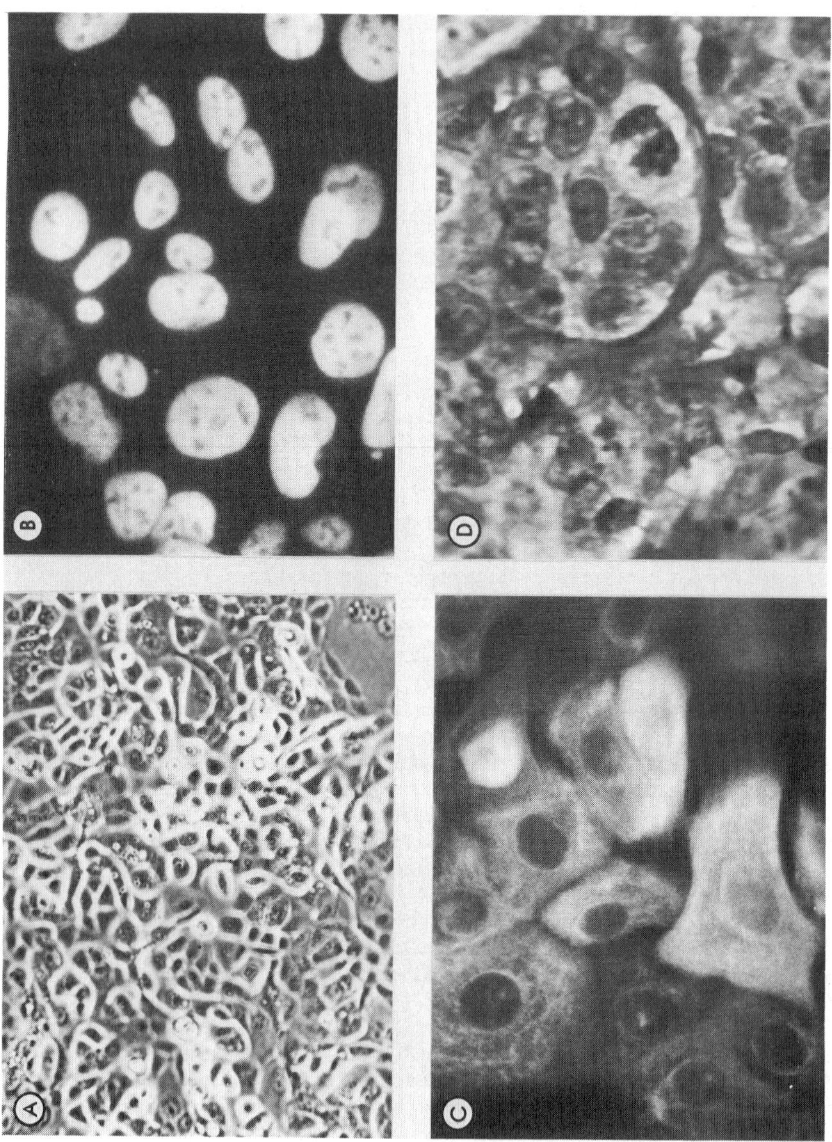

FIGURE 1. (**A**) Phase-contrast photomicrograph of SV40-transformed keratinocytes cultured in a serum-free medium. Immunofluorescence staining pattern of SV 1A2, a transformed neonatal foreskin epidermal keratinocyte cell line, showing (**B**) SV40-specific intranuclear T-antigen and (**C**) cytokeratin 10-staining tonofilaments, characteristic of epidermal keratinocytes. (**D**) Histopathology of a squamous carcinoma tumor formed in a nude mouse by SV 1A2 cells. Magnifications: 150× (**A**); 600× (**B, C**); 750× (**D**), all reproduced at 71%.

One cell line, SV 1A2, was further characterized in detail. FIGURE 1A shows the typical epithelial-cell-colony growth morphology of an early passage culture. FIGURES 1B and 1C present results of immunocytochemical staining reactions, showing that all cells are positive for both large T-antigen and cytokeratin 10, respectively. SV 1A2 was routinely grown in complete MCDB 153 medium, but, like differentiation-defective malignant keratinocytes,[17] and unlike normal keratinocytes,[18] it fails to undergo squamous differentiation when cultured in a serum-free medium containing 1 to 2 m*M* calcium ions and lacking growth factors. Resuspension of dividing SV 1A2 cells in 1.3% methylcellulose medium[10] for 70 hr did not induce terminal differentiation or significant cornified envelope formation. A new subline, SV 1A2-MC, was isolated from methylcellulose suspension culture, and clonal growth experiments were performed with it and with SV 1A2 to determine their growth factor requirements. In this way, two EGF-independent clones were selected from the SV 1A2-MC subline, which could grow in serum-free basal MCDB 153 medium supplemented only with insulin or with insulin and bovine pituitary extract (BPE). Preliminary immunocytochemical experiments suggest that, relative to normal keratinocytes, EGF-independent cells have elevated levels of the EGF receptor.

TABLE 1 presents data showing that early passage SV 1A2 cells formed anchorage-independent colonies in soft agarose and produced tumors (12 of 16 animals) as early as three weeks after 5×10^6 cells were injected subcutaneously into athymic nude mice. Likewise, all (8) of the positive control mice injected with a 3T3 fibroblasts cell line transformed with the human N *ras* gene formed tumors, while all (8) of the negative control mice injected with culture medium (DMEM:F12) were negative. One tumor-bearing mouse was sacrificed at 11 weeks, and the tumor was prepared for cell culture and for histological examination. Figure 1D shows that SV40-transformed keratinocytes induced tumors with the typical appearance of a squamous cell carcinoma, i.e., nests of basal cells surrounded by keratinized squamous cells. A malignant keratinocyte cell line was isolated from this tumor material and, subsequently, found to retain many of the transformed growth characteristic of the parent SV 1A2 cell line, including extended life-span in culture (> 30 passages), ability to grow in serum-free medium without EGF, expression of cytokeratin 10, and uniform retention by all cells of nuclear large T-antigen.

TABLE 1. Anchorage-Independent Growth and Tumorigenicity of SV40-Transformed Human Keratinocytes

Cell Line	Passage No.	Colony Forming Efficiency: Soft Agar[a] (%)	Tumorigenicity[b] Animals (n)	Tumors
Normal[c]	3	0.0	4	0
SV 1A2	6	0.23 ± 0.03	16	12[d]
N-*ras* 3T3	>30	1.60 ± 0.06	8	8[d]
None[e]	—	—	8	0

[a] 7,000 cells were suspended in 0.4% agarose medium and assayed for colony formation at 20 days. The average value ±1 SE is for 4 replicate dishes.

[b] 5×10^6 cells were injected s.c. into 6-9-week-old athymic nude mice, and the time of appearance of tumors was scored weekly for 23 weeks.

[c] Normal epidermal keratinocytes were early passage cells cultured in serum-free complete MCDB 153 medium.

[d] First appearance of tumors was by 3 weeks after injection of cells.

[e] Medium MCDB 153 was injected.

In summary, normal human diploid epidermal cells in serum-free culture can be rapidly and efficiently transformed into malignant keratinocyte cells by brief exposure to whole SV40 virus. The possible cancer risk to human skin of this virus should be reevaluated in the light of these findings.

REFERENCES

1. Chang, S. E. 1986. Biochim. Biophys. Acta **823:** 161-194.
2. Steinberg, M. L. & V. Defendi. 1979. Proc. Natl. Acad. Sci. USA **76:** 801-805.
3. Taylor-Papadimitriou, J., P. Purkis, E. B. Lane, I. A. McKay & S. E. Chang. 1982. Cell Differ. **11:** 169-180.
4. Banks-Schlegel, S. P. & P. M. Howley. 1983. J. Cell Biol. **96:** 330-337.
5. Parkinson, E. K., M. R. Pera, A. Emmerson & P. A. Gorman. 1984. Cancer Res. **44:** 5797-5804.
6. Bernard, B. A., S. M. Robinson, A. Semat & M. Darmon. 1985. Cancer Res. **45:** 1707-1716.
7. Banks-Schlegel, S. P. & J. S. Rhim. 1986. Carcinogenesis **7:** 152-157.
8. Brown,, K. W. & E. K. Parkinson. 1984. Int. J. Cancer **33:** 257-263.
9. Edelman, B., M. L. Steinberg & V. Defendi. 1985. Int. J. Cancer **35:** 219-225.
10. Rheinwald, J. G. & M. A. Beckett. 1980. Cell **22:** 629-632.
11. Rheinwald, J. G. & M. A. Beckett. 1981. Cancer Res. **41:** 1657-1663.
12. Brown, K. W. & E. K. Parkinson. 1985. Int. J. Cancer **35:** 799-807.
13. Brown, K. W. & P. H. Gilmore. 1987. Br. J. Cancer **56:** 545-554.
14. Mertz, J. E. & P. Berg. 1974. Virology **62:** 112-124.
15. Wille, J. J., Jr., M. R. Pittelkow, G. D. Shipley & R. E. Scott. 1984. J. Cell. Physiol. **12:** 31-41.
16. Wille, J. J., Jr., M. R. Pittelkow & R. E. Scott. 1985. Carcinogenesis **6:** 1181-1187.
17. Scott, R. E., M. S. Wilke, J. J. Wille, Jr., M. R. Pittelkow, B. M. Hsu & J. L. Kasperbauer. 1988. Am. J. Pathol. **133:** 374-380.
18. Wilke, M. S., B. M. Hsu, J. J. Wille, Jr., M. R. Pittelkow & R. E. Scott. 1988. Am. J. Pathol. **131:** 171-181.

Friend Erythroleukemia Cell Differentiation: Synergistic Action of Inducers

LALIT C. GARG,[a] APARNA DIXIT,[a] JAY C. BROWN,[b] AND RAJAGOPALAN SRIDHAR[c,d]

[a]*Department of Biochemistry*
Kansas State University
Manhattan, Kansas 66502

[b]*Department of Microbiology*
University of Virginia
School of Medicine
Charlottesville, Virginia 22908

[c]*Department of Basic Pharmaceutical Sciences*
College of Pharmacy
University of South Carolina
Columbia, South Carolina 29208

The Friend murine erythroleukemia (MEL) cell lines are useful for studying mechanisms regulating cell differentiation.[1-4] Several established MEL cell lines exhibit low levels ($< 5\%$ but $> 0\%$) of spontaneous differentiation but quite high (90%-95%) levels of differentiation after treatment with well-defined chemical and physical agents. In response to such inducers, these cells undergo a well-coordinated program of changes reminiscent of a portion of the normal pathway of red cell development *in vivo.* Immature cells at approximately the proerythroblast stage of normal development differentiate, over a five-day culture period, into cells resembling normoblasts. Erythroid differentiation in MEL cells is characterized by terminal cell division, increased accumulation of hemoglobin (Hb)[1] and globin mRNA,[4] as well as by an elevation of intracellular levels of enzymes involved in heme biosynthesis.[5,6] Hemoglobin synthesis and accumulation in MEL cells can be stimulated by a broad spectrum of inducing agents, such as dimethyl sulfoxide (DMSO),[1,2] *N,N*-dimethylformamide (DMF),[2] *N,N*-hexamethylenebisacetamide (HMBA),[2] butyric acid,[2] purine analogs,[7] retinoids,[8] X-rays,[2] and UV radiation.[2]

Among the many MEL lines that have been studied, some are found to be responsive to induction by some agents but not by others. Examples of such clonal variants are a clone that is resistant to DMSO but sensitive to HMBA,[2] one that is responsive to purines but insensitive to DMSO,[7] and two different clones that are inducible by DMSO but not by retinoids.[8]

The above-mentioned features of MEL cell induction and other available evidence in the literature indicate that erythroid differentiation of MEL cells is a multistep

[d] Address correspondence to Rajagopalan Sridhar, Ph.D., Department of Basic Pharmaceutical Sciences, College of Pharmacy, University of South Carolina, Columbia, SC 29208.

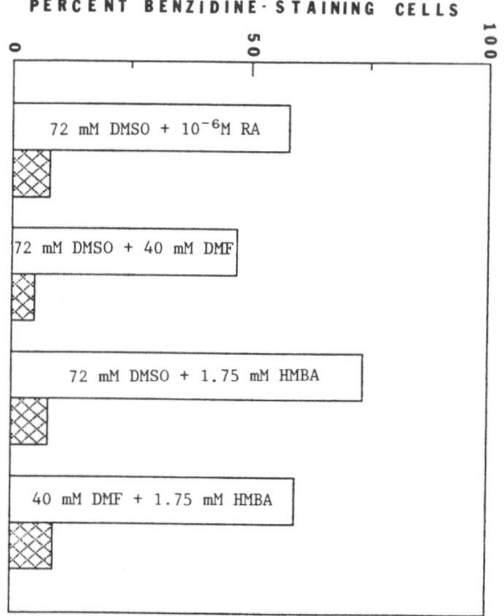

FIGURE 1. Synergistic effect of combining two different inducers of MEL cell differentiation. **Unshaded vertical bars:** percentage of benzidine-staining cells in cultures grown for five days in the presence of the indicated combinations of two inducers, each used at a suboptimal concentration (as indicated) for inducing differentiation by itself. **Shaded vertical bars:** additive value expected on the basis of the individual effects of the two inducers acting independently.

process involving more than one site for regulation of hemoglobin synthesis and of other associated enzymes.[3,4] Bearing this in mind, we have studied the effect of combining two different inducers on MEL cell induction. A synergistic effect was seen with respect to accumulation of hemoglobin when each inducer was present at a suboptimal concentration for inducing erythroid differentiation by itself (FIG. 1 and TABLE 1). The results suggest that the different regulatory sites involved in heme

TABLE 1. Effect of Binary Combinations of Inducers on Erythroid Differentiation of MEL Cells

	Differentiation[b]	
Inducer[a]	Hemoglobin Content (μg/10^6 cells)	Benzidine-Staining Cells (%)
217 m*M* DMSO	10.0	86
72 m*M* DMSO	0.6	2
40 m*M* DMF	0.7	3
1.75 m*M* HMBA	0.8	6
10^{-6} *M* RA	1.0	6
72 m*M* DMSO + 10^{-6} *M* RA	6.8	58
72 m*M* DMSO + 40 m*M* DMF	4.8	47
72 m*M* DMSO + 1.75 m*M* HMBA	9.1	74
40 m*M* DMF + 1.75 m*M* HMBA	7.7	60

[a] All experiments were carried out with 10-ml cultures of clone CV-11 cells initiated at a density of 1×10^5-2×10^5 cells/ml.

[b] Estimations of hemoglobin content and of benzidine-positive cells were made after five days of growth in the presence of the indicated inducer(s) according to previously published procedures.[8] Control cultures grown in the absence of inducers had a hemoglobin content of 0.8 μg/10^6 cells and fewer than 5% benzidine-positive cells.

synthesis interact during the induction of erythroid differentiation in MEL cells. The results are compatible with differential activation of multiple regulatory sites for heme synthesis.

ACKNOWLEDGMENT

The authors thank Mrs. Emily Willingham for her assistance in the preparation of this manuscript.

REFERENCES

1. FRIEND, C., W. SCHER, J. G. HOLLAND & T. SATO. 1971. Hemoglobin synthesis in murine virus-induced leukemic cells in vitro: Stimulation of erythroid differentiation by dimethyl sulfoxide. Proc. Natl. Acad. Sci. USA **68:** 378-382.
2. MARKS, P. A. & R. A. RIFKIND. 1978. Erythroleukemic differentiation. Annu. Rev. Biochem. **47:** 419-448.
3. CHEN, Z., J. BANKS, R. A. RIFKIND & P. A. MARKS. 1982. Inducer-mediated commitment of murine erythroleukemia cells to differentiation: A multistep process. Proc. Natl. Acad. Sci USA **79:** 471-475.
4. ROSS, J., Y. IKAWA & P. LEDER. 1972. Globin messenger-RNA induction during erythroid differentiation of cultured leukemia cells. Proc. Natl. Acad. Sci. USA **69:** 3620-3623.
5. EBERT, P. S. & Y. IKAWA. 1974. Induction of δ-aminolevulinic acid synthetase during erythroid differentiation of cultured leukemia cells. Proc. Soc. Exp. Biol. Med. **146:** 601-604.
6. SASSA, S. 1976. Sequential induction of enzymes of the heme biosynthetic pathway in Friend erythroleukemia cells in culture. J. Exp. Med. **143:** 305-315.
7. GUSELLA, J. F. & D. HOUSMAN. 1976. Induction of erythroid differentiation in vitro by purines and purine analogues. Cell **8:** 263-269.
8. GARG, L. C. & J. C. BROWN. 1983. Friend erythroleukemia cell differentiation: Induction by retinoids. Differentiation **25:** 79-83.

Benzyl Alcohol Reduces the Accumulation of Hemoglobin Minor Compared to Hemoglobin Major in Mouse Erythroleukemia Cells Induced to Differentiate by Dimethyl Sulfoxide or Hexamethylene Bisacetamide[a]

W. SCHER,[b,c] B. M. SCHER,[d] N. HELLINGER,[b] AND S. WAXMAN[b]

Departments of [b]Medicine and [d]Microbiology
Mount Sinai Medical Center
New York, New York 10029

Switching from a relatively high hemoglobin major/hemoglobin minor (Hb mj/Hb mn) ratio to a lower one in Friend leukemia virus-infected MEL cells has been used as a model system for hemoglobin (Hb) switching. Manipulation of this process may be useful in the treatment of some hemoglobinopathies. The control of mouse erythroleukemia (MEL) cell Hb switching is complex. The value of the Hb mj/Hb mn ratio depends not only on the specific inducer or combination of inducers utilized, but also on the concentration of the inducer, the duration of induction, and the cell line.[1] Generally, conditions that lead to relatively low levels of Hb accumulation, *i.e.,* spontaneous induction or treatment with a weak inducer, with a low concentration of a potent inducer, or for a relatively short time, lead to relatively low Hb mj/Hb mn ratios. However, benzyl alcohol (BA) was found to reduce the level of Hb mn more than that of Hb mj while only moderately inhibiting the induction of Hb accumulation. Treatment with BA in the presence of a potent inducer, hexamethylene bisacetamide (HMBA), decreased the Hb mn levels, even at BA concentrations that were not toxic and that did not markedly decrease the accumulation of Hb-containing cells (FIG. 1). BA addition in the presence of dimethyl sulfoxide (DMSO) or HMBA, which induce relatively high Hb mj/Hb mn ratios, increased the ratios further (> 2-fold), while the total Hb and cell yield were only moderately reduced (TABLE 1).

[a]Supported in part by grants from the National Cancer Institute and the American Cancer Society, and by the Chemotherapy Foundation.

[c]Address correspondence to William Scher, M.D., Box 1178, Mount Sinai Medical Center, 1 Gustave L. Levy Place, New York, NY 10029.

TABLE 1. Effect of Benzyl Alcohol on the Hb Phenotype of MEL Cells Treated with Inducers

Inducer[a]	Benzyl alcohol (m*M*)	Hb minor		B$^+$ cells (%)	Total Hb		Cell Yield (no. × 10^{-6}/ml)
		%	% change[b]		pg/cell	% change[b]	
HMBA	0	32.4		88.0	9.9		3.98
	6.0	17.6	−45.7	78.3	6.3	−35.9	3.15
DMSO	0	38.8		88.7	7.5		4.53
	6.1	23.6	−39.2	81.3	5.1	−32.3	3.89
HPX	0	53.4		50.7	3.0		4.35
	6.1	40.4	−24.3	25.7	1.5	−48.5	2.79
Hemin	0	66.4		33.0	3.0		2.13
	6.1	63.1	−5.0	18.7	1.1	−63.0	2.16
Butyrate	0	46.9		53.3	2.4		3.1
	6.1	46.2	−1.5	47.3	1.9	−23.0	1.99

[a] Cells were grown for 5 days in the presence of benzyl alcohol and/or an optimal inducing concentration of an inducer: HMBA, 4 m*M*; DMSO, 253 m*M*; hypoxanthine (HPX), 4 m*M*; hemin, 0.3 m*M*; butyrate, 1.2 m*M*. The Hb phenotype, the percentage of Hb-containing cells (B$^+$), the cellular Hb level, and the cell density were then determined as described.[1]

[b] % change produced by benzyl alcohol treatment.

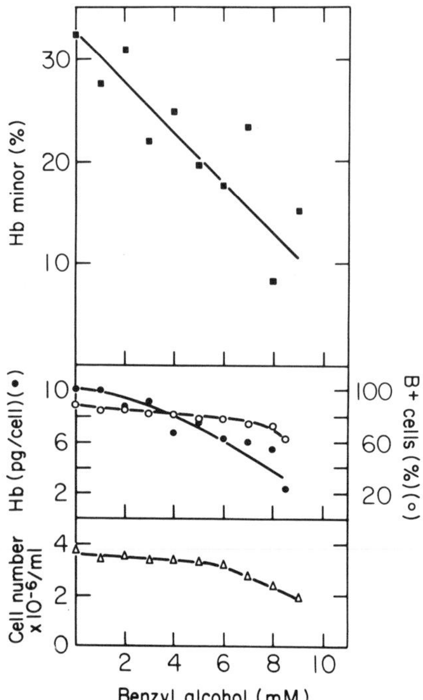

FIGURE 1. Cells in logarithmic growth were seeded at 10^5/ml (as described[1]) in medium containing 4 m*M* HMBA and the concentrations of benzyl alcohol indicated. After 5 days, the percentage of Hb minor was determined by densitometric scanning of 3,3′-dimethoxybenzidine-stained cellulose acetate electrophoretograms[1] of cell lysates; and cell counts, total cellular Hb, and the percentage of Hb-containing, benzidine-positive (B^+) cells were assessed as described.[1]

BA added with hemin or butyrate, which induce relatively low Hb mj/Hb mn ratios, only slightly increased the ratios (14 and 3%, respectively). BA moderately reduced the relative Hb mn concentration in hypoxanthine-treated cells, even though hypoxanthine induction results in a relatively low Hb mj/Hb mn ratio. At the concentration of hypoxanthine used, the cell yield was reduced by the same percentage in BA-treated cultures as in butyrate-treated ones (TABLE 1). In contrast, dexamethasone (6 μM), a known inhibitor of DMSO-, HMBA-, hemin-, and hypoxanthine-induced Hb accumulation,[2] decreased the Hb mj/Hb mn ratio 67% during HMBA induction (not shown). This is in keeping with the findings that suboptimal conditions for Hb induction favor Hb mn accumulation. Therefore, BA is the first agent found that preferentially inhibits production of Hb mn. The effect is so marked that BA reduces the level of HMBA-induced Hb mn to less than 20% of the total Hb present, which is lower than the level of Hb mn (25%) present in the erythrocytes of adult DBA/2 mice (the origin of MEL cells). Since BA is a local anesthetic which increases membrane fluidity, it may influence Hb switching by a membrane-mediated signal.

REFERENCES

1. SCHER, W., B. M. SCHER, N. HELLINGER & S. WAXMAN. 1985. Hemoglobin **9:** 577.
2. SCHER, W. & S. WAXMAN. 1983. Ann. N. Y. Acad. Sci. **411:** 180.

WSU-BL: A New Burkitt's Lymphoma Cell Line with Capacity to Differentiate *In Vitro*

AYAD AL-KATIB,[a] RAMZI M. MOHAMMAD, AND ANWAR N. MOHAMED

Division of Hematology and Oncology
Department of Internal Medicine
Wayne State University School of Medicine
Detroit, Michigan 48201

A new human cell line, WSU-BL, was established from a malignant ascitic fluid occurring in a patient with Burkitt's lymphoma. Immunologic study revealed that WSU-BL cells express IgM/λ both in the cytoplasm and on the surface and react with monoclonal antibodies (MoAb) to B cell antigens. Both fresh tumor and WSU-BL cells had a hyperdiploid karyotype carrying an 8;14 translocation.

WSU-BL cells were treated with the phorbol ester TPA (12-*O*-tetradecanoyl-phorbol-13-acetate: 1.6×10^{-8} *M*) or IFN-γ (500 U/ml) for periods of up to seven days. TPA treatment induced WSU-BL to become mature-looking lymphocytes (FIG. 1) and inhibited their growth by 30%. MoAb binding and flow cytometric analyses indicated that TPA-treated cultures had two populations: small and large cell. The small cell population was approximately the size of normal lymphocytes. As seen in TABLE 1, there was a significant difference between the two populations in their reactivity with the MoAbs. The small cell population showed a dramatic reduction in the expression of B1, B4, BL4, and surface IgM/λ. However, no significant changes were seen in the binding of CALLA and PCA1. B1 and B4 are expressed on B cells at all stages of differentiation except for the most mature B cells. BL4 is an intermediate stage marker.[2] Therefore, a decrease in the expression of these markers is suggestive of a shift to a more mature B cell phenotype. It is generally thought that in the differentiation from early stage B cells to mature B cells, surface Ig fades away.[3] The reduction in the surface IgM/λ is consistent with this interpretation.

An enhancing effect of IFN-γ on mitogen-induced differentiation of normal and malignant B cells has previously been reported.[4] The newly established WSU-BL cells showed no obvious morphological changes or growth inhibition during treatment with IFN-γ. Nevertheless, phenotypic analysis demonstrated that IFN-γ-treated cells started to lose the expression of cell surface antigens B4 and BL4 by approximately 60% and B1 and CALLA by about 20% (TABLE 1). These results suggest that IFN-γ may have induced WSU-BL to enter a more mature state. Total cellular protein

[a] Address correspondence to Ayad Al-Katib, M.D., Assistant Professor of Medicine, Wayne State University, Division of Hematology and Oncology, 3990 John R St., 4 Brush South, Detroit, MI 48201.

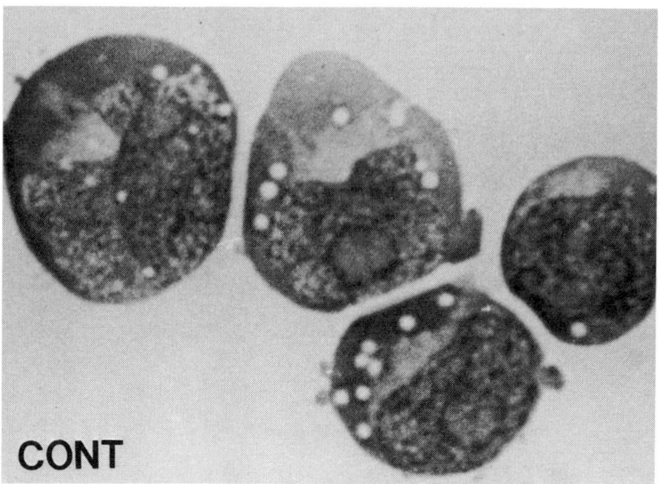

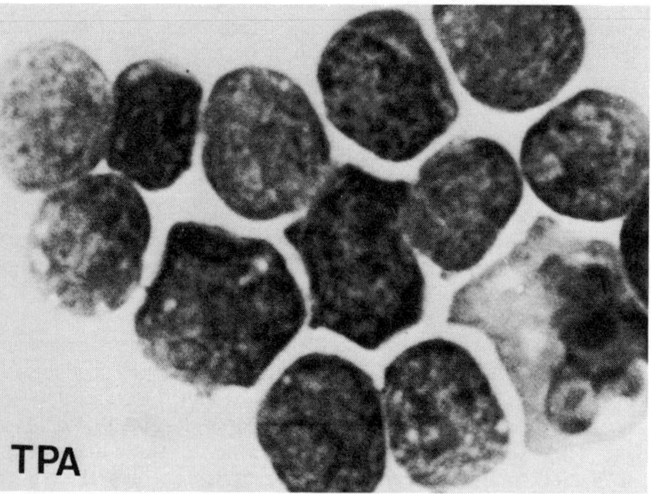

FIGURE 1. Cytospin preparation of the control (**upper panel**) and the TPA-treated (**lower panel**) WSU-BL cells stained with Tetrachrome. WSU-BL cells contain a large nucleus with fine chromatin and one or two nucleoli. The cytoplasm contains vacuoles. TPA-treated cells are smaller, with dark cytoplasm and condensed nuclear chromatin; the vacuoles have disappeared. The percentage of cells showing these changes increased with time and reached 40% on day seven. Magnification: 1000×.

was extracted and analyzed by two-dimensional gel electrophoresis to identify macromolecular changes which accompany the phenotypic changes observed in WSU-BL during induction. Both TPA and IFN-γ induced expression of new cellular proteins and changed the expression of some existing proteins. The gel pattern for the TPA-treated cells showed three new protein spots (M_r 29,000, 31,000, and 35,000) that

TABLE 1. Expression of B Cell Markers on Control Cells and on Cells Treated with TPA or IFN-γ For Seven Days

Marker	Control (%)	TPA-treated Small Cells (%)	TPA-treated Large Cells (%)	IFN-γ-treated (%)
B1	96	32	41	78
B4	98	37	99	30
BL4	74	32	46	18
CALLA	93	87	99	72
PCA1	5	3	7	2
SIgM[a]	99	29	85	85
Sλ[a]	98	63	95	93

[a] SIgM, Sλ: surface IgM and λ chain, respectively.

were not detected in gels of either IFN-γ-treated or control cells. We believe that the three proteins may be related to a more differentiated state, since TPA induced phenotypic and morphological changes consistent with differentiation. At least four protein spots that were consistently present in the gel patterns for control cells were missing in the gel patterns for TPA- or IFN-γ-treated cells. Changes in the kinetics of protein synthesis induced by these two agents may be directly or indirectly involved in lymphoid cell maturation.[1]

REFERENCES

1. NILSSON, K. & G. KLEIN. 1982. Phenotypic and cytogenetic characteristics of human B-lymphoid cell lines and their relevance for the aetiology of Burkitt's lymphoma. Adv. Cancer Res. **37:** 319-380.
2. HASHIMI, L., C. Y. WANG, A. AL-KATIB & B. KOZINER. 1986. Cellular distribution of B-cell specific surface antigen (GP54) detected by a monoclonal antibody (anti-BL4). Cancer Res. **46:** 5431-5437.
3. ANDERSON, K., M. BATES, B. SLAUGHENHOUPT, G. PINKUS, S. SCHLOSSMAN & L. NADLER. 1984. Expression of human B-cell associated antigens on leukemias and lymphomas: A model of human B cell differentiation. Blood **83:** 1424-1433.
4. KISHIMOTO, T. 1985. Factors affecting B cell growth and differentiation. Ann. Rev. Immunol. **3:** 133-157.

One Inducer of Human Promyelocytic Leukemia (HL-60) Cell Differentiation Enhances the Effect of a Second Inducer

LALIT C. GARG,[a] APARNA DIXIT,[a] AND RAJAGOPALAN SRIDHAR [b,c]

[a]*Department of Biochemistry*
Kansas State University
Manhattan, Kansas 66502
and
[b]*Department of Basic Pharmaceutical Sciences*
College of Pharmacy
University of South Carolina
Columbia, South Carolina 29208

The promyelocytic leukemia (HL-60) cell line provides a valuable system for studying human myeloid differentiation *in vitro.* A variety of chemicals can induce functional and morphological differentiation of HL-60 cells to mature granulocytes. These terminally differentiated cells resemble normal peripheral blood granulocytes in their functional attributes, such as chemotaxis, phagocytosis, presence of complement receptors, and the capacity to reduce nitroblue tetrazolium chloride (NBT).[1-2] In the absence of an inducer, the majority of cells in HL-60 cultures are promyelocytes and less than 10% of the cells are terminally differentiated as judged by their morphology or their tendency to be stained as a result of NBT reduction.

The synergistic effect of combining two inducers of HL-60 cell differentiation had been reported earlier by others[2] and by our group.[3] Exponential cultures of HL-60 cells (at an initial density of 6×10^5 cells/ml) treated for 5 days with 210 m*M* dimethyl sulfoxide (DMSO), 120 m*M* *N,N*-dimethylformamide (DMF), 0.5 m*M* N^6,O-2′-dibutyryladenosine 3′,5′-cyclic monophosphate, sodium salt (DBcAMP), 3 m*M* *N,N*-hexamethylenebisacetamide (HMBA), or 10^{-7} *M* retinoic acid (RA) contained 84%, 90%, 66%, 49% and 48%, respectively, of differentiated cells that were stained by NBT. Less than 10% of untreated cells underwent spontaneous differentiation. Less than 15% of the cells were stained by NBT in cultures that had been treated with an inducer at suboptimal concentration, such as 105 m*M* DMSO, 60 m*M* DMF, 0.75 m*M* HMBA, 0.1 m*M* DBcAMP, or 5×10^{-8} *M* RA. A synergistic effect of combining two inducers from the above list was seen with respect to the accumulation of differentiated NBT-staining cells when each inducer was present at

[c]Address correspondence to Rajagopalan Sridhar, Ph.D., College of Pharmacy, University of South Carolina, Columbia, SC 29208.

TABLE 1. Effect of Binary Combinations of Inducers on HL-60 Cell Differentiation

Inducer	NBT-Staining Cells (%)[a]
210 m*M* DMSO	64
105 m*M* DMSO	8
70 m*M* DMSO	5
60 m*M* DMF	8
0.75 m*M* HMBA	7
5×10^{-8} *M* RA	4
0.05 m*M* DBcAMP	6
105 m*M* DMSO + 5×10^{-8} *M RA*	75
60 m*M* DMF + 0.75 m*M* HMBA	87
70 m*M* DMSO + 60 m*M* DMF	85
60 m*M* DMF + 0.05 m*M* DBcAMP	84

[a] Estimate of HL-60 cell induction was made according to the NBT-staining procedure described by Breitman and co-workers.[1] Measurements of NBT-staining cells were made on HL-60 cultures after five days of growth in the presence of the indicated inducer(s). Fewer than 10% of the cells in uninduced control cultures were stained by NBT.

a suboptimal concentration for inducing differentiation by itself. This synergistic effect was observed for several binary combinations of inducing agents (TABLE 1 and FIG. 1).

The ability of chemical inducers to arrest the growth and change the phenotypic expression of neoplastic cells may provide a useful therapeutic strategy.[4] Since RA has shown some promise as an inhibitor of carcinogenesis[5,6] and malignant transformation of cells *in vitro*,[7,8] combinations of inducers that include RA may be particularly useful for effecting remission of certain leukemias.

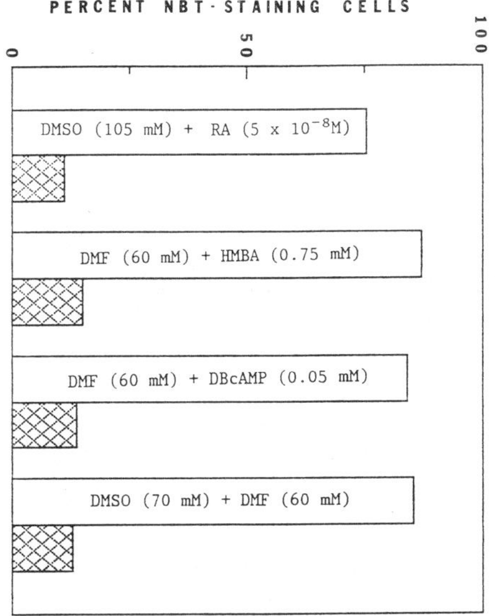

FIGURE 1. Synergistic effect of combining two inducers of HL-60 differentiation. **Unshaded vertical bars:** percentage of NBT-staining cells in cultures grown for five days in the presence of the indicated combinations of two inducers, each used at a suboptimal concentration for inducing differentiation by itself. **Shaded vertical bars:** additive value expected on the basis of the individual effects of the two inducers acting independently.

ACKNOWLEDGMENT

The authors thank Mrs. Emily Willingham for her assistance in the preparation of this manuscript.

REFERENCES

1. BREITMAN, T. R., S. E. SELONICK & S. J. COLLINS. 1980. Induction of differentiation of the human promyelocytic leukemia cell line (HL-60) by retinoic acid. Proc. Natl. Acad. Sci. USA **77:** 2936-2940.
2. CHAPEKAR, M. S., K. D. HARTMAN, M. C. KNODE & R. I. GLAZER. 1987. Synergistic effect of retinoic acid and calcium ionophore A23187 on differentiation, c-*myc* expression, and membrane tyrosine kinase activity in human promyelocytic leukemia cell line HL-60. Molec. Pharmacol. **31:** 140-145.
3. GARG, L. C., A. DIXIT & R. SRIDHAR. 1986. Human promyelocytic leukemia (HL-60) cell differentiation: Synergistic action of inducers. Proc. Am. Assoc. Cancer Res. **27:** 50(Abstract #196).
4. REISS, M., C. GAMBA-VITALO & A. C. SARTORELLI. 1986. Induction of tumor cell differentiation as a therapeutic approach: Preclinical models for hematopoietic and solid neoplasms. Cancer Treat. Rep. **70:** 201-218.
5. MOON, R. C., C. J. GRUBBS, M. B. SPORN & D. G. GOODMAN. 1977. Retinyl acetate inhibits mammary carcinogenesis induced by *N*-methyl-*N*-nitrosourea. Nature **267:** 620-621.
6. MEYSKENS, F. L., JR. & S. E. SALMON. 1979. Inhibition of human melanoma colony formation by retinoids. Cancer Res. **39:** 4055-4057.
7. MERRIMAN, R. L. & J. S. BERTRAM. 1979. Reversible inhibition by retinoids of 3-methylcholanthrene-induced neoplastic transformation in C3H/10T½ clone 8 cells. Cancer Res. **39:** 1661-1666.
8. LOTAN, R. & G. L. NICOLSON. 1977. Inhibitory effects of retinoic acid or retinyl acetate on the growth of untransformed, transformed, and tumor cells *in vitro.* J. Natl. Cancer Inst. **59:** 1717-1722.

Expression of Retinoic Acid Receptor-α-Related mRNA in HL-60 Sublines and Somatic Cell Hybrids

FANA SAID, ISAGANI PUA, AND
ROBERT GALLAGHER[a]

Department of Oncology
Montefiore Medical Center and
Albert Einstein College of Medicine
Bronx, New York 10467

Retinoic acid (RA) is a potent inducer of terminal granulocytic differentiation in the human promyelocytic leukemia cell line HL-60 but not in two other human myeloid leukemia cell lines, KG-1 and K562.[1] HL-60 cells contain a marker chromosome apparently involving a break in the proximal portion of the long arm of chromosome 17 with translocation to a portion of chromosome 5.[2,3] Recently, a gene was identified which encodes a receptor protein for RA (RAR-α) with the expected binding affinity for a physiologically relevant molecule.[4,5] The RAR-α gene has been demonstrated to belong to the steroid-thyroid hormone receptor gene superfamily and has been mapped to chromosome band 17q21.1.[4,5] The present study was designed to determine if the chromosomal translocational breakage in the region of the RAR-α gene might lead to its derepression and account for the unique sensitivity of HL-60 cells to RA-induced differentiation. Additionally, it was asked if sublines of HL-60 cells specifically selected for resistance to differentiation inducers, including RA,[6] or if somatic cell hybrids between RA-sensitive and RA-resistant HL-60 cells with variable resistance to RA (Gallagher, *et al.*, submitted for publication) would manifest variant expression of the RAR-α gene. Total cellular RNA was extracted and purified from these various cell sources by the guanidinium isothiocyanate/cesium chloride procedure and analyzed by Northern blot and dot-blot hybridization to a full-length cDNA probe for the RAR-α gene under stringent conditions.[5] Two radioautographic bands of approximately equal intensity, 4.0-kilobase (kb) and 3.1 kb in size, were observed in all tested sources of HL-60 cell RNA, as well as in K562 and KG-1 cells (FIG. 1 and additional data not shown). As normalized to the signal produced by a an actin gene probe, the expression of the RAR-α gene in the HL-60 cells was only 1.5- to 2-fold greater than the level in RA-non-responsive K562 or KG-1 cells (FIG. 2). An initial extract of RNA from an RA-resistant HL-60 subline (RA-res 1) with ≥ 300-fold higher resistance to RA than that seen in the HL-60 cells was repeatedly determined

[a] Address correspondence to Robert E. Gallagher, M.D., Department of Oncology, Montefiore Medical Center, 111 East 210th Street, Bronx, New York 10467.

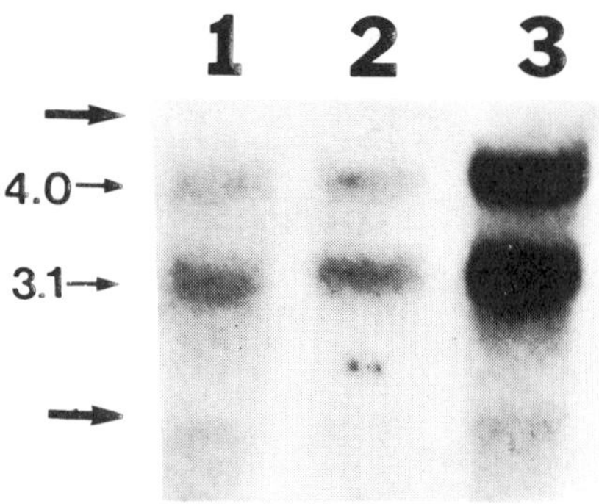

FIGURE 1. Northern blot hybridization of total RNA (15 μg/lane) from wild-type (**lane 1**), universal donor (**lane 2**) and RA-resistant (**lane 3**) HL-60 cells to a full-length RAR-α cDNA probe (kindly provided by V. Giguere, La Jolla, CA). *Heavy arrows* indicate the position of 28S and 18S ribosomal RNA markers and *thin arrows* the positions of 3.1- and 4.0-kilobase bands. Ethidium bromide staining of the gel indicated the presence of intact RNA and approximately equal RNA application for each lane (not shown).

to have a 2- to 5-fold increase in expression of the RAR-α gene compared to that in wild-type HL-60 cells. However, in subsequent extractions of RNA from this subline either no increase or a much lesser degree of increase was observed. Finally, similar levels of RAR-α expression were observed in somatic cell hybrids between wild-type or RA-resistant HL-60 cells and RA-sensitive universal donor (UD) HL-60 cells irrespective of the sensitivity of these hybrids to RA-induced differentiation. These results indicate that the quantitative level of expression of the RAR-α gene alone

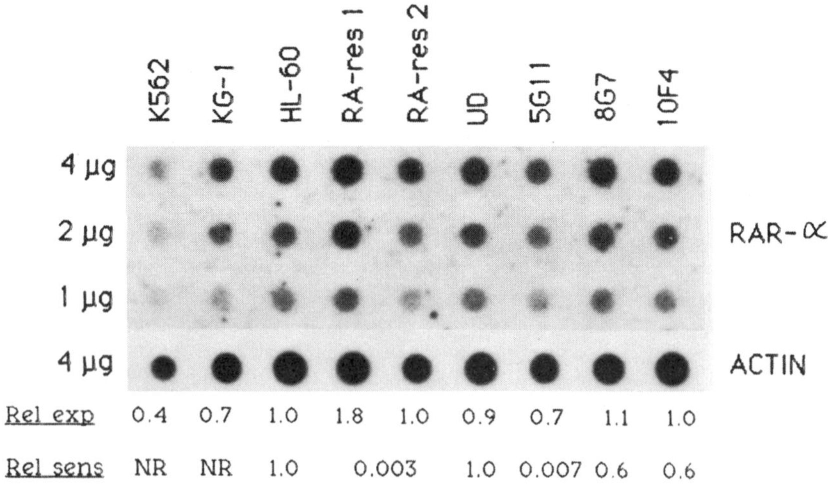

FIGURE 2. Dot-blot hybridization to RAR-α and actin gene probes of total RNA from various HL-60 cell sources and leukemic cell lines K562 and KG-1. RA-res 1 and 2, two separate extractions of RNA from RA-resistant HL-60 cells; UD, universal donor, (i.e., 5-bromo-2′-deoxyuridine/oubain-resistant HL-60 cells); 5G11, a near-tetraploid RA-resistant cell × UD cell HL-60 hybrid; 8G7, a slightly hyperdiploid RA-resistant cell × UD cell HL-60 hybrid; 10F4, a near-tetraploid wild-type cell × UD cell HL-60 hybrid. *Rel exp,* expression of RAR-α relative to level in wild-type HL-60 cells. *Rel sens,* sensitivity to RA-induced differentiation relative to wild-type HL-60 cells. NR, not responsive.

cannot account for the large differences in sensitivity of cultured human myeloid leukemic cells to RA-induced differentiation. Further studies are required to determine if the expression of the RAR-α gene is, nonetheless, essential for RA-mediated differentiation, with differences in the apparent activity of the RA receptor being related to translational/post-translational factors or, for selected RA-resistance, possibly to mutational changes in the RAR-α gene.

REFERENCES

1. Breitman, T. R., S. E. Selonick & S. J. Collins. 1980. Proc. Natl. Acad. Sci. USA **77:** 2936-2940.
2. Gallagher, R. E., A. C. Ferrari, A. W. Zulich, R-W. Chiu-Yen & J. R. Testa. 1984. Cancer Res. **44:** 2542-2653.
3. Wolman, S. R., L. Lanfrancone, R. Dalla-Favera, S. Ripley & A. S. Henderson. 1985. Cancer Genet. Cytogenet. **17:** 133-141.
4. Petkovich, M., N. J. Brand, A. Drust & P. Chambon. 1987. Nature **330:** 444-450.
5. Giguere, V., E. S. Ong, P. Segui & R. M. Evans. 1987. Nature **330:** 624-629.
6. Gallagher, R., P. Bilello, A. Ferrari, C-S. Chang, R-W. Chiu-Yen, W. Nickols & E. Muly, III. 1985. Leukemia Res. **9:** 967-986.

Activation of the Fructose 1,6-Bisphosphatase Gene during Monocytic Differentiation and Maturation

DAVID H. SOLOMON, MARIE-CECILE RAYNAL, AND YVON E. CAYRE[a]

Department of Physiology and Cellular Biophysics and Department of Medicine Columbia University College of Physicians and Surgeons New York, New York 10032

Cells from the human leukemia cell line HL-60 undergo terminal monocyte-like differentiation following exposure to the active, circulating form of vitamin D_3 [1α,25-dihydroxycholecalciferol: 1,25-$(OH)_2D_3$]. Little is known about the genes which regulate monocytic differentiation. Using the 1F10 model system,[1] a clonal variant of HL-60 origin, together with subtraction cDNA cloning, we have shown that the fructose 1,6-bisphosphatase (FBPase) gene, encoding a key enzyme in gluconeogenesis, is activated by 1,25-$(OH)_2D_3$ during monocytic-macrophagic differentiation.[2] This single-copy gene encodes two species of mRNA, one of 1.8 kilobases (kb) and the other of 1.7 kb, that are each regulated at different stages of monocytic maturation.[2] That the 1.7-kb mRNA encodes a protein with FBPase activity is consistent with the fact that this transcript is found as a unique species in kidney, a main source of FBPase, and is considerably induced in 1,25-$(OH)_2D_3$-treated human peripheral blood monocytes (PBMs) which also exhibit FBPase activity.[2]

A high level of the 1.7-kb mRNA is physiologically expressed in normal human alveolar macrophages.[2] This and the fact that mice deficient in 1,25-$(OH)_2D_3$ have a depressed inflammatory response and impairment of phagocytic activity as well as migration of macrophages at the inflammatory site[3] reinforce the view that 1,25-$(OH)_2D_2$ may be a natural inducer of macrophage maturation or activation.

The relationship between induction of FBPase activity and maturation or activation of human macrophages is most interesting. CSF-1 (colony-stimulating factor-1), a cytokine known to be mitogenic to monocytes and to mediate an increased secretion of tumor necrosis factor and IFN-γ (interferon-γ) from these cells during the immune response,[4] activates the expression of the FBPase gene in PBMs (data not shown). Our results suggest that a CSF-1-mediated increase in FBPase activity may play an

[a] Address correspondence to Dr. Yvon E. Cayre, Department of Physiology, Columbia University, College of Physicians and Surgeons, Room P&S 11-431, 630 West 168th Street, New York, NY 10032.

important role in the final stages of monocyte-macrophage maturation. Furthermore, since it is induced by 1,25-$(OH)_2D_3$ only in PBMs and not earlier, expression of the 1.7-kb FBPase mRNA and the concomitant increase in the levels of this protein may serve as an important marker of macrophage maturation, along with the cell surface antigen CD14.[5] Its constitutive expression in normal alveolar macrophages may suggest its involvement in a discrete step in macrophage activation or maturation. Whether it is present in other mature cells of the myeloid lineage, such as peritoneal macrophages, has yet to be studied and is necessary to determine if FBPase is a general marker of the mature, activated macrophage.

IFN-γ, known to be secreted from $CD4^+$ lymphocytes during the immune response,[6] can mediate the conversion of 25-$(OH)D_3$ to 1,25-$(OH)_2D_3$ inside PBMs.[7] We have verified that this generation of intracellular 1,25-$(OH)_2D_3$ gives rise to an increased FBPase mRNA expression and a corresponding increase in FBPase activity (data not shown). This finding suggests a yet undescribed function for FBPase during both the immune response and inflammation, since the increased FBPase activity measured *in vitro* does not correspond to increased gluconeogenic activity in the intact cell. By applying both anti-sense RNA technology and traditional enzymology to an *in vivo* model system of inflammation, we may be able to better understand the function of increased FBPase expression during the inflammation process.

The traditional function attributed to FBPase has been that of a critical regulator of gluconeogenesis. The results of our studies suggest that it also plays an important role in monocytic differentiation and maturation. Elucidating the molecular mechanisms of 1,25-$(OH)_2D_3$-induced monocytic differentiation and maturation and the role of FBPase in these processes may be critical for understanding the inflammatory process as related to the host defense mechanism against infection and the growth and spread of tumor cells.

REFERENCES

1. CAYRE, Y., M. C. RAYNAL, A. DARZYNKIEWICZ & M. DORNER. 1987. Proc. Natl. Acad. Sci. USA **84:** 7619-7623.
2. SOLOMON, D. H., M. C. RAYNAL, G. TEJWANI & Y. E. CAYRE. 1988. Proc. Natl. Acad. Sci. USA **85:** 6904-6908.
3. BAR-SHAVIT, Z., D. NOFF, S. EDELSTEIN, M. MEYER, S. SHIBOLET & R. GOLDMAN. 1981. Calcif. Tissue Int. **33:** 673-696.
4. WARREN, M. K. & P. RALPH. 1986. J. Immunol. **137:** 2281-2285.
5. TODD, R. F., A. K. BHAN, S. E. KABAWAT & S. F. SCHLOSSMAN. 1984. *In* Leukocyte Typing. A. Bernard, A. Boumsell, J. Dausset, C. Milstein & S. F. Schlossman, Eds.: 424. Springer Verlag. New York.
6. TAYLOR, S. & J. BRYSON. 1985. J. Immunol. **134:** 1493-1497.
7. KOEFFLER, H. P., H. REICHEL, J. E. BISHOP & A. W. NORMAN. 1985. Biochem. Biophys. Res. Commun. **127:** 596-603.

Induction of Differentiation in Human Melanoma Cells by the Combination of Different Classes of Interferons or Interferon Plus Mezerein[a]

MOHAMMAD ALMAS AHMED,[b]
LUDOVICO GUARINI,[c] SOLDANO FERRONE,[d] AND
PAUL B. FISHER[b]

[b] *Departments of Neurological Surgery, Pathology and Urology and*
[c] *Division of Hematology/Oncology, Cancer Center/Institute of Cancer Research*
Columbia University
College of Physicians and Surgeons
New York, New York 10032
and
[d] *Department of Microbiology and Immunology*
New York Medical College
Valhalla, New York 10595

Cancer is a disease characterized by alterations in the proliferative control of cells and is often associated with defects in the capacity of tumor cells to undergo normal programs of cellular differentiation (reviewed in Ref. 1). Although improved treatment protocols have been developed, many forms of cancer are still refractile to treatment and this problem is even exacerbated following chemotherapy or radiation therapy.[2] These discouraging findings suggest that newer approaches are required to more effectively treat specific neoplasms and to prevent tumor cells from progressing to a metastatic phenotype. A potential strategy for suppressing tumor cell growth is to utilize single agents or combinations of agents which have the capacity to induce the expression of genes mediating terminal differentiation in tumor cells, thereby resulting in a cessation of tumor cell proliferation. During the process of therapy, one may also exploit those changes that occur in the surface expression of tumor associated antigens (TAA), which may reflect altered states of differentiation of the tumor, as potential targets for monoclonal antibody therapy.[1,3] We have employed these approaches in an attempt to develop improved methods for the detection and, ultimately, the treatment of specific cancers, including breast carcinoma, colon carcinoma, glioblastoma multiforme, and melanoma.[1,3-6]

[a] This research was supported by National Cancer Institute Grants CA35675, CA37959, and CA39559.

To more effectively utilize differentiation therapy as a modality for cancer treatment, it will be necessary to better understand the biochemical and molecular basis of normal cellular differentiation. Although the exact details may differ for specific programs of differentiation, studies employing several model differentiation systems suggest that differentiation is a multistage process, often consisting of an induction, a reversible commitment to differentiation and a terminal differentiation stage.[1,7] Each step of this process is likely to involve a set of specific genes which must be regulated in a coordinated fashion for normal differentiation to occur. For example, recent elegant studies have resulted in the identification, cloning, and expression of genetic elements which can induce expression of the myogenic phenotype when they are transferred and expressed in appropriate target cells.[8,9] The identity and total number of genes which can serve as determinants of differentiation for the different tissue lineages and their temporal relationships of expression have not been determined. In the case of a tumor cell, it is possible that those genes which are required for induction of a normal differentiated phenotype are present but not expressed, or are prevented from functioning normally because of the presence of differentiation-inhibitory molecules, or are defective as a consequence of mutational changes occurring during development of the transformed state. If the appropriate genes for differentiation are present in an inactive form in tumor cells and if treatment with specific agents can activate these genes, it should theoretically be possible to induce terminal differentiation in the tumor cells, resulting in a loss of proliferative capacity.

In recent studies, we have demonstrated that the combination of the biological response modifier fibroblast interferon (IFN-β) with the anti-leukemic compound mezerein (MEZ) is synergistic in suppressing the growth of human melanoma cells.[10–12] Concomitant with this inhibition of cellular growth is induction of differentiation, as indicated by both morphological criteria and an increase in melanin synthesis (melanotic melanoma) or an induction of melanin synthesis (amelanotic melanoma). Detailed studies with the human melanoma cell line HO-1 indicate that specific concentrations of IFN-β plus MEZ result in a reversible commitment to differentiate if cells are treated for 72 or 96 hr, whereas after exposure for 7 days to the same combination of agents, HO-1 cells are terminally differentiated, i.e., they remain viable but lose their proliferative capacity. These results suggest that IFN-β plus MEZ is capable of inducing the appropriate genes required for programming both a reversible commitment to differentiation and terminal differentiation (which includes irreversible loss of proliferative capacity) in HO-1 melanoma cells. In contrast, the combination of IFN-β plus recombinant immune interferon (IFN-γ) results in a potentiation of growth suppression and an increase in melanin synthesis in HO-1 cells, effects which are transient and are reversible when the interferons are removed. The identity and the temporal pattern of expression of the genes involved in human melanoma differentiation (both the reversible commitment and the irreversible terminal stages) have not been defined. Similarly, the cellular antigenic changes associated with the various stages of melanoma differentiation also remain to be determined. The aim of this study was to begin the process of identifying the antigenic and gene expression changes occurring during the early commitment of HO-1 cells to differentiate and during the subsequent reversible step for the commitment to differentiate.

Previous studies have demonstrated that various recombinant human interferons can enhance the expression of HLA class I antigens, induce HLA class II antigens, and modulate TAAs on the cell surface of human melanoma, breast carcinoma, and colon carcinoma cells.[1,3–5,10,13,14] The effect of IFN-β, MEZ, IFN-γ, and the tumor-promoting agent 12-*O*-tetradecanoyl-phorbol-13-acetate (TPA), alone and in various combinations, on the expression of HLA class I antigens, HLA-DR antigens, a high-molecular-weight melanoma-associated antigen (HMW-MAA), and intercellular adhesion molecule (ICAM-1) is shown in FIGURE 1. An increase in the expression of HLA class I antigen was observed 72 hr after exposure of HO-1 cells to IFN-β, IFN-γ, IFN-β + IFN-γ, or IFN-β + TPA, and the greatest increase was observed with IFN-β + MEZ. In the case of HLA-DR antigen expression, a small increase was observed following treatment with IFN-β or IFN-β + MEZ, and the greatest increases were observed with IFN-γ or IFN-β + IFN-γ. In contrast, the various

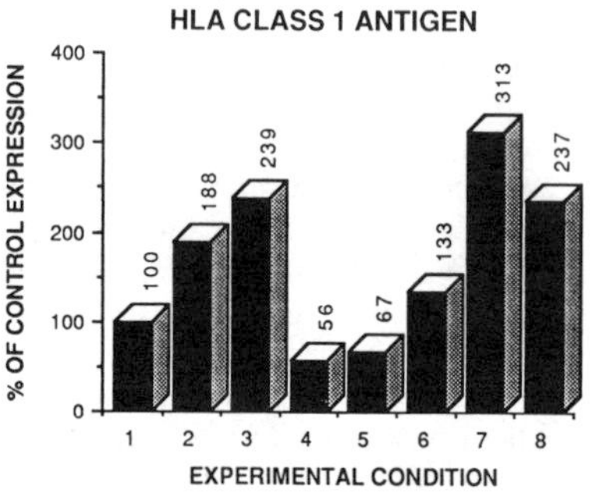

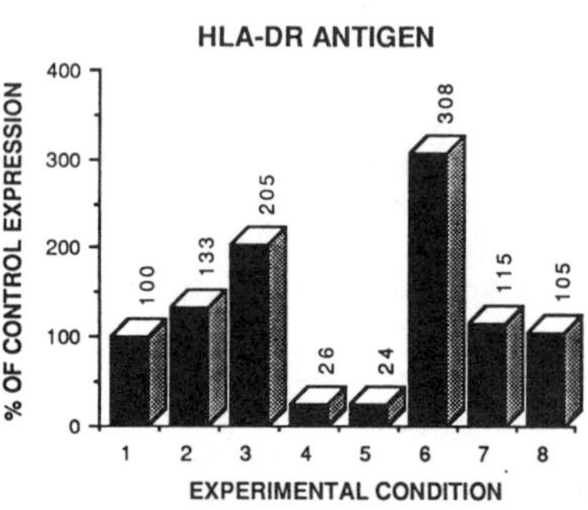

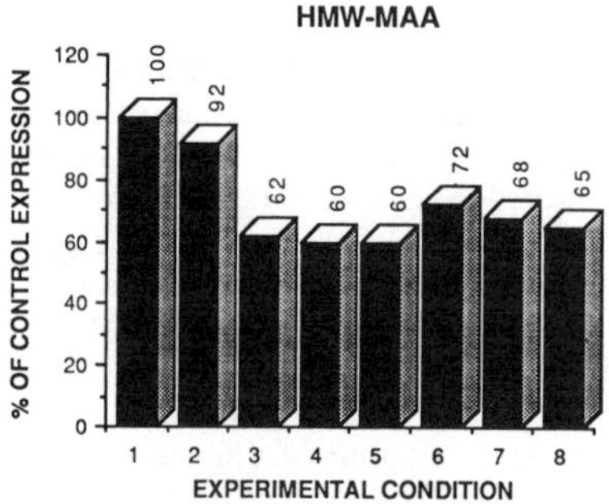

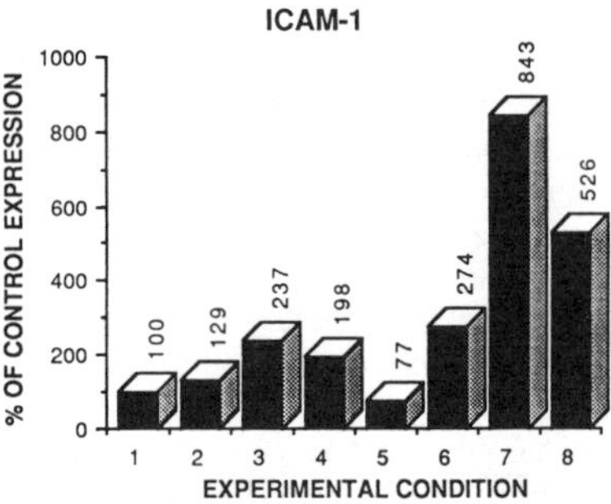

FIGURE 1. Effect of IFN-β, IFN-γ, mezerein (MEZ), and the tumor promoter 12-*O*-tetradecanoyl-phorbol-13-acetate (TPA), alone and in various combinations, on the surface expression of class I HLA antigens, class II HLA-DR antigen, a high-molecular-weight melanoma-associated antigen (HMW-MAA), and an intercellular adhesion molecule (ICAM-1) by the human melanoma cell line, HO-1. Cultures of HO-1 cells in the logarithmic phase of growth were incubated for 72 hr in medium containing the various additions; cells were then washed twice with phosphate-buffered saline containing azide and incubated for 30 min at 4°C with anti-HLA class I mouse monoclonal antibody (MoAb) W6/32, anti-HLA-DR class II MoAb CL 413, anti-HMW-MAA MoAb 225.28, or an anti–96-Kda MAA MoAb which recognizes ICAM-1, MoAb CL 203.4. Cells were then washed and incubated for 30 min at 4°C with fluoresceinated goat anti-mouse antibody (FITC-GaM). At the end of the incubation period, cells were washed and analyzed with a fluorescence-activated cell sorter (FACStar). The results are expressed as relative binding of FITC-GaM to melanoma cells coated with the specific MoAbs for treated versus control cultures. Treatment conditions were as follows: (**1**) control, (**2**) IFN-β (2000 U/ml), (**3**) IFN-γ (2000 U/ml), (**4**) MEZ (10 ng/ml), (**5**) TPA (10 ng/ml), (**6**) IFN-β + IFN-γ (1000 U/ml + 1000 U/ml), (**7**) IFN-β + MEZ (2000 U/ml + 10 ng/ml), (**8**) IFN-β + TPA (2000 U/ml + 10 ng/ml).

compounds either inhibited or did not significantly change the expression of the HMW-MAA. Previous studies have indicated that IFN-γ induces the expression of ICAM-1 on the surface of a variety of cell types.[15] In HO-1 melanoma cells, a 72-hr exposure to IFN-β + MEZ or IFN-β + TPA resulted in a greater induction of ICAM-1 than observed with IFN-γ. These observations with ICAM-1 are particularly intriguing, since it is believed that this molecule is a ligand for the lymphocyte function associated antigen-1 (LFA-1), which is involved in cytotoxic T lymphocyte recognition.[16] Recent studies by Makgoba *et al.*[17] indicate that ICAM-1 is a ligand for antigen-independent conjugates, for antigen-specific cytotoxic T lymphocyte recognition, and for cytolysis of particular target cells. The relationship between ICAM-1 induction and expression of the differentiated phenotype of HO-1 cells following treatment with IFN-β + MEZ is currently under investigation.

To begin to define the changes in gene expression occurring in HO-1 cells following the induction of reversible differentiation, cultures were treated with IFN-β (2000 U/ml), IFN-γ (2000 U/ml), MEZ (10 ng/ml), IFN-β + IFN-γ (1000 U/ml of each), or IFN-β + MEZ (2000 U/ml + 10 ng/ml) for 1 and 4 hr (early phase) or 72 hr (late phase). Messenger RNA was isolated, transferred to nitrocellulose filters, and probed with a series of ^{32}P-labeled, nick-translated, cloned gene probes. Exposure to the different agents for both early (1 and 4 hr) and late (72 hr) times resulted in changes in the expression of several genes. The genes analyzed included a fibroblast interferon-inducible gene (ISG-54)[18], two proto-oncogenes (c-*myc* and c-*fos*), the epidermal growth factor receptor gene, two TPA-regulated genes (TPA-R1 and TPA-S1),[19] the fibronectin gene, and the HLA-DRβ gene. The levels of mRNA for the interferon-responsive gene ISG-54 were elevated following treatment with IFN-β, MEZ, IFN-β + IFN-γ, or IFN-β + MEZ during the early phase of induction of reversible commitment to differentiation, but the effect was less marked during the late phase of reversible induction of differentiation. Maximal enhancement of ISG-54 mRNA levels was observed following treatment with IFN-β + MEZ. In contrast, the highest level of fibronectin mRNA was seen in the late phase of reversible induction of differentiation following treatment with IFN-β + MEZ (FIG. 2). Although we do not yet know if the increase in mRNA for fibronectin is associated with an increase in the level of this protein, the increase observed in the levels of fibronectin mRNA is interesting, because this gene behaves as an early response gene when cells are exposed to various growth factors and tumor promoters.[20] We also observed an increase in mRNA levels for the HLA-DRβ gene during the late phase following treatment with either IFN-γ or IFN-β + IFN-γ (FIG. 2). The latter finding was also correlated with increased levels of HLA-DR protein in cells treated with the appropriate agents (FIG. 1). Results from studies with the human c-*fos* gene indicated no increase in the levels of mRNA in either the early or the late phase of the reversible commitment to differentiation of HO-1 cells, although it is possible that altered expression following treatment with the different agents may be transient and over within 1 hr, as reported previously.[21]

In the present study we have analyzed genes which might be differentially regulated during the early (1 and 4 hr) and later (72 hr) phases of reversible chemically-induced HO-1 human melanoma cell differentiation. Differential expression was observed in the expression of ISG-54, fibronectin, and HLA-DR genes. After 72-hr treatment with the various differentiation modulating agents, we also observed increases in the levels of surface antigens expressed by HO-1 cells, including HLA class I antigen, HLA-DR antigen, and ICAM-1. These results look very promising and further studies using a larger panel of additional gene probes and monoclonal antibodies are planned to identify the genes which are differentially regulated during the induction, reversible commitment, and terminal stages of human melanoma cell differentiation. The system

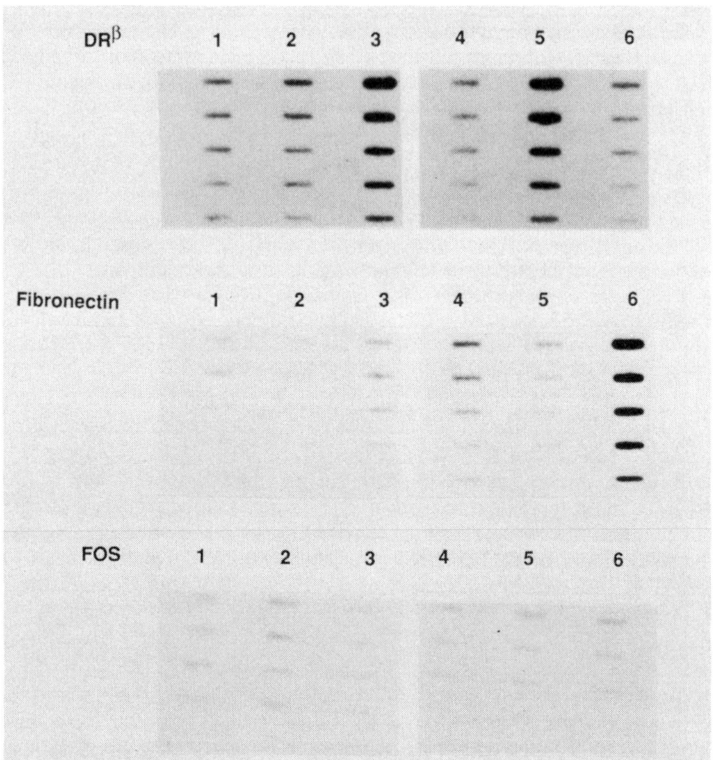

FIGURE 2. Effect of IFN-β, IFN-γ, and mezerein (MEZ), alone and in various combinations, on class II HLA-DR (DRβ), fibronectin, and *fos* mRNA levels in HO-1 cells. Cultures were seeded in 150-cm^2 tissue culture flasks, the indicated compounds were added 24 hr later, and cultures were incubated for 72 hr at 37°C. Total cytoplasmic RNA was isolated, and 2-fold dilutions of RNA were added per slot, beginning with 20 μg of RNA in the upper slot of each lane, and the nylon filters were hybridized using the indicated ^{32}P-labeled, nick-translated probe. Treatment conditions were as follows: (**1**) control, (**2**) IFN-β (2000 U/ml), (**3**) IFN-γ (2000 U/ml), (**4**) MEZ (10 ng/ml), (**5**) IFN-β + IFN-γ (1000 U/ml of each), (**6**) IFN-β + MEZ (2000 U/ml + 10 ng/ml).

described in this report should also be of value in identifying and molecularly cloning the gene(s) which control human melanoma cell differentiation.

REFERENCES

1. Fisher, P. B., J. W. Greiner, R. A. Mufson & J. Schlom. 1989. *In:* Applications of Genetic Engineering. F. Bolivar & P. Balbas, Eds. Marcel Dekker, Inc., New York. In press.
2. Gerlach, J. H., N. Kartner, D. R. Bell & V. Ling. 1986. Cancer Surv. **5:** 25-46.
3. Greiner, J. W., F. Guadagni, P. Noguchi, S. Pestka, D. Colcher, P. B. Fisher & J. Schlom. 1987. Science **235:** 895-898.

4. Greiner, J. W., P. H. Hand, P. Noguchi, P. B. Fisher, S. Pestka & J. Schlom. 1984. Cancer Res. **44:** 3208-3214.
5. Greiner, J. W., J. Schlom, S. Pestka, J. A. Langer, P. Giacomini, M. Kusama, S. Ferrone & P. B. Fisher. 1987. Pharmacol. Therapeut. **31:** 209-236.
6. Vita, J. R., G. M. Edwalds, T. Gorey, E. M. Housepian, M. R. Fetell, L. Guarini, J. A. Langer & P. B. Fisher. 1988. Anticancer Res. **8:** 297-302.
7. Waxman, S., G. B. Rossi & F. Takaku, Eds. 1988. The Status of Differentiation Therapy of Cancer. Serono Symposia Publications **45:** 1-419. Raven Press. New York.
8. Davis, R. L., H. Weintraub & A. B. Lassar. 1987. Cell **51:** 987-1000.
9. Pinney, D. F., S. H. Pearson-White, S. F. Konieczny, K. E. Latham & C. P. Emerson. 1988. Cell **53:** 781-793.
10. Fisher, P. B. & S. Grant. 1985. Pharmacol. Therapeut. **27:** 143-166.
11. Fisher, P. B., D. R. Prignoli, H. Hermo, Jr., I. B. Weinstein & S. Pestka. 1985. Interferon Res. **5:** 11-22.
12. Fisher, P. B., H. Hermo, Jr., W. E. Solowey, M. C. Dietrich, G. M. Edwalds, I. B. Weinstein, J. A. Langer, S. Pestka, P. Giacomini, M. Kusama & S. Ferrone. 1986. Anticancer Res. **6:** 765-774.
13. Giacomini, P., A. Aguzzi, S. Pestka, P. B. Fisher & S. Ferrone. 1984. J. Immunol. **133:** 1649-1655.
14. Giacomini, P., L. Imberti, A. Aguzzi, P. B. Fisher, G. Trinchieri & S. Ferrone. 1985. J. Immunol. **135:** 2887-2894.
15. Dustin, M. L., R. Rothlein, A. K. Bhan, C. A. Dinarello & T. A. Springer. 1986. J. Immunol. **137:** 245-254.
16. Springer, T. A., M. L. Dustin, T. K. Kishimoto & S. D. Marlin. 1987. Annu. Rev. Immunol. **5:** 223-252.
17. Makgoba, M. W., M. E. Sanders, G. E. G. Luce, E. A. Gugel, M. L. Dustin, T. A. Springer & S. Shaw. 1988. Eur. J. Immunol. **18:** 637-640.
18. Levy, D. A., A. Larner, A. Chaudhuri, L. E. Babiss & J. E. Darnell, Jr. 1986. Proc. Natl. Acad. Sci. USA **83:** 8929-8933.
19. Johnson, M. D., G. M. Housey, P. T. Kirschmeier & I. B. Weinstein. 1987. Mol. Cell. Biol. **7:** 2821-2829.
20. Blatti, S. P., D. N. Foster, G. Ranganathan, H. L. Moses & M. J. Getz. 1988. Proc. Natl. Acad. Sci. USA **85:** 1119-1123.
21. Wan, Y. Y., B. Z. Levi & K. Ozato. 1988. J. Interferon Res. **8:** 105-112.

Single-Cell Analysis of DNase I-Sensitive Sites during Neoplastic and Normal Cell Differentiation within Human Bone Marrow[a]

JOHN H. FRENSTER[b]

Departments of Medicine
Stanford University and
Santa Clara Valley Medical Center
San Jose, California 95128

DNase I-sensitive sites in chromatin correspond to points of active gene transcription[1] and can be visualized by high-resolution electron microscopy of intact single cells.[2]

TABLE 1. Contrasts Between Euchromatin and Heterochromatin in Animal Cells[a]

Euchromatin	Heterochromatin
Extended microfibrils	Condensed masses
Active RNA synthesis	No RNA synthesis
Early DNA replication	Late DNA replication
Many DNA helix openings	No DNA helix openings
DNase I-sensitive sites	No DNase I-sensitive sites
Many nuclear polyanions	Few nuclear polyanions
Loose binding of histones to DNA	Tight binding of histones to DNA
Reduced number of nucleosomes	Full number of nucleosomes
Increased binding of steroid hormone	Decreased binding of steroid hormone
Binding of oncogenic viral DNA	No binding of oncogenic viral DNA
Binding of chemical carcinogens	Little binding of chemical carcinogens
Little binding of PHA mitogen[b]	Much binding of PHA mitogen[b]
Decrease during cell differentiation	Increase during cell differentiation
Decrease during cell division	Increase during cell division
Increase during cell neoplasia	Decrease during cell neoplasia
Increase during lymphocyte activation	Decrease during lymphocyte activation
Resistance to added RNA	Response to added RNA

[a] Individual references may be found in Ref. 5.
[b] PHA, phytohemagglutinin.

[a] Supported in part by Research Grants CA-10174 and CA-13524 from the National Cancer Institute, by Research Grant IC-45 from the American Cancer Society, and by a Research Scholar Award from the Leukemia Society.

[b] Address for correspondence: Department of Medicine, Santa Clara Valley Medical Center, 751 South Bascom Avenue, San Jose, CA 95128.

These methods were applied to leukemic and normal human bone marrow spicules, and quantitative analysis revealed an inverse correlation between the advancing stages of granulocytic or erythrocytic cell differentiation and the number and size of DNase I-sensitive sites per cell nucleus. The sites range in size from 25 to 700 nm in length, corresponding to 70-2000 base pairs in length of DNA helix. These DNase I-sensitive sites, which represent localized DNA helix openings,[3] are found exclusively within extended, derepressed euchromatin and never within condensed, repressed heterochromatin.

Detailed studies of the molecular biophysics, biochemistry, and ultrastructure of euchromatin and heterochromatin within animal cells[4] have revealed a striking partition of function[5] between the two states of chromatin (TABLE 1). Since oncogenic viral DNA requires DNA helix openings within complementary host DNA sequences for effective viral oncogenesis[6] (FIGURE 1), these sequences in euchromatin[7] also allow gene transcription characteristic of the neoplastic state,[8] often involving derepression of previously inactive embryonic genes;[9] loss of viral DNA from these integration sites correlates with reversion of the transformed cells to the normal state.[10]

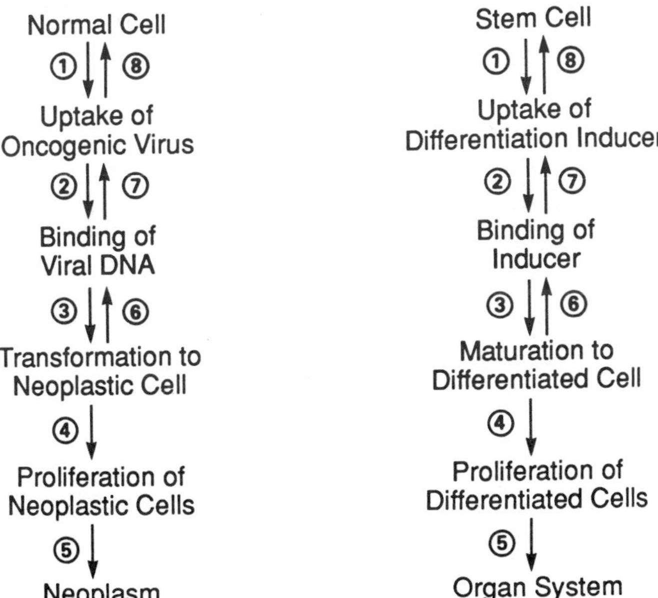

FIGURE 1. Comparison of viral oncogenesis and cell differentiation in animal cells. If normal cells are susceptible, they may be infected by an oncogenic virus (**step 1**). If the normal cells contain cell DNA sequences complementary to sequences in the viral DNA, the viral DNA may be bound and integrated (**step 2**). Bound viral DNA may then induce synthesis of RNA species usually repressed in a normal cell (**step 3**). The resultant transformed cell may enter the G_1 and S phases of the proliferation cycle (**step 4**). An excess of cell proliferation over cell destruction results in a growing neoplasm (**step 5**). Cell differentiation processes pass through similar steps.[9] Steps 3, 2, and 1 may be reversible, as steps 6, 7, and 8, in both systems.[10]

REFERENCES

1. Frenster, J. H. 1971. Electron microscopic localization of acridine orange binding to DNA within human leukemic bone marrow cells. Cancer Res. **31:** 1128-1133.
2. Frenster, J. H., M. M. Papalian, M. A. Masek & J. A. Frenster. 1979. Electron microscopic analysis of lymph node cellular activity in Hodgkin's disease. J. Natl. Cancer Inst. **63:** 331-335.
3. Frenster, J. H. 1976. Selective control of DNA helix openings during gene regulation. Cancer Res. **36:** 3394-3398.
4. Frenster, J. H. 1974. Ultrastructure and function of heterochromatin and euchromatin. *In* The Cell Nucleus. H. Busch, Ed. Vol. 1: 565-580. Academic Press. New York.
5. Frenster, J. H. 1980. Selective gene de-repression by de-repressor RNA. *In* Eukaryotic Gene Regulation. G. M. Kolodny, Ed. Vol. 1: 131-143. CRC Press. Boca Raton, FL.
6. Tereba, A., L. Skoog & P. K. Vogt. 1975. RNA tumor virus specific sequences in nuclear DNA of several avian species. Virology **65:** 524-534.
7. De La Maza, L. M., A. Faras, H. Varmus, P. K. Vogt & J. J. Yunis. 1975. Integration of avian sarcoma specific DNA in mammalian chromatin. Exp. Cell Res. **93:** 484-489.
8. Van Dyke, M. W., R. G. Roeder & M. Sawadogo. 1988. Physical analysis of transcription preinitiation complex assembly on a class II gene promoter. Science **241:** 1335-1338.
9. Frenster, J. H. & P. R. Herstein. 1973. Gene de-repression. New Engl. J. Med. **288:** 1224-1229.
10. Nomura, S., P. J. Fischinger, C. F. T. Mattern, B. I. Gerwin & K. J. Dunn. 1973. Revertants of mouse cells transformed by murine sarcoma virus: Flat variants induced by FUDR and colcemide. Virology **56:** 152-163.

Changes in Chromatin Structure Temporally Relate to Tumorigenicity and Inducibility of Friend Cell Types

KATHLEEN E. LEONARDSON AND
STUART B. LEVY

Department of Medicine (Hematology/Oncology)
New England Medical Center
Tufts University Medical School
Boston, Massachusetts 02111

In a manner similar to human and animal leukemias which commonly progress through a series of stages, Friend virus-induced erythroleukemia begins with a rapid proliferation of differentiating erythroid precursors in the spleen and bone marrow, followed by the appearance of cells capable of tumorigenic growth.[1,2] Our laboratory has derived and propagated a set of relatively stable Friend tumors at different levels of malignancy from the same subcutaneous tumor.[2] Although these tumors are all proerythroid and identical at the light and electron microscope levels,[3] they differ in their ability to grow *in vitro,*[2] their clonability,[2] their level of virus expression,[3] and their response to chemical inducers of differentiation.[2] In addition, we have identified differences between the chromatins of these long-term propagated Friend tumors, including decreased amounts of the non-allelic histone variant H2A.1 in proportion to the level of malignancy,[4,5] different nucleosome repeat lengths (NRL),[6] and different levels of globin gene enrichment in a minor chromatin fraction (K. Leonardson and S. B. Levy, manuscript in preparation).

We sought to determine the temporal relationship of the chromatin changes to tumor phenotype and here report the results of serial analysis of five newly derived Friend tumors during early subcutaneous establishment. Our data show that upon placement of splenic or omentum foci in a subcutaneous environment, the histone variants H2A.1 and H2B.2 decrease continually over the first 10 passages (while the H2A.2 and H2B.1 levels increase) and then stabilize between passages 10 and 20 in all five tumors. Extrapolation of the H2A variant ratios to the time of initial subcutaneous passage suggests that all tumors began with ratios characteristic of erythroleukemic spleen (3.1-3.3).[4] The nucleosome repeat length also decreased over the first 10 passages but increased after passage 10 in four of the five tumors. These results show that certain predictable chromatin changes are initiated immediately upon placement of the foci into the subcutaneous site. The lowest H2A.1/H2A.2 ratio was observed in OM 1, correlating with a high level of malignancy, while the other tumors, with ratios between 1.7 and 2.1, showed lower levels of malignancy (TABLE 1). The ability to be induced to differentiate by dimethyl sulfoxide (DMSO) treatment was lowest in the least tumorigenic tumor (17% induction in SP6) and highest in the most malignant tumor (40% in OM1). Although the H2B.2/H2B.1 variant ratio also decreased in all tumors, the stabilized values appeared unrelated to either the H2A variant ratio or the malignant potential (TABLE 1).

While chromosomal change and DNA alterations have been previously described as important in tumor development,[7] our results identifying a burst of chromatin changes in new tumors suggest that large-scale chromatin reorganization is also an important feature in early tumor establishment and is related to the emergent tumor phenotype.

TABLE 1. Characteristics of Friend Tumors

	Characteristic[b]			
	Histone Variant Ratio[c]			
Tumor[a]	H2A.1/H2A.2	H2B.2/H2B.1	NRL[d]	Hemoglobin Induction with DMSO[e]
SP6	2.0 ± 0.2 (4)	1.3 ± 0.1 (3)	186 ± 6 (3)	+
SP1	2.1 ± 0.1 (4)	1.2 ± 0.1 (5)	182 ± 3 (3)	++
SP2	1.9 ± 0.1 (4)	1.6 ± 0.1 (5)	193 ± 4 (3)	++
SP5	1.7 ± 0.2 (4)	1.2 ± 0.1 (4)	195 ± 6 (3)	ND[f]
OM1	1.0 ± 0.1 (5)	1.2 ± 0.2 (5)	186 (2)	+++

[a] Tumors are listed in increasing order of malignancy, measured as the rate of the appearance of tumors produced by subcutaneous injection of 10^3 cells at a single site in DBA/2J mice. Six animals were used to test each tumor, and they were monitored for 30 days. Tumorigenicity studies of SP6 at passage 20 indicated it was 10-fold less tumorigenic than the other tumors.

[b] The mean values and standard deviations reported were obtained from analysis of cells at tumor passages 39-40, with the exception of SP6, which was examined at tumor passage 29, after which it failed to propagate. The number of determinations is given in parenthesis.

[c] To obtain variant ratios, purified tumor nuclei were applied to gels, and the variants were resolved by Triton X-100-acetic acid-urea polyacrylamide gel electrophoresis. Gels were stained with amido black,[8] and peaks were quantitated as described.[5]

[d] NRL, nucleosome repeat length.

[e] Relative DMSO (dimethyl sulfoxide) inducibility: cells which became benzidine-positive after 5 and 7 days of culture in 1.2 or 1.5% DMSO.

[f] ND, analysis not performed.

REFERENCES

1. FRIEND, C. 1957. J. Exp. Med. **105:** 307-318.
2. LEVY, S. B., L. A. BLANKSTEIN, E. C. VINTON & T. J. CHAMBERS. 1979. *In* Oncogenic Viruses and Host Cell Genes. Y. Ikawa & T. Odaka, Eds.: 409-428. Academic Press. New York.
3. WOYTOWICZ, J. M., P. R. DAOUST, J. ANDRE-SCHWARTZ & S. B. LEVY. 1983. Blood **62:** 425-432.
4. BLANKSTEIN, L. A. & S. B. LEVY. 1976. Nature **260:** 638-640.

5. Blankstein, L. A., B. D. Stollar, S. G. Franklin, A. Zweidler & S. B. Levy. 1977. Biochemistry **16:** 4557-4562.
6. Leonardson, K. E. & S. B. Levy. 1980. Nucleic Acids Res. **8:** 5317-5331.
7. Bishop, J. M. 1987. Science **235:** 305-311.
8. Froussard, P., L. D. Tempelis & S. B. Levy. 1981. Br. J. Haematol. **49:** 275-282.

Methylation of Repetitive DNA Sequences and Differentiation of Friend Erythroleukemia Cells[a]

NATALIE SCHNEIDERMAN,[b] ZEE-FEN CHANG,[c] AND JUDITH K. CHRISTMAN[c,d]

[c]*Department of Molecular Biology*
Michigan Cancer Foundation
Detroit, Michigan 48201
and
[b]*Department of Biochemistry*
Mount Sinai School of Medicine
New York, New York 10029

Erythroid differentiation of Friend leukemia (FL) cells is accompanied by a decrease in methylation of cytosine residues in the DNA.[1-3] However, since no changes occur in methylation of the *Hpa* II and *Hha* I sites within and flanking the α- and β-globin genes,[4] the relationship between hypomethylation and changes in gene regulation during FL cell differentiation has remained obscure. Here, we report an association between the ability of FL cell clones to respond to inducing agents and the level of DNA methylation as reflected in overall 5-methylcytosine (5mC) content of DNA, methylation of *Hpa* II and *Hha* I sites in total genomic DNA, and methylation of *Hpa* II sites in a class of minor mouse satellite sequences.

Clones compared were DR-10, DS-19 and 745A.[5,6] Virtually all DS-19 cells in a population undergo erythroid differentiation when exposed to dimethyl sulfoxide (DMSO), while 20-40% of 745A cells fail to respond. In contrast, DR-10 cells are cultured continually in the presence of DMSO without induction of differentiation. The percentage of cytosine residues methylated in DNA from these clones is 3.2 $\pm$ 0.11 (DS-19), 3.7 $\pm$ 0.06 (745A), and 4.0 $\pm$ 0.01 (DR-10). Southern blots of *Hpa* II- and *Msp* I-cleaved DNA from these cells probed with the mouse repetitive sequences cloned in pMR150[7] (MR150 sequences) reveal extensive hypomethylation of CCGG sites in minor satellite DNA in DS-19 cells and 745A cells and virtually complete methylation in DR-10 cells. These differences are not detected in the CCGG and GCGC sites flanking and within the α- and β-globin genes.

Hexamethylene bisacetamide (HMBA), a potent inducer of DS-19 and 745A differentiation, fails to trigger differentiation of the DR-10 cells employed in these studies. As would be predicted if loss of methyl groups from MR150 sequences in

[a]Supported in part by NCI Grant CA25985 and the Marilyn and Lloyd Smith Fund.

[d]Address correspondence to Judith K. Christman, Ph.D., Michigan Cancer Foundation, 110 East Warren Avenue, Detroit, MI 48201.

FL cells is linked to differentiation, HMBA treatment causes detectable decreases of methylation in MR150 sequences in DS-19 and 745A cell DNA but no loss of methylation in those sequences in DR-10 cells. In addition, we have found that DS-19 cells produce large (> 10 kb) poly(A)$^+$ RNAs that contain sequences homologous to MR150. The level of these transcripts is increased more than 10-fold when the cells are induced to differentiate by exposure to HMBA for 5 days. RNA containing MR150 sequences is not detectable in DR-10 cells, nor is it induced by growing them in the presence of HMBA.

The observation that *Hpa* II sites flanking MR150 sequences are significantly undermethylated in germline tissues of the mouse and become fully methylated during embryonic development[8] suggests that MR150 sequences may act as indicators for changes in methylation associated with commitment of cells to particular pathways of differentiation. However, the detection of these sequences in RNA transcripts that accumulate during FL cell differentiation points to the possibility of a more direct involvement for them in the differentiation process. Determination of the coding potential of transcripts with MR150 sequences, as well as the relationship between their synthesis, the methylation status of MR150 sequences, and the ability of murine cells to differentiate, should help to elucidate the role of MR150 sequences.

ACKNOWLEDGMENTS

We are grateful to Drs. J. Sanford and V. Chapman for providing pMR150 and to Dr. P. Leder for α- and β-globin clones.

REFERENCES

1. CHRISTMAN, J. K., P. PRICE, L. PEDRINAN & G. ACS. 1977. Eur. J. Biochem. **8:** 53-61.
2. CHRISTMAN, J. K., N. WEICH, B. SCHOENBRUN, N. SCHNEIDERMAN & G. ACS. 1980. J. Cell. Biol. **86:** 366-370.
3. CREUSOT, F., G. ACS & J. K. CHRISTMAN. 1982. J. Biol. Chem. **257:** 2041-2048.
4. SHEFFREY, M., R. RIFKIND & P. MARKS. 1982. Proc. Natl. Acad. Sci. USA **82:** 1180-1184.
5. OHTA, T., M. TANAKA, M. TERADA, O. MILLER, A. BANKS, P. MARKS & R. RIFKIND. 1976. Proc. Natl. Acad. Sci. USA **73:** 1232-1236.
6. PATULEIA, M. C. & C. FRIEND. 1967. Cancer Res. **27:** 726-730.
7. PIETRAS, D. F., K. L. BENNET, L. D. SIRACUSA, M. WOODWORTH-GUTAI, V. M. CHAPMAN, K. W. GROSS, C. KANE-HAASE & N. D. HASTIE. 1983. Nucleic Acids Res. **11:** 6965-6979.
8. CHAPMAN, V., L. FORRESTER, J. SANFORD, N. HASTIE & J. ROSSANT. 1984. Nature **307:** 284-286.

Modification of the Effects of Ionizing Radiation by Differentiation-Induction[a]

JOHN T. LEITH AND ARVIN S. GLICKSMAN

Department of Radiation Medicine and Biology Research
Brown University and
Rhode Island Hospital
Providence, Rhode Island 02903

The use of differentiation-inducing agents (DIAs) has been proposed as a possible means of altering the phenotypic expression of neoplastic cells; such alterations might then have an impact on the choice of therapeutic strategy.[1] We have investigated the effects of two types of such agents (sodium butyrate: NAB; *N,N*-dimethylformamide or *N*-methylformamide: DMF or NMF) on the responses of both rodent and human tumor cells to X-irradiation, both *in vitro* and *in vivo*.[2–7]

These agents do possess significant activity with regard to modification of cellular radiation sensitivity (TABLE 1). The most important effect *in vitro* of both NAB and DMF/NMF is the decrease produced in the D_q value of the tumor survival curve.[b] Since radiotherapy is given in multiple small doses (e.g., 30 fractions), this increased sensitivity is precisely in the right dose region. If such increased killing were carried throughout a clinical treatment, even a small enhancement (e.g., 5%) could produce marked effects (about four logarithmic units increase in the number of cells killed). *In vivo,* an important result has been the observation that chronic administration of NAB or NMF results in essentially complete removal of hypoxic cells.[7] Electrode measurements *in vitro* of NAB-adapted tumor cells suggest that the NAB treatment may be reducing metabolism; this reduction could then lead to effective "reoxygenation" *in vivo* (J. Leith, unpublished data).

In summary, the increased radiosentization, decreased proliferation, and altered hypoxic cell physiology observed in tumor cells treated with DIAs indicate that continued preclinical research into the combinations of DIAs with conventional cytotoxic agents is worth pursuing. Still, DIAs must be well characterized, as it is likely that individual agents will have unique properties. For example, DMF and NMF produce reductions of intracellular glutathione,[8] while NAB produces a marked increase in such levels.[5] As glutathione metabolism may be an important factor in the extent of multi-drug resistance which occurs,[9] this difference may have clinically important implications for strategies of therapy.

[a] Supported by ACS Grant PDT 243C.

[b] The D_q and D_o values refer to the low-dose "shoulder" and high-dose exponential regions, respectively, of the mammalian X-ray survival curve.

TABLE 1. Effects of Sodium Butyrate (NAB) or Polar Solvents (*N,N*-Dimethylformamide or *N*-Dimethylformamide: NMF or DMF) on the Response of Tumor Cells to X-Irradiation

Endpoint	Character of Response
In vitro responses	
Effect on D_q parameter	Both NAB and NMF/DMF reduce magnitude of D_q value in concentration-dependent manner. Effect is very relevant to radiation therapy, because treatments are given in multiple small fractions.
Effect on D_o parameter	Agents have little effect; there is occasionally an increase.
Effect on sublethal damage	DMF and NMF have no effect on recovery from radiation-induced sublethal damage; NAB inhibits this recovery in a dose-dependent manner.
Effect on potentially lethal damage	Both agents increase recovery.
In vivo responses	
Effects on growth	In multiple administration experiments, both agents inhibit solid tumor growth in a dose-dependent manner.
Interaction with X-irradiation	DMF produces a greater than additive delay in tumor growth and increased tumor cell killing.
Effects on hypoxic cells	Both NMF and NAB remove hypoxic cells.

REFERENCES

1. REISS, M., C. GAMBA-VITALO, & A. C. SARTORELLI. 1986. Induction of tumor cell differentiation as a therapeutic approach: Preclinical models for hematopoietic and solid neoplasms. Cancer Treat. Rep. **70:** 201.
2. LEITH, J. T., L. A. GASKINS, D. L. DEXTER, P. CALABRESI & A. S. GLICKSMAN. 1982. Alteration of the survival response of two human colon carcinoma subpopulations to X-irradiation by *N,N*-dimethylformamide. Cancer Res. **42:** 30.
3. DEXTER, D. L., E. S. LEE, S. F. BLIVEN, A. S. GLICKSMAN & J. T. LEITH. 1984. Enhancement by *N*-methylformamide of the effect of ionizing radiation on a human colon tumor xenografted in nude mice. Cancer Res. **44:** 4942.
4. ARUNDEL, C. M., S. M. KENNEY, J. T. LEITH & A. S. GLICKSMAN. 1986. Contrasting effects of the differentiating agent sodium butyrate on recovery processes after x-irradiation in heterogeneous human colon tumor cells. Int. J. Radiat. Oncol. Biol. Phys. **12:** 959.
5. LEITH, J. T., K. T. HALLOWS, C. M. ARUNDEL & S. F. BLIVEN. 1988. Changes in X-ray sensitivity and glutathione content of human colon tumor cells after exposure to the differentiation-inducing agent sodium butyrate. Radiat. Res. **114:** 579.
6. HALLOWS, K. R., S. F. BLIVEN & J. T. LEITH. 1988. Effects of the differentiating agents sodium butyrate and *N*-methylformamide on the oxygen enhancement ratio of human colon tumor cells. Radiat. Res. **113:** 191.
7. LEITH, J. T. 1988. Modification of the hypoxic fraction of a xenografted human colon tumor by differentiation-inducing agents. J. Natl. Cancer Inst. **80:** 444.
8. CORDEIRO, R. M. & T. M. SAVARES. 1986. Role of glutathione depletion in the mechanism of action of *N*-methylformamide and *N,N*-dimethylformamide in a cultured human colon carcinoma cell line. Cancer Res. **46:** 1297.
9. MOSCOW, J. A. & K. H. COWAN. 1988. Multidrug resistance. J. Natl. Cancer Inst. **80:** 14.

Anti-viral Therapy Induces T Cells Which Protect against Viral Challenge

R. M. RUPRECHT, S. MULLANEY, M. GAMA SOSA,
R. HOM, AND R. FINBERG

Dana-Farber Cancer Institute and
Harvard Medical School
Boston, Massachusetts 02115

Rauscher murine leukemia virus (RLV) causes a lethal infection of hematopoietic cells in mice. Infected animals develop splenomegaly proportional to the virus titer. We have previously shown that the combination of 3′-azido-3′-deoxythymidine (AZT) and recombinant human interferonαA/D (rHuIFNαA/D) is highly synergistic in mice infected *de novo* with RLV.[1] Here we show that animals treated promptly with the combination of AZT + rHuIFNαA/D following exposure to RLV can be protected from viremia and disease. When rechallenged with live virus after cessation of therapy, these mice are resistant due to a protective cellular immune response.

TABLE 1. Protocol for Combination Anti-viral Therapy and Effects on RLV-Induced Splenomegaly and Viremia

		Protocol[a]				Splenomegaly[b]		
Group No.	Mice (*n*)	RLV	Saline	AZT (mg/ml)	IFNα (10 kU, i.p.)	Spleen Weight (mg)	Inhibition (%)	Viremia[c]
1, 2	16	+	−	0	−	1478 ± 122		+
3	4	−	−	0	−	102 ± 16		−
4	4	−	+	0.1	twice daily	83 ± 7		
5	7	+	−	0.1	twice daily	136 ± 13	96.2	−
6	4	−	+	0.1	daily	82 ± 13		
7	7	+	−	0.1	daily	128 ± 12	96.7	−
8	4	−	+	0.1	every other day	86 ± 9		
9	7	+	−	0.1	every other day	149 ± 32	95.4	−

[a] Groups of young female BALB/c mice were exposed to RLV intravenously as outlined (appropriate controls received saline). AZT was administered orally in the drinking water at the concentration indicated. Recombinant human interferonαA/D was administered to the mice intraperitoneally (i.p.) at 10,000 U/20 g body weight at the frequency indicated.

[b] After 20 days of therapy, the animals were sacrificed; there mean spleen weights and the % inhibition of splenomegaly are given.

[c] The results of the immunoblot analysis for the p30 *gag* antigen are indicated.

The protocol for virus inoculation and post-exposure chemoprophylaxis with AZT + rHuIFNαA/D is outlined in FIGURE 1. When combination therapy at the dose outlined in TABLE 1 was administered from 4 hr to 20 days post-inoculation, neither viremia nor splenomegaly was detectable in treated animals.[2] Five days after cessation of therapy, the mice were challenged with live virus. After several weeks of follow-up, no antigenemia was detected by immunoblot assay. The animals were sacrificed, and single cell suspensions were prepared from their spleens. Adoptive transfer of these cells to naive recipients was fully protective against challenge with live RLV. To identify the protective cell population, single-cell suspensions from RLV-immunized

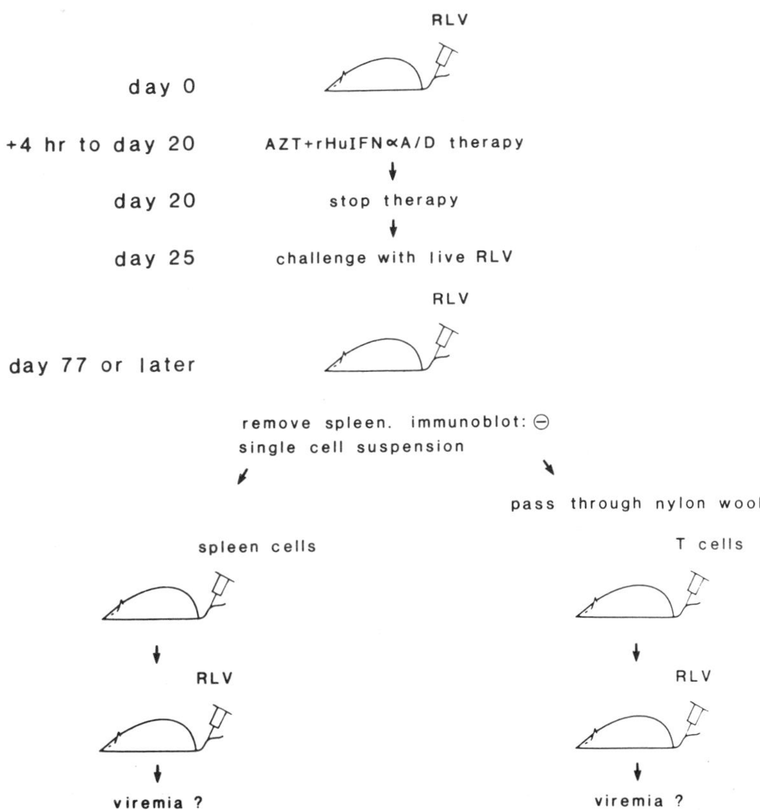

FIGURE 1. Spleen cell transfer from RLV-immunized mice. Groups of young female BALB/c mice were inoculated with 1×10^4 pfu (plaque-forming units) of RLV on day 0. Combination therapy with AZT (0.1 mg/ml) plus rHuIFNαA/D (10 kU/20 g body weight, i.p., every other day) was administered to the mice as indicated. At the end of therapy, all animals gave negative results when tested for the presence of p30 *gag* antigen by immunoblot analysis. On day 25, they were challenged with live RLV and subsequently examined for viremia or disease. 92% of the RLV-challenged mice had no evidence of viremia. Their spleen cells were isolated and transferred into naive recipient mice according to the schema. One hour after adoptive spleen cell transfer, the recipient mice were challenged with 10^4 pfu of live RLV. Three weeks later, they were examined for viremia and splenomegaly.

mice were further fractionated by passage through nylon wool, which effectively removes B cells and macrophages (FIG. 1). The remaining T cells were injected intravenously into naive recipient mice. A dose of 4×10^7 T cells fully protected against subsequent challenge with live RLV.

We conclude from these observations that the anti-viral coverage provided by AZT + rHuIFNαA/D is highly effective in mice exposed *de novo* to RLV. It allows RLV-inoculated animals to mount an effective immune response to live, pharmacologically attentuated RLV. Specifically, we found that (1) AZT combined with rHuIFNαA/D is highly synergistic in this animal/retrovirus system; (2) initiation of therapy with AZT + rHuIFNαA/D in effective dosage 4 hr after exposure to virus can prevent infection, viremia and disease; (3) a 20-day course of therapy is sufficient; (4) the combination regimens were neither toxic nor immunosuppressive; (5) RLV-exposed mice given 20 days of combination therapy acquired immunity to RLV, and, after cessation of therapy, these animals were resistant to challenge with live virus; (6) protective immunity resides in the T-cell fraction of splenocytes.

REFERENCES

1. RUPRECHT, R., F. CHIPTY, M. GAMA SOSA & H. ROSAS. 1988. Proc. Am. Assoc. Cancer Res. **29:** 1859.
2. RUPRECHT, R. M., M. A. GAMA SOSA & H. D. ROSAS. 1988. Lancet **i:** 239-240.

Studies on the DNA Ligase of Mouse Erythroleukemia Cells: Therapeutic Implications[a]

BARBARA M. SCHER,[b,c] WILLIAM SCHER,[d] AND SAMUEL WAXMAN[d]

Departments of [b]Microbiology and [d]Medicine
Mount Sinai Medical Center
City University of New York
New York, New York 10029

The DNA ligase activity present in cell-free extracts of mouse erythroleukemia (MEL) cells could be inhibited up to 90% by preincubation with hemin. The concentration of hemin required to inhibit 50% of the enzymatic activity was about 90 μM.[1] Since DNA ligase activity is required for both DNA replication and repair, the effect of hemin on cell growth in the absence or presence of DNA-damaging agents was determined. The concentration of hemin required to decrease the yield of viable cells by 50% (I.D.$_{50}$) after five days of growth was about 250 μM (FIG. 1). Hemin also acted in a synergistic fashion in the inhibition of cell growth due to DNA-damaging agents such as mitomycin C (FIG. 1 and data not shown). Mitomycin C inhibited the viable cell yield by 16% at 120 nM, and its I.D.$_{50}$ was 240 nM. The combination of hemin and mitomycin C reduced the cell yield to nearly zero at concentrations of the two agents that were at or below the I.D.$_{50}$ of each. Mitomycin C at 120 nM and at 240 nM reduced the I.D.$_{50}$ of hemin from 250 μM to about 100 and 56 μM, respectively. Results indicating similar synergistic activity were obtained with combinations of hemin and another DNA-damaging agent, bleomycin, but not with other exogenous toxic agents, i.e., cytosine arabinoside, a DNA polymerase inhibitor; and ATP, a membrane-active agent (data not shown). Partial characterization of the DNA ligase activity present in MEL cell-free extracts indicated that the enzyme had a M_r of 86,000, an $s_{20,w}$ of 5.5, and marked heat lability, with a $t_{1/2}$ at 45°C of 8-9 min. Since mild hyperthermia has been used in conjunction with other antineoplastic therapies to augment tumor cell death and since the MEL cell DNA ligase is heat-sensitive and inhibited by hemin, the effects of combinations of hemin and hyperthermia on cell yield were studied. In an apparently similar fashion to that of the DNA-damaging agents tested, supranormal temperatures sensitized the cells to the cytotoxic action of

[a]Supported in part by Grants from the American Cancer Society (CH-144 and CH-303), U.S. Public Health Service (AM16690 and CA2440), the Chemotherapy Foundation, Gar Reichman Foundation, C. E. Merrill Trust, H. Goldman Foundation, and Samuel Waxman Foundation.

[c]Address correspondence to Barbara M. Scher, Ph.D., Box 1178, Mount Sinai Medical Center, 1 Gustave L. Levy Place, New York, NY 10029.

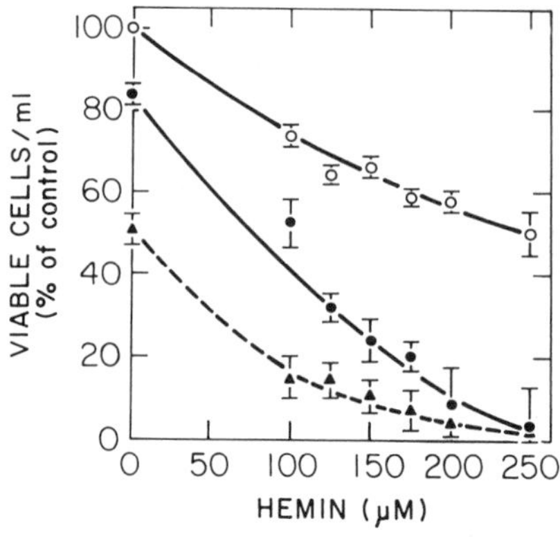

FIGURE 1. Effect of mitomycin C and hemin on the yield of MEL cells. MEL cells (line DS-19) were seeded at 10^5 cells/ml and grown in the absence (○) and presence of mitomycin C, 120 n*M* (●) and 240 n*M* (▲), and in the presence of the indicated concentrations of hemin chloride for 5 days. Then the viable (trypan blue-excluding) cell concentration and the standard error of the mean were determined.[1] The viable cell concentration in untreated cultures after 5 days was 3.45 ± 0.035 × 10^6 cells/ml. In both this figure and FIGURE 2, representative experiments are shown. The *error bars* indicate the standard error of the mean of at least three experiments.

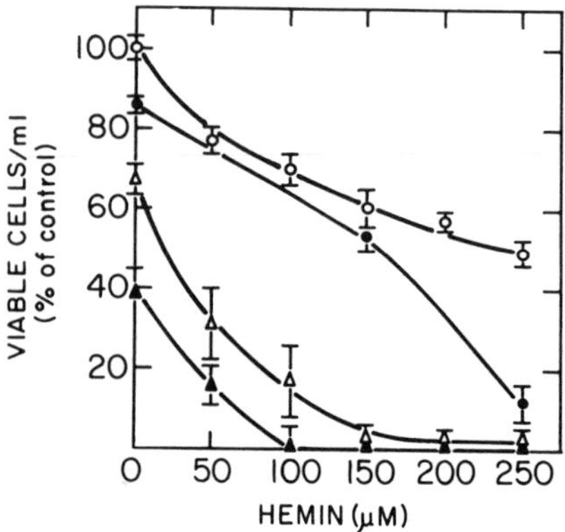

FIGURE 2. Effect of temperature and hemin on the yield of MEL cells. MEL cells were grown and cell concentrations determined as in FIGURE 1, but the cells in media containing the indicated hemin concentrations were at 37°C (○), 41°C (●), 42°C (△), or 43°C (▲). The viable cell concentration in untreated cultures grown at 37°C for 5 days was 3.27 ± 0.07 × 10^6 cells/ml. The I.D.$_{50}$ determined at each temperature is the hemin concentration that yielded 50% of the number of viable cells present in cultures grown at that same temperature in the absence of hemin.

hemin (FIG. 2). The I.D.$_{50}$ of hemin for cells grown at 41° and 42°C were 175 and 45 μ*M*, respectively, i.e., 30% and 82% decreases when compared to the I.D.$_{50}$ at 37°C. Since hemin has effects on many cellular processes, including DNA cleavage (see Ref. 2 for a review), it may be acting at multiple sites. The results presented here indicate that treatment which inhibits DNA ligase activity in cells undergoing active DNA synthesis, particularly in combination with DNA-cleaving agents, may yield a new and powerful type of cancer chemotherapy.

REFERENCES

1. SCHER, B. M., W. SCHER & S. WAXMAN. 1988. Cancer Res. **48:** 6278–6284.
2. WAXMAN, S., W. SCHER & B. M. SCHER. 1986. Cancer Detect. Prevent. **9:** 395–407.

KEYNOTE ADDRESS

The Friend Legacy: From Mouse to Man

FRED RAPP

Department of Microbiology and Immunology
The Pennsylvania State University
College of Medicine
Hershey, Pennsylvania 17033

The history of tumor virology had its inception with the pioneering work of Ellermann and Bang[1] and that of Rous,[2] who demonstrated that filtrates free of bacteria and cells were capable of inducing leukemia and sarcomas, respectively, in chickens. These seminal observations, made 80 years ago, were largely ignored for almost 40 years while a large number of investigators struggled with ways to demonstrate that viruses were the cause of naturally occurring cancers. Although some important observations were made on the papillomaviruses and on mouse mammary carcinomas in the 1930s,[3] the field was in general disarray until virology entered its quantitative phase and became a science, circa 1950.

Enders, Weller and Robbins[4] discovered that poliovirus could replicate in non-neural tissue. They observed that poliovirus replication could be monitored by cell destruction (cytopathology), which led to the development, by Dulbecco, of a plaque assay for animal viruses.[5] Prior to that time, the only available system for quantitating virus replication was pock formation on the membranes of embryonated chickens. The use of animals, employing lethality as an endpoint, was clearly too expensive and too cumbersome for routine monitoring of viral replication and was, for practical purposes, only applicable to those viruses able to cause disease in an animal host system.

The observation by Dalldorf and his colleagues[6,7] that Coxsackie viruses could replicate in newborn mice led to the isolation of a variety of animal viruses and paved the way for the isolation, by Gross, of the first mouse leukemia viruses.[8] It remained for Friend to isolate the first virus shown to cause leukemia in adult Swiss mice, an observation first published in 1957.[9] Her original observations, reported to a skeptical scientific community, had immediate and major impact on the burgeoning field of leukemia and sarcoma tumor viruses. One of the first papers on the subject appeared in the *Annals of the New York Academy of Sciences* in 1957[10] and was soon followed by a large number of publications describing the properties of the newly named Friend leukemia virus, the host response to virus infection, and the development of disease.[11–17]

It is of special interest that the first description of the Friend virus reported the importance of the genetic makeup of the host animal in viral pathogenesis.[9] Serial transmission of leukemia could be readily achieved in adult Swiss mice or DBA/2 mice but not in a number of other strains of adult mice, including the widely used C3H and C57 black mice. Interestingly, almost any route of injection caused disease in susceptible mice.[9] Early reports preferred to use the phrase "virus-like," testimony to the fact that in the 1950s virologists were wary of basing their reputations on work with tumor viruses.

Friend immediately saw the importance of the immune system in disease progression. Early studies reported that antibodies could be raised in mice and rabbits injected with filtrates from leukemic spleens.[18] Amazingly, the first articles published by Friend on this subject demonstrated that a formalinized vaccine prepared against such filtrates protected 80% of mice against challenge with live virus.[18] Thus, Friend developed an inactivated virus vaccine that immunized mice against challenge with live leukemia virus as early as 1959. The vaccine, clearly patterned after the early poliovirus (Salk) vaccine, is a striking example of Friend's efforts to relate theoretical virology with practical application. Her work was far ahead of its time. Thirty years have since elapsed, and no effective vaccine has yet been produced against any of the retroviruses to prevent the large variety of neoplasias associated with this virus group.

In a paper co-authored by Rapp and Friend,[19] it was demonstrated that ascites cells and impression smears of solid tumors from animals with Friend leukemia contained DNA in the cytoplasm, as measured by acridine orange techniques or with anti-nuclear serum obtained from patients with systemic lupus erythematosus. The significance of this observation has been lost in scientific antiquity (defined by this author as 3 to 5 years after an observation is made), but it may well have been the first demonstration of a DNA intermediate involved in the replication of a retrovirus. The observation, made years before the discovery of reverse transcriptase by Baltimore[20] and Temin and Mizutani,[21] represents one of those lost opportunities so common in the annals of science.

The last 20 years of Friend's career were spent studying cell differentiation induced by Friend leukemia virus,[22–24] made possible with the use of dimethyl sulfoxide.[25–27] This compound greatly catalyzed the differentiation of cells from solid leukemic tumors produced by subcutaneous inoculation of Friend virus-induced leukemic cells.

Studies by Friend and others on mouse retroviruses were paralleled by investigations with similar retroviruses of cats and monkeys. A huge amount of information concerning the transforming properties of tumor viruses was derived from work with polyoma and simian virus 40 (SV40), which demonstrated that a single gene and its product were capable of transforming normal cells to a malignant phenotype.[28] Therefore, the subsequent demonstration that a single retrovirus gene[29] was capable of causing sarcomas in chickens (the *src* gene, a phenomenon also observed for other viruses) should not have been surprising.

The difficulty in finding human retroviruses finally was overcome by Gallo[30,31] and by Hinuma,[32] who independently isolated such agents from human T cell leukemias. Their observations were made possible by the addition of various growth factors, in particular the T cell growth factor (now known as interleukin-2), which enabled maintenance and growth of T cells in culture for extended periods of time. This ended decades of frustration by many investigators attempting to isolate such viruses. Moreover, the methodology came at an opportune moment, because it was immediately employed to isolate[33–35] human immunodeficiency virus (HIV), the cause of acquired immunodeficiency syndrome (AIDS). These retroviruses, the first of many we expect to be isolated in the future, have provided insight into the type and scope of the problems likely to be faced by scientists in dealing with human retrovirus infections.

The well-documented efficacy of the early vaccines against smallpox and yellow fever, as well as those against acute infections by poliovirus, rubeola virus, rubella virus, and mumps virus, caused many in the medical community to believe that vaccines could prevent all virus diseases. Friend herself felt that this might be an answer and developed an early vaccine against the virus she had isolated. Unfortunately, this did not prove to be the case. The results in attempting to produce vaccines against, for example, herpes simplex viruses clearly demonstrate the difficulties involved. These include variation in virus glycoproteins (especially significant for HIV) and the ability of these viruses to become latent and to integrate their genetic information into that of the host, thus protecting them from the host's immune response. The need to vaccinate at a very early age in order to control chronic or latent viral infections (i.e., infection with retroviruses) presents complex and difficult problems. In fact, once viruses establish latency, vaccines are not likely to prevent disease. This means that vaccination would have to take place prior to the time of primary infection. In effect, the vaccine would have to block the virus at the portal of entry (something that no current vaccine is able to do). Poliovirus vaccine does not prevent infection in the gastrointestinal tract; it prevents movement of the virus to the central nervous system. Thus, a totally new concept will be required to prevent entry of a retrovirus into the target cells of the host. The mere fact that a virus or virus precursor protein can elicit an antibody or a T cell response is of little value in attempting to control disease caused by viruses that can integrate their genome or undergo latency in a protected cell.

Charlotte Friend, in a relatively short time span, bridged the gap between the knowledge that retroviruses were responsible for leukemias as well as other tumors of mice and the now almost certain conclusion that many human neoplasias are caused by similar microorganisms. She opened new pathways of investigation to many other researchers and helped end the years of frustration in which a viral etiology for naturally occurring tumors was in doubt. In pioneering this work and in searching for a solution to the problems of leukemia, Charlotte Friend reached for the stars. The many milestones she achieved helped lay the groundwork for current scientific endeavor.

SUMMARY

The origins of retrovirology began in the primordial laboratories of Ellermann and Bang and of Rous in the first decade of the twentieth century. More than 40 frustrating years were to elapse before this early work with chickens was to lead to experiments with mice, made possible by the use of inbred strains and catalyzed by the observations of Dalldorf and of Gross that newborn animals were susceptible targets for pathogenesis by, respectively, Coxsackie viruses, and polyoma and retroviruses. Seminal observations by Charlotte Friend that retroviruses caused neoplasia in adult mice and her studies investigating the properties and pathogenesis of the Friend leukemia virus, as well as the role of the host immune response in development of disease, helped lay the groundwork of modern retrovirology. The use of retroviruses to study cell differentiation became the foundation on which many more recent discoveries rest. Above all, the information supplied by Friend and her colleagues and investigators in other laboratories finally enabled unequivocal isolation of the first human retroviruses long after most investigators had given up hope of finding such agents in man. Moreover, the techniques developed and the rapid characterization of these newly discovered human pathogens enabled the isolation of human immunodeficiency virus, the cause of acquired immunodeficiency syndrome. It is a challenge to current investigators to extend and expand upon the original work of Friend concerning the pathogenesis of retroviruses, as only a fuller understanding of the complex virus-host disease patterns induced by these viruses will ultimately lead to their control and prevention.

REFERENCES

1. Ellermann, V. & O. Bang. 1908. Experimentelle Leukämie bei Hünern. Centralbl. Bakteriol. Abt. I (Orig.) **46:** 595-609.
2. Rous, P. 1911. A sarcoma of the fowl transmissible by an agent separable from the tumor cells. J. Exp. Med. **13:** 397-411.
3. Gross, L. Ed. 1983. Oncogenic Viruses, 3rd ed. Vols. 1 and 2: 1-1124. Pergamon Press. New York.
4. Enders, J. F., T. H. Weller & F. C. Robbins. 1949. Cultivation of the Lansing strain of poliomyelitis virus in cultures of various human embryonic tissues. Science **109:** 85-87.
5. Dulbecco, R. 1952. Production of plaques in monolayer tissue cultures by single particles of an animal virus. Proc. Natl. Acad. Sci. USA **38:** 747-752.
6. Dalldorf, G. & G. Sickles. 1948. An unidentified, filterable agent isolated from the feces of children with paralysis. Science **108:** 61-62.
7. Dalldorf, G. 1949. The Coxsackie group of viruses. Science **110:** 594.
8. Gross, L. 1951. "Spontaneous" leukemia developing in C3H mice following inoculation, in infancy, with Ak-leukemic extracts, or Ak-embryos. Proc. Soc. Exp. Biol. Med. **76:** 27-32.
9. Friend, C. 1957. Cell-free transmission in adult Swiss mice of a disease having the character of a leukemia. J. Exp. Med. **105:** 307-318.
10. Friend, C. 1957. Leukemia of adult mice caused by transmissible agent. Ann. N. Y. Acad. Sci. **68:** 522-532.
11. De Harven, E. & C. Friend. 1958. Electron microscope study of a cell-free induced leukemia of the mouse: A preliminary report. J. Biophys. Biochem. Cytol. **4:** 151-156.
12. De Harven, E. & C. Friend. 1960. Further electron microscope studies of a mouse leukemia induced by cell-free filtrates. J. Biophys. Biochem. Cytol. **7:** 747-752.
13. Friend, C., E. De Harven & J. R. Haddad. 1963. Studies on several lines of murine lymphomas associated with intracytoplasmic particles. Acta Un. Int. Cancer **19:** 344-347.
14. Rapp, F. & C. Friend. 1963. Early detection and localization of Swiss mouse leukemia virus. Acta Un. Int. Cancer **19:** 348-350.
15. De Harven, E. & C. Friend. 1964. Structure of virus particles partially purified from the blood of leukemic mice. Virology **23:** 119-124.
16. Patuleia, M. C. & C. Friend. 1967. Tissue culture studies on murine virus-induced leukemia cells: Isolation of single cells in agar-liquid medium. Cancer Res. **27:** 726-730.
17. Silber, R., B. Goldstein, E. Berman, J. Decter & C. Friend. 1967. The effect of a murine leukemia virus on RNA metabolism. Cancer Res. **27:** 1264-1269.
18. Friend, C. 1959. Immunological relationships of a filterable agent causing a leukemia in adult mice. I. The neutralization of infectivity by specific antiserum. J. Exp. Med. **109:** 217-228.
19. Rapp, F. & C. Friend. 1962. Detection of cytoplasmic deoxyribonucleic acid and nucleoproteins with antinuclear serum. Virology **17:** 497-499.
20. Baltimore, D. 1970. Viral RNA-dependent DNA polymerase. Nature **226:** 1209-1211.
21. Temin, H. M. & S. Mizutani. 1970. RNA-dependent polymerase in virions of Rous sarcoma virus. Nature **226:** 1211-1213.
22. Rossi, G. B. & C. Friend. 1967. Erythrocytic maturation of (Friend) virus-induced leukemic cells in spleen clones. Proc. Natl. Acad. Sci. USA **58:** 1373-1380.
23. Rossi, G. B. & C. Friend. 1970. Further studies on the biological properties of Friend virus-induced leukemic cells differentiating along the erythrocytic pathway. J. Cell. Physiol. **76:** 159-166.
24. Scher, W., J. G. Holland & C. Friend. 1971. Hemoglobin synthesis in murine virus-induced leukemic cells *in vitro:* Partial purification and identification of hemoglobins. Blood **37:** 428-437.
25. Friend, C., W. Scher, J. G. Holland & T. Sato. 1971. Hemoglobin synthesis in murine virus-induced leukemic cells *in vitro:* Stimulation of erythroid differentiation by dimethyl sulfoxide. Proc. Natl. Acad. Sci. USA **68:** 378-382.
26. Harel, L., C. Blat, F. Lacour & C. Friend. 1981. Altered RNA/protein ratio associated with the induction of differentiation of Friend erythroleukemia cells. Proc. Natl. Acad. Sci. USA **78:** 3882-3886.

27. ZAJAC-KAYE, M., E. BROWN & C. FRIEND. 1986. Induction of differentiation in Friend erythroleukemia cells with dimethyl sulfoxide, hexamethylene bisacetamide and sodium butyrate is not accompanied by changes in proviral DNA or its expression. Virus Res. **6:** 45-55.

28. RAPP, F. & H. C. ISOM. 1985. Etiology of cancer: Viral. *In* Medical Oncology: Basic Principles and Clinical Management of Cancer. P. Calabresi, P. S. Schein, S. A. Rosenberg, Eds.: 103-128. Macmillan Publishing Co., New York.

29. BRUGGE, J. S. & R. L. ERIKSON. 1977. Identification of a transformation-specific antigen induced by an avian sarcoma virus. Nature **269:** 346-347.

30. POIESZ, B. J., F. W. RUSCETTI, A. F. GAZDAR, P. A. BUNN, J. D. MINNA & R. C. GALLO. 1980. Detection and isolation of type C retrovirus particles from fresh and cultured lymphocytes of a patient with cutaneous T-cell lymphoma. Proc. Natl. Acad. Sci. USA **77:** 7415-7419.

31. POIESZ, B. J., F. W. RUSSETTI, M. S. REITZ, V. S. KALYANARAMAN & R. C. GALLO. 1981. Isolation of a new type C retrovirus (HTLV) in primary uncultured cells of a patient with Sezary T-cell leukemia. Nature **294:** 268-271.

32. YOSHIDA, M., I. MIYOSHI & Y. HINUMA. 1982. Isolation and characterization of retrovirus from cell lines of human adult T-cell leukemia and its implication in the disease. Proc. Natl. Acad. Sci. USA **79:** 2031-2035.

33. BARRE-SINOUSSI, F., J. C. CHERMANN, F. REY, M. T. NUGEYRE, S. CHAMARET, J. GRUEST, C. DAUGUET, C. AXLER-BLIN, F. VEZINET-BRUN, C. ROUZIOUX, W. ROZENBAUM & L. MONTAGNIER. 1983. Isolation of a T-lymphotropic retrovirus from a patient at risk for acquired immunodeficiency syndrome (AIDS). Science **220:** 868-871.

34. POPOVIC, M., M. G. SARNGADHARAN, E. READ & R. C. GALLO. 1984. Detection, isolation and continuous production of cytopathic human T lymphotropic retrovirus (HTLV-III) from patients with AIDS and pre-AIDS. Science **224:** 497-500.

35. GALLO, R. C., S. Z. SALAHUDDIN, M. POPOVIC, G. M. SHEARER, M. KAPLAN, B. F. HAYNES, T. J. PALKER, R. REDFIELD, J. OLESKE, B. SAFAI, G. WHITE, P. FOSTER & P. D. MARKHAM. 1984. Frequent detection and isolation of cytopathic retroviruses (HTLV-III) from patients with AIDS and at risk for AIDS. Science **224:** 500-503.

Index of Contributors